ALFRED A. KNOPF
1915 · 100 YEARS · 2015

ANN TENNA

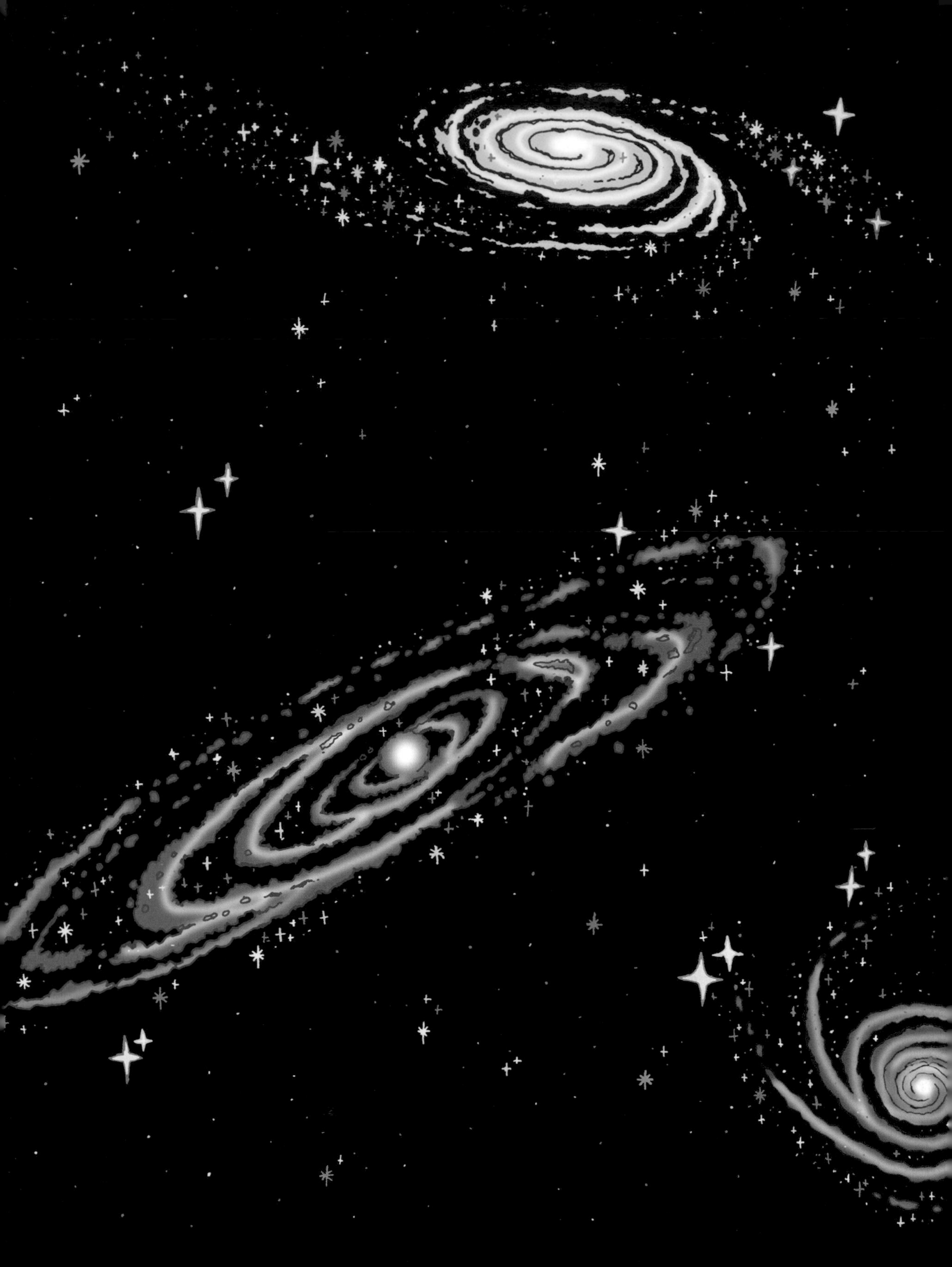

ANN TENNA

A NOVEL

MARISA ACOCELLA MARCHETTO

ALFRED A. KNOPF
NEW YORK
2015

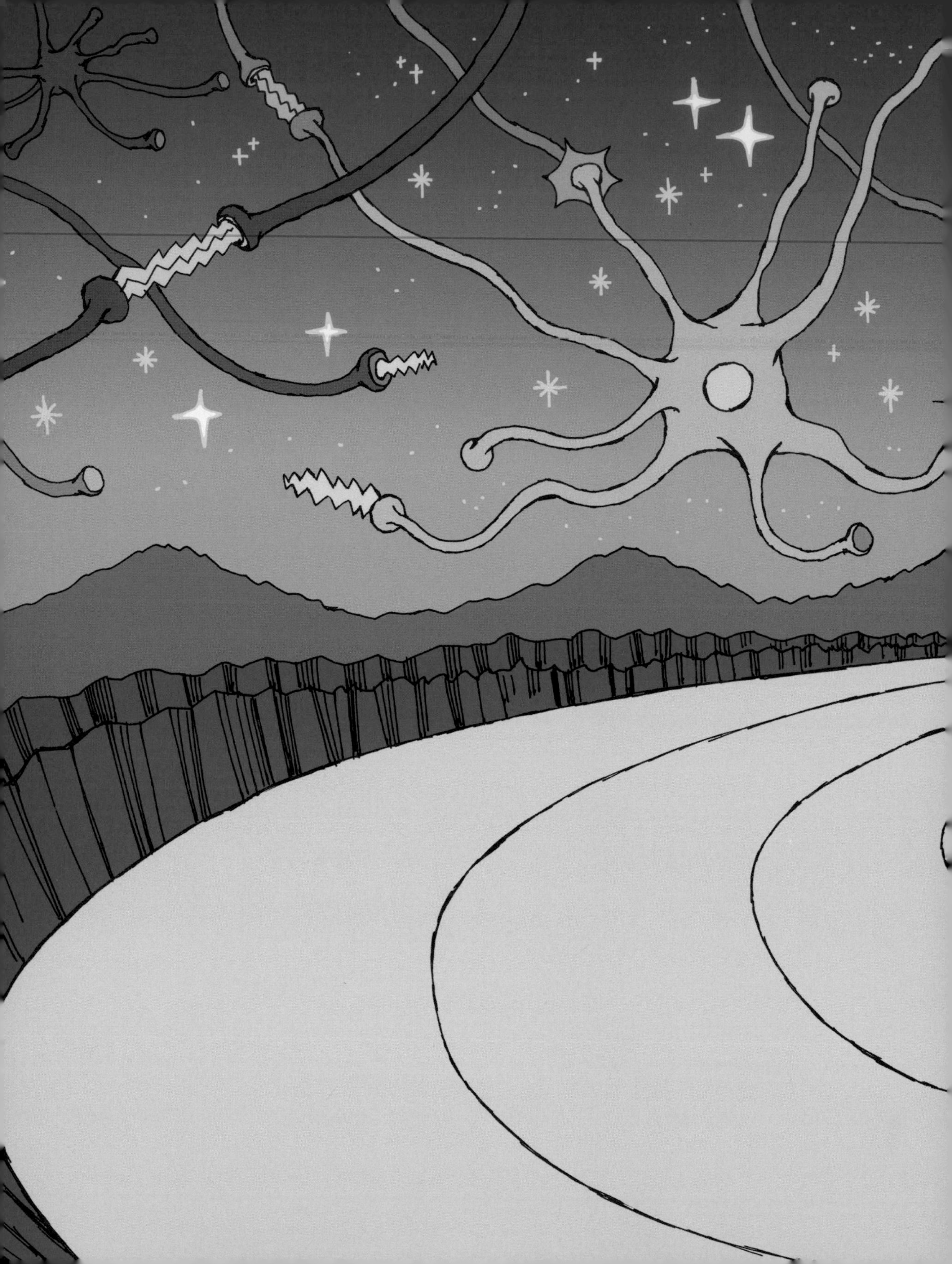

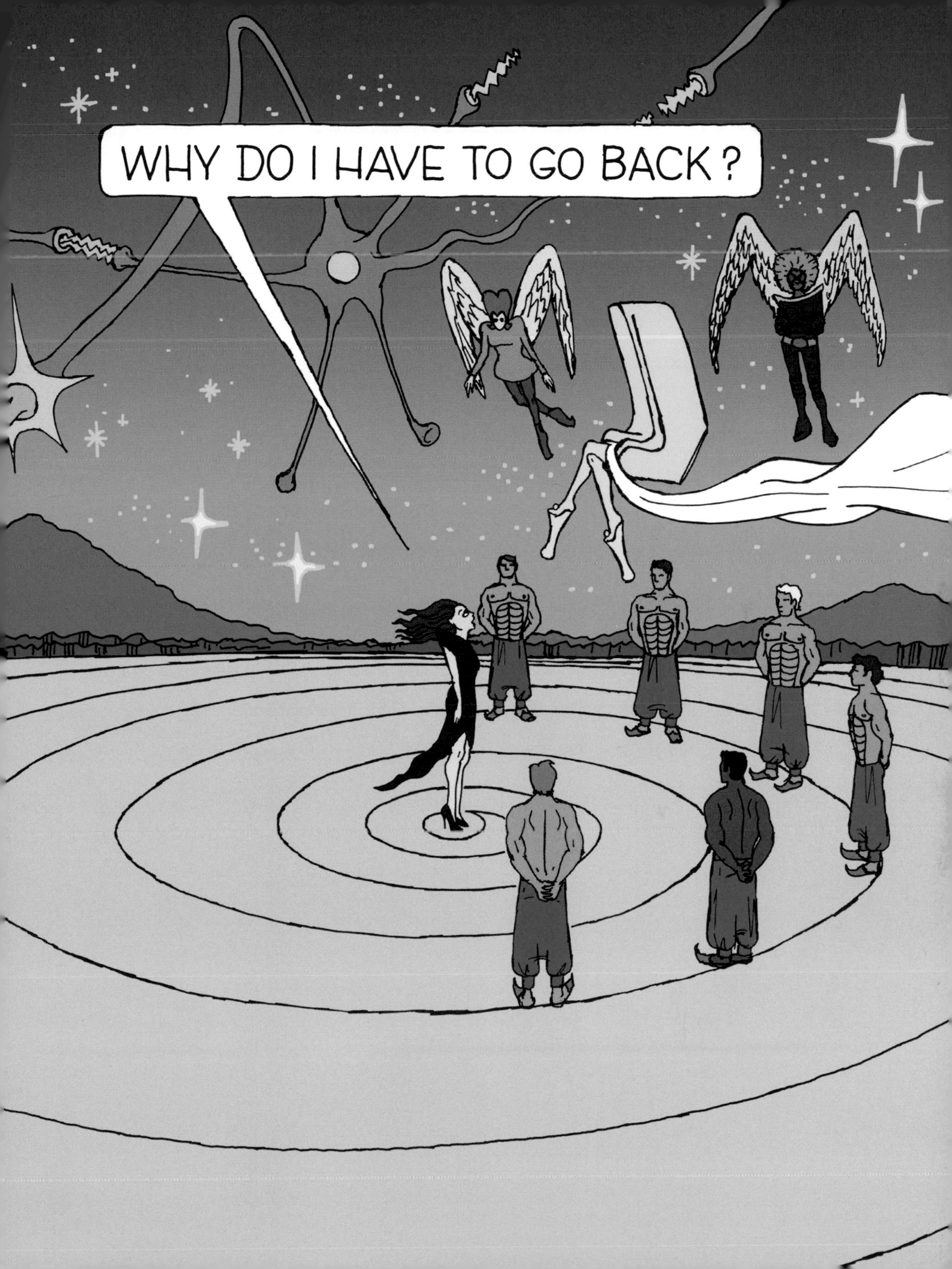
WHY DO I HAVE TO GO BACK?

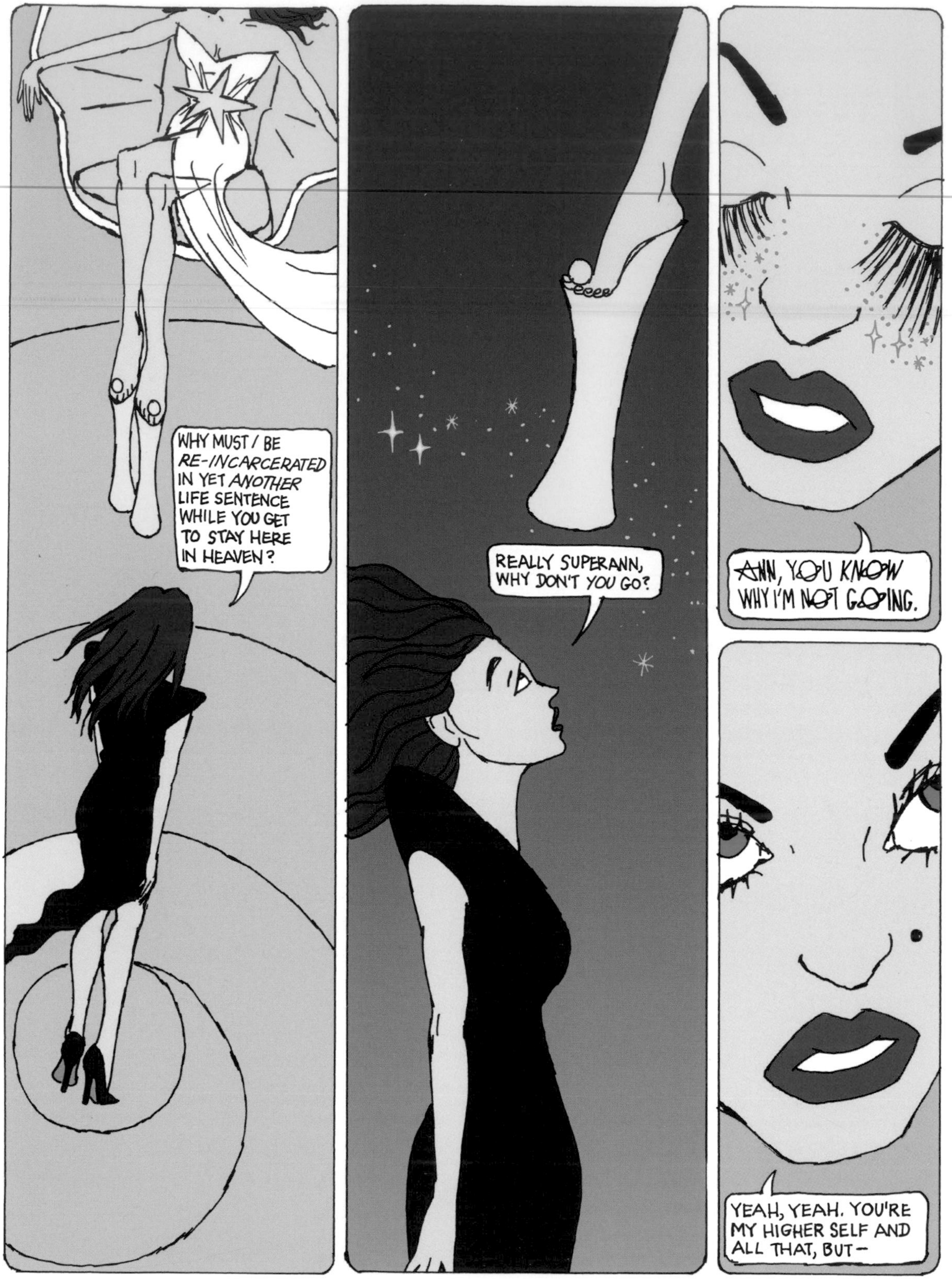
WHY MUST I BE RE-INCARCERATED IN YET ANOTHER LIFE SENTENCE WHILE YOU GET TO STAY HERE IN HEAVEN?
REALLY SUPERANN, WHY DON'T YOU GO?
ANN, YOU KNOW WHY I'M NOT GOING.
YEAH, YEAH. YOU'RE MY HIGHER SELF AND ALL THAT, BUT—

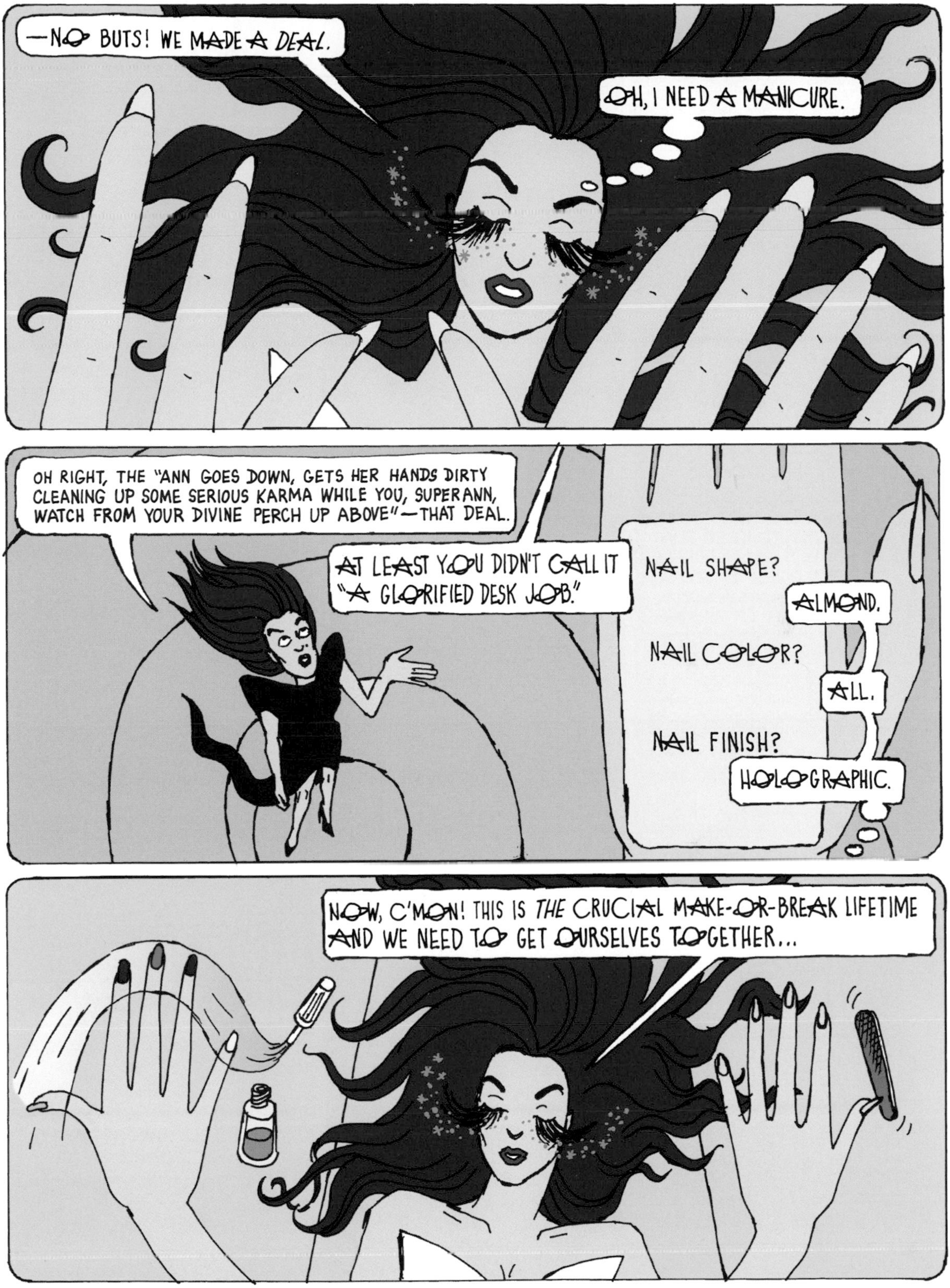
—NO BUTS! WE MADE A *DEAL.*
OH, I NEED A MANICURE.
OH RIGHT, THE "ANN GOES DOWN, GETS HER HANDS DIRTY CLEANING UP SOME SERIOUS KARMA WHILE YOU, SUPERANN, WATCH FROM YOUR DIVINE PERCH UP ABOVE"—THAT DEAL.
AT LEAST YOU DIDN'T CALL IT "A GLORIFIED DESK JOB."
NAIL SHAPE?
ALMOND.
NAIL COLOR?
ALL.
NAIL FINISH?
HOLOGRAPHIC.
NOW, C'MON! THIS IS *THE* CRUCIAL MAKE-OR-BREAK LIFETIME AND WE NEED TO GET OURSELVES TOGETHER...

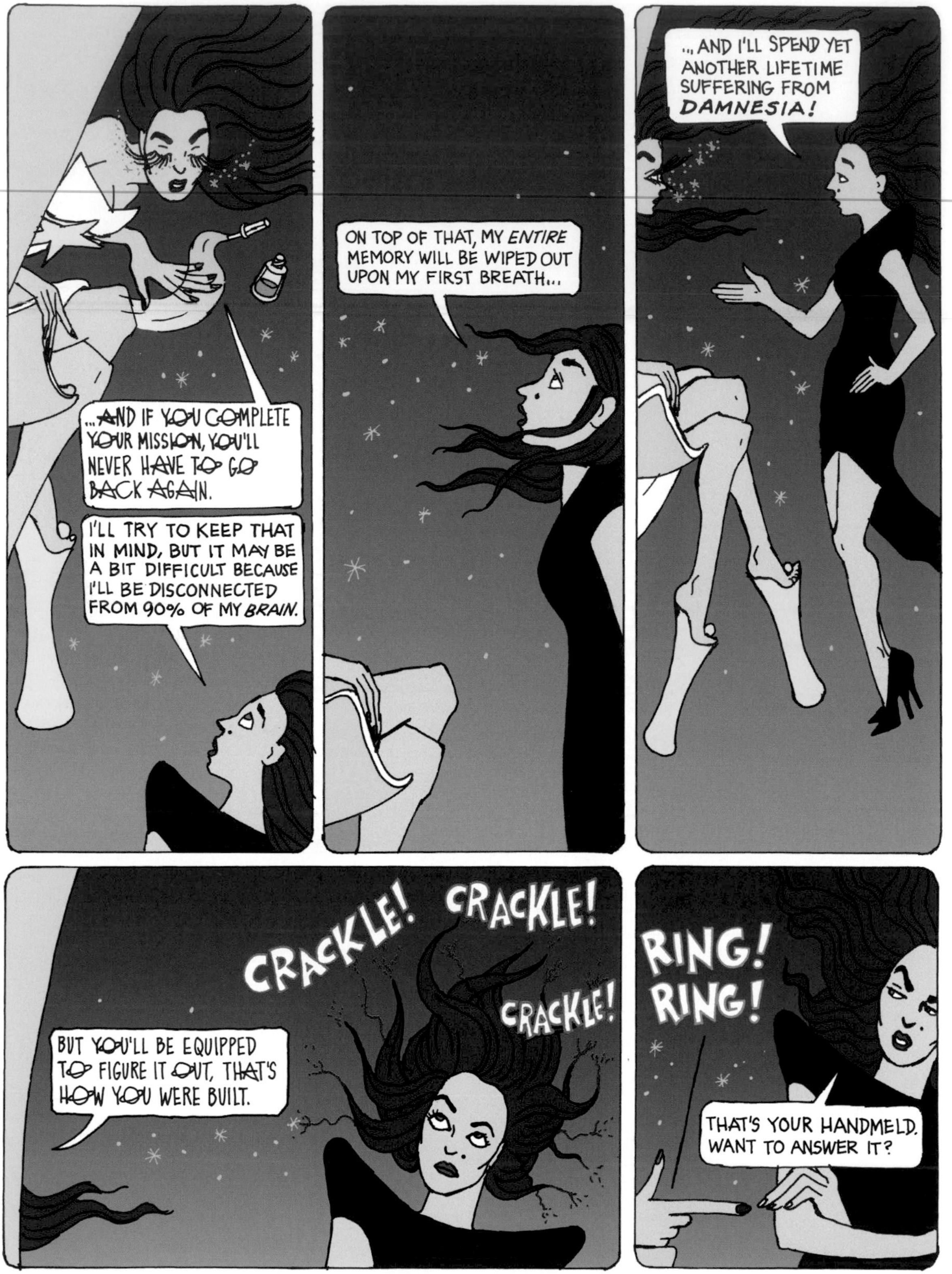
...AND IF YOU COMPLETE YOUR MISSION, YOU'LL NEVER HAVE TO GO BACK AGAIN.
I'LL TRY TO KEEP THAT IN MIND, BUT IT MAY BE A BIT DIFFICULT BECAUSE I'LL BE DISCONNECTED FROM 90% OF MY BRAIN.
ON TOP OF THAT, MY ENTIRE MEMORY WILL BE WIPED OUT UPON MY FIRST BREATH...
...AND I'LL SPEND YET ANOTHER LIFETIME SUFFERING FROM DAMNESIA!
CRACKLE! CRACKLE!
CRACKLE!
BUT YOU'LL BE EQUIPPED TO FIGURE IT OUT, THAT'S HOW YOU WERE BUILT.
RING! RING!
THAT'S YOUR HANDMELD. WANT TO ANSWER IT?

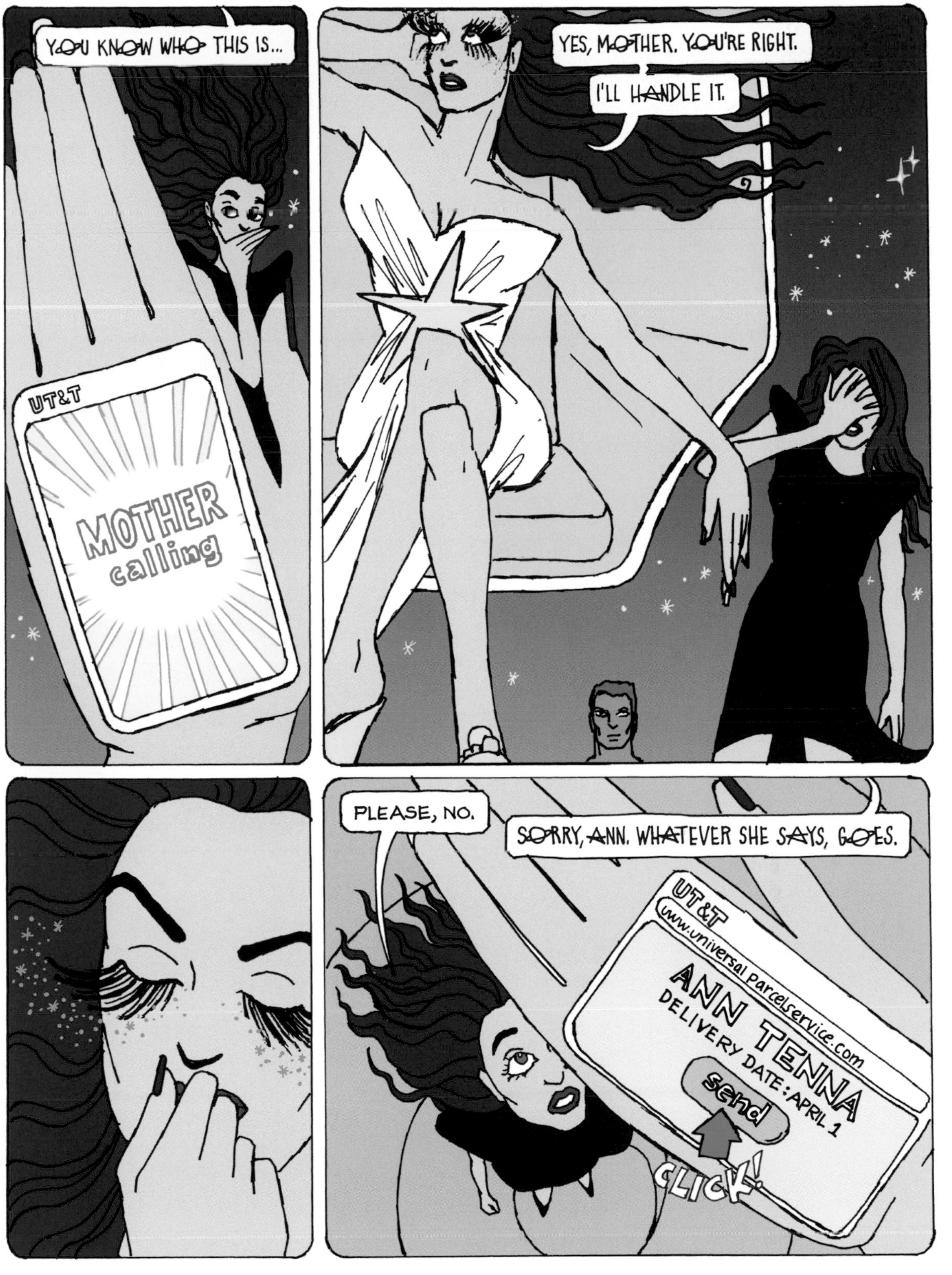
YOU KNOW WHO THIS IS...
UT&T
MOTHER
calling
YES, MOTHER. YOU'RE RIGHT.
I'LL HANDLE IT.
PLEASE, NO.
SORRY, ANN. WHATEVER SHE SAYS, GOES.
UT&T
www.universalparcelservice.com
ANN TENNA
DELIVERY DATE: APRIL 1
send
CLICK!

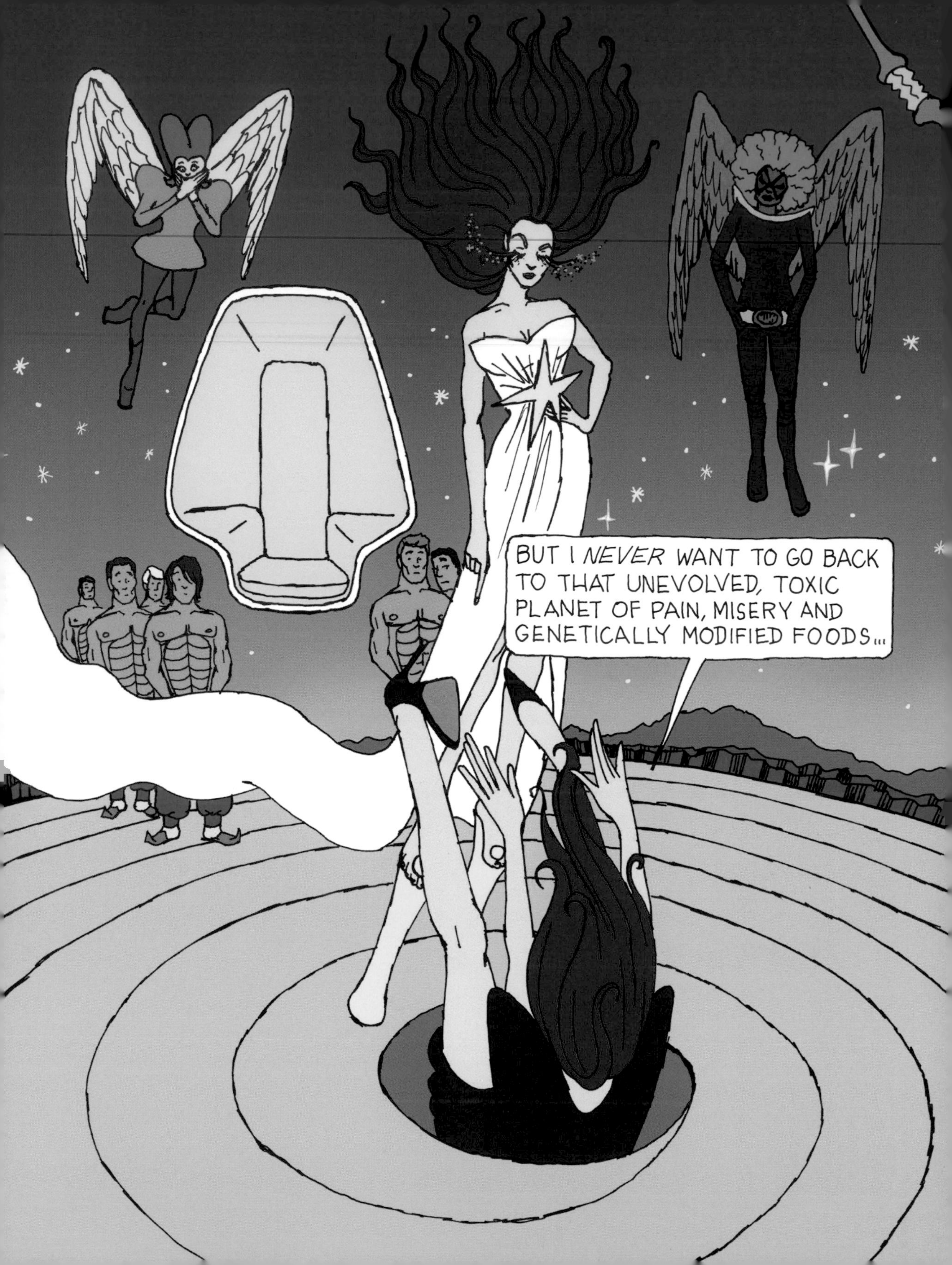
BUT I NEVER WANT TO GO BACK TO THAT UNEVOLVED, TOXIC PLANET OF PAIN, MISERY AND GENETICALLY MODIFIED FOODS...

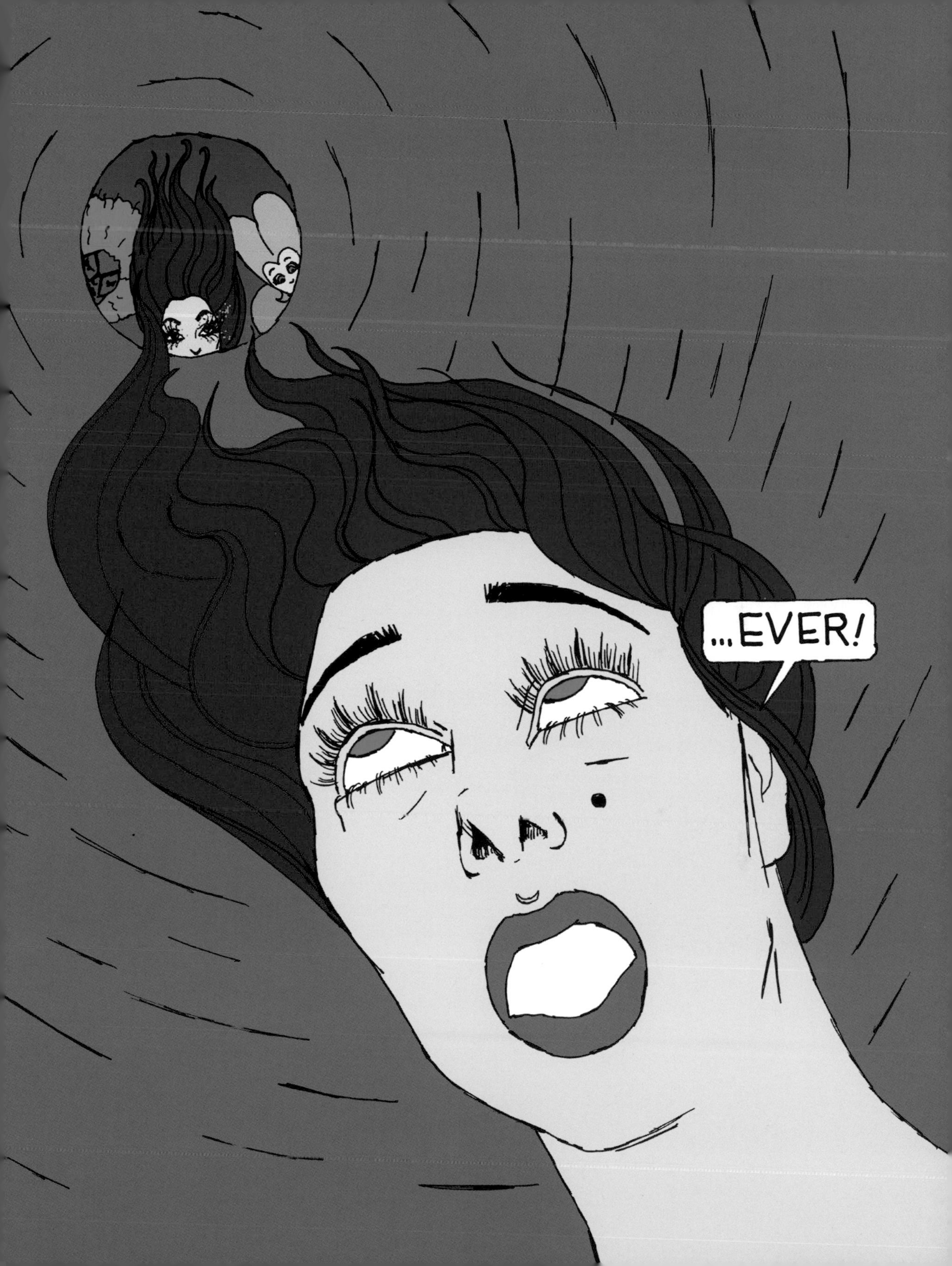
...EVER!

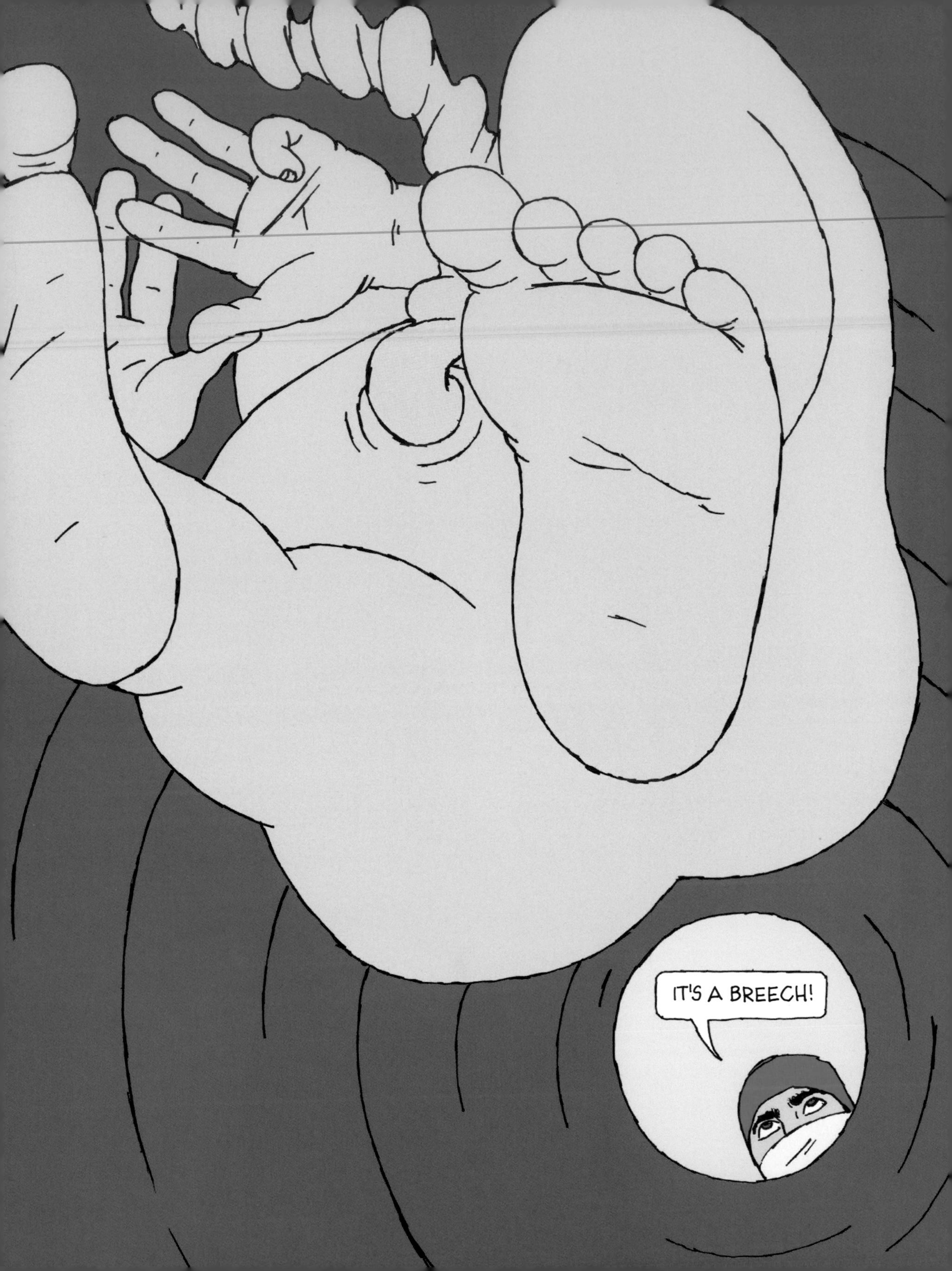
IT'S A BREECH!

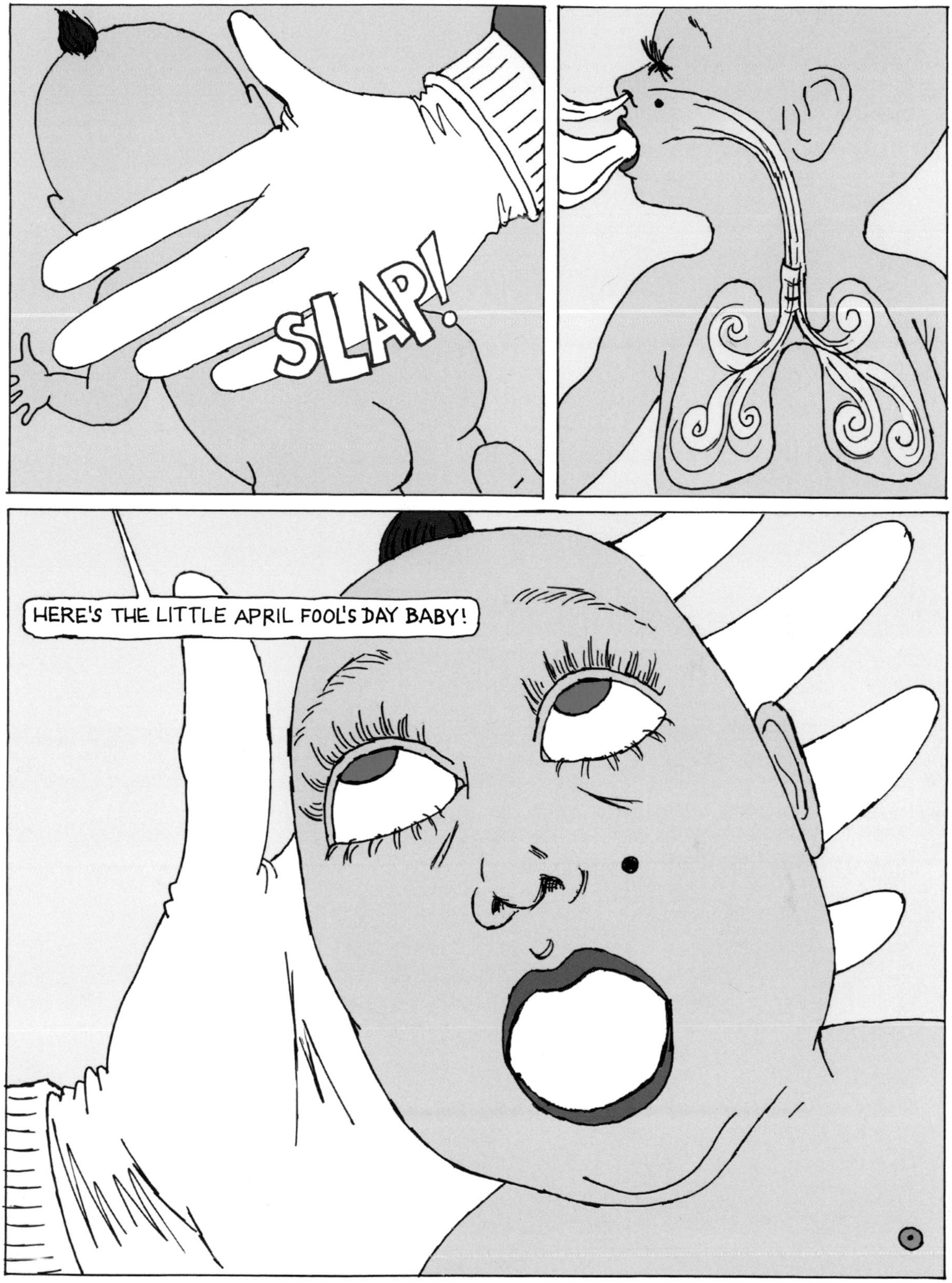
SLAP!
HERE'S THE LITTLE APRIL FOOL'S DAY BABY!

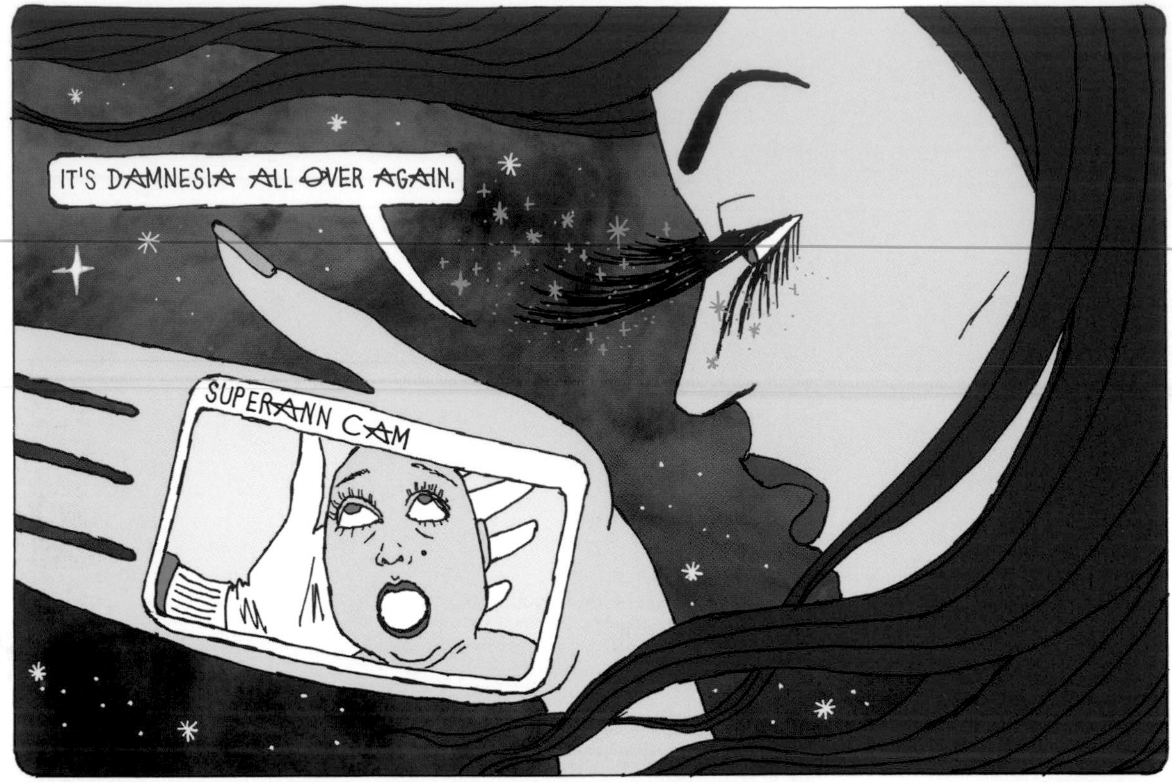
IT'S DAMNESIA ALL OVER AGAIN.
SUPERANN CAM

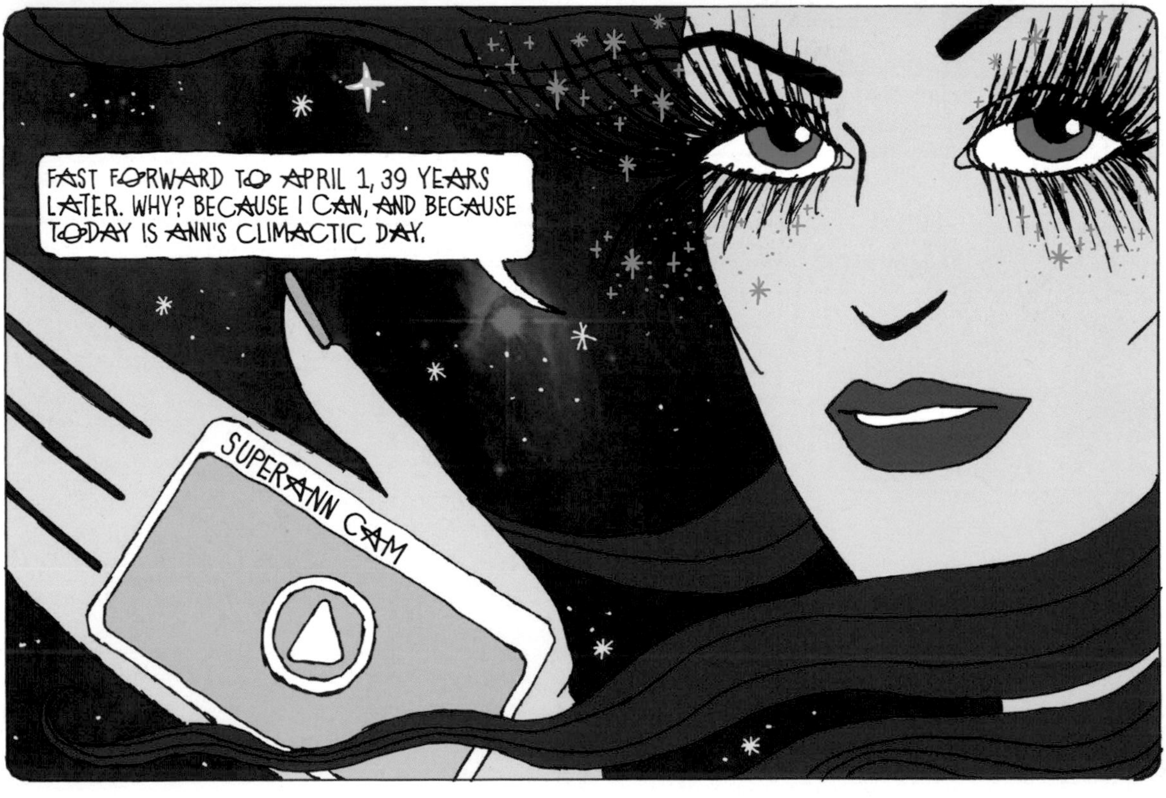
FAST FORWARD TO APRIL 1, 39 YEARS LATER. WHY? BECAUSE I CAN, AND BECAUSE TODAY IS ANN'S CLIMACTIC DAY.
SUPERANN CAM

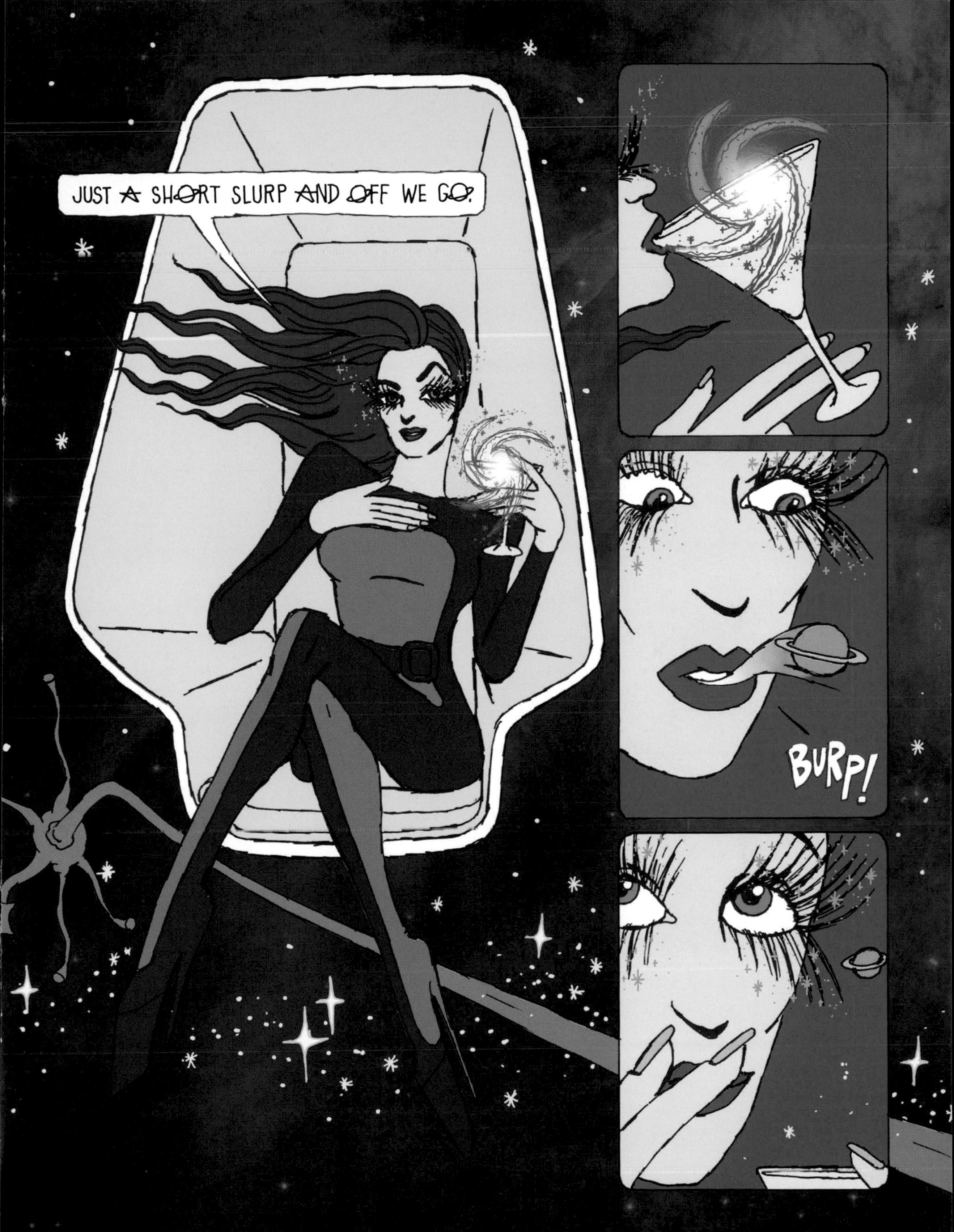
JUST A SHORT SLURP AND OFF WE GO.
BURP!

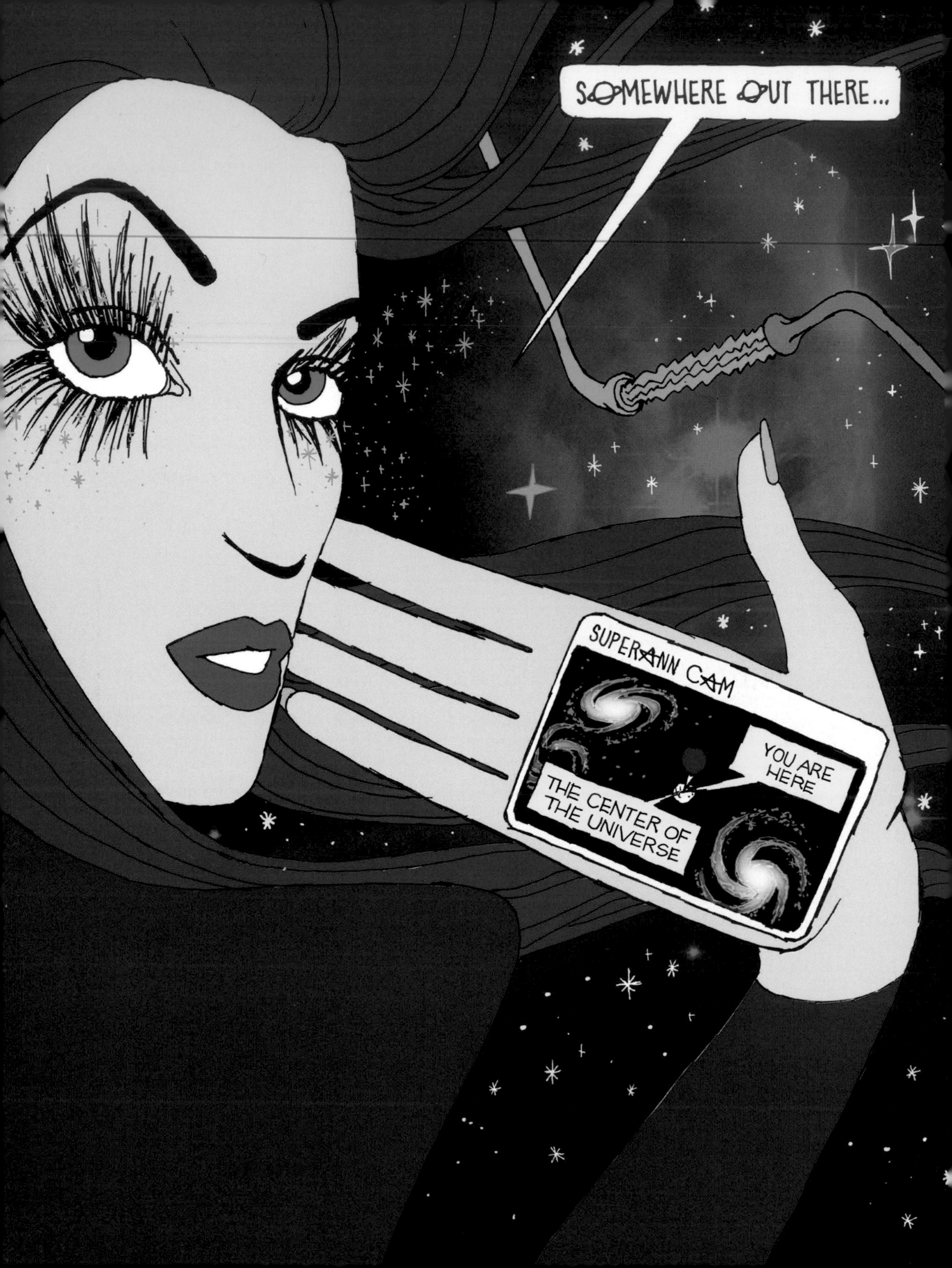
SOMEWHERE OUT THERE...
SUPERANN CAM
YOU ARE HERE
THE CENTER OF THE UNIVERSE

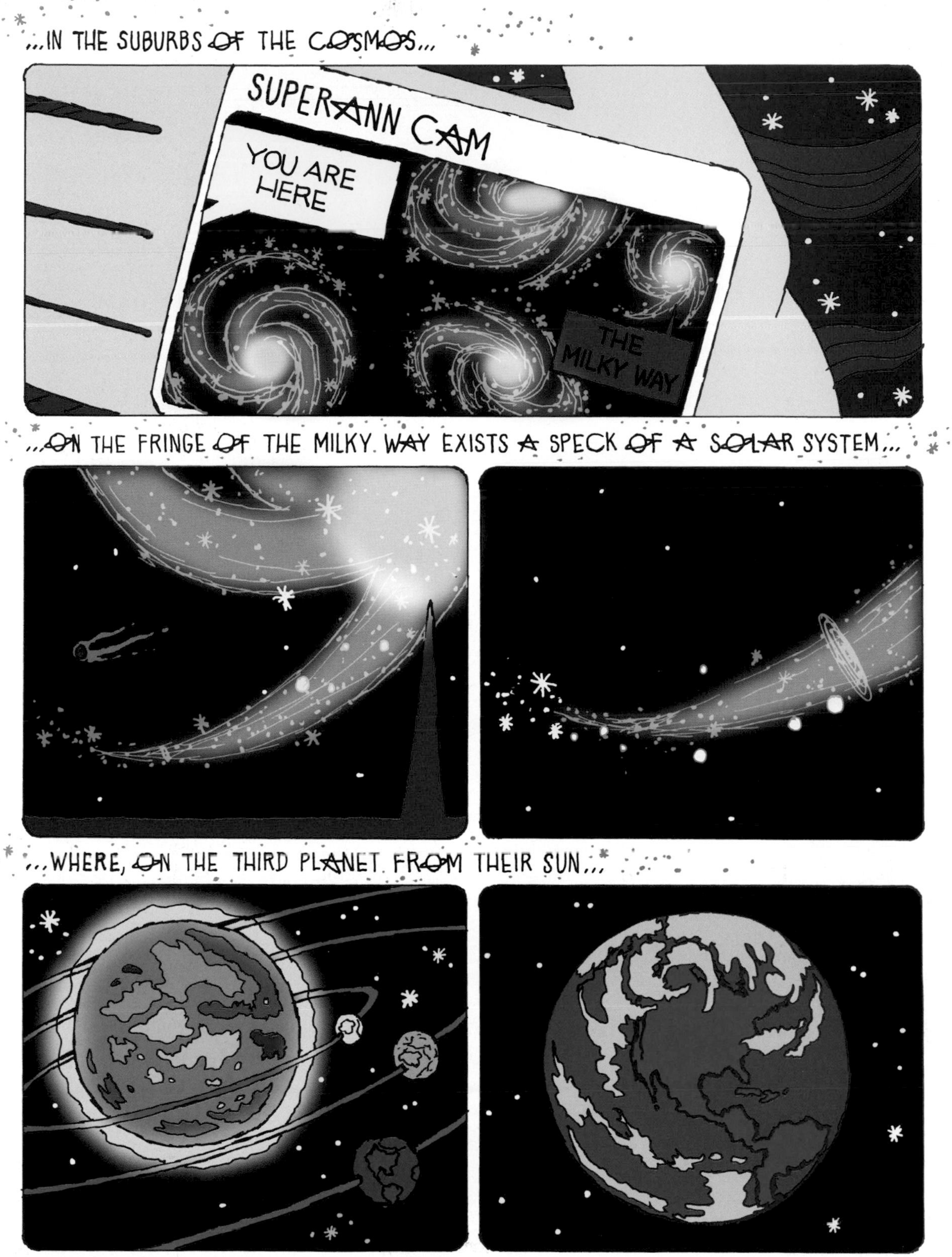
...IN THE SUBURBS OF THE COSMOS...
SUPERANN CAM
YOU ARE HERE
THE MILKY WAY
...ON THE FRINGE OF THE MILKY WAY EXISTS A SPECK OF A SOLAR SYSTEM...
...WHERE, ON THE THIRD PLANET FROM THEIR SUN...

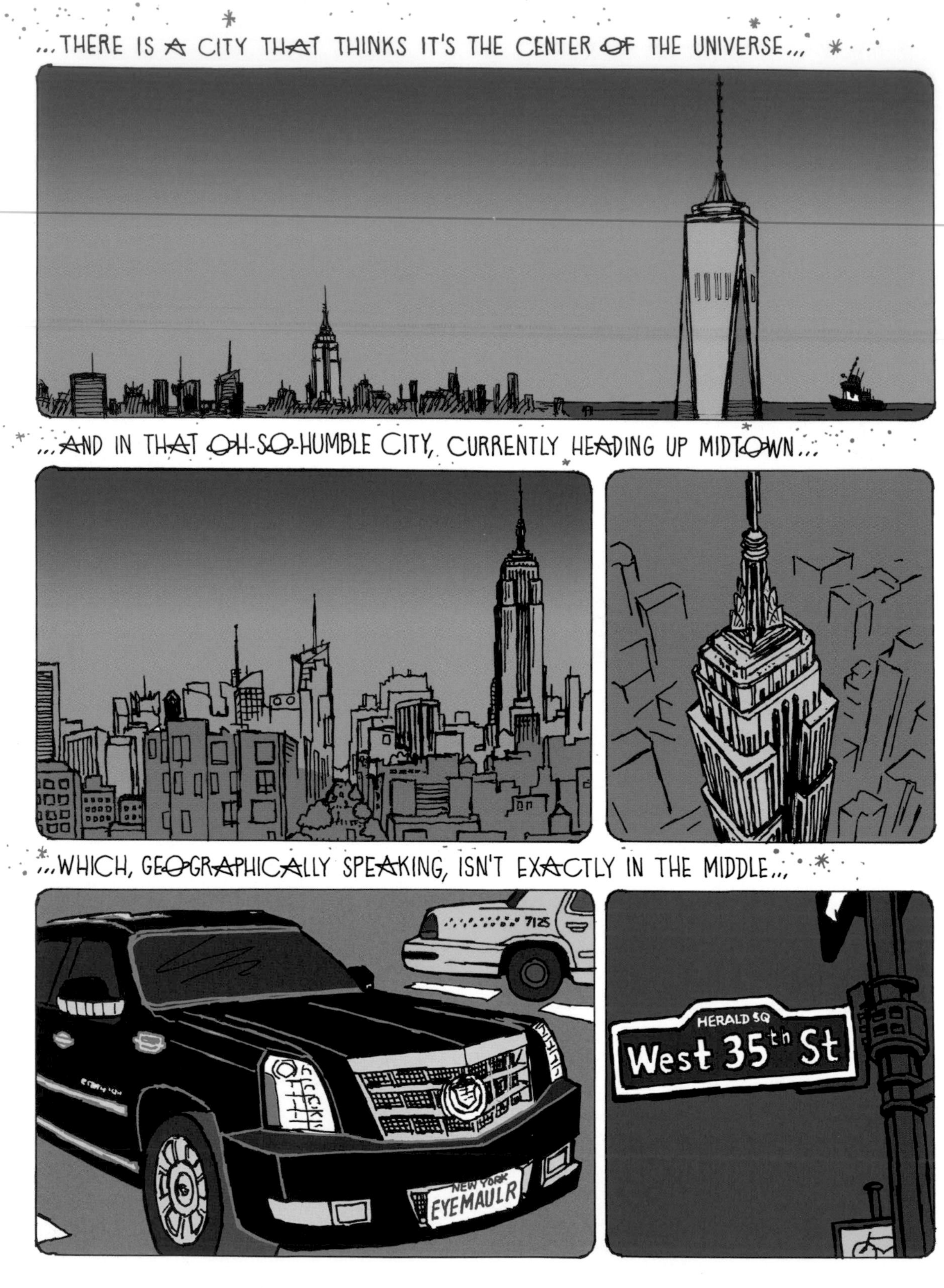
...THERE IS A CITY THAT THINKS IT'S THE CENTER OF THE UNIVERSE...
...AND IN THAT OH-SO-HUMBLE CITY, CURRENTLY HEADING UP MIDTOWN...
...WHICH, GEOGRAPHICALLY SPEAKING, ISN'T EXACTLY IN THE MIDDLE...
7125
NEW YORK
EYEMAULR
HERALD SQ
West 35th St

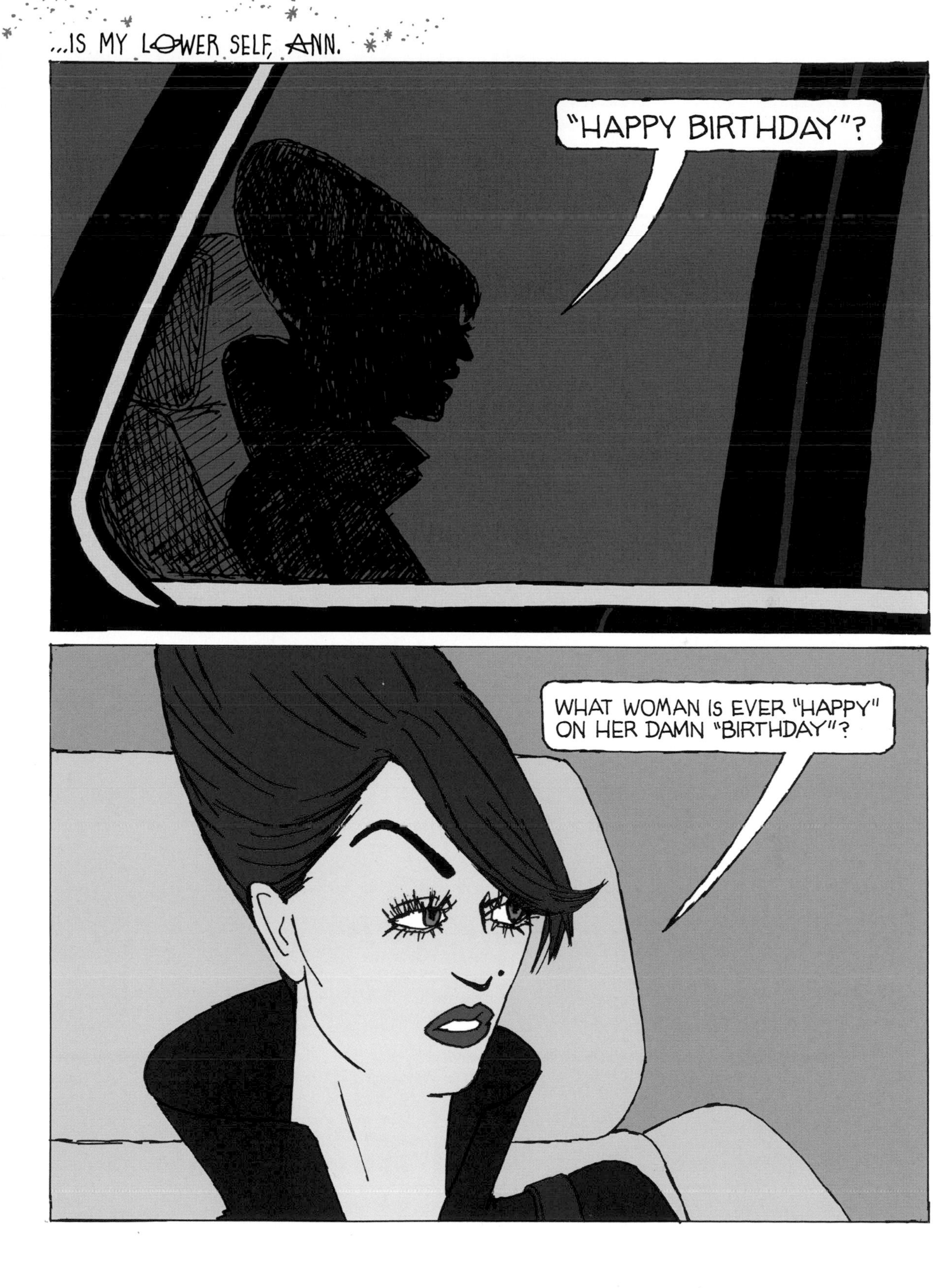
...IS MY LOWER SELF, ANN.
"HAPPY BIRTHDAY"?
WHAT WOMAN IS EVER "HAPPY" ON HER DAMN "BIRTHDAY"?

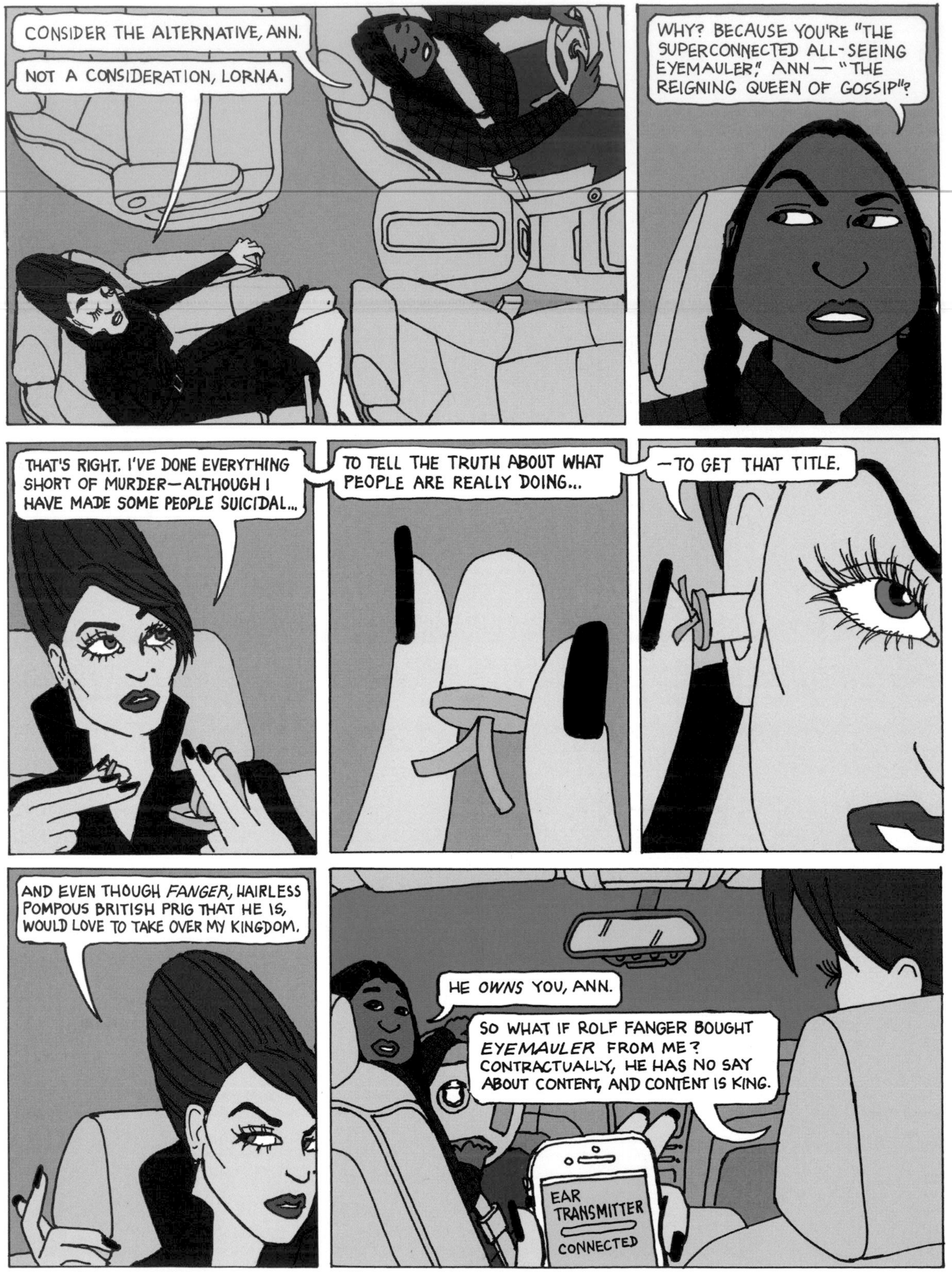

CONSIDER THE ALTERNATIVE, ANN.
NOT A CONSIDERATION, LORNA.
WHY? BECAUSE YOU'RE "THE SUPERCONNECTED ALL-SEEING EYEMAULER," ANN — "THE REIGNING QUEEN OF GOSSIP"?
THAT'S RIGHT. I'VE DONE EVERYTHING SHORT OF MURDER—ALTHOUGH I HAVE MADE SOME PEOPLE SUICIDAL...
TO TELL THE TRUTH ABOUT WHAT PEOPLE ARE REALLY DOING...
—TO GET THAT TITLE.
AND EVEN THOUGH *FANGER*, HAIRLESS POMPOUS BRITISH PRIG THAT HE IS, WOULD LOVE TO TAKE OVER MY KINGDOM.
HE *OWNS* YOU, ANN.
SO WHAT IF ROLF FANGER BOUGHT *EYEMAULER* FROM ME? CONTRACTUALLY, HE HAS NO SAY ABOUT CONTENT, AND CONTENT IS KING.
EAR TRANSMITTER
CONNECTED

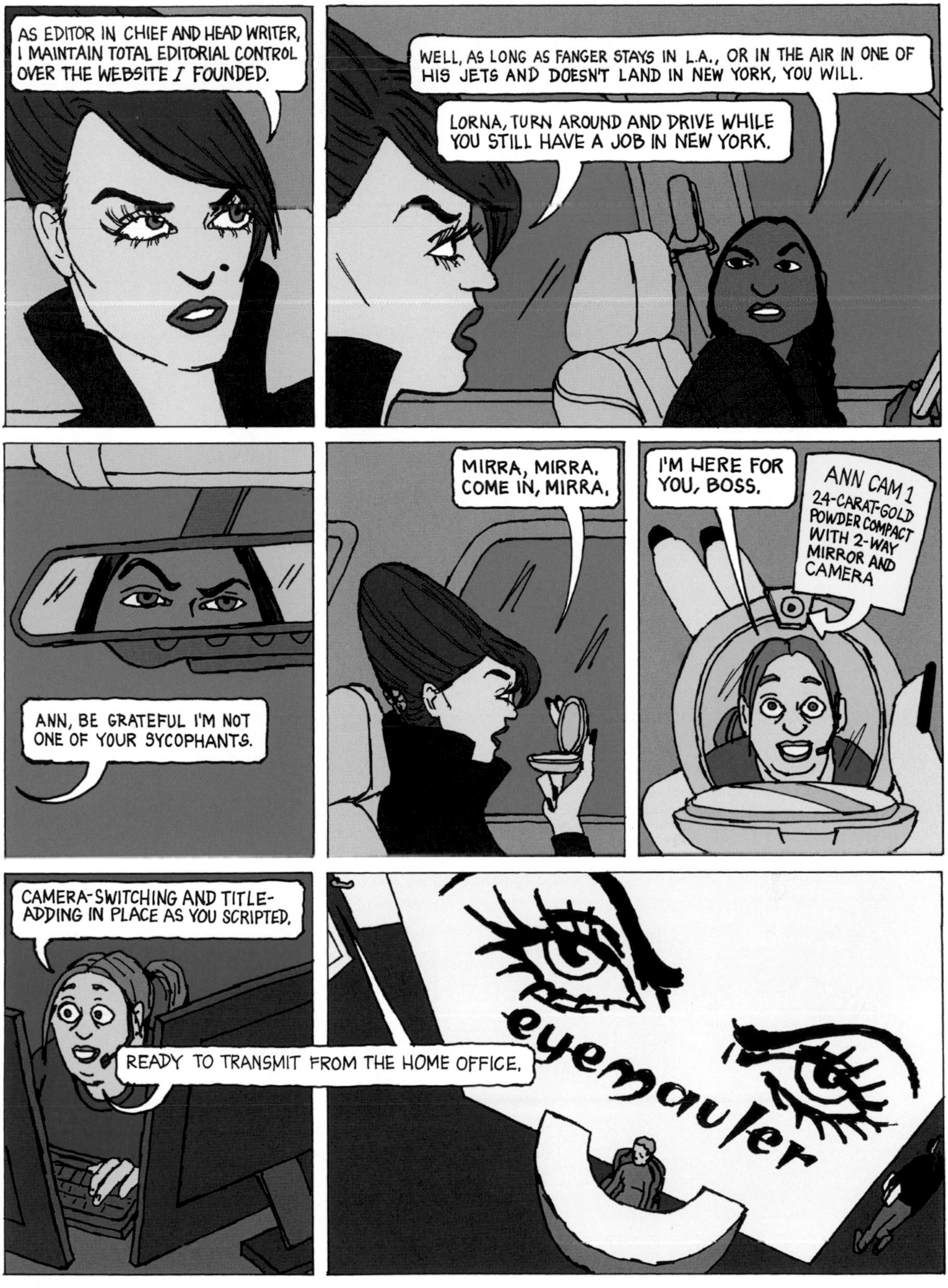
AS EDITOR IN CHIEF AND HEAD WRITER, I MAINTAIN TOTAL EDITORIAL CONTROL OVER THE WEBSITE I FOUNDED.
WELL, AS LONG AS FANGER STAYS IN L.A., OR IN THE AIR IN ONE OF HIS JETS AND DOESN'T LAND IN NEW YORK, YOU WILL.
LORNA, TURN AROUND AND DRIVE WHILE YOU STILL HAVE A JOB IN NEW YORK.
ANN, BE GRATEFUL I'M NOT ONE OF YOUR SYCOPHANTS.
MIRRA, MIRRA. COME IN, MIRRA.
I'M HERE FOR YOU, BOSS.
ANN CAM 1 24-CARAT-GOLD POWDER COMPACT WITH 2-WAY MIRROR AND CAMERA
CAMERA-SWITCHING AND TITLE-ADDING IN PLACE AS YOU SCRIPTED.
READY TO TRANSMIT FROM THE HOME OFFICE.
eyemauler

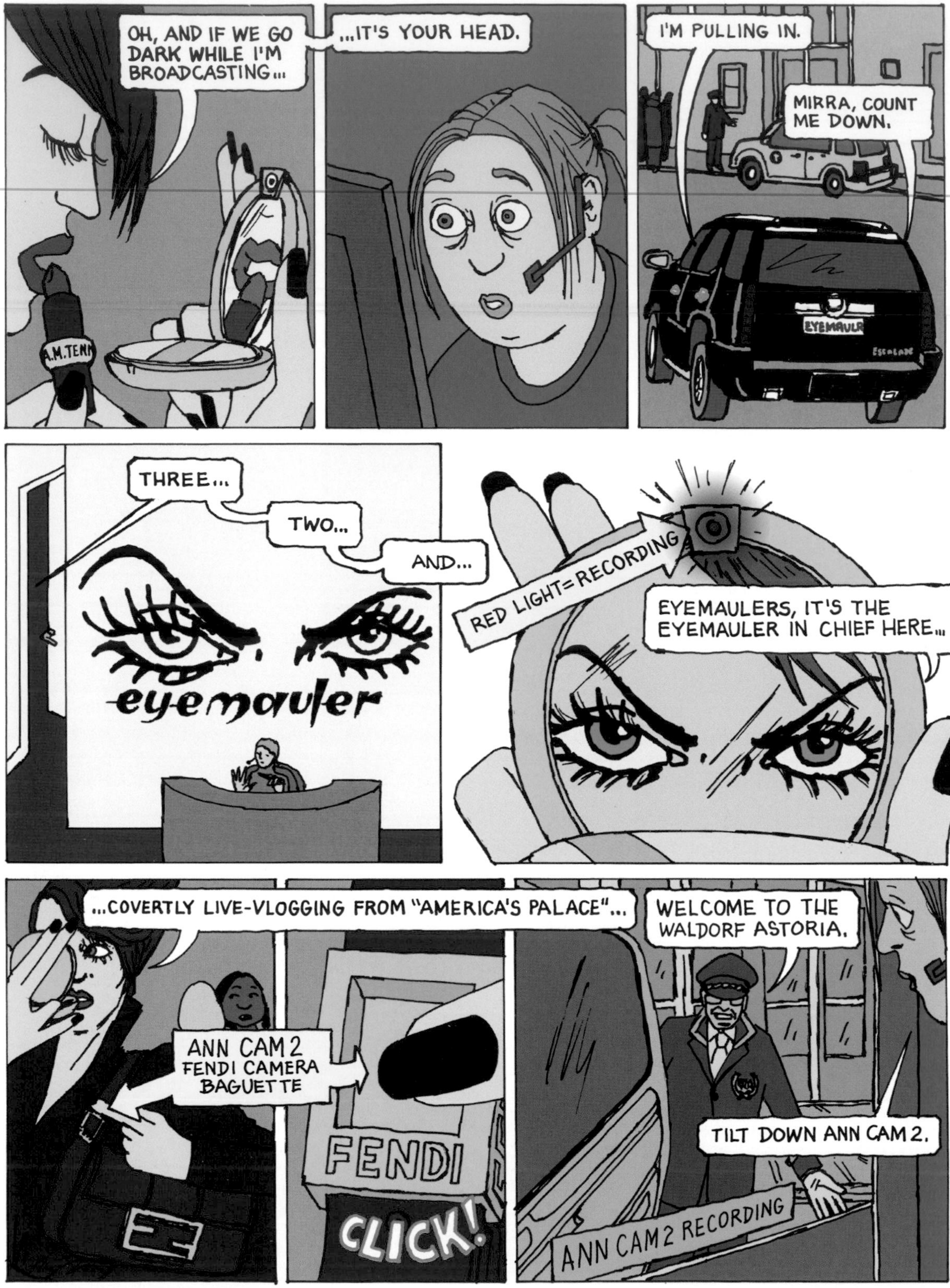
OH, AND IF WE GO DARK WHILE I'M BROADCASTING...
A.M.TENN
...IT'S YOUR HEAD.
I'M PULLING IN.
MIRRA, COUNT ME DOWN.
EYEMAULR
ESCALADE
THREE...
TWO...
AND...
eyemauler
RED LIGHT=RECORDING
EYEMAULERS, IT'S THE EYEMAULER IN CHIEF HERE...
...COVERTLY LIVE-VLOGGING FROM "AMERICA'S PALACE"...
ANN CAM 2 FENDI CAMERA BAGUETTE
FENDI
CLICK!
WELCOME TO THE WALDORF ASTORIA.
TILT DOWN ANN CAM 2.
ANN CAM 2 RECORDING

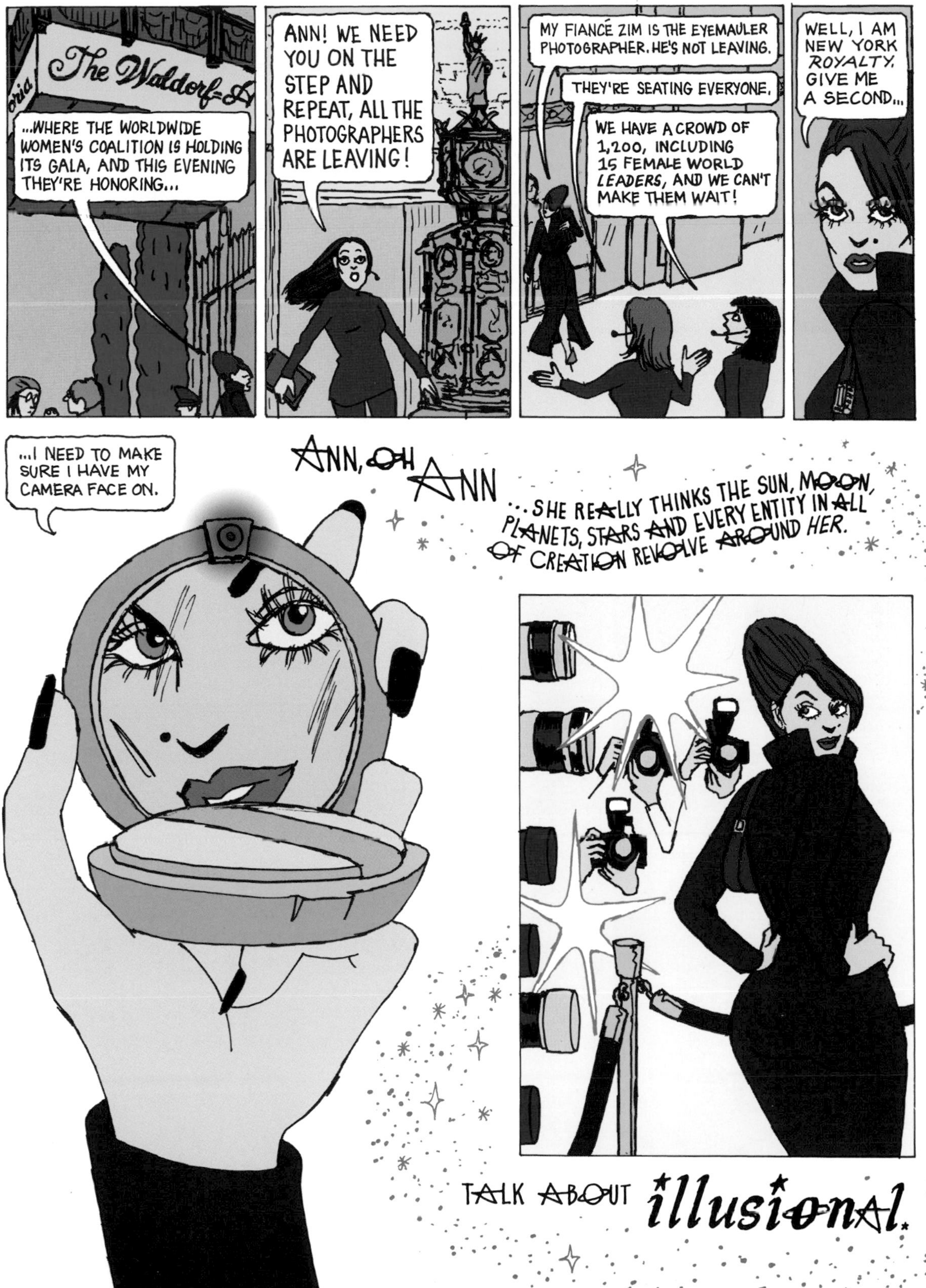
The Waldorf-A
...WHERE THE WORLDWIDE WOMEN'S COALITION IS HOLDING ITS GALA, AND THIS EVENING THEY'RE HONORING...
ANN! WE NEED YOU ON THE STEP AND REPEAT, ALL THE PHOTOGRAPHERS ARE LEAVING!
MY FIANCÉ ZIM IS THE EYEMAULER PHOTOGRAPHER. HE'S NOT LEAVING.
THEY'RE SEATING EVERYONE.
WE HAVE A CROWD OF 1,200, INCLUDING 15 FEMALE WORLD LEADERS, AND WE CAN'T MAKE THEM WAIT!
WELL, I AM NEW YORK ROYALTY. GIVE ME A SECOND...
...I NEED TO MAKE SURE I HAVE MY CAMERA FACE ON.
ANN, OH ANN
...SHE REALLY THINKS THE SUN, MOON, PLANETS, STARS AND EVERY ENTITY IN ALL OF CREATION REVOLVE AROUND HER.
TALK ABOUT illusional.

SPEAKING OF WHICH...

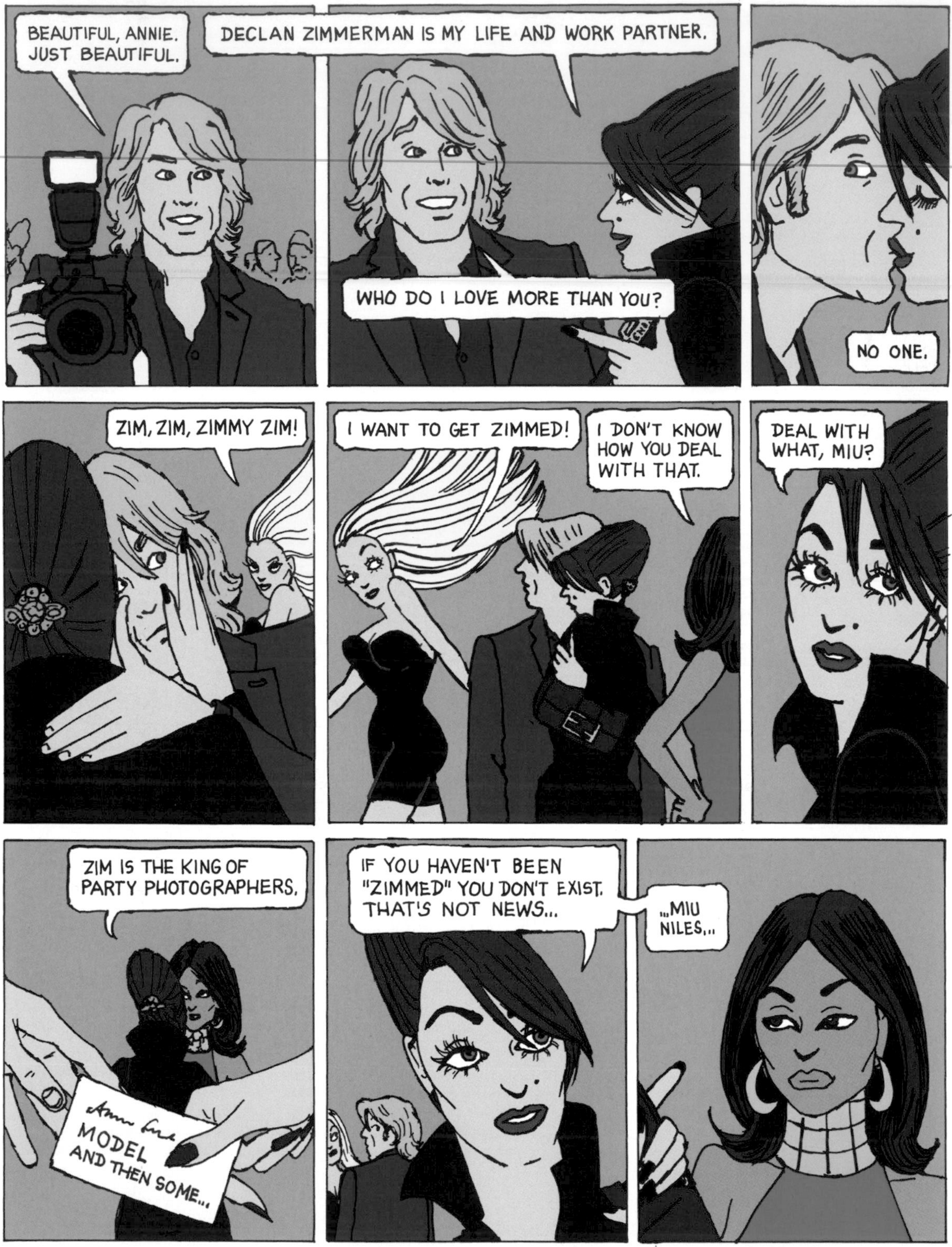
BEAUTIFUL, ANNIE. JUST BEAUTIFUL.
DECLAN ZIMMERMAN IS MY LIFE AND WORK PARTNER.
WHO DO I LOVE MORE THAN YOU?
NO ONE.
ZIM, ZIM, ZIMMY ZIM!
I WANT TO GET ZIMMED!
I DON'T KNOW HOW YOU DEAL WITH THAT.
DEAL WITH WHAT, MIU?
ZIM IS THE KING OF PARTY PHOTOGRAPHERS.
MODEL AND THEN SOME...
IF YOU HAVEN'T BEEN "ZIMMED" YOU DON'T EXIST. THAT'S NOT NEWS...
...MIU NILES,...

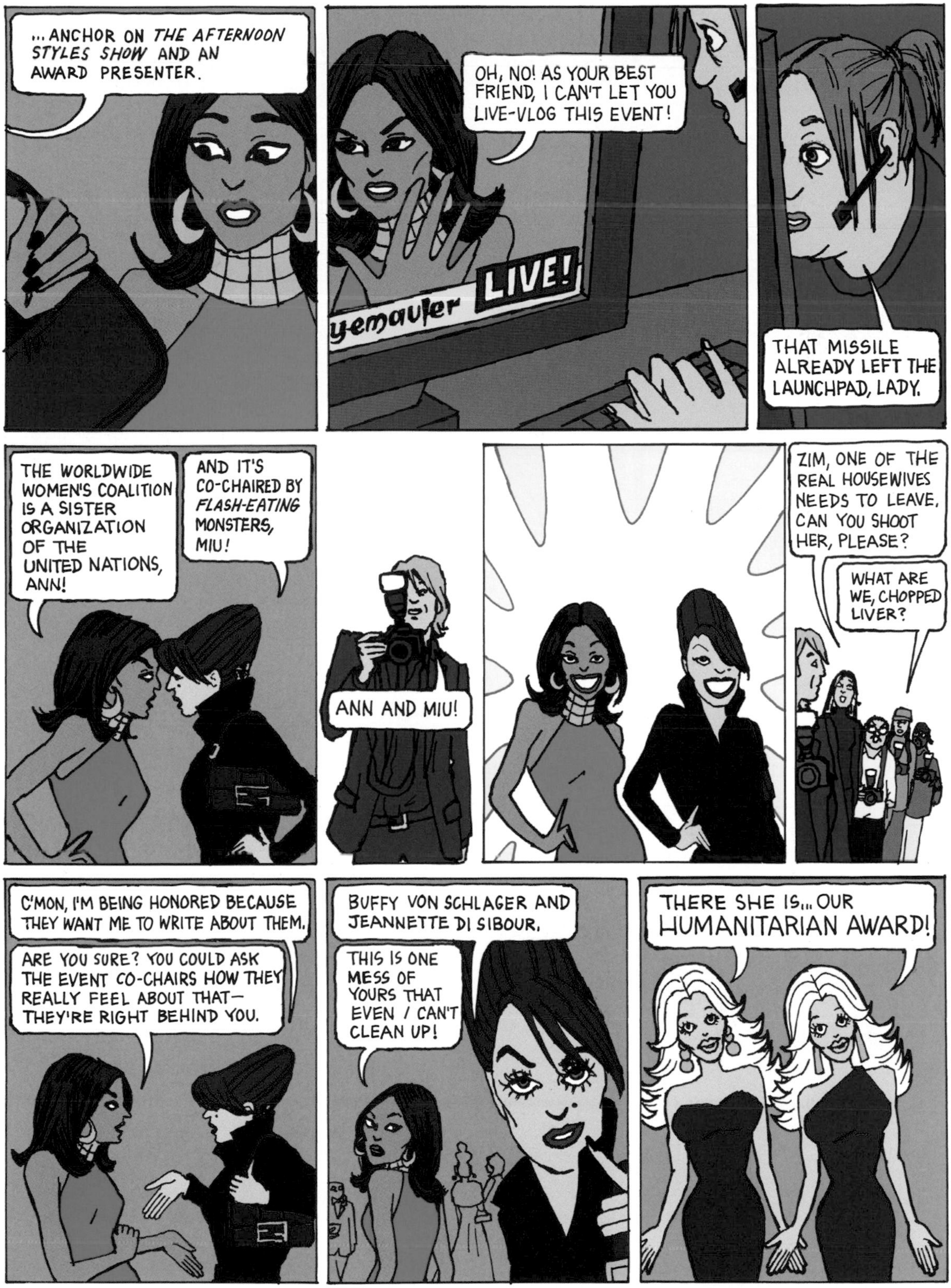
...ANCHOR ON *THE AFTERNOON STYLES SHOW* AND AN AWARD PRESENTER.
OH, NO! AS YOUR BEST FRIEND, I CAN'T LET YOU LIVE-VLOG THIS EVENT!
LIVE!
THAT MISSILE ALREADY LEFT THE LAUNCHPAD, LADY.
THE WORLDWIDE WOMEN'S COALITION IS A SISTER ORGANIZATION OF THE UNITED NATIONS, ANN!
AND IT'S CO-CHAIRED BY *FLASH-EATING* MONSTERS, MIU!
ANN AND MIU!
ZIM, ONE OF THE REAL HOUSEWIVES NEEDS TO LEAVE. CAN YOU SHOOT HER, PLEASE?
WHAT ARE WE, CHOPPED LIVER?
C'MON, I'M BEING HONORED BECAUSE THEY WANT ME TO WRITE ABOUT THEM.
ARE YOU SURE? YOU COULD ASK THE EVENT CO-CHAIRS HOW THEY REALLY FEEL ABOUT THAT— THEY'RE RIGHT BEHIND YOU.
BUFFY VON SCHLAGER AND JEANNETTE DI SIBOUR.
THIS IS ONE MESS OF YOURS THAT EVEN *I* CAN'T CLEAN UP!
THERE SHE IS... OUR HUMANITARIAN AWARD!

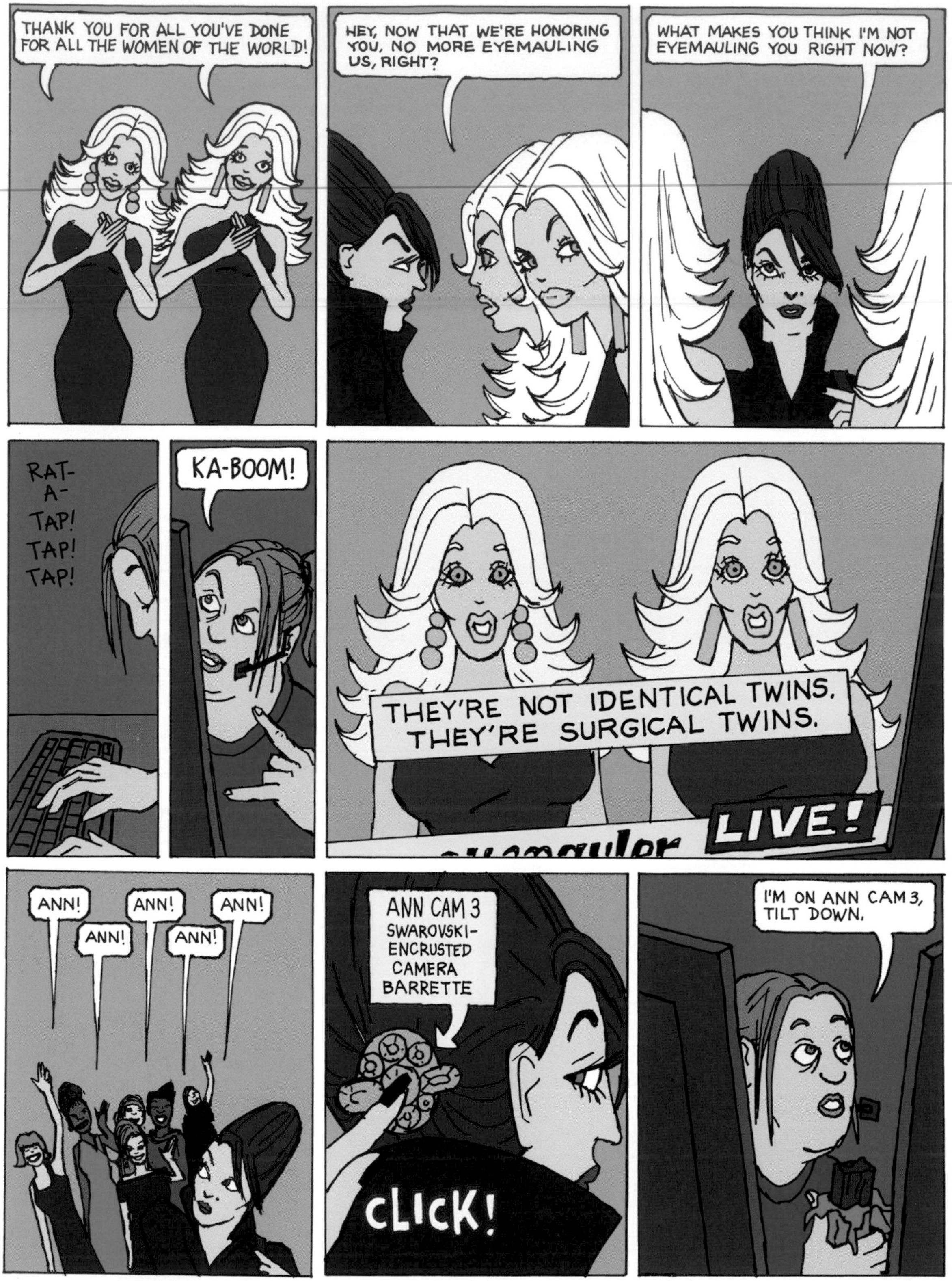
THANK YOU FOR ALL YOU'VE DONE FOR ALL THE WOMEN OF THE WORLD!
HEY, NOW THAT WE'RE HONORING YOU, NO MORE EYEMAULING US, RIGHT?
WHAT MAKES YOU THINK I'M NOT EYEMAULING YOU RIGHT NOW?
RAT-A-TAP! TAP! TAP!
KA-BOOM!
THEY'RE NOT IDENTICAL TWINS. THEY'RE SURGICAL TWINS.
LIVE!
ANN!
ANN!
ANN!
ANN!
ANN!
ANN CAM 3 SWAROVSKI-ENCRUSTED CAMERA BARRETTE
CLICK!
I'M ON ANN CAM 3, TILT DOWN.

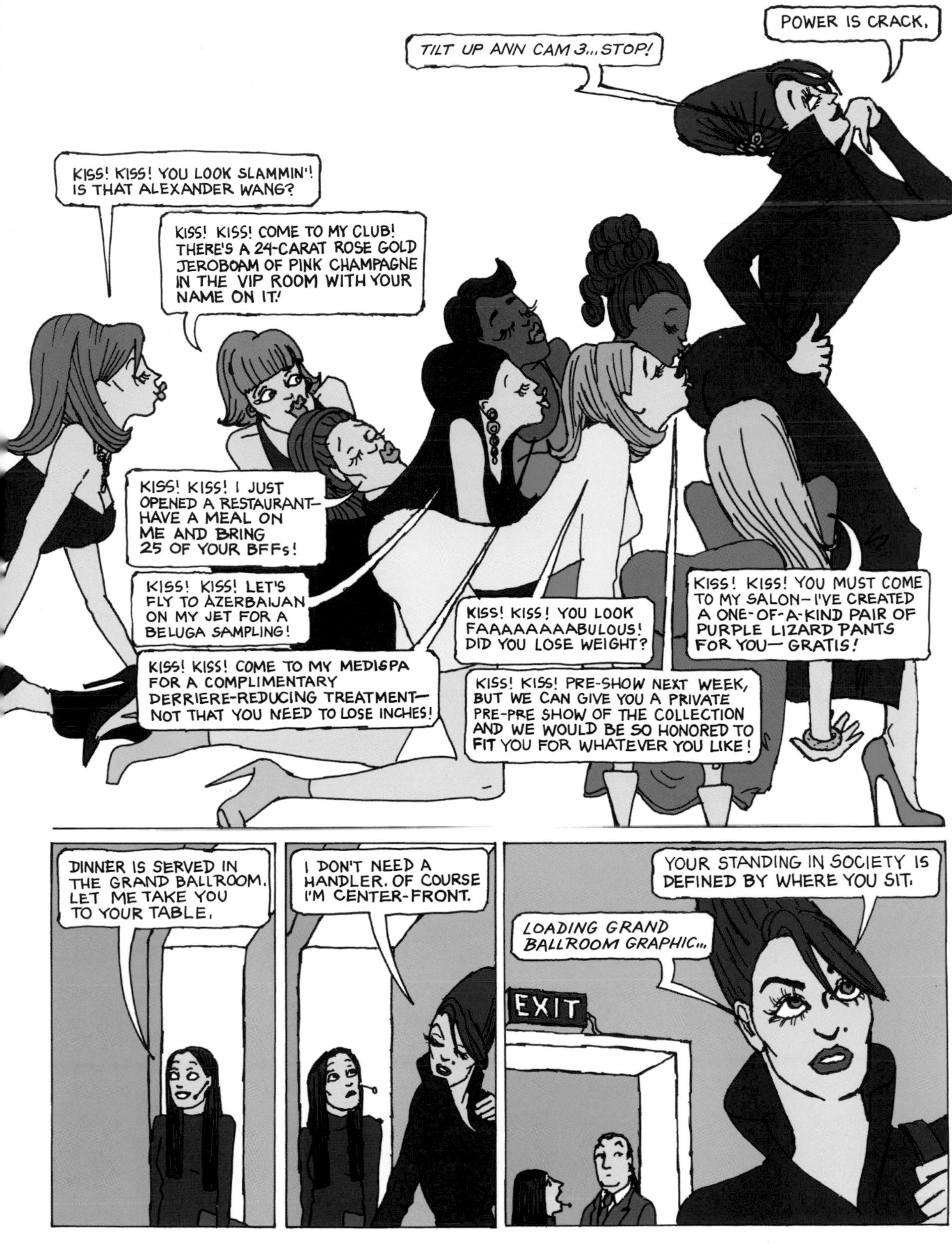
TILT UP ANN CAM 3...STOP!
POWER IS CRACK.
KISS! KISS! YOU LOOK SLAMMIN'! IS THAT ALEXANDER WANG?
KISS! KISS! COME TO MY CLUB! THERE'S A 24-CARAT ROSE GOLD JEROBOAM OF PINK CHAMPAGNE IN THE VIP ROOM WITH YOUR NAME ON IT!
KISS! KISS! I JUST OPENED A RESTAURANT— HAVE A MEAL ON ME AND BRING 25 OF YOUR BFFs!
KISS! KISS! LET'S FLY TO AZERBAIJAN ON MY JET FOR A BELUGA SAMPLING!
KISS! KISS! COME TO MY MEDISPA FOR A COMPLIMENTARY DERRIERE-REDUCING TREATMENT— NOT THAT YOU NEED TO LOSE INCHES!
KISS! KISS! YOU LOOK FAAAAAAAABULOUS! DID YOU LOSE WEIGHT?
KISS! KISS! PRE-SHOW NEXT WEEK, BUT WE CAN GIVE YOU A PRIVATE PRE-PRE SHOW OF THE COLLECTION AND WE WOULD BE SO HONORED TO FIT YOU FOR WHATEVER YOU LIKE!
KISS! KISS! YOU MUST COME TO MY SALON— I'VE CREATED A ONE-OF-A-KIND PAIR OF PURPLE LIZARD PANTS FOR YOU— GRATIS!
DINNER IS SERVED IN THE GRAND BALLROOM. LET ME TAKE YOU TO YOUR TABLE.
I DON'T NEED A HANDLER. OF COURSE I'M CENTER-FRONT.
YOUR STANDING IN SOCIETY IS DEFINED BY WHERE YOU SIT.
LOADING GRAND BALLROOM GRAPHIC...
EXIT

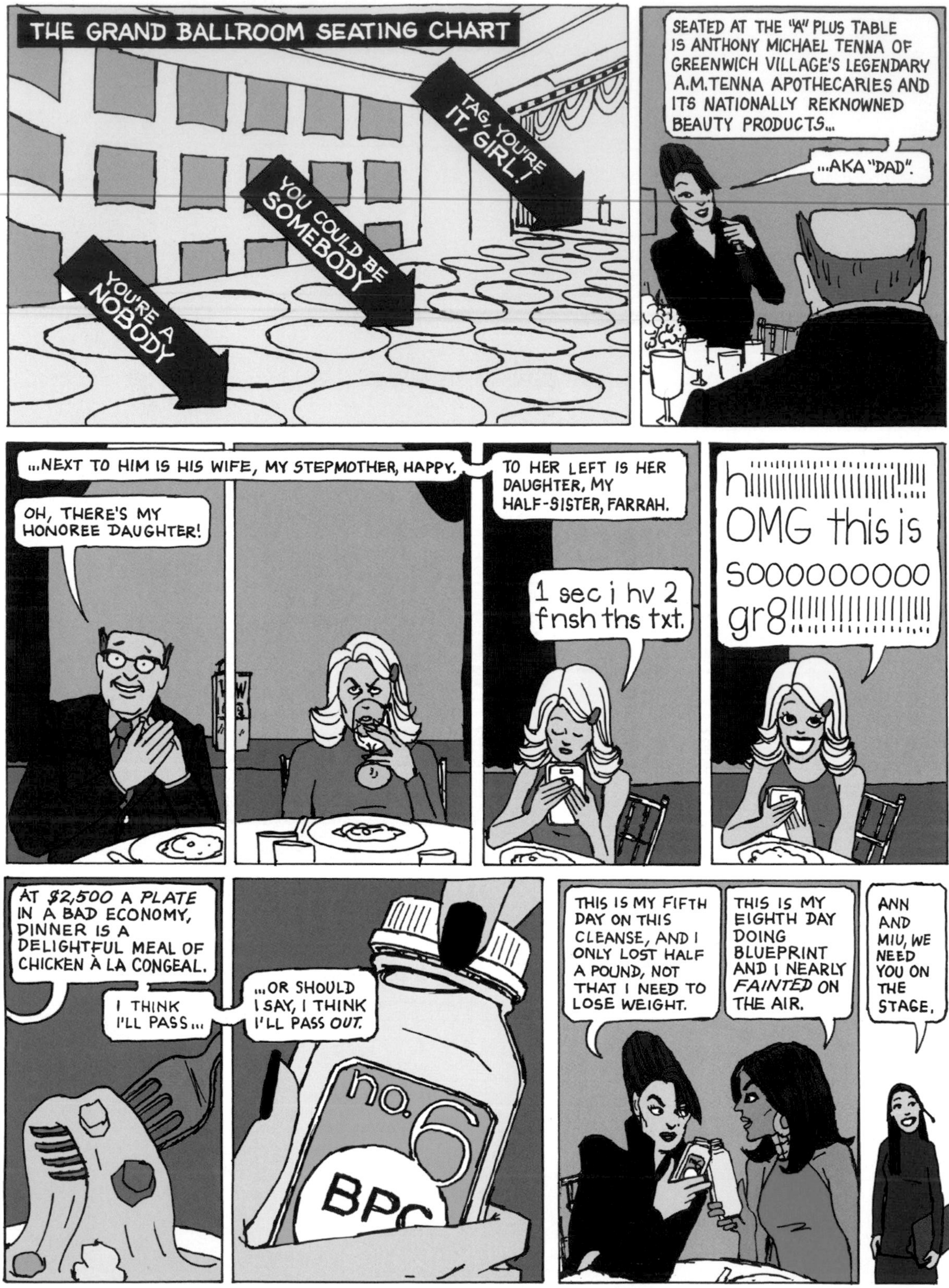
THE GRAND BALLROOM SEATING CHART
TAG, YOU'RE IT, GIRL!
YOU COULD BE SOMEBODY
YOU'RE A NOBODY
SEATED AT THE "A" PLUS TABLE IS ANTHONY MICHAEL TENNA OF GREENWICH VILLAGE'S LEGENDARY A.M.TENNA APOTHECARIES AND ITS NATIONALLY REKNOWNED BEAUTY PRODUCTS...
...AKA "DAD".
...NEXT TO HIM IS HIS WIFE, MY STEPMOTHER, HAPPY.
OH, THERE'S MY HONOREE DAUGHTER!
TO HER LEFT IS HER DAUGHTER, MY HALF-SISTER, FARRAH.
1 sec i hv 2 fnsh ths txt.
hiiiiiiiiiiiiiiiiiiiiii!!!!!! OMG this is sooooooooo gr8!!!!!!!!!!!!!!!!!!!!!
AT $2,500 A PLATE IN A BAD ECONOMY, DINNER IS A DELIGHTFUL MEAL OF CHICKEN À LA CONGEAL.
I THINK I'LL PASS...
...OR SHOULD I SAY, I THINK I'LL PASS OUT.
no. 6
BPC
THIS IS MY FIFTH DAY ON THIS CLEANSE, AND I ONLY LOST HALF A POUND, NOT THAT I NEED TO LOSE WEIGHT.
THIS IS MY EIGHTH DAY DOING BLUEPRINT AND I NEARLY FAINTED ON THE AIR.
ANN AND MIU, WE NEED YOU ON THE STAGE.

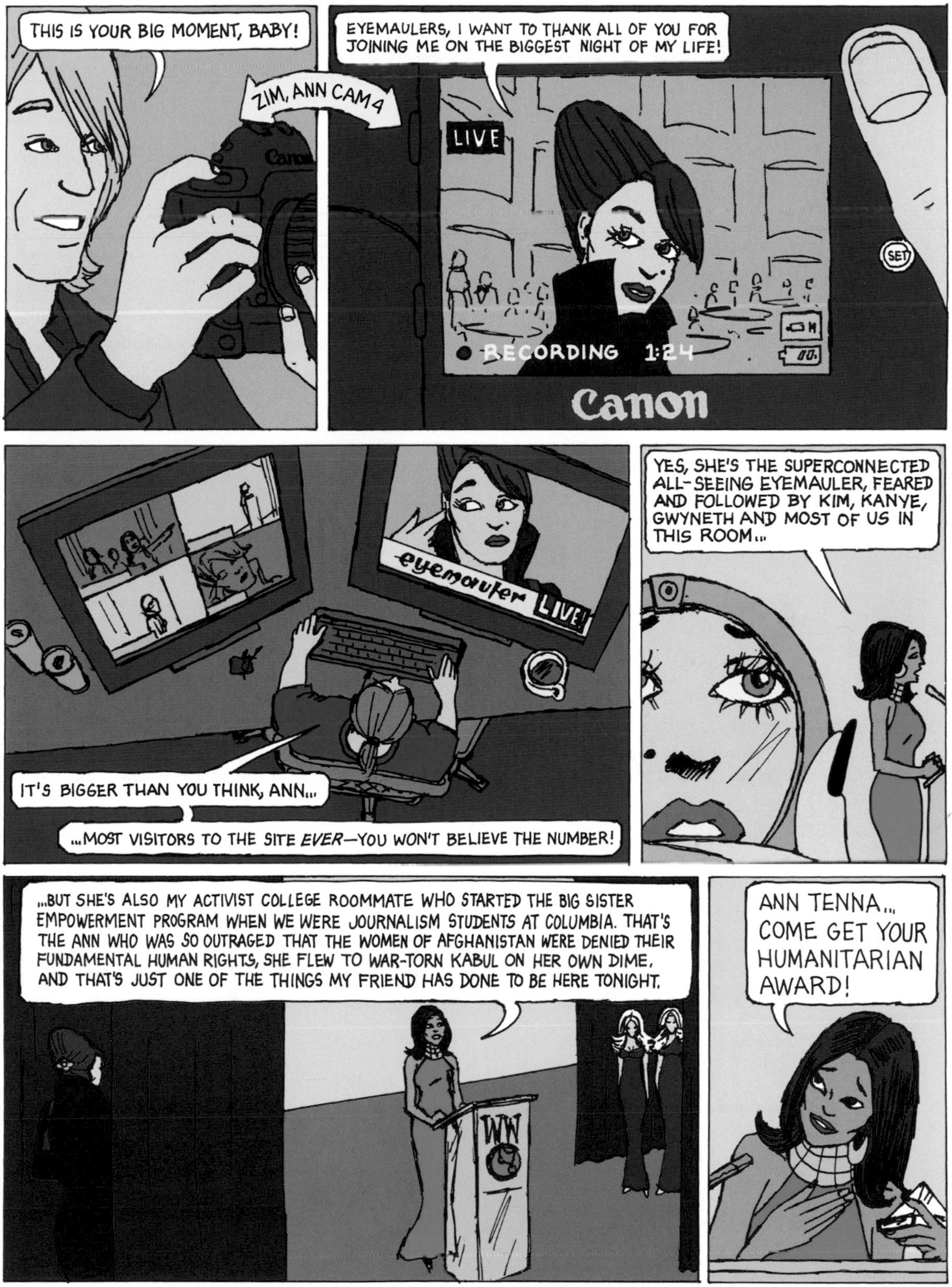
THIS IS YOUR BIG MOMENT, BABY!
ZIM, ANN CAM 4
EYEMAULERS, I WANT TO THANK ALL OF YOU FOR JOINING ME ON THE BIGGEST NIGHT OF MY LIFE!
LIVE
RECORDING 1:24
SET
Canon
eyemauler LIVE
IT'S BIGGER THAN YOU THINK, ANN...
...MOST VISITORS TO THE SITE *EVER*—YOU WON'T BELIEVE THE NUMBER!
YES, SHE'S THE SUPERCONNECTED ALL-SEEING EYEMAULER, FEARED AND FOLLOWED BY KIM, KANYE, GWYNETH AND MOST OF US IN THIS ROOM...
...BUT SHE'S ALSO MY ACTIVIST COLLEGE ROOMMATE WHO STARTED THE BIG SISTER EMPOWERMENT PROGRAM WHEN WE WERE JOURNALISM STUDENTS AT COLUMBIA. THAT'S THE ANN WHO WAS SO OUTRAGED THAT THE WOMEN OF AFGHANISTAN WERE DENIED THEIR FUNDAMENTAL HUMAN RIGHTS, SHE FLEW TO WAR-TORN KABUL ON HER OWN DIME, AND THAT'S JUST ONE OF THE THINGS MY FRIEND HAS DONE TO BE HERE TONIGHT.
WW
ANN TENNA... COME GET YOUR HUMANITARIAN AWARD!

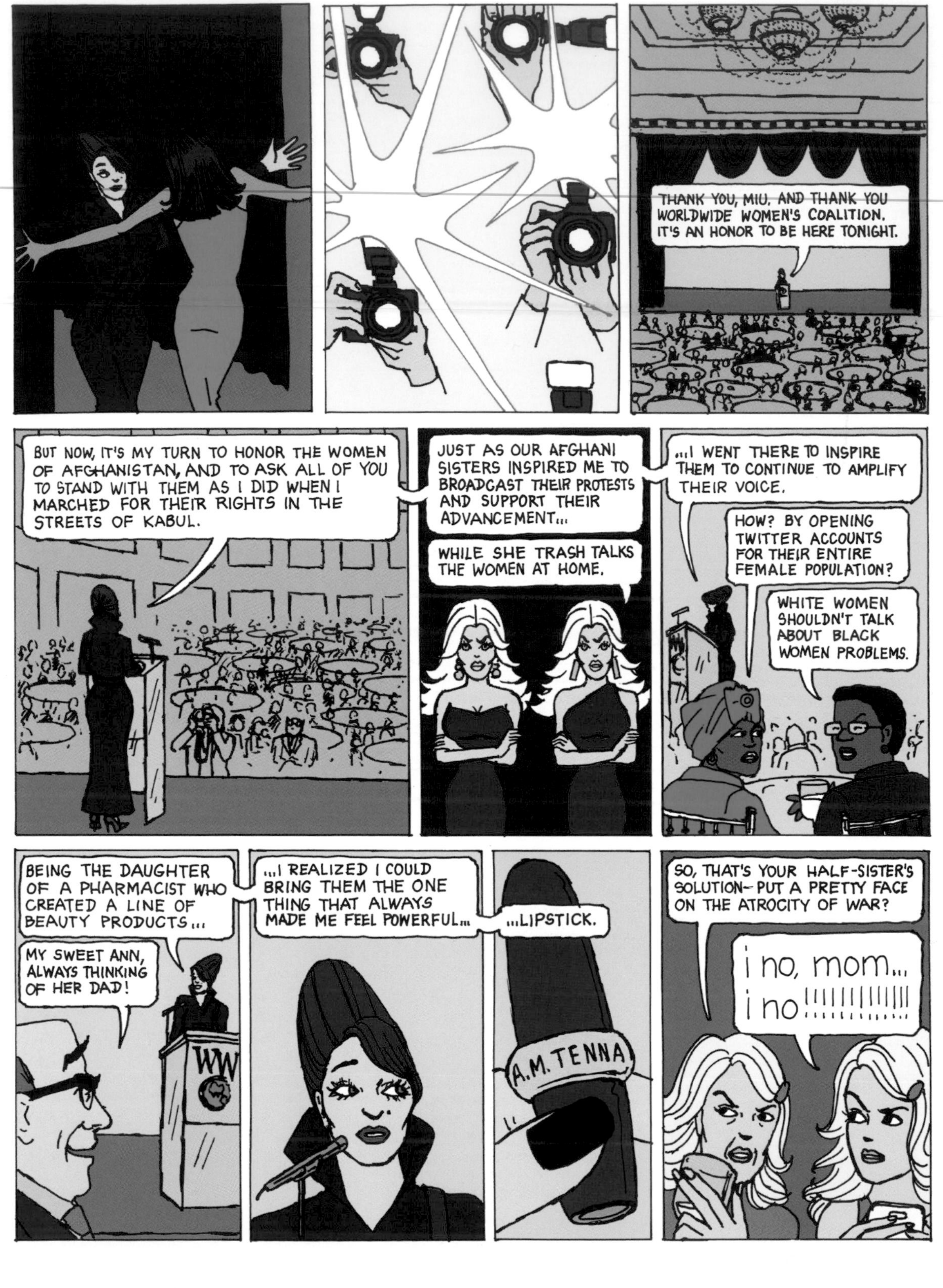

THANK YOU, MIU, AND THANK YOU WORLDWIDE WOMEN'S COALITION. IT'S AN HONOR TO BE HERE TONIGHT.
BUT NOW, IT'S MY TURN TO HONOR THE WOMEN OF AFGHANISTAN, AND TO ASK ALL OF YOU TO STAND WITH THEM AS I DID WHEN I MARCHED FOR THEIR RIGHTS IN THE STREETS OF KABUL.
JUST AS OUR AFGHANI SISTERS INSPIRED ME TO BROADCAST THEIR PROTESTS AND SUPPORT THEIR ADVANCEMENT...
WHILE SHE TRASH TALKS THE WOMEN AT HOME.
...I WENT THERE TO INSPIRE THEM TO CONTINUE TO AMPLIFY THEIR VOICE.
HOW? BY OPENING TWITTER ACCOUNTS FOR THEIR ENTIRE FEMALE POPULATION?
WHITE WOMEN SHOULDN'T TALK ABOUT BLACK WOMEN PROBLEMS.
BEING THE DAUGHTER OF A PHARMACIST WHO CREATED A LINE OF BEAUTY PRODUCTS...
MY SWEET ANN, ALWAYS THINKING OF HER DAD!
WW
...I REALIZED I COULD BRING THEM THE ONE THING THAT ALWAYS MADE ME FEEL POWERFUL...
...LIPSTICK.
A.M. TENNA
SO, THAT'S YOUR HALF-SISTER'S SOLUTION-- PUT A PRETTY FACE ON THE ATROCITY OF WAR?
i no, mom...
i no!!!!!!!!!!!!

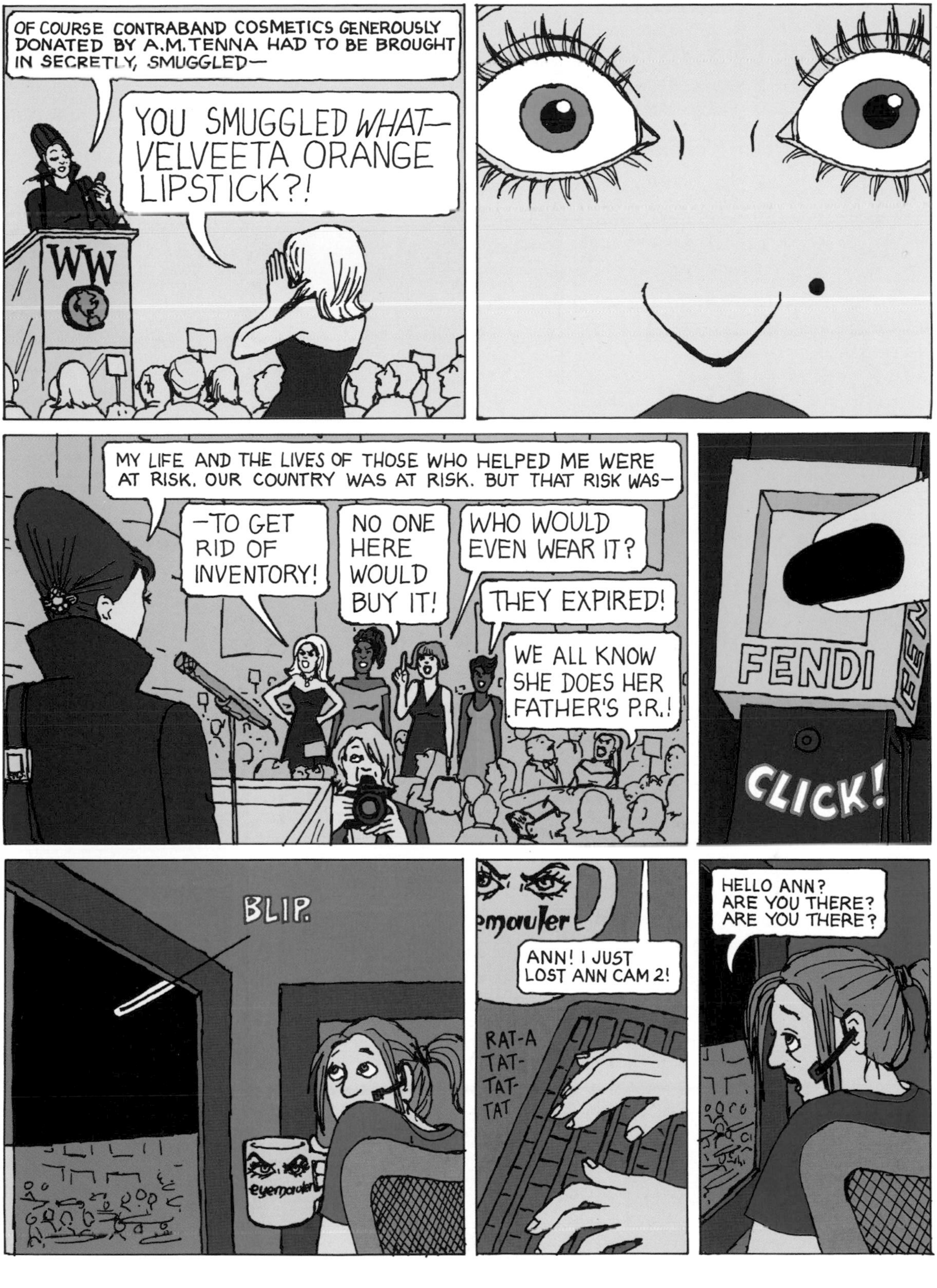

OF COURSE CONTRABAND COSMETICS GENEROUSLY DONATED BY A.M.TENNA HAD TO BE BROUGHT IN SECRETLY, SMUGGLED—
YOU SMUGGLED WHAT—VELVEETA ORANGE LIPSTICK?!
WW
MY LIFE AND THE LIVES OF THOSE WHO HELPED ME WERE AT RISK. OUR COUNTRY WAS AT RISK. BUT THAT RISK WAS—
—TO GET RID OF INVENTORY!
NO ONE HERE WOULD BUY IT!
WHO WOULD EVEN WEAR IT?
THEY EXPIRED!
WE ALL KNOW SHE DOES HER FATHER'S P.R.!
FENDI
CLICK!
BLIP.
eyemauler
ANN! I JUST LOST ANN CAM 2!
RAT-A TAT-TAT-TAT
HELLO ANN? ARE YOU THERE? ARE YOU THERE?

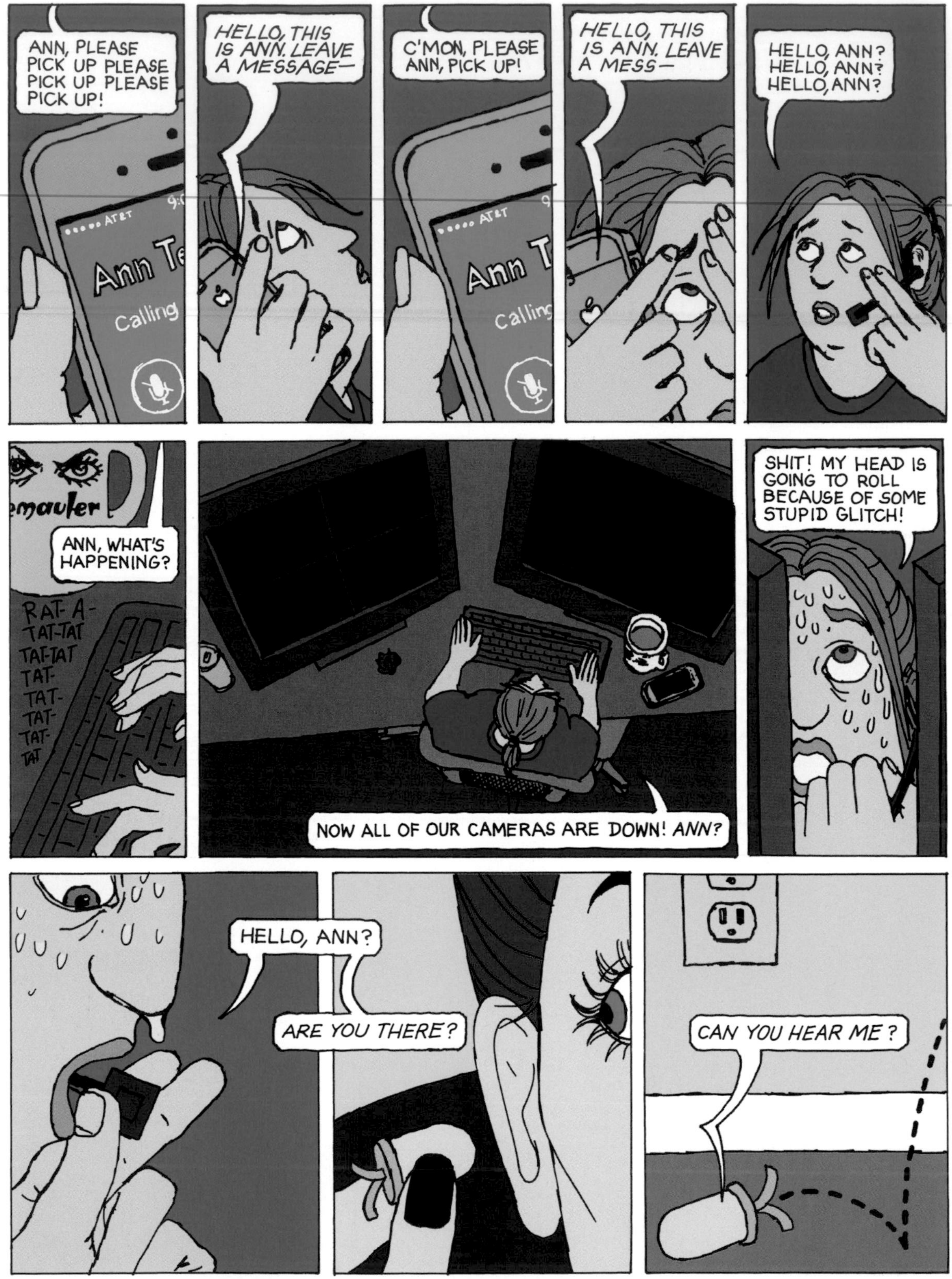
ANN, PLEASE PICK UP PLEASE PICK UP PLEASE PICK UP!
HELLO, THIS IS ANN. LEAVE A MESSAGE—
C'MON, PLEASE ANN, PICK UP!
HELLO, THIS IS ANN. LEAVE A MESS—
HELLO, ANN? HELLO, ANN? HELLO, ANN?
mauler
ANN, WHAT'S HAPPENING?
RAT-A-TAT-TAT TAT-TAT TAT-TAT-TAT-TAT-TAT
NOW ALL OF OUR CAMERAS ARE DOWN! ANN?
SHIT! MY HEAD IS GOING TO ROLL BECAUSE OF SOME STUPID GLITCH!
HELLO, ANN?
ARE YOU THERE?
CAN YOU HEAR ME?

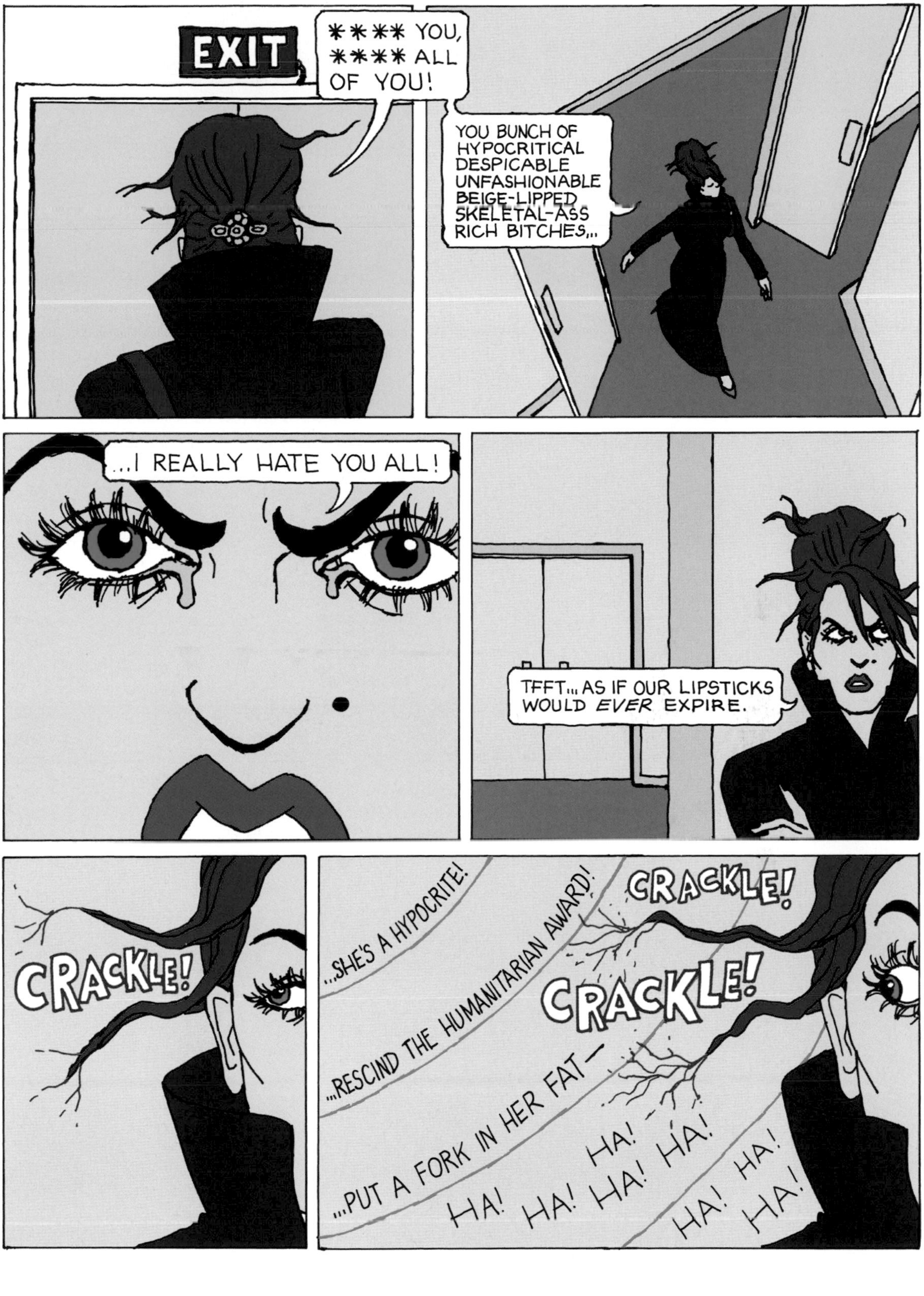
EXIT
**** YOU, **** ALL OF YOU!
YOU BUNCH OF HYPOCRITICAL DESPICABLE UNFASHIONABLE BEIGE-LIPPED SKELETAL-ASS RICH BITCHES,..
...I REALLY HATE YOU ALL!
TFFT... AS IF OUR LIPSTICKS WOULD EVER EXPIRE.
CRACKLE!
...SHE'S A HYPOCRITE!
...RESCIND THE HUMANITARIAN AWARD!
...PUT A FORK IN HER FAT—
CRACKLE!
CRACKLE!
HA! HA! HA! HA! HA! HA! HA! HA! HA!

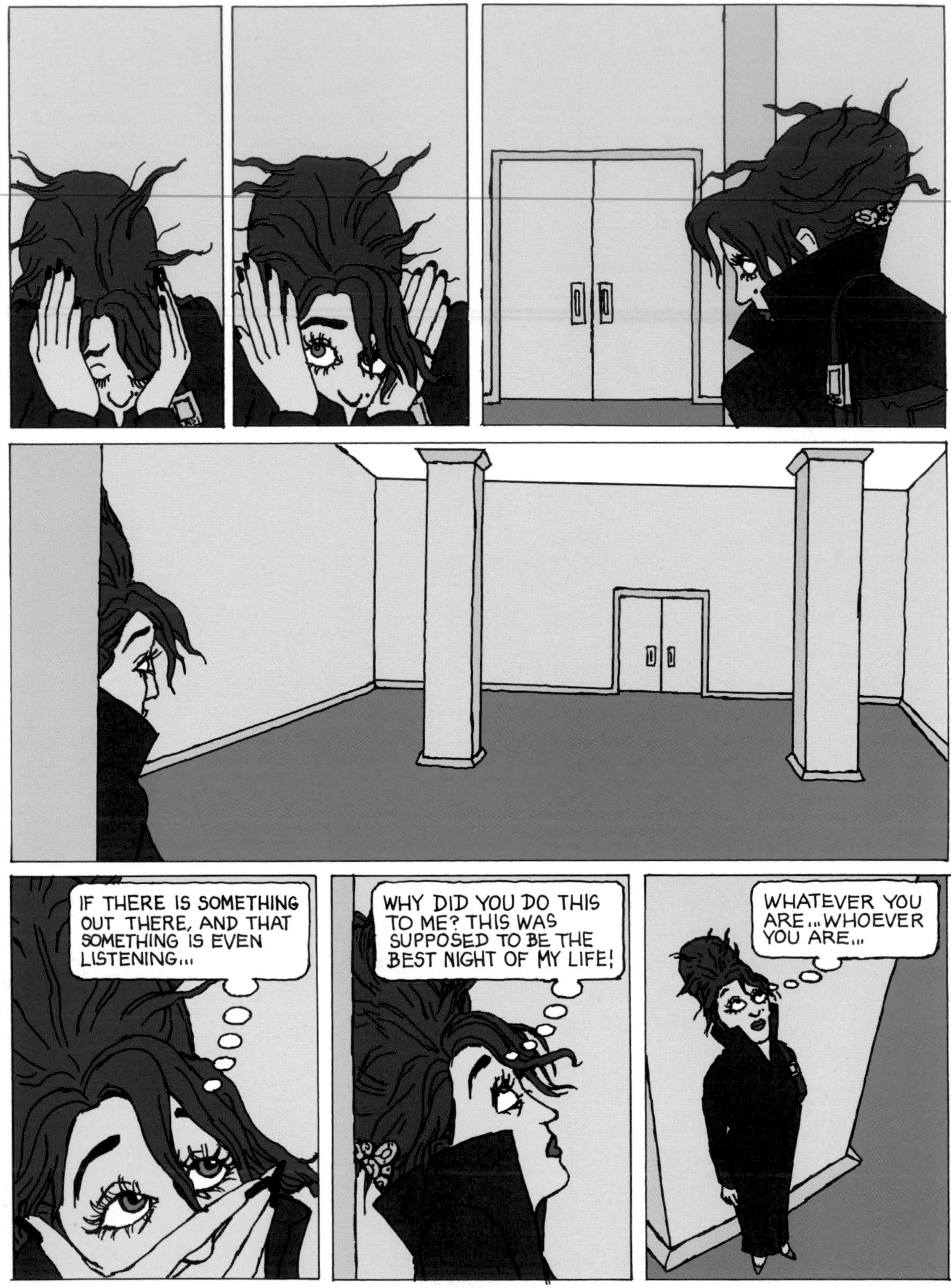
IF THERE IS SOMETHING OUT THERE, AND THAT SOMETHING IS EVEN LISTENING...
WHY DID YOU DO THIS TO ME? THIS WAS SUPPOSED TO BE THE BEST NIGHT OF MY LIFE!
WHATEVER YOU ARE...WHOEVER YOU ARE...

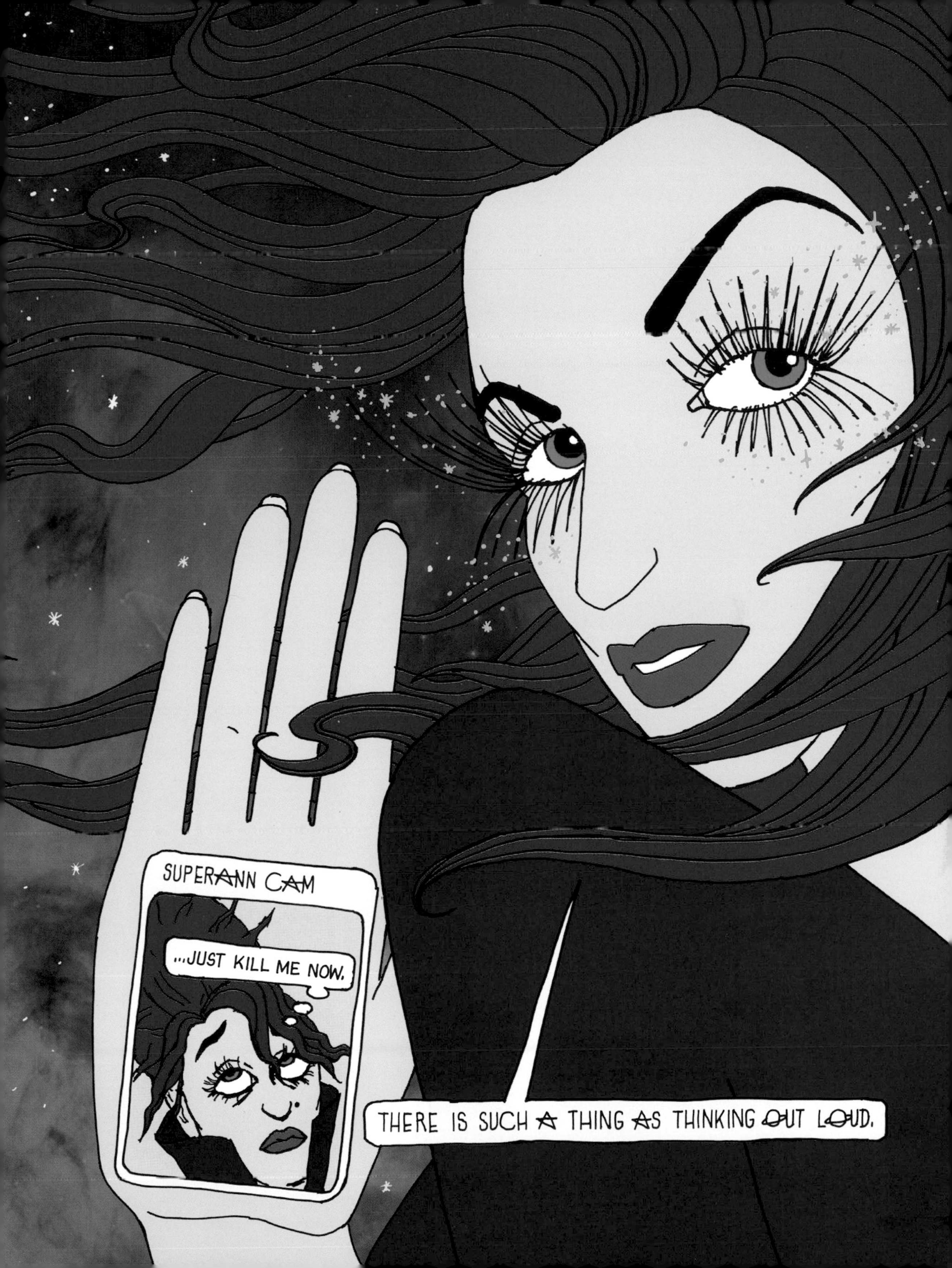
SUPERANN CAM
...JUST KILL ME NOW.
THERE IS SUCH A THING AS THINKING OUT LOUD.

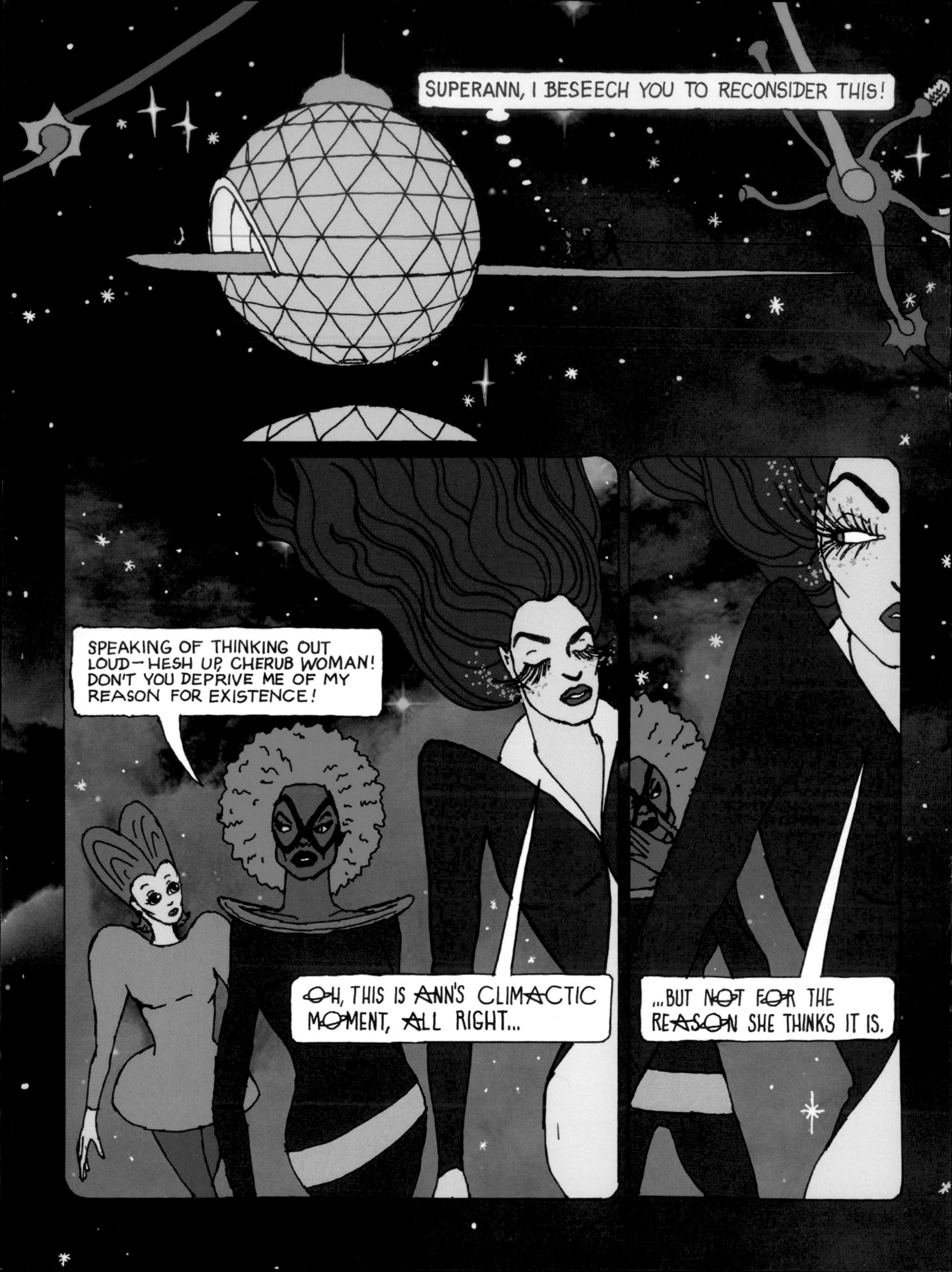
SUPERANN, I BESEECH YOU TO RECONSIDER THIS!
SPEAKING OF THINKING OUT LOUD—HESH UP, CHERUB WOMAN! DON'T YOU DEPRIVE ME OF MY REASON FOR EXISTENCE!
OH, THIS IS ANN'S CLIMACTIC MOMENT, ALL RIGHT...
...BUT NOT FOR THE REASON SHE THINKS IT IS.

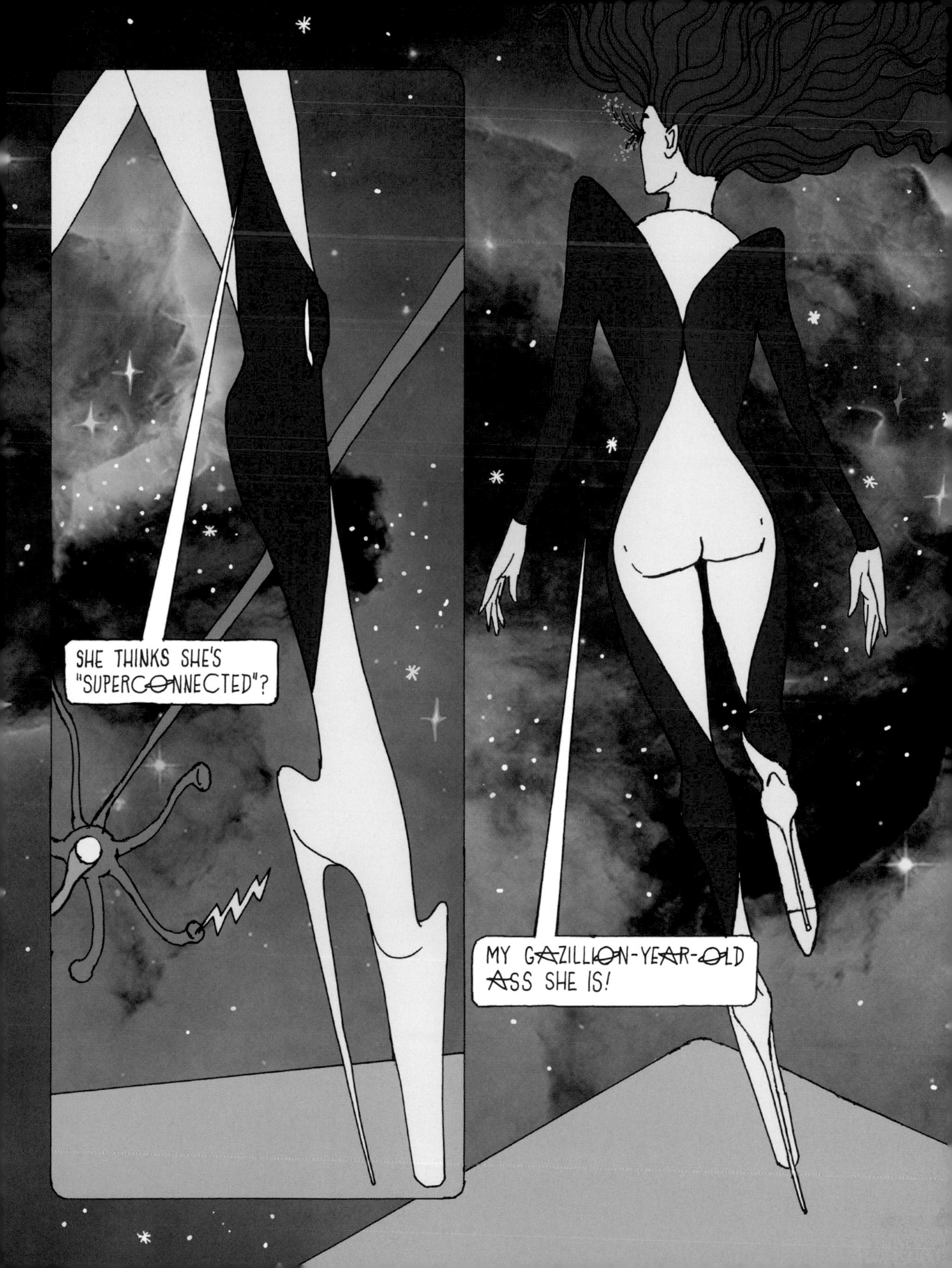
SHE THINKS SHE'S "SUPERCONNECTED"?
MY GAZILLION-YEAR-OLD ASS SHE IS!

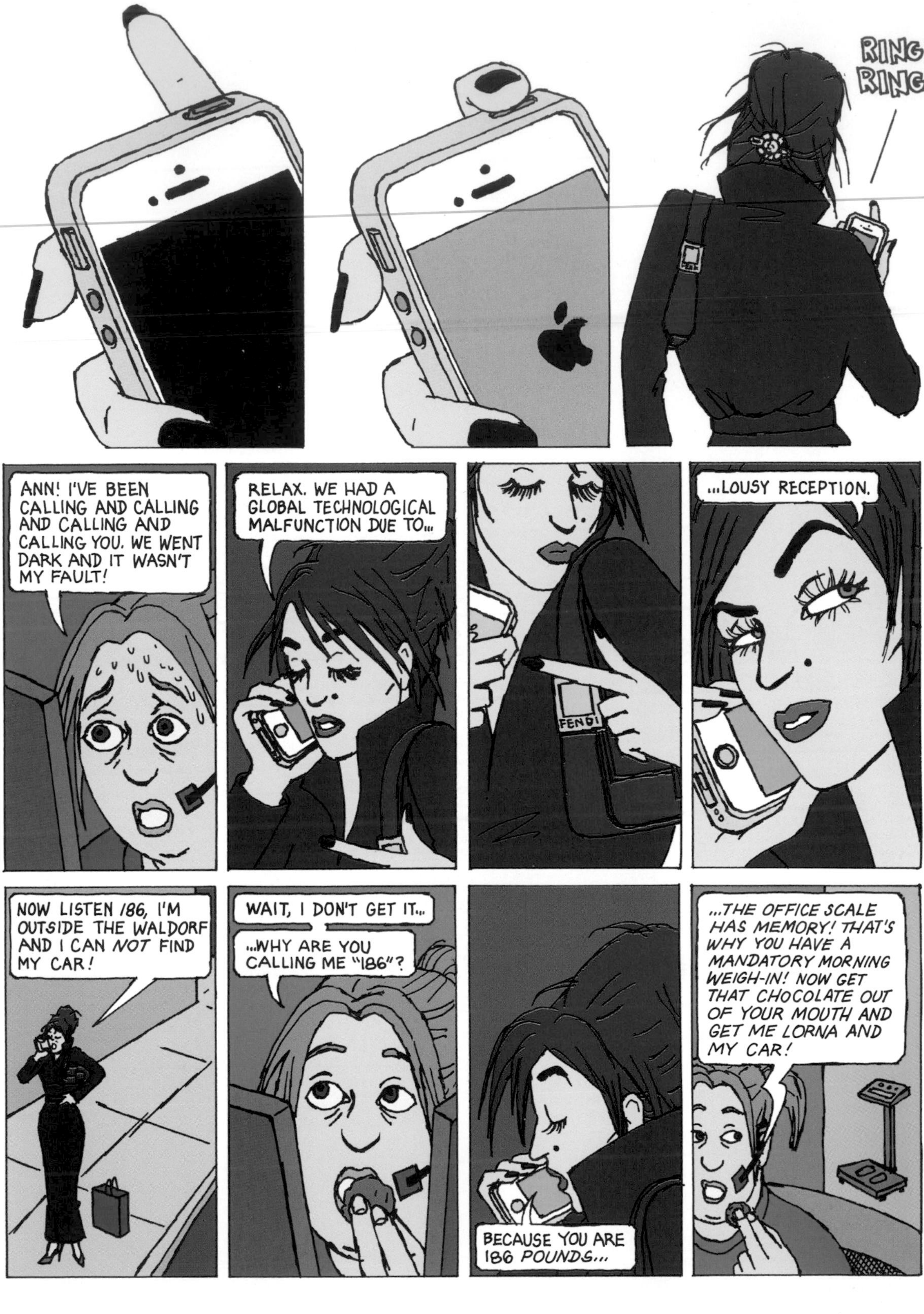
RING! RING!
ANN! I'VE BEEN CALLING AND CALLING AND CALLING AND CALLING YOU. WE WENT DARK AND IT WASN'T MY FAULT!
RELAX. WE HAD A GLOBAL TECHNOLOGICAL MALFUNCTION DUE TO...
FENDI
...LOUSY RECEPTION.
NOW LISTEN 186, I'M OUTSIDE THE WALDORF AND I CAN *NOT* FIND MY CAR!
WAIT, I DON'T GET IT...
...WHY ARE YOU CALLING ME "186"?
BECAUSE YOU ARE 186 *POUNDS...*
...THE OFFICE SCALE HAS MEMORY! THAT'S WHY YOU HAVE A MANDATORY MORNING WEIGH-IN! NOW GET THAT CHOCOLATE OUT OF YOUR MOUTH AND GET ME LORNA AND MY CAR!

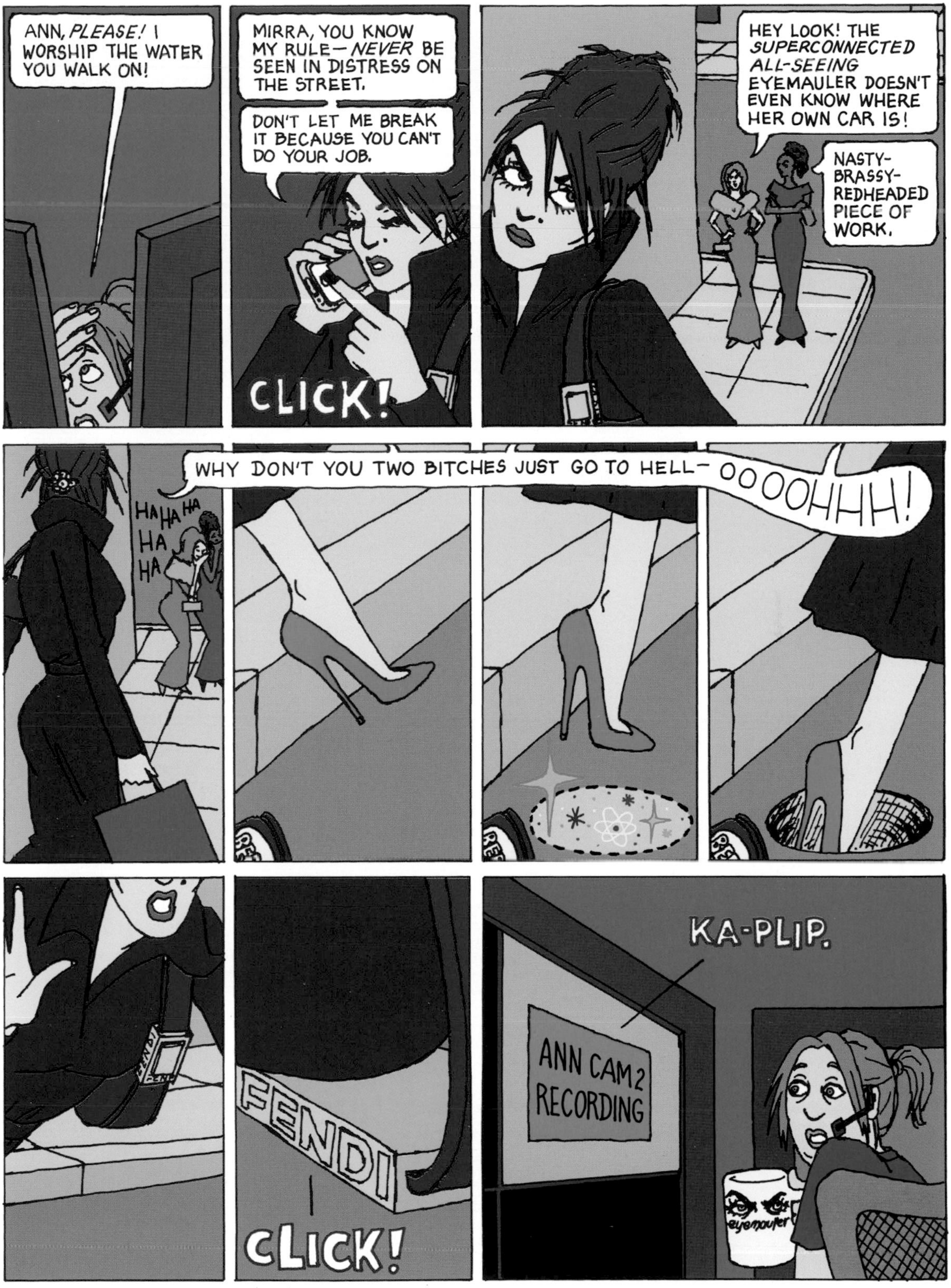
ANN, *PLEASE!* I WORSHIP THE WATER YOU WALK ON!
MIRRA, YOU KNOW MY RULE—*NEVER* BE SEEN IN DISTRESS ON THE STREET.
DON'T LET ME BREAK IT BECAUSE YOU CAN'T DO YOUR JOB.
CLICK!
HEY LOOK! THE *SUPERCONNECTED ALL-SEEING* EYEMAULER DOESN'T EVEN KNOW WHERE HER OWN CAR IS!
NASTY-BRASSY-REDHEADED PIECE OF WORK.
HA HA HA HA HA
WHY DON'T YOU TWO BITCHES JUST GO TO HELL—OOOOHHH!
FENDI
CLICK!
KA-PLIP.
ANN CAM 2 RECORDING
eyemauler

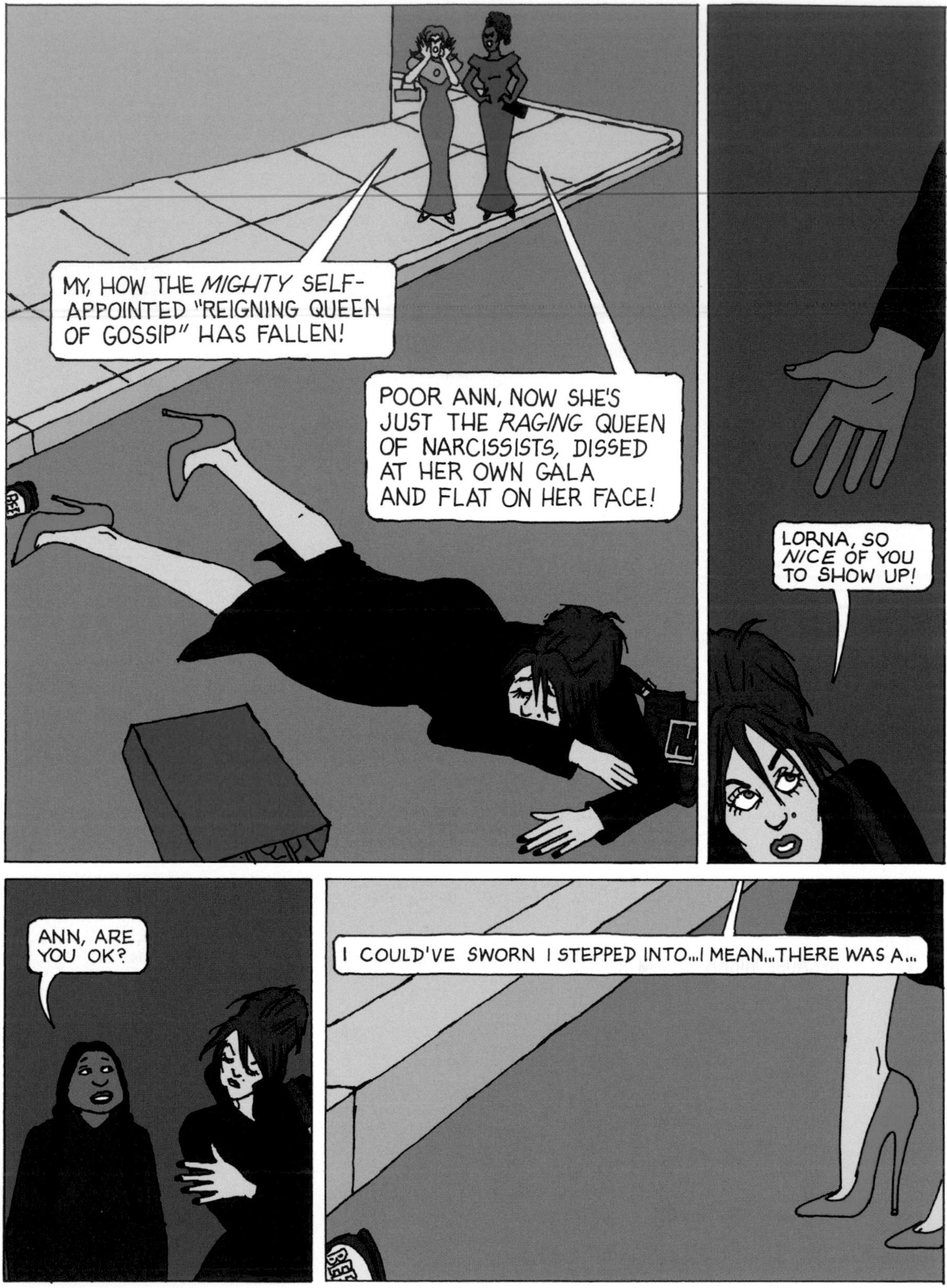
MY, HOW THE *MIGHTY* SELF-APPOINTED "REIGNING QUEEN OF GOSSIP" HAS FALLEN!
POOR ANN, NOW SHE'S JUST THE *RAGING* QUEEN OF NARCISSISTS, DISSED AT HER OWN GALA AND FLAT ON HER FACE!
LORNA, SO *NICE* OF YOU TO SHOW UP!
ANN, ARE YOU OK?
I COULD'VE SWORN I STEPPED INTO...I MEAN...THERE WAS A...

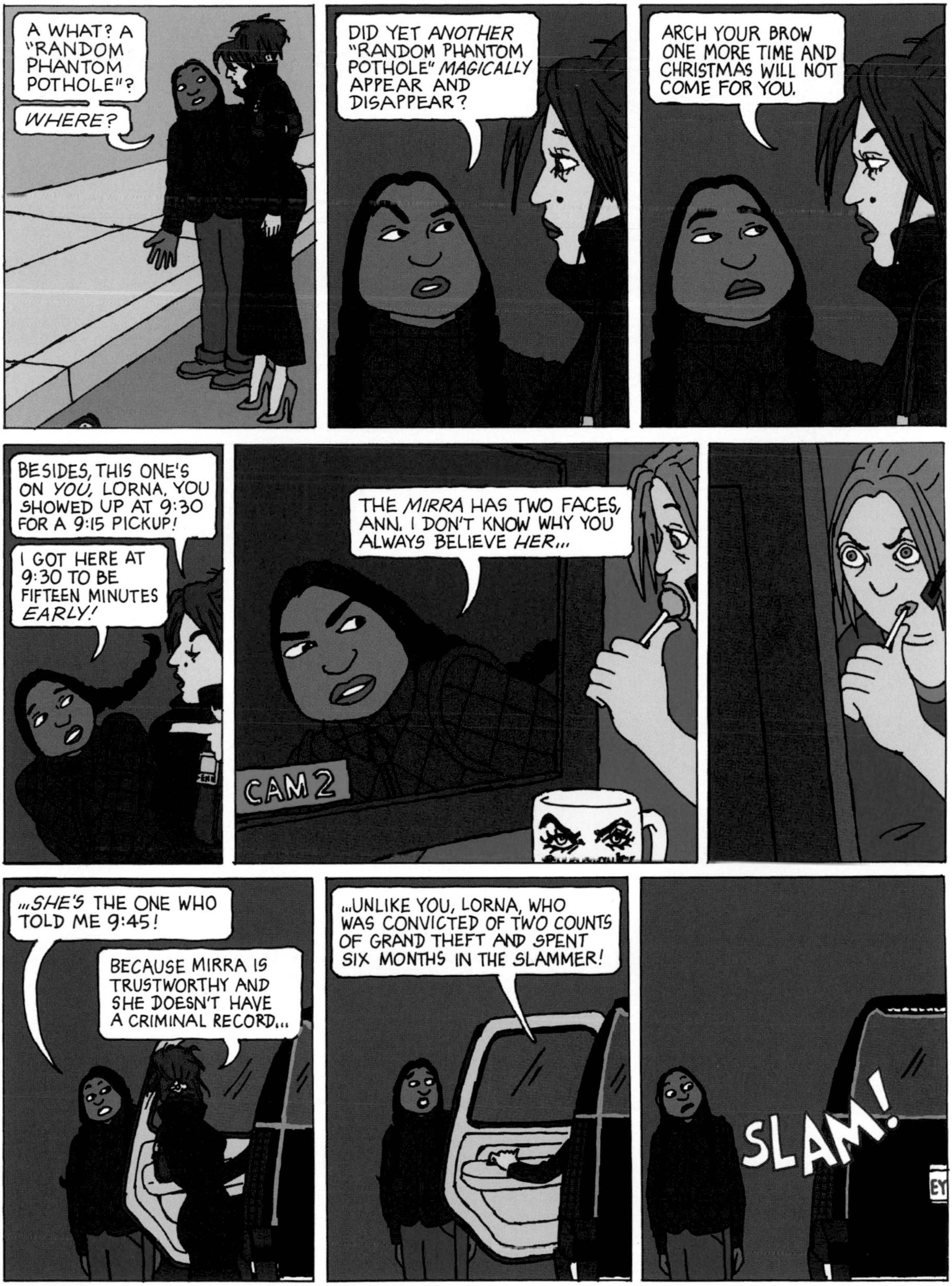
A WHAT? A "RANDOM PHANTOM POTHOLE"?
WHERE?
DID YET ANOTHER "RANDOM PHANTOM POTHOLE" MAGICALLY APPEAR AND DISAPPEAR?
ARCH YOUR BROW ONE MORE TIME AND CHRISTMAS WILL NOT COME FOR YOU.
BESIDES, THIS ONE'S ON YOU, LORNA. YOU SHOWED UP AT 9:30 FOR A 9:15 PICKUP!
I GOT HERE AT 9:30 TO BE FIFTEEN MINUTES EARLY!
THE MIRRA HAS TWO FACES, ANN. I DON'T KNOW WHY YOU ALWAYS BELIEVE HER...
CAM 2
...SHE'S THE ONE WHO TOLD ME 9:45!
BECAUSE MIRRA IS TRUSTWORTHY AND SHE DOESN'T HAVE A CRIMINAL RECORD...
...UNLIKE YOU, LORNA, WHO WAS CONVICTED OF TWO COUNTS OF GRAND THEFT AND SPENT SIX MONTHS IN THE SLAMMER!
SLAM!

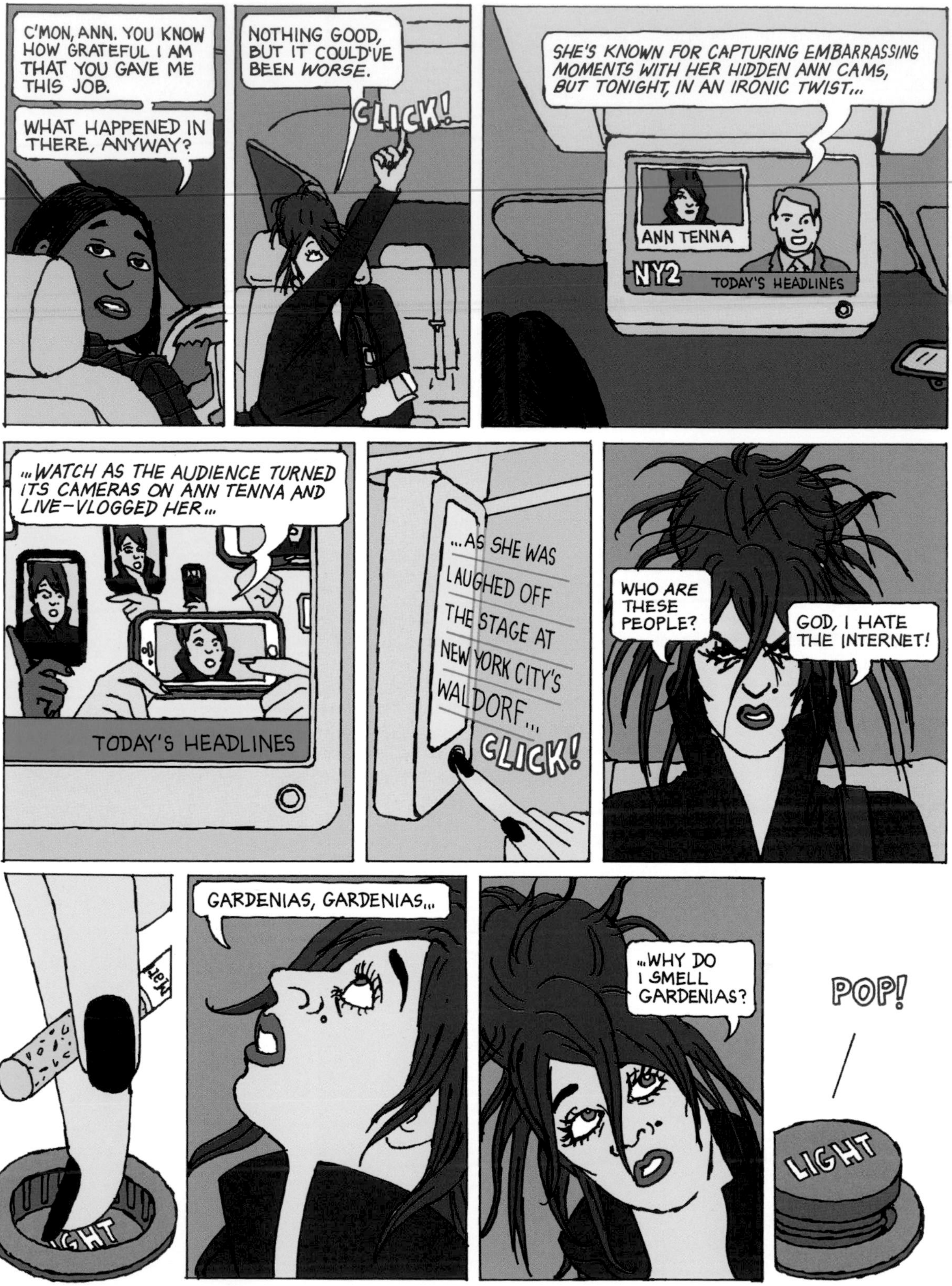

C'MON, ANN. YOU KNOW HOW GRATEFUL I AM THAT YOU GAVE ME THIS JOB.
WHAT HAPPENED IN THERE, ANYWAY?
NOTHING GOOD, BUT IT COULD'VE BEEN *WORSE.*
CLICK!
SHE'S KNOWN FOR CAPTURING EMBARRASSING MOMENTS WITH HER HIDDEN ANN CAMS, BUT TONIGHT, IN AN IRONIC TWIST...
ANN TENNA
NY2
TODAY'S HEADLINES
...WATCH AS THE AUDIENCE TURNED ITS CAMERAS ON ANN TENNA AND LIVE-VLOGGED HER...
TODAY'S HEADLINES
...AS SHE WAS LAUGHED OFF THE STAGE AT NEW YORK CITY'S WALDORF...
CLICK!
WHO *ARE* THESE PEOPLE?
GOD, I HATE THE INTERNET!
GARDENIAS, GARDENIAS...
...WHY DO I SMELL GARDENIAS?
POP!
LIGHT

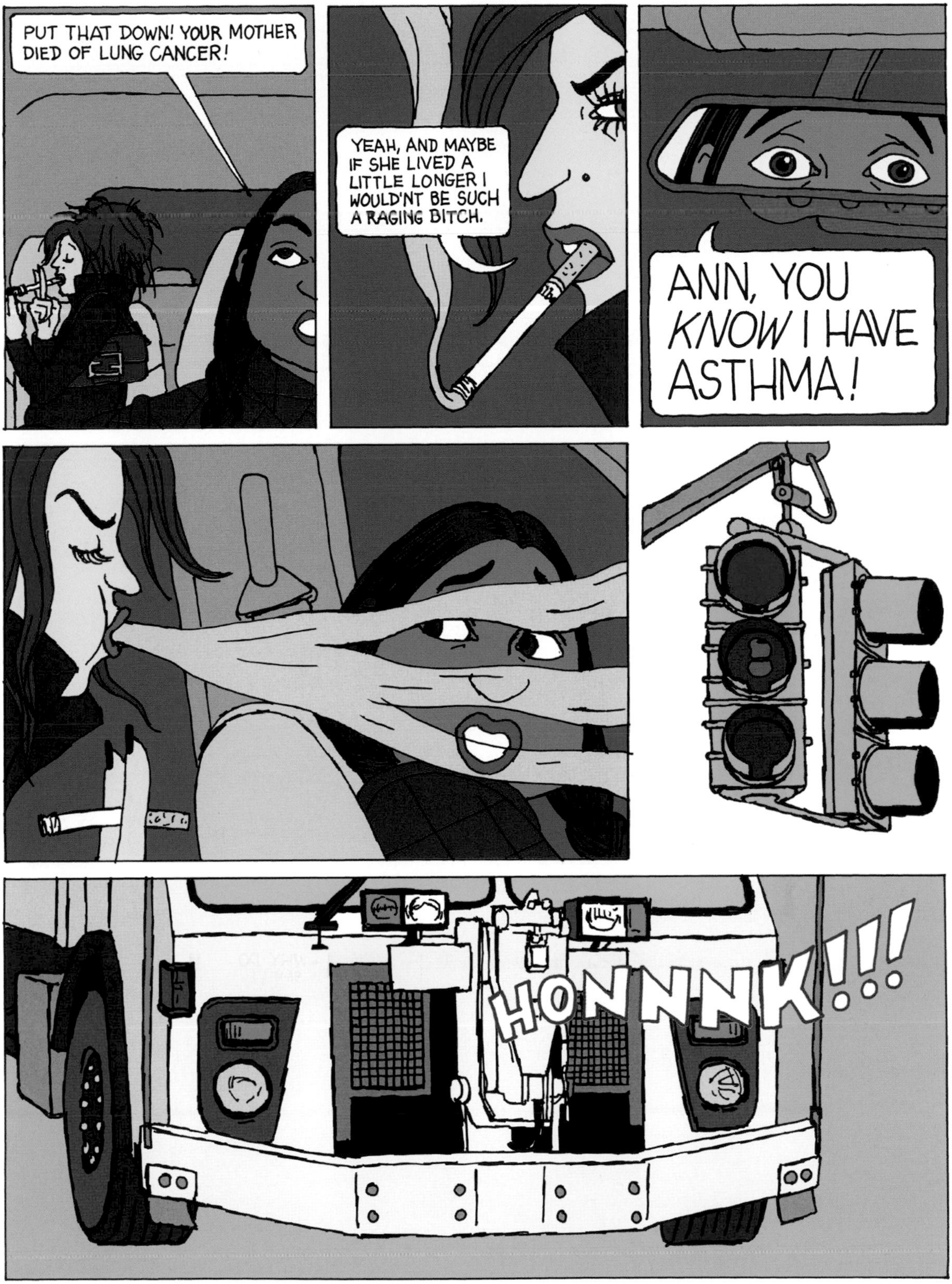
PUT THAT DOWN! YOUR MOTHER DIED OF LUNG CANCER!
YEAH, AND MAYBE IF SHE LIVED A LITTLE LONGER I WOULD'NT BE SUCH A RAGING BITCH.
ANN, YOU *KNOW* I HAVE ASTHMA!
HONNNK!!!!

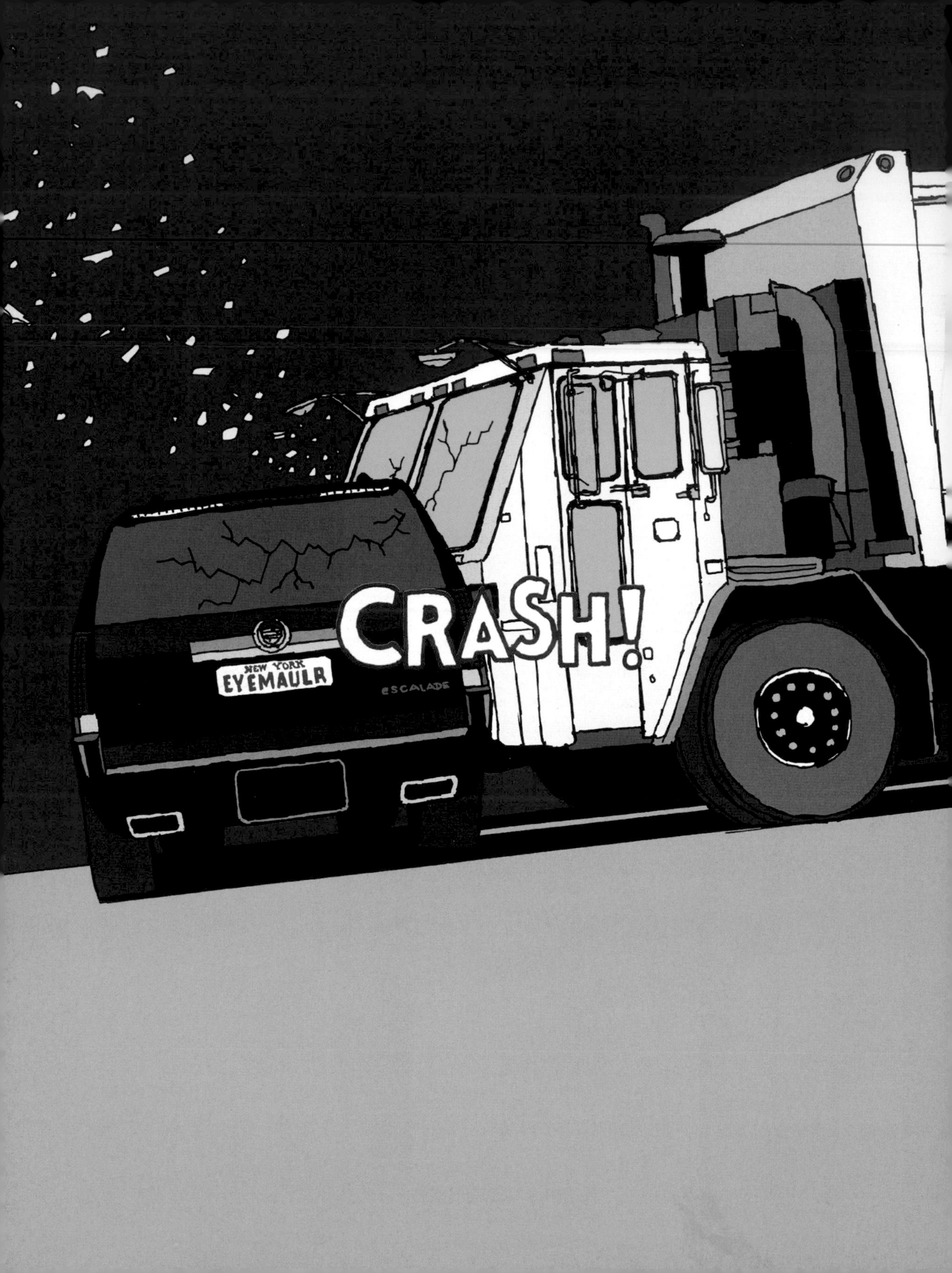
CRASH!
NEW YORK
EYEMAULR
ESCALADE

sanitation

SCREEEEEEEEEECH!

ANN CAM 2

ANN...?

mauler

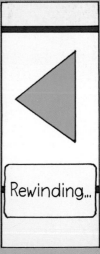

Rewinding...

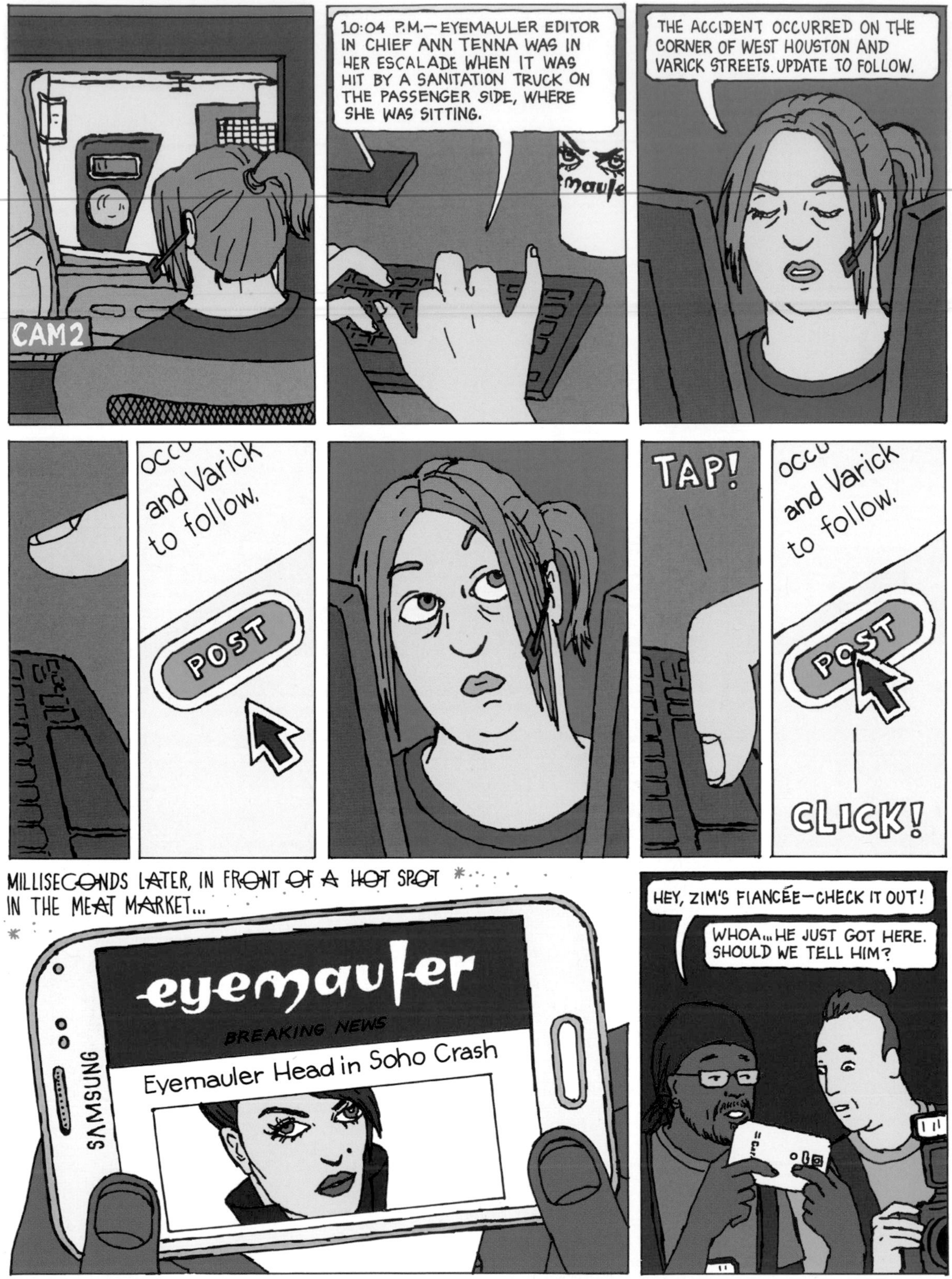
CAM 2
10:04 P.M.—EYEMAULER EDITOR IN CHIEF ANN TENNA WAS IN HER ESCALADE WHEN IT WAS HIT BY A SANITATION TRUCK ON THE PASSENGER SIDE, WHERE SHE WAS SITTING.
THE ACCIDENT OCCURRED ON THE CORNER OF WEST HOUSTON AND VARICK STREETS. UPDATE TO FOLLOW.
and Varick
to follow.
POST
TAP!
and Varick
to follow.
POST
CLICK!
MILLISECONDS LATER, IN FRONT OF A HOT SPOT IN THE MEAT MARKET...
eyemauler
BREAKING NEWS
Eyemauler Head in Soho Crash
SAMSUNG
HEY, ZIM'S FIANCÉE—CHECK IT OUT!
WHOA... HE JUST GOT HERE. SHOULD WE TELL HIM?

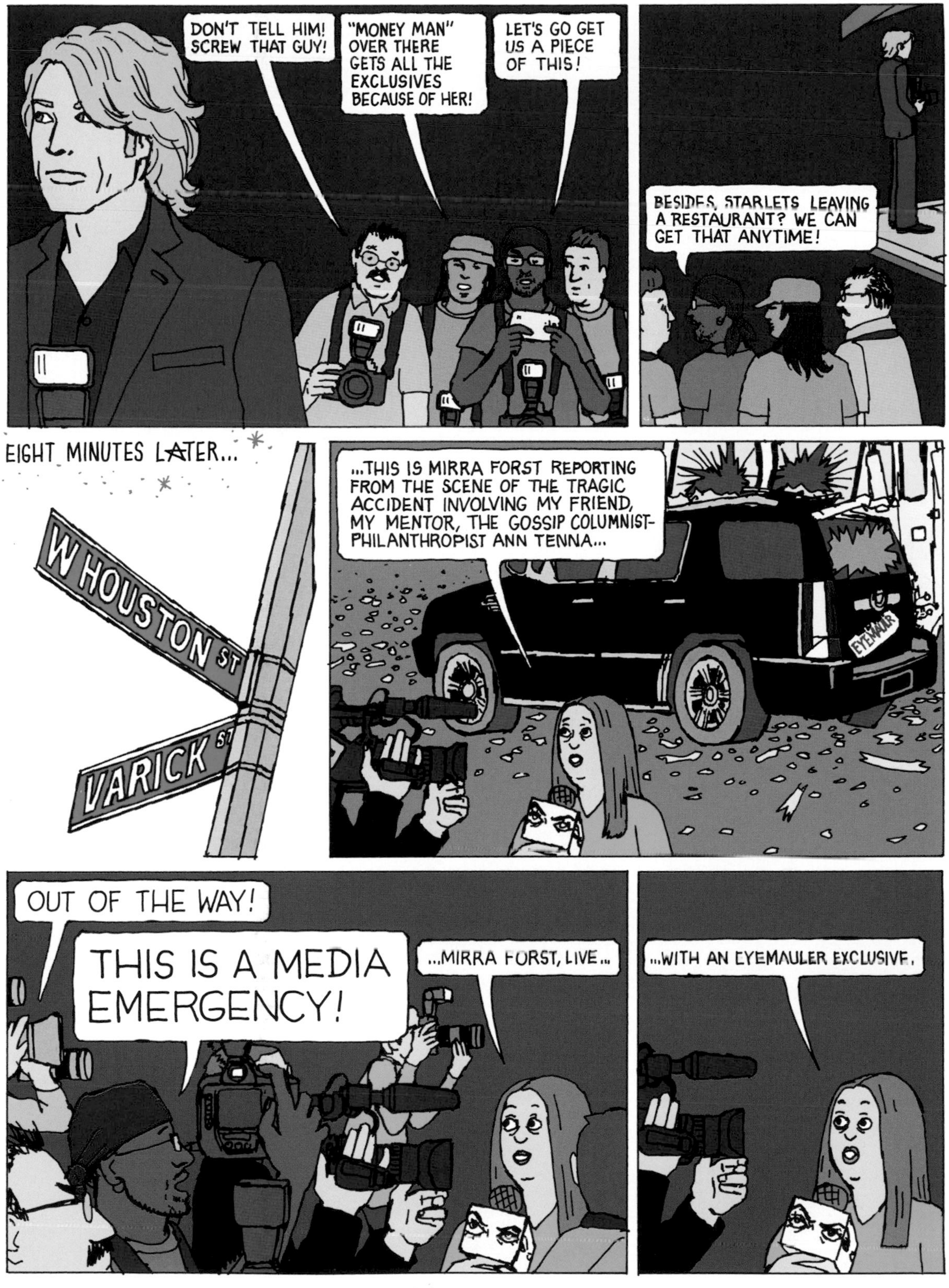
DON'T TELL HIM! SCREW THAT GUY!
"MONEY MAN" OVER THERE GETS ALL THE EXCLUSIVES BECAUSE OF HER!
LET'S GO GET US A PIECE OF THIS!
BESIDES, STARLETS LEAVING A RESTAURANT? WE CAN GET THAT ANYTIME!
EIGHT MINUTES LATER...
W HOUSTON ST
VARICK ST
...THIS IS MIRRA FORST REPORTING FROM THE SCENE OF THE TRAGIC ACCIDENT INVOLVING MY FRIEND, MY MENTOR, THE GOSSIP COLUMNIST-PHILANTHROPIST ANN TENNA...
EYEMAULER
OUT OF THE WAY!
THIS IS A MEDIA EMERGENCY!
...MIRRA FORST, LIVE...
...WITH AN EYEMAULER EXCLUSIVE.

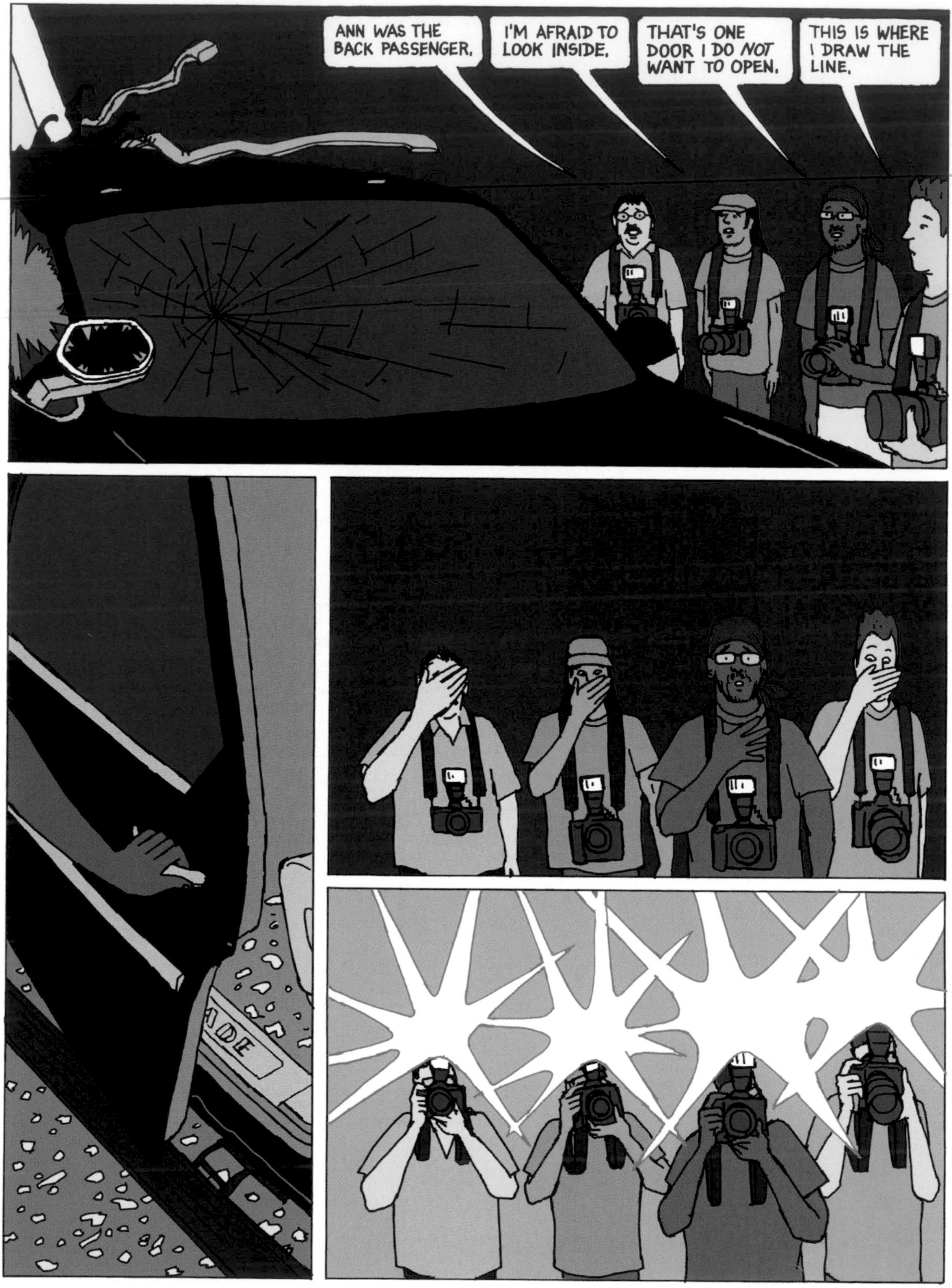
ANN WAS THE BACK PASSENGER.
I'M AFRAID TO LOOK INSIDE.
THAT'S ONE DOOR I DO *NOT* WANT TO OPEN.
THIS IS WHERE I DRAW THE LINE.

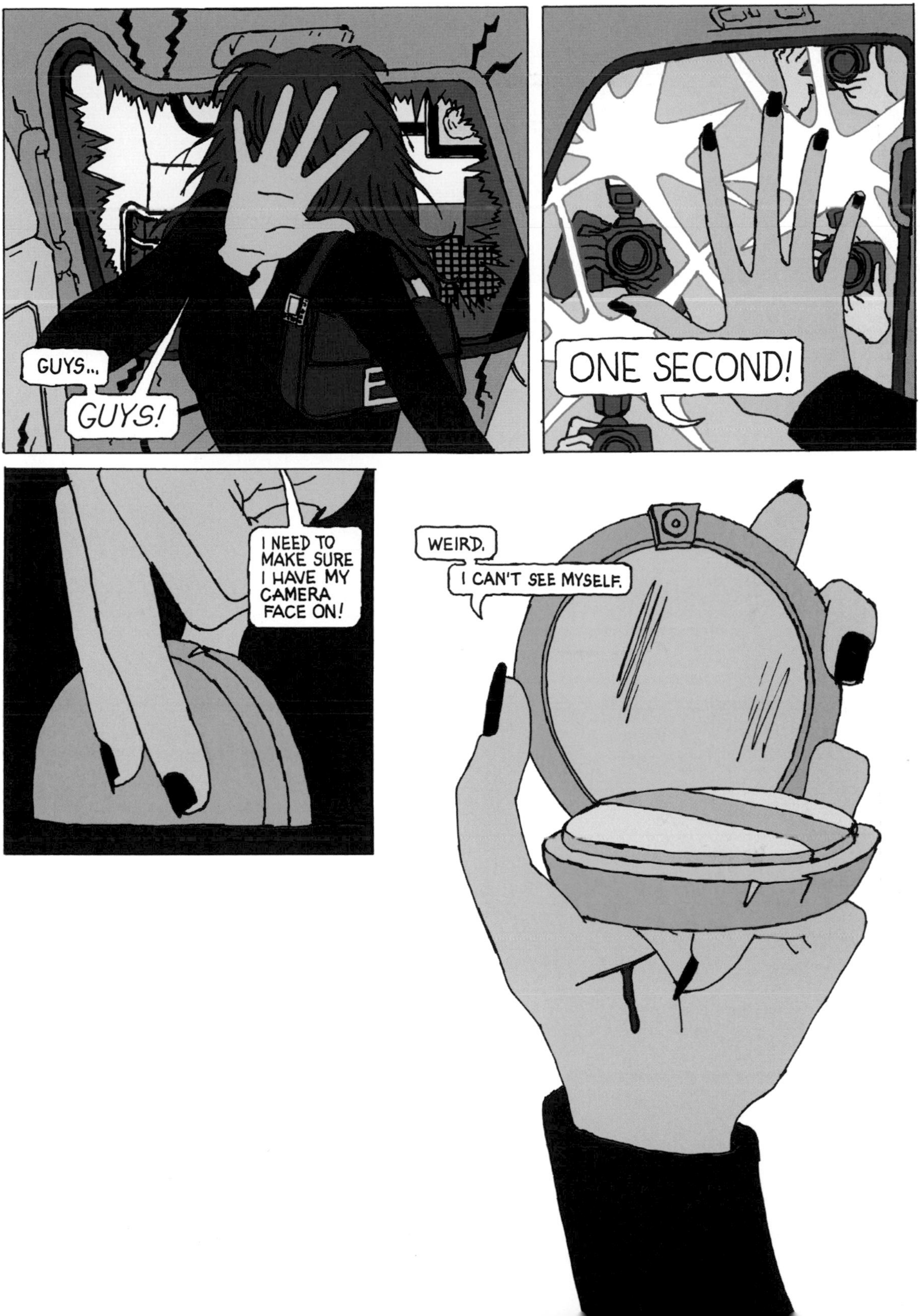
GUYS...
GUYS!
ONE SECOND!
I NEED TO MAKE SURE I HAVE MY CAMERA FACE ON!
WEIRD.
I CAN'T SEE MYSELF.

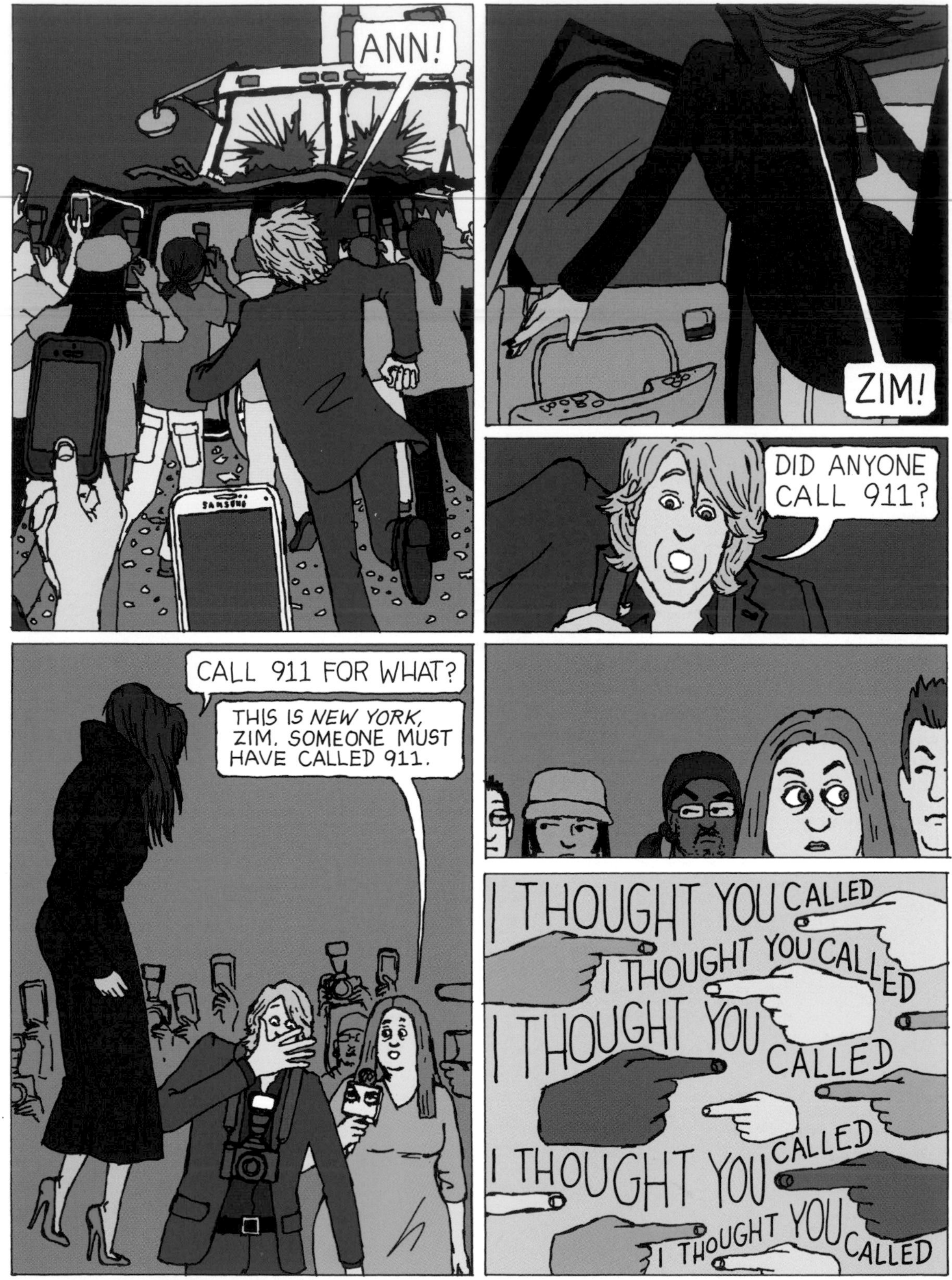
ANN!
ZIM!
DID ANYONE CALL 911?
CALL 911 FOR WHAT?
THIS IS *NEW YORK*, ZIM. SOMEONE MUST HAVE CALLED 911.
I THOUGHT YOU CALLED
I THOUGHT YOU CALLED
I THOUGHT YOU CALLED
I THOUGHT YOU CALLED
I THOUGHT YOU CALLED

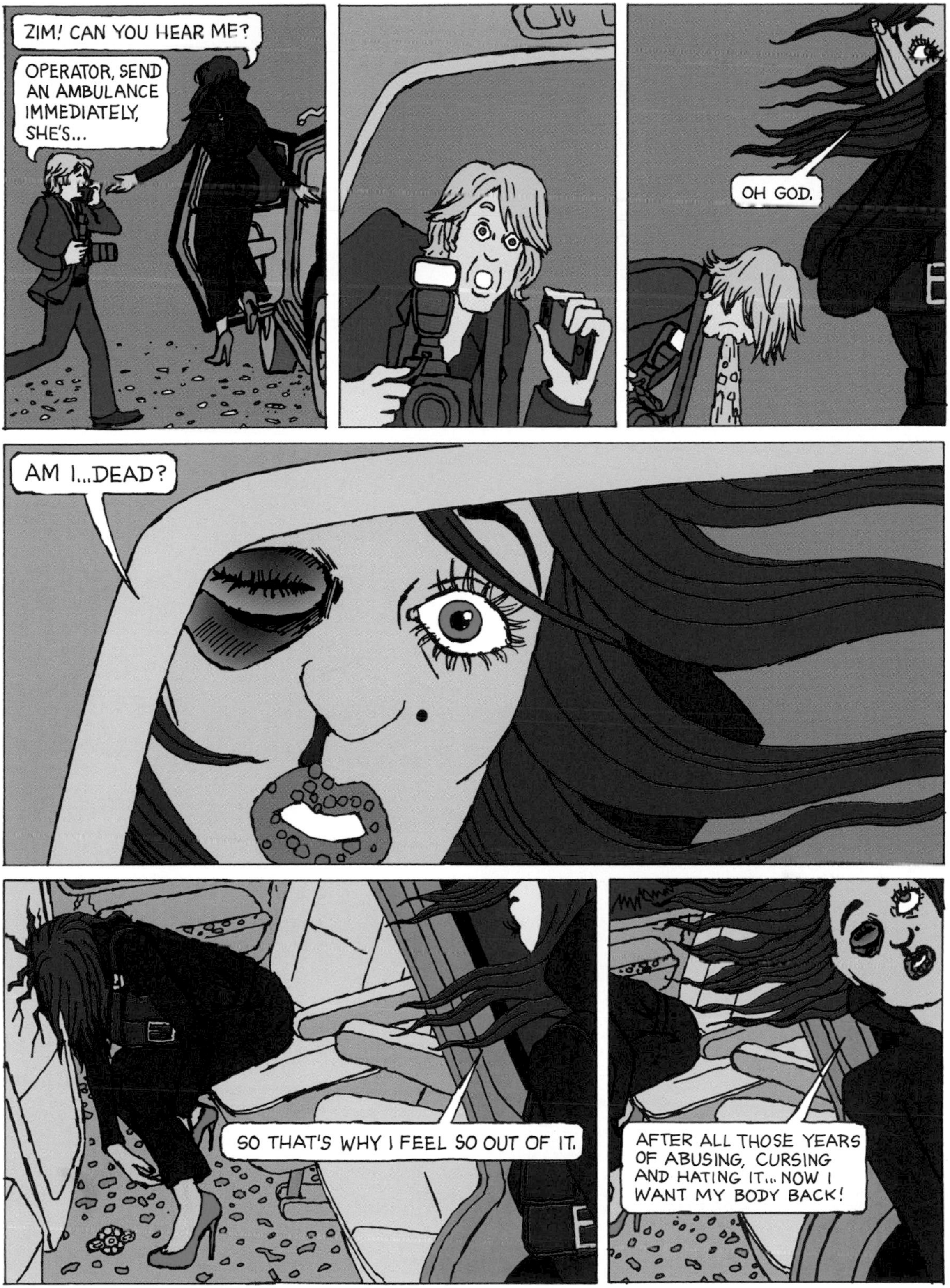
ZIM! CAN YOU HEAR ME?
OPERATOR, SEND AN AMBULANCE IMMEDIATELY, SHE'S...
OH GOD.
AM I...DEAD?
SO THAT'S WHY I FEEL SO OUT OF IT.
AFTER ALL THOSE YEARS OF ABUSING, CURSING AND HATING IT... NOW I WANT MY BODY BACK!

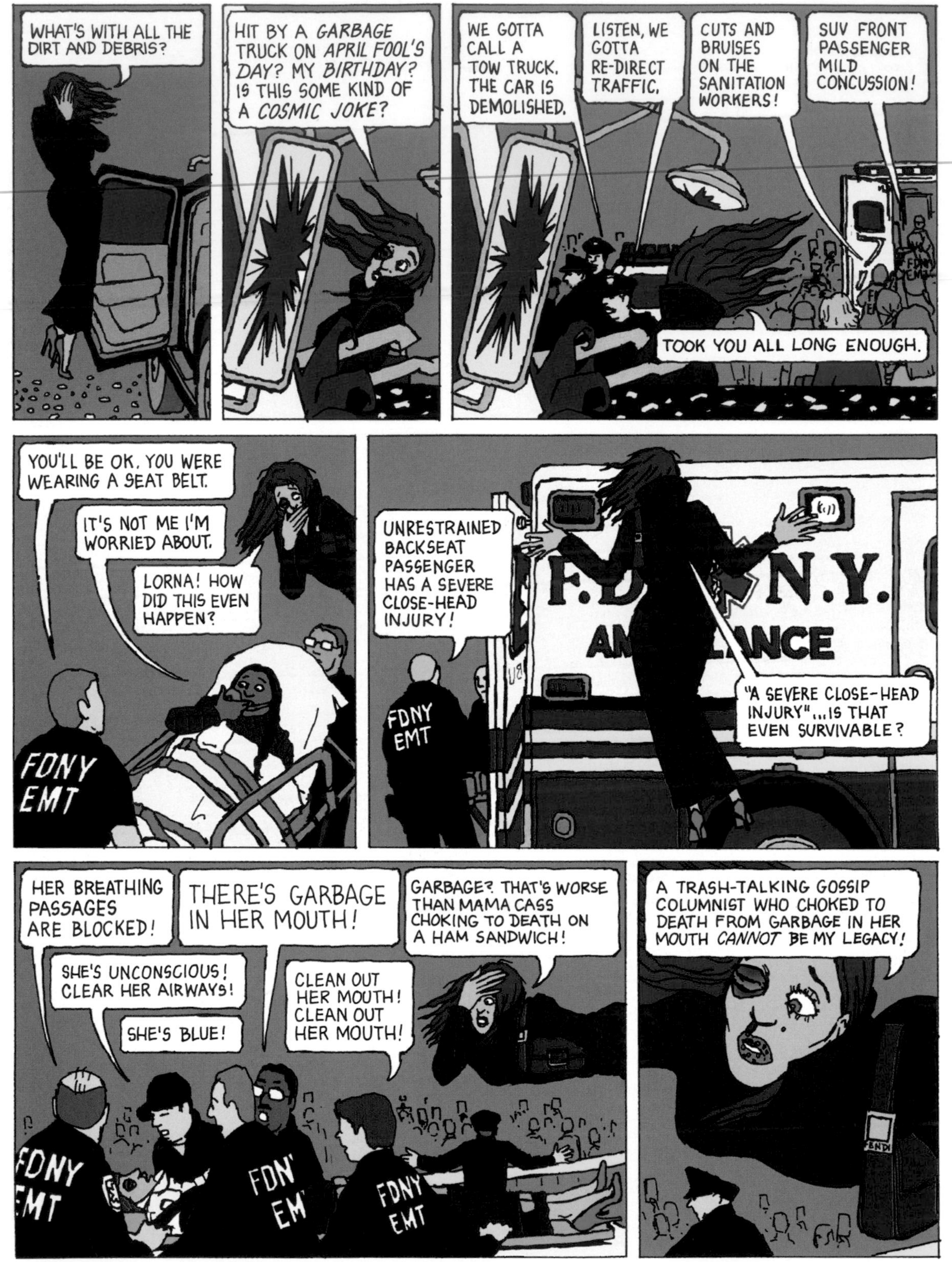

WHAT'S WITH ALL THE DIRT AND DEBRIS?
HIT BY A *GARBAGE* TRUCK ON *APRIL FOOL'S DAY*? MY *BIRTHDAY*? IS THIS SOME KIND OF A *COSMIC JOKE*?
WE GOTTA CALL A TOW TRUCK. THE CAR IS DEMOLISHED.
LISTEN, WE GOTTA RE-DIRECT TRAFFIC.
CUTS AND BRUISES ON THE SANITATION WORKERS!
SUV FRONT PASSENGER MILD CONCUSSION!
TOOK YOU ALL LONG ENOUGH.
YOU'LL BE OK. YOU WERE WEARING A SEAT BELT.
IT'S NOT ME I'M WORRIED ABOUT.
LORNA! HOW DID THIS EVEN HAPPEN?
FDNY EMT
UNRESTRAINED BACKSEAT PASSENGER HAS A SEVERE CLOSE-HEAD INJURY!
FDNY EMT
F.D N.Y.
AM LANCE
"A SEVERE CLOSE-HEAD INJURY"... IS THAT EVEN SURVIVABLE?
HER BREATHING PASSAGES ARE BLOCKED!
SHE'S UNCONSCIOUS! CLEAR HER AIRWAYS!
SHE'S BLUE!
THERE'S GARBAGE IN HER MOUTH!
CLEAN OUT HER MOUTH! CLEAN OUT HER MOUTH!
GARBAGE? THAT'S WORSE THAN MAMA CASS CHOKING TO DEATH ON A HAM SANDWICH!
FDNY EMT
FDN EM
FDNY EMT
A TRASH-TALKING GOSSIP COLUMNIST WHO CHOKED TO DEATH FROM GARBAGE IN HER MOUTH *CANNOT* BE MY LEGACY!
FENDI

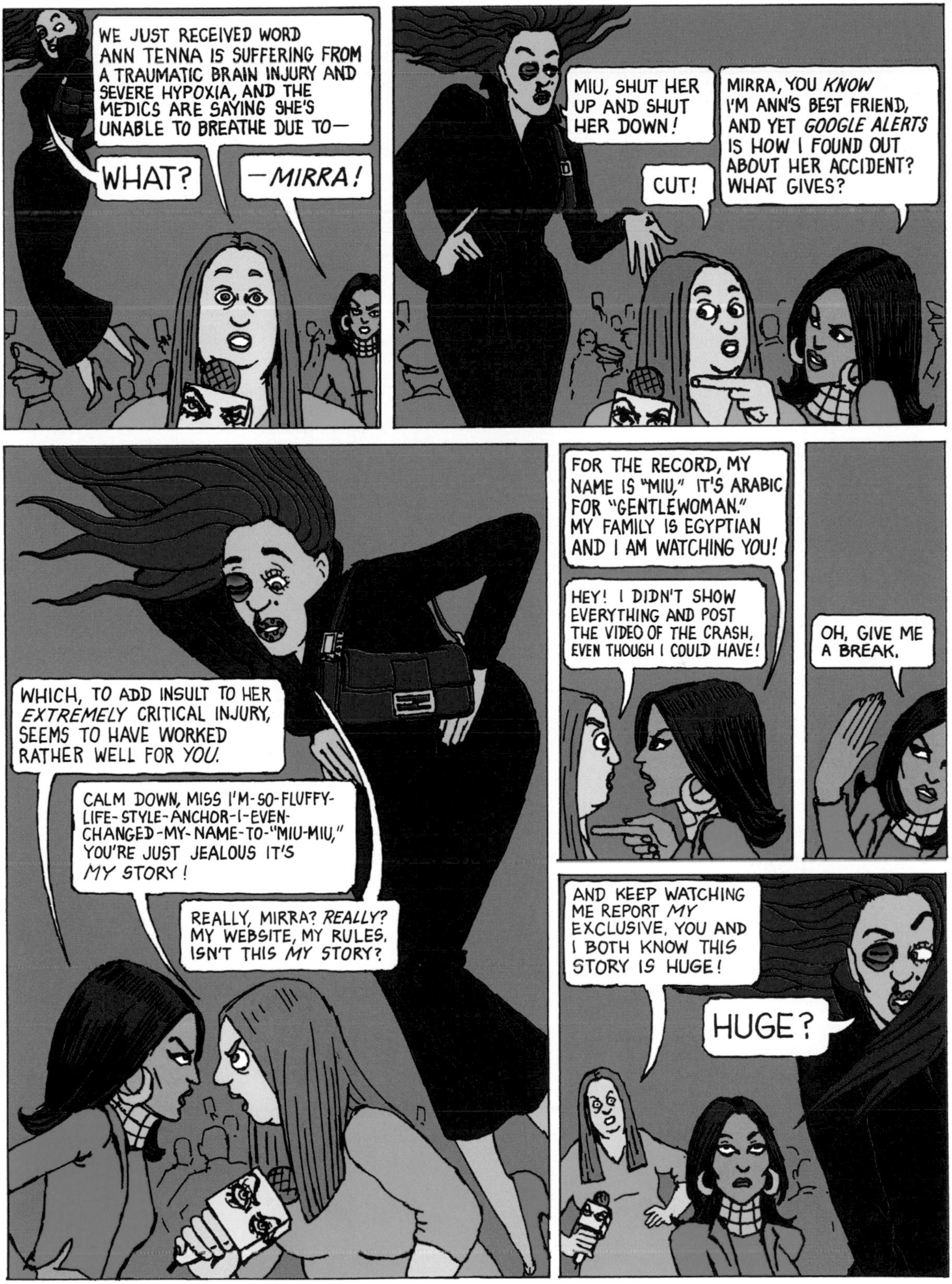
WE JUST RECEIVED WORD ANN TENNA IS SUFFERING FROM A TRAUMATIC BRAIN INJURY AND SEVERE HYPOXIA, AND THE MEDICS ARE SAYING SHE'S UNABLE TO BREATHE DUE TO—
WHAT?
—MIRRA!
MIU, SHUT HER UP AND SHUT HER DOWN!
CUT!
MIRRA, YOU KNOW I'M ANN'S BEST FRIEND, AND YET GOOGLE ALERTS IS HOW I FOUND OUT ABOUT HER ACCIDENT? WHAT GIVES?
WHICH, TO ADD INSULT TO HER EXTREMELY CRITICAL INJURY, SEEMS TO HAVE WORKED RATHER WELL FOR YOU.
CALM DOWN, MISS I'M-SO-FLUFFY-LIFE-STYLE-ANCHOR-I-EVEN-CHANGED-MY-NAME-TO-"MIU-MIU," YOU'RE JUST JEALOUS IT'S MY STORY!
REALLY, MIRRA? REALLY? MY WEBSITE, MY RULES. ISN'T THIS MY STORY?
FOR THE RECORD, MY NAME IS "MIU," IT'S ARABIC FOR "GENTLEWOMAN." MY FAMILY IS EGYPTIAN AND I AM WATCHING YOU!
HEY! I DIDN'T SHOW EVERYTHING AND POST THE VIDEO OF THE CRASH, EVEN THOUGH I COULD HAVE!
OH, GIVE ME A BREAK.
AND KEEP WATCHING ME REPORT MY EXCLUSIVE. YOU AND I BOTH KNOW THIS STORY IS HUGE!
HUGE?

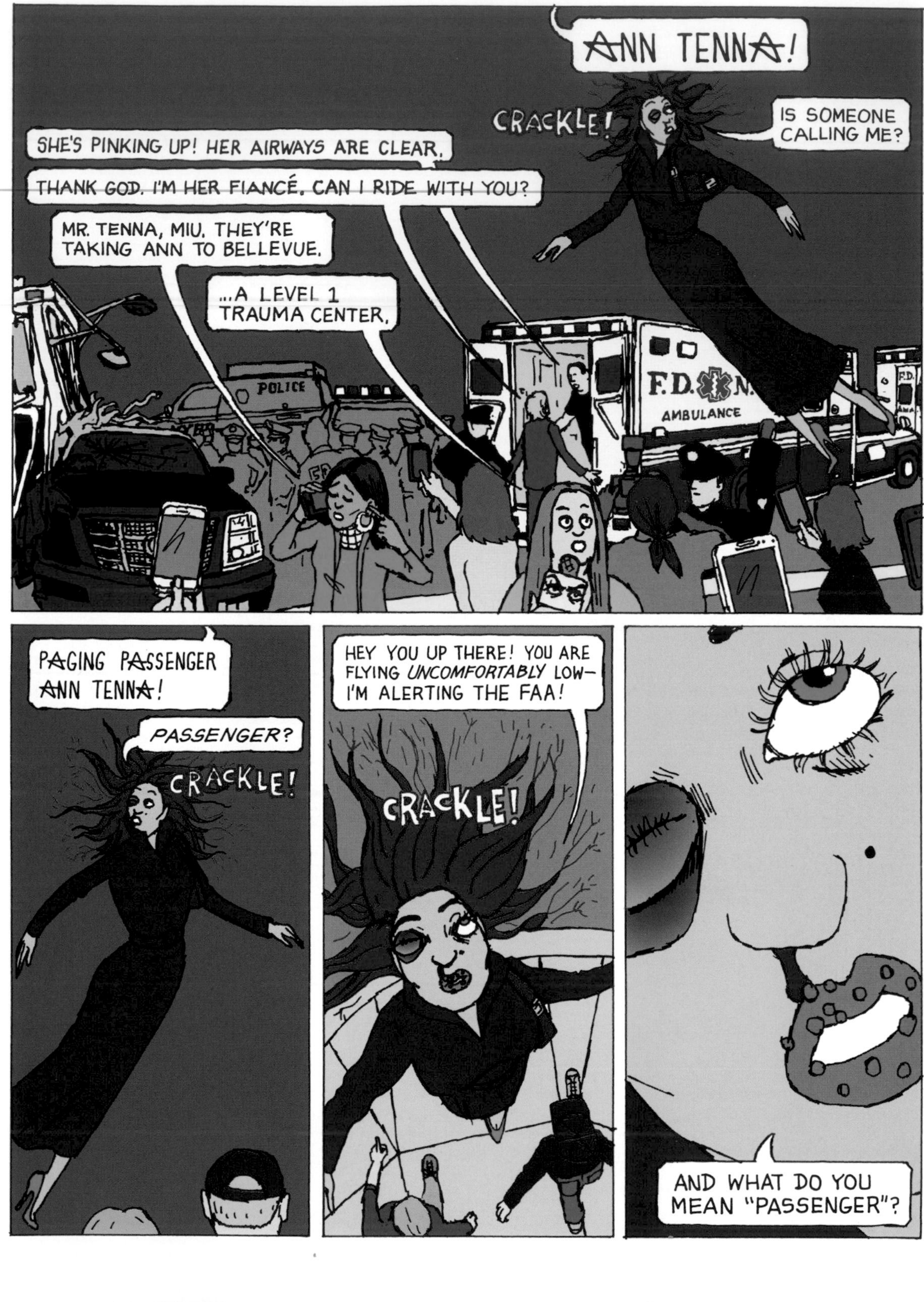
ANN TENNA!
CRACKLE!
IS SOMEONE CALLING ME?
SHE'S PINKING UP! HER AIRWAYS ARE CLEAR.
THANK GOD. I'M HER FIANCÉ. CAN I RIDE WITH YOU?
MR. TENNA, MIU. THEY'RE TAKING ANN TO BELLEVUE.
...A LEVEL 1 TRAUMA CENTER.
POLICE
F.D.N.
AMBULANCE
PAGING PASSENGER ANN TENNA!
PASSENGER?
CRACKLE!
HEY YOU UP THERE! YOU ARE FLYING *UNCOMFORTABLY* LOW—I'M ALERTING THE FAA!
CRACKLE!
AND WHAT DO YOU MEAN "PASSENGER"?

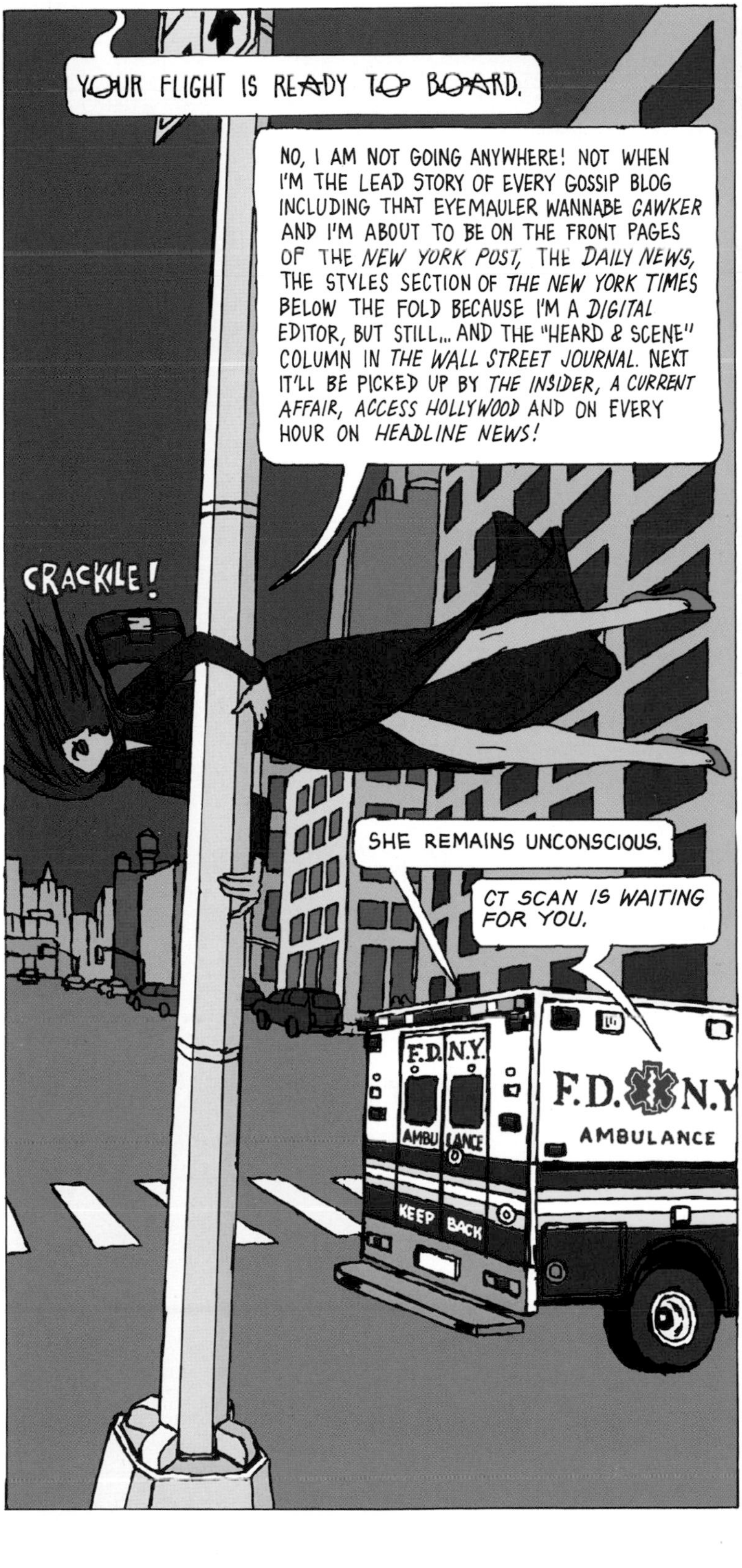
YOUR FLIGHT IS READY TO BOARD.
NO, I AM NOT GOING ANYWHERE! NOT WHEN I'M THE LEAD STORY OF EVERY GOSSIP BLOG INCLUDING THAT EYEMAULER WANNABE *GAWKER* AND I'M ABOUT TO BE ON THE FRONT PAGES OF THE *NEW YORK POST*, THE *DAILY NEWS*, THE STYLES SECTION OF *THE NEW YORK TIMES* BELOW THE FOLD BECAUSE I'M A *DIGITAL* EDITOR, BUT STILL... AND THE "HEARD & SCENE" COLUMN IN *THE WALL STREET JOURNAL*. NEXT IT'LL BE PICKED UP BY *THE INSIDER*, *A CURRENT AFFAIR*, *ACCESS HOLLYWOOD* AND ON EVERY HOUR ON *HEADLINE NEWS*!
CRACKLE!
SHE REMAINS UNCONSCIOUS.
CT SCAN IS WAITING FOR YOU.
F.D.N.Y.
AMBULANCE
KEEP BACK

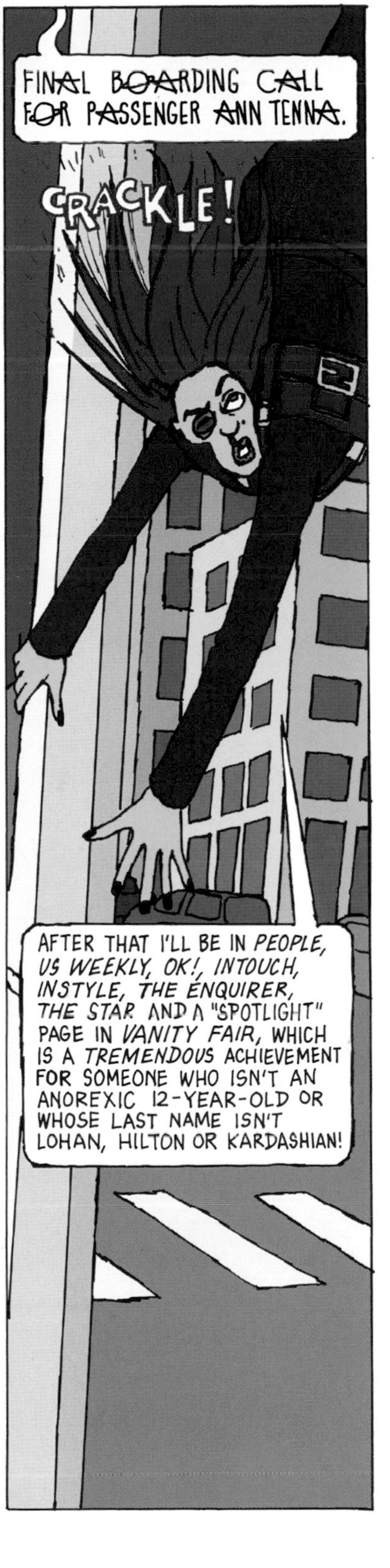
FINAL BOARDING CALL FOR PASSENGER ANN TENNA.
CRACKLE!
AFTER THAT I'LL BE IN *PEOPLE*, *US WEEKLY*, *OK!*, *INTOUCH*, *INSTYLE*, *THE ENQUIRER*, *THE STAR* AND A "SPOTLIGHT" PAGE IN *VANITY FAIR*, WHICH IS A *TREMENDOUS* ACHIEVEMENT FOR SOMEONE WHO ISN'T AN ANOREXIC 12-YEAR-OLD OR WHOSE LAST NAME ISN'T LOHAN, HILTON OR KARDASHIAN!

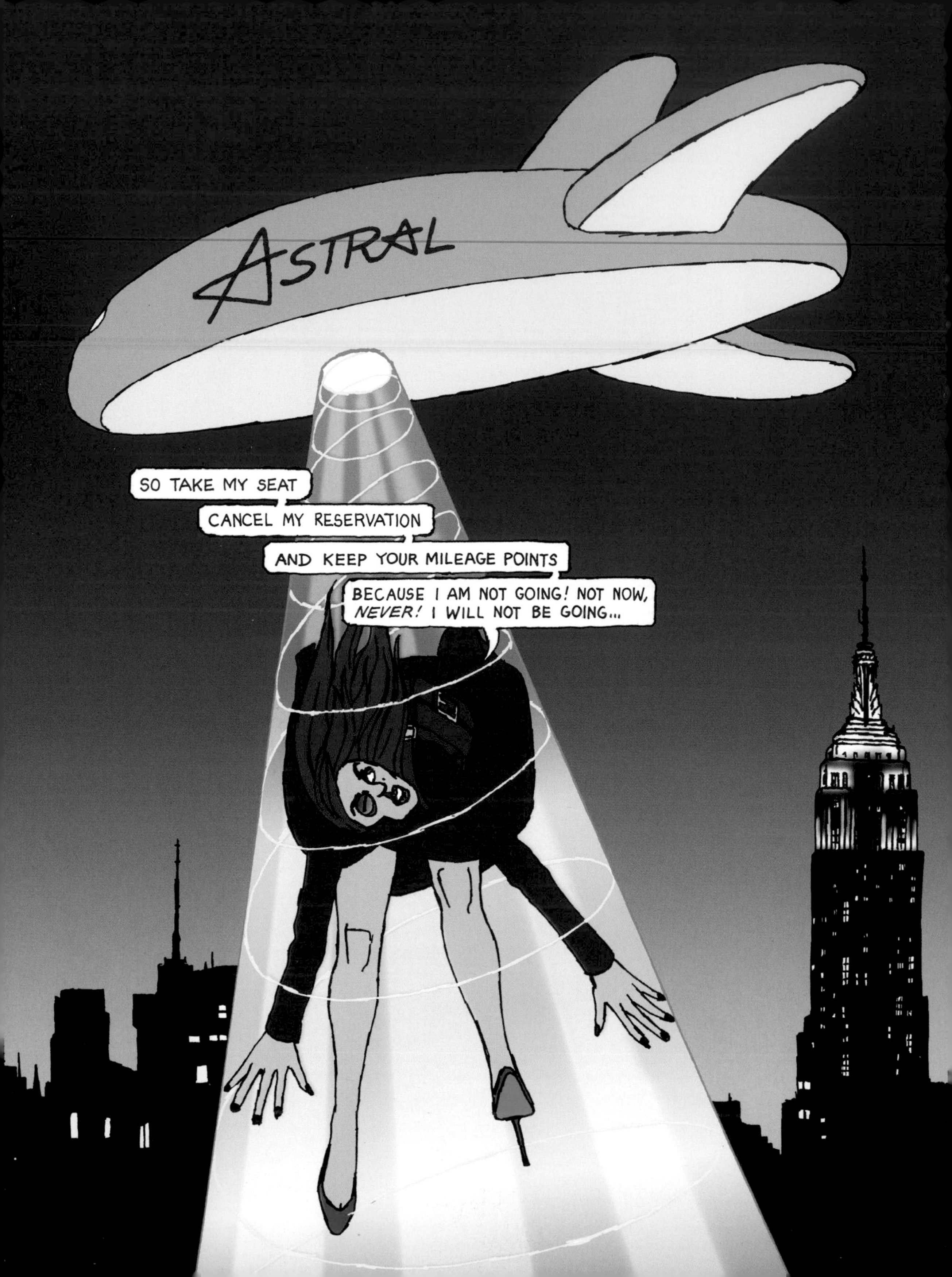
ASTRAL
SO TAKE MY SEAT
CANCEL MY RESERVATION
AND KEEP YOUR MILEAGE POINTS
BECAUSE I AM NOT GOING! NOT NOW, NEVER! I WILL NOT BE GOING...

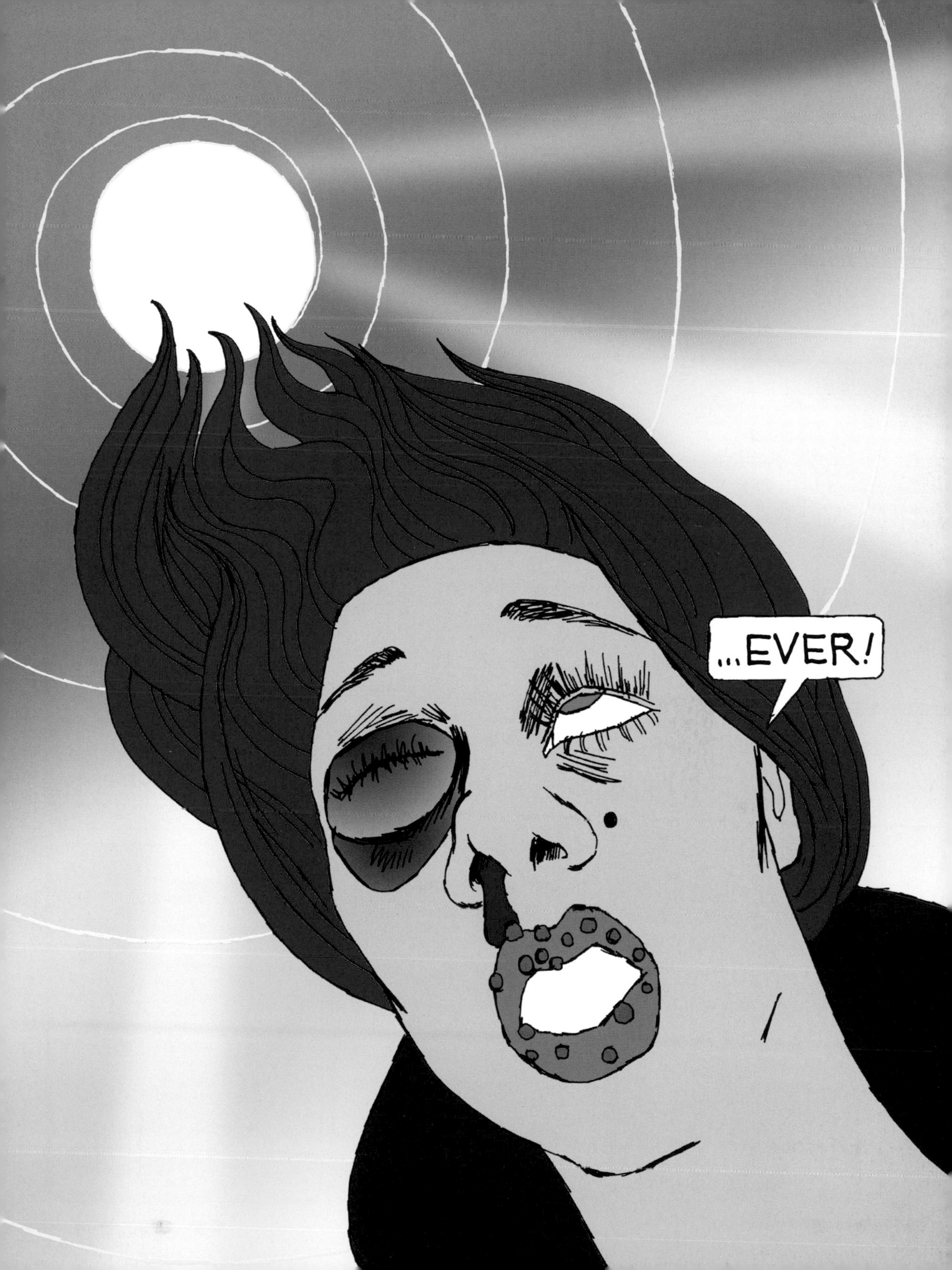
...EVER!

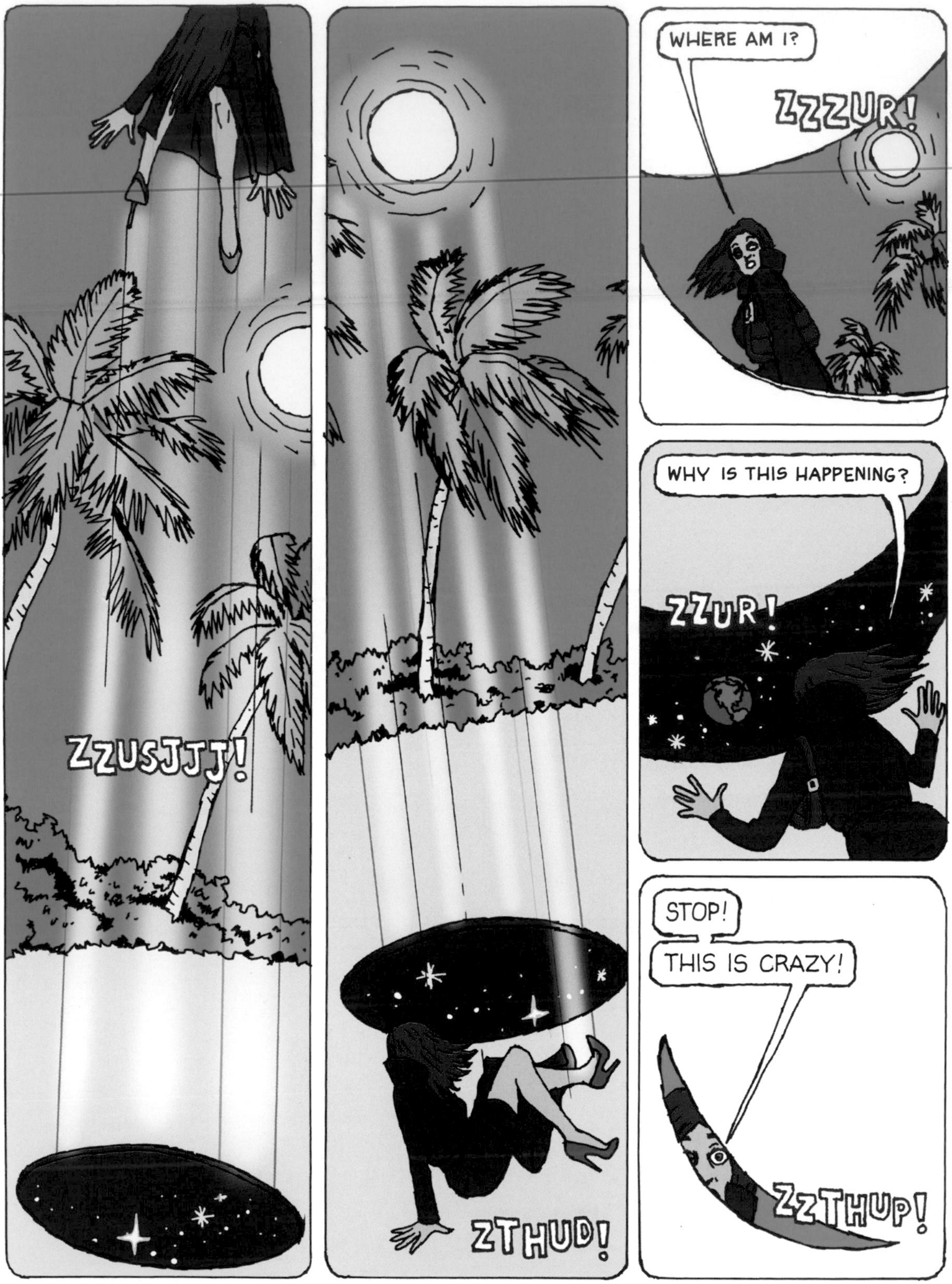
ZZUSJJJ!
ZTHUD!
WHERE AM I?
ZZZUR!
WHY IS THIS HAPPENING?
ZZUR!
STOP!
THIS IS CRAZY!
ZZTHUP!

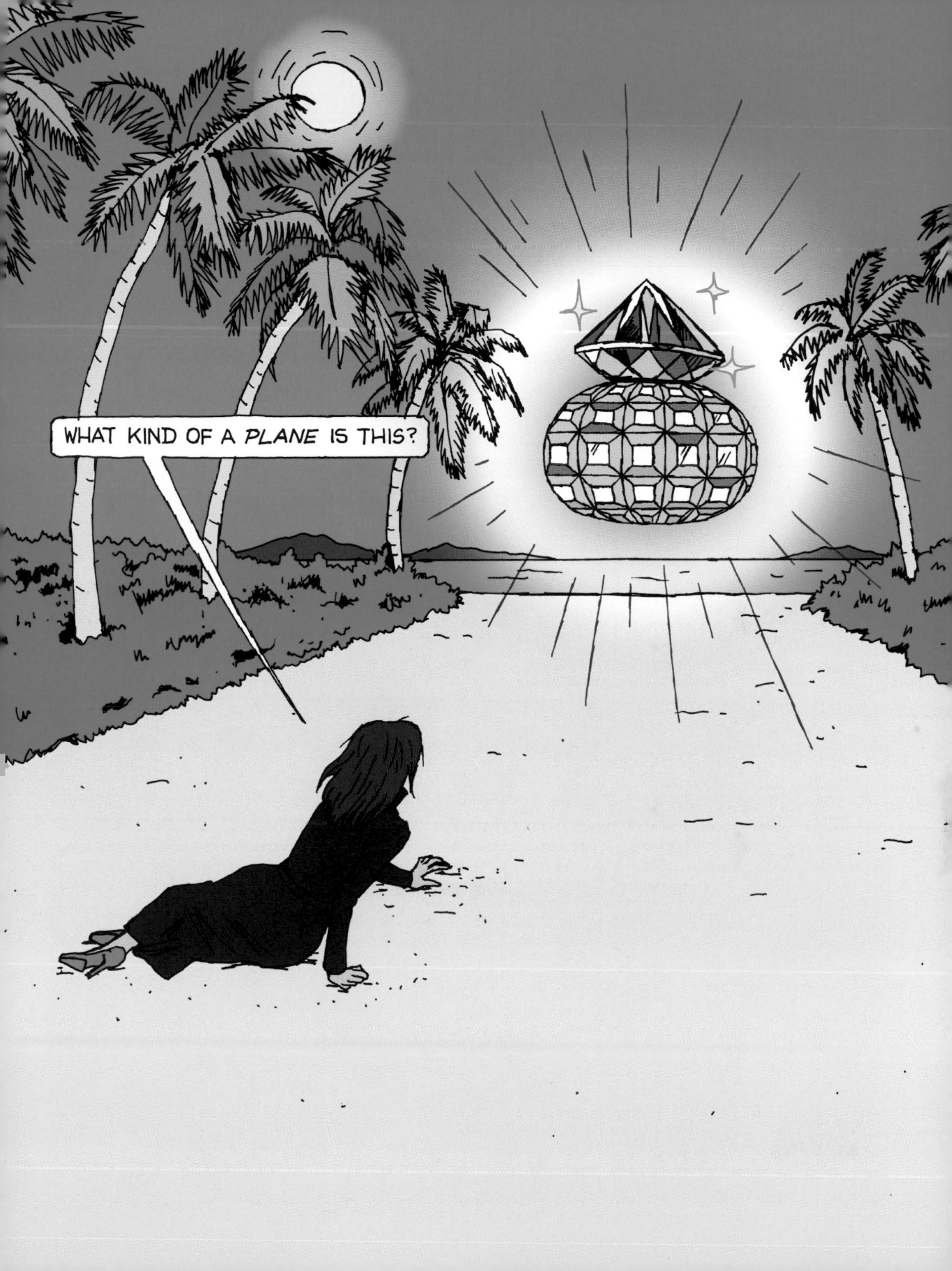
WHAT KIND OF A *PLANE* IS THIS?

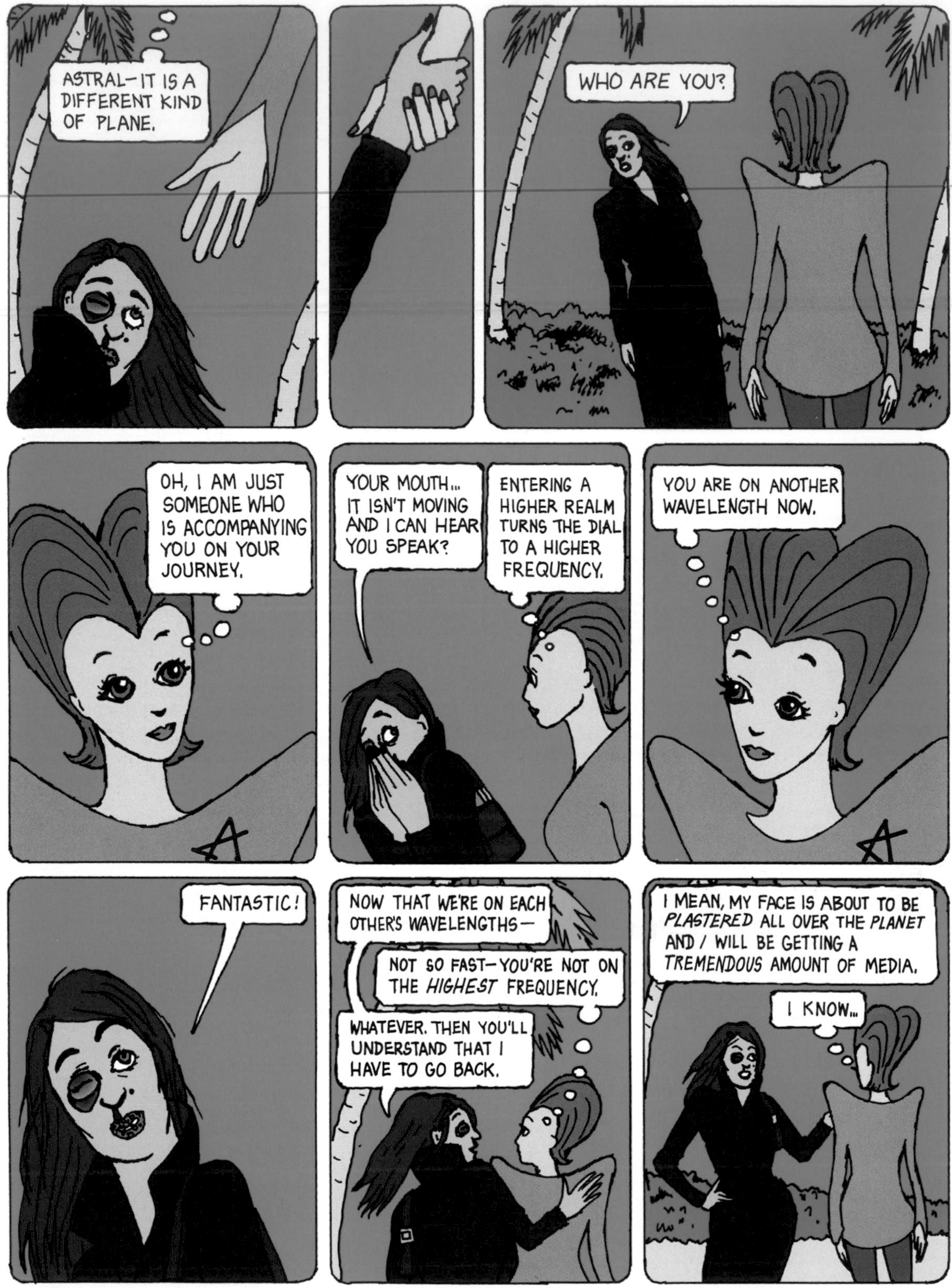
ASTRAL—IT IS A DIFFERENT KIND OF PLANE.
WHO ARE YOU?
OH, I AM JUST SOMEONE WHO IS ACCOMPANYING YOU ON YOUR JOURNEY.
YOUR MOUTH... IT ISN'T MOVING AND I CAN HEAR YOU SPEAK?
ENTERING A HIGHER REALM TURNS THE DIAL TO A HIGHER FREQUENCY.
YOU ARE ON ANOTHER WAVELENGTH NOW.
FANTASTIC!
NOW THAT WE'RE ON EACH OTHER'S WAVELENGTHS—
NOT SO FAST—YOU'RE NOT ON THE *HIGHEST* FREQUENCY.
WHATEVER. THEN YOU'LL UNDERSTAND THAT I HAVE TO GO BACK.
I MEAN, MY FACE IS ABOUT TO BE *PLASTERED* ALL OVER THE *PLANET* AND *I* WILL BE GETTING A *TREMENDOUS* AMOUNT OF MEDIA.
I KNOW...

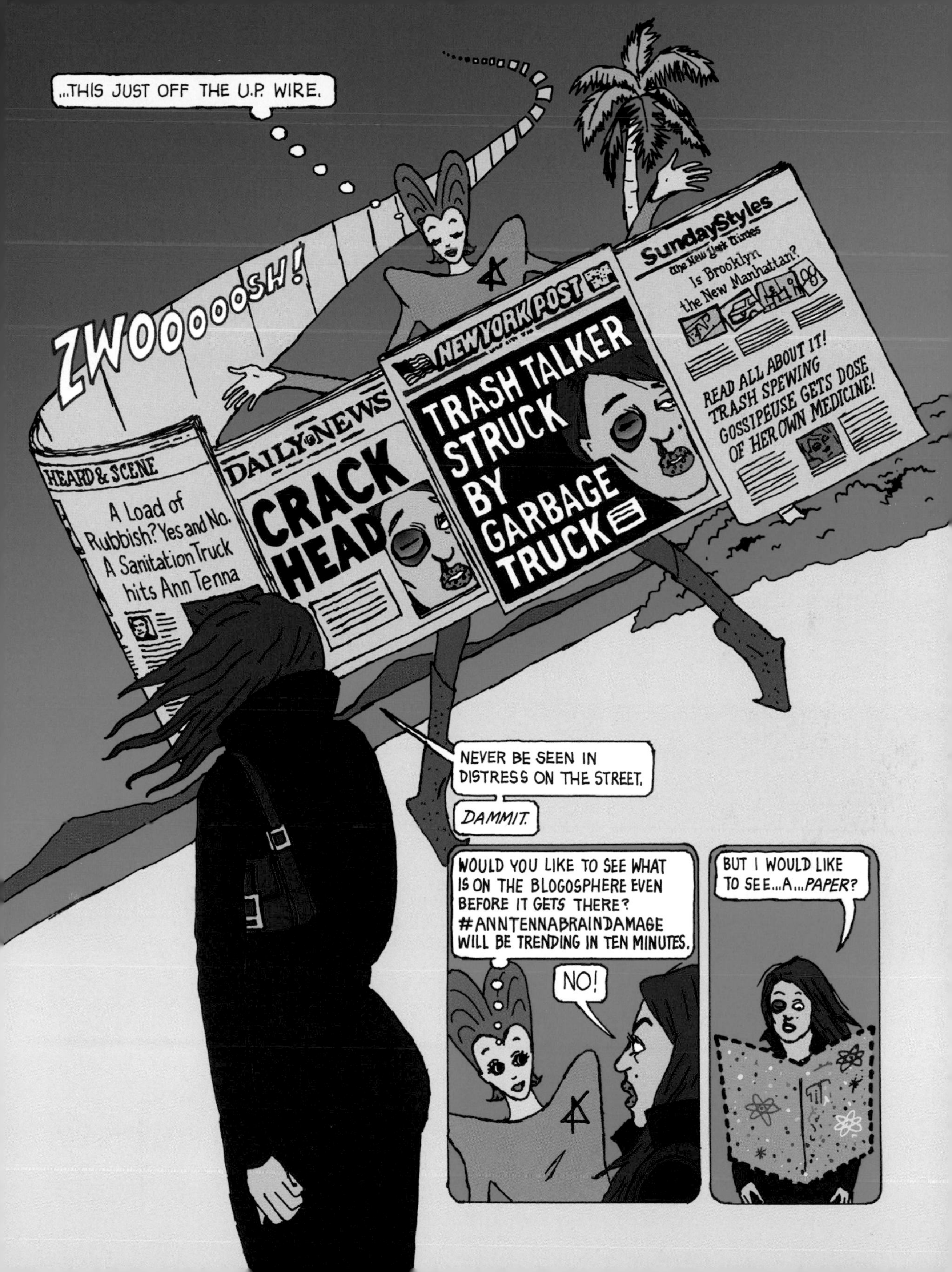
...THIS JUST OFF THE U.P. WIRE.
ZWOOOOOOSH!
HEARD & SCENE
A Load of Rubbish? Yes and No. A Sanitation Truck hits Ann Tenna
DAILY NEWS
CRACK HEAD
NEW YORK POST
TRASH TALKER STRUCK BY GARBAGE TRUCK
SundayStyles
The New York Times
Is Brooklyn the New Manhattan?
READ ALL ABOUT IT! TRASH SPEWING GOSSIPEUSE GETS DOSE OF HER OWN MEDICINE!
NEVER BE SEEN IN DISTRESS ON THE STREET.
DAMMIT.
WOULD YOU LIKE TO SEE WHAT IS ON THE BLOGOSPHERE EVEN BEFORE IT GETS THERE? #ANNTENNABRAINDAMAGE WILL BE TRENDING IN TEN MINUTES.
NO!
BUT I WOULD LIKE TO SEE...A...PAPER?

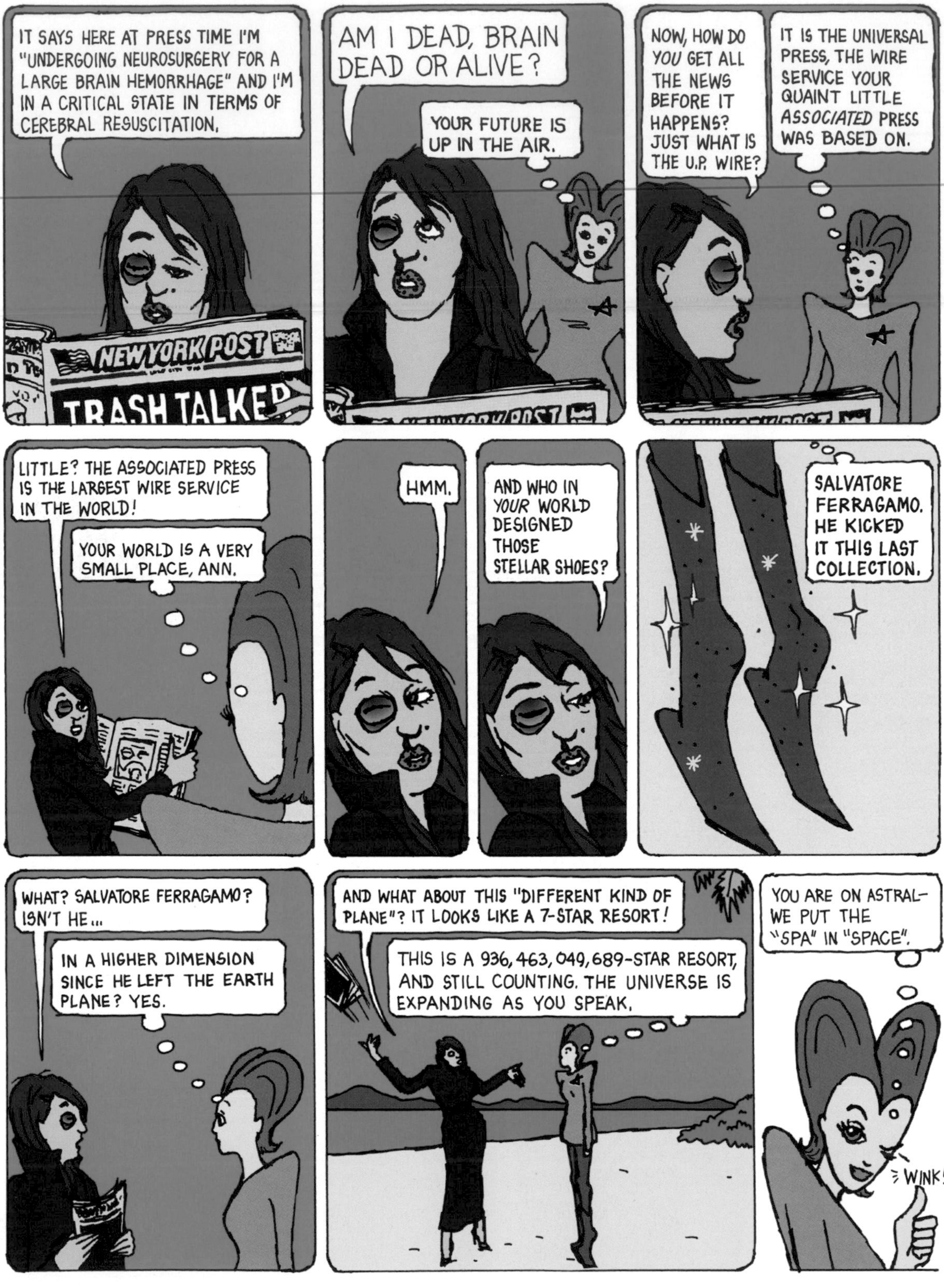
IT SAYS HERE AT PRESS TIME I'M "UNDERGOING NEUROSURGERY FOR A LARGE BRAIN HEMORRHAGE" AND I'M IN A CRITICAL STATE IN TERMS OF CEREBRAL RESUSCITATION.
NEW YORK POST
TRASH TALKER
AM I DEAD, BRAIN DEAD OR ALIVE?
YOUR FUTURE IS UP IN THE AIR.
NOW, HOW DO *YOU* GET ALL THE NEWS BEFORE IT HAPPENS? JUST WHAT IS THE U.P. WIRE?
IT IS THE UNIVERSAL PRESS, THE WIRE SERVICE YOUR QUAINT LITTLE *ASSOCIATED* PRESS WAS BASED ON.
LITTLE? THE ASSOCIATED PRESS IS THE LARGEST WIRE SERVICE IN THE WORLD!
YOUR WORLD IS A VERY SMALL PLACE, ANN.
HMM.
AND WHO IN *YOUR* WORLD DESIGNED THOSE STELLAR SHOES?
SALVATORE FERRAGAMO. HE KICKED IT THIS LAST COLLECTION.
WHAT? SALVATORE FERRAGAMO? ISN'T HE...
IN A HIGHER DIMENSION SINCE HE LEFT THE EARTH PLANE? YES.
AND WHAT ABOUT THIS "DIFFERENT KIND OF PLANE"? IT LOOKS LIKE A 7-STAR RESORT!
THIS IS A 936,463,049,689-STAR RESORT, AND STILL COUNTING. THE UNIVERSE IS EXPANDING AS YOU SPEAK.
YOU ARE ON ASTRAL— WE PUT THE "SPA" IN "SPACE".
WINK!

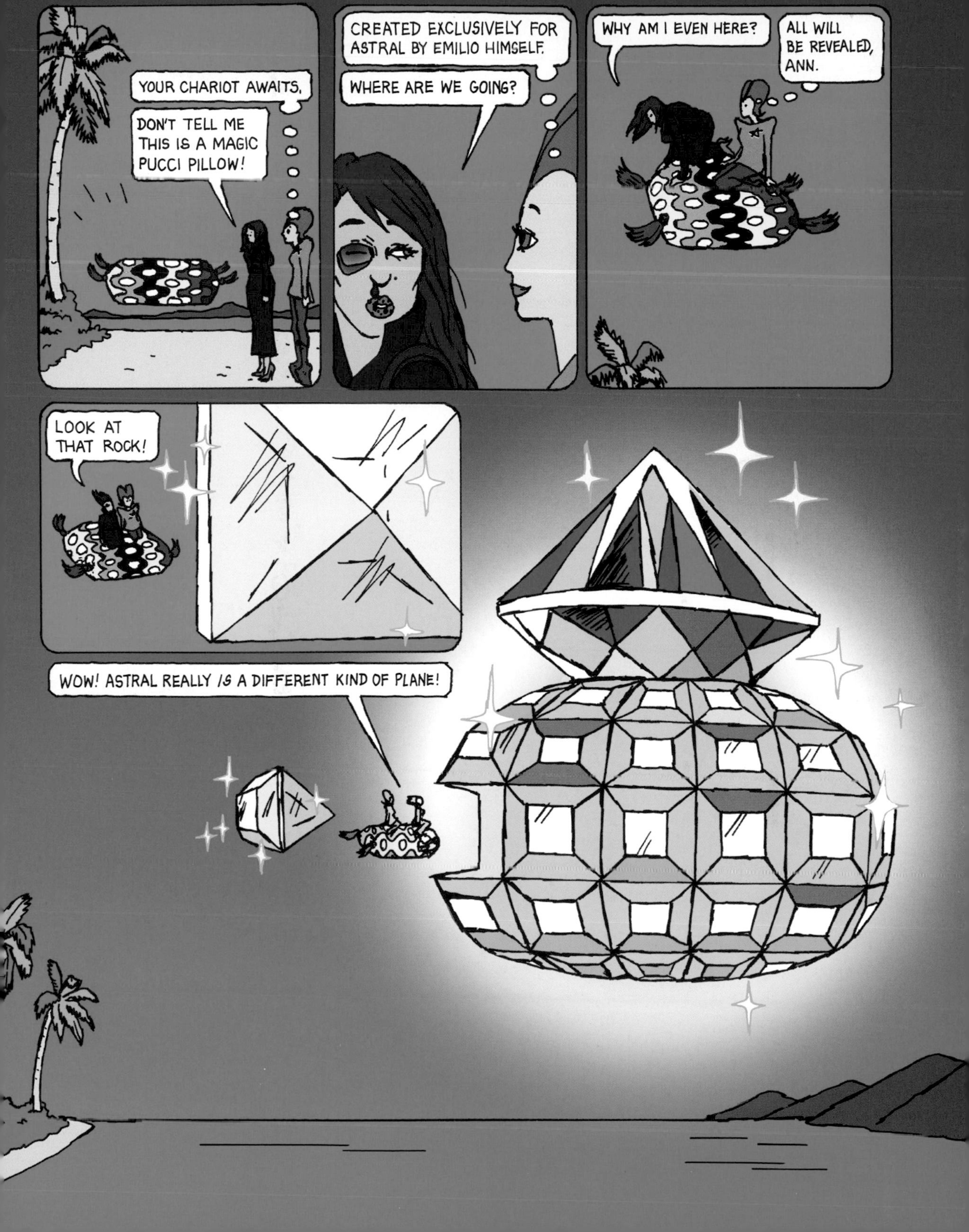
YOUR CHARIOT AWAITS,
DON'T TELL ME THIS IS A MAGIC PUCCI PILLOW!
CREATED EXCLUSIVELY FOR ASTRAL BY EMILIO HIMSELF.
WHERE ARE WE GOING?
WHY AM I EVEN HERE?
ALL WILL BE REVEALED, ANN.
LOOK AT THAT ROCK!
WOW! ASTRAL REALLY IS A DIFFERENT KIND OF PLANE!

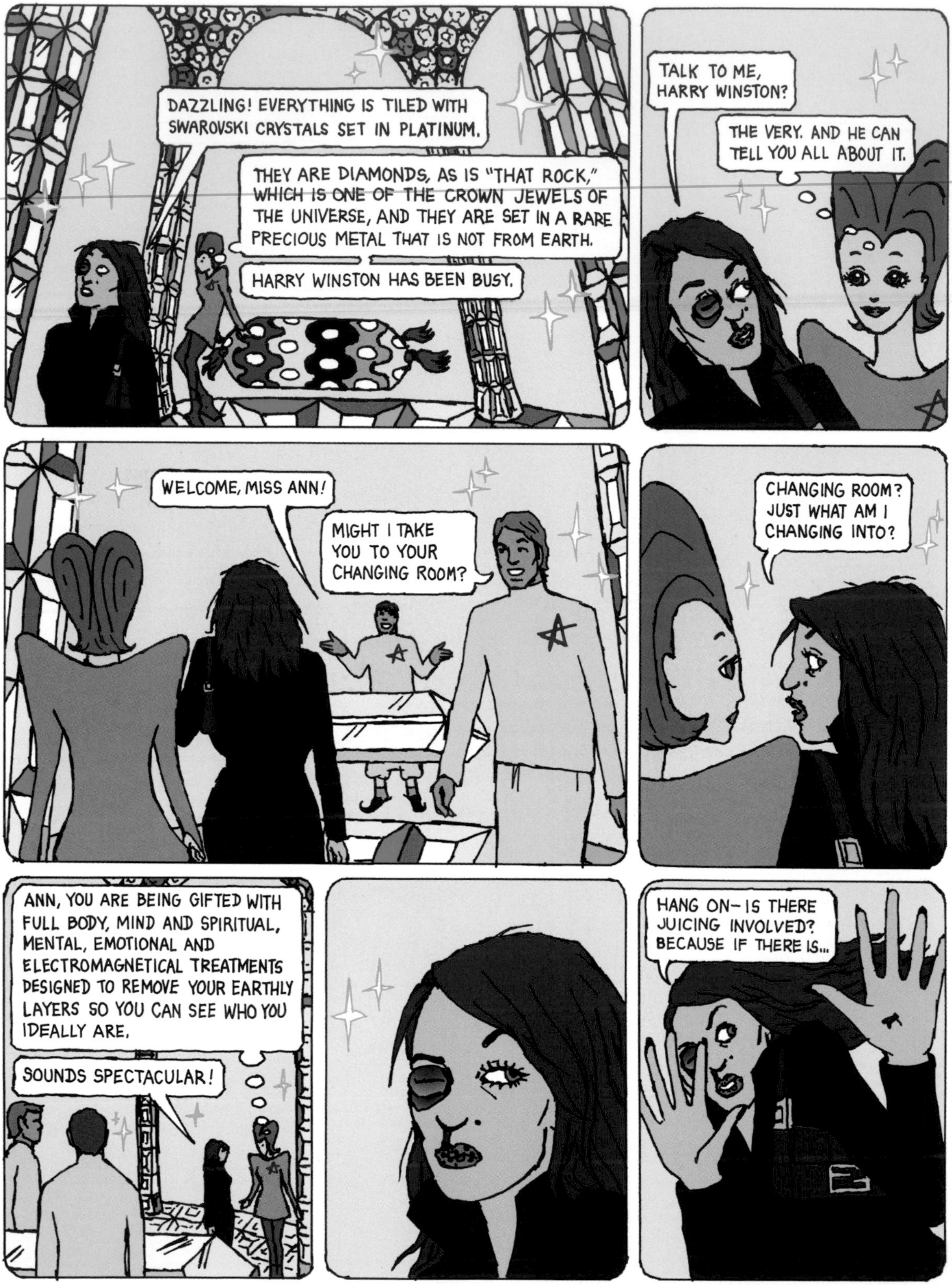
DAZZLING! EVERYTHING IS TILED WITH SWAROVSKI CRYSTALS SET IN PLATINUM.
THEY ARE DIAMONDS, AS IS "THAT ROCK," WHICH IS ONE OF THE CROWN JEWELS OF THE UNIVERSE, AND THEY ARE SET IN A RARE PRECIOUS METAL THAT IS NOT FROM EARTH.
HARRY WINSTON HAS BEEN BUSY.
TALK TO ME, HARRY WINSTON?
THE VERY. AND HE CAN TELL YOU ALL ABOUT IT.
WELCOME, MISS ANN!
MIGHT I TAKE YOU TO YOUR CHANGING ROOM?
CHANGING ROOM? JUST WHAT AM I CHANGING INTO?
ANN, YOU ARE BEING GIFTED WITH FULL BODY, MIND AND SPIRITUAL, MENTAL, EMOTIONAL AND ELECTROMAGNETICAL TREATMENTS DESIGNED TO REMOVE YOUR EARTHLY LAYERS SO YOU CAN SEE WHO YOU IDEALLY ARE.
SOUNDS SPECTACULAR!
HANG ON— IS THERE JUICING INVOLVED? BECAUSE IF THERE IS...

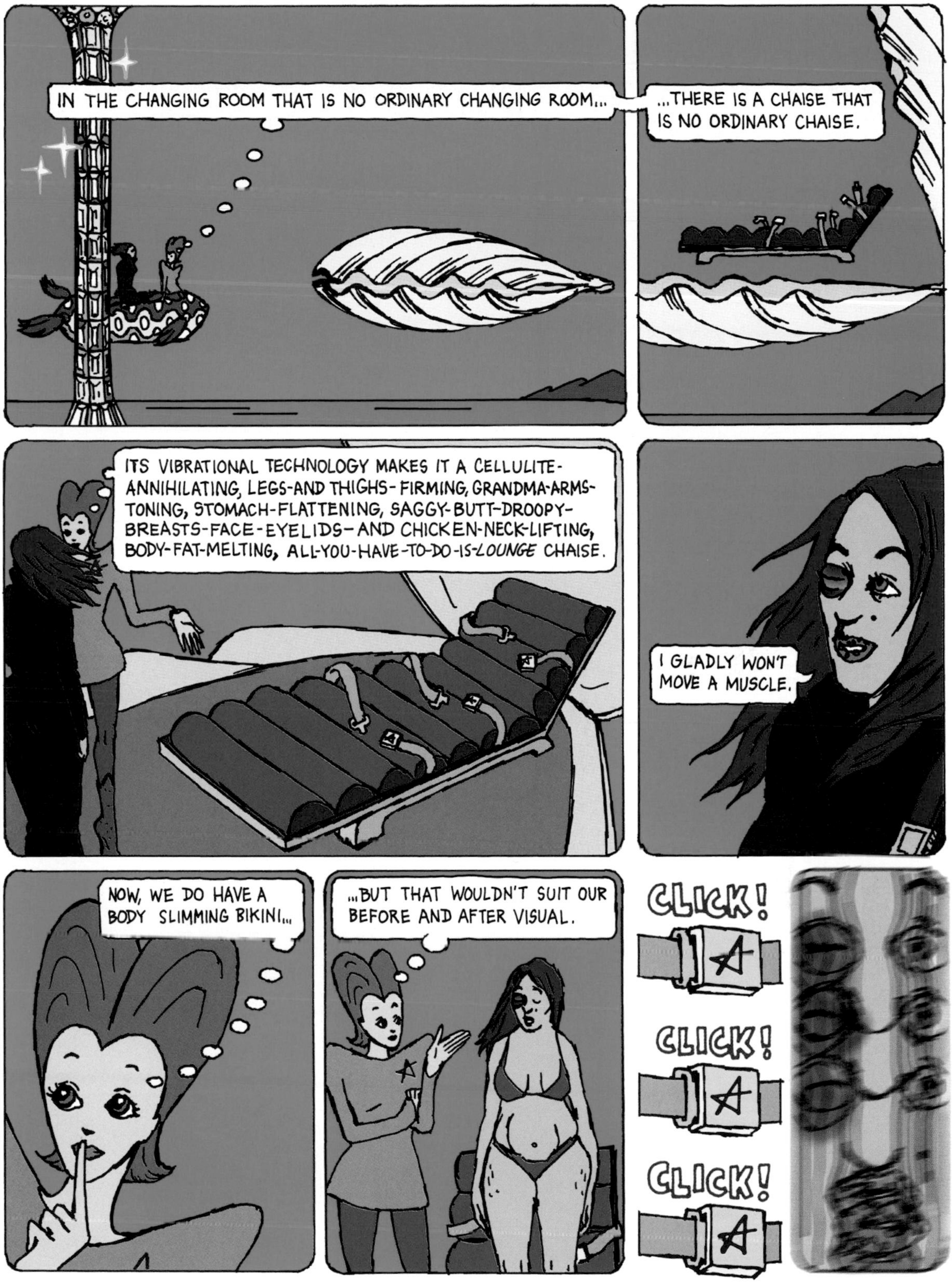
IN THE CHANGING ROOM THAT IS NO ORDINARY CHANGING ROOM...
...THERE IS A CHAISE THAT IS NO ORDINARY CHAISE.
ITS VIBRATIONAL TECHNOLOGY MAKES IT A CELLULITE-ANNIHILATING, LEGS-AND THIGHS-FIRMING, GRANDMA-ARMS-TONING, STOMACH-FLATTENING, SAGGY-BUTT-DROOPY-BREASTS-FACE-EYELIDS-AND CHICKEN-NECK-LIFTING, BODY-FAT-MELTING, ALL-YOU-HAVE-TO-DO-IS-*LOUNGE* CHAISE.
I GLADLY WON'T MOVE A MUSCLE.
NOW, WE DO HAVE A BODY SLIMMING BIKINI...
...BUT THAT WOULDN'T SUIT OUR BEFORE AND AFTER VISUAL.
CLICK!
CLICK!
CLICK!

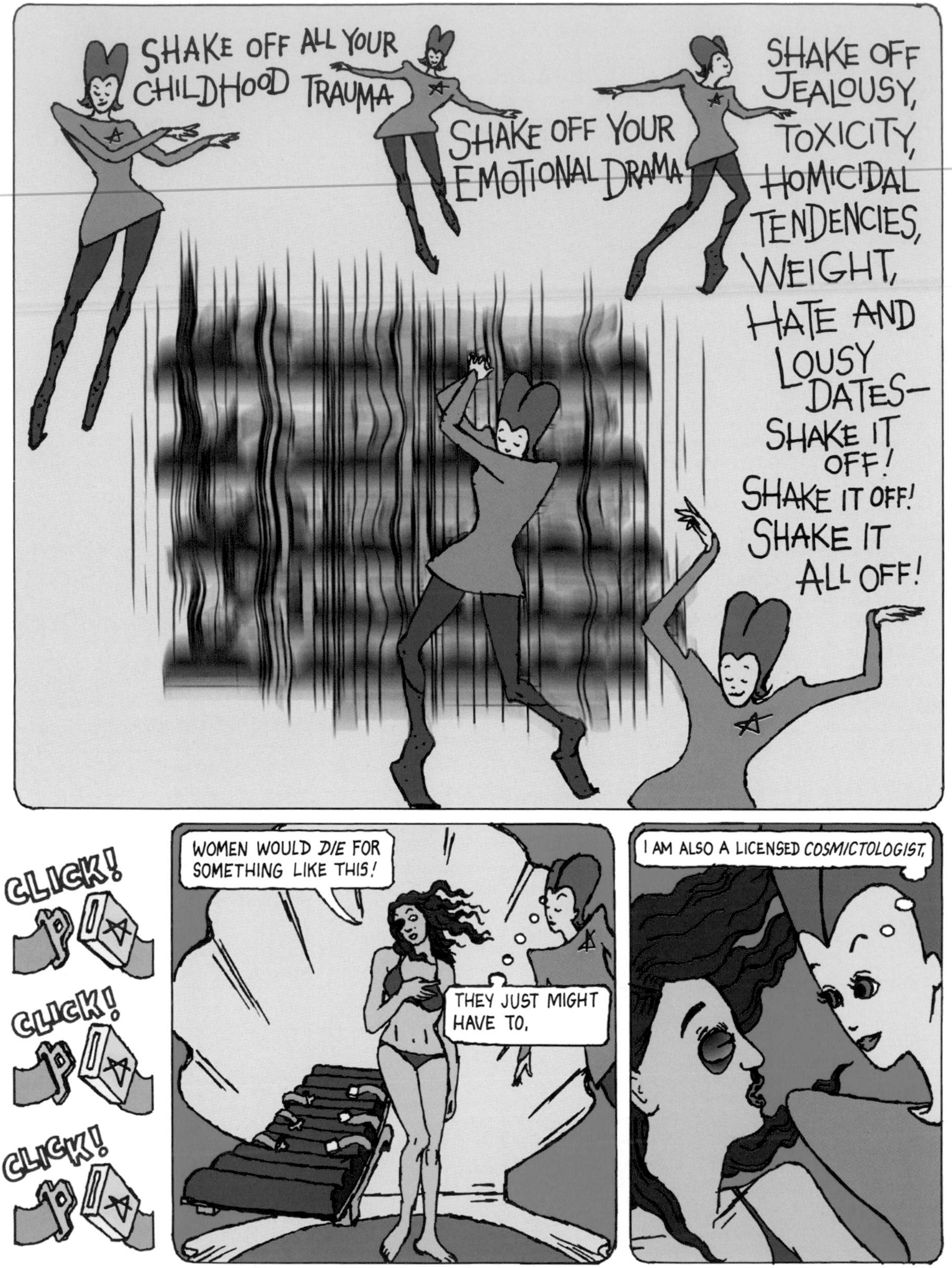
SHAKE OFF ALL YOUR CHILDHOOD TRAUMA
SHAKE OFF YOUR EMOTIONAL DRAMA
SHAKE OFF JEALOUSY, TOXICITY, HOMICIDAL TENDENCIES, WEIGHT, HATE AND LOUSY DATES—
SHAKE IT OFF! SHAKE IT OFF! SHAKE IT ALL OFF!
CLICK!
CLICK!
CLICK!
WOMEN WOULD *DIE* FOR SOMETHING LIKE THIS!
THEY JUST MIGHT HAVE TO.
I AM ALSO A LICENSED *COSMICTOLOGIST.*

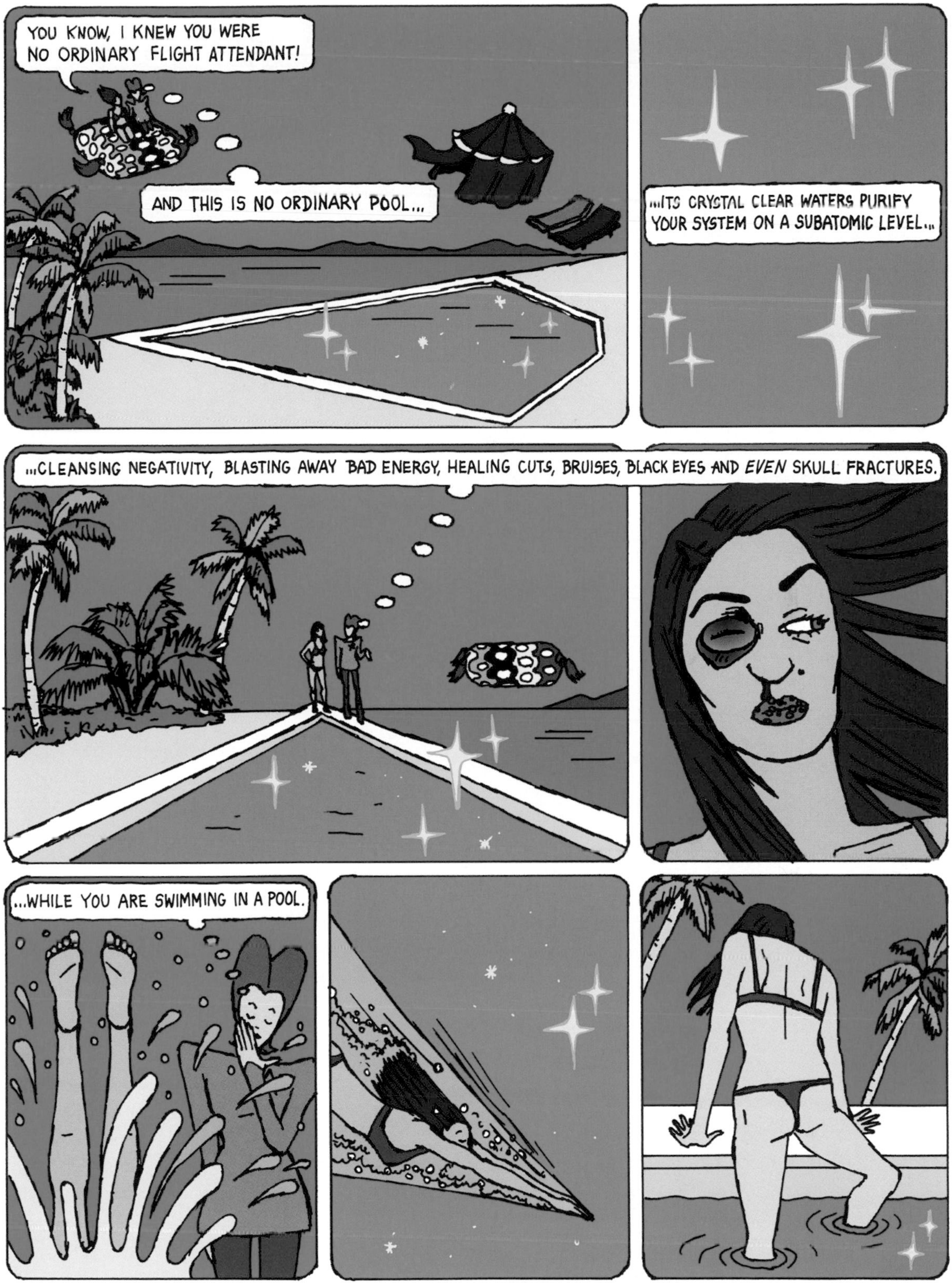
YOU KNOW, I KNEW YOU WERE NO ORDINARY FLIGHT ATTENDANT!
AND THIS IS NO ORDINARY POOL...
...ITS CRYSTAL CLEAR WATERS PURIFY YOUR SYSTEM ON A SUBATOMIC LEVEL...
...CLEANSING NEGATIVITY, BLASTING AWAY BAD ENERGY, HEALING CUTS, BRUISES, BLACK EYES AND *EVEN* SKULL FRACTURES.
...WHILE YOU ARE SWIMMING IN A POOL.

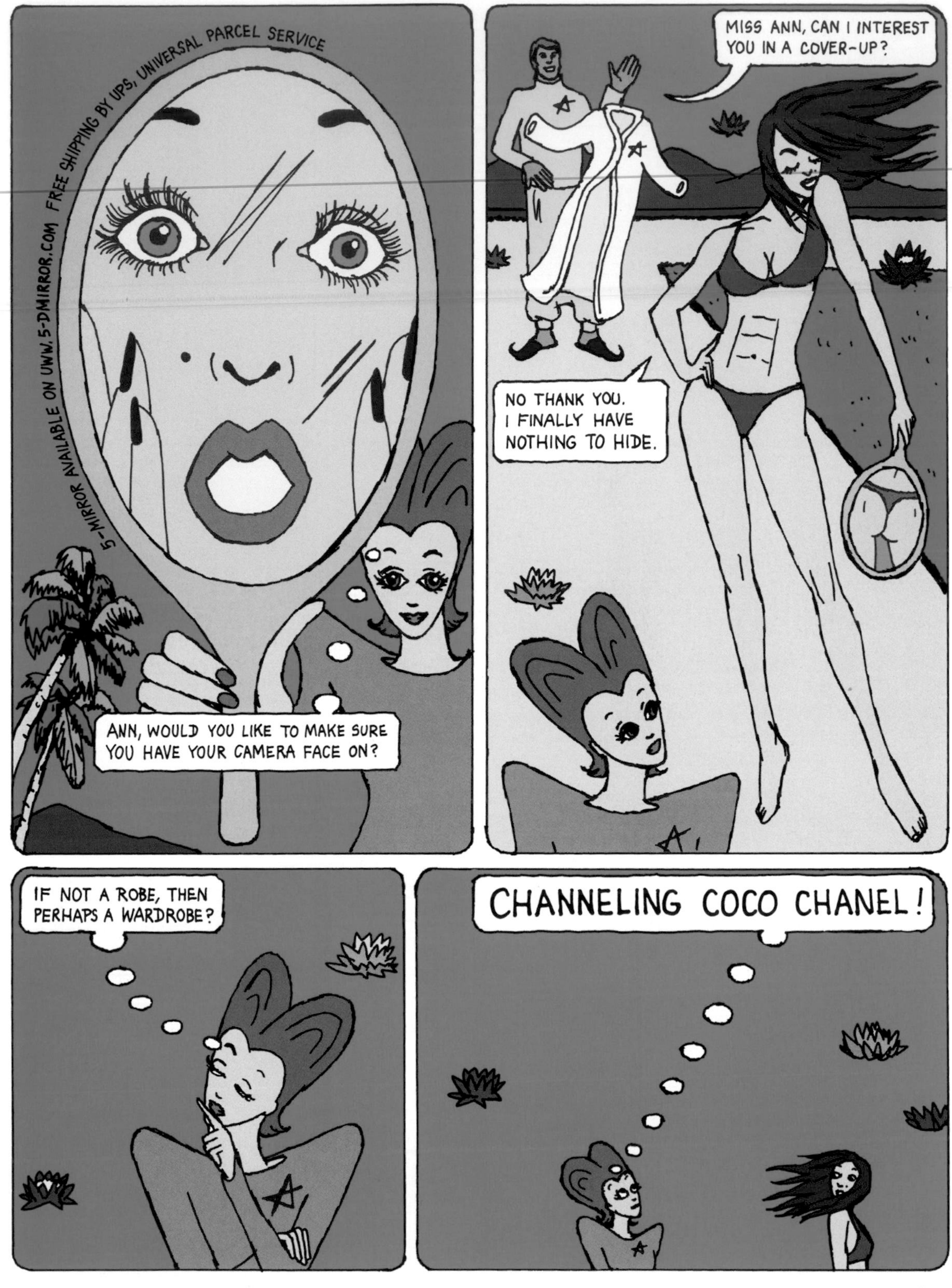
5-MIRROR AVAILABLE ON UWW.5-DMIRROR.COM FREE SHIPPING BY UPS, UNIVERSAL PARCEL SERVICE
ANN, WOULD YOU LIKE TO MAKE SURE YOU HAVE YOUR CAMERA FACE ON?
MISS ANN, CAN I INTEREST YOU IN A COVER-UP?
NO THANK YOU. I FINALLY HAVE NOTHING TO HIDE.
IF NOT A ROBE, THEN PERHAPS A WARDROBE?
CHANNELING COCO CHANEL!

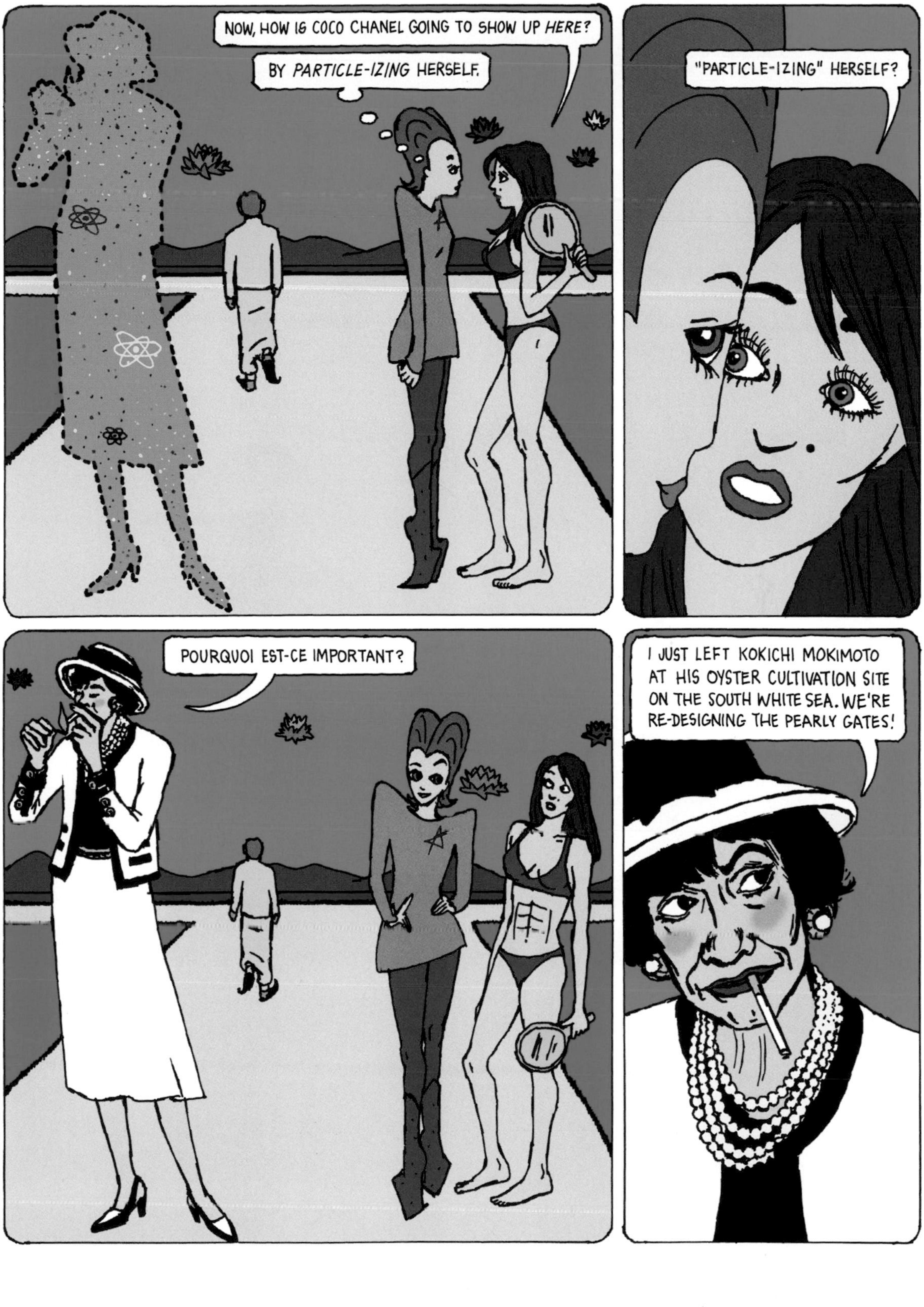
NOW, HOW IS COCO CHANEL GOING TO SHOW UP *HERE?*
BY *PARTICLE-IZING* HERSELF.
"PARTICLE-IZING" HERSELF?
POURQUOI EST-CE IMPORTANT?
I JUST LEFT KOKICHI MOKIMOTO AT HIS OYSTER CULTIVATION SITE ON THE SOUTH WHITE SEA. WE'RE RE-DESIGNING THE PEARLY GATES!

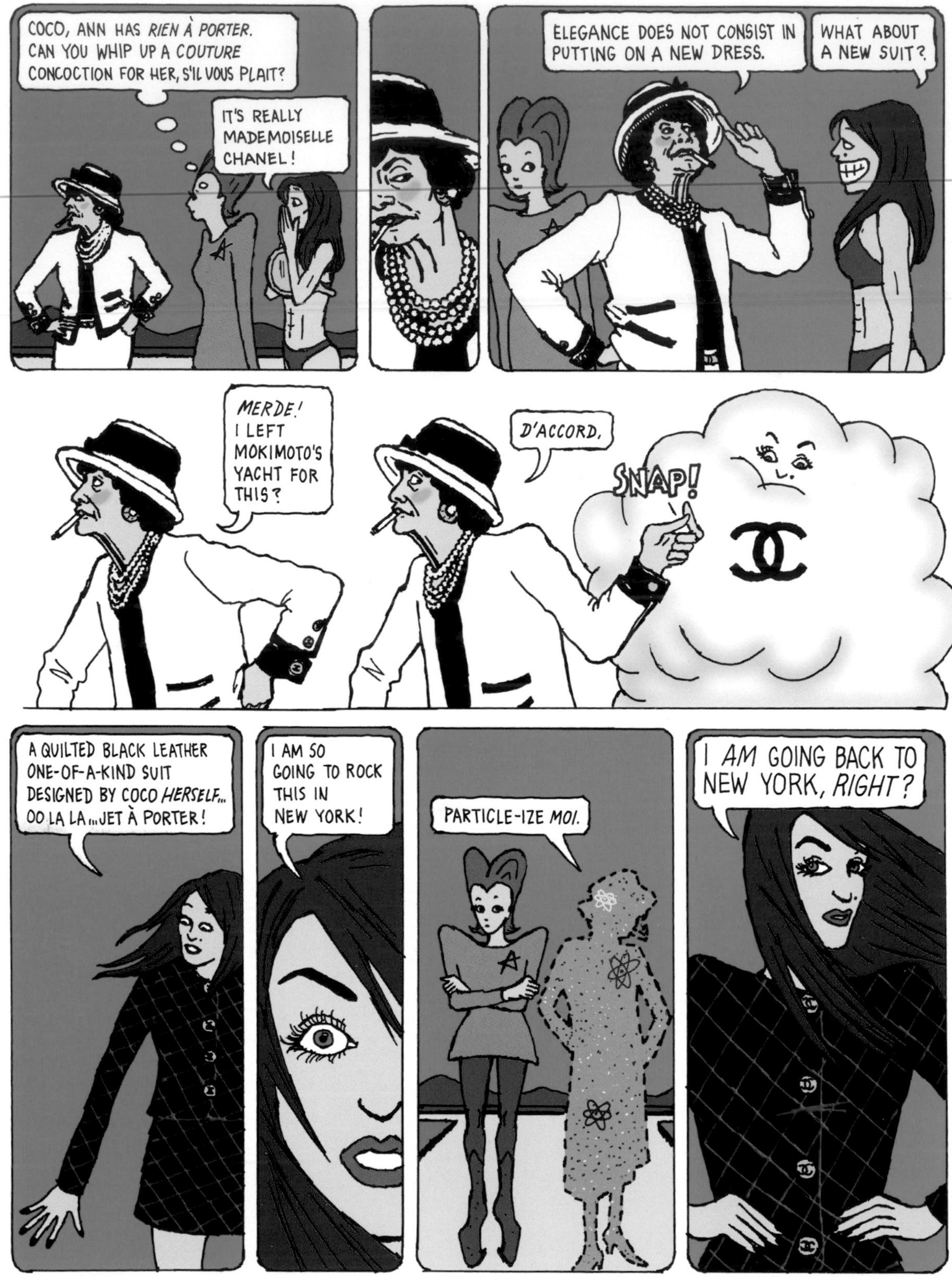
COCO, ANN HAS *RIEN À PORTER*. CAN YOU WHIP UP A *COUTURE* CONCOCTION FOR HER, S'IL VOUS PLAIT?
IT'S REALLY MADEMOISELLE CHANEL!
ELEGANCE DOES NOT CONSIST IN PUTTING ON A NEW DRESS.
WHAT ABOUT A NEW SUIT?
MERDE! I LEFT MOKIMOTO'S YACHT FOR THIS?
D'ACCORD.
SNAP!
A QUILTED BLACK LEATHER ONE-OF-A-KIND SUIT DESIGNED BY COCO *HERSELF*... OO LA LA...JET À PORTER!
I AM SO GOING TO ROCK THIS IN NEW YORK!
PARTICLE-IZE *MOI*.
I *AM* GOING BACK TO NEW YORK, *RIGHT*?

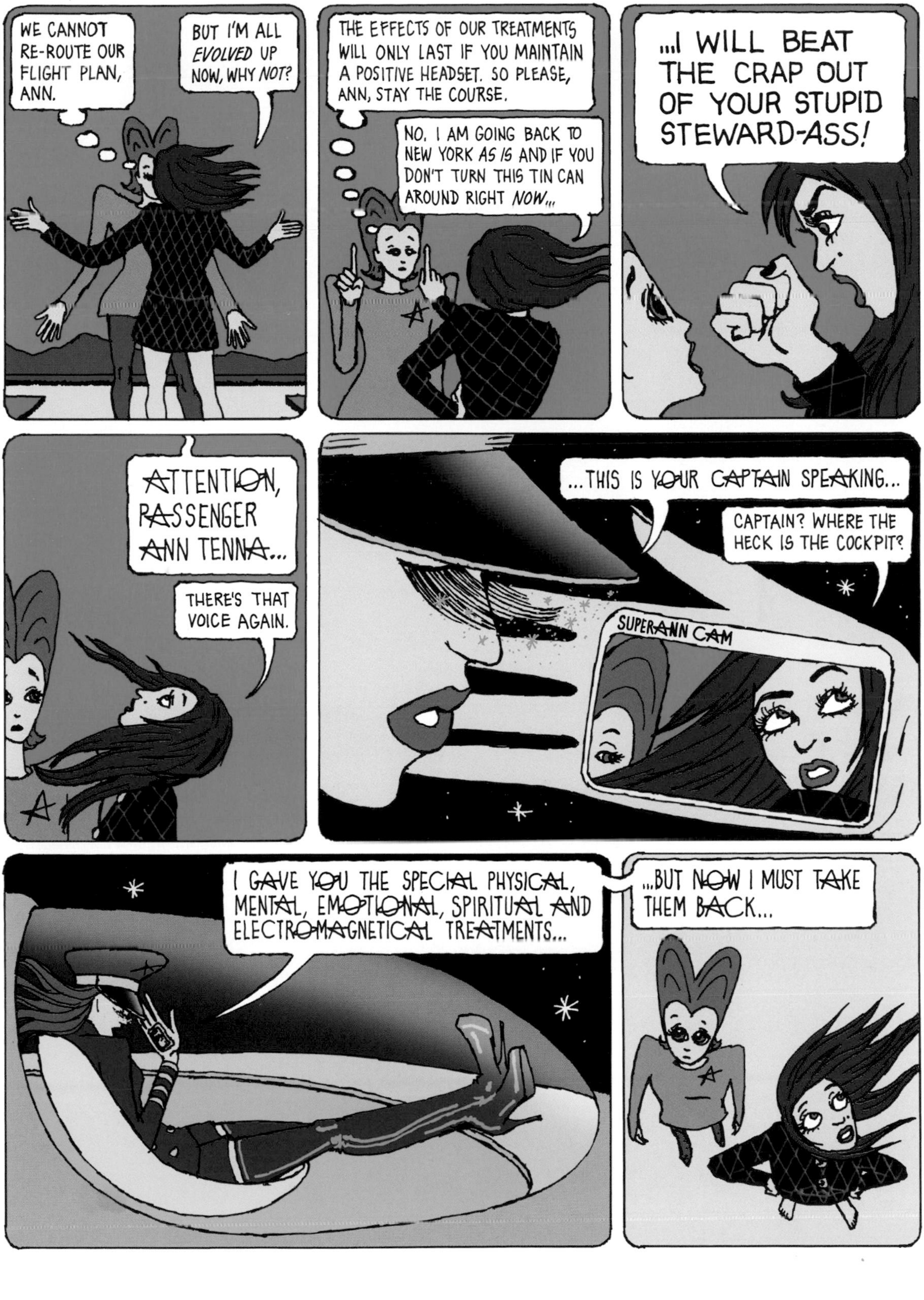
WE CANNOT RE-ROUTE OUR FLIGHT PLAN, ANN.
BUT I'M ALL *EVOLVED* UP NOW, WHY *NOT*?
THE EFFECTS OF OUR TREATMENTS WILL ONLY LAST IF YOU MAINTAIN A POSITIVE HEADSET. SO PLEASE, ANN, STAY THE COURSE.
NO. I AM GOING BACK TO NEW YORK *AS IS* AND IF YOU DON'T TURN THIS TIN CAN AROUND RIGHT *NOW*...
...I WILL BEAT THE CRAP OUT OF YOUR STUPID STEWARD-ASS!
ATTENTION, PASSENGER ANN TENNA...
THERE'S THAT VOICE AGAIN.
...THIS IS YOUR CAPTAIN SPEAKING...
CAPTAIN? WHERE THE HECK IS THE COCKPIT?
SUPERANN CAM
I GAVE YOU THE SPECIAL PHYSICAL, MENTAL, EMOTIONAL, SPIRITUAL AND ELECTROMAGNETICAL TREATMENTS...
...BUT NOW I MUST TAKE THEM BACK...

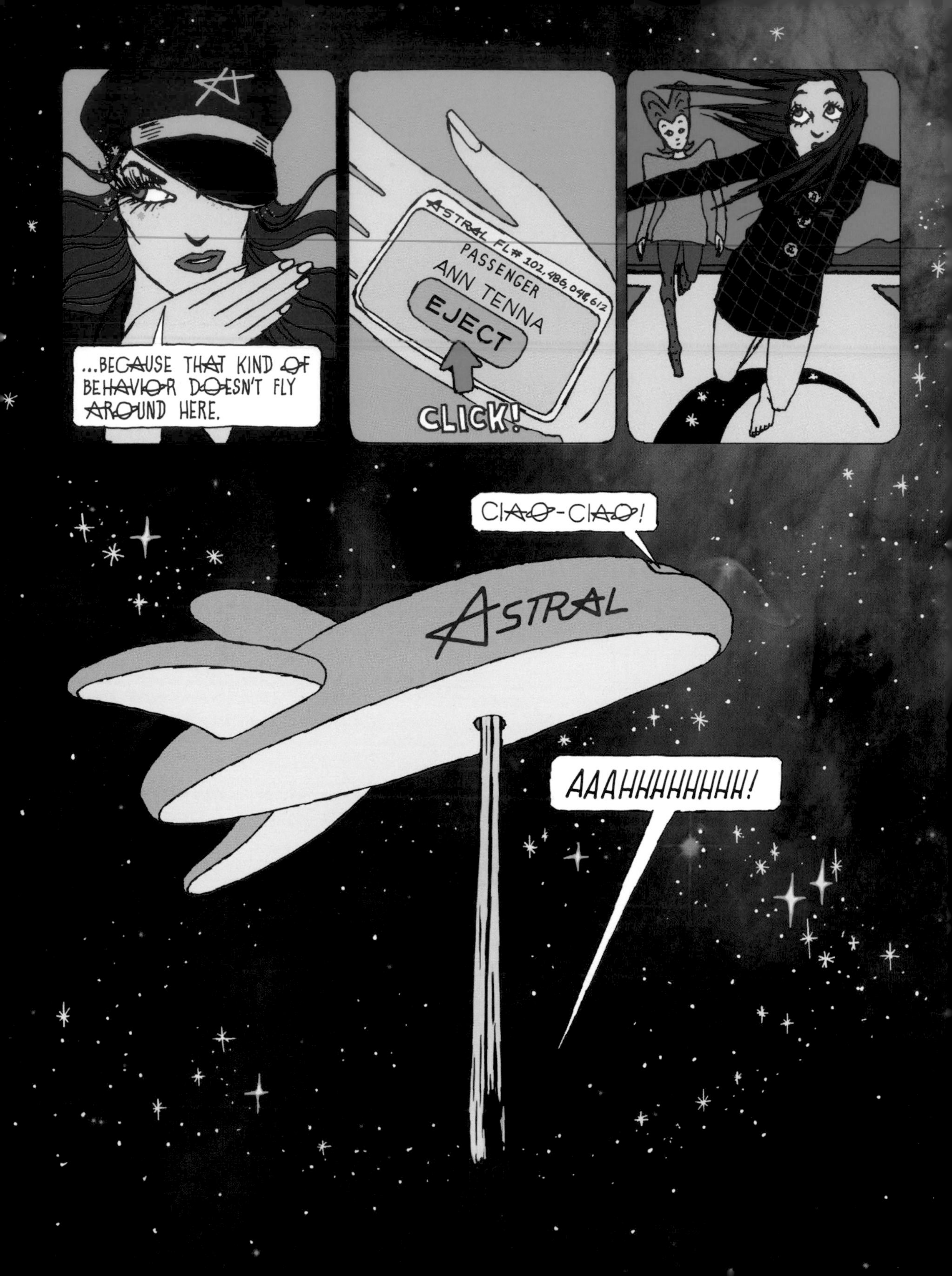
...BECAUSE THAT KIND OF BEHAVIOR DOESN'T FLY AROUND HERE.
ASTRAL FL# 102,486,048,612
PASSENGER
ANN TENNA
EJECT
CLICK!
CIAO-CIAO!
ASTRAL
AAAHHHHHHHH!

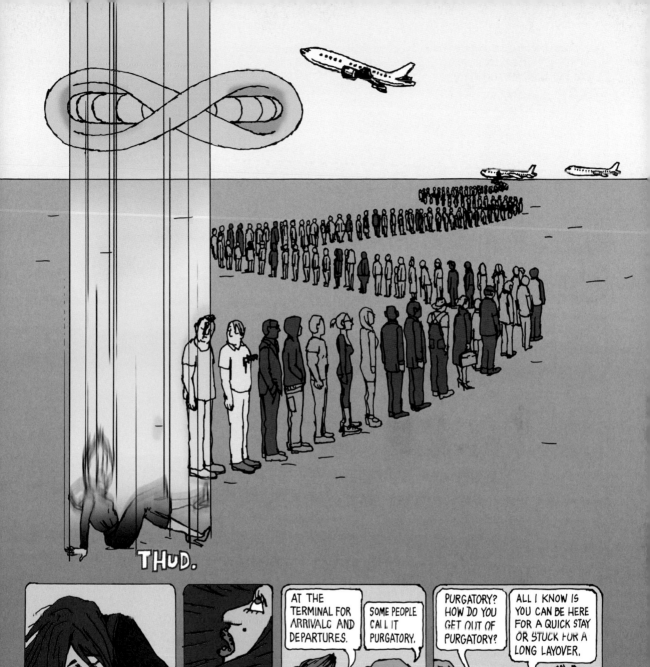

THUD.

I GAINED 21 POUNDS AND LOST MY ONE-OF-A-KIND CHANEL SUIT ALL IN THE SAME MILLISECOND.

NOW WHERE AM I?

AT THE TERMINAL FOR ARRIVALS AND DEPARTURES.

SOME PEOPLE CALL IT PURGATORY.

PURGATORY? HOW DO YOU GET OUT OF PURGATORY?

ALL I KNOW IS YOU CAN BE HERE FOR A QUICK STAY OR STUCK FOR A LONG LAYOVER.

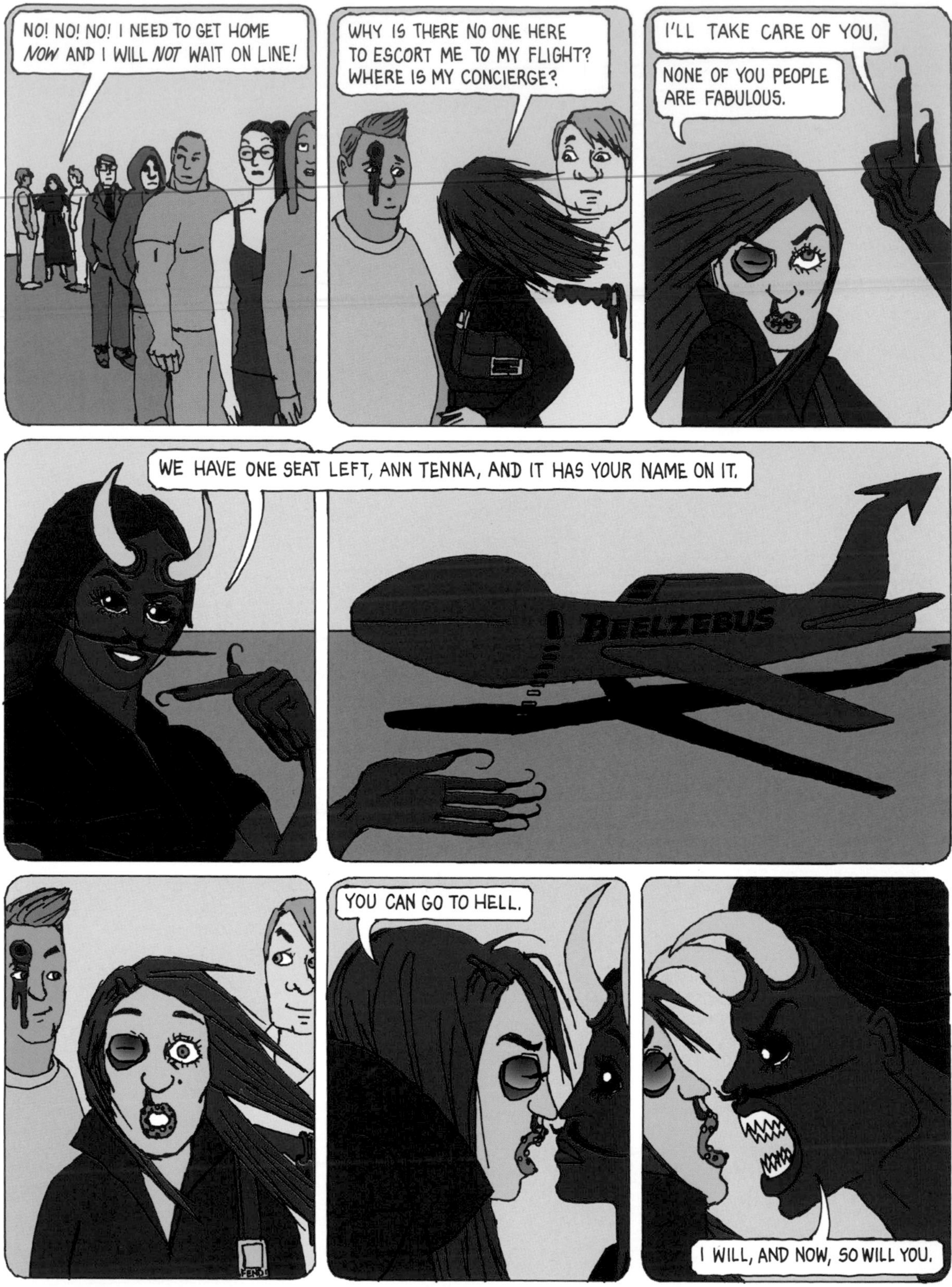
NO! NO! NO! I NEED TO GET HOME NOW AND I WILL NOT WAIT ON LINE!
WHY IS THERE NO ONE HERE TO ESCORT ME TO MY FLIGHT? WHERE IS MY CONCIERGE?
I'LL TAKE CARE OF YOU.
NONE OF YOU PEOPLE ARE FABULOUS.
WE HAVE ONE SEAT LEFT, ANN TENNA, AND IT HAS YOUR NAME ON IT.
BEELZEBUS
YOU CAN GO TO HELL.
I WILL, AND NOW, SO WILL YOU.

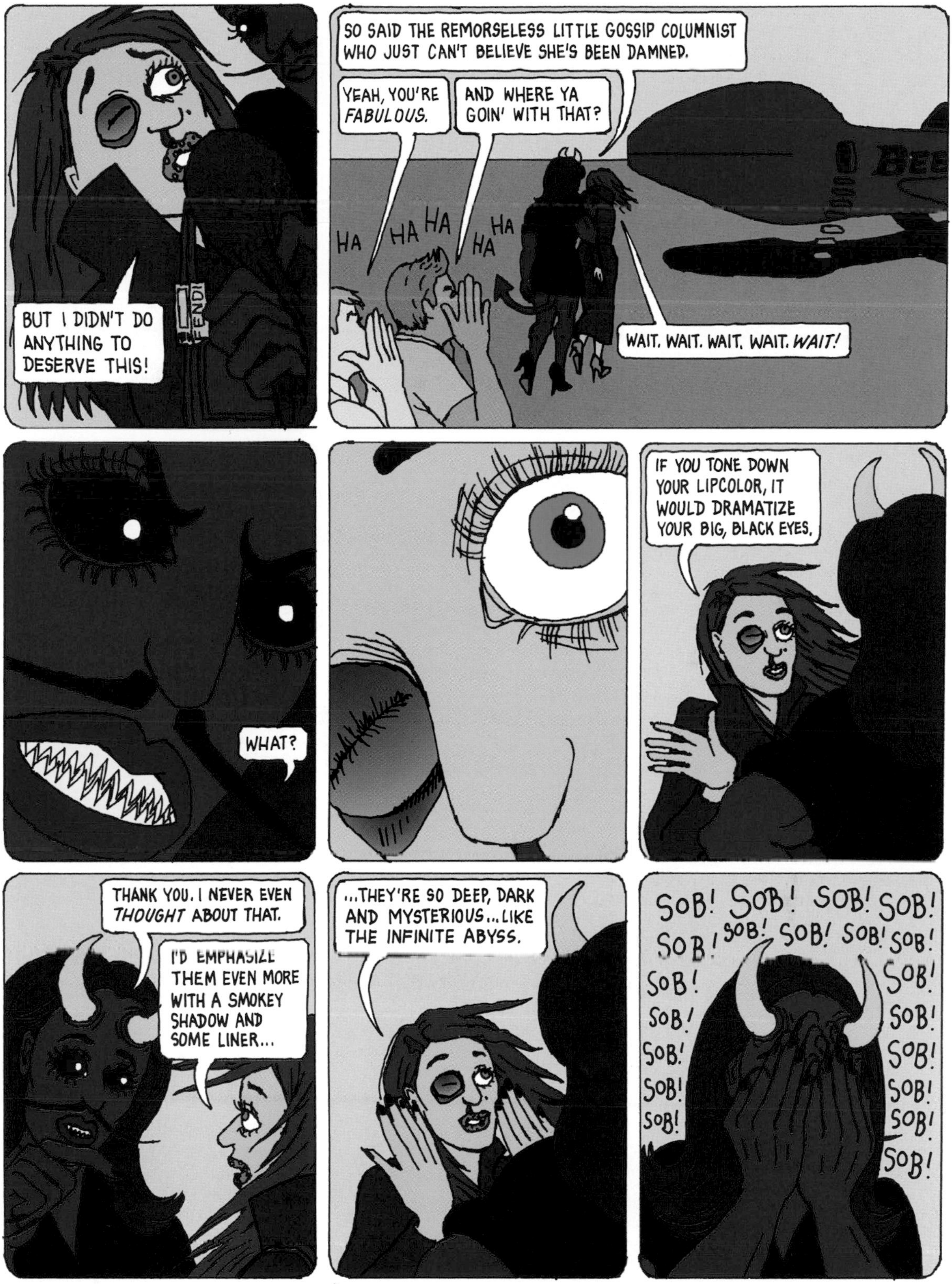
BUT I DIDN'T DO ANYTHING TO DESERVE THIS!
FENDI
SO SAID THE REMORSELESS LITTLE GOSSIP COLUMNIST WHO JUST CAN'T BELIEVE SHE'S BEEN DAMNED.
YEAH, YOU'RE *FABULOUS.*
AND WHERE YA GOIN' WITH THAT?
HA HA HA HA HA
WAIT. WAIT. WAIT. WAIT. *WAIT!*
WHAT?
IF YOU TONE DOWN YOUR LIPCOLOR, IT WOULD DRAMATIZE YOUR BIG, BLACK EYES.
THANK YOU. I NEVER EVEN *THOUGHT* ABOUT THAT.
I'D EMPHASIZE THEM EVEN MORE WITH A SMOKEY SHADOW AND SOME LINER...
...THEY'RE SO DEEP, DARK AND MYSTERIOUS... LIKE THE INFINITE ABYSS.
SOB! SOB! SOB! SOB! SOB! SOB! SOB! SOB! SOB! SOB! SOB! SOB! SOB! SOB! SOB! SOB! SOB! SOB! SOB! SOB! SOB! SOB!

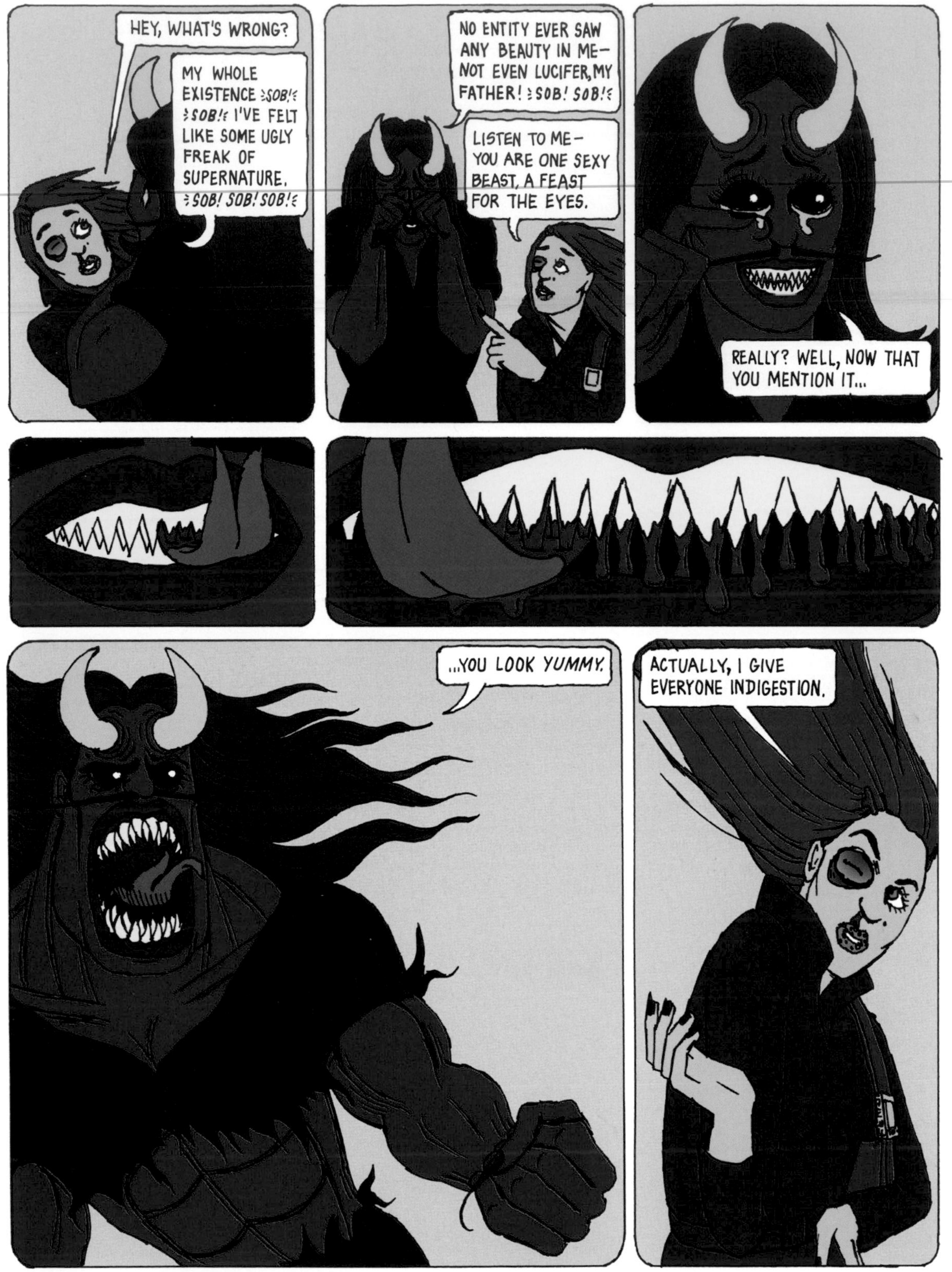
HEY, WHAT'S WRONG?
MY WHOLE EXISTENCE ≷SOB!≶ ≷SOB!≶ I'VE FELT LIKE SOME UGLY FREAK OF SUPERNATURE. ≷SOB! SOB! SOB!≶
NO ENTITY EVER SAW ANY BEAUTY IN ME—NOT EVEN LUCIFER, MY FATHER! ≷SOB! SOB!≶
LISTEN TO ME—YOU ARE ONE SEXY BEAST, A FEAST FOR THE EYES.
REALLY? WELL, NOW THAT YOU MENTION IT...
...YOU LOOK YUMMY.
ACTUALLY, I GIVE EVERYONE INDIGESTION.

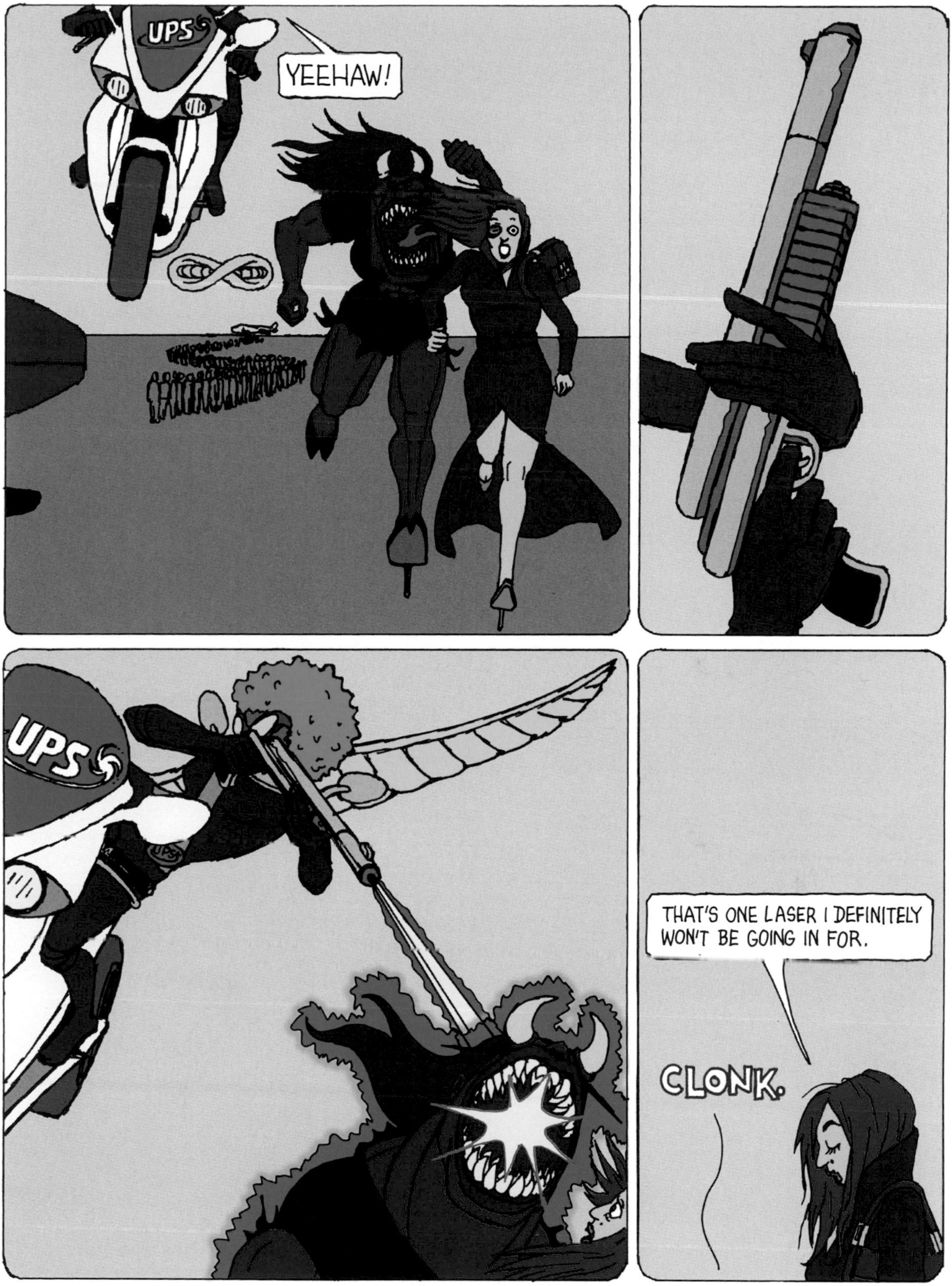
YEEHAW!
UPS
UPS
THAT'S ONE LASER I DEFINITELY WON'T BE GOING IN FOR.
CLONK.

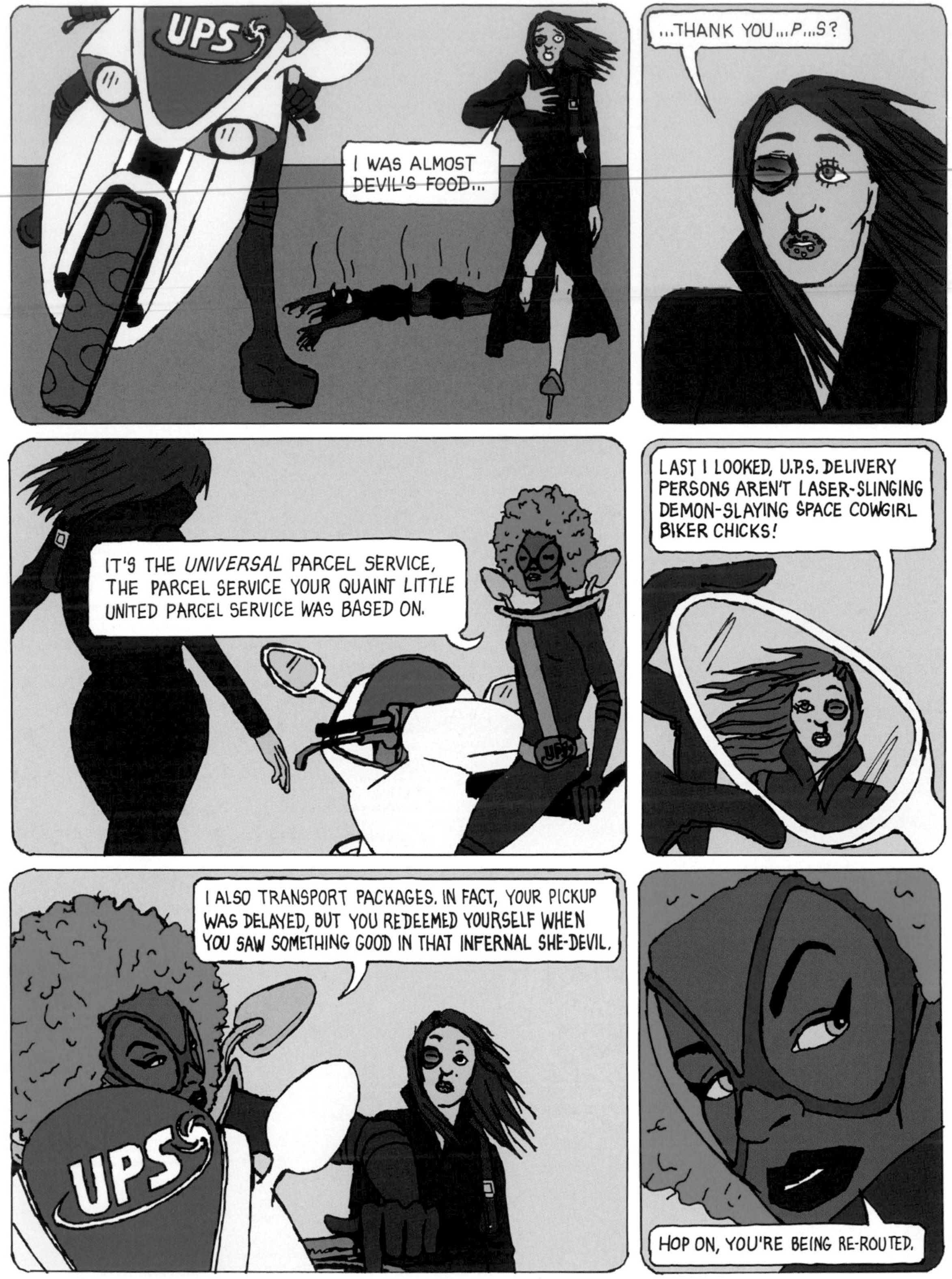
I WAS ALMOST DEVIL'S FOOD...
...THANK YOU...*P*...*S*?
IT'S THE *UNIVERSAL* PARCEL SERVICE, THE PARCEL SERVICE YOUR QUAINT LITTLE UNITED PARCEL SERVICE WAS BASED ON.
LAST I LOOKED, U.P.S. DELIVERY PERSONS AREN'T LASER-SLINGING DEMON-SLAYING SPACE COWGIRL BIKER CHICKS!
I ALSO TRANSPORT PACKAGES. IN FACT, YOUR PICKUP WAS DELAYED, BUT YOU REDEEMED YOURSELF WHEN YOU SAW SOMETHING GOOD IN THAT INFERNAL SHE-DEVIL.
HOP ON, YOU'RE BEING RE-ROUTED.

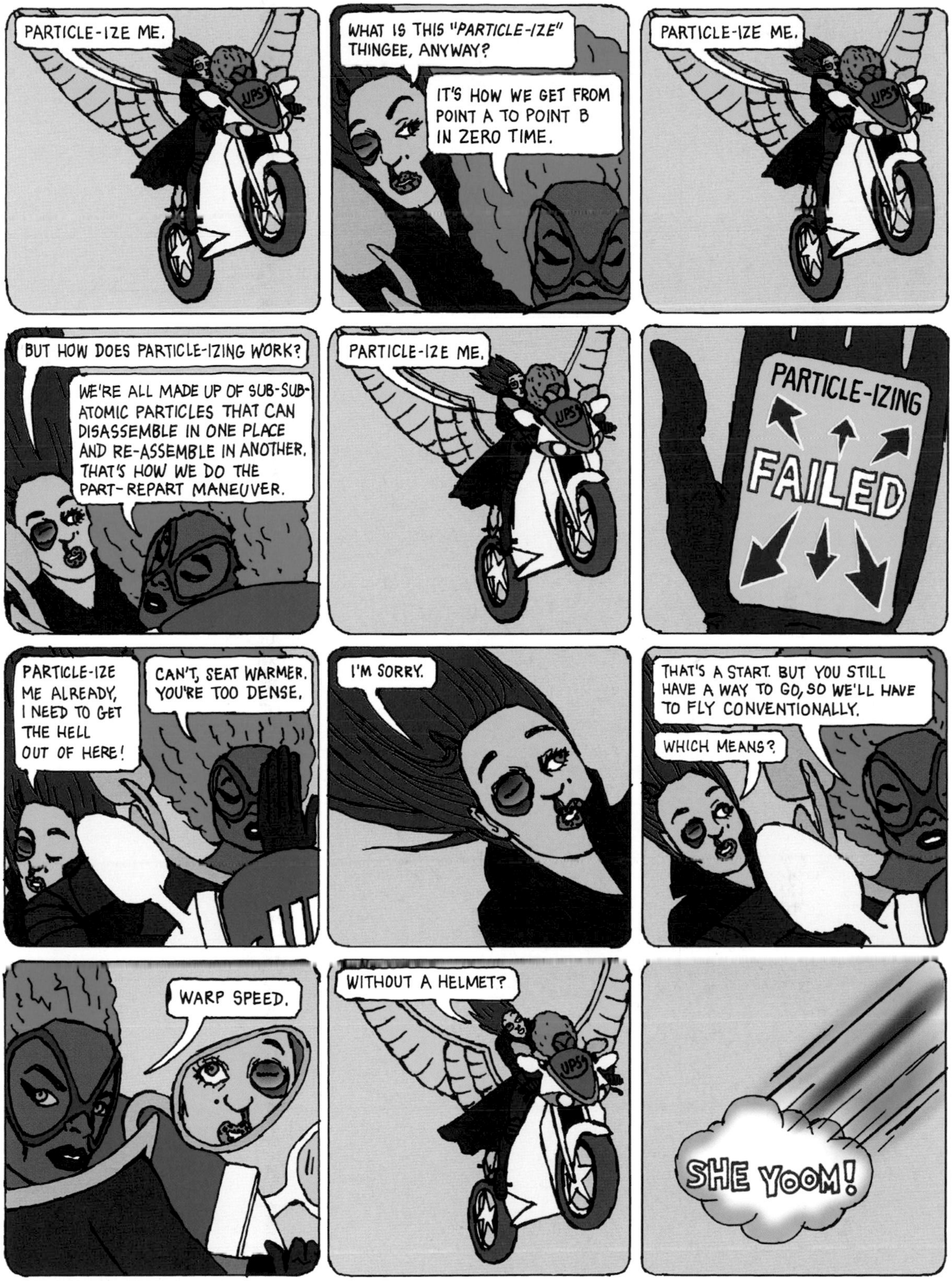
PARTICLE-IZE ME.
WHAT IS THIS "PARTICLE-IZE" THINGEE, ANYWAY?
IT'S HOW WE GET FROM POINT A TO POINT B IN ZERO TIME.
PARTICLE-IZE ME.
BUT HOW DOES PARTICLE-IZING WORK?
WE'RE ALL MADE UP OF SUB-SUB-ATOMIC PARTICLES THAT CAN DISASSEMBLE IN ONE PLACE AND RE-ASSEMBLE IN ANOTHER. THAT'S HOW WE DO THE PART-REPART MANEUVER.
PARTICLE-IZE ME.
PARTICLE-IZING
FAILED
PARTICLE-IZE ME ALREADY, I NEED TO GET THE HELL OUT OF HERE!
CAN'T, SEAT WARMER. YOU'RE TOO DENSE.
I'M SORRY.
THAT'S A START. BUT YOU STILL HAVE A WAY TO GO, SO WE'LL HAVE TO FLY CONVENTIONALLY.
WHICH MEANS?
WARP SPEED.
WITHOUT A HELMET?
SHE YOOM!

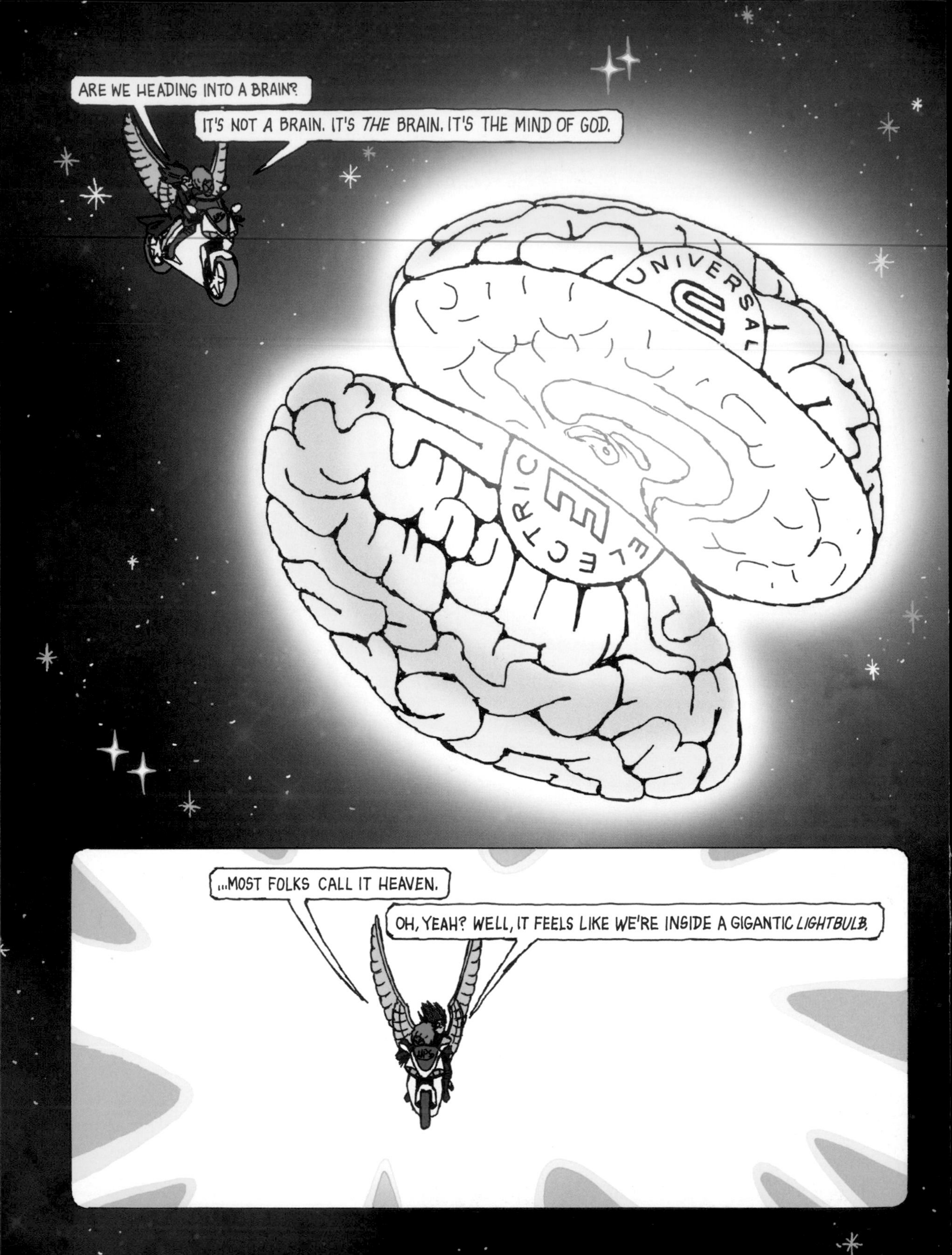

ARE WE HEADING INTO A BRAIN?
IT'S NOT A BRAIN. IT'S *THE* BRAIN. IT'S THE MIND OF GOD.
UNIVERSAL
U
ELECTRIC
E
...MOST FOLKS CALL IT HEAVEN.
OH, YEAH? WELL, IT FEELS LIKE WE'RE INSIDE A GIGANTIC *LIGHTBULB*.

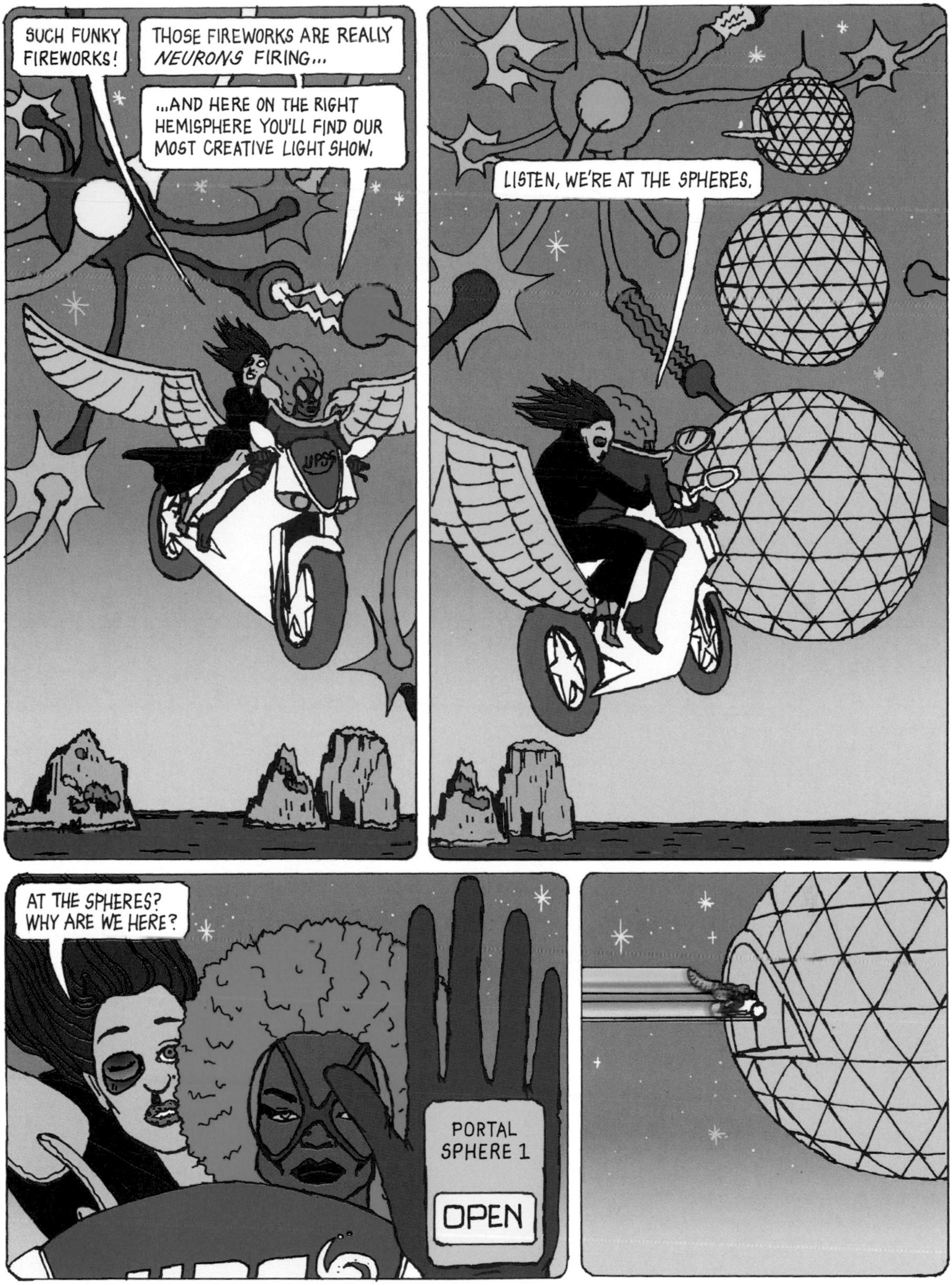
SUCH FUNKY FIREWORKS!
THOSE FIREWORKS ARE REALLY *NEURONS* FIRING...
...AND HERE ON THE RIGHT HEMISPHERE YOU'LL FIND OUR MOST CREATIVE LIGHT SHOW.
LISTEN, WE'RE AT THE SPHERES.
AT THE SPHERES? WHY ARE WE HERE?
PORTAL SPHERE 1
OPEN

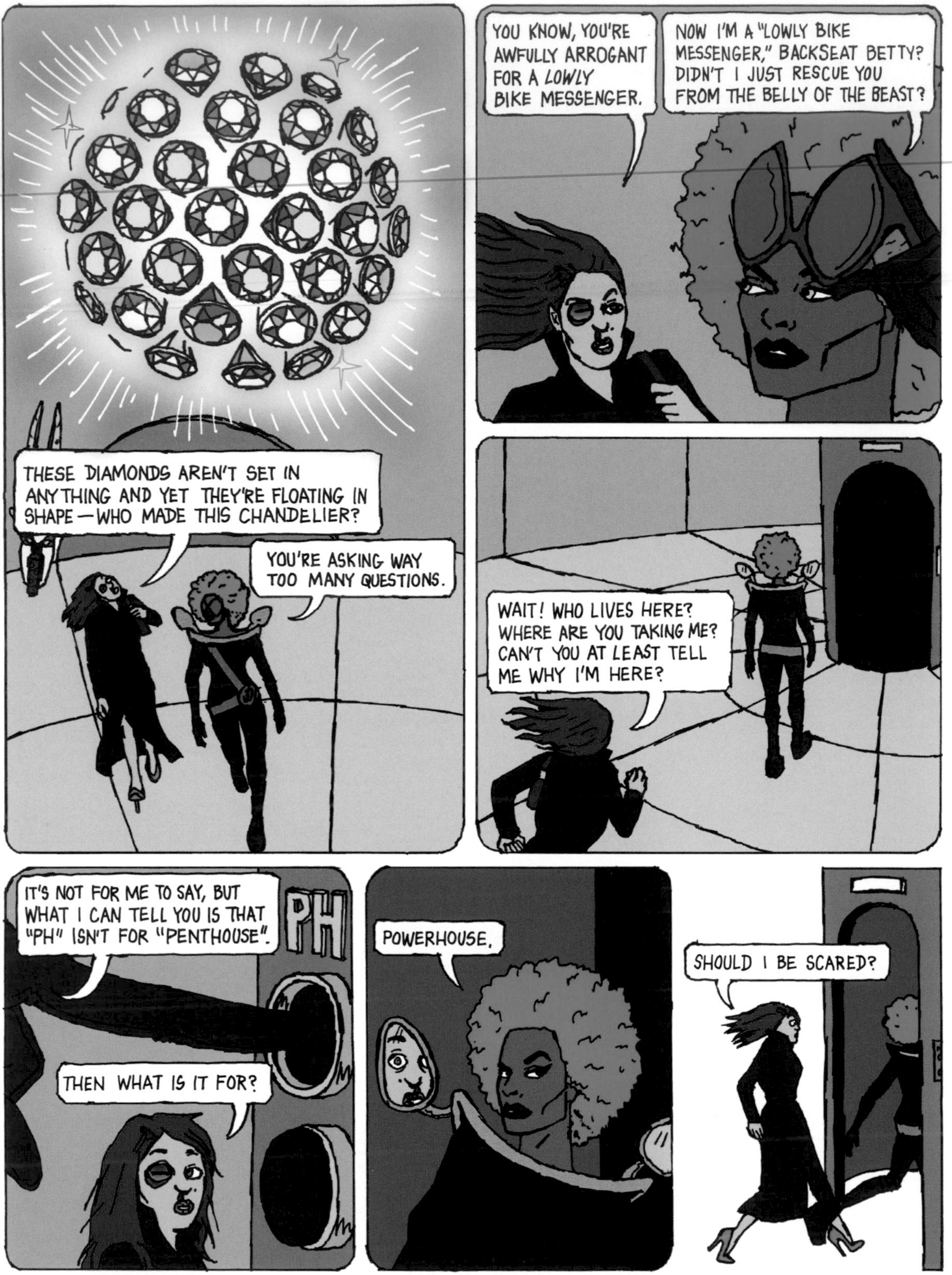
THESE DIAMONDS AREN'T SET IN ANYTHING AND YET THEY'RE FLOATING IN SHAPE—WHO MADE THIS CHANDELIER?
YOU'RE ASKING WAY TOO MANY QUESTIONS.
YOU KNOW, YOU'RE AWFULLY ARROGANT FOR A *LOWLY* BIKE MESSENGER.
NOW I'M A "LOWLY BIKE MESSENGER," BACKSEAT BETTY? DIDN'T I JUST RESCUE YOU FROM THE BELLY OF THE BEAST?
WAIT! WHO LIVES HERE? WHERE ARE YOU TAKING ME? CAN'T YOU AT LEAST TELL ME WHY I'M HERE?
IT'S NOT FOR ME TO SAY, BUT WHAT I CAN TELL YOU IS THAT "PH" ISN'T FOR "PENTHOUSE".
PH
THEN WHAT IS IT FOR?
POWERHOUSE.
SHOULD I BE SCARED?

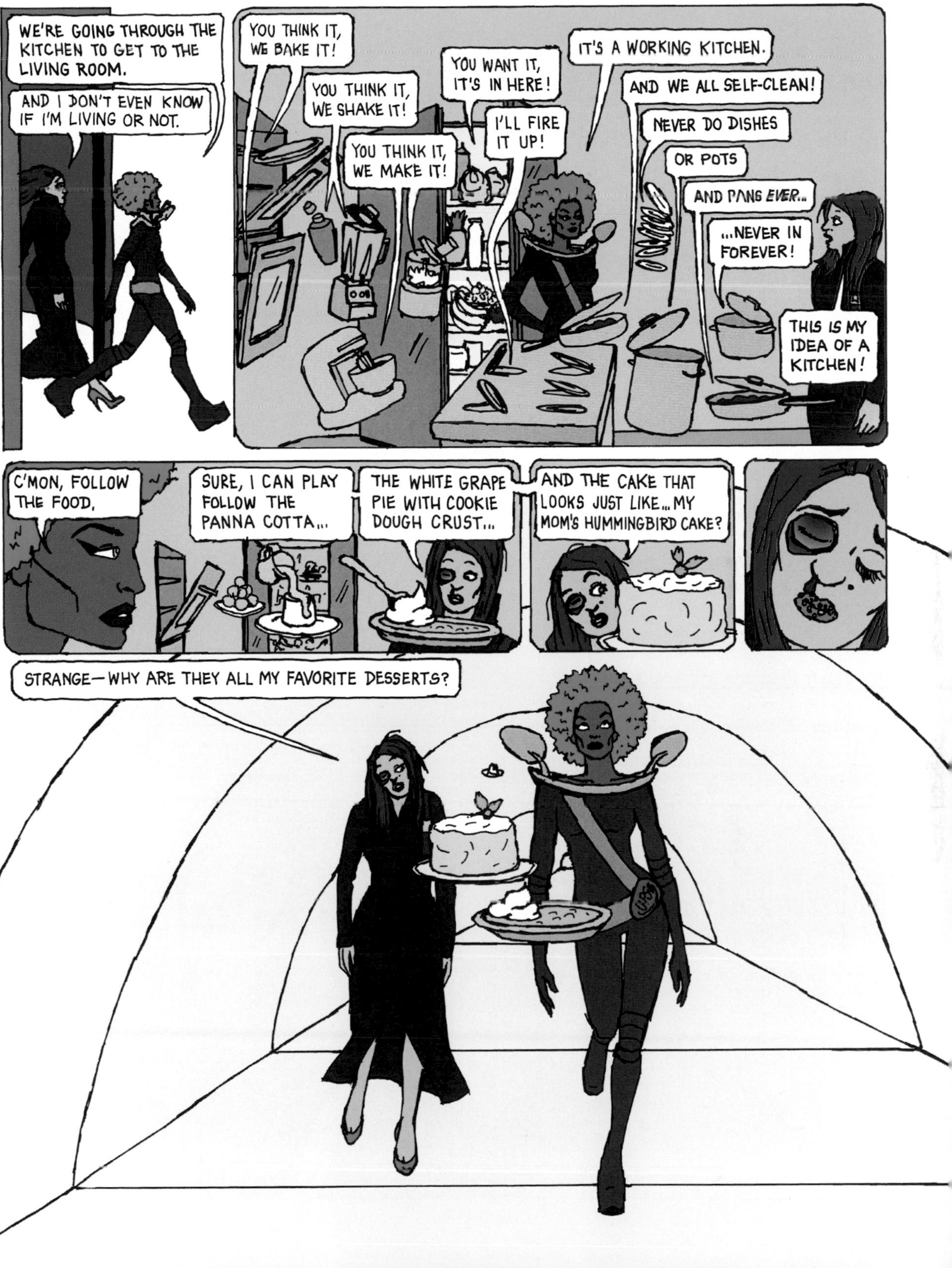
WE'RE GOING THROUGH THE KITCHEN TO GET TO THE LIVING ROOM.
AND I DON'T EVEN KNOW IF I'M LIVING OR NOT.
YOU THINK IT, WE BAKE IT!
YOU THINK IT, WE SHAKE IT!
YOU THINK IT, WE MAKE IT!
YOU WANT IT, IT'S IN HERE!
I'LL FIRE IT UP!
IT'S A WORKING KITCHEN.
AND WE ALL SELF-CLEAN!
NEVER DO DISHES
OR POTS
AND PANS EVER...
...NEVER IN FOREVER!
THIS IS MY IDEA OF A KITCHEN!
C'MON, FOLLOW THE FOOD.
SURE, I CAN PLAY FOLLOW THE PANNA COTTA...
THE WHITE GRAPE PIE WITH COOKIE DOUGH CRUST...
AND THE CAKE THAT LOOKS JUST LIKE... MY MOM'S HUMMINGBIRD CAKE?
STRANGE—WHY ARE THEY ALL MY FAVORITE DESSERTS?

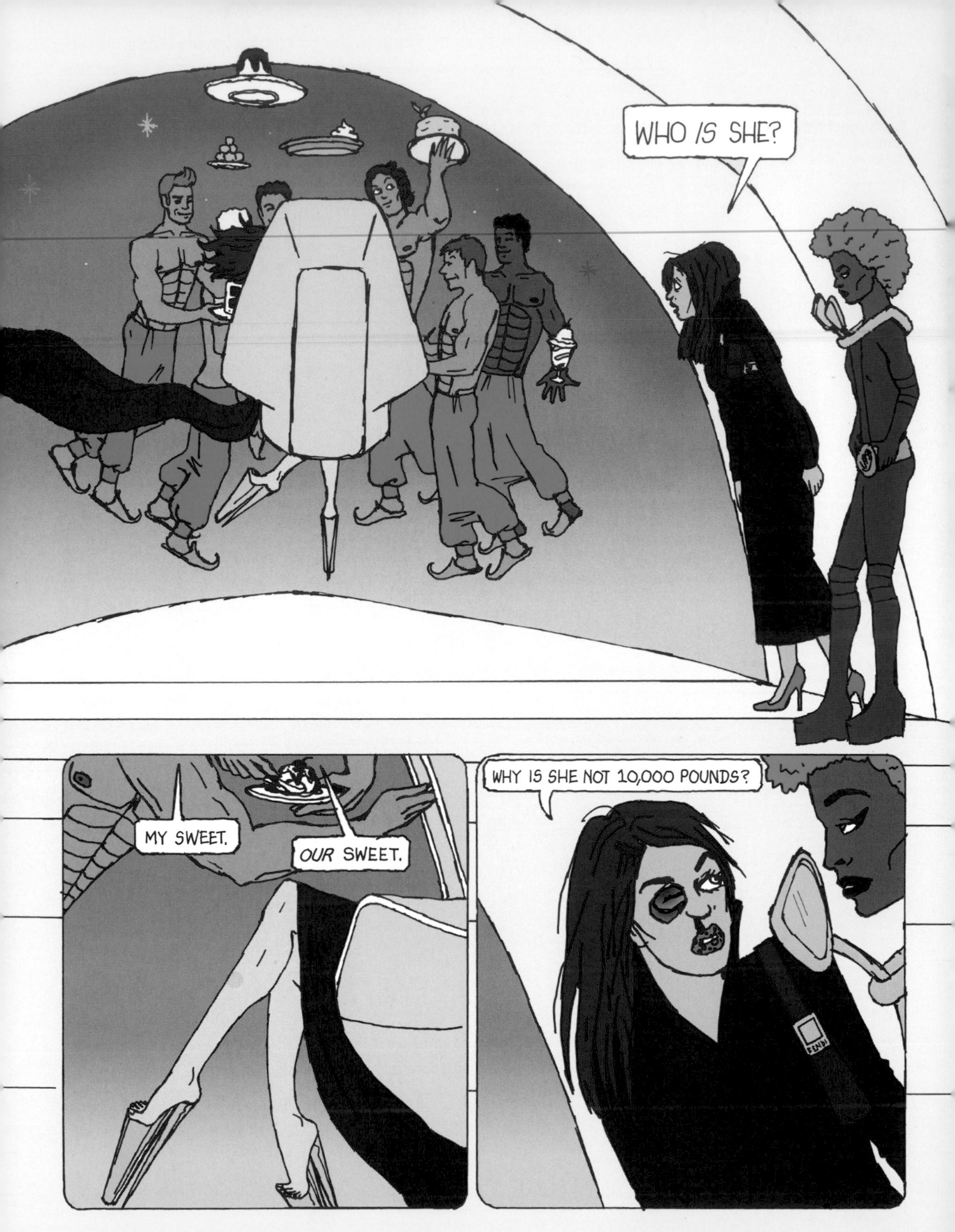
WHO IS SHE?
MY SWEET.
OUR SWEET.
WHY IS SHE NOT 10,000 POUNDS?

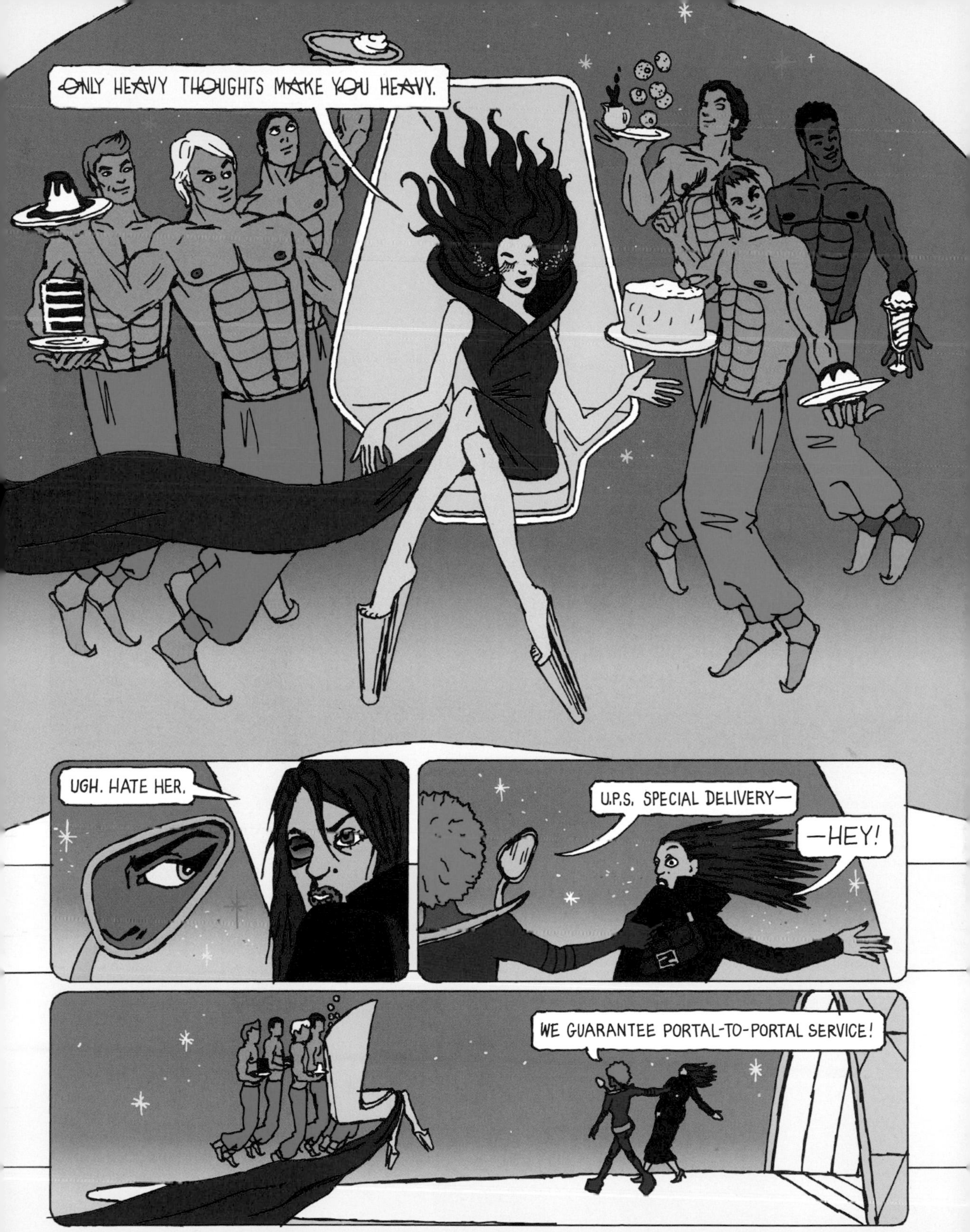
ONLY HEAVY THOUGHTS MAKE YOU HEAVY.
UGH. HATE HER.
U.P.S. SPECIAL DELIVERY—
—HEY!
WE GUARANTEE PORTAL-TO-PORTAL SERVICE!

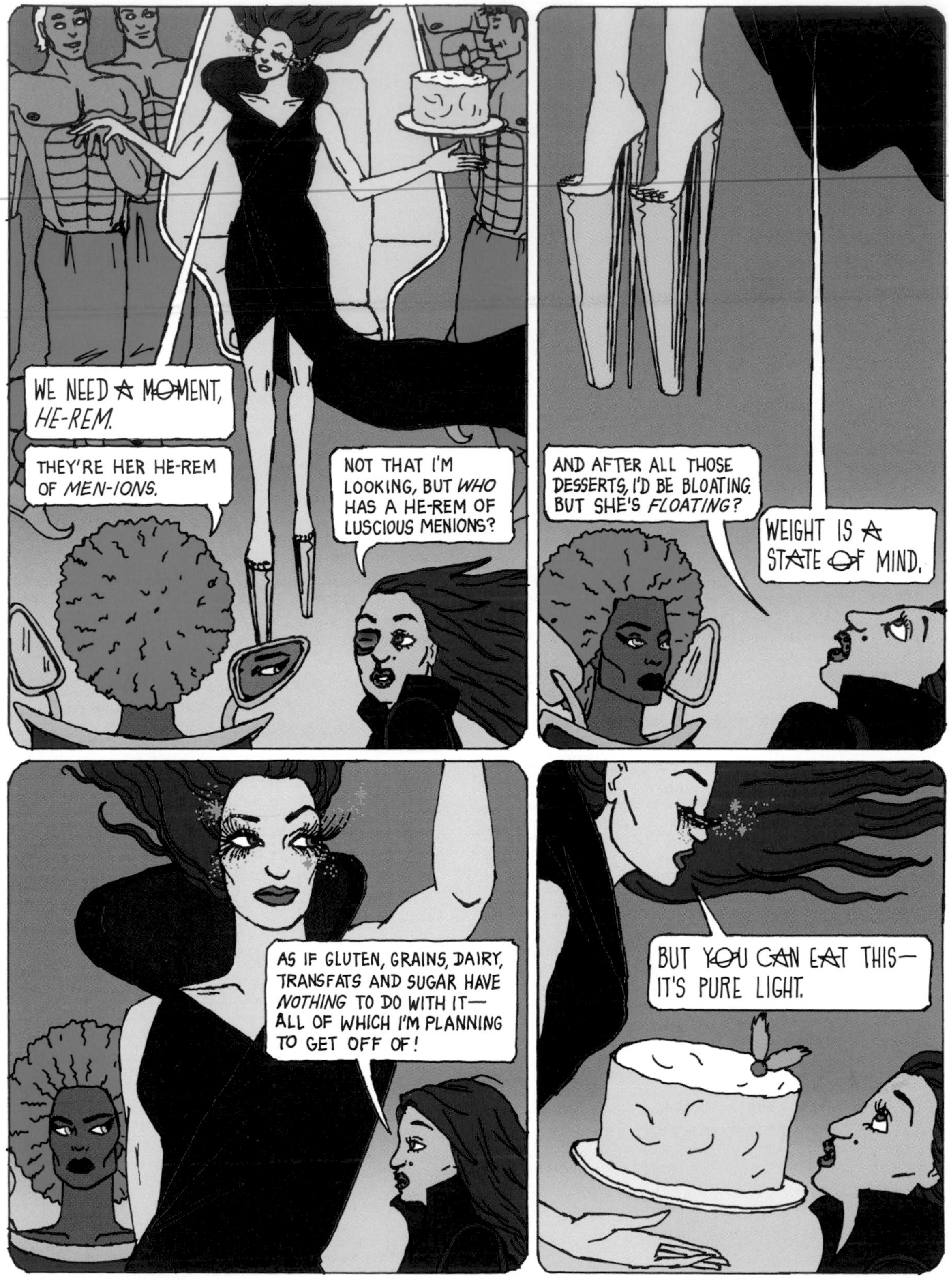
WE NEED A MOMENT, HE-REM.
THEY'RE HER HE-REM OF MEN-IONS.
NOT THAT I'M LOOKING, BUT WHO HAS A HE-REM OF LUSCIOUS MENIONS?
AND AFTER ALL THOSE DESSERTS, I'D BE BLOATING. BUT SHE'S FLOATING?
WEIGHT IS A STATE OF MIND.
AS IF GLUTEN, GRAINS, DAIRY, TRANSFATS AND SUGAR HAVE NOTHING TO DO WITH IT— ALL OF WHICH I'M PLANNING TO GET OFF OF!
BUT YOU CAN EAT THIS— IT'S PURE LIGHT.

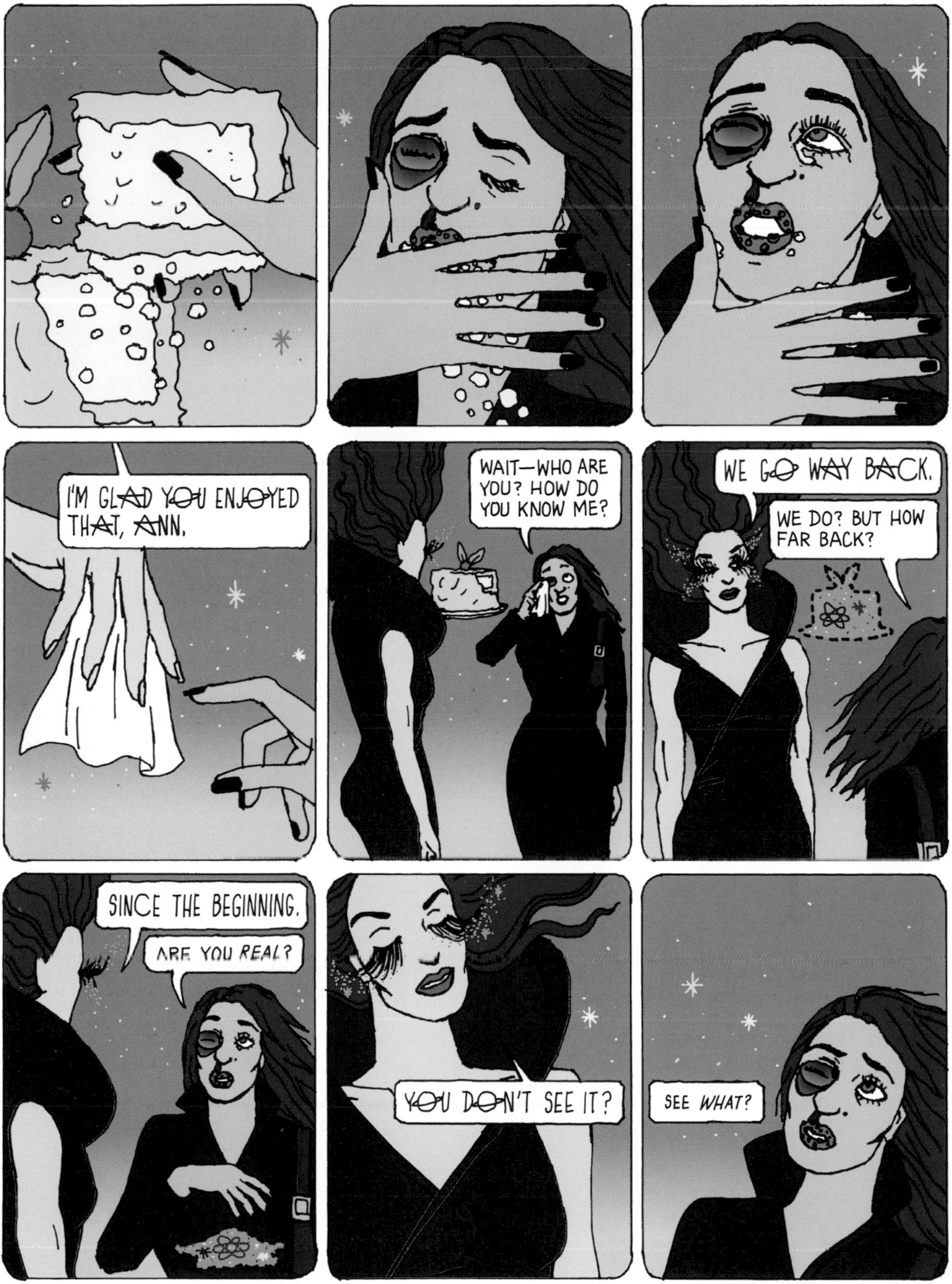
I'M GLAD YOU ENJOYED THAT, ANN.
WAIT—WHO ARE YOU? HOW DO YOU KNOW ME?
WE GO WAY BACK.
WE DO? BUT HOW FAR BACK?
SINCE THE BEGINNING.
ARE YOU *REAL*?
YOU DON'T SEE IT?
SEE *WHAT*?

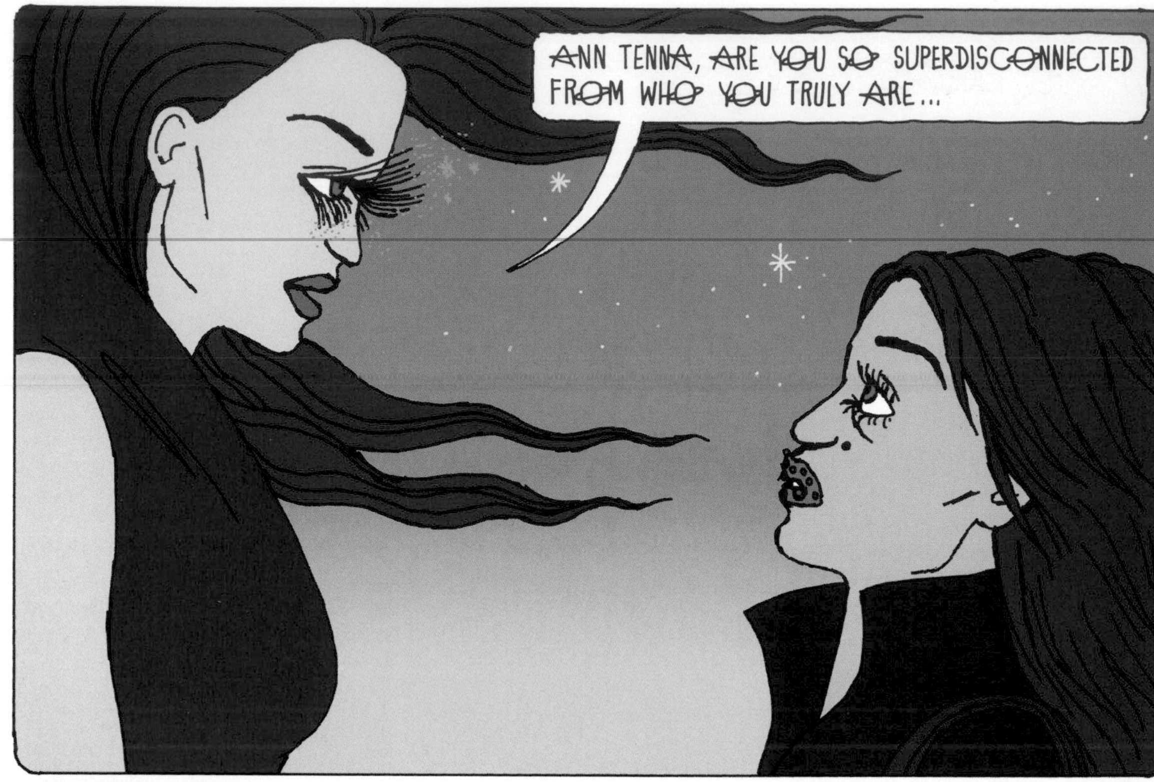
ANN TENNA, ARE YOU SO SUPERDISCONNECTED FROM WHO YOU TRULY ARE...

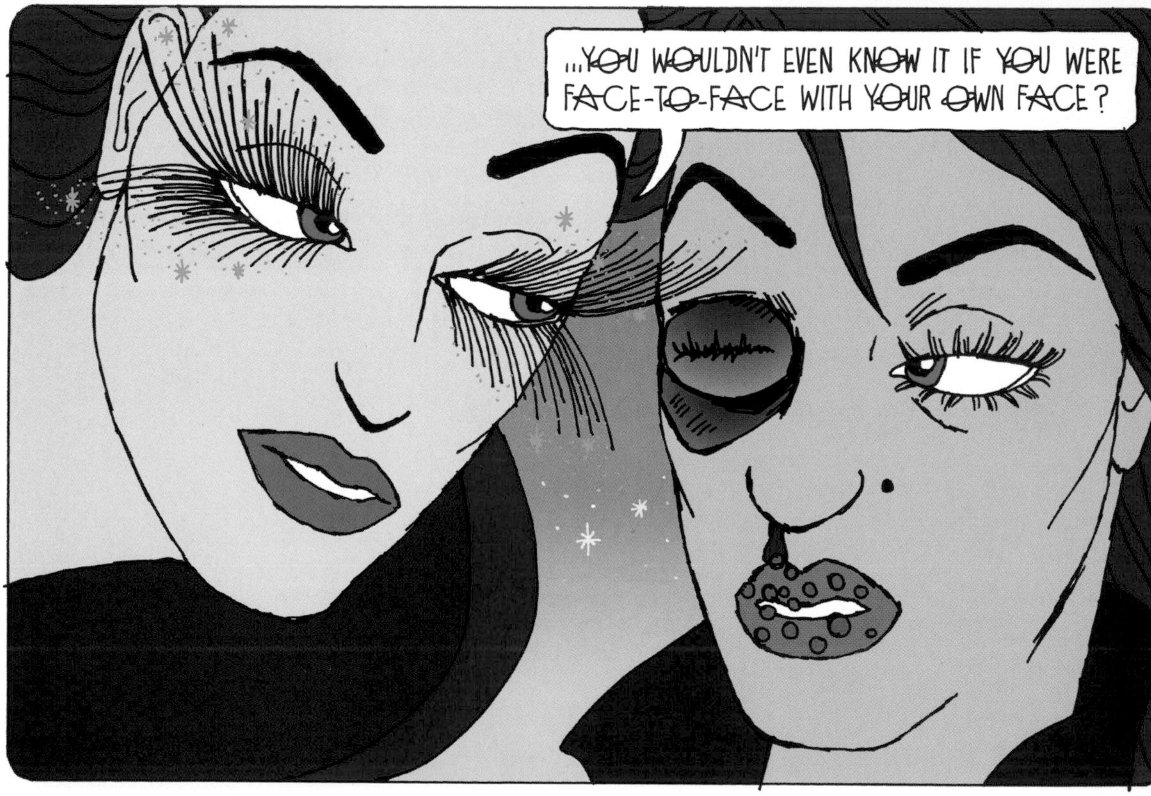
...YOU WOULDN'T EVEN KNOW IT IF YOU WERE FACE-TO-FACE WITH YOUR OWN FACE?

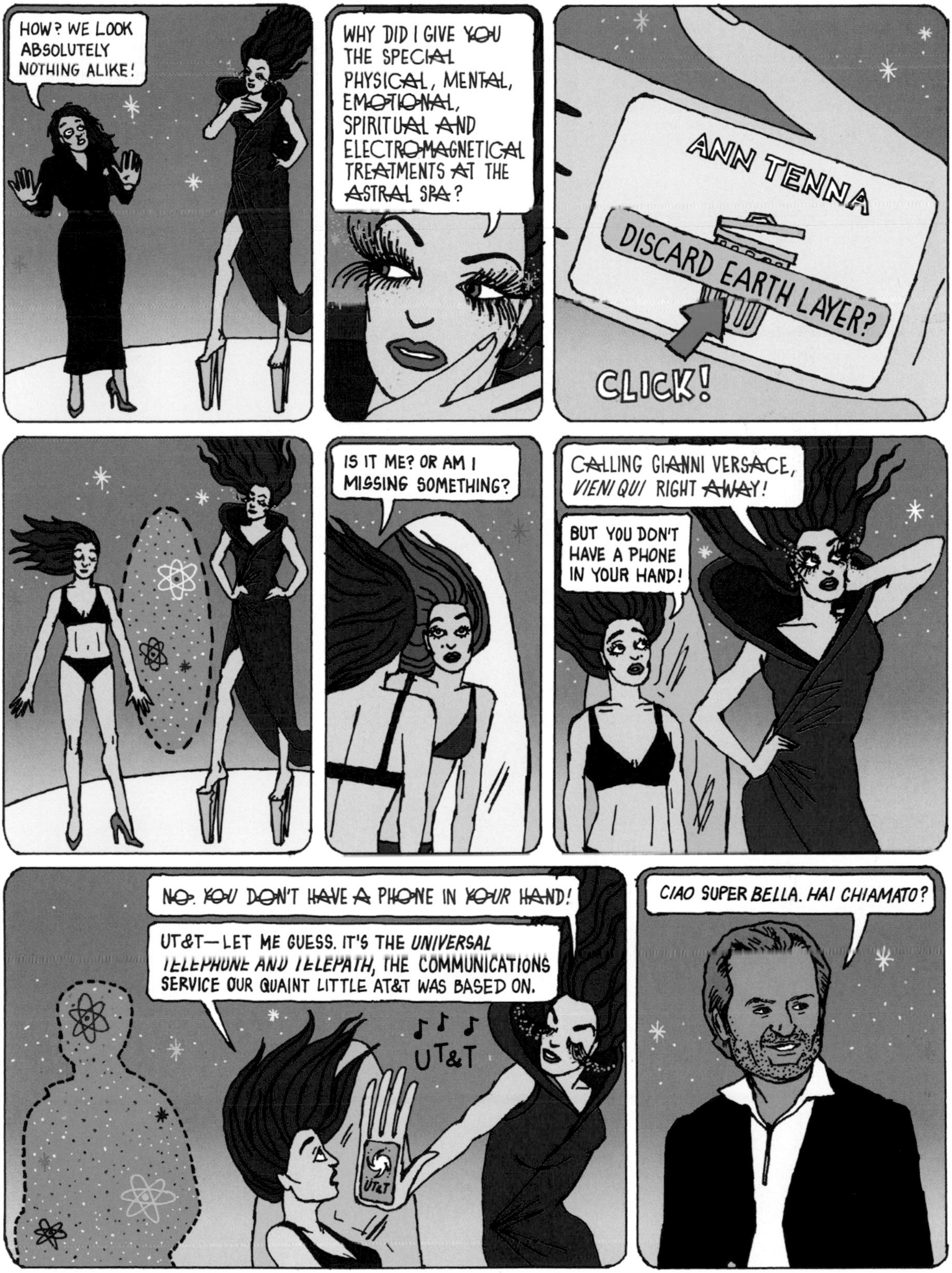
HOW? WE LOOK ABSOLUTELY NOTHING ALIKE!
WHY DID I GIVE YOU THE SPECIAL PHYSICAL, MENTAL, EMOTIONAL, SPIRITUAL AND ELECTROMAGNETICAL TREATMENTS AT THE ASTRAL SPA?
ANN TENNA
DISCARD EARTH LAYER?
CLICK!
IS IT ME? OR AM I MISSING SOMETHING?
CALLING GIANNI VERSACE, *VIENI QUI* RIGHT AWAY!
BUT YOU DON'T HAVE A PHONE IN YOUR HAND!
NO. *YOU* DON'T HAVE A PHONE IN *YOUR* HAND!
UT&T—LET ME GUESS. IT'S THE *UNIVERSAL TELEPHONE AND TELEPATH*, THE COMMUNICATIONS SERVICE OUR QUAINT LITTLE AT&T WAS BASED ON.
UT&T
UT&T
CIAO SUPER *BELLA. HAI CHIAMATO?*

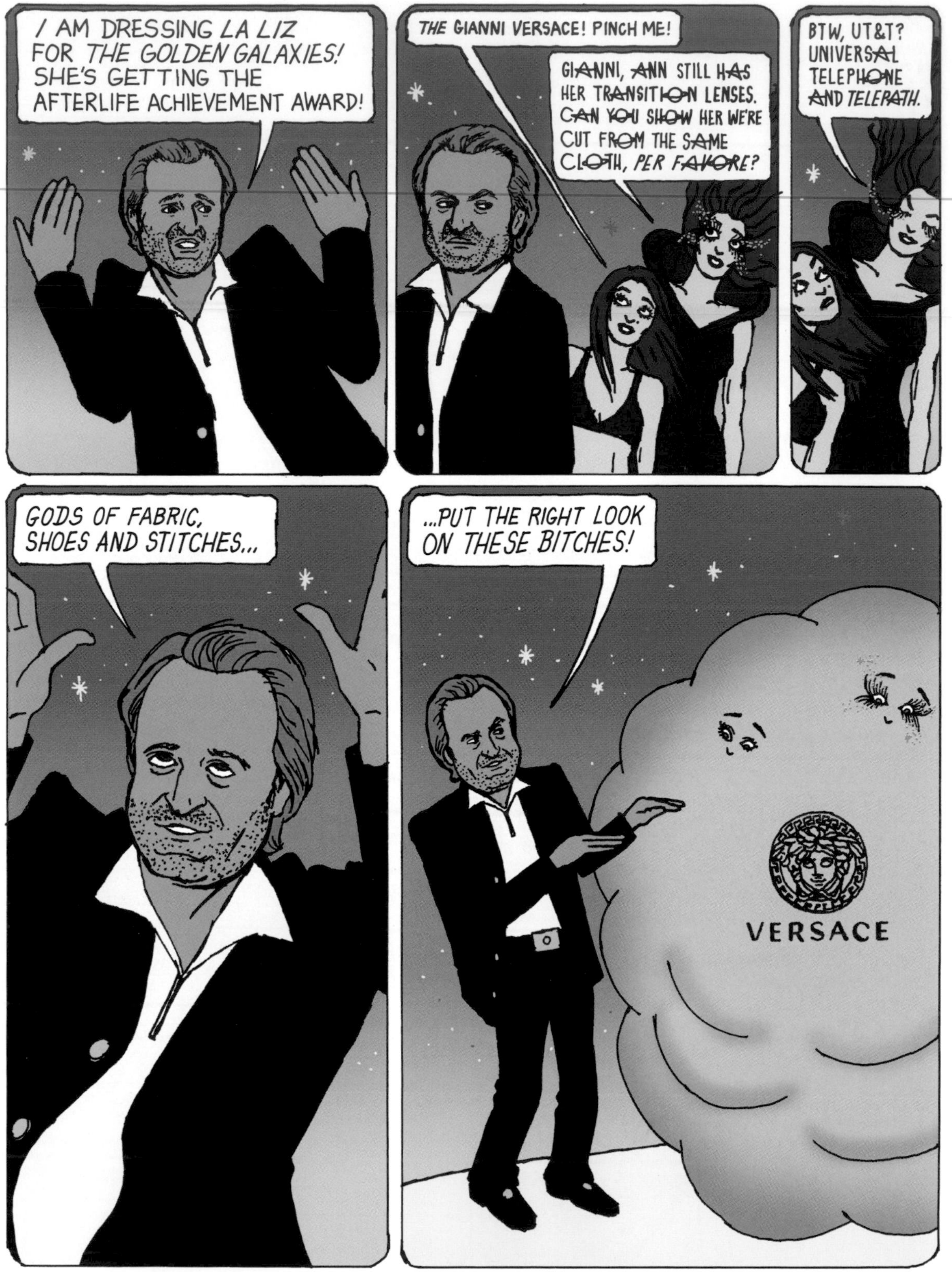
I AM DRESSING *LA LIZ* FOR *THE GOLDEN GALAXIES!* SHE'S GETTING THE AFTERLIFE ACHIEVEMENT AWARD!
THE GIANNI VERSACE! PINCH ME!
GIANNI, ANN STILL HAS HER TRANSITION LENSES. CAN YOU SHOW HER WE'RE CUT FROM THE SAME CLOTH, *PER FAVORE?*
BTW, UT&T? UNIVERSAL TELEPHONE AND *TELEPATH.*
GODS OF FABRIC, SHOES AND STITCHES...
...PUT THE RIGHT LOOK ON THESE BITCHES!
VERSACE

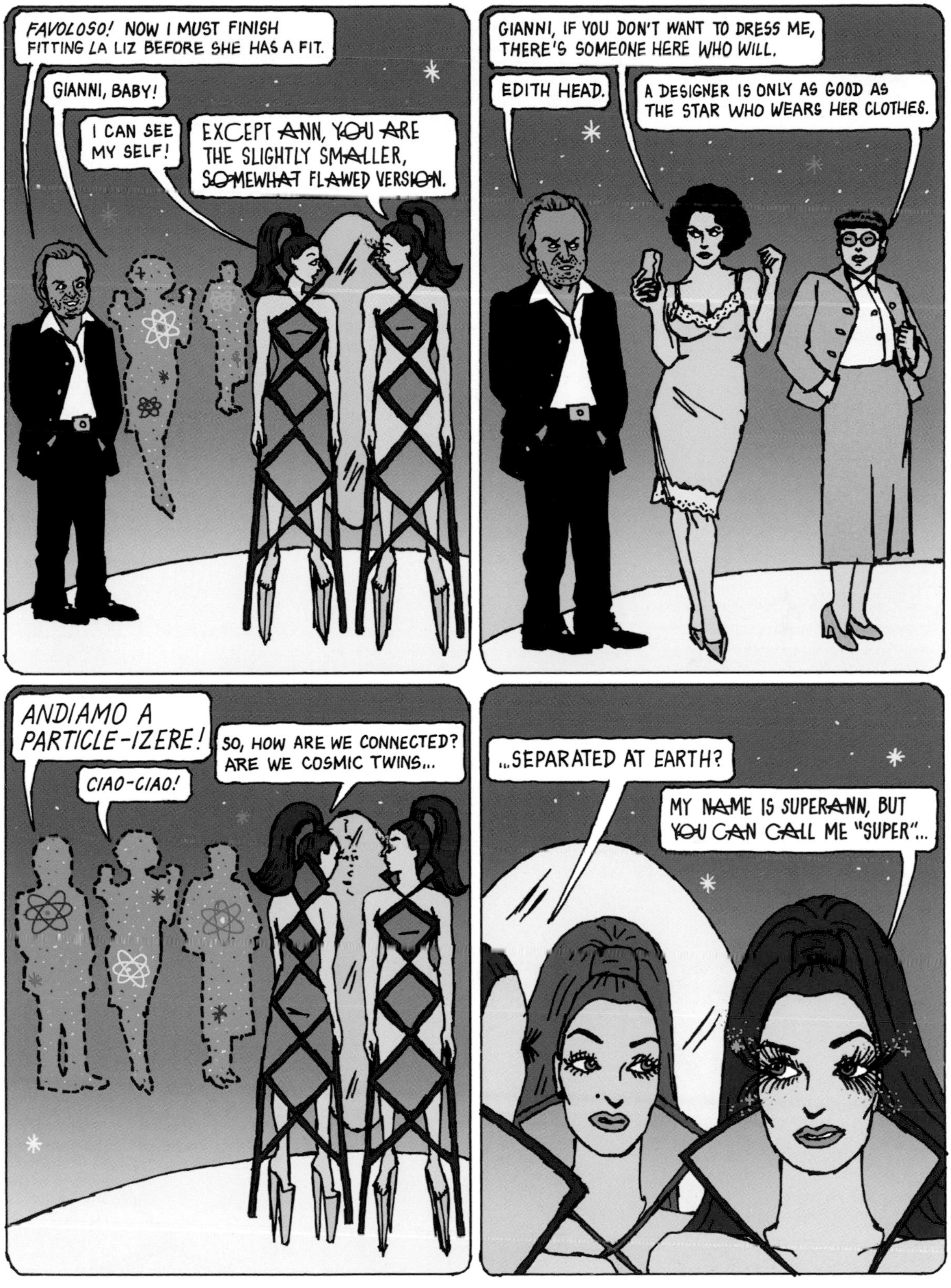
FAVOLOSO! NOW I MUST FINISH FITTING LA LIZ BEFORE SHE HAS A FIT.
GIANNI, BABY!
I CAN SEE MY SELF!
EXCEPT ANN, YOU ARE THE SLIGHTLY SMALLER, SOMEWHAT FLAWED VERSION.
GIANNI, IF YOU DON'T WANT TO DRESS ME, THERE'S SOMEONE HERE WHO WILL.
EDITH HEAD.
A DESIGNER IS ONLY AS GOOD AS THE STAR WHO WEARS HER CLOTHES.
ANDIAMO A PARTICLE-IZERE!
CIAO-CIAO!
SO, HOW ARE WE CONNECTED? ARE WE COSMIC TWINS...
...SEPARATED AT EARTH?
MY NAME IS SUPERANN, BUT YOU CAN CALL ME "SUPER"...

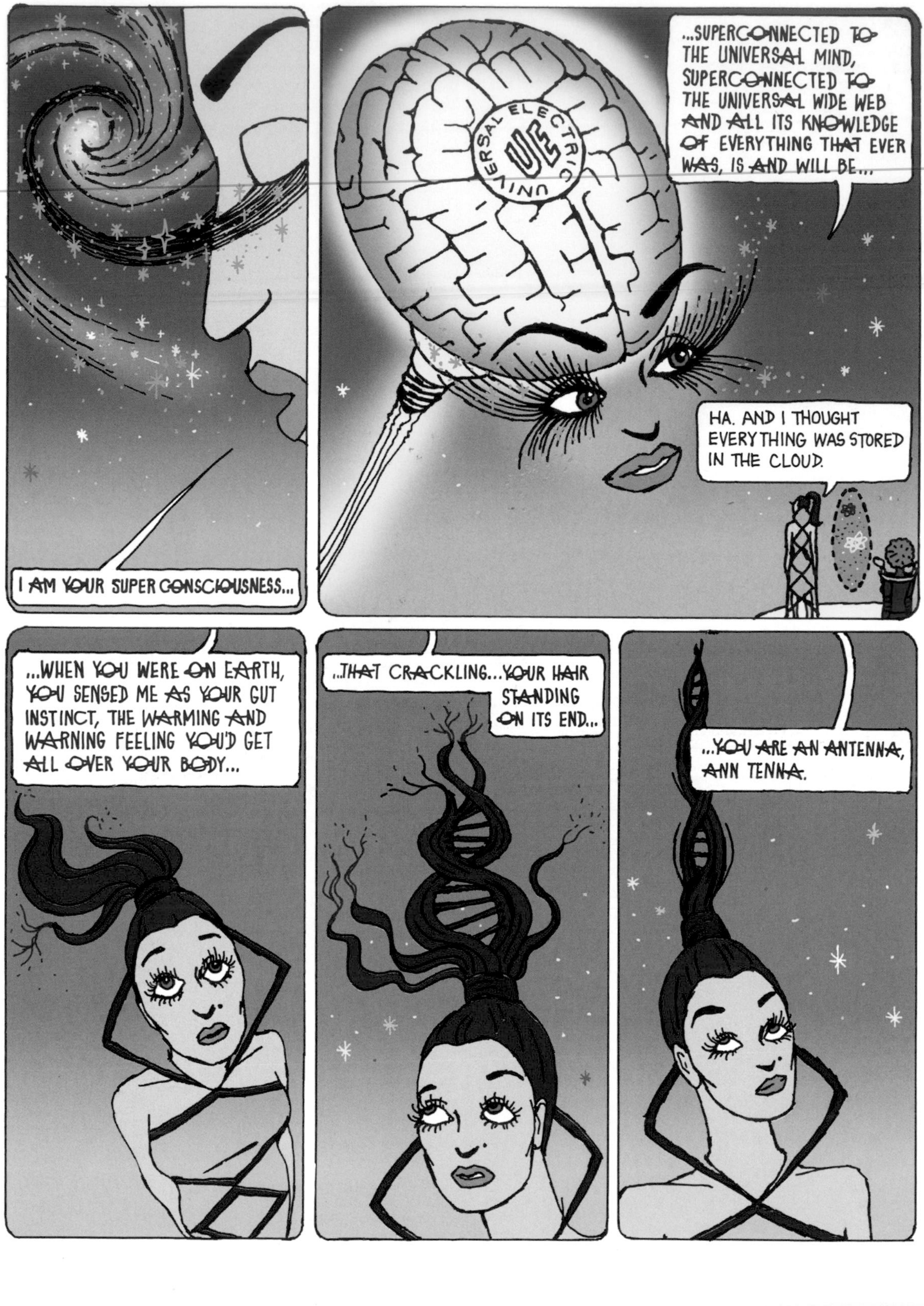
I AM YOUR SUPER CONSCIOUSNESS...
UNIVERSAL ELECTRIC UE
...SUPERCONNECTED TO THE UNIVERSAL MIND, SUPERCONNECTED TO THE UNIVERSAL WIDE WEB AND ALL ITS KNOWLEDGE OF EVERYTHING THAT EVER WAS, IS AND WILL BE...
HA. AND I THOUGHT EVERYTHING WAS STORED IN THE CLOUD.
...WHEN YOU WERE ON EARTH, YOU SENSED ME AS YOUR GUT INSTINCT, THE WARMING AND WARNING FEELING YOU'D GET ALL OVER YOUR BODY...
...THAT CRACKLING...YOUR HAIR STANDING ON ITS END...
...YOU ARE AN ANTENNA, ANN TENNA.

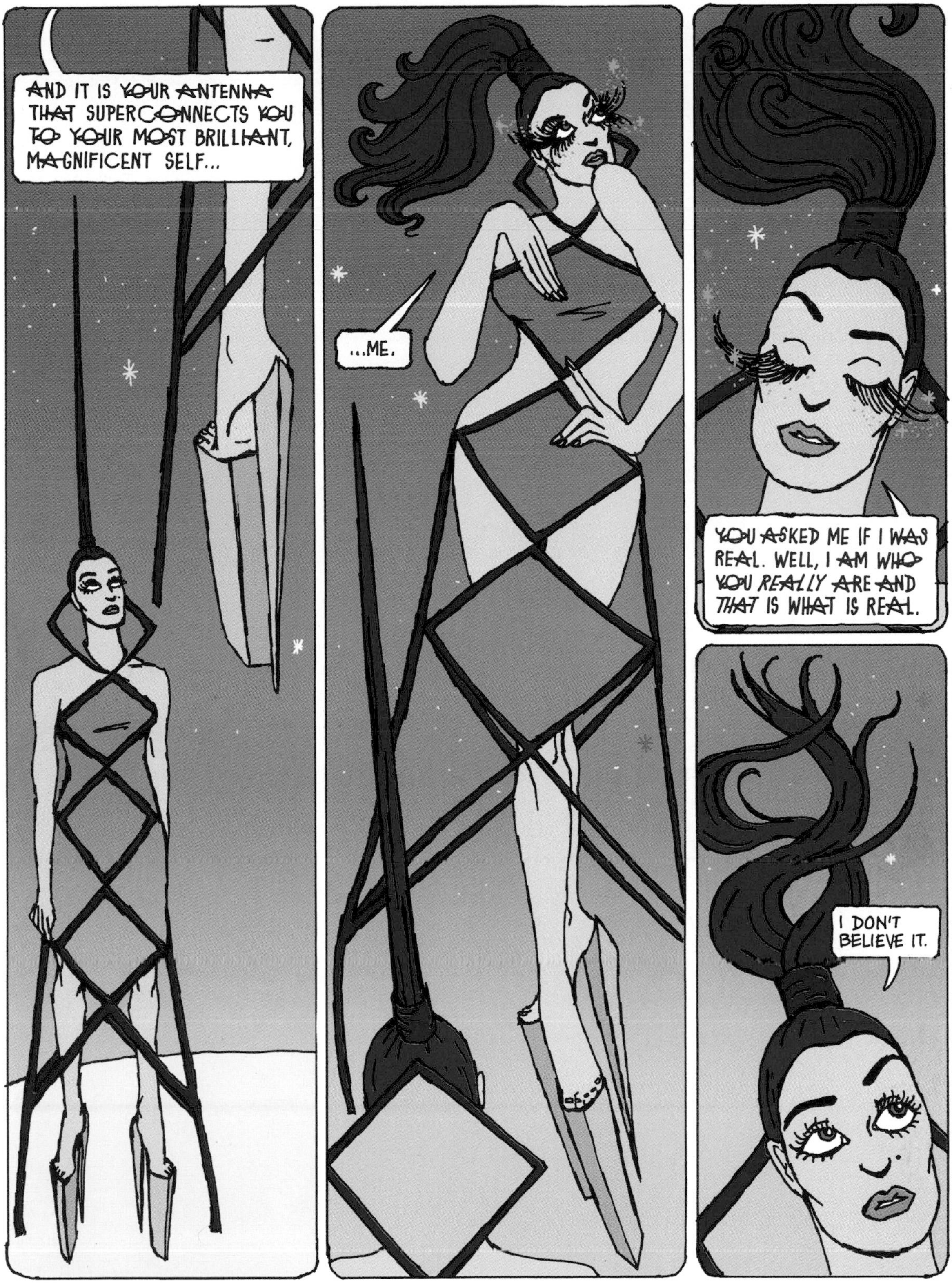
AND IT IS YOUR ANTENNA THAT SUPERCONNECTS YOU TO YOUR MOST BRILLIANT, MAGNIFICENT SELF...
...ME.
YOU ASKED ME IF I WAS REAL. WELL, I AM WHO YOU *REALLY* ARE AND *THAT* IS WHAT IS REAL.
I DON'T BELIEVE IT.

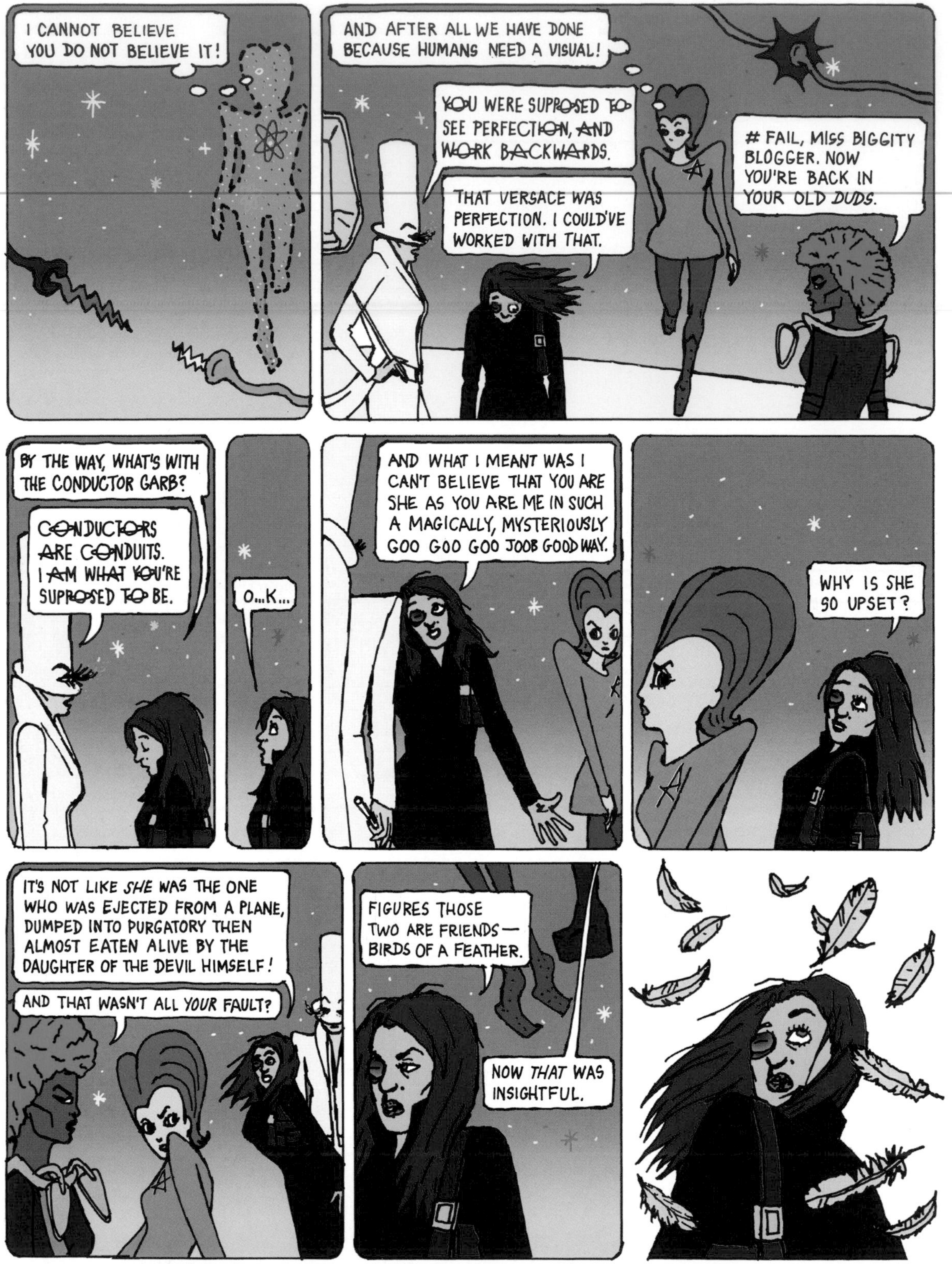
I CANNOT BELIEVE YOU DO NOT BELIEVE IT!
AND AFTER ALL WE HAVE DONE BECAUSE HUMANS NEED A VISUAL!
YOU WERE SUPPOSED TO SEE PERFECTION, AND WORK BACKWARDS.
THAT VERSACE WAS PERFECTION. I COULD'VE WORKED WITH THAT.
FAIL, MISS BIGGITY BLOGGER. NOW YOU'RE BACK IN YOUR OLD DUDS.
BY THE WAY, WHAT'S WITH THE CONDUCTOR GARB?
CONDUCTORS ARE CONDUITS. I AM WHAT YOU'RE SUPPOSED TO BE.
O...K...
AND WHAT I MEANT WAS I CAN'T BELIEVE THAT YOU ARE SHE AS YOU ARE ME IN SUCH A MAGICALLY, MYSTERIOUSLY GOO GOO GOO JOOB GOOD WAY.
WHY IS SHE SO UPSET?
IT'S NOT LIKE SHE WAS THE ONE WHO WAS EJECTED FROM A PLANE, DUMPED INTO PURGATORY THEN ALMOST EATEN ALIVE BY THE DAUGHTER OF THE DEVIL HIMSELF!
AND THAT WASN'T ALL YOUR FAULT?
FIGURES THOSE TWO ARE FRIENDS— BIRDS OF A FEATHER.
NOW THAT WAS INSIGHTFUL.

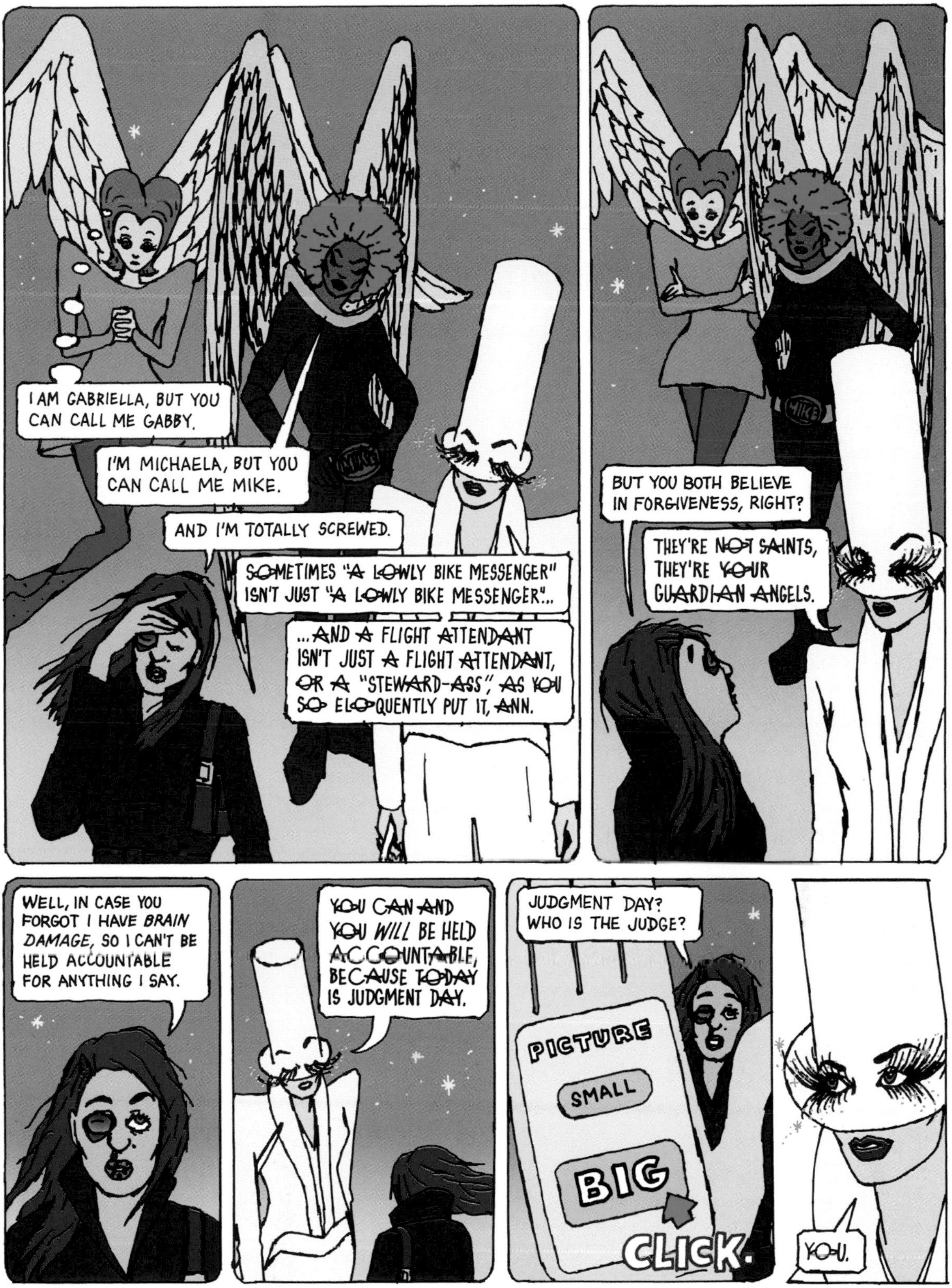
I AM GABRIELLA, BUT YOU CAN CALL ME GABBY.
I'M MICHAELA, BUT YOU CAN CALL ME MIKE.
AND I'M TOTALLY SCREWED.
SOMETIMES "A LOWLY BIKE MESSENGER" ISN'T JUST "A LOWLY BIKE MESSENGER"...
...AND A FLIGHT ATTENDANT ISN'T JUST A FLIGHT ATTENDANT, OR A "STEWARD-ASS," AS YOU SO ELOQUENTLY PUT IT, ANN.
MIKE
BUT YOU BOTH BELIEVE IN FORGIVENESS, RIGHT?
THEY'RE NOT SAINTS, THEY'RE YOUR GUARDIAN ANGELS.
MIKE
WELL, IN CASE YOU FORGOT I HAVE BRAIN DAMAGE, SO I CAN'T BE HELD ACCOUNTABLE FOR ANYTHING I SAY.
YOU CAN AND YOU WILL BE HELD ACCOUNTABLE, BECAUSE TODAY IS JUDGMENT DAY.
JUDGMENT DAY? WHO IS THE JUDGE?
PICTURE
SMALL
BIG
CLICK.
YOU.

WE HAVE A CHANNEL THAT ARCHIVES THE COMPLETE HISTORY OF THE COSMOS, AND EACH AND EVERY ENTITY IN ALL OF ITS INCARNATIONS SINCE THE BEGINNING OF ALL TIME, FOR ALL TIME.

U Tube

UNIVERSAL TUBE — OUR QUAINT, LITTLE YOUTUBE WAS BASED ON THIS, RIGHT?

IT'S MUCH DEEPER THAN THAT. EVERYTHING YOU'VE EVER DONE, EVERYTHING YOU'VE EVER SAID, AND EVERYTHING YOU'VE EVER THOUGHT HAS BEEN, IS BEING AND WILL BE RECORDED.

SERIOUSLY? EVERY THOUGHT? LIKE I'VE BEEN BRAIN-BUGGED BY SOME KIND OF COSMIC NSA?

U Tube

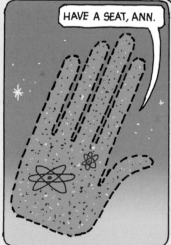

HAVE A SEAT, ANN.

COMFY?

I'VE NEVER BEEN LESS COMFY IN MY ENTIRE LIVING NON-LIVING LIFE!

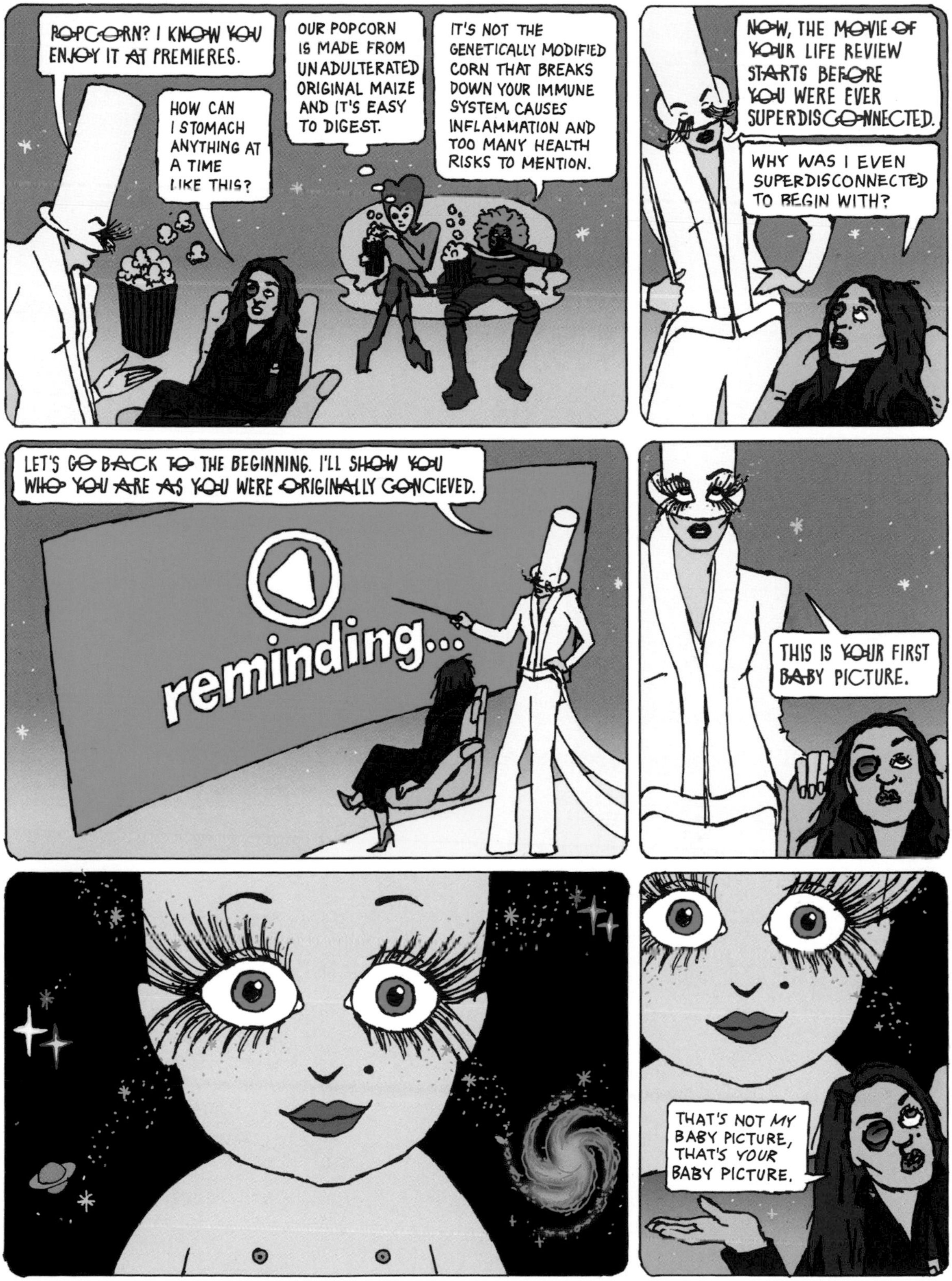
POPCORN? I KNOW YOU ENJOY IT AT PREMIERES.
HOW CAN I STOMACH ANYTHING AT A TIME LIKE THIS?
OUR POPCORN IS MADE FROM UNADULTERATED ORIGINAL MAIZE AND IT'S EASY TO DIGEST.
IT'S NOT THE GENETICALLY MODIFIED CORN THAT BREAKS DOWN YOUR IMMUNE SYSTEM, CAUSES INFLAMMATION AND TOO MANY HEALTH RISKS TO MENTION.
NOW, THE MOVIE OF YOUR LIFE REVIEW STARTS BEFORE YOU WERE EVER SUPERDISCONNECTED.
WHY WAS I EVEN SUPERDISCONNECTED TO BEGIN WITH?
LET'S GO BACK TO THE BEGINNING. I'LL SHOW YOU WHO YOU ARE AS YOU WERE ORIGINALLY CONCIEVED.
reminding...
THIS IS YOUR FIRST BABY PICTURE.
THAT'S NOT MY BABY PICTURE, THAT'S YOUR BABY PICTURE.

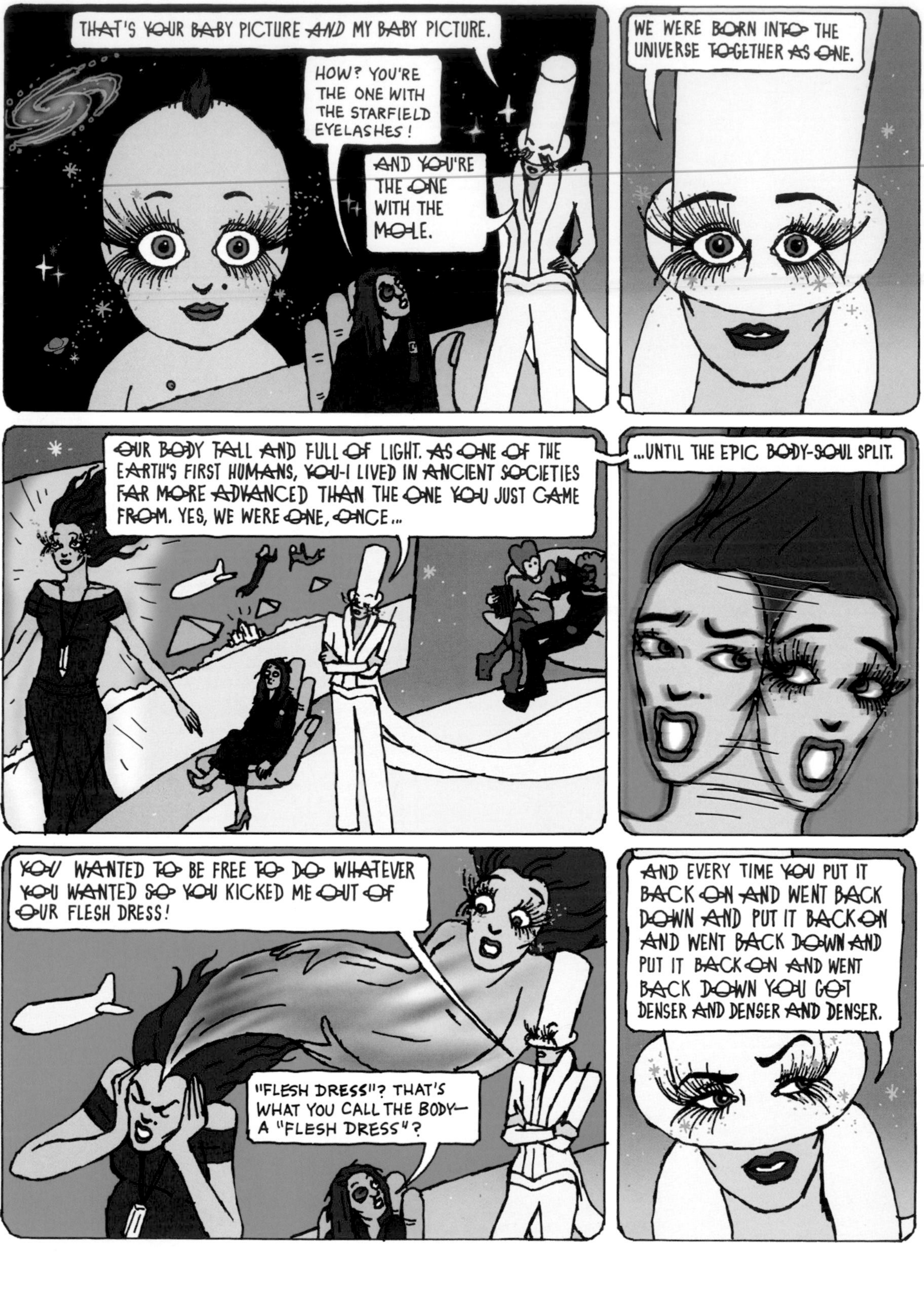
THAT'S YOUR BABY PICTURE AND MY BABY PICTURE.
HOW? YOU'RE THE ONE WITH THE STARFIELD EYELASHES!
AND YOU'RE THE ONE WITH THE MOLE.
WE WERE BORN INTO THE UNIVERSE TOGETHER AS ONE.
OUR BODY TALL AND FULL OF LIGHT. AS ONE OF THE EARTH'S FIRST HUMANS, YOU-I LIVED IN ANCIENT SOCIETIES FAR MORE ADVANCED THAN THE ONE YOU JUST CAME FROM. YES, WE WERE ONE, ONCE...
...UNTIL THE EPIC BODY-SOUL SPLIT.
YOU WANTED TO BE FREE TO DO WHATEVER YOU WANTED SO YOU KICKED ME OUT OF OUR FLESH DRESS!
"FLESH DRESS"? THAT'S WHAT YOU CALL THE BODY— A "FLESH DRESS"?
AND EVERY TIME YOU PUT IT BACK ON AND WENT BACK DOWN AND PUT IT BACK ON AND WENT BACK DOWN AND PUT IT BACK ON AND WENT BACK DOWN YOU GOT DENSER AND DENSER AND DENSER.

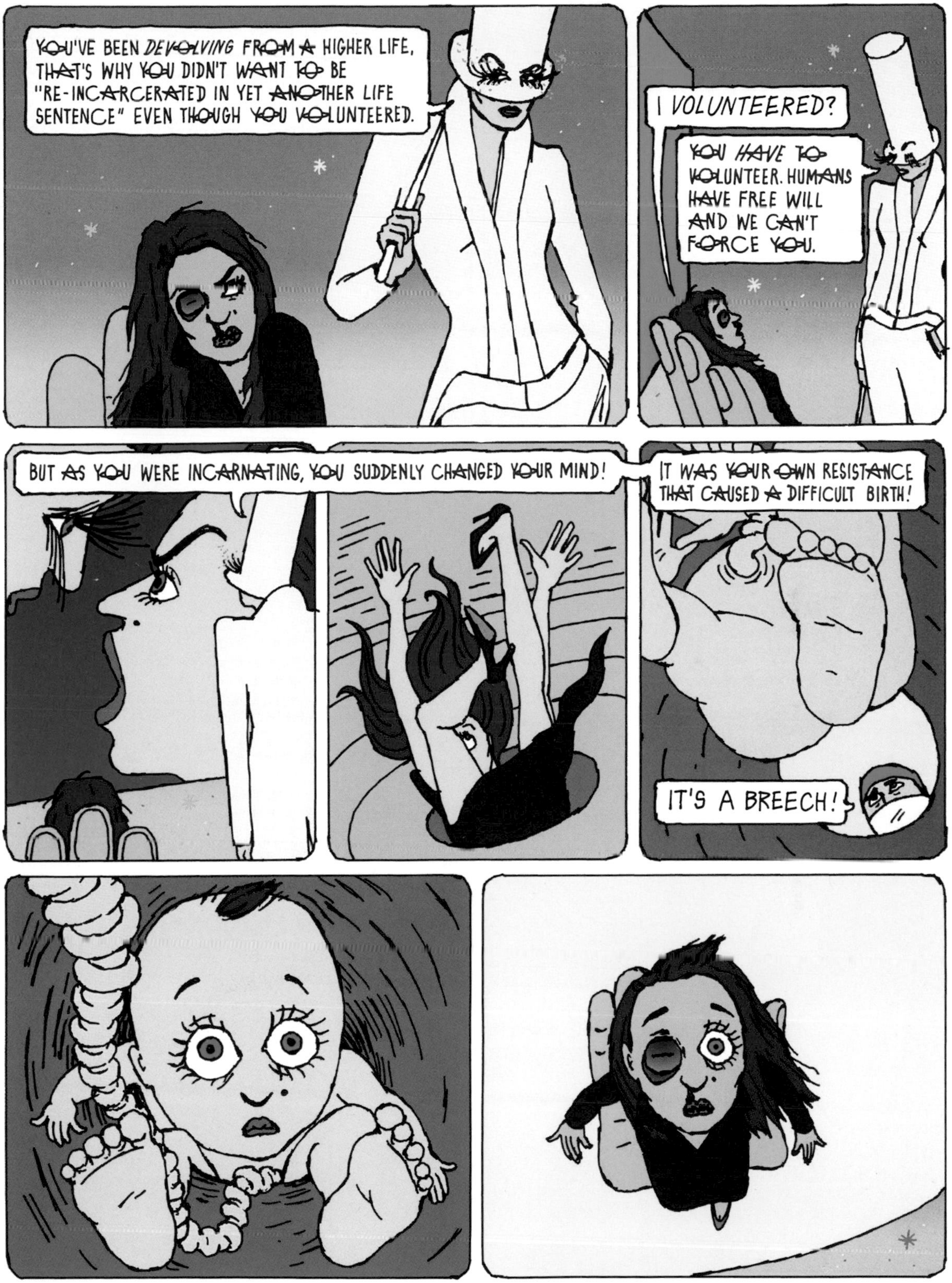
YOU'VE BEEN DEVOLVING FROM A HIGHER LIFE, THAT'S WHY YOU DIDN'T WANT TO BE "RE-INCARCERATED IN YET ANOTHER LIFE SENTENCE" EVEN THOUGH YOU VOLUNTEERED.
I VOLUNTEERED?
YOU HAVE TO VOLUNTEER. HUMANS HAVE FREE WILL AND WE CAN'T FORCE YOU.
BUT AS YOU WERE INCARNATING, YOU SUDDENLY CHANGED YOUR MIND!
IT WAS YOUR OWN RESISTANCE THAT CAUSED A DIFFICULT BIRTH!
IT'S A BREECH!

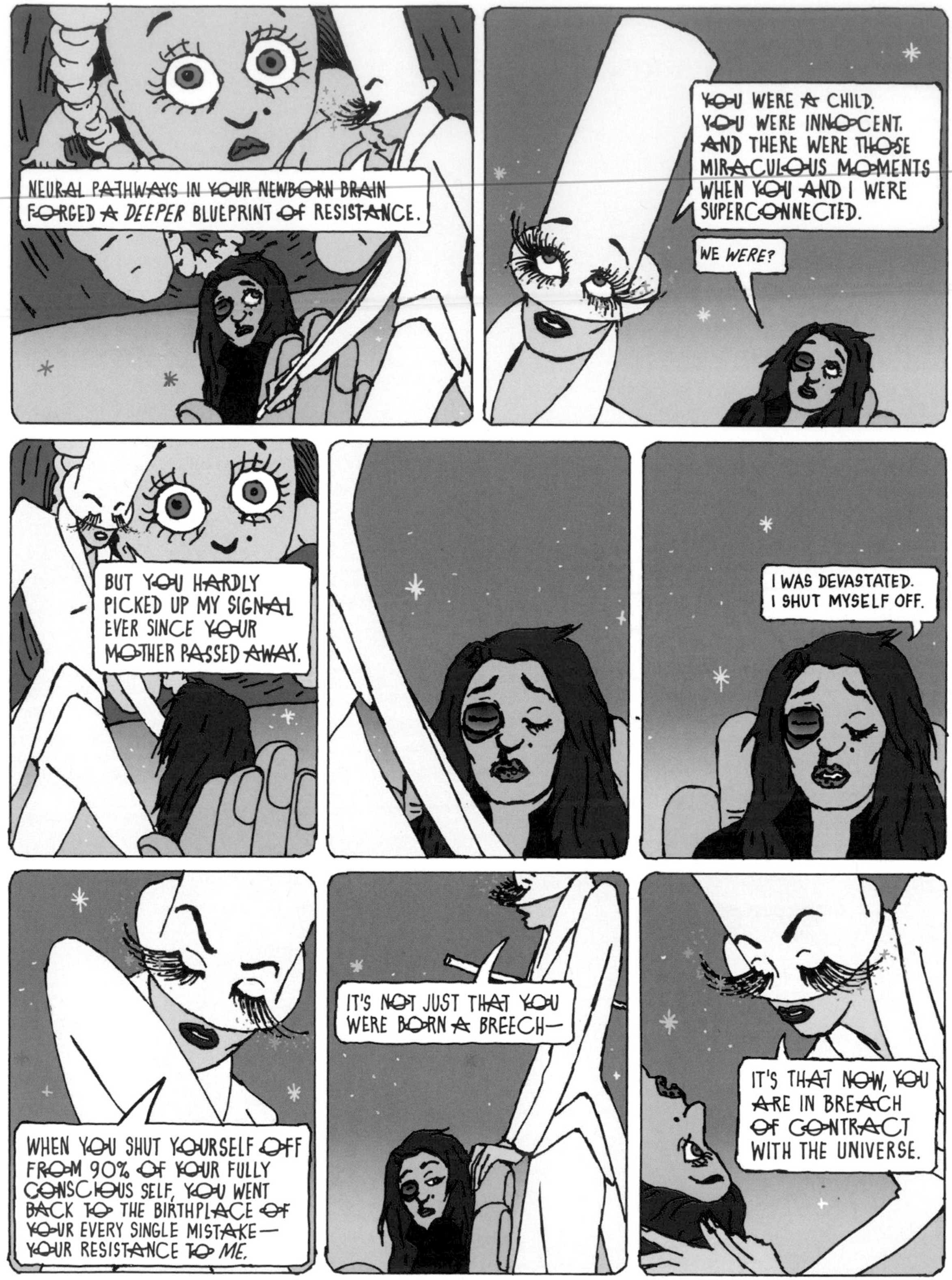
NEURAL PATHWAYS IN YOUR NEWBORN BRAIN FORGED A *DEEPER* BLUEPRINT OF RESISTANCE.
YOU WERE A CHILD. YOU WERE INNOCENT. AND THERE WERE THOSE MIRACULOUS MOMENTS WHEN YOU AND I WERE SUPERCONNECTED.
WE *WERE?*
BUT YOU HARDLY PICKED UP MY SIGNAL EVER SINCE YOUR MOTHER PASSED AWAY.
I WAS DEVASTATED. I SHUT MYSELF OFF.
WHEN YOU SHUT YOURSELF OFF FROM 90% OF YOUR FULLY CONSCIOUS SELF, YOU WENT BACK TO THE BIRTHPLACE OF YOUR EVERY SINGLE MISTAKE— YOUR RESISTANCE TO *ME.*
IT'S NOT JUST THAT YOU WERE BORN A BREECH—
IT'S THAT NOW, YOU ARE IN BREACH OF CONTRACT WITH THE UNIVERSE.

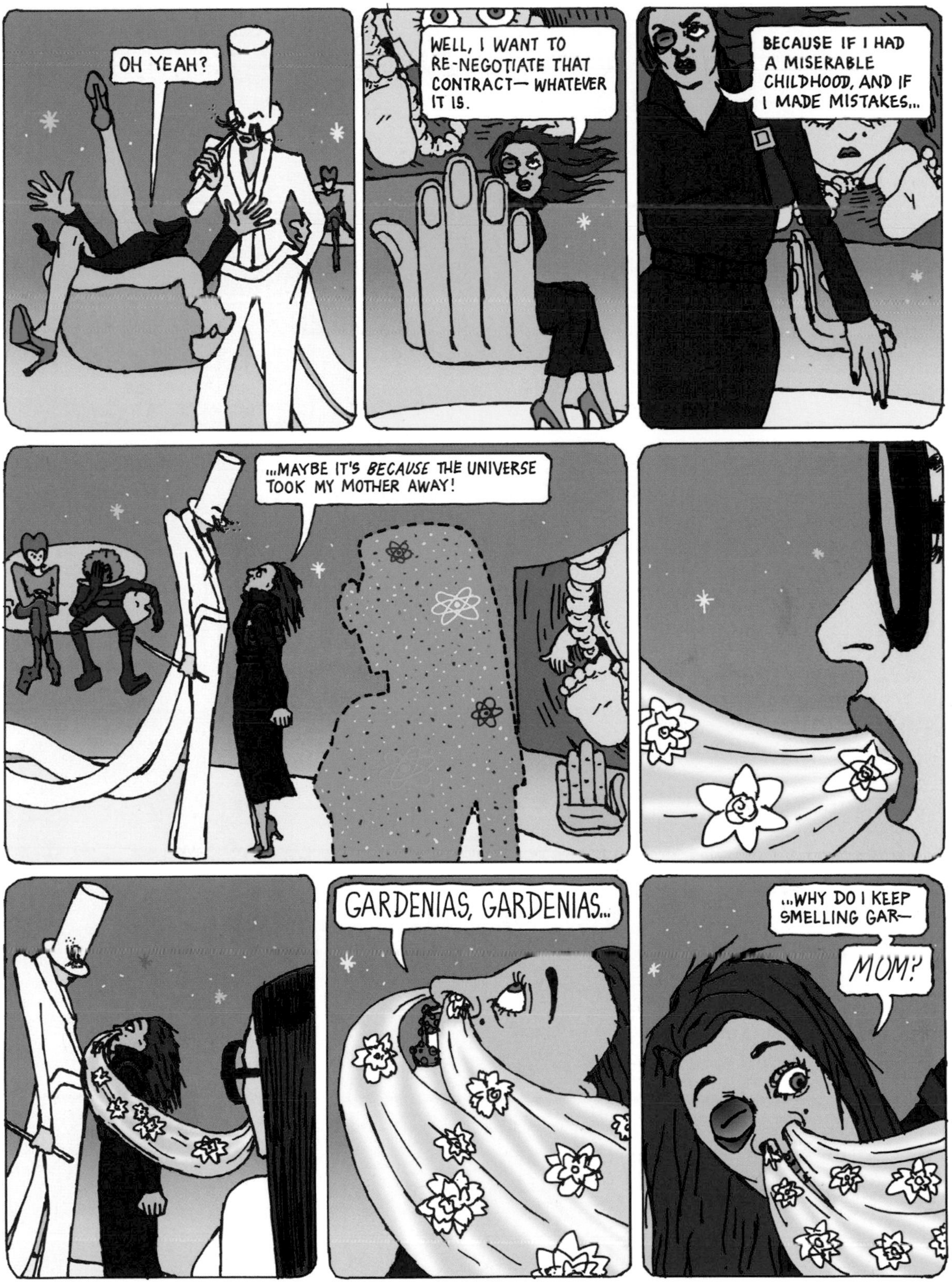
OH YEAH?
WELL, I WANT TO RE-NEGOTIATE THAT CONTRACT— WHATEVER IT IS.
BECAUSE IF I HAD A MISERABLE CHILDHOOD, AND IF I MADE MISTAKES...
...MAYBE IT'S *BECAUSE* THE UNIVERSE TOOK MY MOTHER AWAY!
GARDENIAS, GARDENIAS...
...WHY DO I KEEP SMELLING GAR—
MOM?

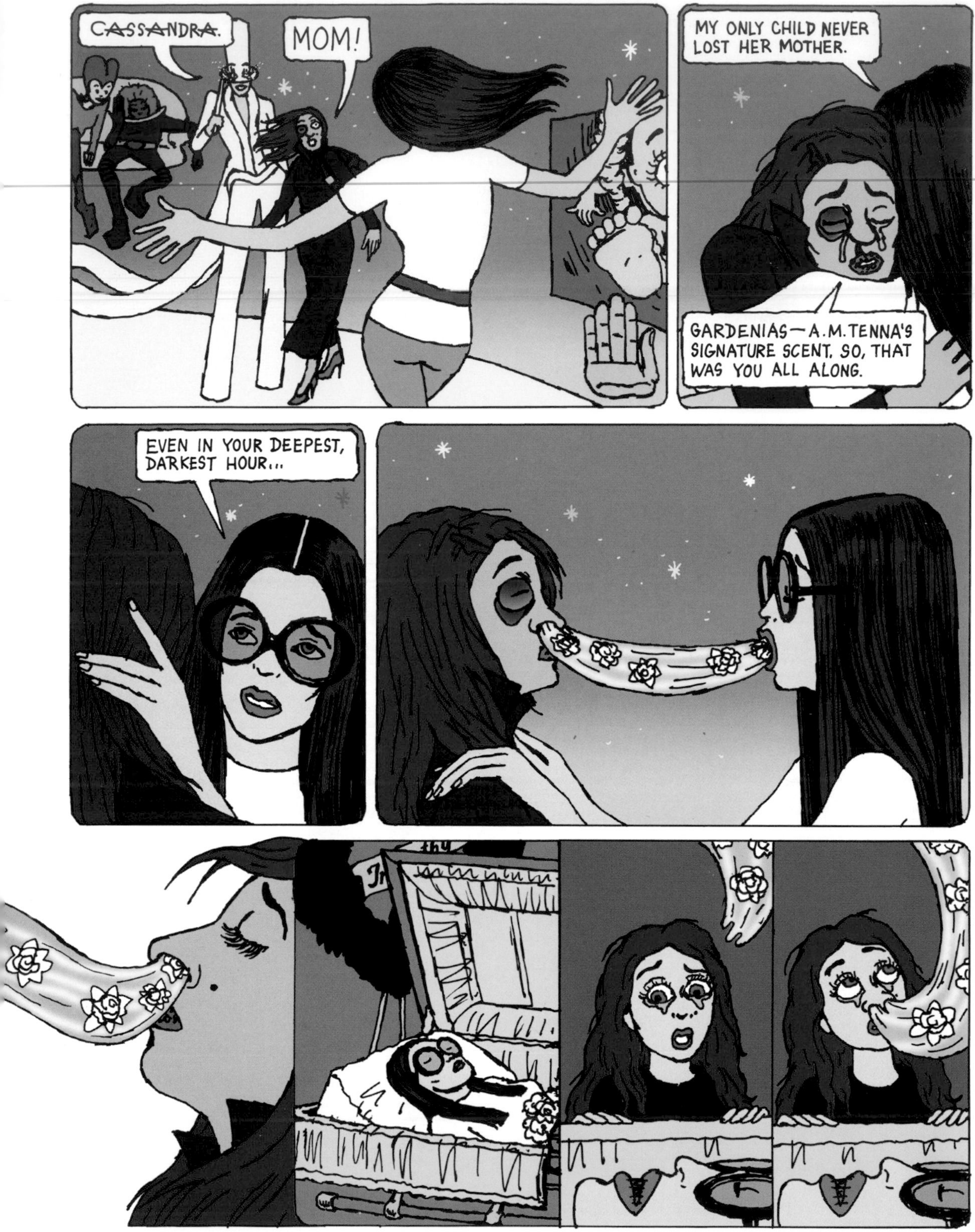
CASSANDRA.
MOM!
MY ONLY CHILD NEVER LOST HER MOTHER.
GARDENIAS—A.M.TENNA'S SIGNATURE SCENT. SO, THAT WAS YOU ALL ALONG.
EVEN IN YOUR DEEPEST, DARKEST HOUR...

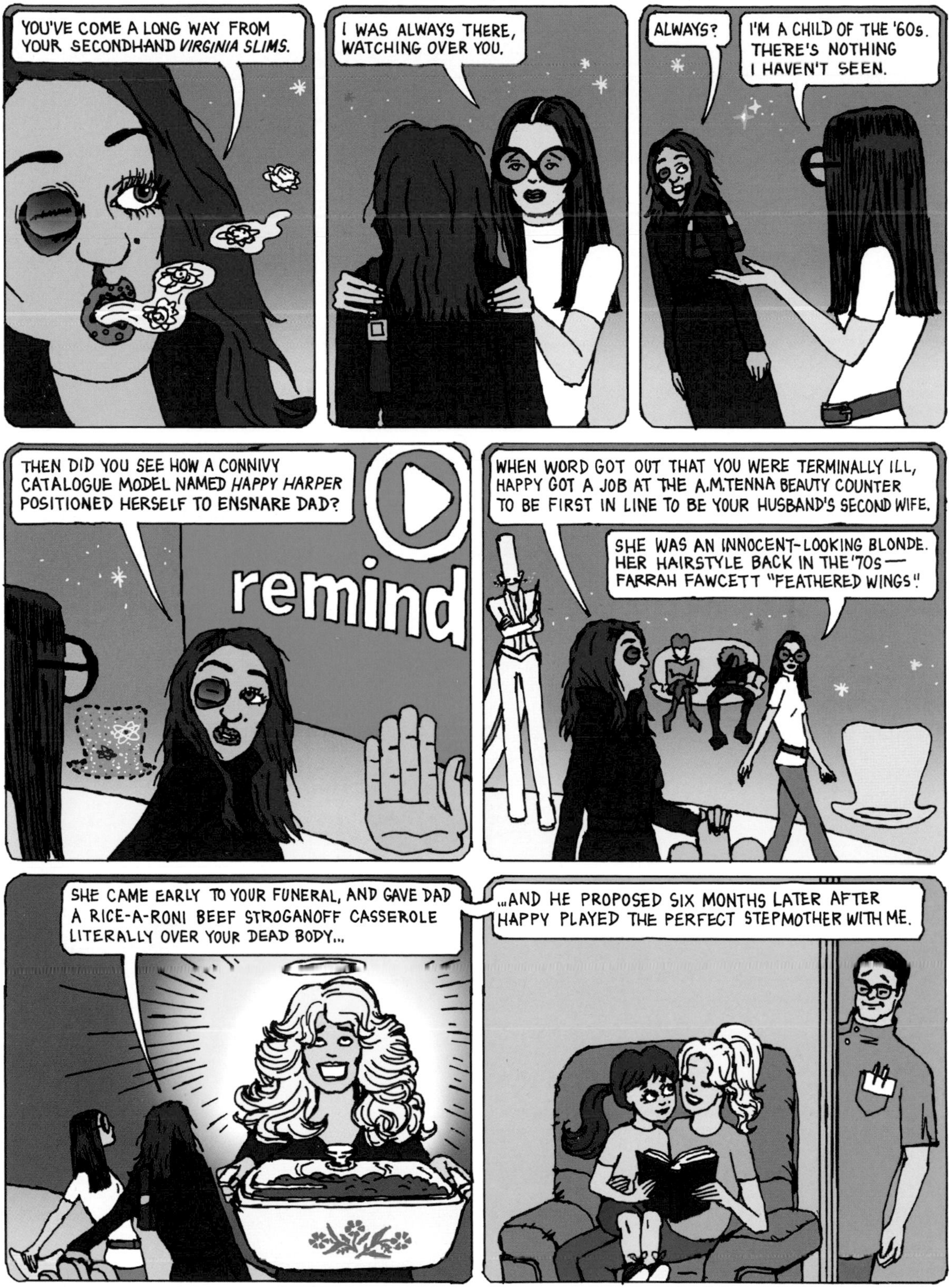
YOU'VE COME A LONG WAY FROM YOUR SECONDHAND *VIRGINIA SLIMS*.
I WAS ALWAYS THERE, WATCHING OVER YOU.
ALWAYS?
I'M A CHILD OF THE '60s. THERE'S NOTHING I HAVEN'T SEEN.
THEN DID YOU SEE HOW A CONNIVY CATALOGUE MODEL NAMED *HAPPY HARPER* POSITIONED HERSELF TO ENSNARE DAD?
remind
WHEN WORD GOT OUT THAT YOU WERE TERMINALLY ILL, HAPPY GOT A JOB AT THE A.M.TENNA BEAUTY COUNTER TO BE FIRST IN LINE TO BE YOUR HUSBAND'S SECOND WIFE.
SHE WAS AN INNOCENT-LOOKING BLONDE. HER HAIRSTYLE BACK IN THE '70s— FARRAH FAWCETT "FEATHERED WINGS."
SHE CAME EARLY TO YOUR FUNERAL, AND GAVE DAD A RICE-A-RONI BEEF STROGANOFF CASSEROLE LITERALLY OVER YOUR DEAD BODY...
...AND HE PROPOSED SIX MONTHS LATER AFTER HAPPY PLAYED THE PERFECT STEPMOTHER WITH ME.

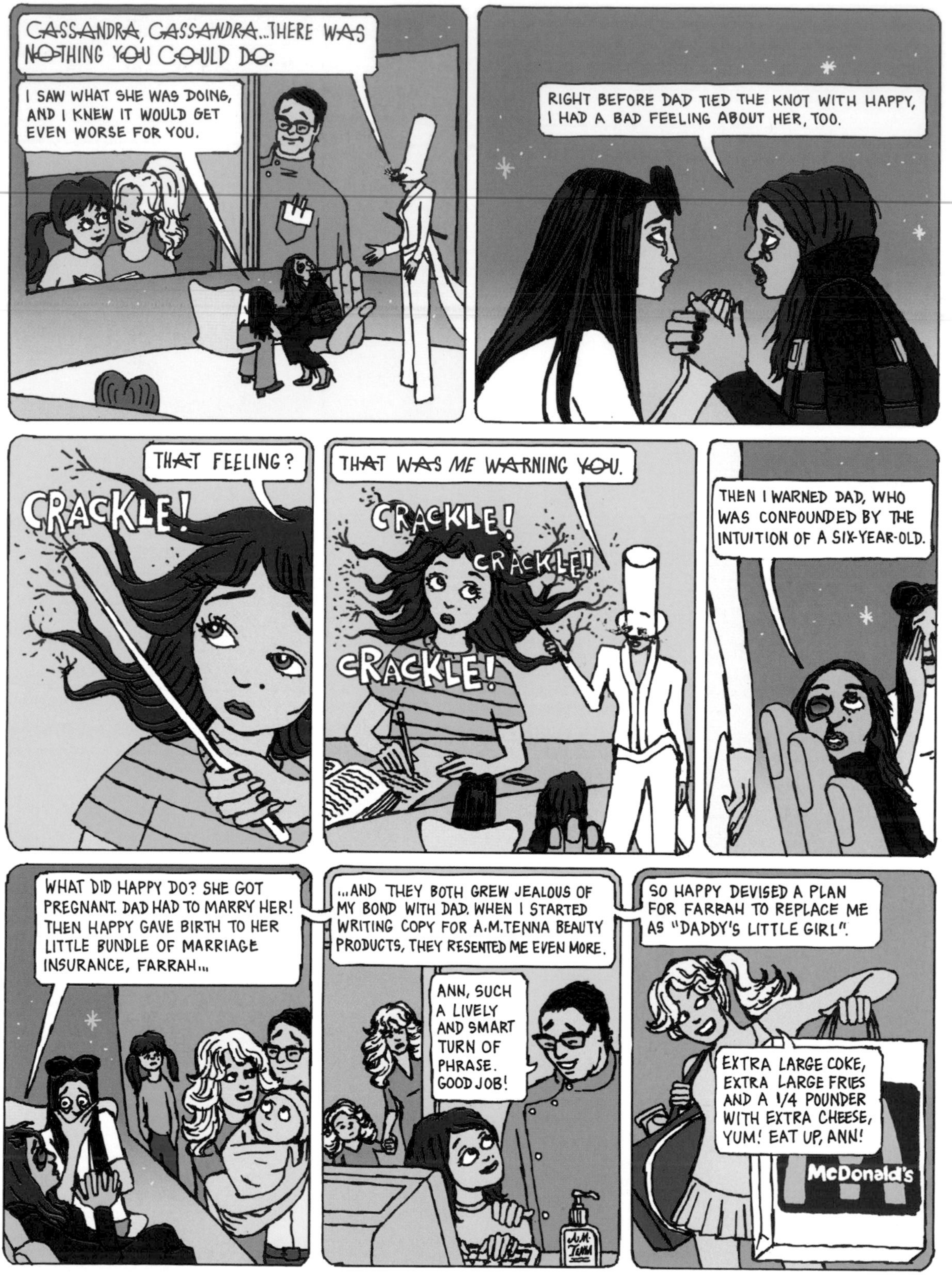
CASSANDRA, CASSANDRA...THERE WAS NOTHING YOU COULD DO.
I SAW WHAT SHE WAS DOING, AND I KNEW IT WOULD GET EVEN WORSE FOR YOU.
RIGHT BEFORE DAD TIED THE KNOT WITH HAPPY, I HAD A BAD FEELING ABOUT HER, TOO.
THAT FEELING?
CRACKLE!
THAT WAS ME WARNING YOU.
CRACKLE!
CRACKLE!
CRACKLE!
THEN I WARNED DAD, WHO WAS CONFOUNDED BY THE INTUITION OF A SIX-YEAR-OLD.
WHAT DID HAPPY DO? SHE GOT PREGNANT. DAD HAD TO MARRY HER! THEN HAPPY GAVE BIRTH TO HER LITTLE BUNDLE OF MARRIAGE INSURANCE, FARRAH...
...AND THEY BOTH GREW JEALOUS OF MY BOND WITH DAD. WHEN I STARTED WRITING COPY FOR A.M.TENNA BEAUTY PRODUCTS, THEY RESENTED ME EVEN MORE.
ANN, SUCH A LIVELY AND SMART TURN OF PHRASE. GOOD JOB!
A.M. TENNA
SO HAPPY DEVISED A PLAN FOR FARRAH TO REPLACE ME AS "DADDY'S LITTLE GIRL".
EXTRA LARGE COKE, EXTRA LARGE FRIES AND A 1/4 POUNDER WITH EXTRA CHEESE, YUM! EAT UP, ANN!
McDonald's

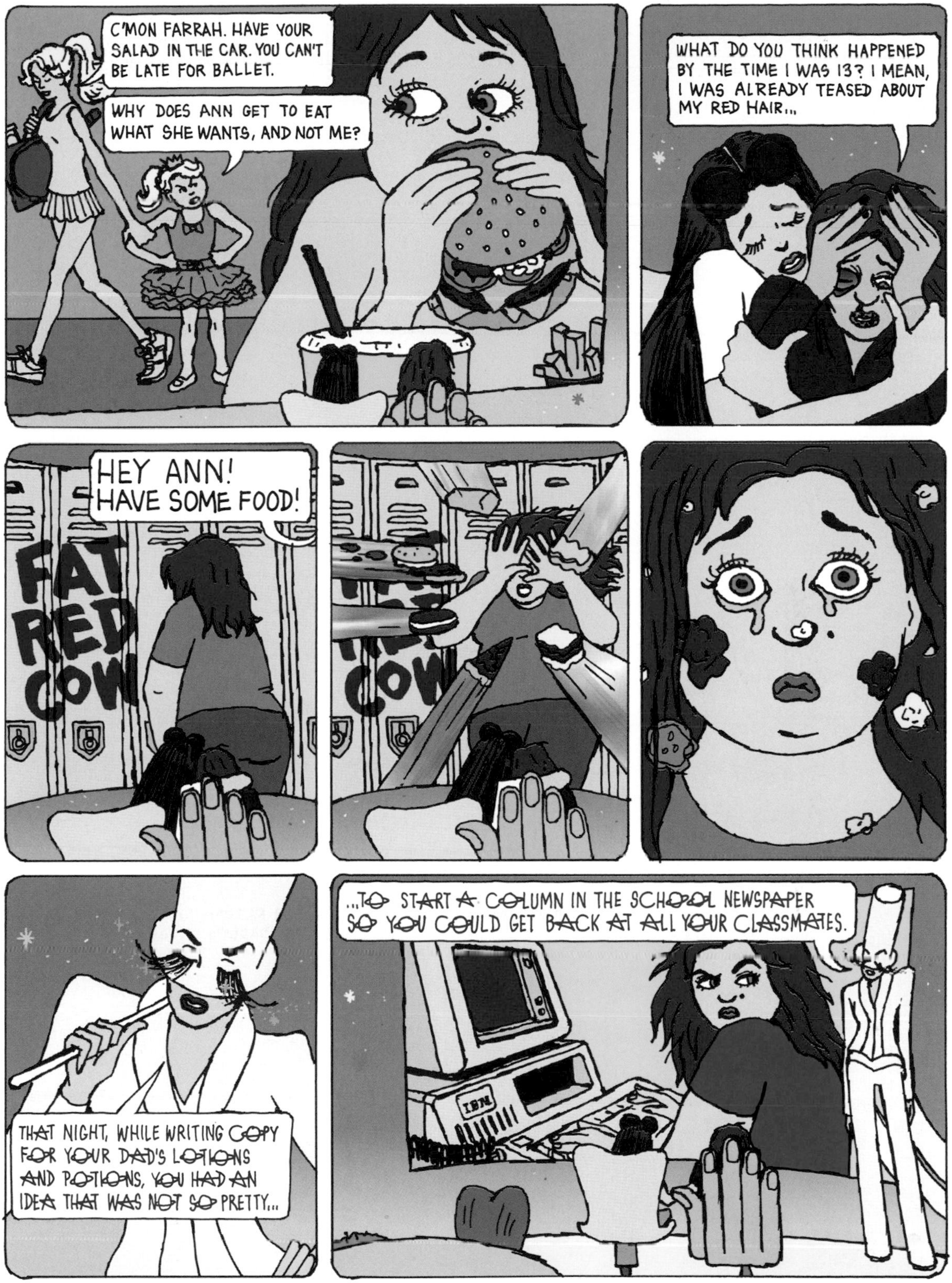
C'MON FARRAH. HAVE YOUR SALAD IN THE CAR. YOU CAN'T BE LATE FOR BALLET.
WHY DOES ANN GET TO EAT WHAT SHE WANTS, AND NOT ME?
WHAT DO YOU THINK HAPPENED BY THE TIME I WAS 13? I MEAN, I WAS ALREADY TEASED ABOUT MY RED HAIR...
HEY ANN! HAVE SOME FOOD!
FAT RED COW
THAT NIGHT, WHILE WRITING COPY FOR YOUR DAD'S LOTIONS AND POTIONS, YOU HAD AN IDEA THAT WAS NOT SO PRETTY...
...TO START A COLUMN IN THE SCHOOL NEWSPAPER SO YOU COULD GET BACK AT ALL YOUR CLASSMATES.
IBM

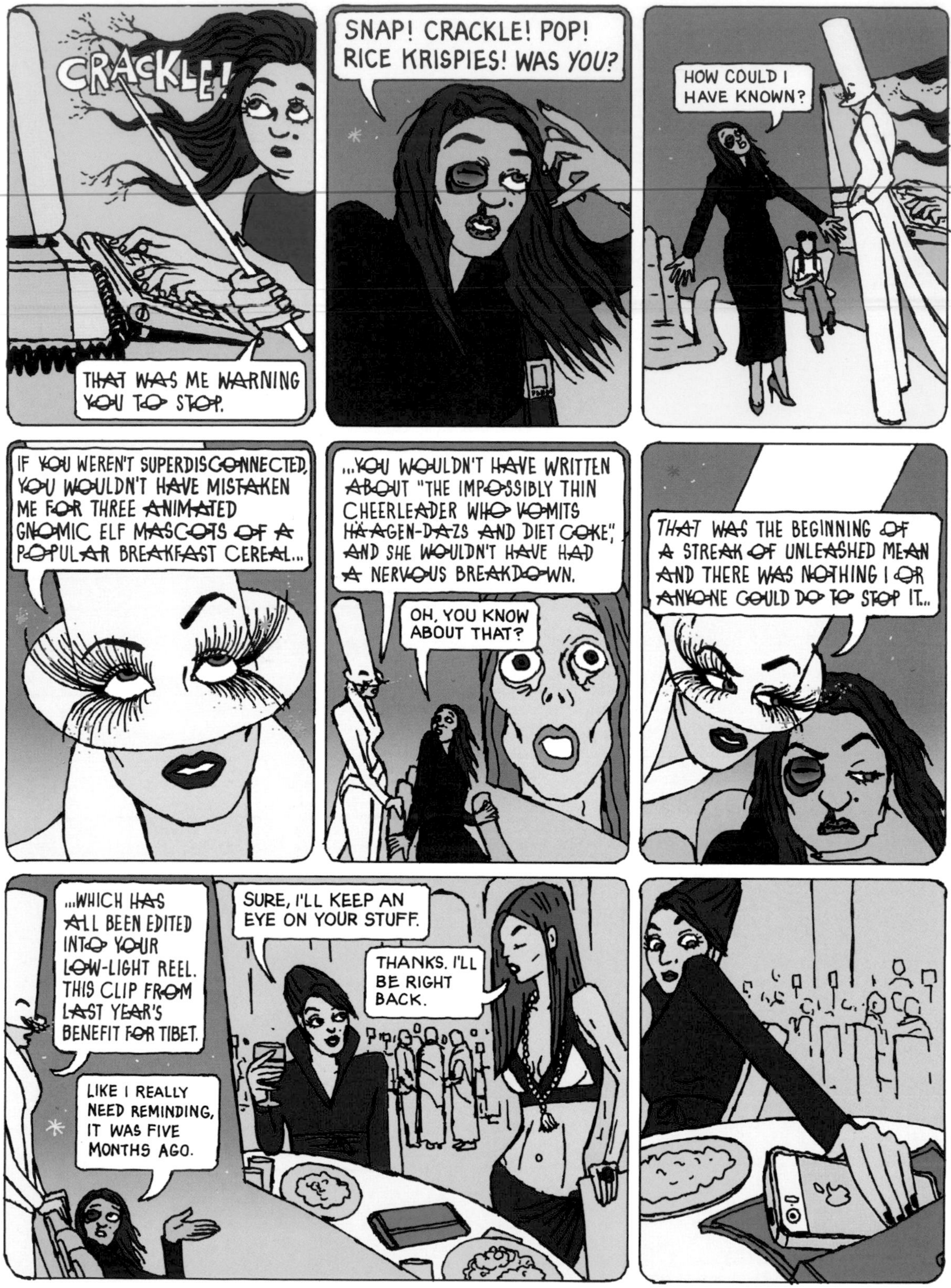
CRACKLE!
THAT WAS ME WARNING YOU TO STOP.
SNAP! CRACKLE! POP! RICE KRISPIES! WAS *YOU*?
HOW COULD I HAVE KNOWN?
IF YOU WEREN'T SUPERDISCONNECTED, YOU WOULDN'T HAVE MISTAKEN ME FOR THREE ANIMATED GNOMIC ELF MASCOTS OF A POPULAR BREAKFAST CEREAL...
...YOU WOULDN'T HAVE WRITTEN ABOUT "THE IMPOSSIBLY THIN CHEERLEADER WHO VOMITS HÄAGEN-DAZS AND DIET COKE," AND SHE WOULDN'T HAVE HAD A NERVOUS BREAKDOWN.
OH, YOU KNOW ABOUT THAT?
THAT WAS THE BEGINNING OF A STREAK OF UNLEASHED MEAN AND THERE WAS NOTHING I OR ANYONE COULD DO TO STOP IT...
...WHICH HAS ALL BEEN EDITED INTO YOUR LOW-LIGHT REEL. THIS CLIP FROM LAST YEAR'S BENEFIT FOR TIBET.
LIKE I REALLY NEED REMINDING, IT WAS FIVE MONTHS AGO.
SURE, I'LL KEEP AN EYE ON YOUR STUFF.
THANKS. I'LL BE RIGHT BACK.

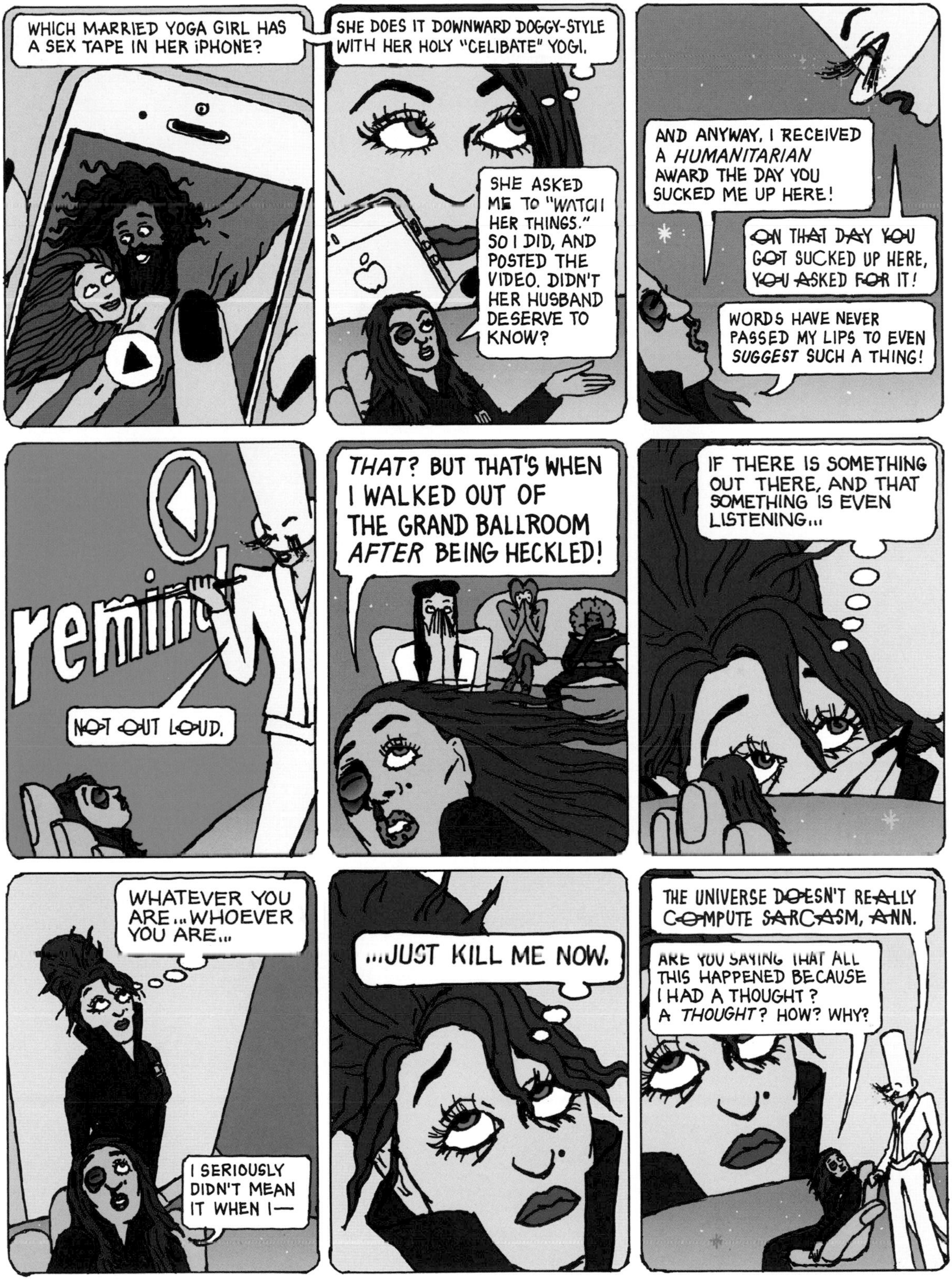

WHICH MARRIED YOGA GIRL HAS A SEX TAPE IN HER iPHONE?
SHE DOES IT DOWNWARD DOGGY-STYLE WITH HER HOLY "CELIBATE" YOGI.
SHE ASKED ME TO "WATCH HER THINGS." SO I DID, AND POSTED THE VIDEO. DIDN'T HER HUSBAND DESERVE TO KNOW?
AND ANYWAY, I RECEIVED A *HUMANITARIAN* AWARD THE DAY YOU SUCKED ME UP HERE!
ON THAT DAY YOU GOT SUCKED UP HERE, YOU ASKED FOR IT!
WORDS HAVE NEVER PASSED MY LIPS TO EVEN *SUGGEST* SUCH A THING!
remind
NOT OUT LOUD.
THAT? BUT THAT'S WHEN I WALKED OUT OF THE GRAND BALLROOM *AFTER* BEING HECKLED!
IF THERE IS SOMETHING OUT THERE, AND THAT SOMETHING IS EVEN LISTENING...
WHATEVER YOU ARE... WHOEVER YOU ARE...
I SERIOUSLY DIDN'T MEAN IT WHEN I—
...JUST KILL ME NOW.
THE UNIVERSE DOESN'T REALLY COMPUTE SARCASM, ANN.
ARE YOU SAYING THAT ALL THIS HAPPENED BECAUSE I HAD A THOUGHT? A *THOUGHT*? HOW? WHY?

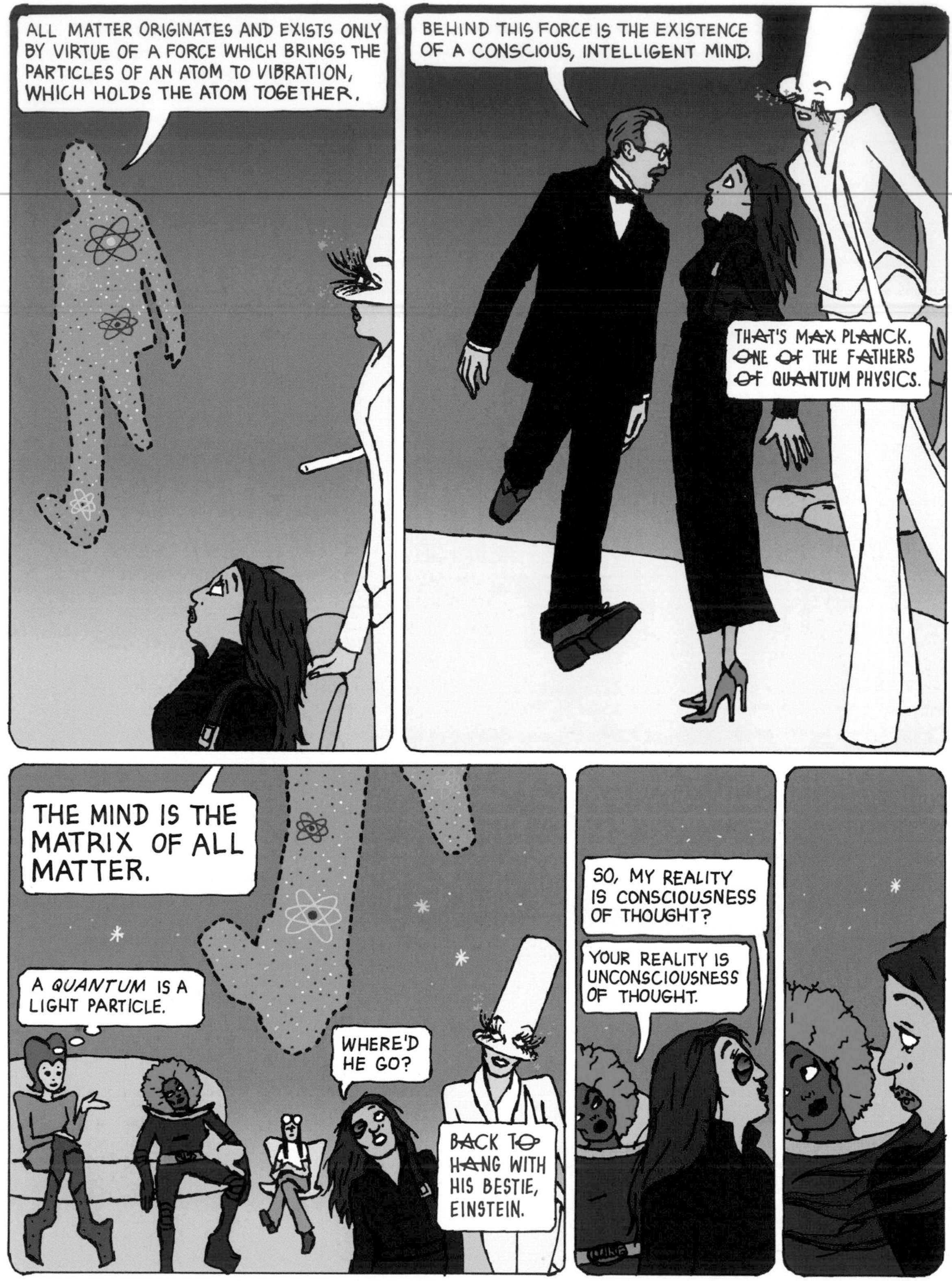
ALL MATTER ORIGINATES AND EXISTS ONLY BY VIRTUE OF A FORCE WHICH BRINGS THE PARTICLES OF AN ATOM TO VIBRATION, WHICH HOLDS THE ATOM TOGETHER.
BEHIND THIS FORCE IS THE EXISTENCE OF A CONSCIOUS, INTELLIGENT MIND.
THAT'S MAX PLANCK. ONE OF THE FATHERS OF QUANTUM PHYSICS.
THE MIND IS THE MATRIX OF ALL MATTER.
A *QUANTUM* IS A LIGHT PARTICLE.
WHERE'D HE GO?
BACK TO HANG WITH HIS BESTIE, EINSTEIN.
SO, MY REALITY IS CONSCIOUSNESS OF THOUGHT?
YOUR REALITY IS UNCONSCIOUSNESS OF THOUGHT.

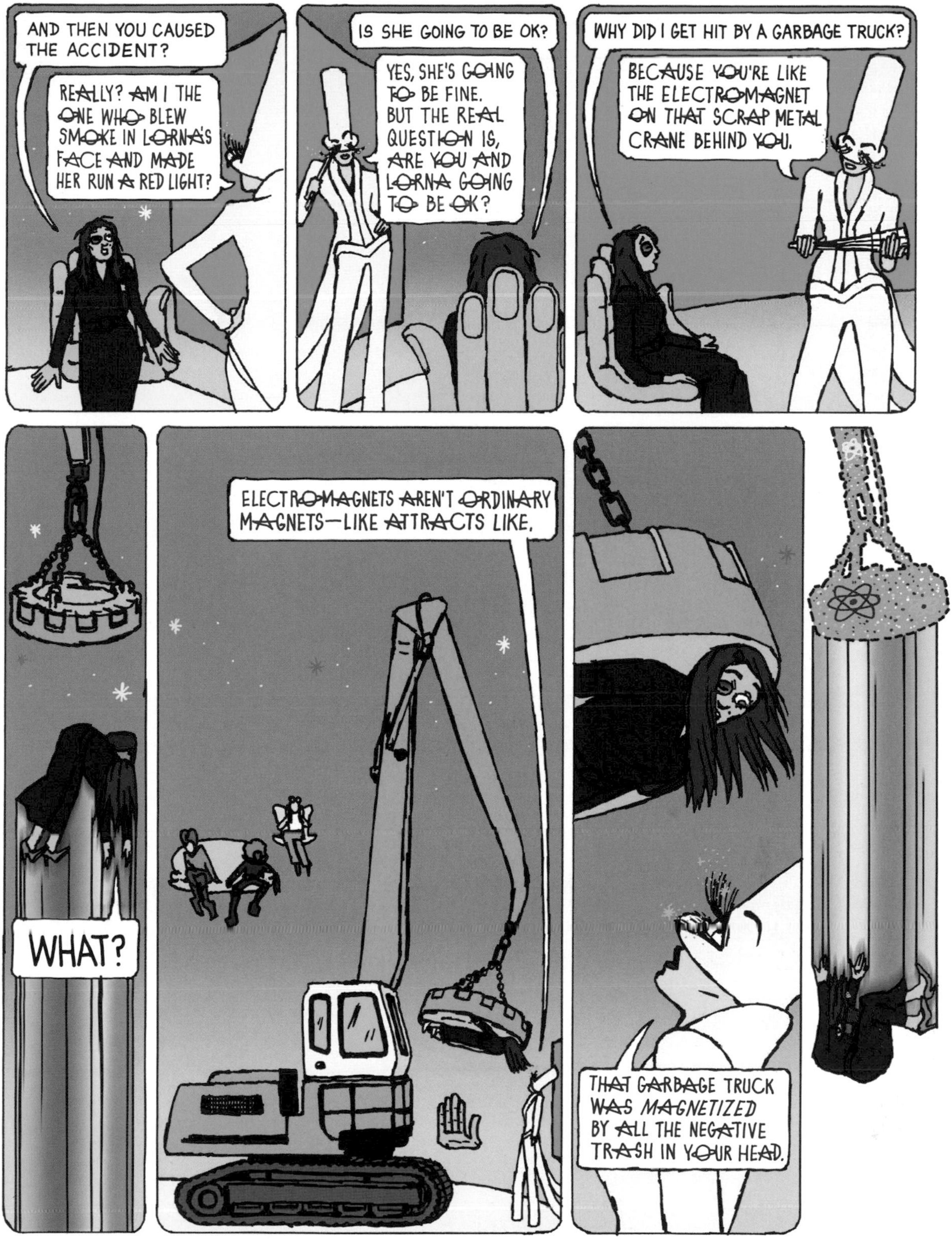

AND THEN YOU CAUSED THE ACCIDENT?
REALLY? AM I THE ONE WHO BLEW SMOKE IN LORNA'S FACE AND MADE HER RUN A RED LIGHT?
IS SHE GOING TO BE OK?
YES, SHE'S GOING TO BE FINE. BUT THE REAL QUESTION IS, ARE YOU AND LORNA GOING TO BE OK?
WHY DID I GET HIT BY A GARBAGE TRUCK?
BECAUSE YOU'RE LIKE THE ELECTROMAGNET ON THAT SCRAP METAL CRANE BEHIND YOU.
WHAT?
ELECTROMAGNETS AREN'T ORDINARY MAGNETS—LIKE ATTRACTS LIKE.
THAT GARBAGE TRUCK WAS *MAGNETIZED* BY ALL THE NEGATIVE TRASH IN YOUR HEAD.

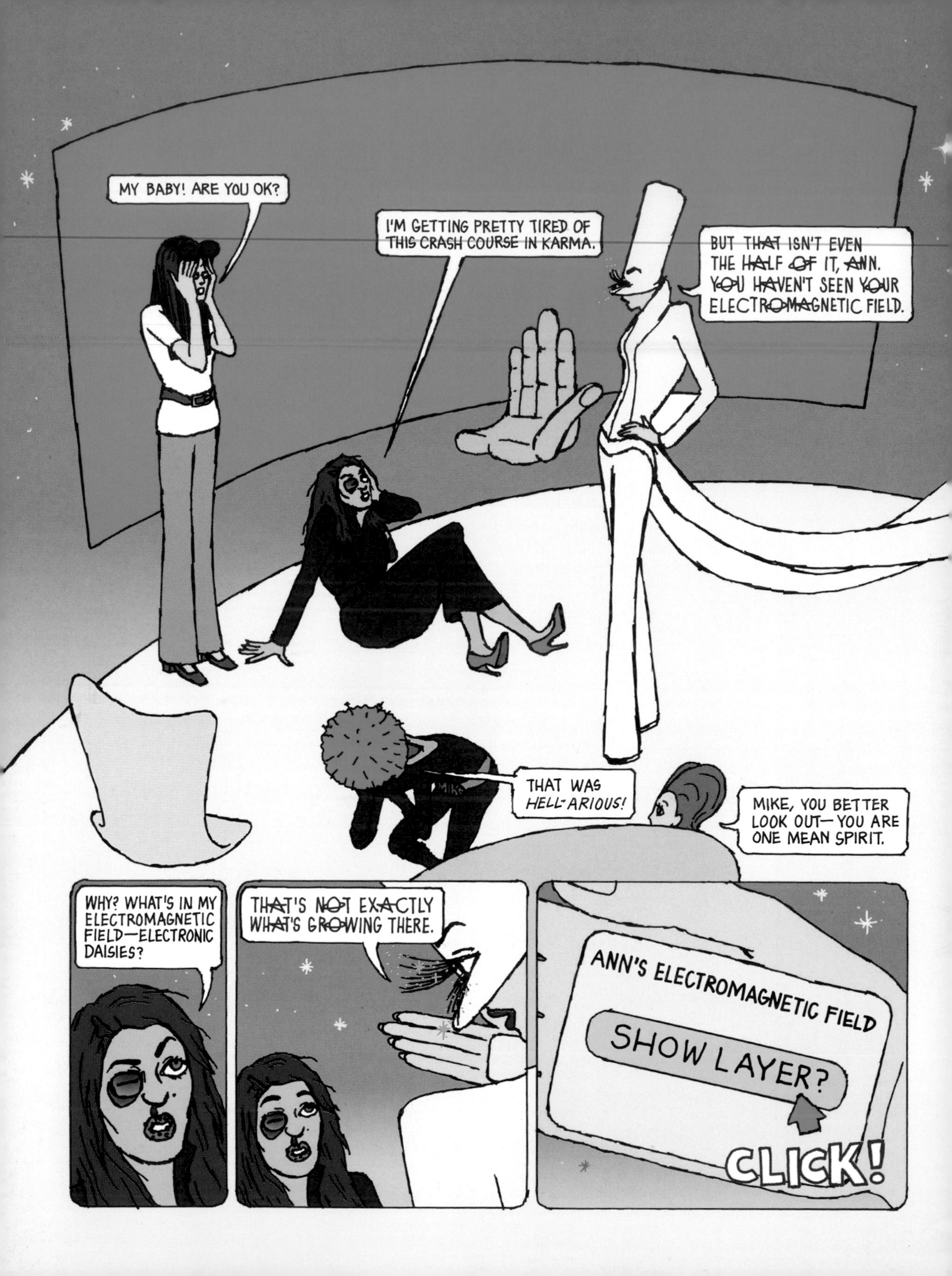
MY BABY! ARE YOU OK?
I'M GETTING PRETTY TIRED OF THIS CRASH COURSE IN KARMA.
BUT THAT ISN'T EVEN THE HALF OF IT, ANN. YOU HAVEN'T SEEN YOUR ELECTROMAGNETIC FIELD.
MIKE
THAT WAS *HELL-ARIOUS!*
MIKE, YOU BETTER LOOK OUT— YOU ARE ONE MEAN SPIRIT.
WHY? WHAT'S IN MY ELECTROMAGNETIC FIELD—ELECTRONIC DAISIES?
THAT'S NOT EXACTLY WHAT'S GROWING THERE.
ANN'S ELECTROMAGNETIC FIELD
SHOW LAYER?
CLICK!

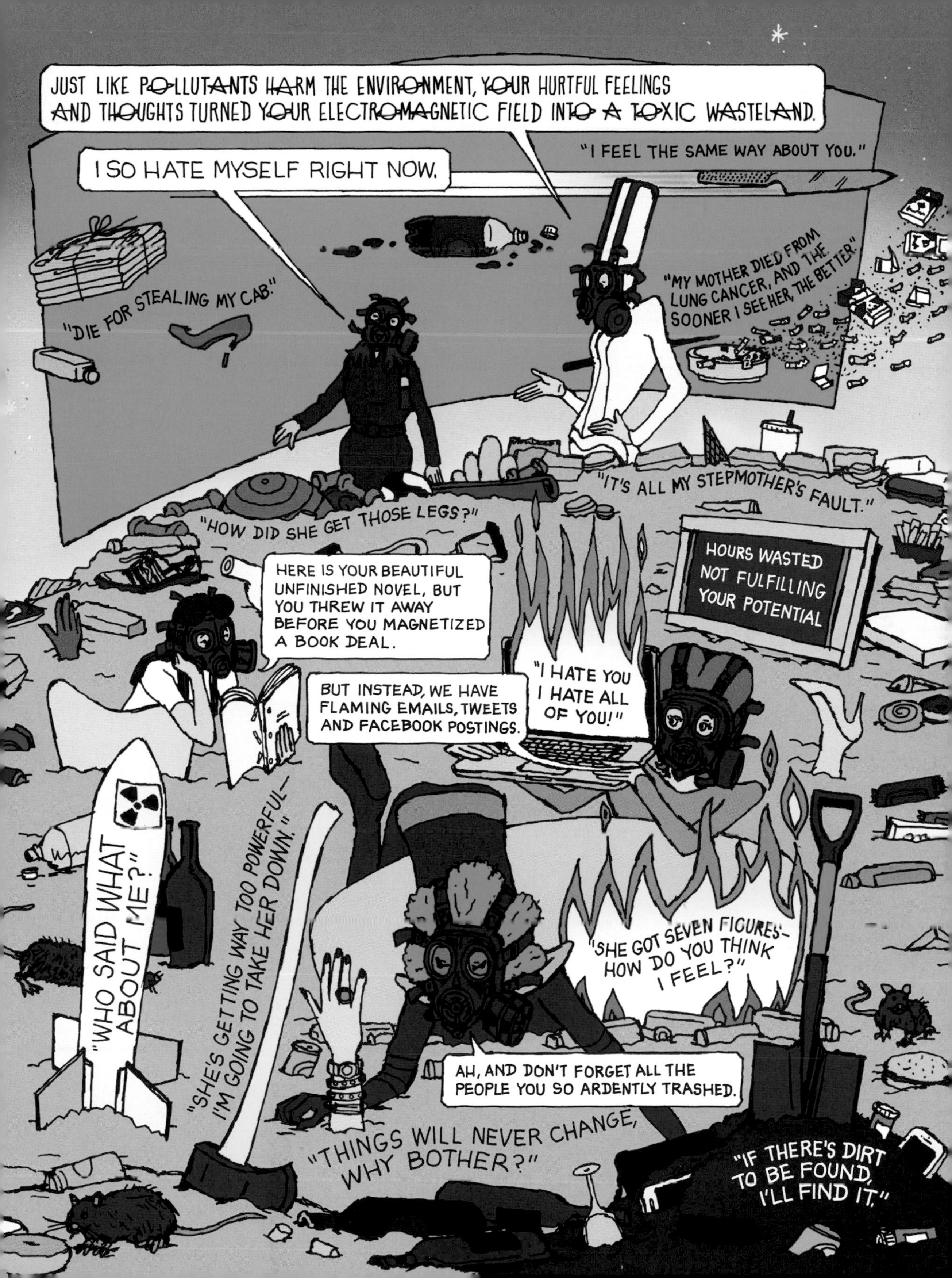
JUST LIKE POLLUTANTS HARM THE ENVIRONMENT, YOUR HURTFUL FEELINGS AND THOUGHTS TURNED YOUR ELECTROMAGNETIC FIELD INTO A TOXIC WASTELAND.
I SO HATE MYSELF RIGHT NOW.
"I FEEL THE SAME WAY ABOUT YOU."
"DIE FOR STEALING MY CAB."
"MY MOTHER DIED FROM LUNG CANCER, AND THE SOONER I SEE HER, THE BETTER."
"HOW DID SHE GET THOSE LEGS?"
"IT'S ALL MY STEPMOTHER'S FAULT."
HERE IS YOUR BEAUTIFUL UNFINISHED NOVEL, BUT YOU THREW IT AWAY BEFORE YOU MAGNETIZED A BOOK DEAL.
HOURS WASTED NOT FULFILLING YOUR POTENTIAL
BUT INSTEAD, WE HAVE FLAMING EMAILS, TWEETS AND FACEBOOK POSTINGS.
"I HATE YOU I HATE ALL OF YOU!"
"WHO SAID WHAT ABOUT ME?"
"SHE'S GETTING WAY TOO POWERFUL— I'M GOING TO TAKE HER DOWN."
"SHE GOT SEVEN FIGURES— HOW DO YOU THINK I FEEL?"
AH, AND DON'T FORGET ALL THE PEOPLE YOU SO ARDENTLY TRASHED.
"THINGS WILL NEVER CHANGE, WHY BOTHER?"
"IF THERE'S DIRT TO BE FOUND, I'LL FIND IT."

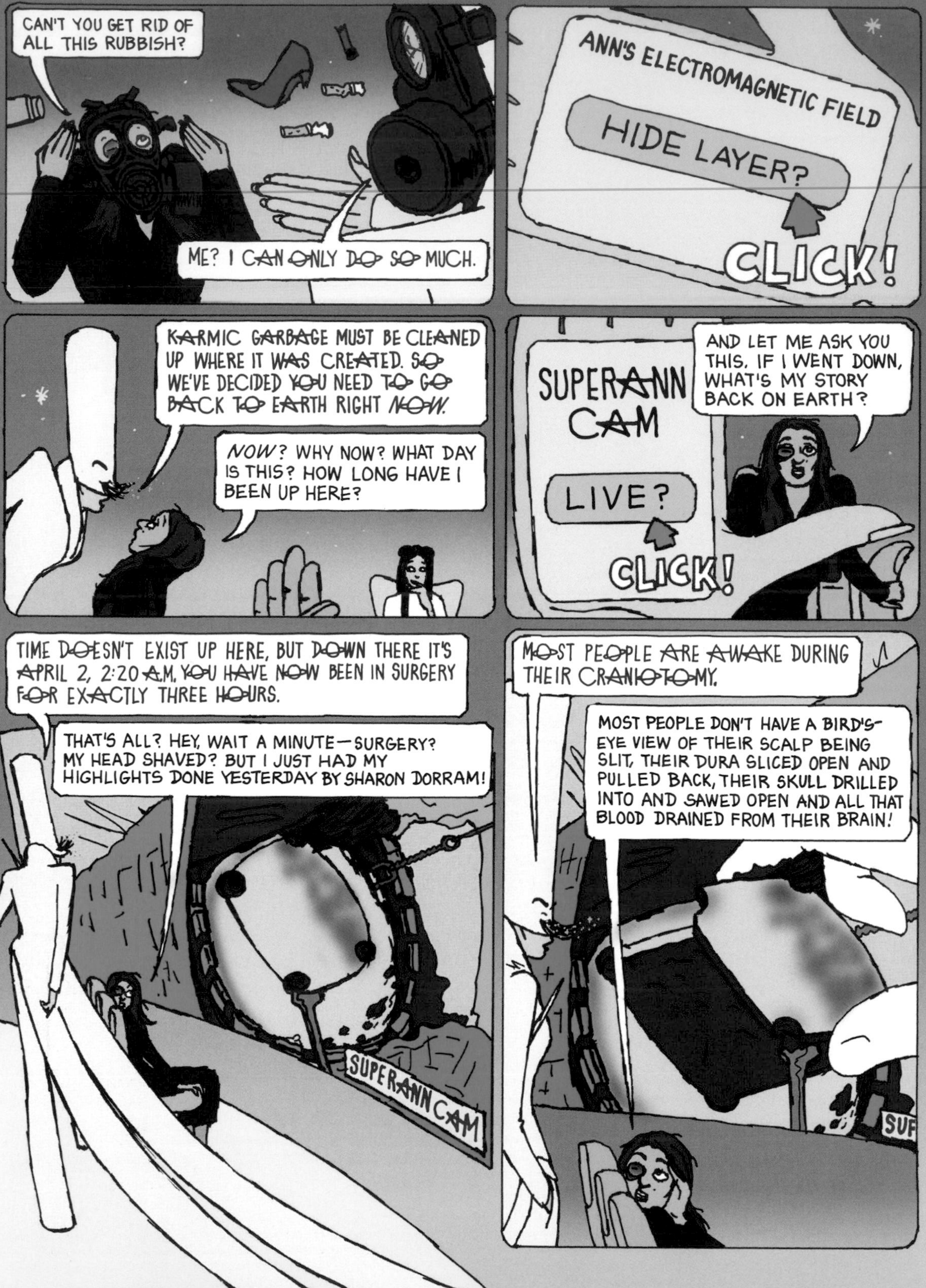
CAN'T YOU GET RID OF ALL THIS RUBBISH?
ME? I CAN ONLY DO SO MUCH.
ANN'S ELECTROMAGNETIC FIELD
HIDE LAYER?
CLICK!
KARMIC GARBAGE MUST BE CLEANED UP WHERE IT WAS CREATED. SO WE'VE DECIDED YOU NEED TO GO BACK TO EARTH RIGHT NOW.
NOW? WHY NOW? WHAT DAY IS THIS? HOW LONG HAVE I BEEN UP HERE?
SUPERANN CAM
LIVE?
CLICK!
AND LET ME ASK YOU THIS. IF I WENT DOWN, WHAT'S MY STORY BACK ON EARTH?
TIME DOESN'T EXIST UP HERE, BUT DOWN THERE IT'S APRIL 2, 2:20 A.M. YOU HAVE NOW BEEN IN SURGERY FOR EXACTLY THREE HOURS.
THAT'S ALL? HEY, WAIT A MINUTE—SURGERY? MY HEAD SHAVED? BUT I JUST HAD MY HIGHLIGHTS DONE YESTERDAY BY SHARON DORRAM!
SUPERANN CAM
MOST PEOPLE ARE AWAKE DURING THEIR CRANIOTOMY.
MOST PEOPLE DON'T HAVE A BIRD'S-EYE VIEW OF THEIR SCALP BEING SLIT, THEIR DURA SLICED OPEN AND PULLED BACK, THEIR SKULL DRILLED INTO AND SAWED OPEN AND ALL THAT BLOOD DRAINED FROM THEIR BRAIN!
SUP

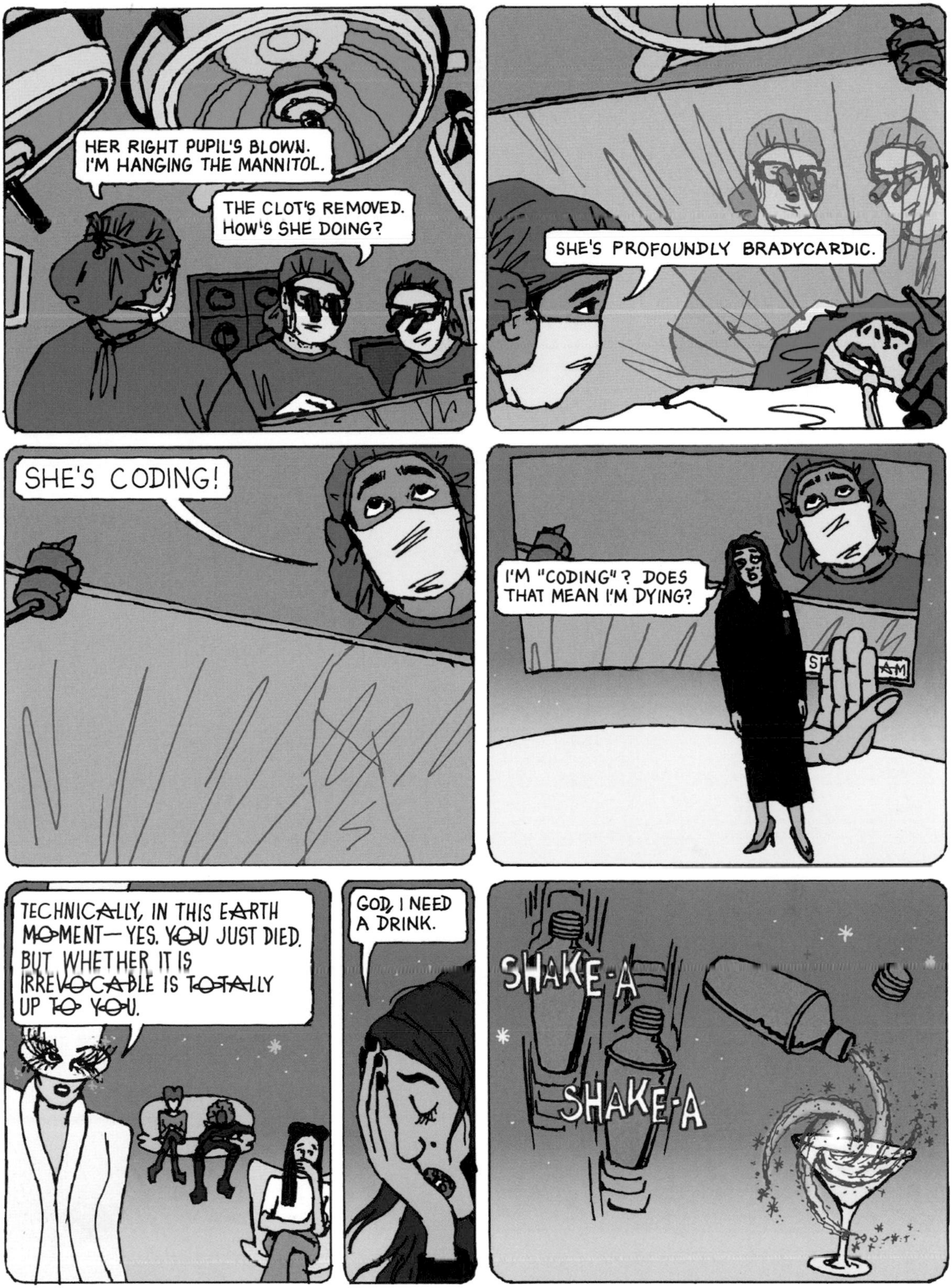
HER RIGHT PUPIL'S BLOWN. I'M HANGING THE MANNITOL.
THE CLOT'S REMOVED. HOW'S SHE DOING?
SHE'S PROFOUNDLY BRADYCARDIC.
SHE'S CODING!
I'M "CODING"? DOES THAT MEAN I'M DYING?
TECHNICALLY, IN THIS EARTH MOMENT— YES. YOU JUST DIED. BUT WHETHER IT IS IRREVOCABLE IS TOTALLY UP TO YOU.
GOD, I NEED A DRINK.
SHAKE-A
SHAKE-A

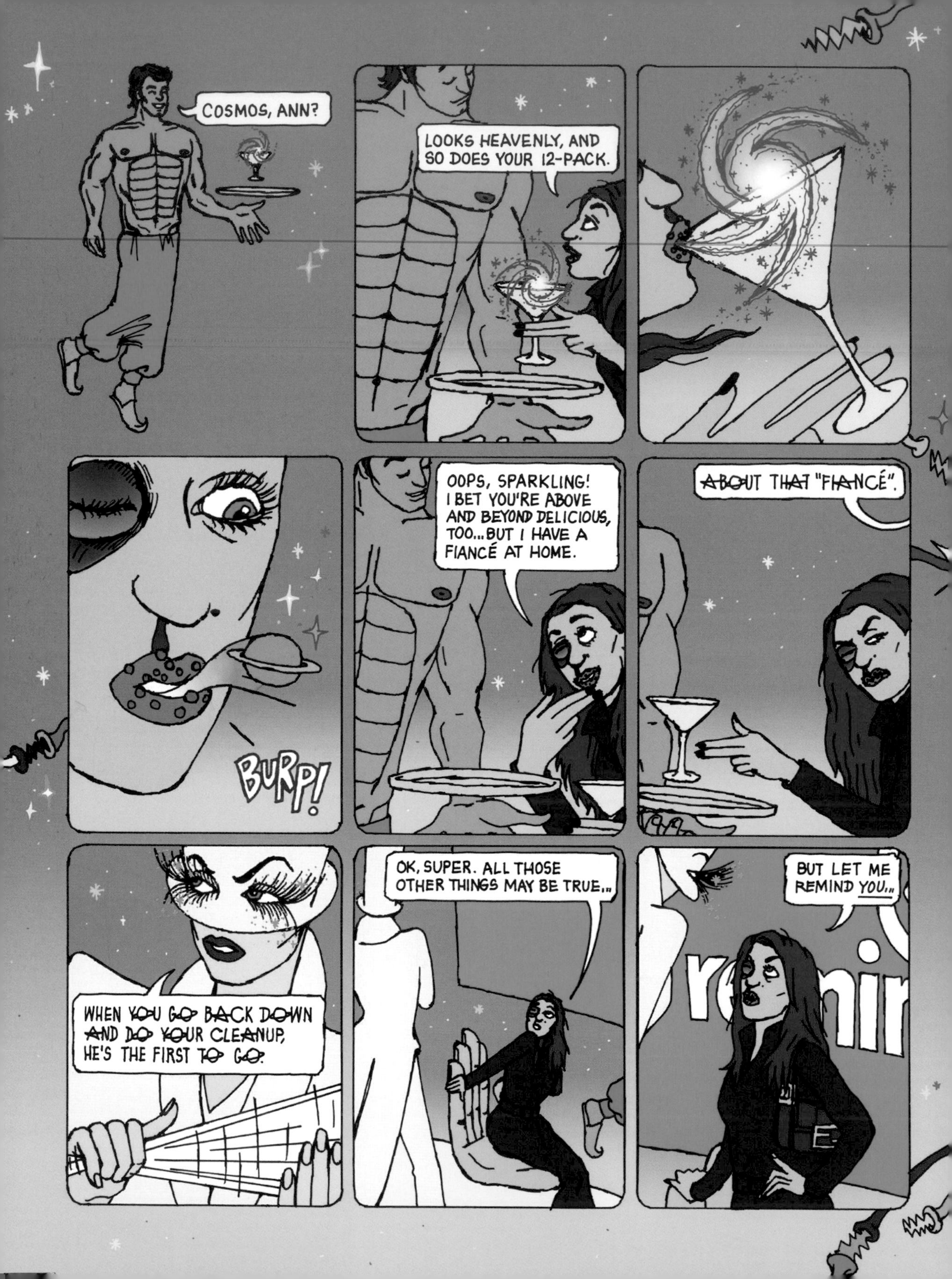
COSMOS, ANN?
LOOKS HEAVENLY, AND SO DOES YOUR 12-PACK.
BURP!
OOPS, SPARKLING! I BET YOU'RE ABOVE AND BEYOND DELICIOUS, TOO...BUT I HAVE A FIANCÉ AT HOME.
ABOUT THAT "FIANCÉ".
WHEN YOU GO BACK DOWN AND DO YOUR CLEANUP, HE'S THE FIRST TO GO.
OK, SUPER. ALL THOSE OTHER THINGS MAY BE TRUE...
BUT LET ME REMIND YOU...
remin

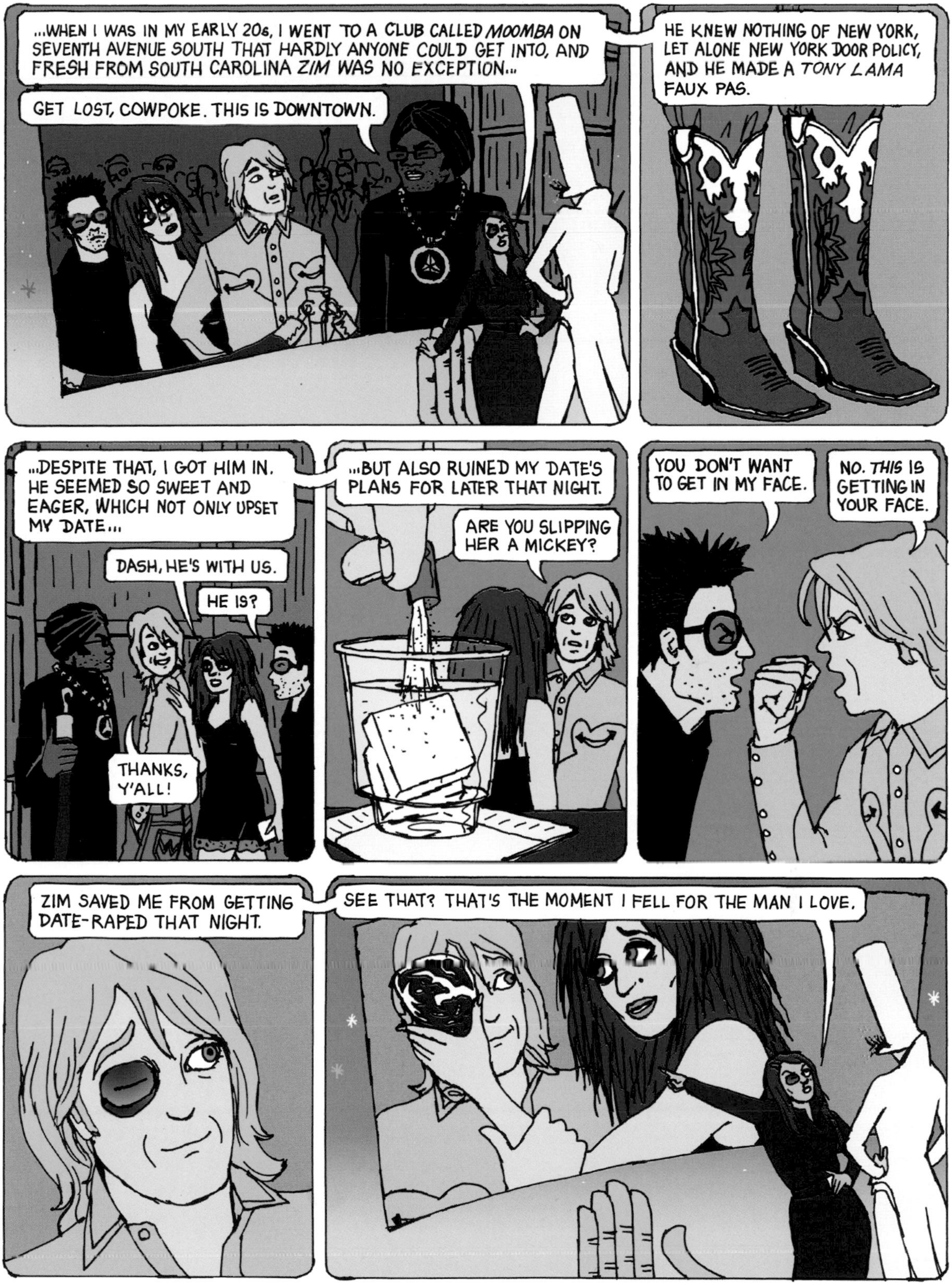
...WHEN I WAS IN MY EARLY 20s, I WENT TO A CLUB CALLED MOOMBA ON SEVENTH AVENUE SOUTH THAT HARDLY ANYONE COULD GET INTO, AND FRESH FROM SOUTH CAROLINA ZIM WAS NO EXCEPTION...
GET LOST, COWPOKE. THIS IS DOWNTOWN.
HE KNEW NOTHING OF NEW YORK, LET ALONE NEW YORK DOOR POLICY, AND HE MADE A TONY LAMA FAUX PAS.
...DESPITE THAT, I GOT HIM IN. HE SEEMED SO SWEET AND EAGER, WHICH NOT ONLY UPSET MY DATE...
DASH, HE'S WITH US.
HE IS?
THANKS, Y'ALL!
...BUT ALSO RUINED MY DATE'S PLANS FOR LATER THAT NIGHT.
ARE YOU SLIPPING HER A MICKEY?
YOU DON'T WANT TO GET IN MY FACE.
NO. THIS IS GETTING IN YOUR FACE.
ZIM SAVED ME FROM GETTING DATE-RAPED THAT NIGHT.
SEE THAT? THAT'S THE MOMENT I FELL FOR THE MAN I LOVE.

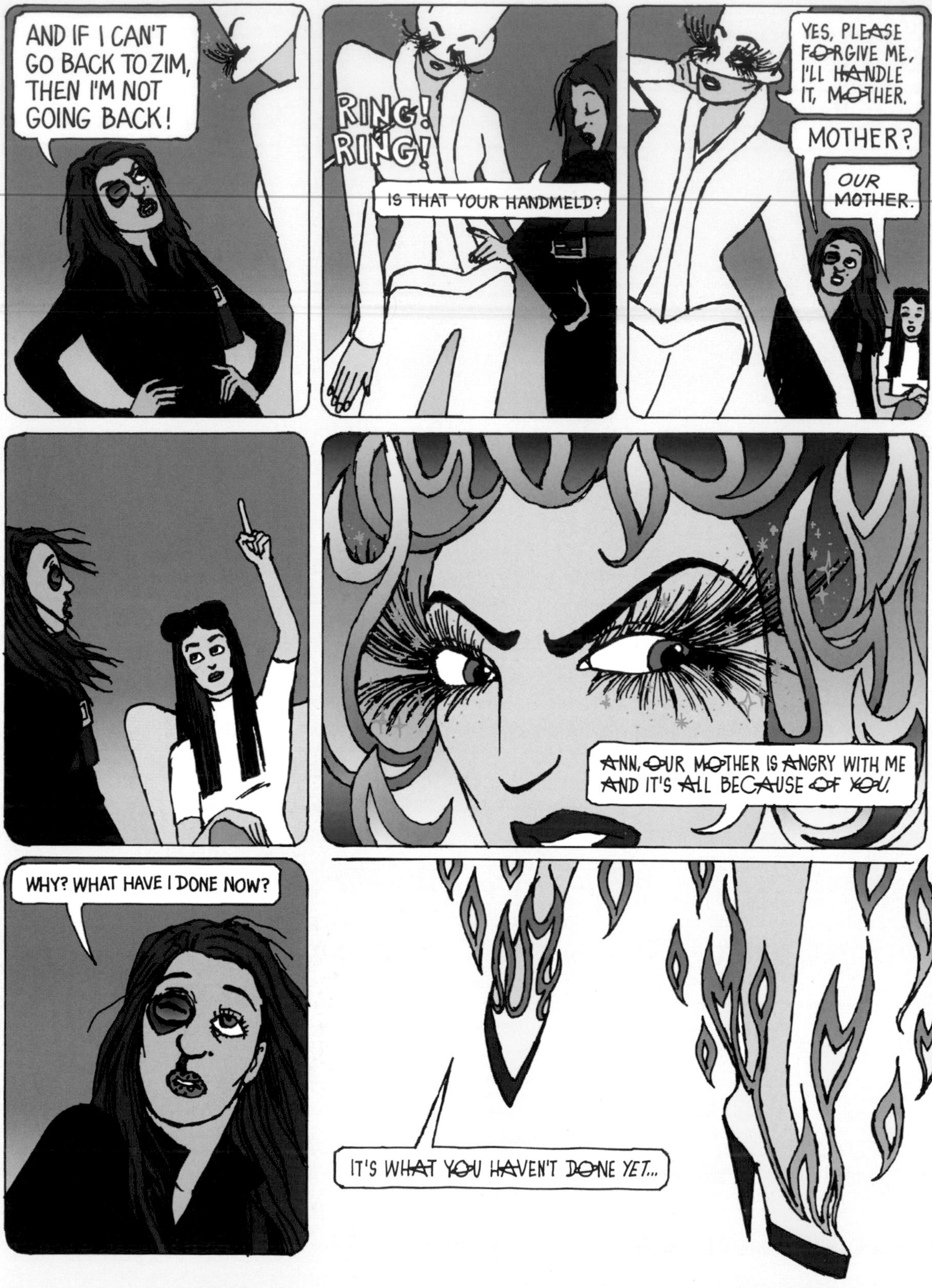
AND IF I CAN'T GO BACK TO ZIM, THEN I'M NOT GOING BACK!
RING! RING!
IS THAT YOUR HANDMELD?
YES, PLEASE FORGIVE ME, I'LL HANDLE IT, MOTHER.
MOTHER?
OUR MOTHER.
ANN, OUR MOTHER IS ANGRY WITH ME AND IT'S ALL BECAUSE OF YOU.
WHY? WHAT HAVE I DONE NOW?
IT'S WHAT YOU HAVEN'T DONE YET...

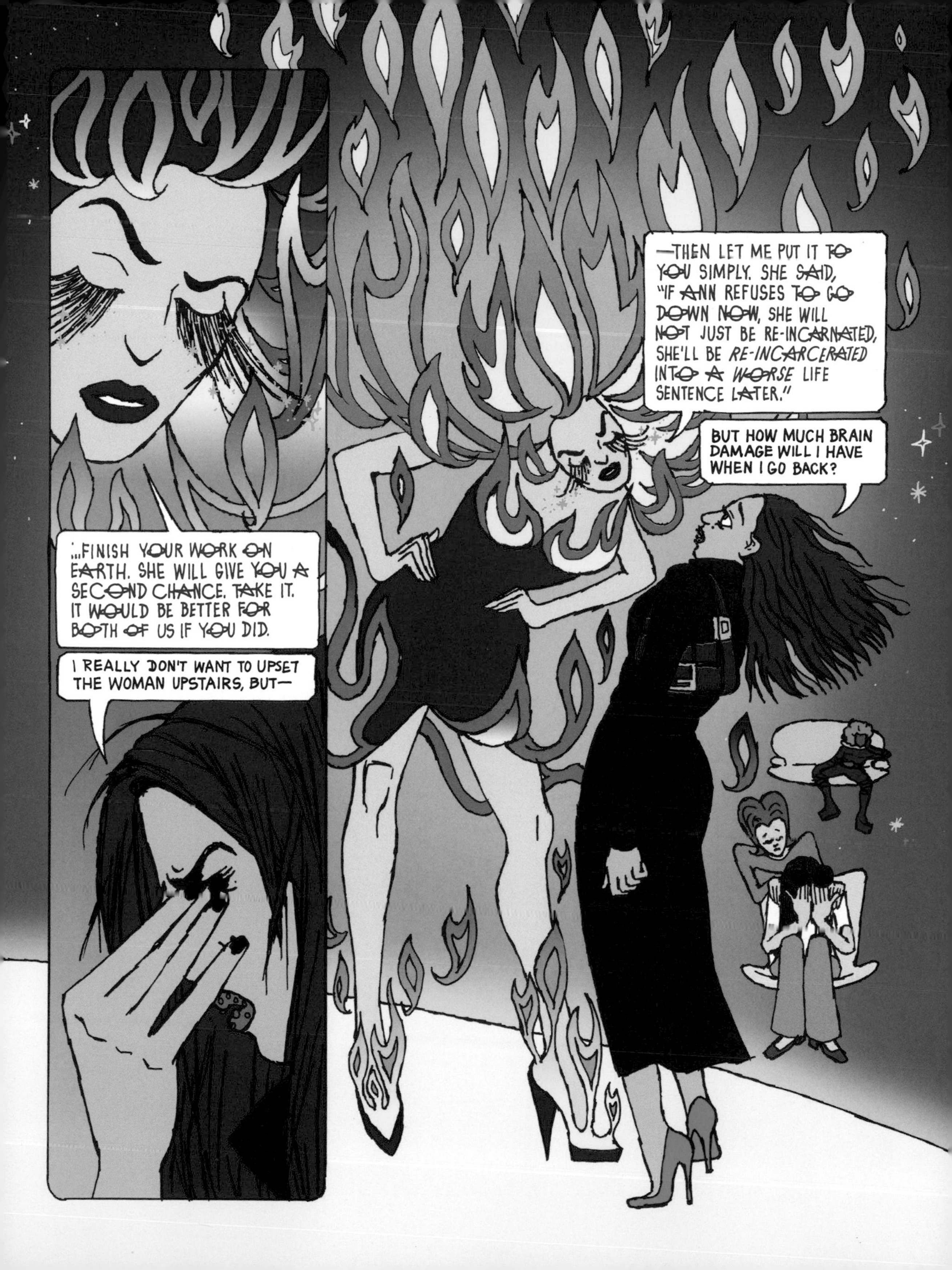
...FINISH YOUR WORK ON EARTH. SHE WILL GIVE YOU A SECOND CHANCE. TAKE IT. IT WOULD BE BETTER FOR BOTH OF US IF YOU DID.
I REALLY DON'T WANT TO UPSET THE WOMAN UPSTAIRS, BUT—
—THEN LET ME PUT IT TO YOU SIMPLY. SHE SAID, "IF ANN REFUSES TO GO DOWN NOW, SHE WILL NOT JUST BE RE-INCARNATED, SHE'LL BE *RE-INCARCERATED* INTO A *WORSE* LIFE SENTENCE LATER."
BUT HOW MUCH BRAIN DAMAGE WILL I HAVE WHEN I GO BACK?

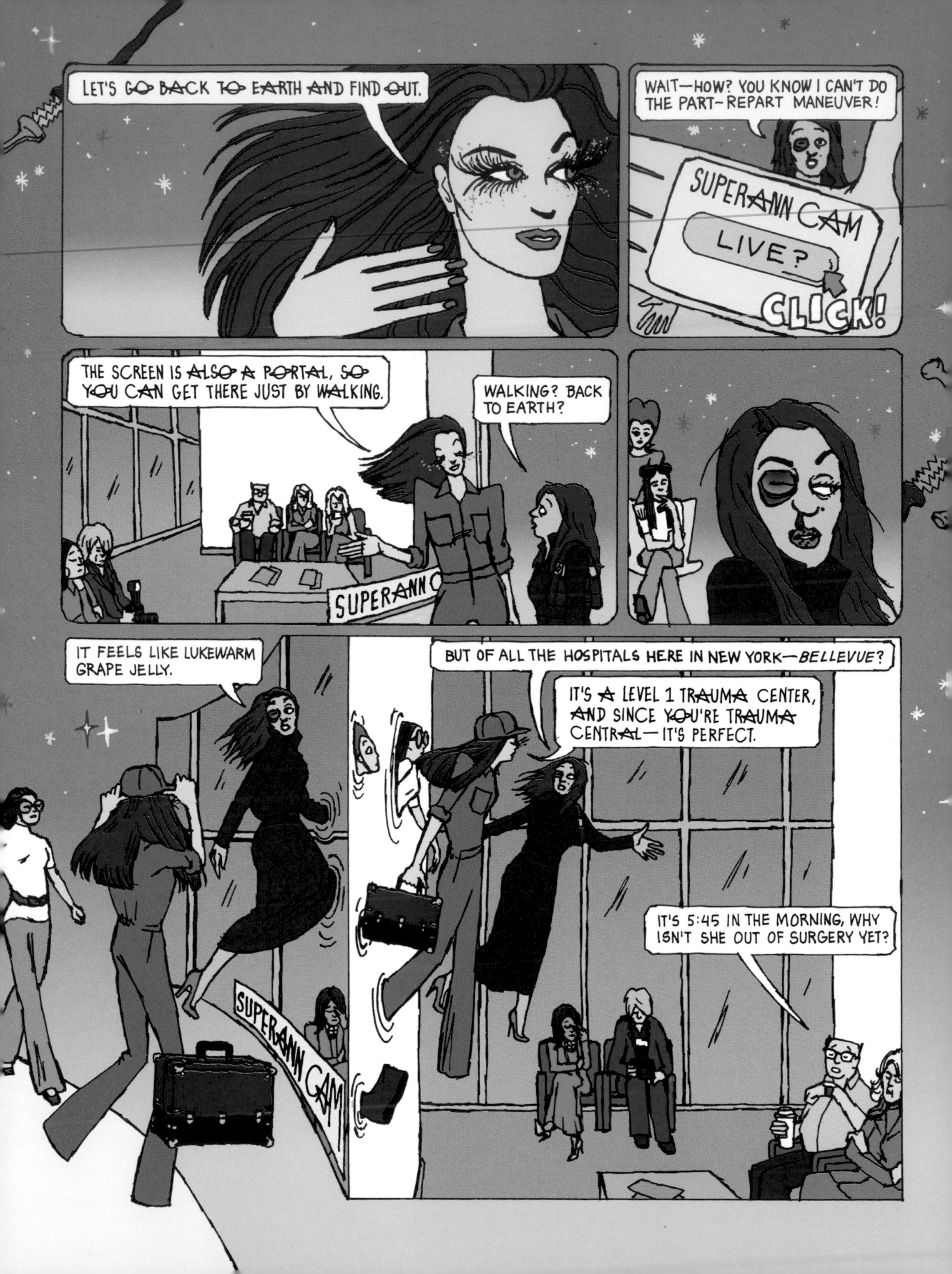
LET'S GO BACK TO EARTH AND FIND OUT.
WAIT—HOW? YOU KNOW I CAN'T DO THE PART-REPART MANEUVER!
SUPERANN CAM
LIVE?
CLICK!
THE SCREEN IS ALSO A PORTAL, SO YOU CAN GET THERE JUST BY WALKING.
WALKING? BACK TO EARTH?
SUPERANN C
IT FEELS LIKE LUKEWARM GRAPE JELLY.
BUT OF ALL THE HOSPITALS HERE IN NEW YORK—*BELLEVUE*?
IT'S A LEVEL 1 TRAUMA CENTER, AND SINCE YOU'RE TRAUMA CENTRAL—IT'S PERFECT.
SUPERANN CAM
IT'S 5:45 IN THE MORNING, WHY ISN'T SHE OUT OF SURGERY YET?

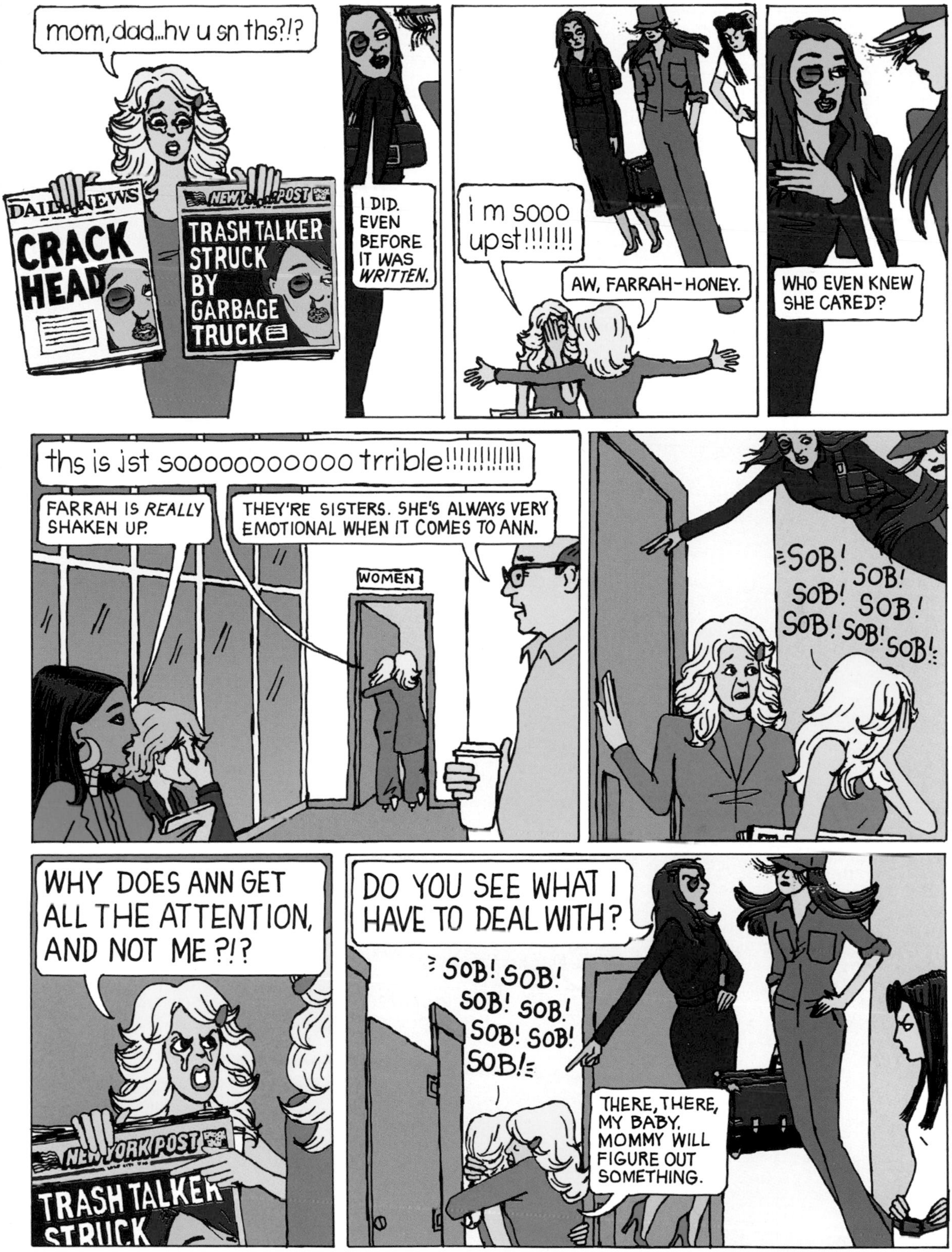
mom, dad...hv u sn ths?!?
DAILY NEWS
CRACK HEAD
NEW YORK POST
TRASH TALKER STRUCK BY GARBAGE TRUCK
I DID. EVEN BEFORE IT WAS *WRITTEN*.
i m sooo upst!!!!!!!
AW, FARRAH-HONEY.
WHO EVEN KNEW SHE CARED?
ths is jst soooooooooooo trrible!!!!!!!!!!!
FARRAH IS *REALLY* SHAKEN UP.
THEY'RE SISTERS. SHE'S ALWAYS VERY EMOTIONAL WHEN IT COMES TO ANN.
WOMEN
SOB! SOB! SOB! SOB! SOB! SOB! SOB!
WHY DOES ANN GET ALL THE ATTENTION, AND NOT ME ?!?
NEW YORK POST
TRASH TALKER STRUCK
DO YOU SEE WHAT I HAVE TO DEAL WITH?
SOB! SOB! SOB! SOB! SOB! SOB! SOB!
THERE, THERE, MY BABY. MOMMY WILL FIGURE OUT SOMETHING.

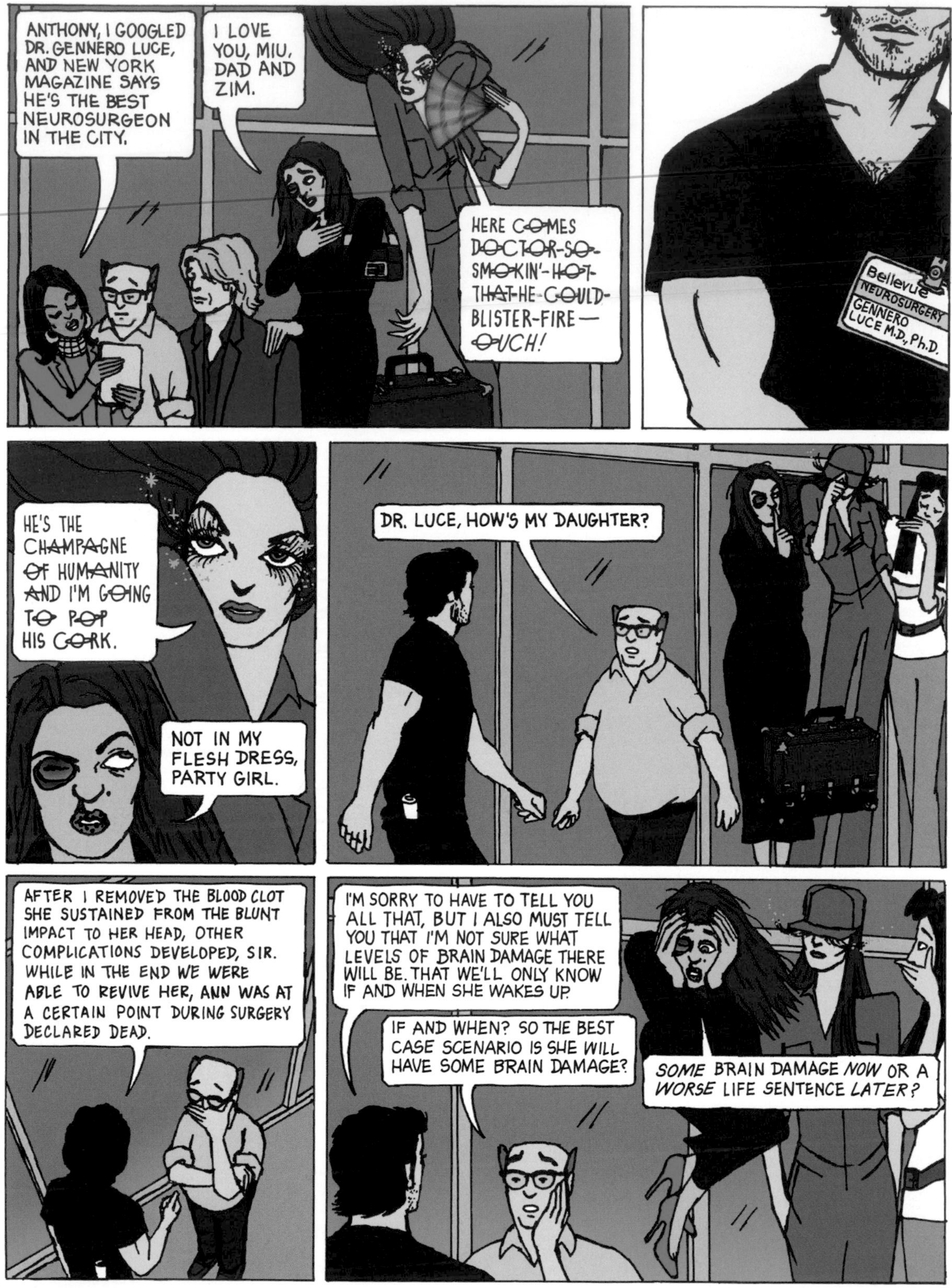
ANTHONY, I GOOGLED DR. GENNERO LUCE, AND NEW YORK MAGAZINE SAYS HE'S THE BEST NEUROSURGEON IN THE CITY.
I LOVE YOU, MIU, DAD AND ZIM.
HERE COMES DOCTOR-SO-SMOKIN'-HOT-THAT-HE-COULD-BLISTER-FIRE— OUCH!
Bellevue NEUROSURGERY GENNERO LUCE M.D., Ph.D.
HE'S THE CHAMPAGNE OF HUMANITY AND I'M GOING TO POP HIS CORK.
NOT IN MY FLESH DRESS, PARTY GIRL.
DR. LUCE, HOW'S MY DAUGHTER?
AFTER I REMOVED THE BLOOD CLOT SHE SUSTAINED FROM THE BLUNT IMPACT TO HER HEAD, OTHER COMPLICATIONS DEVELOPED, SIR. WHILE IN THE END WE WERE ABLE TO REVIVE HER, ANN WAS AT A CERTAIN POINT DURING SURGERY DECLARED DEAD.
I'M SORRY TO HAVE TO TELL YOU ALL THAT, BUT I ALSO MUST TELL YOU THAT I'M NOT SURE WHAT LEVELS OF BRAIN DAMAGE THERE WILL BE. THAT WE'LL ONLY KNOW IF AND WHEN SHE WAKES UP.
IF AND WHEN? SO THE BEST CASE SCENARIO IS SHE WILL HAVE SOME BRAIN DAMAGE?
SOME BRAIN DAMAGE *NOW* OR A *WORSE* LIFE SENTENCE *LATER*?

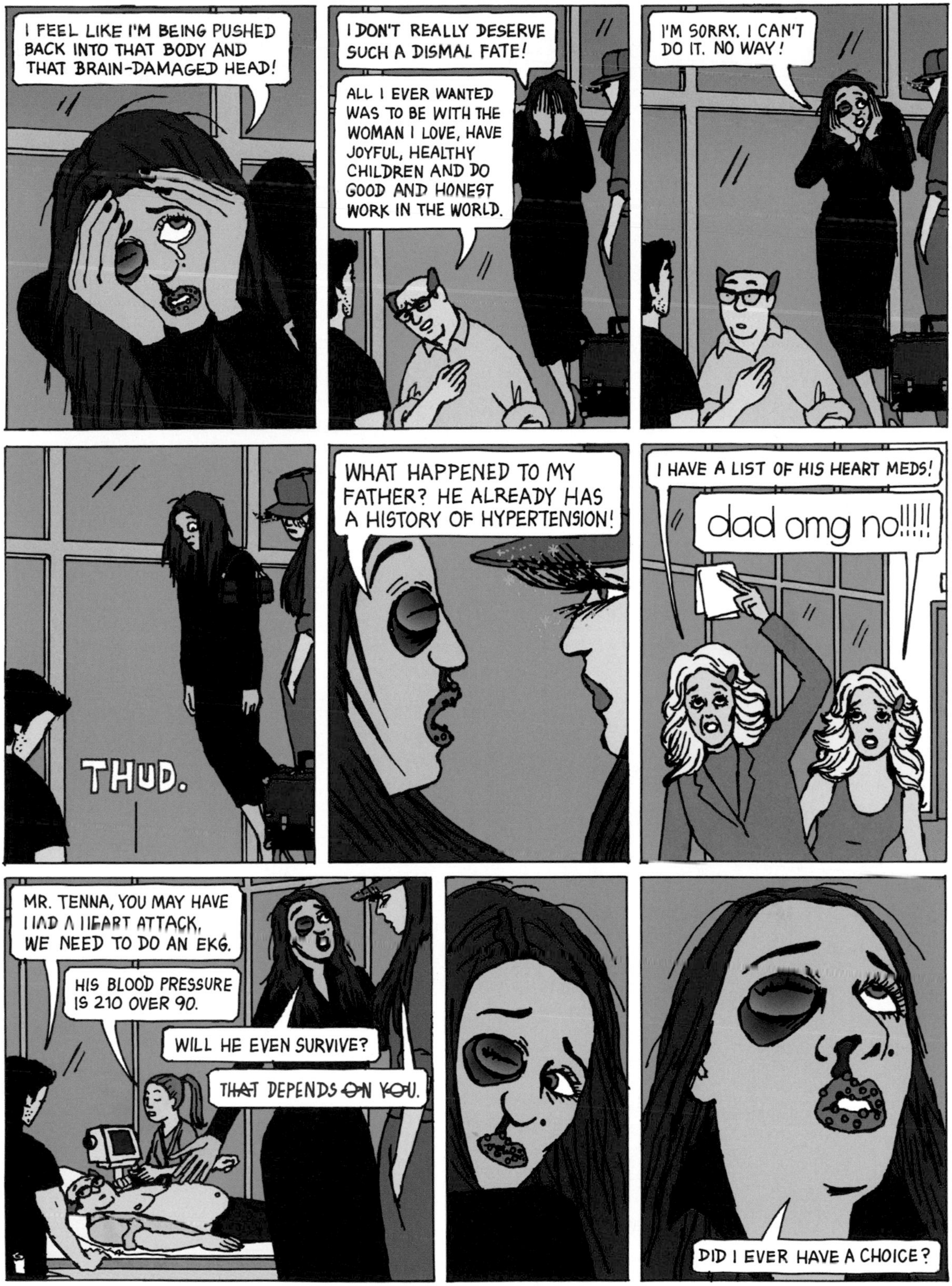
I FEEL LIKE I'M BEING PUSHED BACK INTO THAT BODY AND THAT BRAIN-DAMAGED HEAD!
I DON'T REALLY DESERVE SUCH A DISMAL FATE!
ALL I EVER WANTED WAS TO BE WITH THE WOMAN I LOVE, HAVE JOYFUL, HEALTHY CHILDREN AND DO GOOD AND HONEST WORK IN THE WORLD.
I'M SORRY. I CAN'T DO IT. NO WAY!
THUD.
WHAT HAPPENED TO MY FATHER? HE ALREADY HAS A HISTORY OF HYPERTENSION!
I HAVE A LIST OF HIS HEART MEDS!
dad omg no!!!!!
MR. TENNA, YOU MAY HAVE HAD A HEART ATTACK, WE NEED TO DO AN EKG.
HIS BLOOD PRESSURE IS 210 OVER 90.
WILL HE EVEN SURVIVE?
THAT DEPENDS ON YOU.
DID I EVER HAVE A CHOICE?

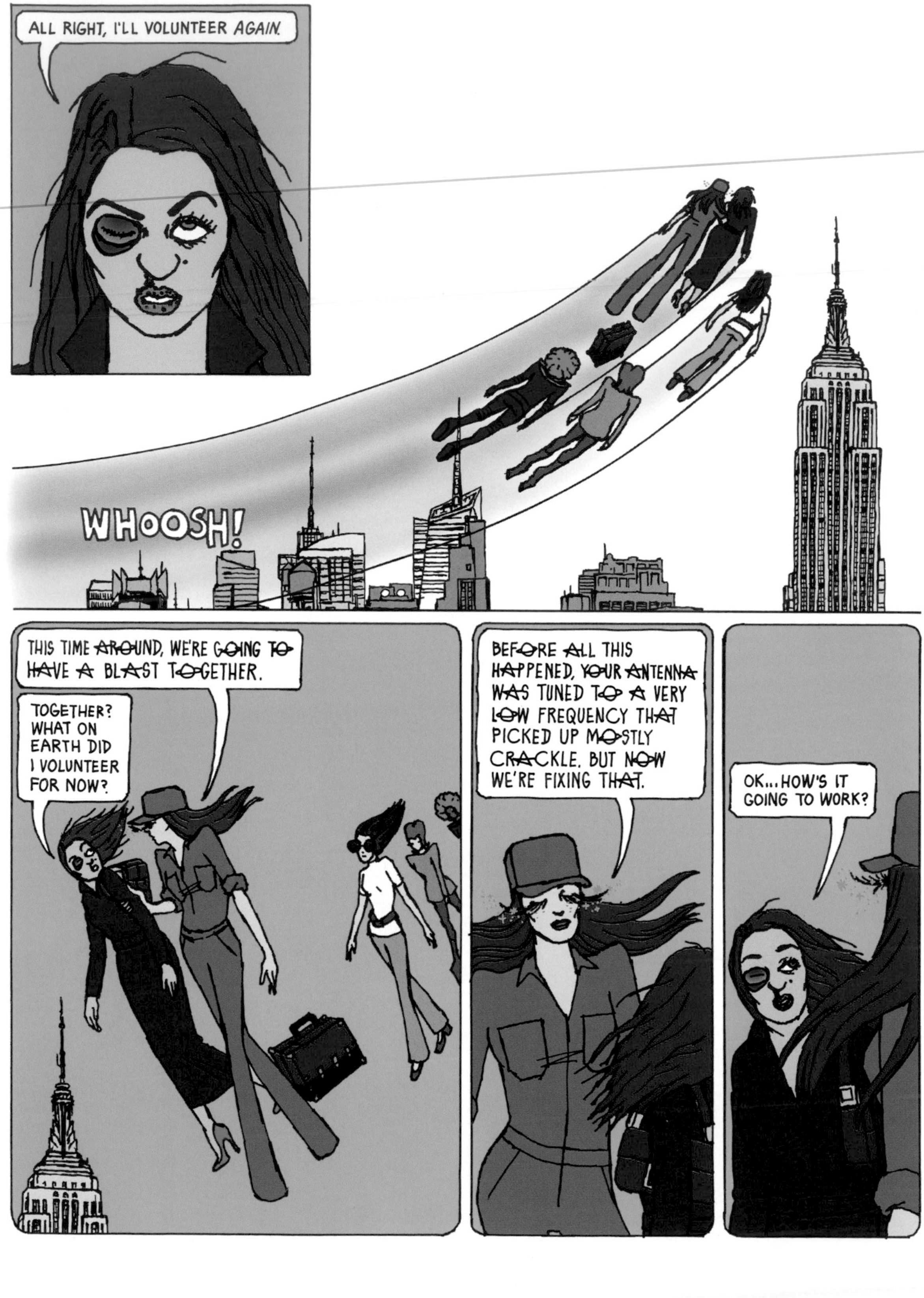
ALL RIGHT, I'LL VOLUNTEER AGAIN.
WHOOSH!
THIS TIME AROUND, WE'RE GOING TO HAVE A BLAST TOGETHER.
TOGETHER? WHAT ON EARTH DID I VOLUNTEER FOR NOW?
BEFORE ALL THIS HAPPENED, YOUR ANTENNA WAS TUNED TO A VERY LOW FREQUENCY THAT PICKED UP MOSTLY CRACKLE. BUT NOW WE'RE FIXING THAT.
OK... HOW'S IT GOING TO WORK?

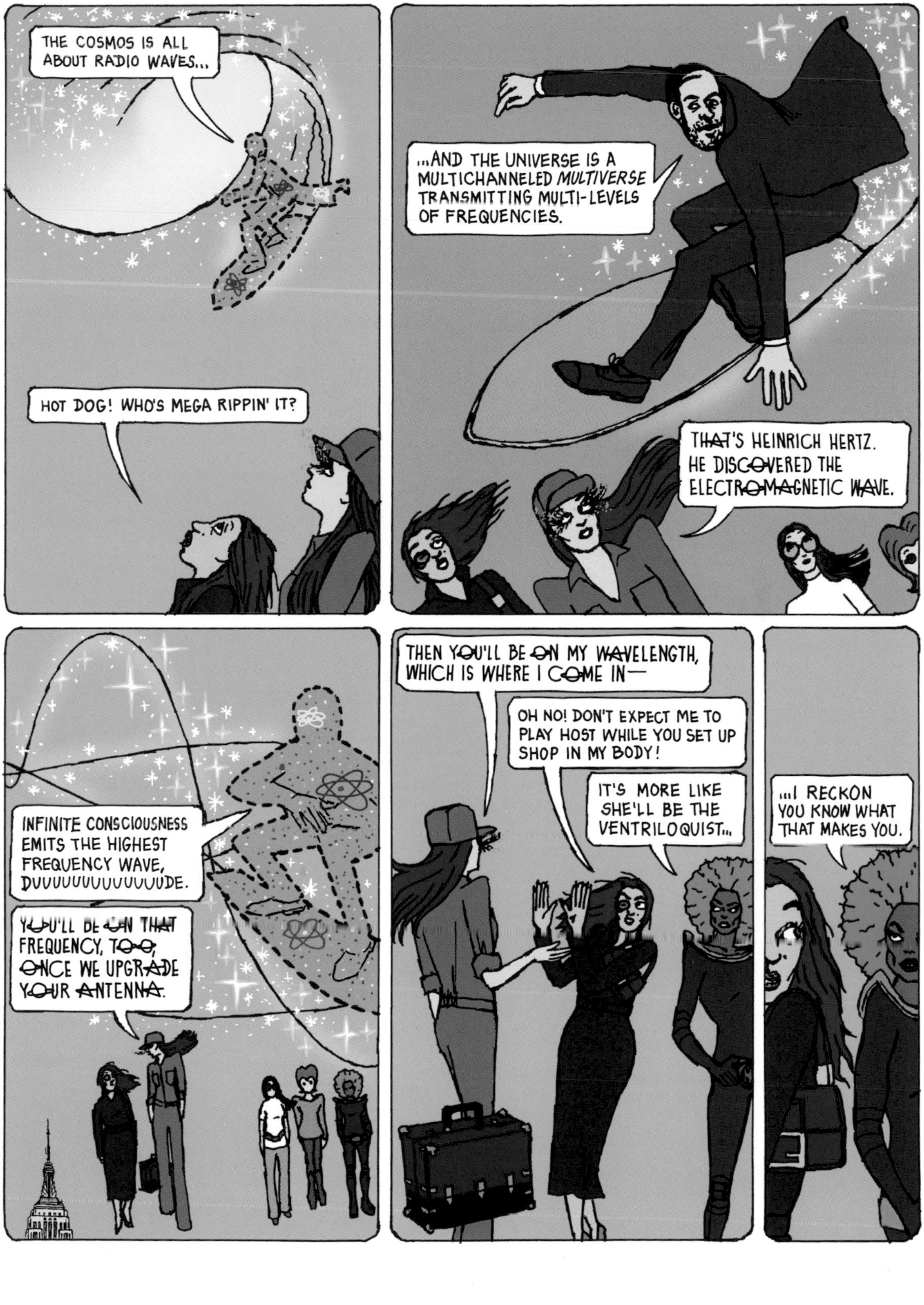
THE COSMOS IS ALL ABOUT RADIO WAVES...
HOT DOG! WHO'S MEGA RIPPIN' IT?
...AND THE UNIVERSE IS A MULTICHANNELED *MULTIVERSE* TRANSMITTING MULTI-LEVELS OF FREQUENCIES.
THAT'S HEINRICH HERTZ. HE DISCOVERED THE ELECTROMAGNETIC WAVE.
INFINITE CONSCIOUSNESS EMITS THE HIGHEST FREQUENCY WAVE, DUUUUUUUUUUUUUDE.
YOU'LL BE ON THAT FREQUENCY, TOO, ONCE WE UPGRADE YOUR ANTENNA.
THEN YOU'LL BE ON MY WAVELENGTH, WHICH IS WHERE I COME IN—
OH NO! DON'T EXPECT ME TO PLAY HOST WHILE YOU SET UP SHOP IN MY BODY!
IT'S MORE LIKE SHE'LL BE THE VENTRILOQUIST...
...I RECKON YOU KNOW WHAT THAT MAKES YOU.

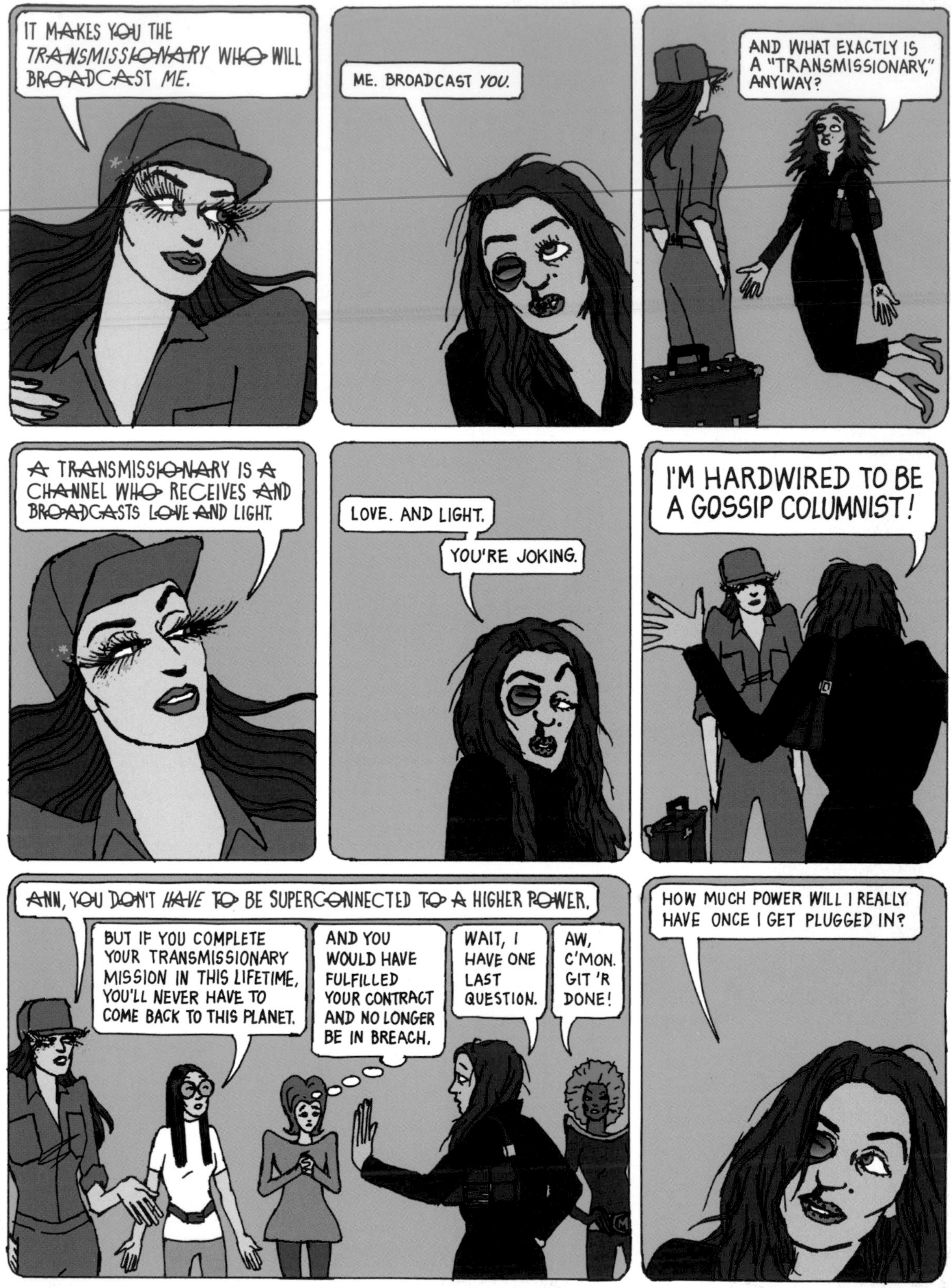
IT MAKES YOU THE TRANSMISSIONARY WHO WILL BROADCAST ME.
ME. BROADCAST YOU.
AND WHAT EXACTLY IS A "TRANSMISSIONARY," ANYWAY?
A TRANSMISSIONARY IS A CHANNEL WHO RECEIVES AND BROADCASTS LOVE AND LIGHT.
LOVE. AND LIGHT.
YOU'RE JOKING.
I'M HARDWIRED TO BE A GOSSIP COLUMNIST!
ANN, YOU DON'T HAVE TO BE SUPERCONNECTED TO A HIGHER POWER,
BUT IF YOU COMPLETE YOUR TRANSMISSIONARY MISSION IN THIS LIFETIME, YOU'LL NEVER HAVE TO COME BACK TO THIS PLANET.
AND YOU WOULD HAVE FULFILLED YOUR CONTRACT AND NO LONGER BE IN BREACH.
WAIT, I HAVE ONE LAST QUESTION.
AW, C'MON. GIT 'R DONE!
HOW MUCH POWER WILL I REALLY HAVE ONCE I GET PLUGGED IN?

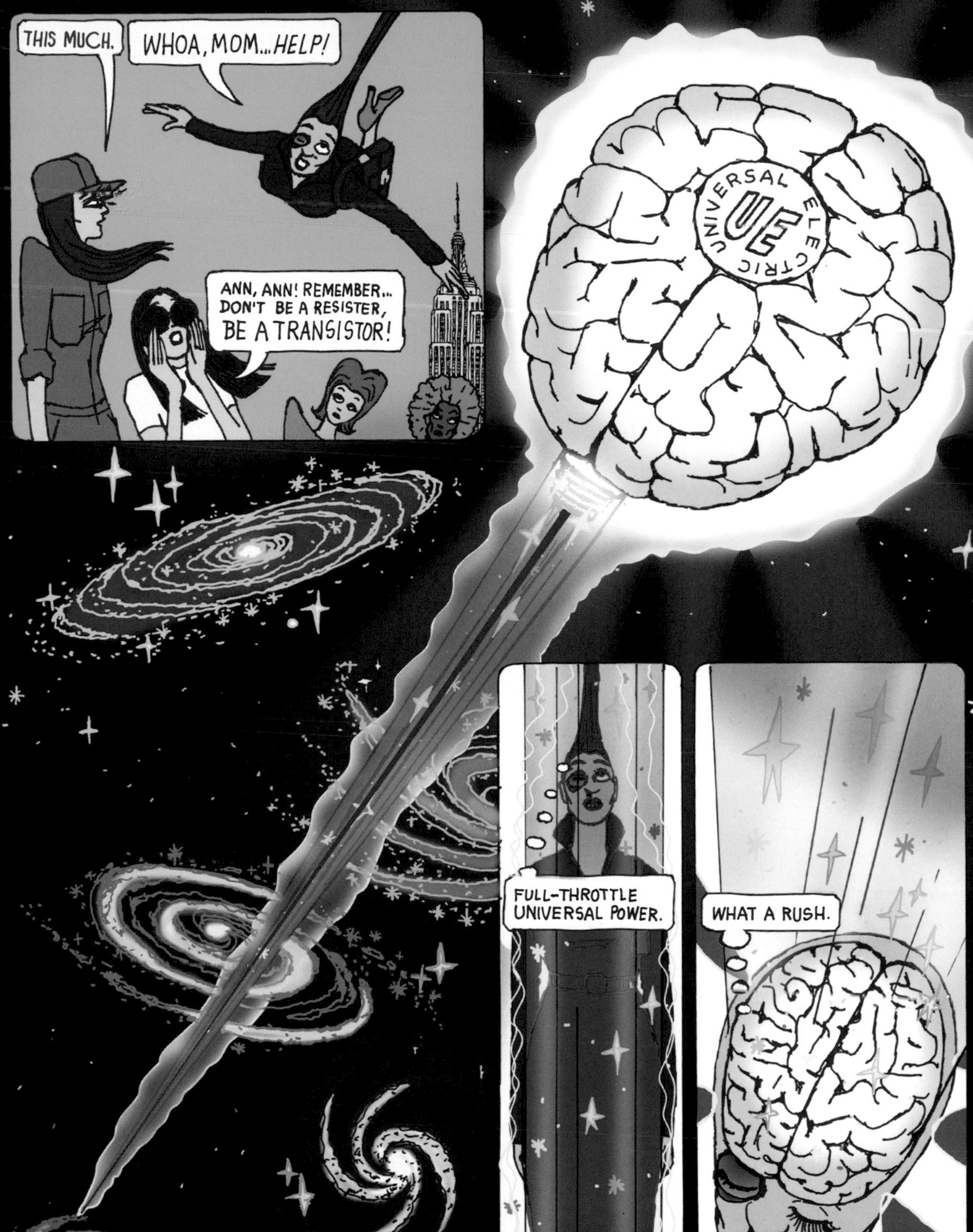
THIS MUCH.
WHOA, MOM...HELP!
ANN, ANN! REMEMBER... DON'T BE A RESISTER, BE A TRANSISTOR!
UNIVERSAL ELECTRIC
UE
FULL-THROTTLE UNIVERSAL POWER.
WHAT A RUSH.

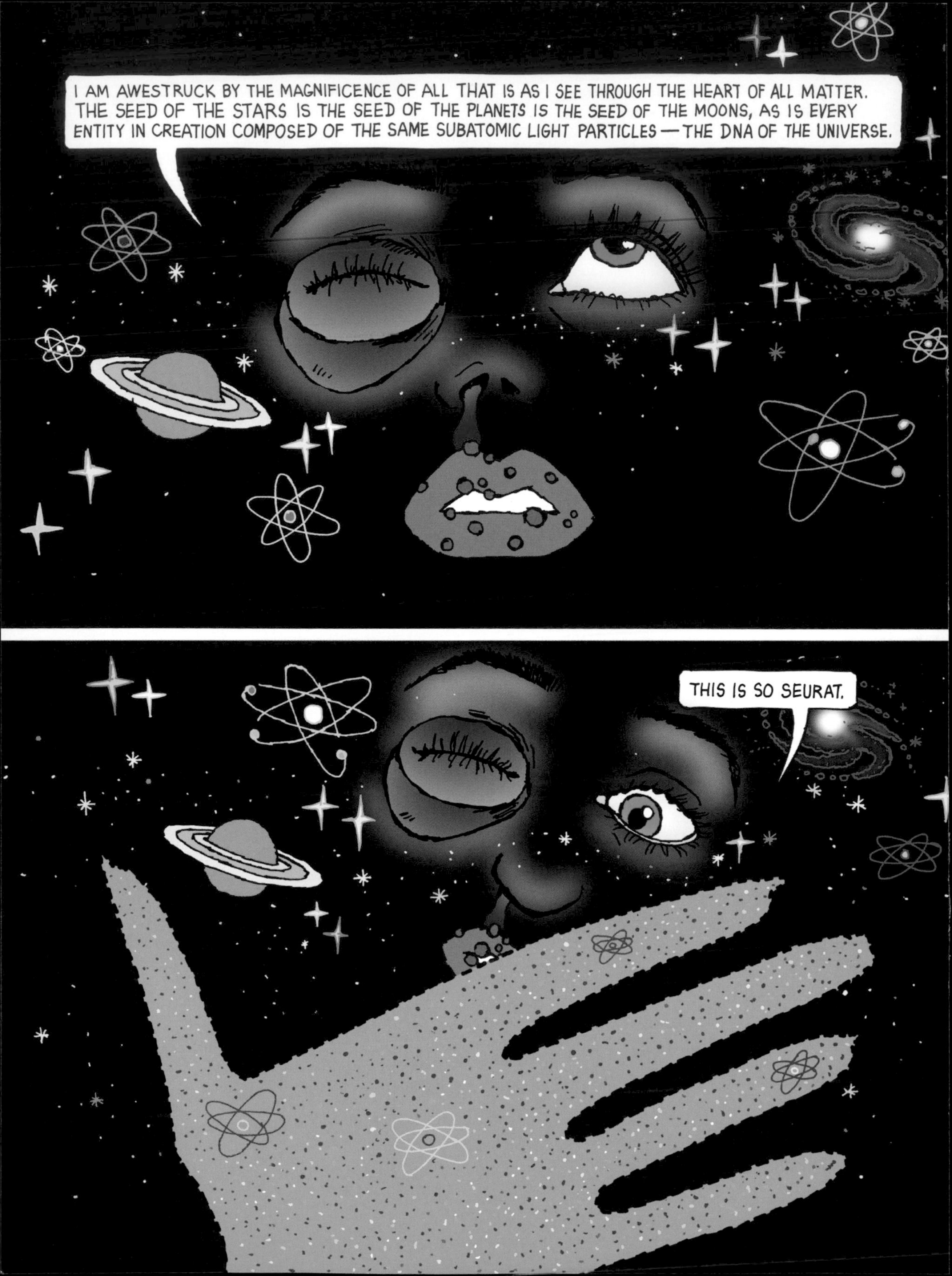
I AM AWESTRUCK BY THE MAGNIFICENCE OF ALL THAT IS AS I SEE THROUGH THE HEART OF ALL MATTER. THE SEED OF THE STARS IS THE SEED OF THE PLANETS IS THE SEED OF THE MOONS, AS IS EVERY ENTITY IN CREATION COMPOSED OF THE SAME SUBATOMIC LIGHT PARTICLES — THE DNA OF THE UNIVERSE.
THIS IS SO SEURAT.

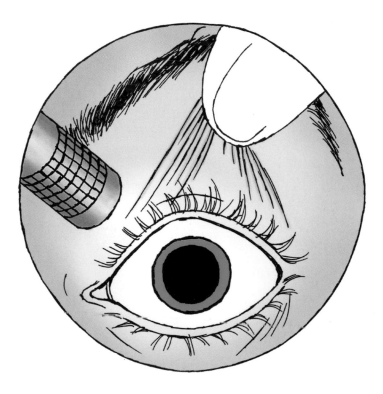

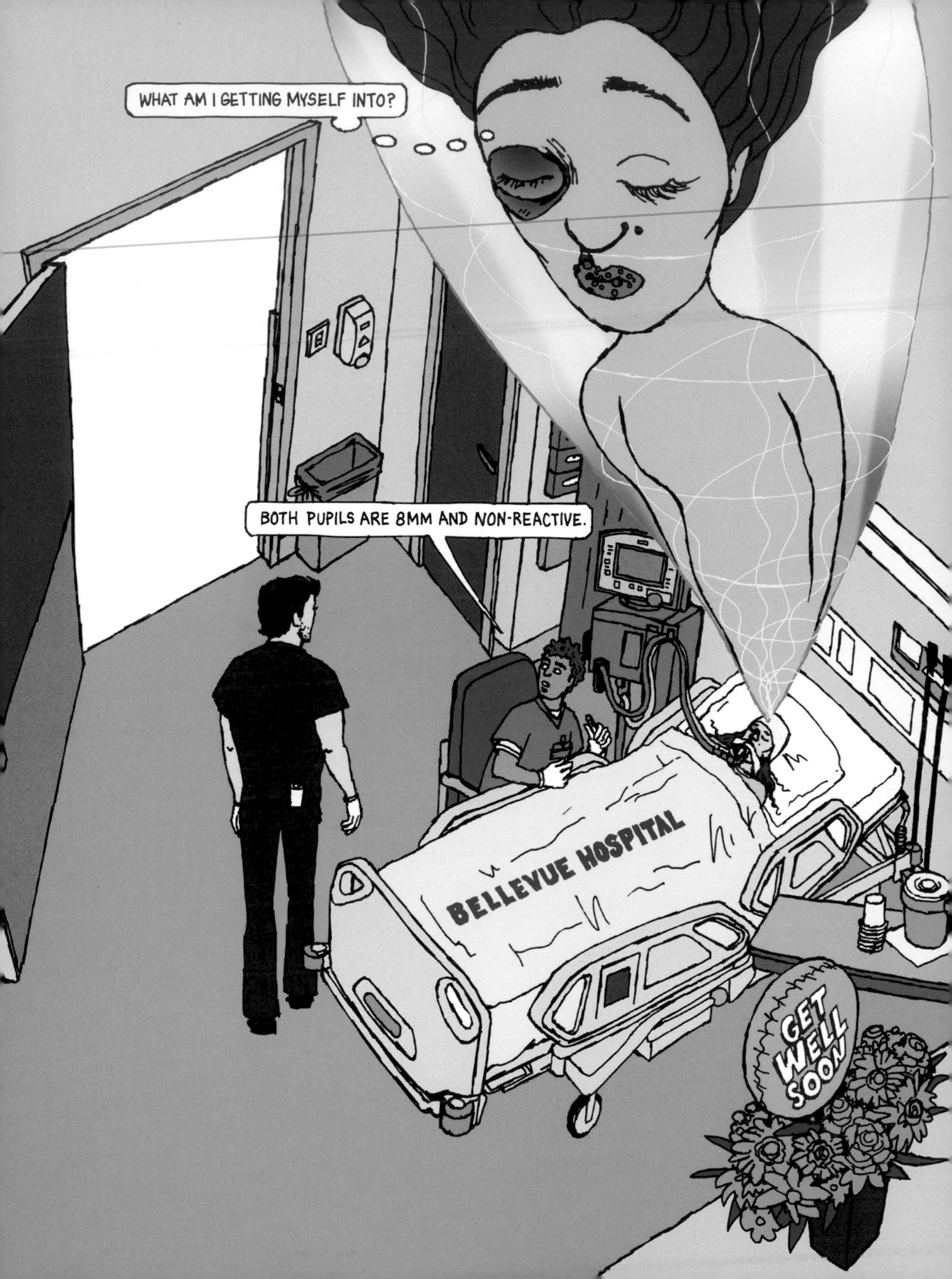
WHAT AM I GETTING MYSELF INTO?
BOTH PUPILS ARE 8MM AND NON-REACTIVE.
BELLEVUE HOSPITAL
GET WELL SOON

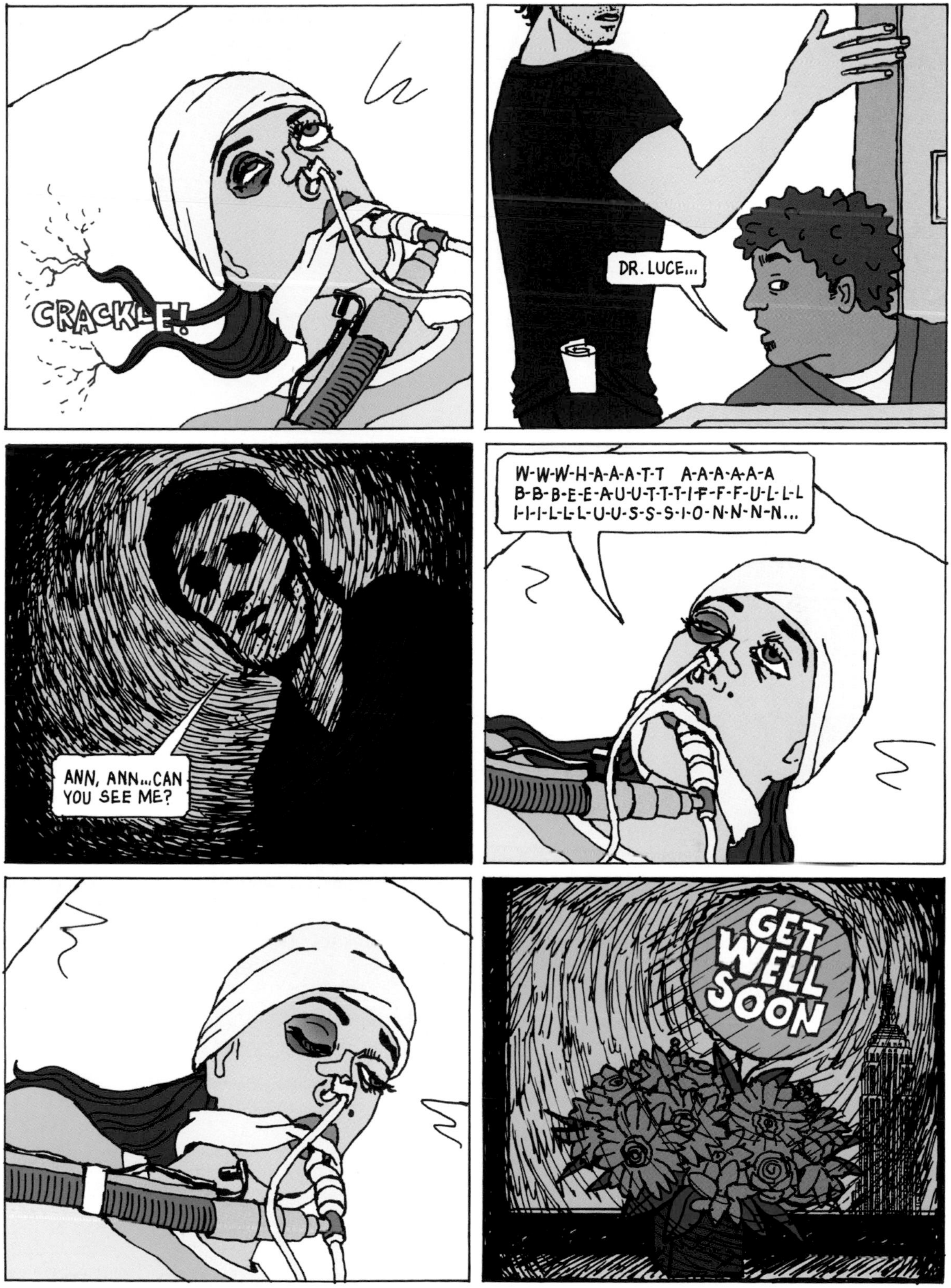
CRACKLE!
DR. LUCE...
ANN, ANN...CAN YOU SEE ME?
W-W-W-H-A-A-A-T-T A-A-A-A-A-A B-B-B-E-E-A-U-T-T-T-I-F-F-F-U-L-L-L I-I-I-L-L-L-U-U-S-S-S-I-O-N-N-N-N...
GET WELL SOON

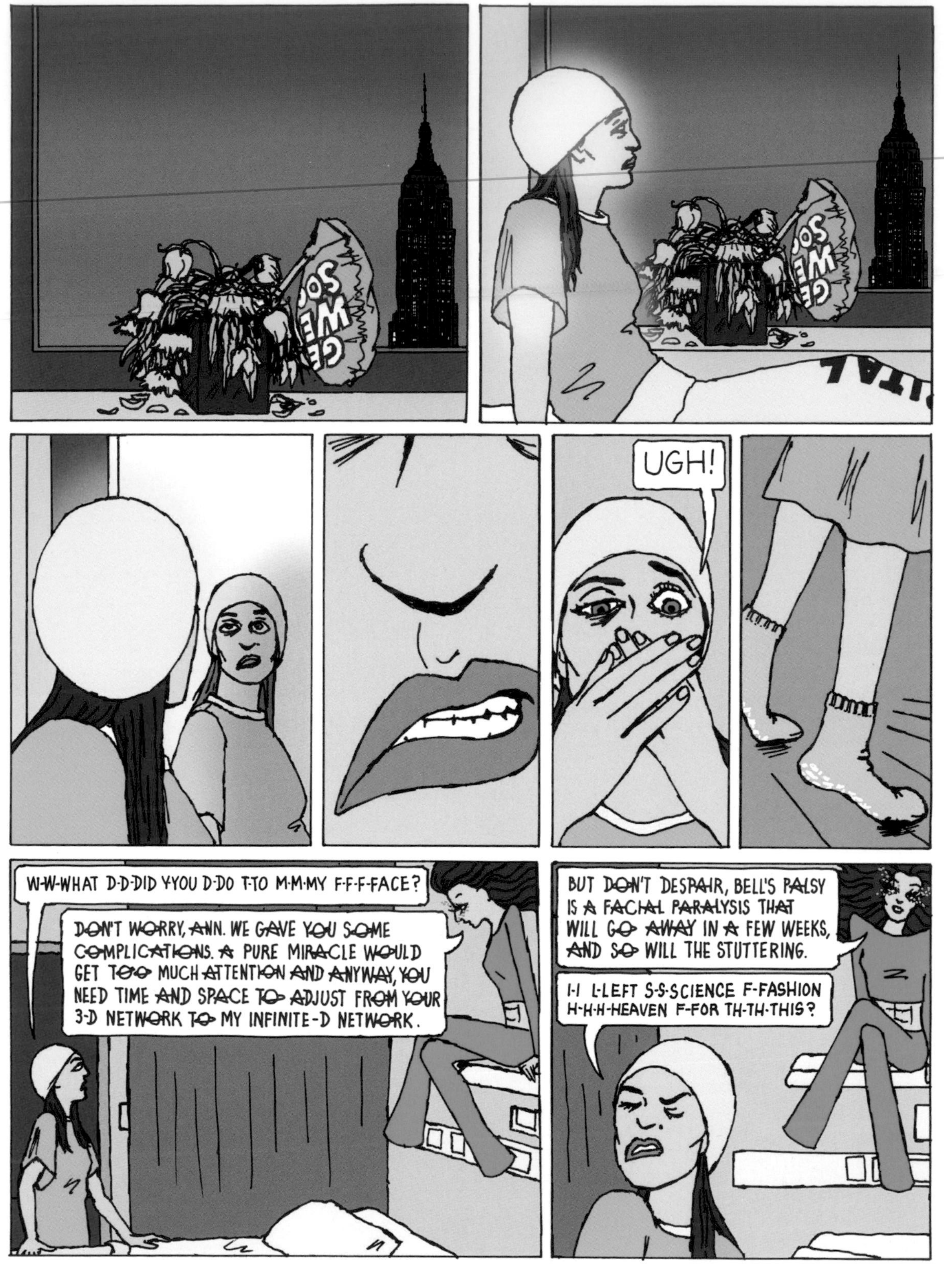
UGH!
W-W-WHAT D-D-DID Y-YOU D-DO T-TO M-M-MY F-F-F-FACE?
DON'T WORRY, ANN. WE GAVE YOU SOME COMPLICATIONS. A PURE MIRACLE WOULD GET TOO MUCH ATTENTION AND ANYWAY, YOU NEED TIME AND SPACE TO ADJUST FROM YOUR 3-D NETWORK TO MY INFINITE-D NETWORK.
BUT DON'T DESPAIR, BELL'S PALSY IS A FACIAL PARALYSIS THAT WILL GO AWAY IN A FEW WEEKS, AND SO WILL THE STUTTERING.
I-I L-LEFT S-S-SCIENCE F-FASHION H-H-H-HEAVEN F-FOR TH-TH-THIS?

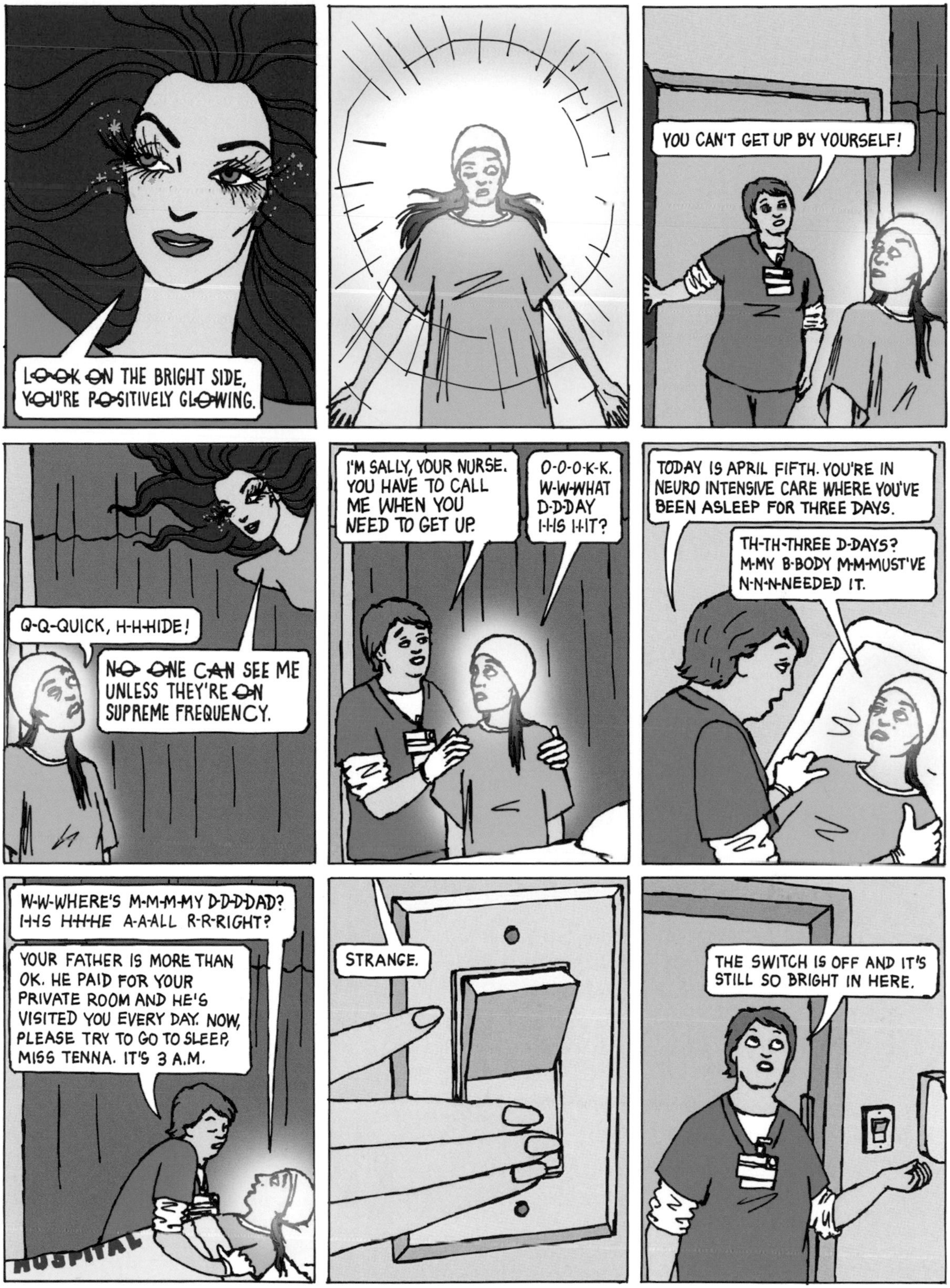
LOOK ON THE BRIGHT SIDE, YOU'RE POSITIVELY GLOWING.
YOU CAN'T GET UP BY YOURSELF!
Q-Q-QUICK, H-H-HIDE!
NO ONE CAN SEE ME UNLESS THEY'RE ON SUPREME FREQUENCY.
I'M SALLY, YOUR NURSE. YOU HAVE TO CALL ME WHEN YOU NEED TO GET UP.
O-O-O-K-K. W-W-WHAT D-D-DAY I-I-IS I-I-IT?
TODAY IS APRIL FIFTH. YOU'RE IN NEURO INTENSIVE CARE WHERE YOU'VE BEEN ASLEEP FOR THREE DAYS.
TH-TH-THREE D-DAYS? M-MY B-BODY M-M-MUST'VE N-N-N-NEEDED IT.
W-W-WHERE'S M-M-M-MY D-D-D-DAD? I-I-IS H-H-HE A-A-ALL R-R-RIGHT?
YOUR FATHER IS MORE THAN OK. HE PAID FOR YOUR PRIVATE ROOM AND HE'S VISITED YOU EVERY DAY. NOW, PLEASE TRY TO GO TO SLEEP, MISS TENNA. IT'S 3 A.M.
HOSPITAL
STRANGE.
THE SWITCH IS OFF AND IT'S STILL SO BRIGHT IN HERE.

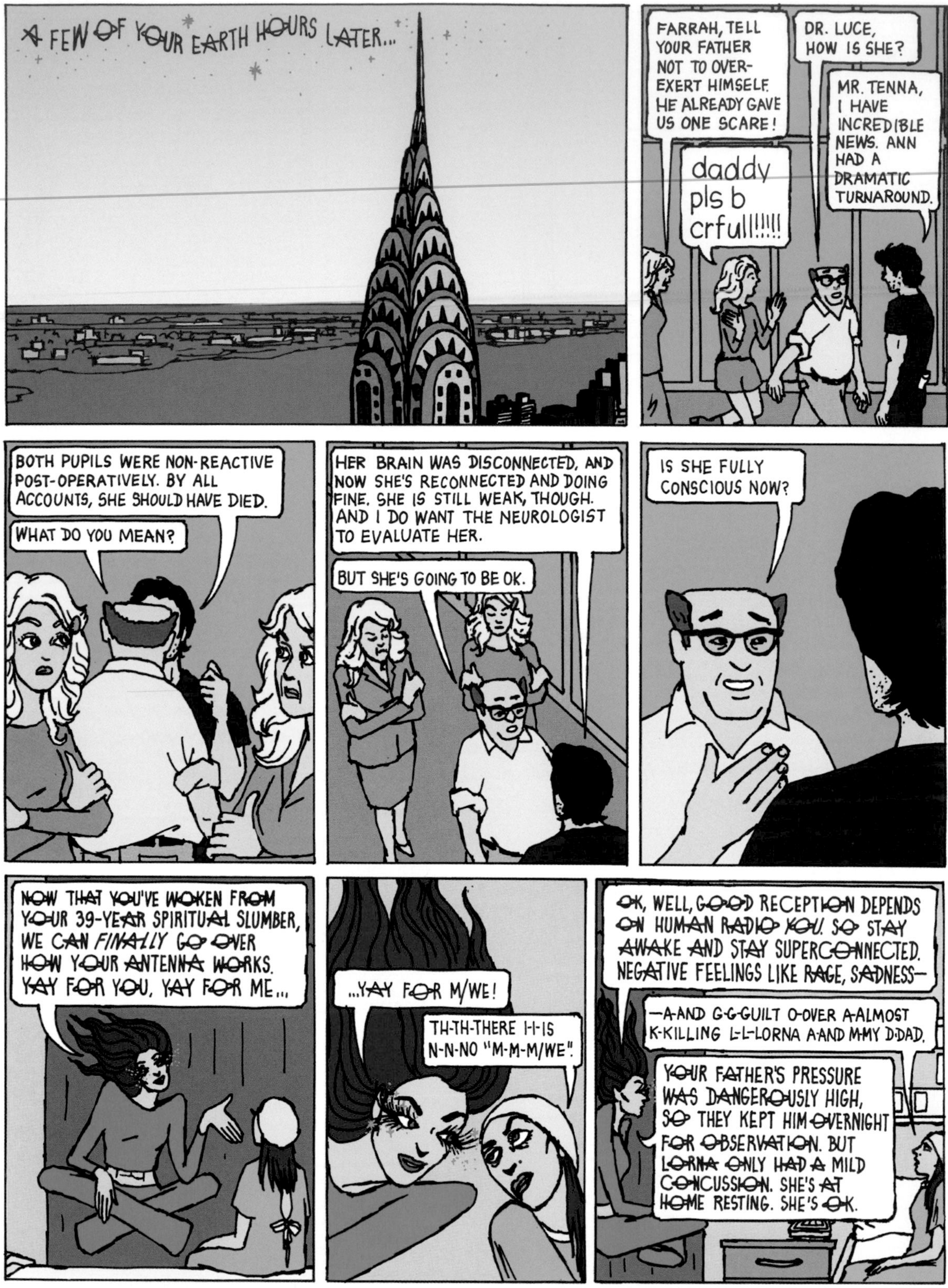
A FEW OF YOUR EARTH HOURS LATER...
FARRAH, TELL YOUR FATHER NOT TO OVER-EXERT HIMSELF. HE ALREADY GAVE US ONE SCARE!
daddy pls b crfull!!!!!
DR. LUCE, HOW IS SHE?
MR. TENNA, I HAVE INCREDIBLE NEWS. ANN HAD A DRAMATIC TURNAROUND.
BOTH PUPILS WERE NON-REACTIVE POST-OPERATIVELY. BY ALL ACCOUNTS, SHE SHOULD HAVE DIED.
WHAT DO YOU MEAN?
HER BRAIN WAS DISCONNECTED, AND NOW SHE'S RECONNECTED AND DOING FINE. SHE IS STILL WEAK, THOUGH. AND I DO WANT THE NEUROLOGIST TO EVALUATE HER.
BUT SHE'S GOING TO BE OK.
IS SHE FULLY CONSCIOUS NOW?
NOW THAT YOU'VE WOKEN FROM YOUR 39-YEAR SPIRITUAL SLUMBER, WE CAN FINALLY GO OVER HOW YOUR ANTENNA WORKS. YAY FOR YOU, YAY FOR ME...
...YAY FOR M/WE!
TH-TH-THERE I-I-IS N-N-NO "M-M-M/WE".
OK, WELL, GOOD RECEPTION DEPENDS ON HUMAN RADIO YOU. SO STAY AWAKE AND STAY SUPERCONNECTED. NEGATIVE FEELINGS LIKE RAGE, SADNESS—
—A-AND G-G-GUILT O-OVER A-ALMOST K-KILLING L-L-LORNA A-AND M-MY D-DAD.
YOUR FATHER'S PRESSURE WAS DANGEROUSLY HIGH, SO THEY KEPT HIM OVERNIGHT FOR OBSERVATION. BUT LORNA ONLY HAD A MILD CONCUSSION. SHE'S AT HOME RESTING. SHE'S OK.

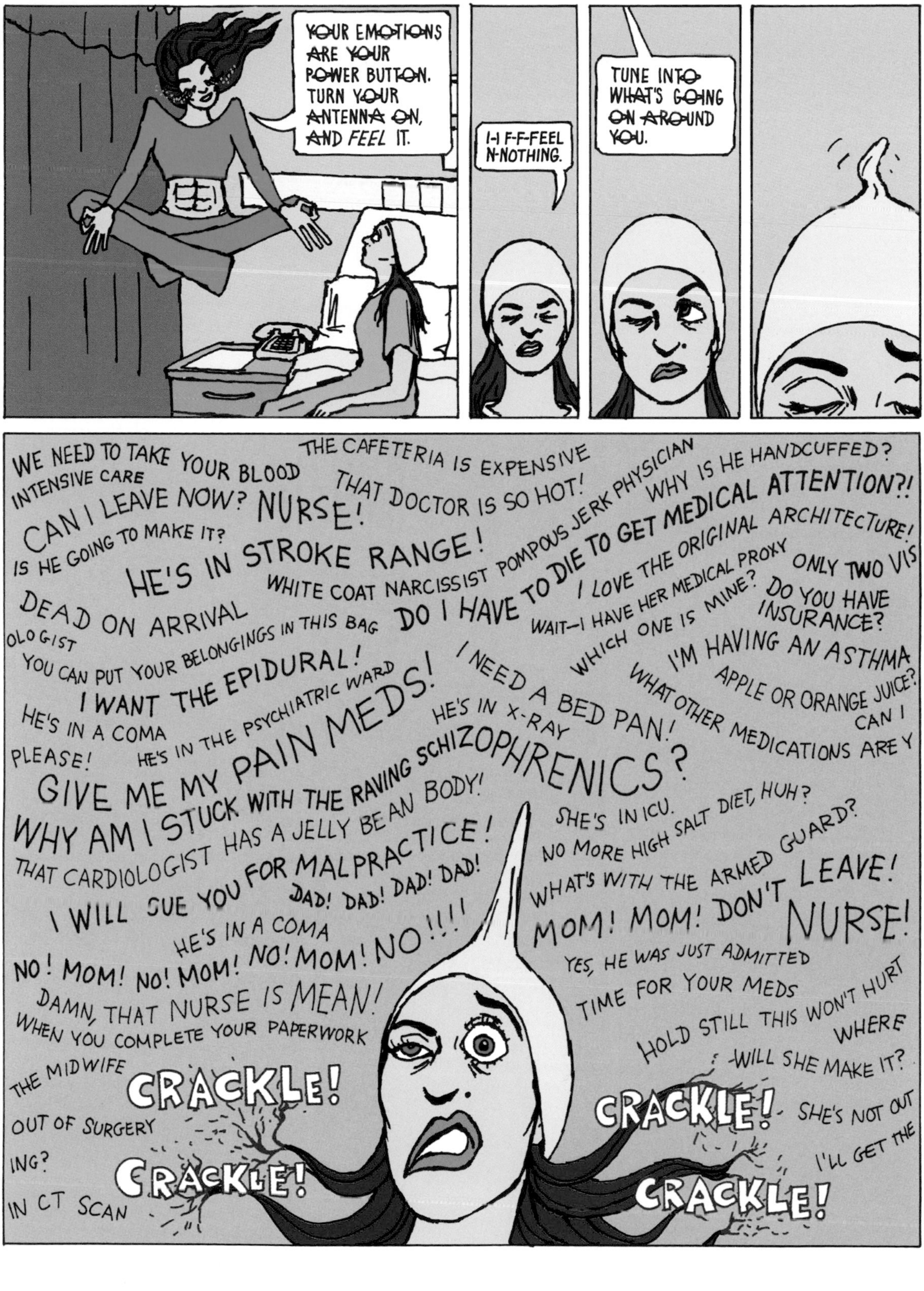
YOUR EMOTIONS ARE YOUR POWER BUTTON. TURN YOUR ANTENNA ON, AND *FEEL* IT.
I-I F-F-FEEL N-NOTHING.
TUNE INTO WHAT'S GOING ON AROUND YOU.
WE NEED TO TAKE YOUR BLOOD
THE CAFETERIA IS EXPENSIVE
WHY IS HE HANDCUFFED?
INTENSIVE CARE
THAT DOCTOR IS SO HOT!
POMPOUS JERK PHYSICIAN
CAN I LEAVE NOW?
NURSE!
DO I HAVE TO DIE TO GET MEDICAL ATTENTION?!
IS HE GOING TO MAKE IT?
HE'S IN STROKE RANGE!
I LOVE THE ORIGINAL ARCHITECTURE!
WHITE COAT NARCISSIST
ONLY TWO VIS
WAIT—I HAVE HER MEDICAL PROXY
DO YOU HAVE INSURANCE?
DEAD ON ARRIVAL
WHICH ONE IS MINE?
OLOGIST
YOU CAN PUT YOUR BELONGINGS IN THIS BAG
I'M HAVING AN ASTHMA
I NEED A BED PAN!
I WANT THE EPIDURAL!
WHAT OTHER MEDICATIONS ARE Y
APPLE OR ORANGE JUICE?
HE'S IN A COMA
HE'S IN THE PSYCHIATRIC WARD
HE'S IN X-RAY
CAN I
PLEASE!
GIVE ME MY PAIN MEDS!
WHY AM I STUCK WITH THE RAVING SCHIZOPHRENICS?
THAT CARDIOLOGIST HAS A JELLY BEAN BODY!
SHE'S IN ICU.
NO MORE HIGH SALT DIET, HUH?
I WILL SUE YOU FOR MALPRACTICE!
WHAT'S WITH THE ARMED GUARD?
DAD! DAD! DAD! DAD!
MOM! MOM! DON'T LEAVE!
NURSE!
HE'S IN A COMA
NO! MOM! NO! MOM! NO! MOM! NO!!!!
YES, HE WAS JUST ADMITTED
DAMN, THAT NURSE IS MEAN!
TIME FOR YOUR MEDS
WHEN YOU COMPLETE YOUR PAPERWORK
HOLD STILL THIS WON'T HURT
WHERE
WILL SHE MAKE IT?
THE MIDWIFE
CRACKLE!
CRACKLE!
SHE'S NOT OUT
OUT OF SURGERY
I'LL GET THE
ING?
CRACKLE!
CRACKLE!
IN CT SCAN

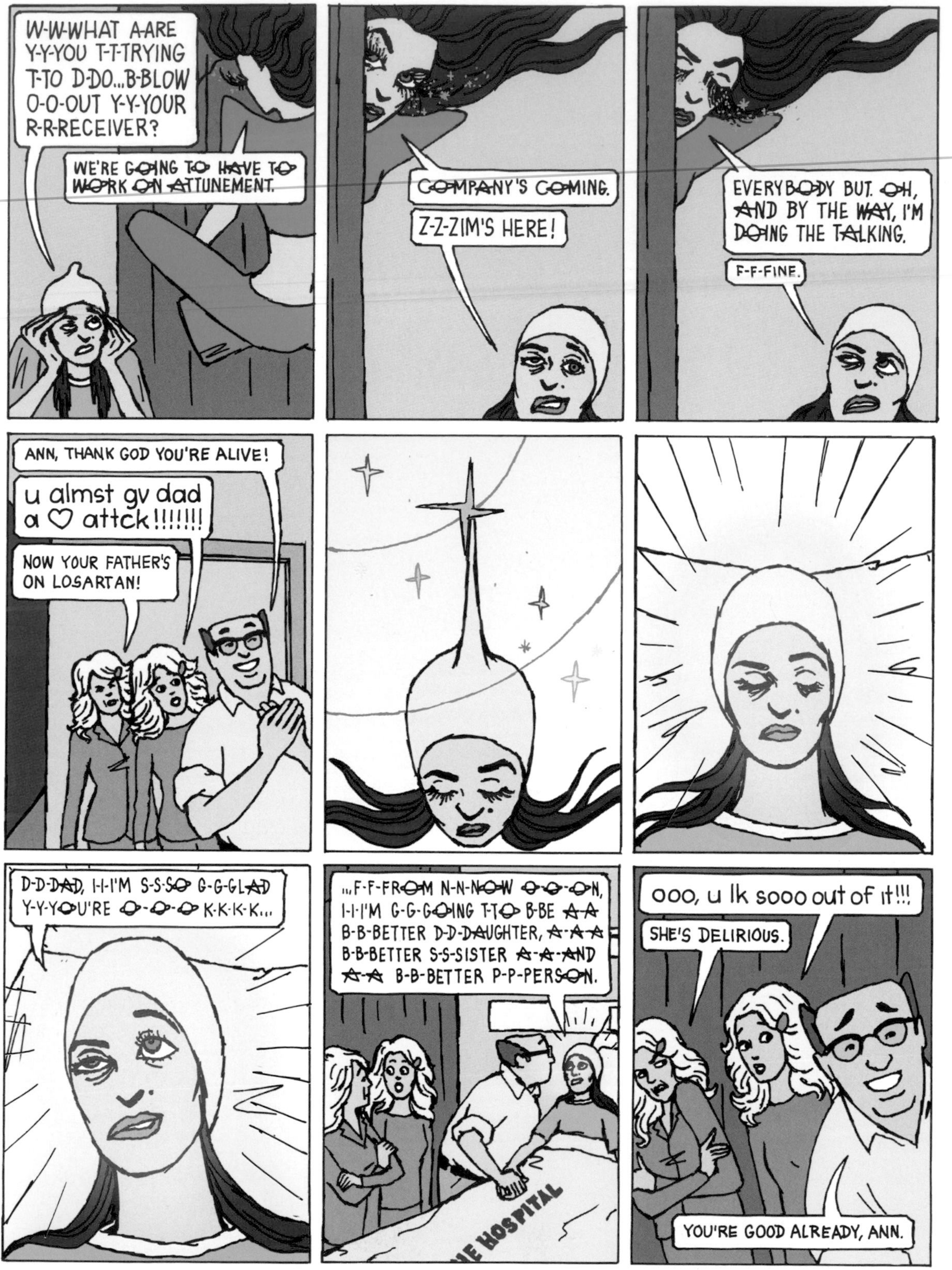
W-W-WHAT A-ARE Y-Y-YOU T-T-TRYING T-TO D-DO...B-BLOW O-O-OUT Y-Y-YOUR R-R-RECEIVER?
WE'RE GOING TO HAVE TO WORK ON ATTUNEMENT.
COMPANY'S COMING.
Z-Z-ZIM'S HERE!
EVERYBODY BUT. OH, AND BY THE WAY, I'M DOING THE TALKING.
F-F-FINE.
ANN, THANK GOD YOU'RE ALIVE!
u almst gv dad a ♡ attck!!!!!!!
NOW YOUR FATHER'S ON LOSARTAN!
D-D-DAD, I-I-I'M S-S-SO G-G-GLAD Y-Y-YOU'RE O-O-O K-K-K-K...
...F-F-FROM N-N-NOW O-O-ON, I-I-I'M G-G-GOING T-TO B-BE A-A B-B-BETTER D-D-DAUGHTER, A-A-A B-B-BETTER S-S-SISTER A-A-AND A-A B-B-BETTER P-P-PERSON.
HOSPITAL
OOO, u lk sooo out of it!!!
SHE'S DELIRIOUS.
YOU'RE GOOD ALREADY, ANN.

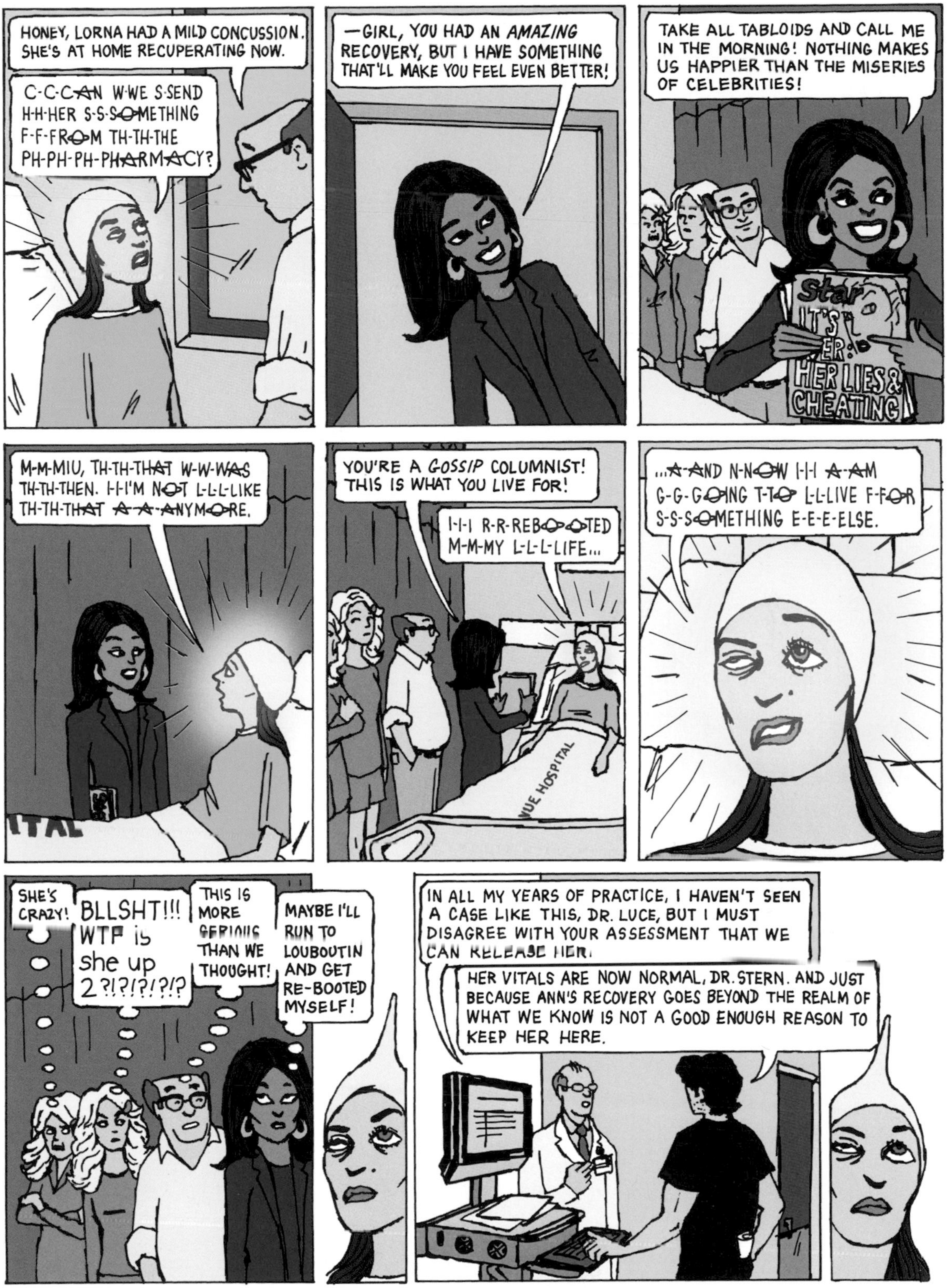
HONEY, LORNA HAD A MILD CONCUSSION. SHE'S AT HOME RECUPERATING NOW.
C-C-CAN W-WE S-SEND H-H-HER S-S-SOMETHING F-F-FROM TH-TH-THE PH-PH-PH-PHARMACY?
—GIRL, YOU HAD AN *AMAZING* RECOVERY, BUT I HAVE SOMETHING THAT'LL MAKE YOU FEEL EVEN BETTER!
TAKE ALL TABLOIDS AND CALL ME IN THE MORNING! NOTHING MAKES US HAPPIER THAN THE MISERIES OF CELEBRITIES!
Star
HER LIES & CHEATING
M-M-MIU, TH-TH-THAT W-W-WAS TH-TH-THEN. I-I-I'M NOT L-L-LIKE TH-TH-THAT A-A-ANYMORE.
YOU'RE A *GOSSIP* COLUMNIST! THIS IS WHAT YOU LIVE FOR!
I-I-I R-R-REBOOOTED M-M-MY L-L-LIFE...
...A-AND N-NOW I-I-I A-AM G-G-GOING T-TO L-L-LIVE F-FOR S-S-SOMETHING E-E-E-ELSE.
SHE'S CRAZY!
BLLSHT!!! WTF is she up 2?!?!?!?!?
THIS IS MORE SERIOUS THAN WE THOUGHT!
MAYBE I'LL RUN TO LOUBOUTIN AND GET RE-BOOTED MYSELF!
IN ALL MY YEARS OF PRACTICE, I HAVEN'T SEEN A CASE LIKE THIS, DR. LUCE, BUT I MUST DISAGREE WITH YOUR ASSESSMENT THAT WE CAN RELEASE HER.
HER VITALS ARE NOW NORMAL, DR. STERN. AND JUST BECAUSE ANN'S RECOVERY GOES BEYOND THE REALM OF WHAT WE KNOW IS NOT A GOOD ENOUGH REASON TO KEEP HER HERE.

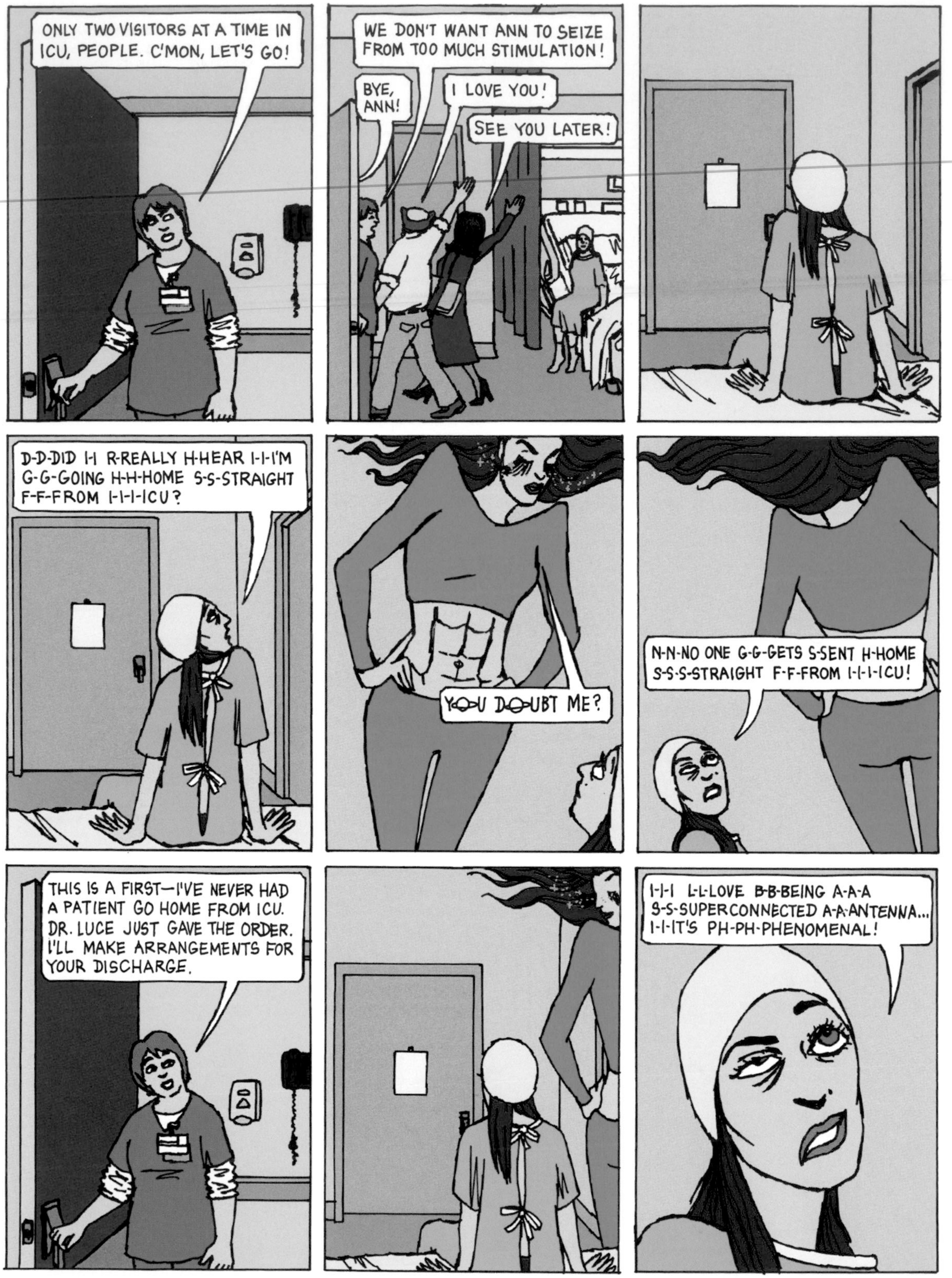
ONLY TWO VISITORS AT A TIME IN ICU, PEOPLE. C'MON, LET'S GO!
WE DON'T WANT ANN TO SEIZE FROM TOO MUCH STIMULATION!
BYE, ANN!
I LOVE YOU!
SEE YOU LATER!
D-D-DID I-I R-REALLY H-HEAR I-I-I'M G-G-GOING H-H-HOME S-S-STRAIGHT F-F-FROM I-I-I-ICU?
YOU DOUBT ME?
N-N-NO ONE G-G-GETS S-SENT H-HOME S-S-S-STRAIGHT F-F-FROM I-I-I-ICU!
THIS IS A FIRST—I'VE NEVER HAD A PATIENT GO HOME FROM ICU. DR. LUCE JUST GAVE THE ORDER. I'LL MAKE ARRANGEMENTS FOR YOUR DISCHARGE.
I-I-I L-L-LOVE B-B-BEING A-A-A S-S-SUPERCONNECTED A-A-ANTENNA... I-I-IT'S PH-PH-PHENOMENAL!

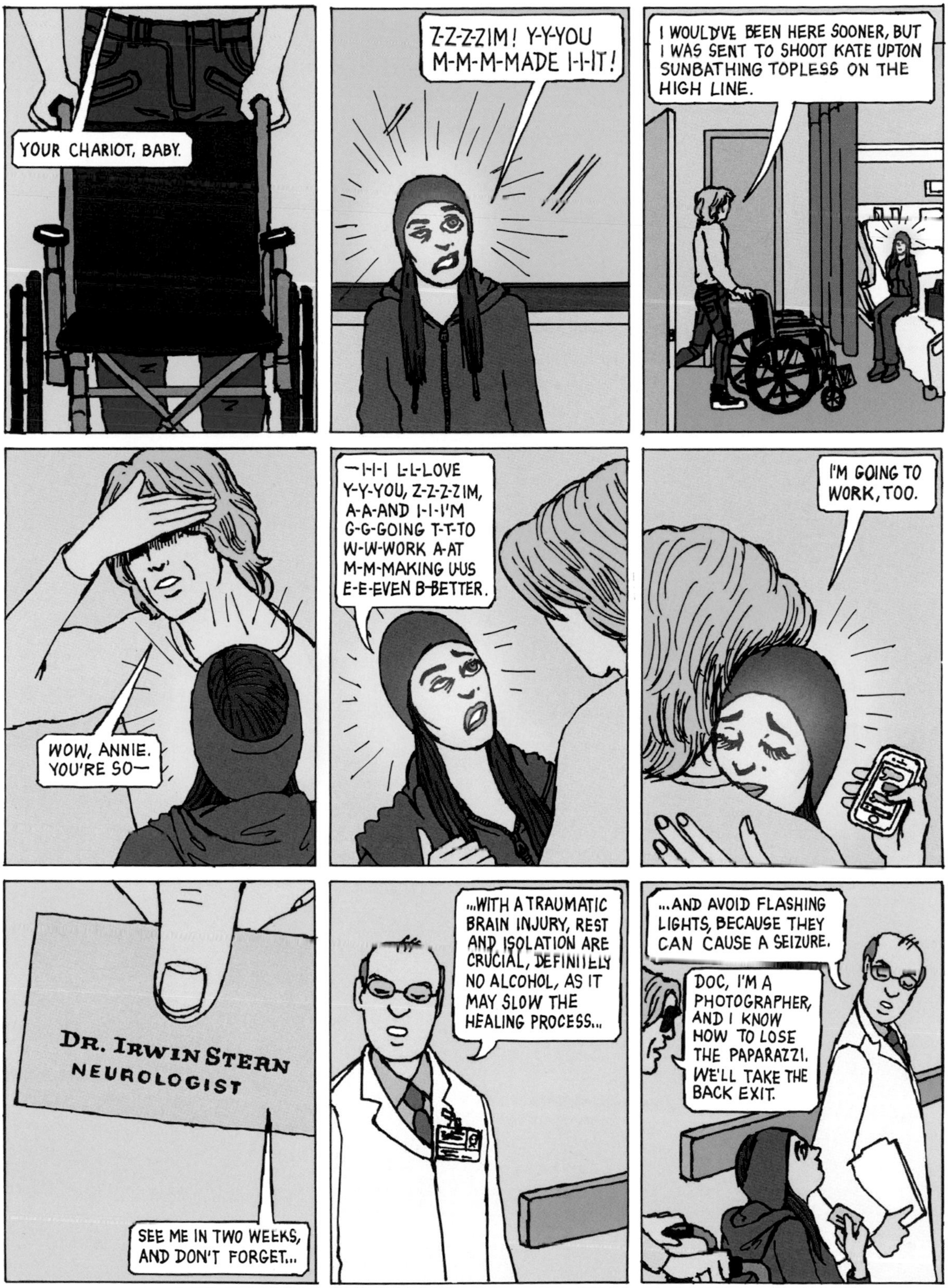
YOUR CHARIOT, BABY.
Z-Z-Z-ZIM! Y-Y-YOU M-M-M-MADE I-I-IT!
I WOULD'VE BEEN HERE SOONER, BUT I WAS SENT TO SHOOT KATE UPTON SUNBATHING TOPLESS ON THE HIGH LINE.
WOW, ANNIE. YOU'RE SO—
—I-I-I L-L-LOVE Y-Y-YOU, Z-Z-Z-ZIM, A-A-AND I-I-I'M G-G-GOING T-T-TO W-W-WORK A-AT M-M-MAKING U-US E-E-EVEN B-BETTER.
I'M GOING TO WORK, TOO.
DR. IRWIN STERN
NEUROLOGIST
SEE ME IN TWO WEEKS, AND DON'T FORGET...
...WITH A TRAUMATIC BRAIN INJURY, REST AND ISOLATION ARE CRUCIAL, DEFINITELY NO ALCOHOL, AS IT MAY SLOW THE HEALING PROCESS...
...AND AVOID FLASHING LIGHTS, BECAUSE THEY CAN CAUSE A SEIZURE.
DOC, I'M A PHOTOGRAPHER, AND I KNOW HOW TO LOSE THE PAPARAZZI. WE'LL TAKE THE BACK EXIT.

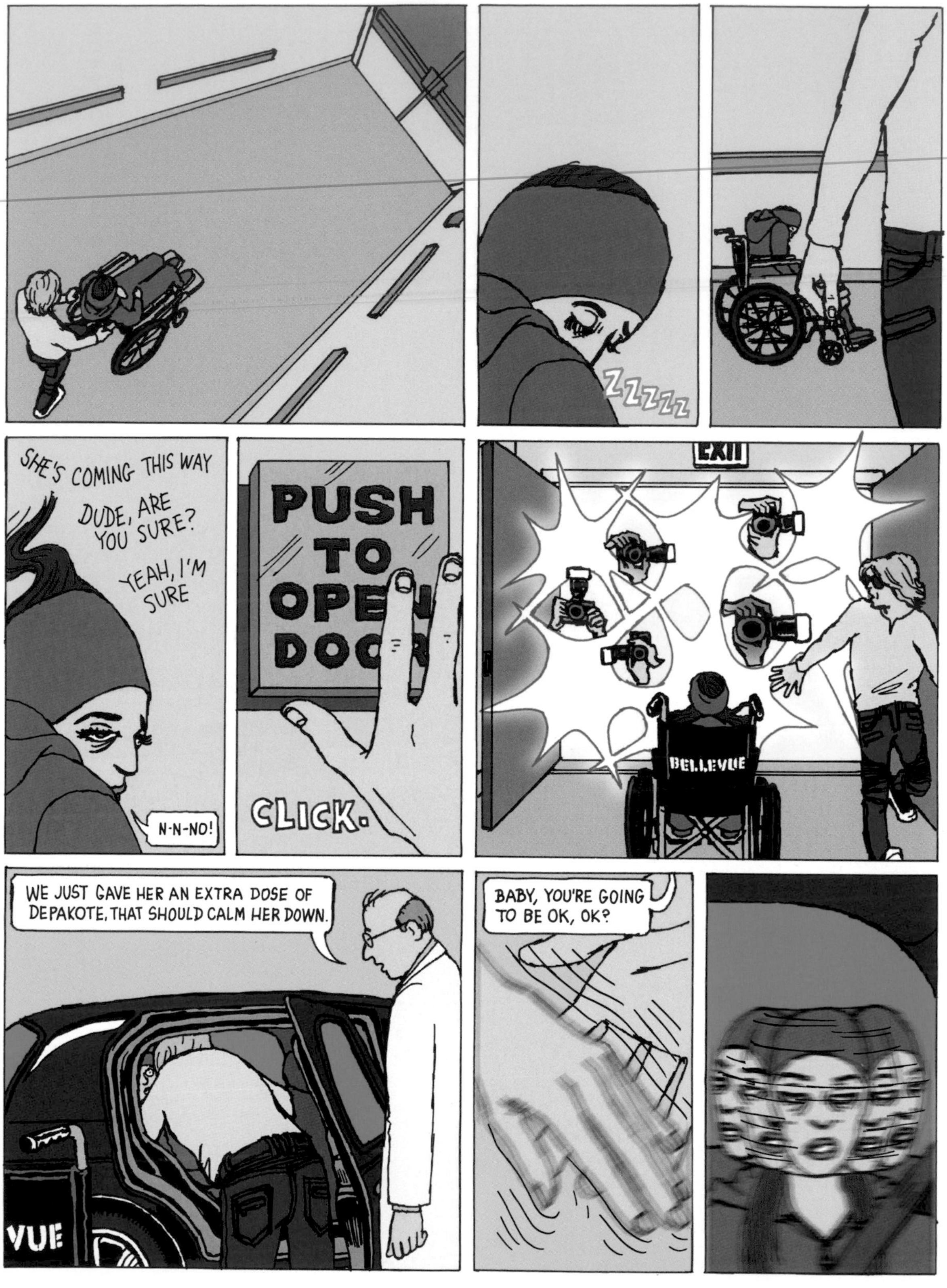
ZZZZZ
SHE'S COMING THIS WAY
DUDE, ARE YOU SURE?
YEAH, I'M SURE
N-N-NO!
PUSH TO OPEN DOOR
CLICK.
EXIT
BELLEVUE
WE JUST GAVE HER AN EXTRA DOSE OF DEPAKOTE, THAT SHOULD CALM HER DOWN.
VUE
BABY, YOU'RE GOING TO BE OK, OK?

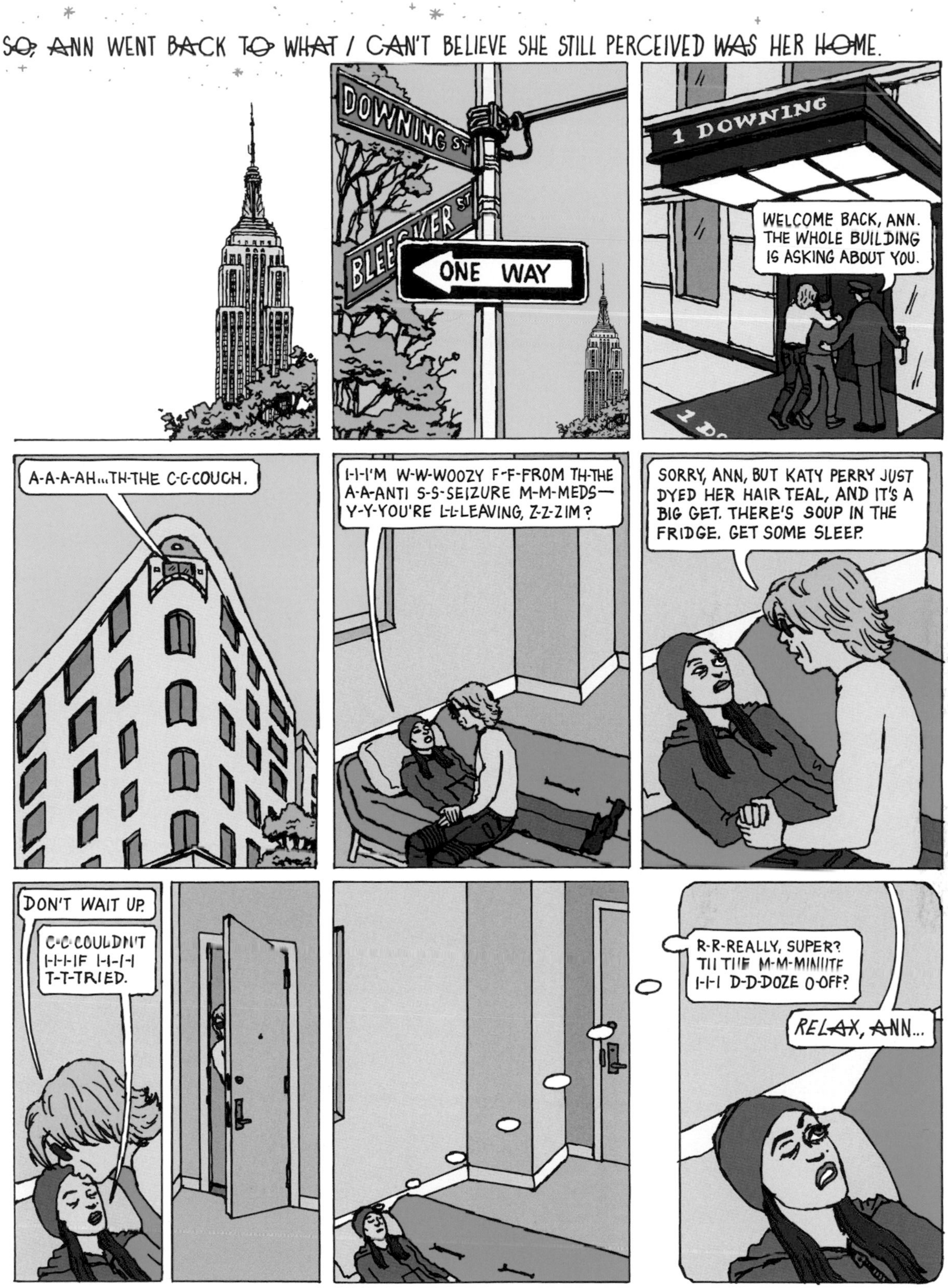
SO, ANN WENT BACK TO WHAT I CAN'T BELIEVE SHE STILL PERCEIVED WAS HER HOME.
DOWNING ST
BLEECKER ST
ONE WAY
1 DOWNING
WELCOME BACK, ANN. THE WHOLE BUILDING IS ASKING ABOUT YOU.
A-A-A-AH...TH-THE C-C-COUCH.
I-I-I'M W-W-WOOZY F-F-FROM TH-THE A-A-ANTI S-S-SEIZURE M-M-MEDS— Y-Y-YOU'RE L-L-LEAVING, Z-Z-ZIM?
SORRY, ANN, BUT KATY PERRY JUST DYED HER HAIR TEAL, AND IT'S A BIG GET. THERE'S SOUP IN THE FRIDGE. GET SOME SLEEP.
DON'T WAIT UP.
C-C-COULDN'T I-I-I-IF I-I-I-I T-T-TRIED.
R-R-REALLY, SUPER? TIL THE M-M-MINUTE I-I-I D-D-DOZE O-OFF?
RELAX, ANN...

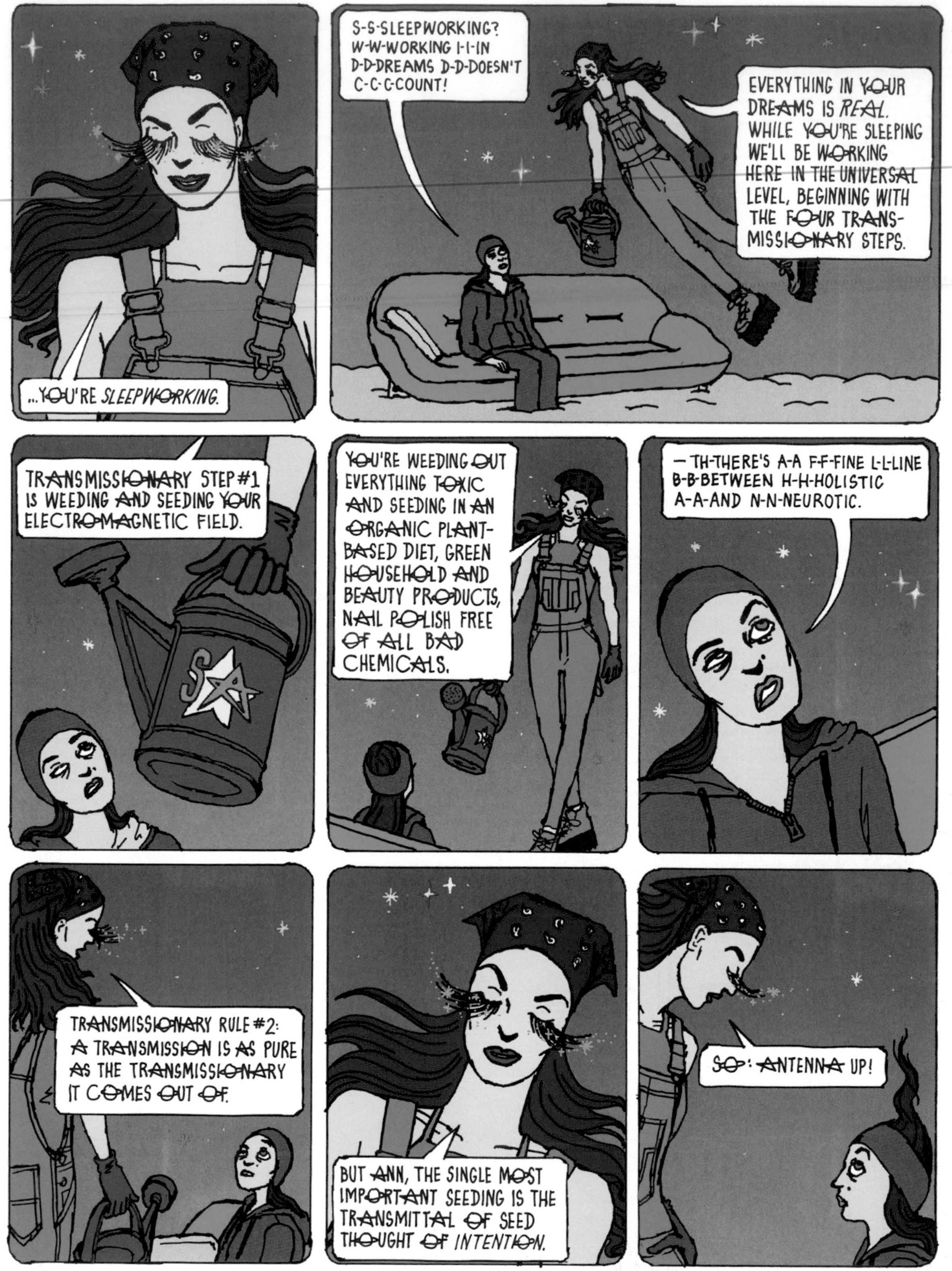
...YOU'RE SLEEPWORKING.
S-S-SLEEPWORKING? W-W-WORKING I-I-IN D-D-DREAMS D-D-DOESN'T C-C-C-COUNT!
EVERYTHING IN YOUR DREAMS IS REAL. WHILE YOU'RE SLEEPING WE'LL BE WORKING HERE IN THE UNIVERSAL LEVEL, BEGINNING WITH THE FOUR TRANSMISSIONARY STEPS.
TRANSMISSIONARY STEP #1 IS WEEDING AND SEEDING YOUR ELECTROMAGNETIC FIELD.
YOU'RE WEEDING OUT EVERYTHING TOXIC AND SEEDING IN AN ORGANIC PLANT-BASED DIET, GREEN HOUSEHOLD AND BEAUTY PRODUCTS, NAIL POLISH FREE OF ALL BAD CHEMICALS.
— TH-THERE'S A-A F-F-FINE L-L-LINE B-B-BETWEEN H-H-HOLISTIC A-A-AND N-N-NEUROTIC.
TRANSMISSIONARY RULE #2: A TRANSMISSION IS AS PURE AS THE TRANSMISSIONARY IT COMES OUT OF.
BUT ANN, THE SINGLE MOST IMPORTANT SEEDING IS THE TRANSMITTAL OF SEED THOUGHT OF INTENTION.
SO: ANTENNA UP!

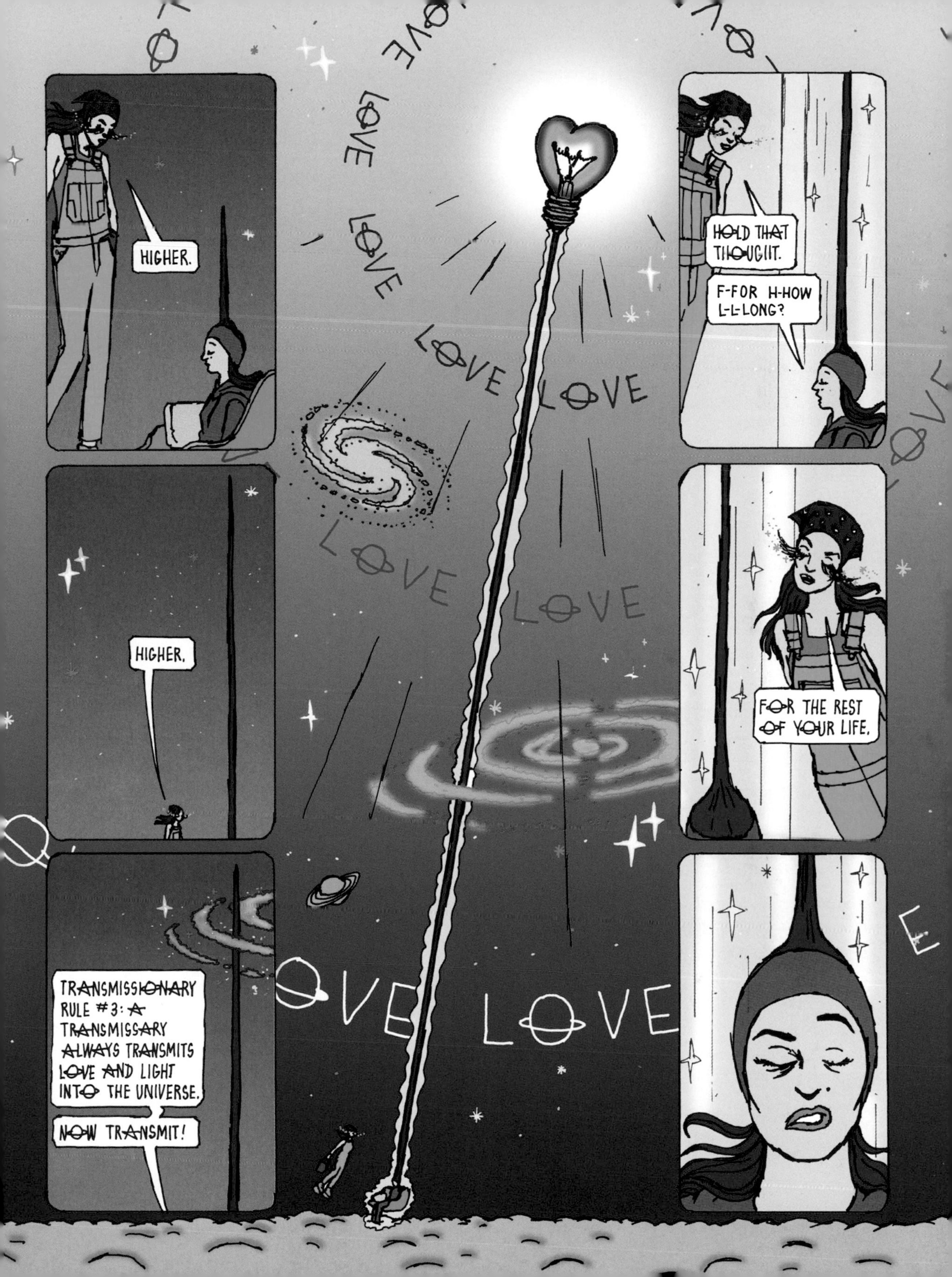
HIGHER.
HOLD THAT THOUGHT.
F-FOR H-HOW L-L-LONG?
HIGHER.
FOR THE REST OF YOUR LIFE.
TRANSMISSIONARY RULE #3: A TRANSMISSARY ALWAYS TRANSMITS LOVE AND LIGHT INTO THE UNIVERSE.
NOW TRANSMIT!
LOVE
LOVE
LOVE
LOVE
LOVE
LOVE
LOVE
LOVE
LOVE

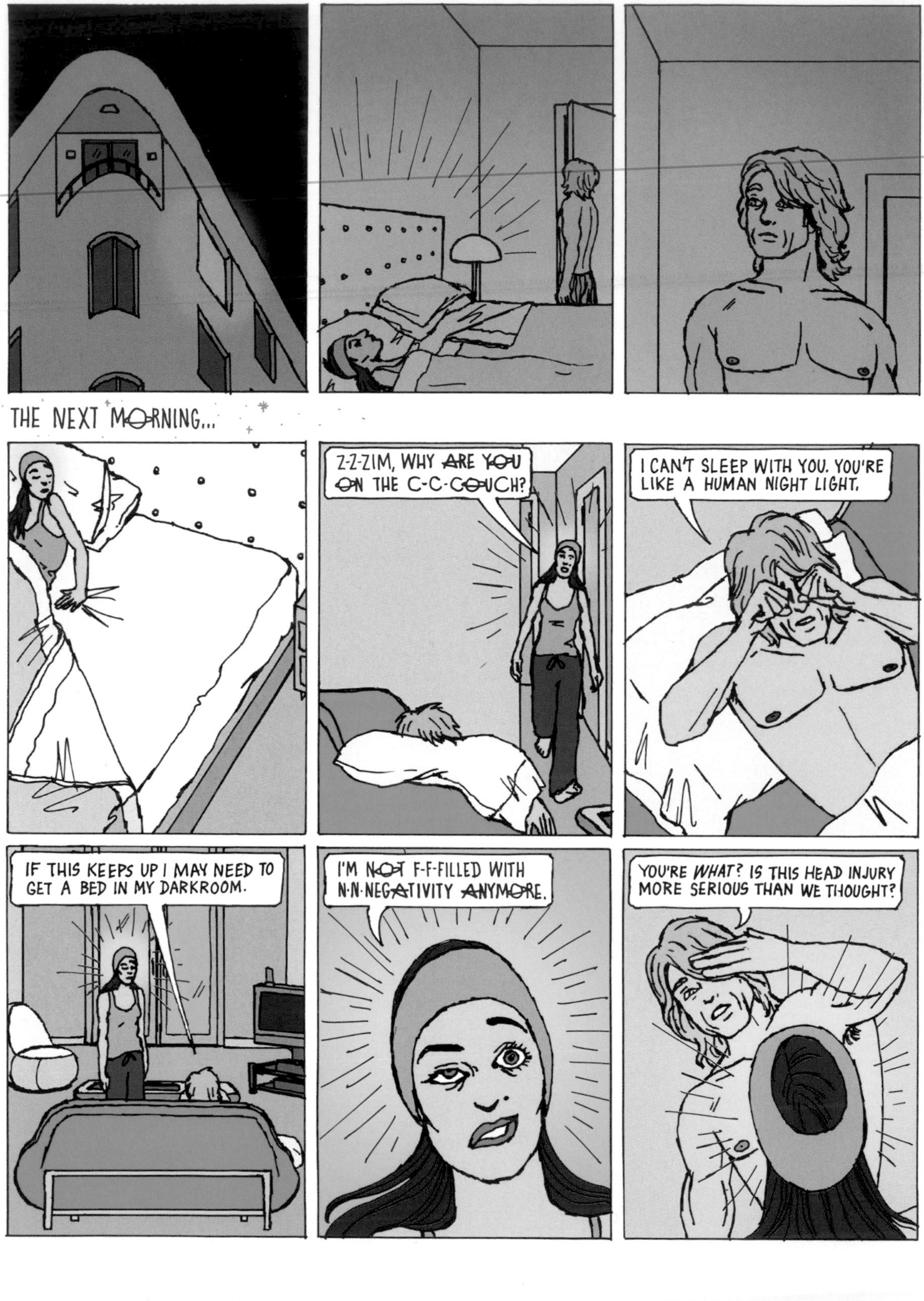
THE NEXT MORNING...
Z-Z-ZIM, WHY ARE YOU ON THE C-C-COUCH?
I CAN'T SLEEP WITH YOU. YOU'RE LIKE A HUMAN NIGHT LIGHT.
IF THIS KEEPS UP I MAY NEED TO GET A BED IN MY DARKROOM.
I'M NOT F-F-FILLED WITH N-N-NEGATIVITY ANYMORE.
YOU'RE WHAT? IS THIS HEAD INJURY MORE SERIOUS THAN WE THOUGHT?

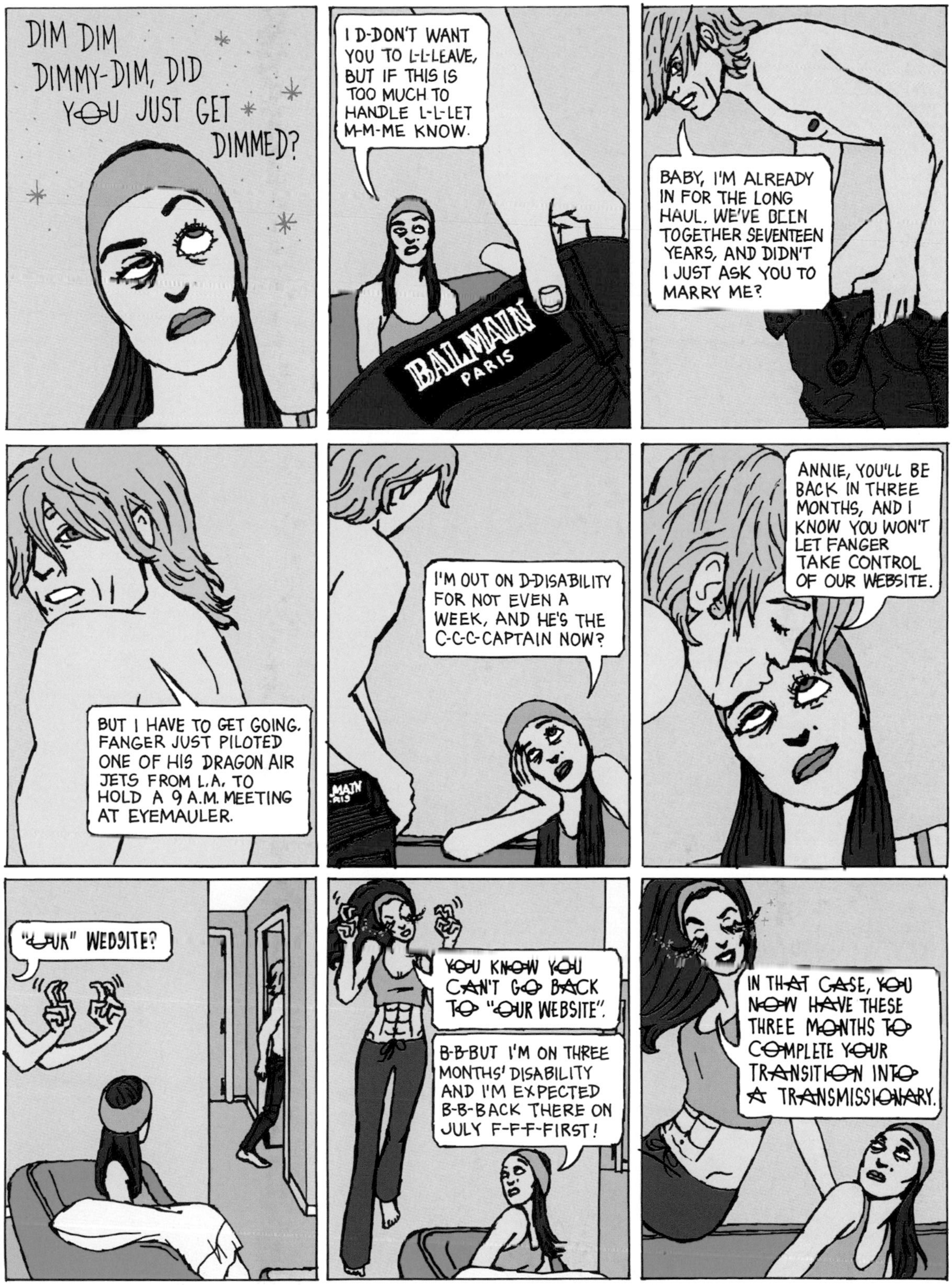
DIM DIM DIMMY-DIM, DID YOU JUST GET DIMMED?
I D-DON'T WANT YOU TO L-L-LEAVE, BUT IF THIS IS TOO MUCH TO HANDLE L-L-LET M-M-ME KNOW.
BALMAIN PARIS
BABY, I'M ALREADY IN FOR THE LONG HAUL. WE'VE BEEN TOGETHER SEVENTEEN YEARS, AND DIDN'T I JUST ASK YOU TO MARRY ME?
BUT I HAVE TO GET GOING. FANGER JUST PILOTED ONE OF HIS DRAGON AIR JETS FROM L.A. TO HOLD A 9 A.M. MEETING AT EYEMAULER.
I'M OUT ON D-DISABILITY FOR NOT EVEN A WEEK, AND HE'S THE C-C-CAPTAIN NOW?
ANNIE, YOU'LL BE BACK IN THREE MONTHS, AND I KNOW YOU WON'T LET FANGER TAKE CONTROL OF OUR WEBSITE.
"OUR" WEBSITE?
YOU KNOW YOU CAN'T GO BACK TO "OUR WEBSITE".
B-B-BUT I'M ON THREE MONTHS' DISABILITY AND I'M EXPECTED B-B-BACK THERE ON JULY F-F-F-FIRST!
IN THAT CASE, YOU NOW HAVE THESE THREE MONTHS TO COMPLETE YOUR TRANSITION INTO A TRANSMISSIONARY.

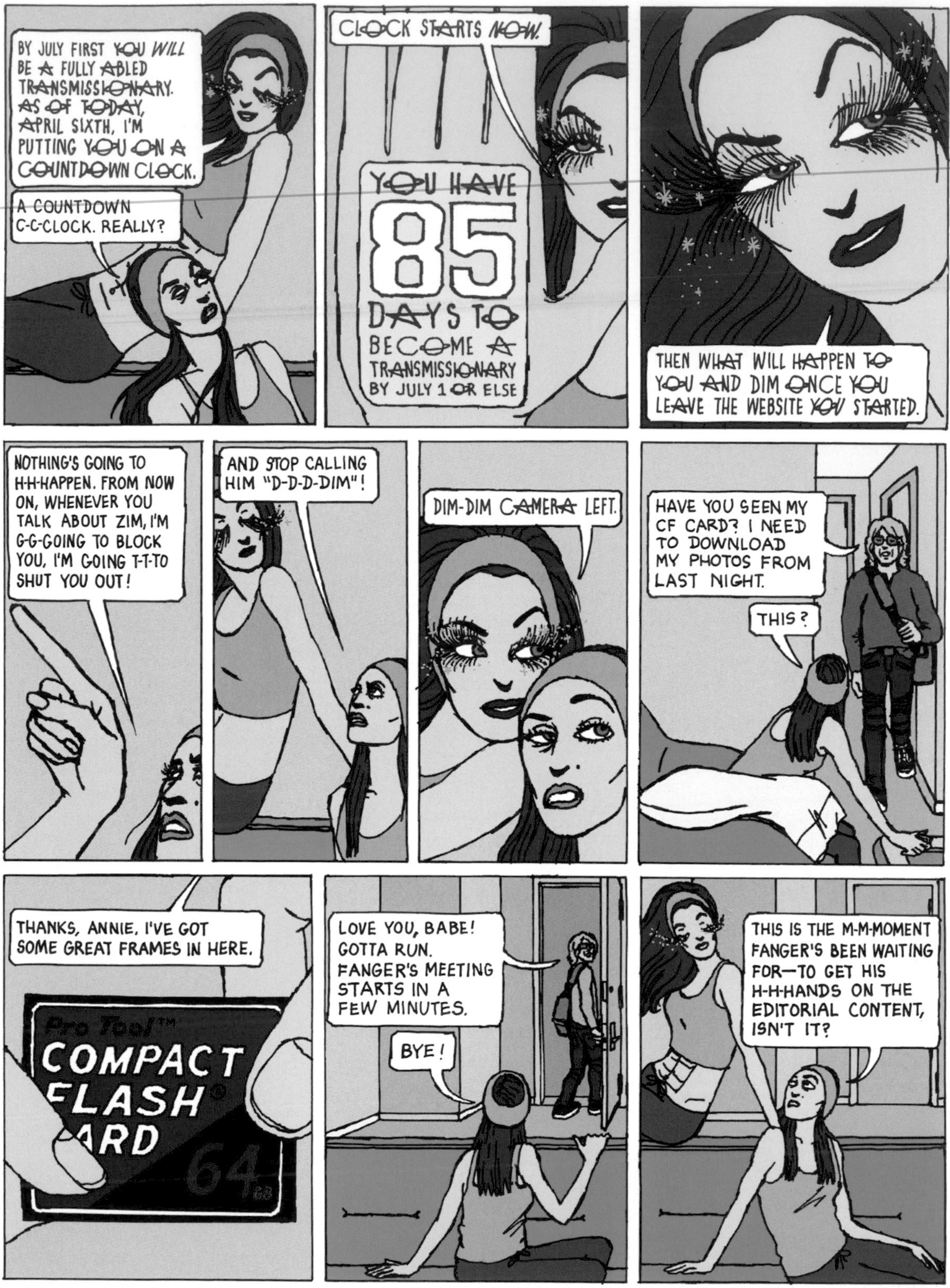
BY JULY FIRST YOU WILL BE A FULLY ABLED TRANSMISSIONARY. AS OF TODAY, APRIL SIXTH, I'M PUTTING YOU ON A COUNTDOWN CLOCK.
A COUNTDOWN C-C-CLOCK. REALLY?
CLOCK STARTS NOW.
YOU HAVE 85 DAYS TO BECOME A TRANSMISSIONARY BY JULY 1 OR ELSE
THEN WHAT WILL HAPPEN TO YOU AND DIM ONCE YOU LEAVE THE WEBSITE YOU STARTED.
NOTHING'S GOING TO H-H-HAPPEN. FROM NOW ON, WHENEVER YOU TALK ABOUT ZIM, I'M G-G-GOING TO BLOCK YOU, I'M GOING T-T-TO SHUT YOU OUT!
AND STOP CALLING HIM "D-D-D-DIM"!
DIM-DIM CAMERA LEFT.
HAVE YOU SEEN MY CF CARD? I NEED TO DOWNLOAD MY PHOTOS FROM LAST NIGHT.
THIS?
THANKS, ANNIE. I'VE GOT SOME GREAT FRAMES IN HERE.
Pro Tool™
COMPACT FLASH® ARD
64GB
LOVE YOU, BABE! GOTTA RUN. FANGER'S MEETING STARTS IN A FEW MINUTES.
BYE!
THIS IS THE M-M-MOMENT FANGER'S BEEN WAITING FOR—TO GET HIS H-H-HANDS ON THE EDITORIAL CONTENT, ISN'T IT?

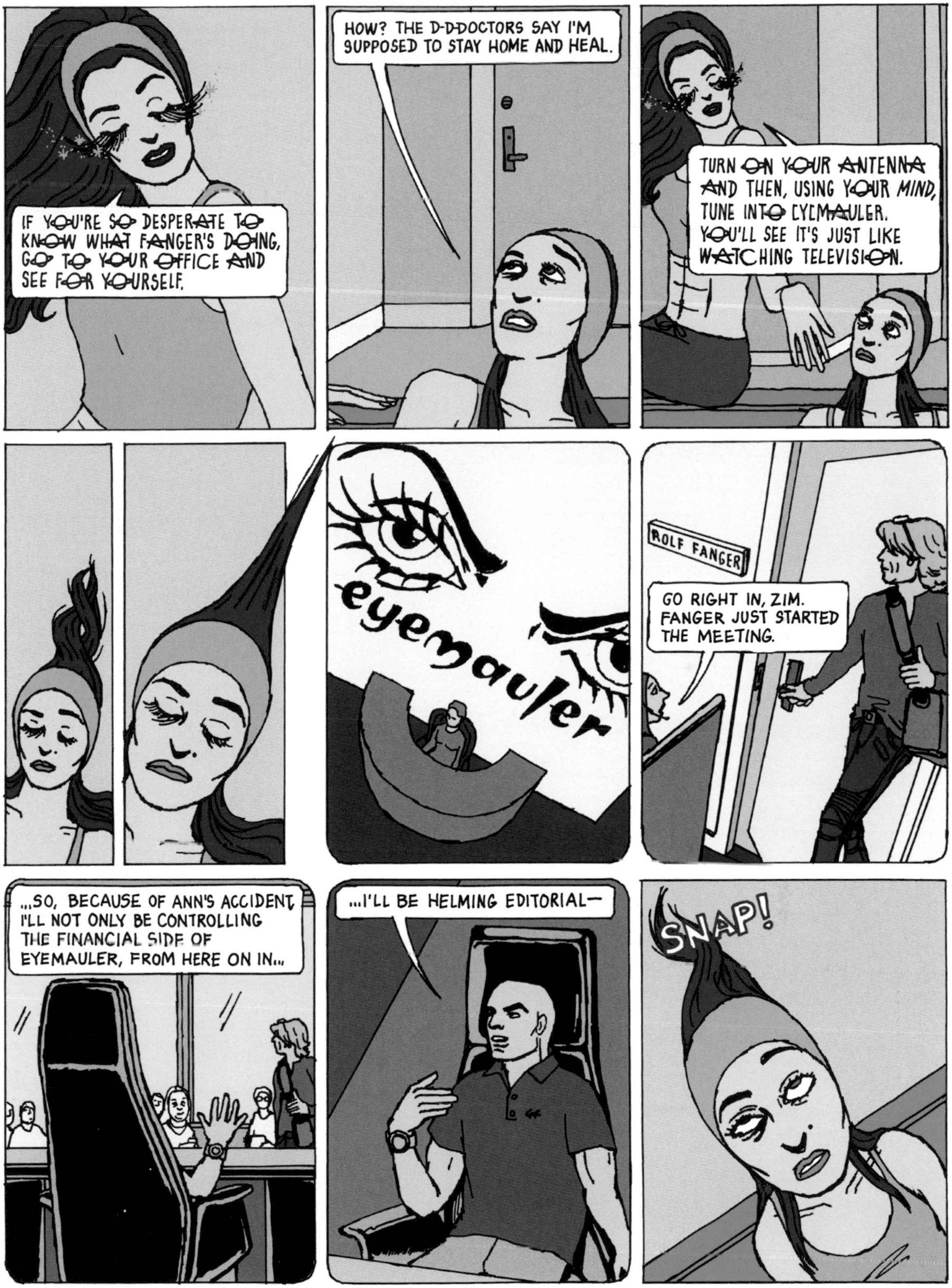
IF YOU'RE SO DESPERATE TO KNOW WHAT FANGER'S DOING, GO TO YOUR OFFICE AND SEE FOR YOURSELF.
HOW? THE D-D-DOCTORS SAY I'M SUPPOSED TO STAY HOME AND HEAL.
TURN ON YOUR ANTENNA AND THEN, USING YOUR MIND, TUNE INTO EYEMAULER. YOU'LL SEE IT'S JUST LIKE WATCHING TELEVISION.
eyemauler
ROLF FANGER
GO RIGHT IN, ZIM. FANGER JUST STARTED THE MEETING.
...SO, BECAUSE OF ANN'S ACCIDENT, I'LL NOT ONLY BE CONTROLLING THE FINANCIAL SIDE OF EYEMAULER, FROM HERE ON IN...
...I'LL BE HELMING EDITORIAL—
SNAP!

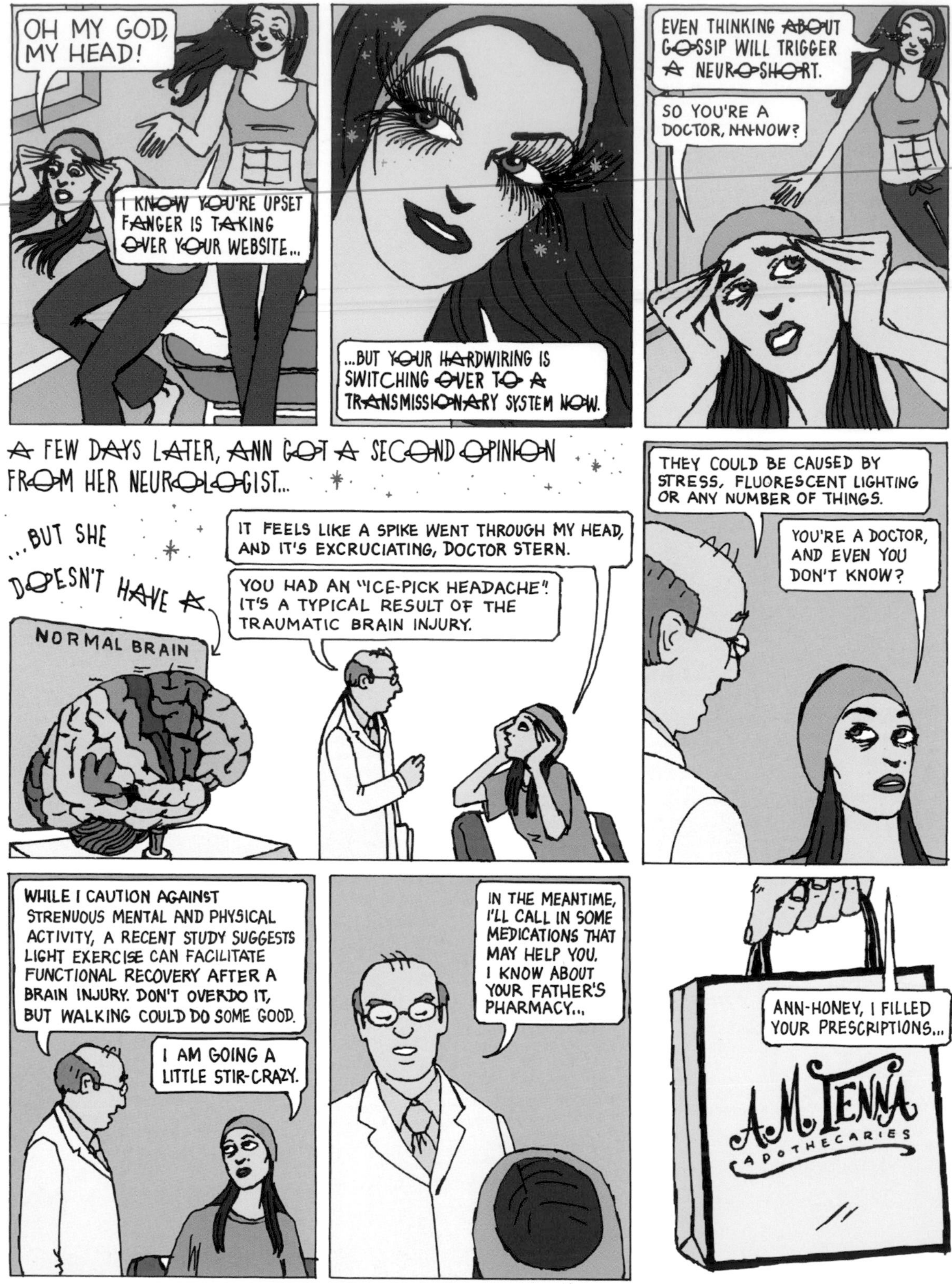
OH MY GOD, MY HEAD!
I KNOW YOU'RE UPSET FANGER IS TAKING OVER YOUR WEBSITE...
...BUT YOUR HARDWIRING IS SWITCHING OVER TO A TRANSMISSIONARY SYSTEM NOW.
EVEN THINKING ABOUT GOSSIP WILL TRIGGER A NEURO-SHORT.
SO YOU'RE A DOCTOR, N-N-NOW?
A FEW DAYS LATER, ANN GOT A SECOND OPINION FROM HER NEUROLOGIST...
...BUT SHE DOESN'T HAVE A
NORMAL BRAIN
IT FEELS LIKE A SPIKE WENT THROUGH MY HEAD, AND IT'S EXCRUCIATING, DOCTOR STERN.
YOU HAD AN "ICE-PICK HEADACHE". IT'S A TYPICAL RESULT OF THE TRAUMATIC BRAIN INJURY.
THEY COULD BE CAUSED BY STRESS, FLUORESCENT LIGHTING OR ANY NUMBER OF THINGS.
YOU'RE A DOCTOR, AND EVEN YOU DON'T KNOW?
WHILE I CAUTION AGAINST STRENUOUS MENTAL AND PHYSICAL ACTIVITY, A RECENT STUDY SUGGESTS LIGHT EXERCISE CAN FACILITATE FUNCTIONAL RECOVERY AFTER A BRAIN INJURY. DON'T OVERDO IT, BUT WALKING COULD DO SOME GOOD.
I AM GOING A LITTLE STIR-CRAZY.
IN THE MEANTIME, I'LL CALL IN SOME MEDICATIONS THAT MAY HELP YOU. I KNOW ABOUT YOUR FATHER'S PHARMACY...
ANN-HONEY, I FILLED YOUR PRESCRIPTIONS...
A.M. TENNA
APOTHECARIES

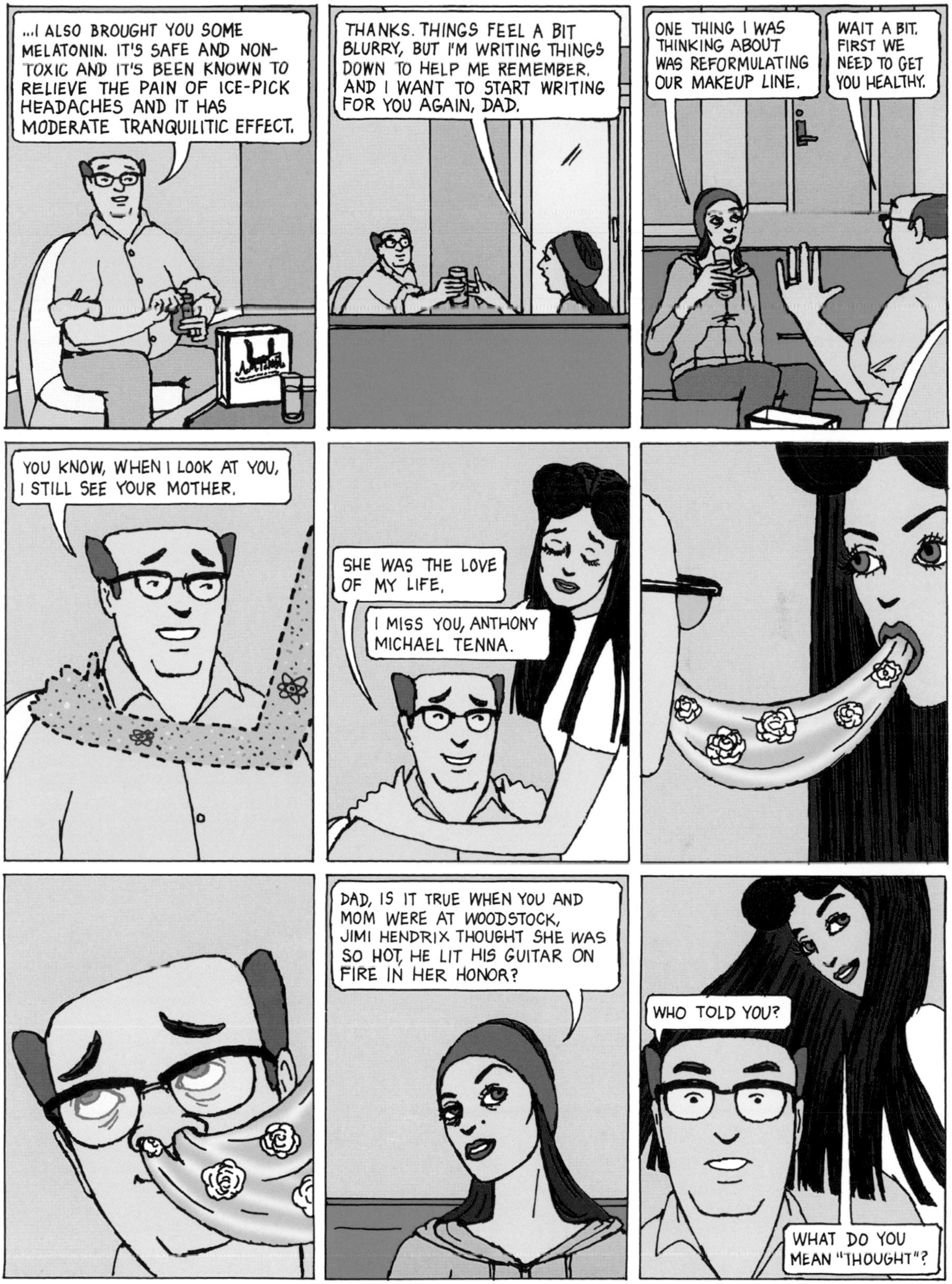
...I ALSO BROUGHT YOU SOME MELATONIN. IT'S SAFE AND NON-TOXIC AND IT'S BEEN KNOWN TO RELIEVE THE PAIN OF ICE-PICK HEADACHES AND IT HAS MODERATE TRANQUILITIC EFFECT.
THANKS. THINGS FEEL A BIT BLURRY, BUT I'M WRITING THINGS DOWN TO HELP ME REMEMBER. AND I WANT TO START WRITING FOR YOU AGAIN, DAD.
ONE THING I WAS THINKING ABOUT WAS REFORMULATING OUR MAKEUP LINE.
WAIT A BIT. FIRST WE NEED TO GET YOU HEALTHY.
YOU KNOW, WHEN I LOOK AT YOU, I STILL SEE YOUR MOTHER.
SHE WAS THE LOVE OF MY LIFE.
I MISS YOU, ANTHONY MICHAEL TENNA.
DAD, IS IT TRUE WHEN YOU AND MOM WERE AT WOODSTOCK, JIMI HENDRIX THOUGHT SHE WAS SO HOT, HE LIT HIS GUITAR ON FIRE IN HER HONOR?
WHO TOLD YOU?
WHAT DO YOU MEAN "THOUGHT"?

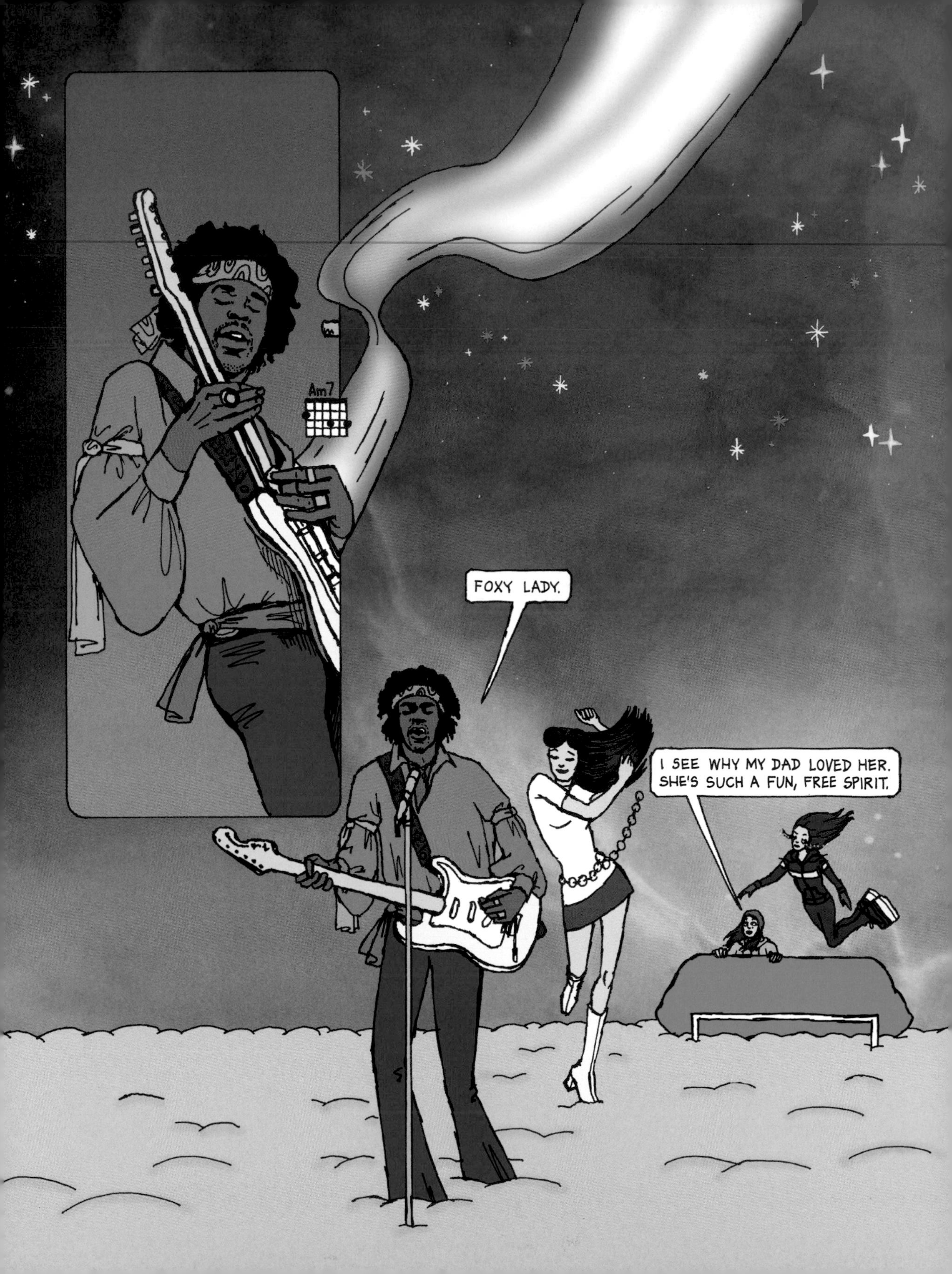
Am7
FOXY LADY.
I SEE WHY MY DAD LOVED HER. SHE'S SUCH A FUN, FREE SPIRIT.

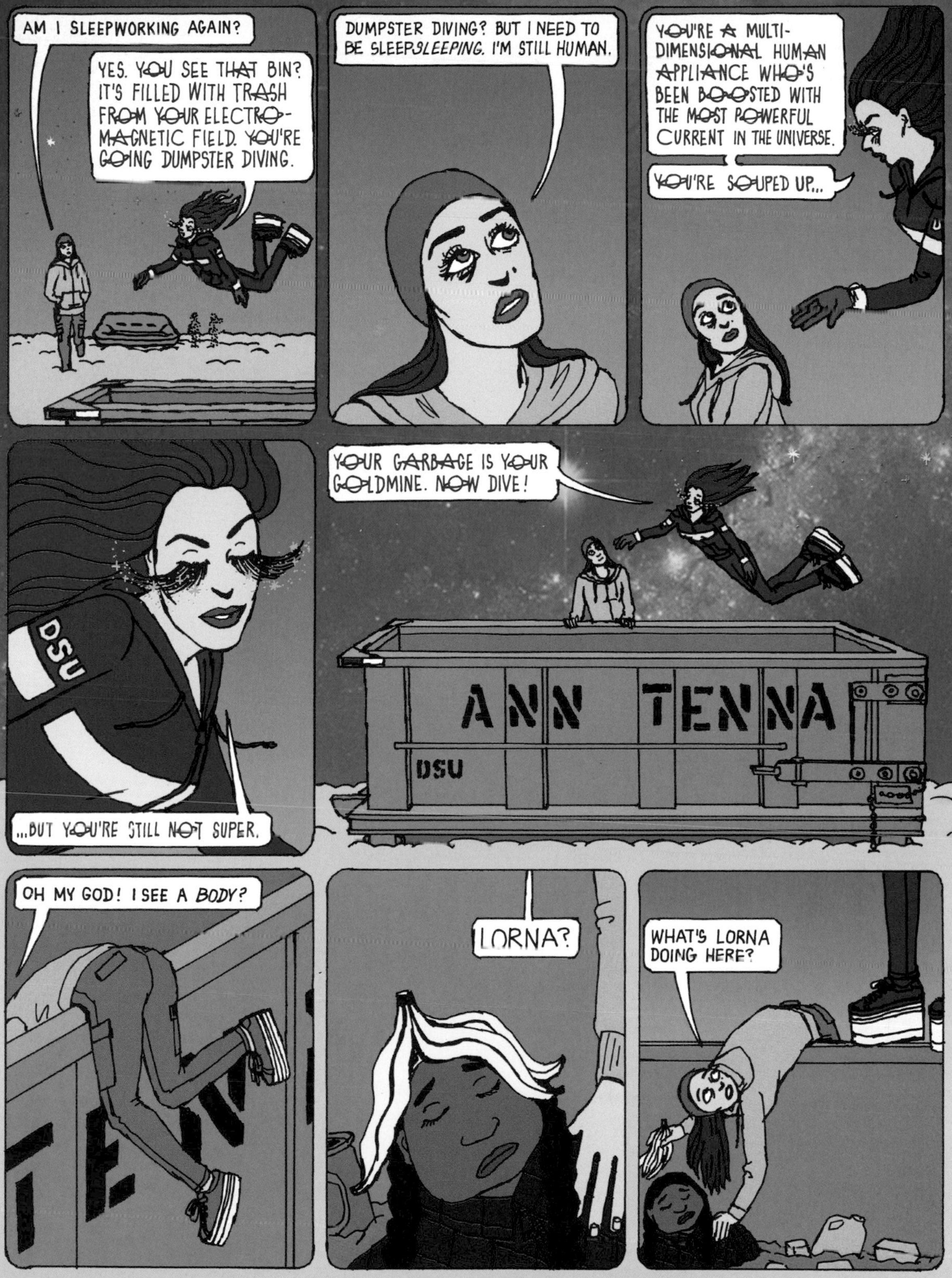
AM I SLEEPWORKING AGAIN?
YES. YOU SEE THAT BIN? IT'S FILLED WITH TRASH FROM YOUR ELECTROMAGNETIC FIELD. YOU'RE GOING DUMPSTER DIVING.
DUMPSTER DIVING? BUT I NEED TO BE SLEEP*SLEEPING*. I'M STILL HUMAN.
YOU'RE A MULTI-DIMENSIONAL HUMAN APPLIANCE WHO'S BEEN BOOSTED WITH THE MOST POWERFUL CURRENT IN THE UNIVERSE.
YOU'RE SOUPED UP...
...BUT YOU'RE STILL NOT SUPER.
YOUR GARBAGE IS YOUR GOLDMINE. NOW DIVE!
ANN TENNA
DSU
DSU
OH MY GOD! I SEE A *BODY*?
LORNA?
WHAT'S LORNA DOING HERE?

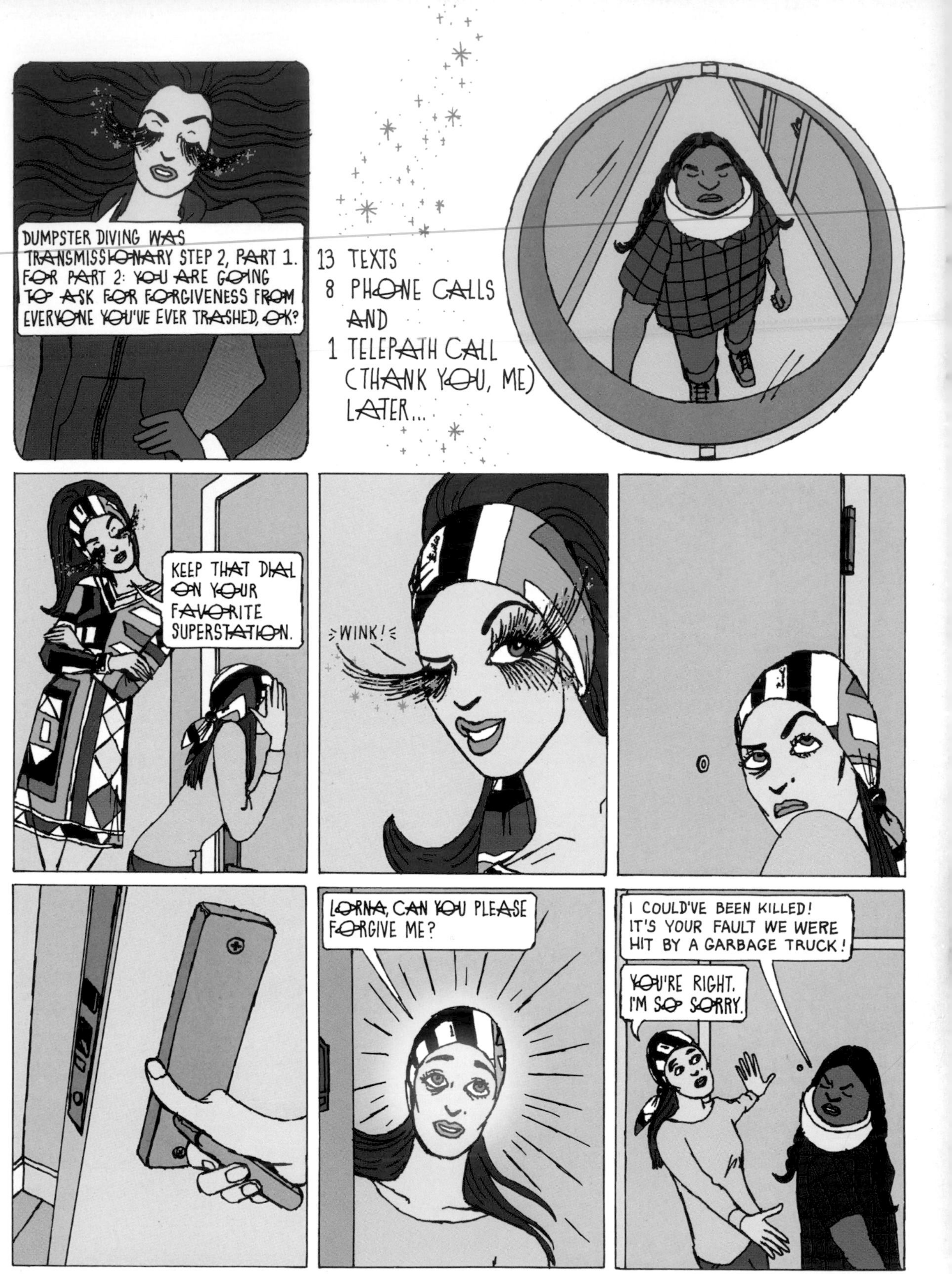
DUMPSTER DIVING WAS TRANSMISSIONARY STEP 2, PART 1. FOR PART 2: YOU ARE GOING TO ASK FOR FORGIVENESS FROM EVERYONE YOU'VE EVER TRASHED, OK?
13 TEXTS
8 PHONE CALLS
AND
1 TELEPATH CALL (THANK YOU, ME)
LATER...
KEEP THAT DIAL ON YOUR FAVORITE SUPERSTATION.
WINK!
LORNA, CAN YOU PLEASE FORGIVE ME?
I COULD'VE BEEN KILLED! IT'S YOUR FAULT WE WERE HIT BY A GARBAGE TRUCK!
YOU'RE RIGHT. I'M SO SORRY.

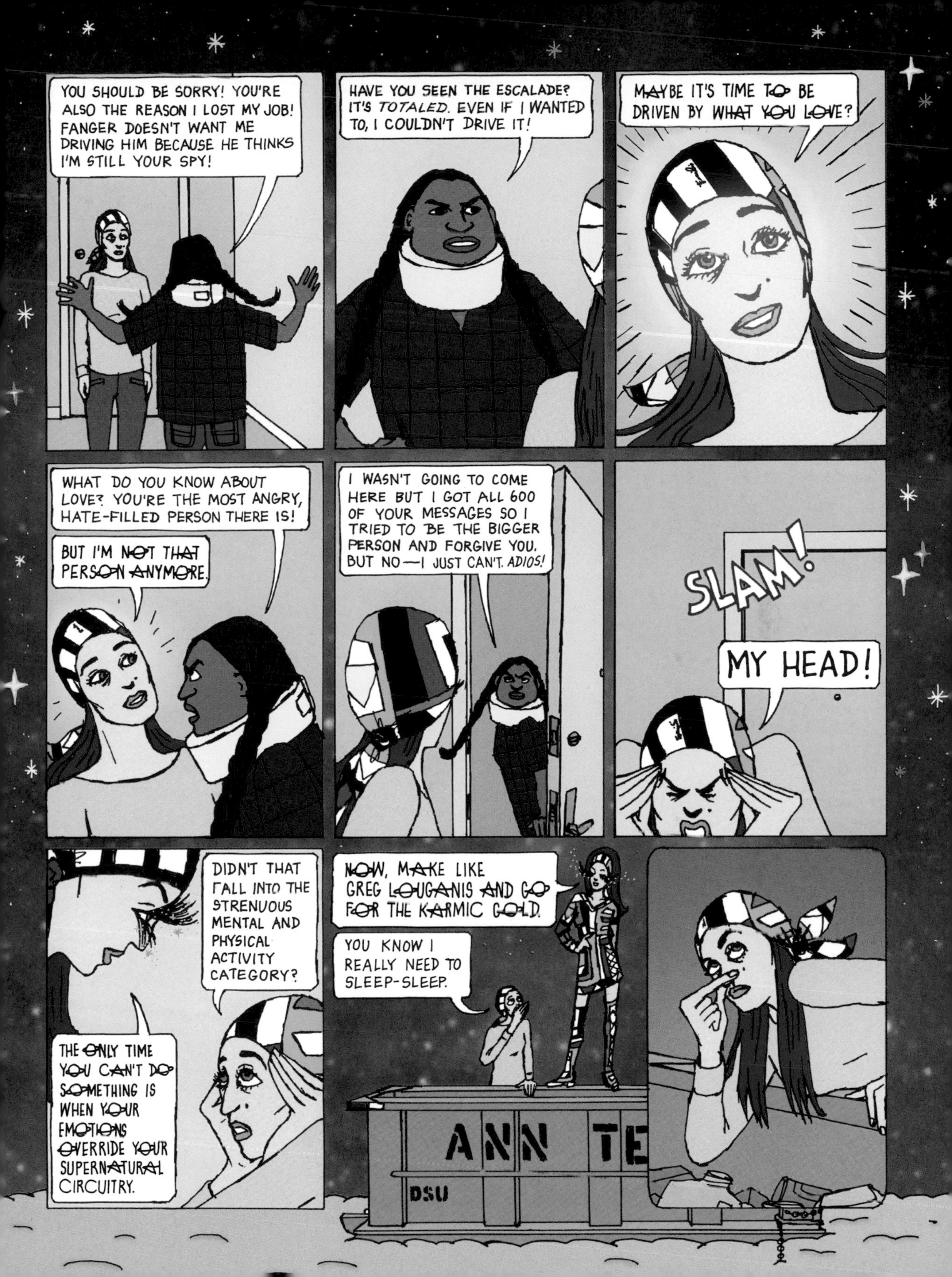

YOU SHOULD BE SORRY! YOU'RE ALSO THE REASON I LOST MY JOB! FANGER DOESN'T WANT ME DRIVING HIM BECAUSE HE THINKS I'M STILL YOUR SPY!
HAVE YOU SEEN THE ESCALADE? IT'S *TOTALED*. EVEN IF I WANTED TO, I COULDN'T DRIVE IT!
MAYBE IT'S TIME TO BE DRIVEN BY WHAT YOU LOVE?
WHAT DO YOU KNOW ABOUT LOVE? YOU'RE THE MOST ANGRY, HATE-FILLED PERSON THERE IS!
BUT I'M NOT THAT PERSON ANYMORE.
I WASN'T GOING TO COME HERE BUT I GOT ALL 600 OF YOUR MESSAGES SO I TRIED TO BE THE BIGGER PERSON AND FORGIVE YOU. BUT NO—I JUST CAN'T. *ADIOS!*
SLAM!
MY HEAD!
DIDN'T THAT FALL INTO THE STRENUOUS MENTAL AND PHYSICAL ACTIVITY CATEGORY?
THE ONLY TIME YOU CAN'T DO SOMETHING IS WHEN YOUR EMOTIONS OVERRIDE YOUR SUPERNATURAL CIRCUITRY.
NOW, MAKE LIKE GREG LOUGANIS AND GO FOR THE KARMIC GOLD.
YOU KNOW I REALLY NEED TO SLEEP-SLEEP.
ANN TE
DSU

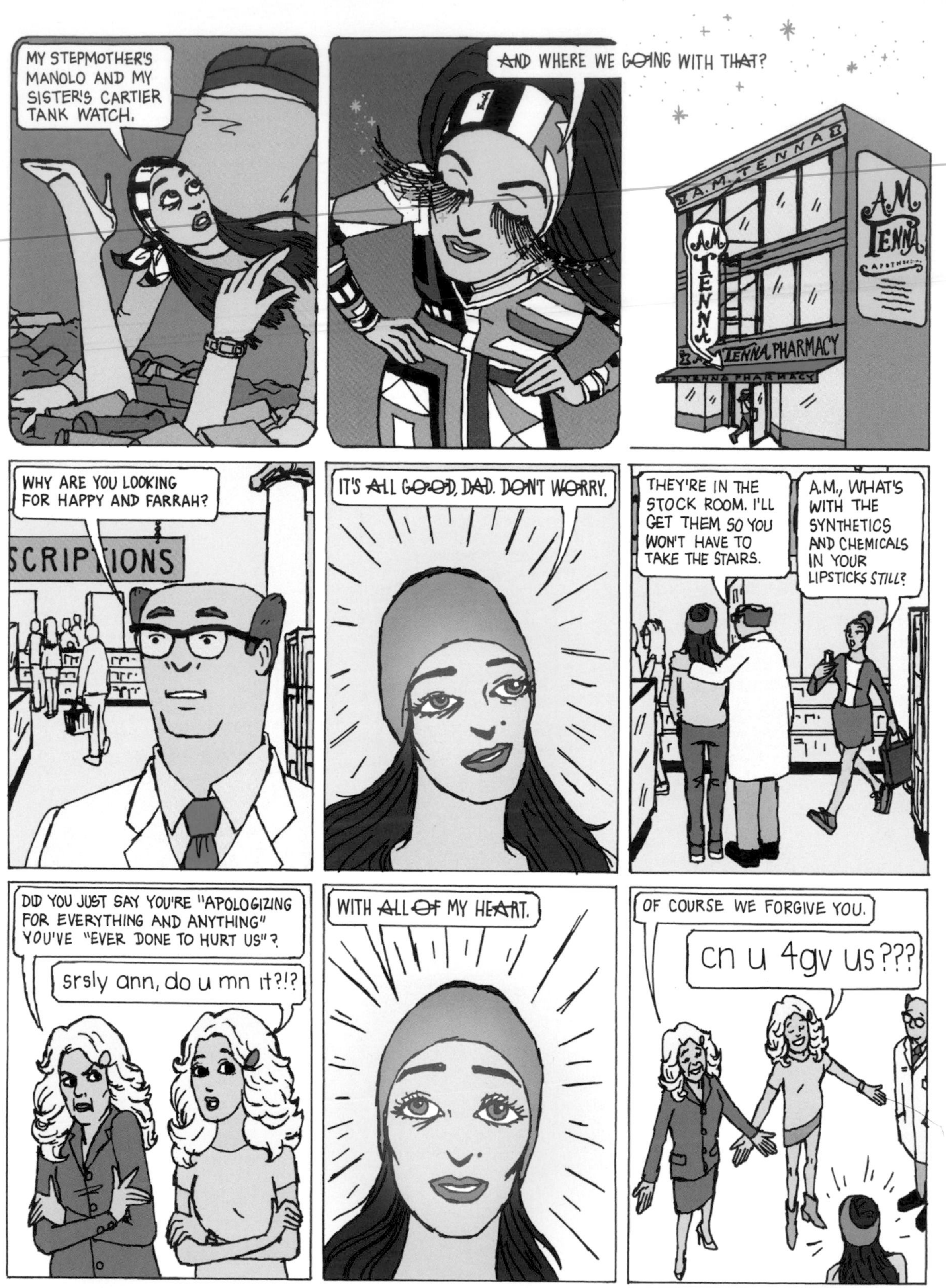
MY STEPMOTHER'S MANOLO AND MY SISTER'S CARTIER TANK WATCH.
AND WHERE WE GOING WITH THAT?
A.M. TENNA
A.M. TENNA
A.M. TENNA APOTHECARY
A.M. TENNA PHARMACY
A.M. TENNA PHARMACY
WHY ARE YOU LOOKING FOR HAPPY AND FARRAH?
SCRIPTIONS
IT'S ALL GOOD, DAD. DON'T WORRY.
THEY'RE IN THE STOCK ROOM. I'LL GET THEM SO YOU WON'T HAVE TO TAKE THE STAIRS.
A.M., WHAT'S WITH THE SYNTHETICS AND CHEMICALS IN YOUR LIPSTICKS STILL?
DID YOU JUST SAY YOU'RE "APOLOGIZING FOR EVERYTHING AND ANYTHING" YOU'VE "EVER DONE TO HURT US"?
srsly ann, do u mn it?!?
WITH ALL OF MY HEART.
OF COURSE WE FORGIVE YOU.
cn u 4gv us???

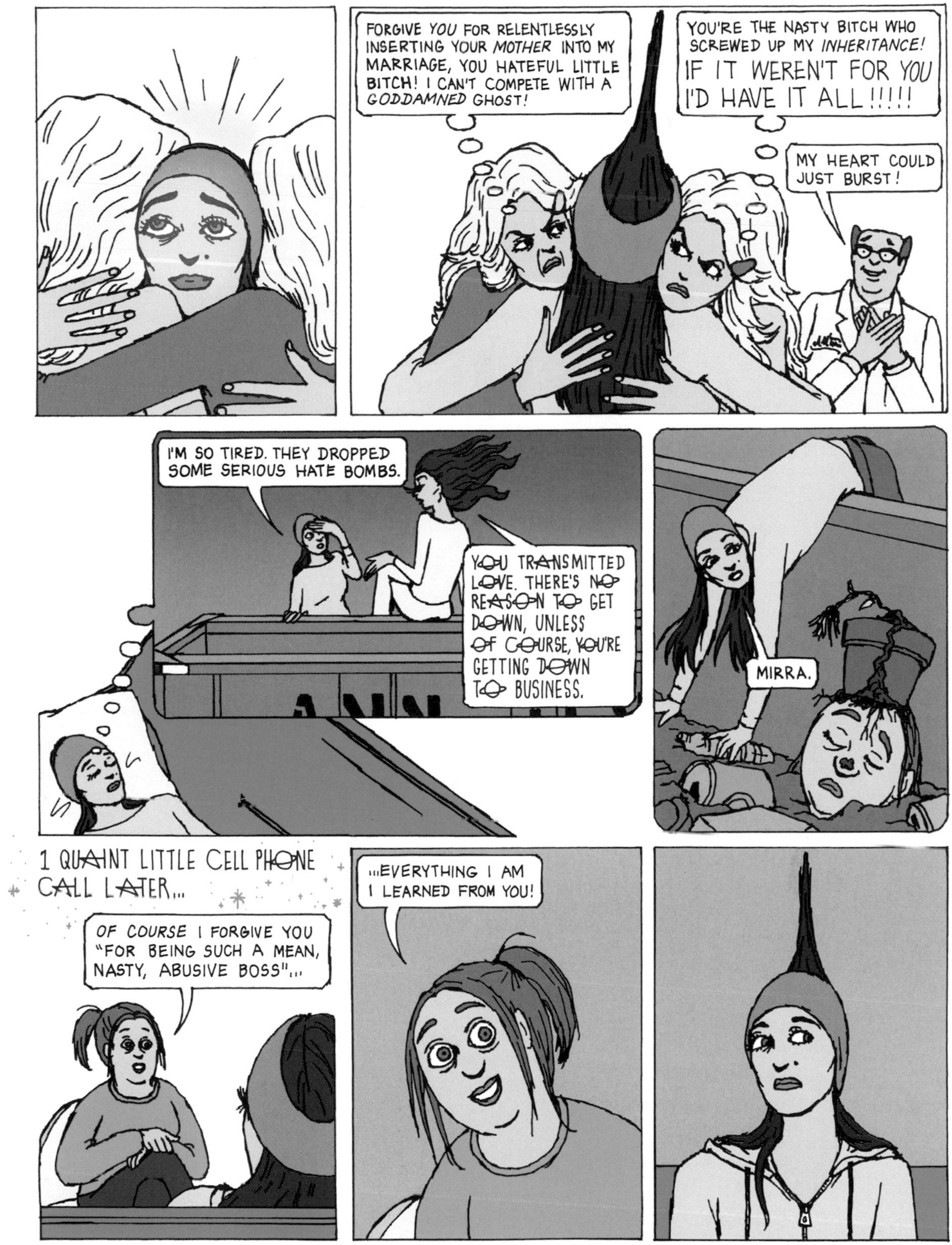
FORGIVE YOU FOR RELENTLESSLY INSERTING YOUR MOTHER INTO MY MARRIAGE, YOU HATEFUL LITTLE BITCH! I CAN'T COMPETE WITH A GODDAMNED GHOST!
YOU'RE THE NASTY BITCH WHO SCREWED UP MY INHERITANCE! IF IT WEREN'T FOR YOU I'D HAVE IT ALL!!!!!
MY HEART COULD JUST BURST!
I'M SO TIRED. THEY DROPPED SOME SERIOUS HATE BOMBS.
YOU TRANSMITTED LOVE. THERE'S NO REASON TO GET DOWN, UNLESS OF COURSE, YOU'RE GETTING DOWN TO BUSINESS.
MIRRA.
1 QUAINT LITTLE CELL PHONE CALL LATER...
OF COURSE I FORGIVE YOU "FOR BEING SUCH A MEAN, NASTY, ABUSIVE BOSS"...
...EVERYTHING I AM I LEARNED FROM YOU!

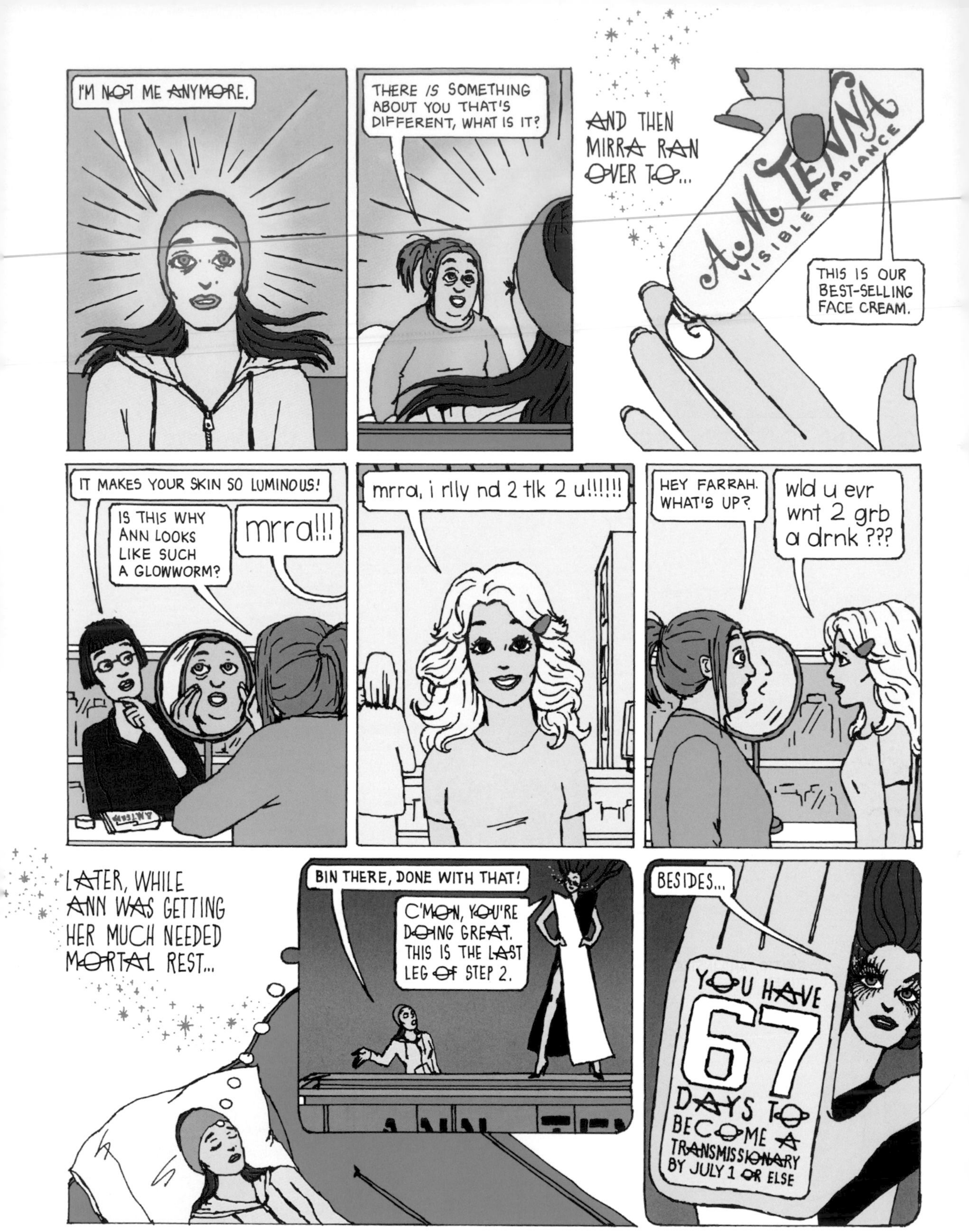
I'M NOT ME ANYMORE.
THERE IS SOMETHING ABOUT YOU THAT'S DIFFERENT, WHAT IS IT?
AND THEN MIRRA RAN OVER TO...
A.M. TENNA VISIBLE RADIANCE
THIS IS OUR BEST-SELLING FACE CREAM.
IT MAKES YOUR SKIN SO LUMINOUS!
IS THIS WHY ANN LOOKS LIKE SUCH A GLOWWORM?
mrra!!!
mrra, i rlly nd 2 tlk 2 u!!!!!!
HEY FARRAH. WHAT'S UP?
wld u evr wnt 2 grb a drnk ???
LATER, WHILE ANN WAS GETTING HER MUCH NEEDED MORTAL REST...
BIN THERE, DONE WITH THAT!
C'MON, YOU'RE DOING GREAT. THIS IS THE LAST LEG OF STEP 2.
BESIDES...
YOU HAVE 67 DAYS TO BECOME A TRANSMISSIONARY BY JULY 1 OR ELSE

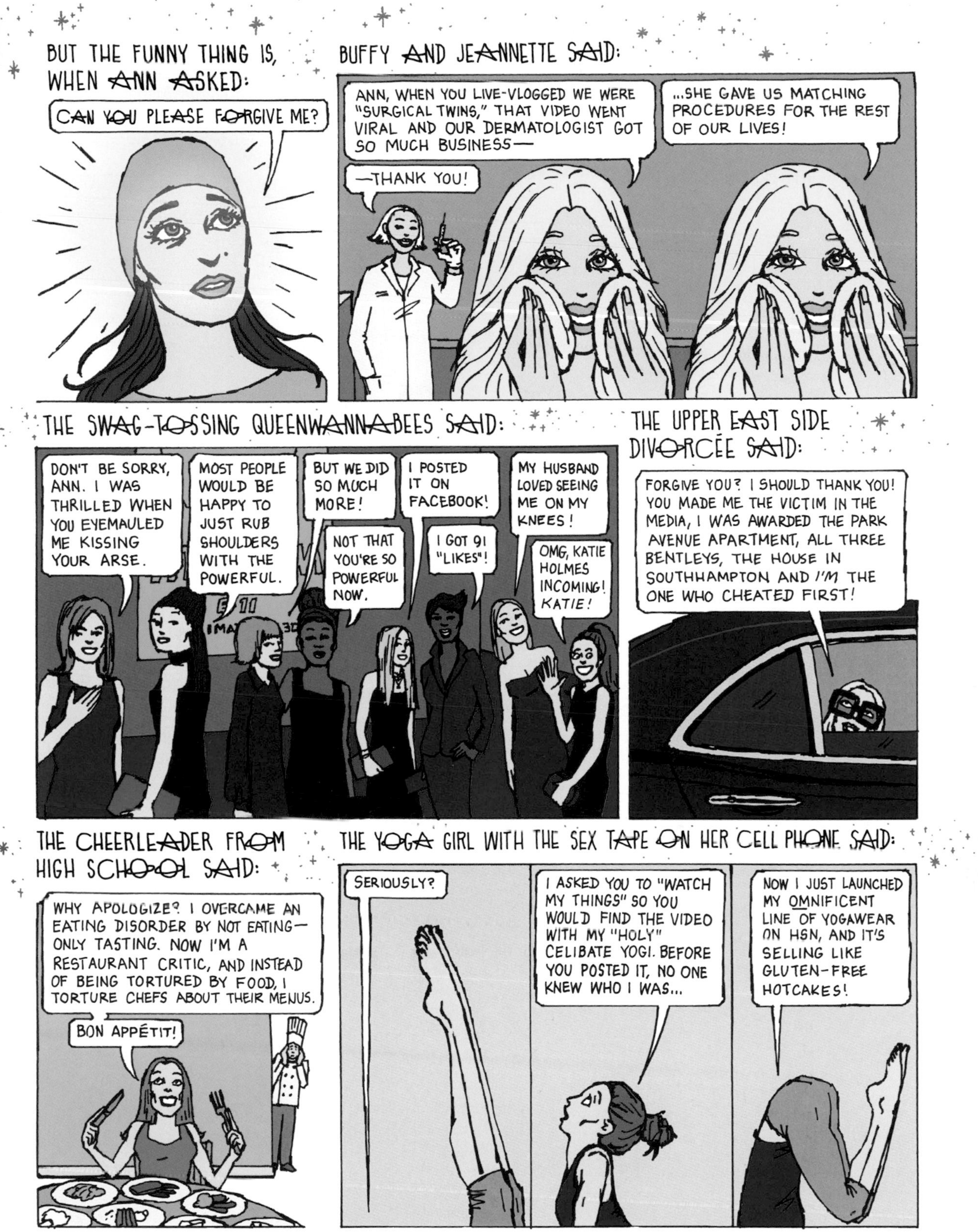
BUT THE FUNNY THING IS, WHEN ANN ASKED:
CAN YOU PLEASE FORGIVE ME?
BUFFY AND JEANNETTE SAID:
ANN, WHEN YOU LIVE-VLOGGED WE WERE "SURGICAL TWINS," THAT VIDEO WENT VIRAL AND OUR DERMATOLOGIST GOT SO MUCH BUSINESS—
—THANK YOU!
...SHE GAVE US MATCHING PROCEDURES FOR THE REST OF OUR LIVES!
THE SWAG-TOSSING QUEENWANNABEES SAID:
DON'T BE SORRY, ANN. I WAS THRILLED WHEN YOU EYEMAULED ME KISSING YOUR ARSE.
MOST PEOPLE WOULD BE HAPPY TO JUST RUB SHOULDERS WITH THE POWERFUL.
BUT WE DID SO MUCH MORE!
NOT THAT YOU'RE SO POWERFUL NOW.
I POSTED IT ON FACEBOOK!
I GOT 91 "LIKES"!
MY HUSBAND LOVED SEEING ME ON MY KNEES!
OMG, KATIE HOLMES INCOMING! KATIE!
THE UPPER EAST SIDE DIVORCÉE SAID:
FORGIVE YOU? I SHOULD THANK YOU! YOU MADE ME THE VICTIM IN THE MEDIA, I WAS AWARDED THE PARK AVENUE APARTMENT, ALL THREE BENTLEYS, THE HOUSE IN SOUTHHAMPTON AND I'M THE ONE WHO CHEATED FIRST!
THE CHEERLEADER FROM HIGH SCHOOL SAID:
WHY APOLOGIZE? I OVERCAME AN EATING DISORDER BY NOT EATING—ONLY TASTING. NOW I'M A RESTAURANT CRITIC, AND INSTEAD OF BEING TORTURED BY FOOD, I TORTURE CHEFS ABOUT THEIR MENUS.
BON APPÉTIT!
THE YOGA GIRL WITH THE SEX TAPE ON HER CELL PHONE SAID:
SERIOUSLY?
I ASKED YOU TO "WATCH MY THINGS" SO YOU WOULD FIND THE VIDEO WITH MY "HOLY" CELIBATE YOGI. BEFORE YOU POSTED IT, NO ONE KNEW WHO I WAS...
NOW I JUST LAUNCHED MY OMNIFICENT LINE OF YOGAWEAR ON HSN, AND IT'S SELLING LIKE GLUTEN-FREE HOTCAKES!

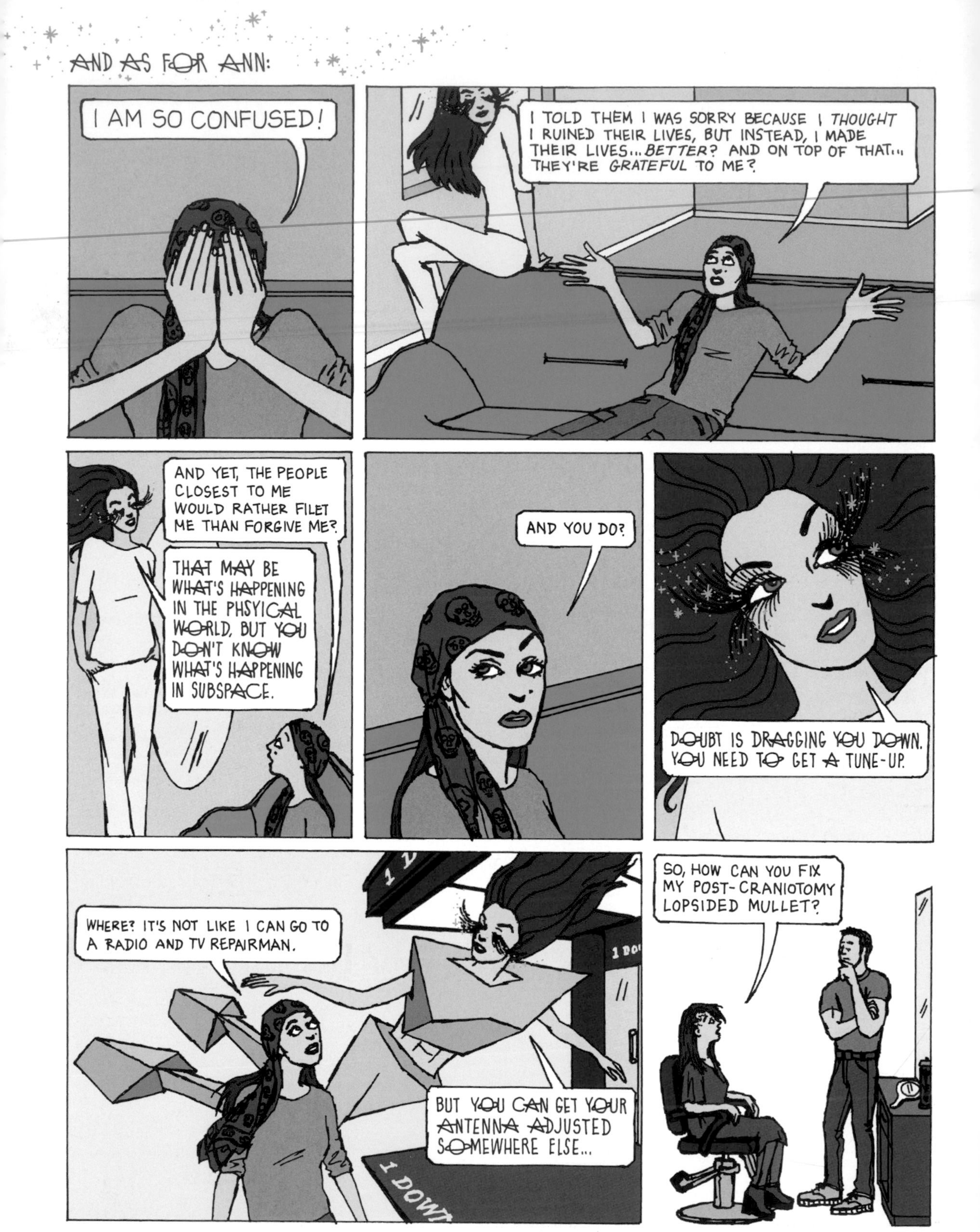
AND AS FOR ANN:
I AM SO CONFUSED!
I TOLD THEM I WAS SORRY BECAUSE I THOUGHT I RUINED THEIR LIVES, BUT INSTEAD, I MADE THEIR LIVES... BETTER? AND ON TOP OF THAT... THEY'RE GRATEFUL TO ME?
AND YET, THE PEOPLE CLOSEST TO ME WOULD RATHER FILET ME THAN FORGIVE ME?
THAT MAY BE WHAT'S HAPPENING IN THE PHSYICAL WORLD, BUT YOU DON'T KNOW WHAT'S HAPPENING IN SUBSPACE.
AND YOU DO?
DOUBT IS DRAGGING YOU DOWN. YOU NEED TO GET A TUNE-UP.
WHERE? IT'S NOT LIKE I CAN GO TO A RADIO AND TV REPAIRMAN.
BUT YOU CAN GET YOUR ANTENNA ADJUSTED SOMEWHERE ELSE...
SO, HOW CAN YOU FIX MY POST-CRANIOTOMY LOPSIDED MULLET?

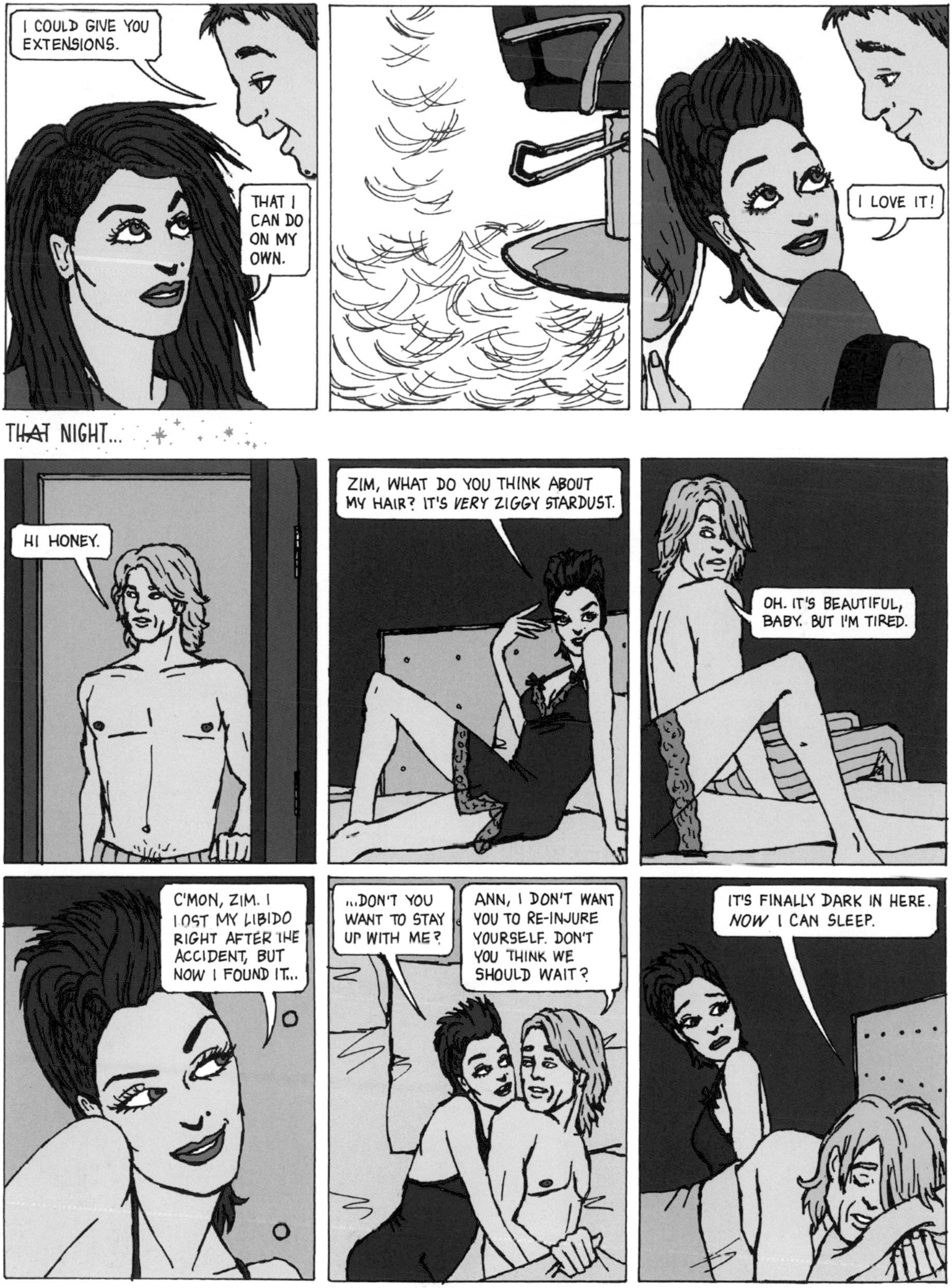
I COULD GIVE YOU EXTENSIONS.
THAT I CAN DO ON MY OWN.
I LOVE IT!
THAT NIGHT...
HI HONEY.
ZIM, WHAT DO YOU THINK ABOUT MY HAIR? IT'S VERY ZIGGY STARDUST.
OH. IT'S BEAUTIFUL, BABY. BUT I'M TIRED.
C'MON, ZIM. I LOST MY LIBIDO RIGHT AFTER THE ACCIDENT, BUT NOW I FOUND IT...
...DON'T YOU WANT TO STAY UP WITH ME?
ANN, I DON'T WANT YOU TO RE-INJURE YOURSELF. DON'T YOU THINK WE SHOULD WAIT?
IT'S FINALLY DARK IN HERE. NOW I CAN SLEEP.

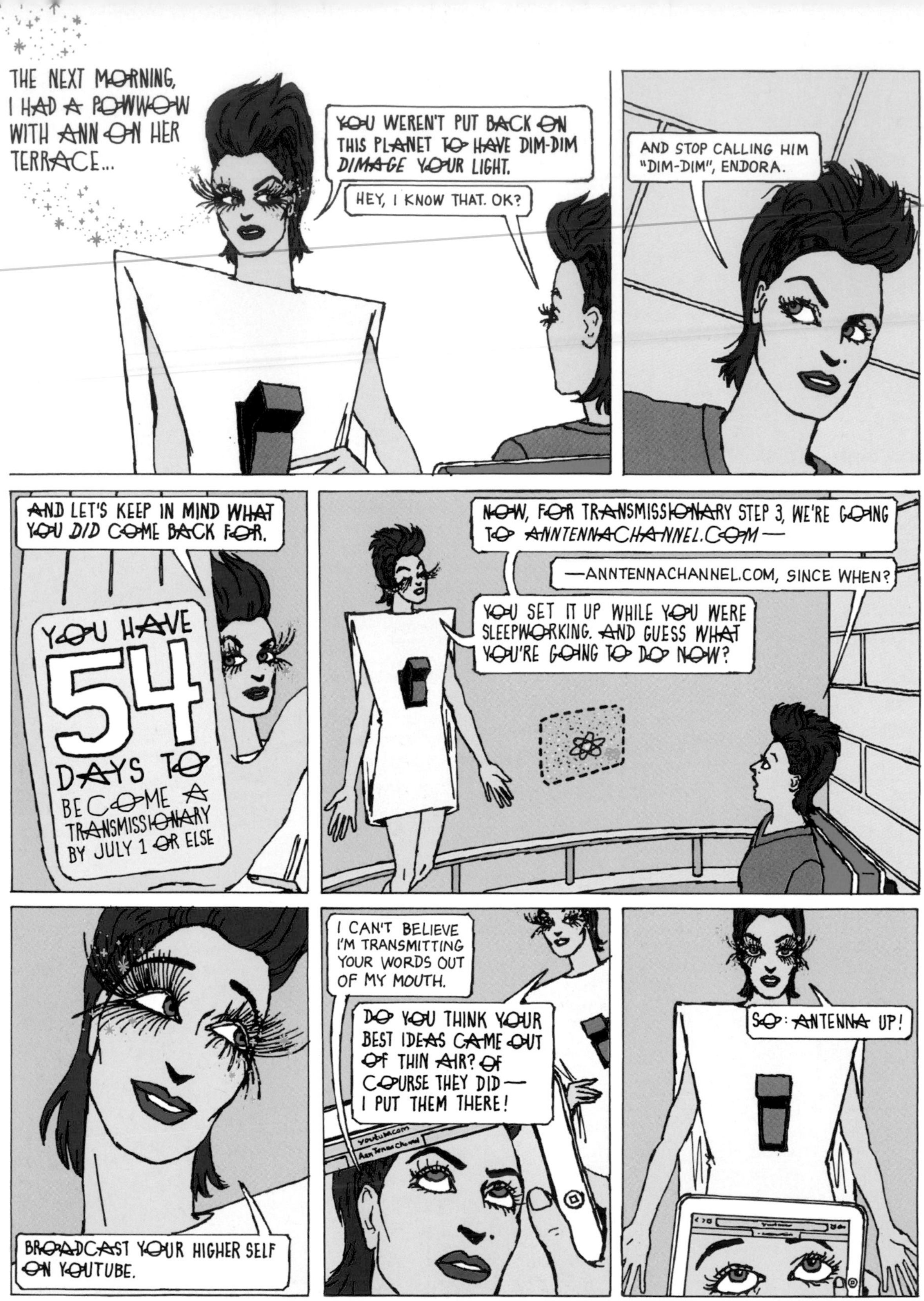
THE NEXT MORNING, I HAD A POWWOW WITH ANN ON HER TERRACE...
YOU WEREN'T PUT BACK ON THIS PLANET TO HAVE DIM-DIM *DIMAGE* YOUR LIGHT.
HEY, I KNOW THAT. OK?
AND STOP CALLING HIM "DIM-DIM", ENDORA.
AND LET'S KEEP IN MIND WHAT YOU *DID* COME BACK FOR.
YOU HAVE 54 DAYS TO BECOME A TRANSMISSIONARY BY JULY 1 OR ELSE
NOW, FOR TRANSMISSIONARY STEP 3, WE'RE GOING TO *ANNTENNACHANNEL.COM*—
—ANNTENNACHANNEL.COM, SINCE WHEN?
YOU SET IT UP WHILE YOU WERE SLEEPWORKING. AND GUESS WHAT YOU'RE GOING TO DO NOW?
BROADCAST YOUR HIGHER SELF ON YOUTUBE.
I CAN'T BELIEVE I'M TRANSMITTING YOUR WORDS OUT OF MY MOUTH.
DO YOU THINK YOUR BEST IDEAS CAME OUT OF THIN AIR? OF COURSE THEY DID— I PUT THEM THERE!
SO: ANTENNA UP!

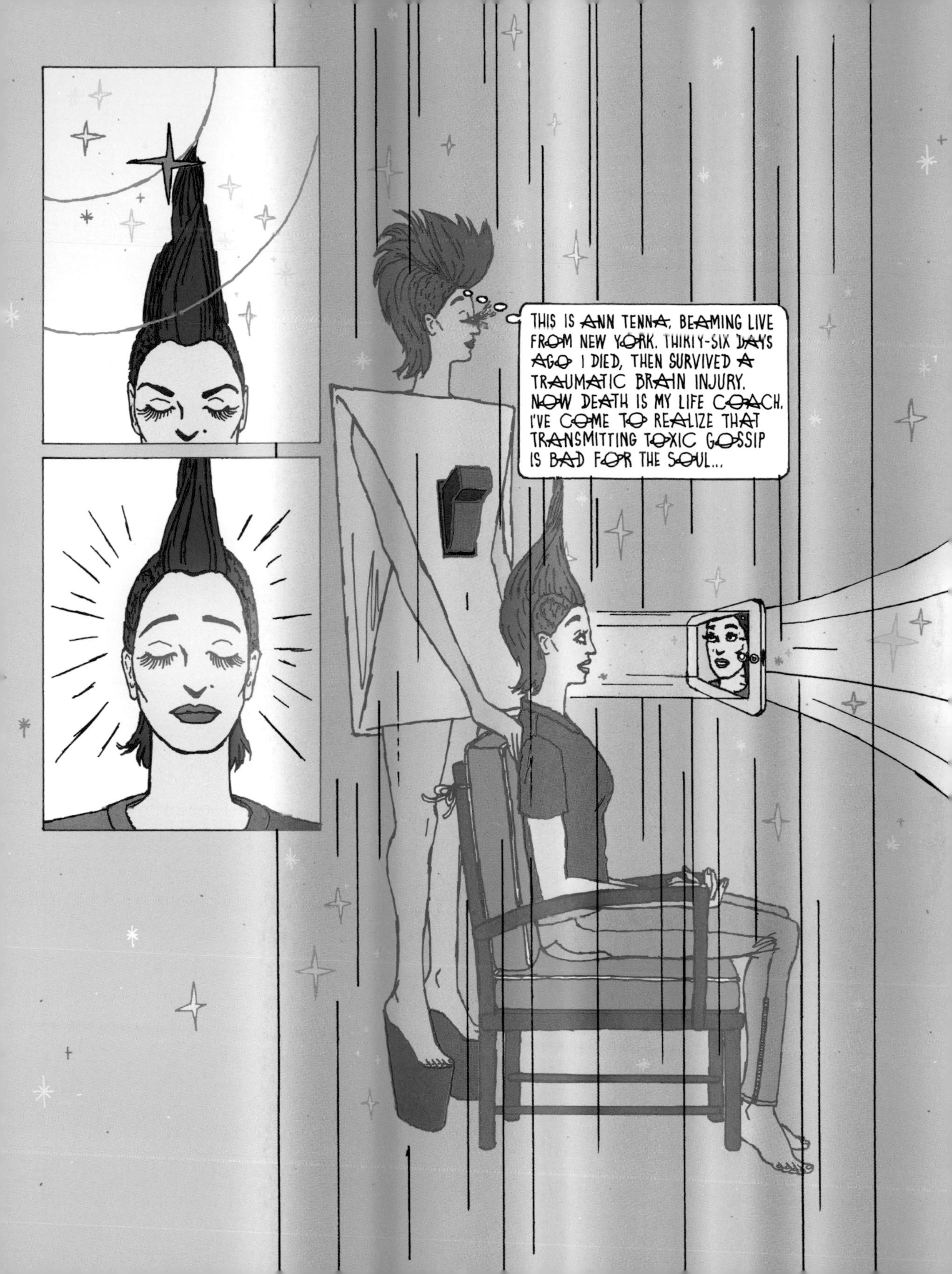
THIS IS ANN TENNA, BEAMING LIVE FROM NEW YORK. THIRTY-SIX DAYS AGO I DIED, THEN SURVIVED A TRAUMATIC BRAIN INJURY. NOW DEATH IS MY LIFE COACH. I'VE COME TO REALIZE THAT TRANSMITTING TOXIC GOSSIP IS BAD FOR THE SOUL...

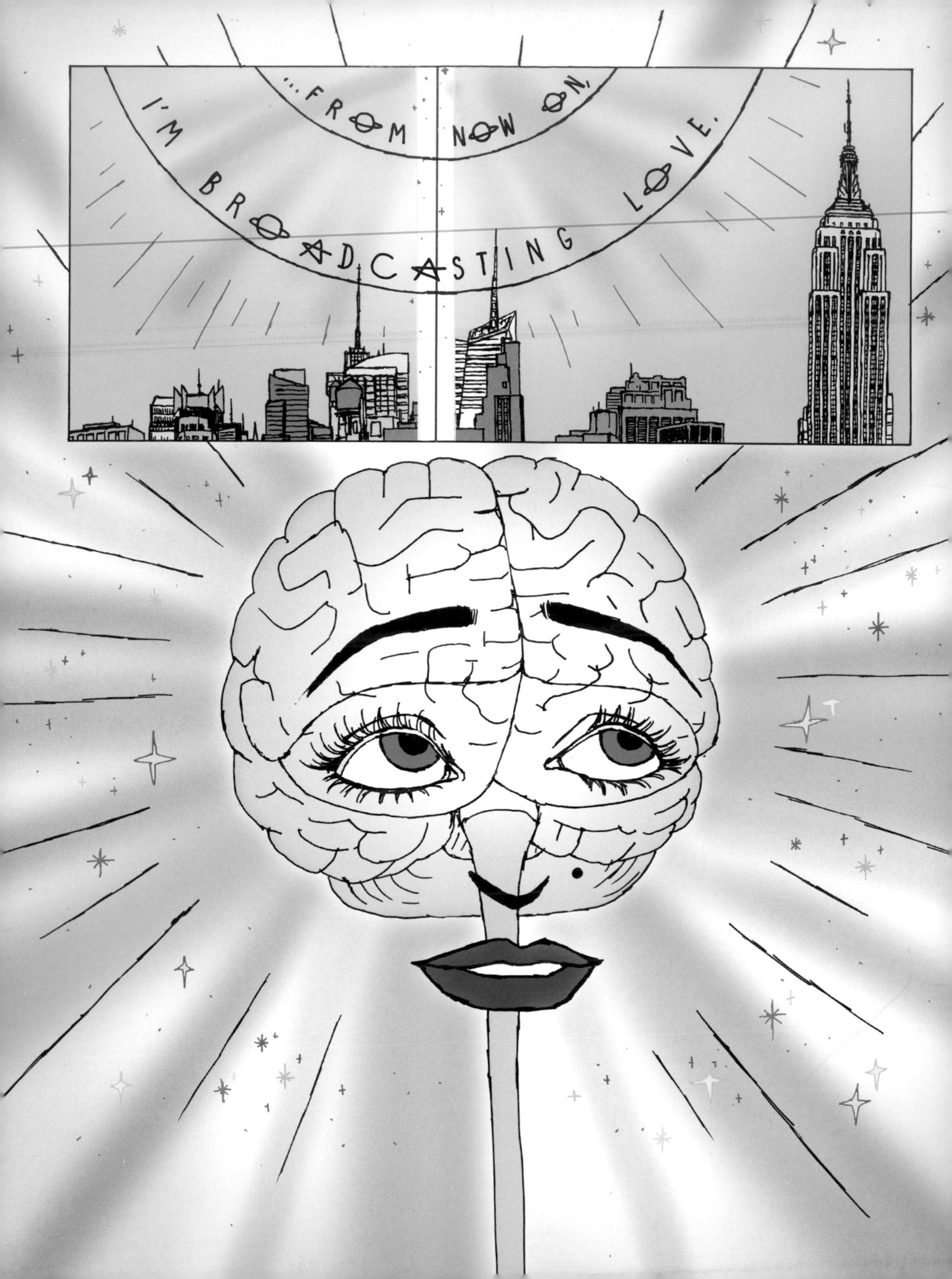
...FROM NOW ON,
I'M BROADCASTING LOVE.

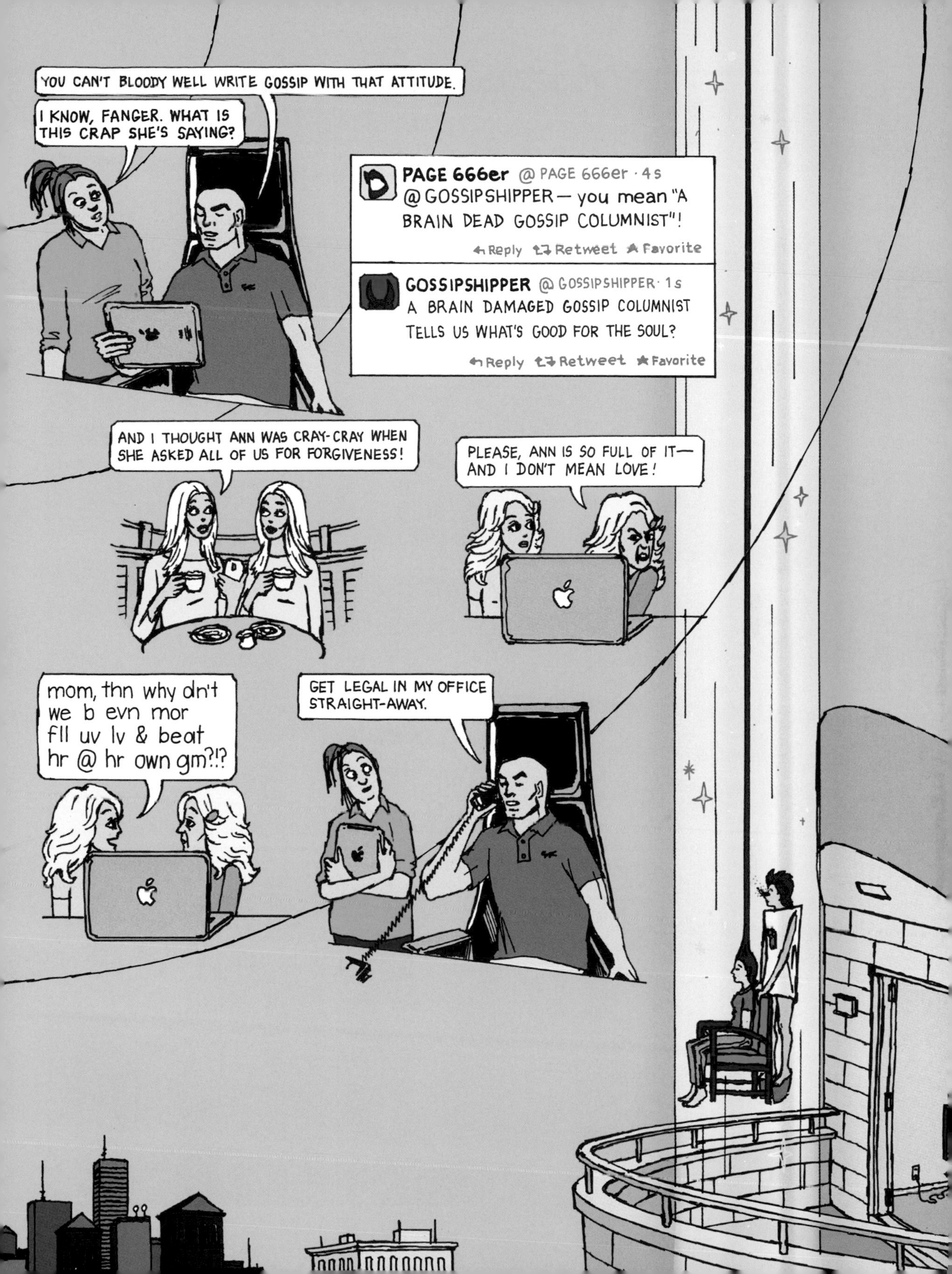

YOU CAN'T BLOODY WELL WRITE GOSSIP WITH THAT ATTITUDE.
I KNOW, FANGER. WHAT IS THIS CRAP SHE'S SAYING?
PAGE 666er @PAGE 666er · 4s
@GOSSIPSHIPPER — you mean "A BRAIN DEAD GOSSIP COLUMNIST"!
Reply Retweet Favorite
GOSSIPSHIPPER @GOSSIPSHIPPER · 1s
A BRAIN DAMAGED GOSSIP COLUMNIST TELLS US WHAT'S GOOD FOR THE SOUL?
Reply Retweet Favorite
AND I THOUGHT ANN WAS CRAY-CRAY WHEN SHE ASKED ALL OF US FOR FORGIVENESS!
PLEASE, ANN IS SO FULL OF IT— AND I DON'T MEAN LOVE!
mom, thn why dn't we b evn mor fll uv lv & beat hr @ hr own gm?!?
GET LEGAL IN MY OFFICE STRAIGHT-AWAY.

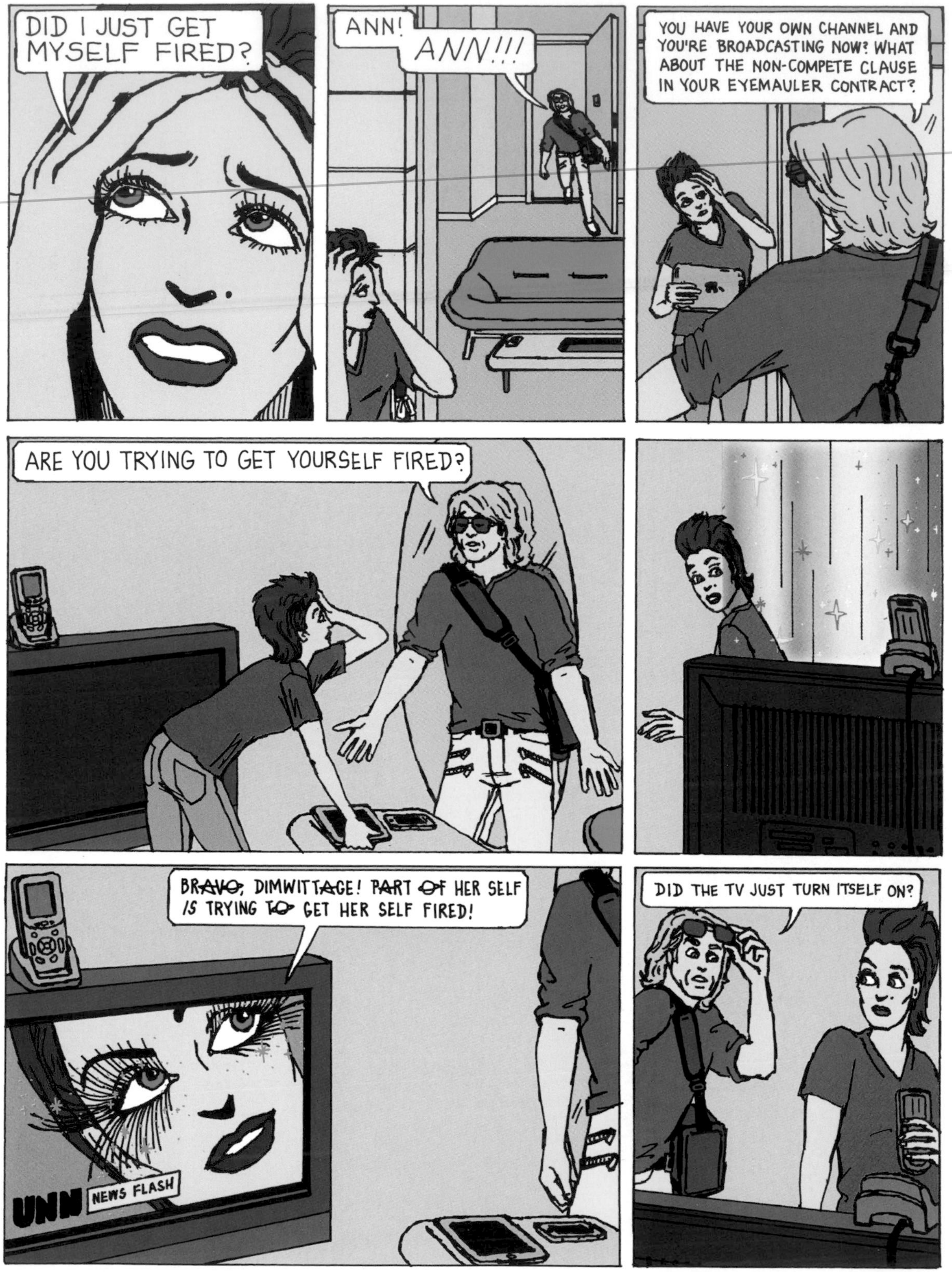
DID I JUST GET MYSELF FIRED?
ANN!
ANN!!!
YOU HAVE YOUR OWN CHANNEL AND YOU'RE BROADCASTING NOW? WHAT ABOUT THE NON-COMPETE CLAUSE IN YOUR EYEMAULER CONTRACT?
ARE YOU TRYING TO GET YOURSELF FIRED?
BRAVO, DIMWITTAGE! PART OF HER SELF IS TRYING TO GET HER SELF FIRED!
UNN NEWS FLASH
DID THE TV JUST TURN ITSELF ON?

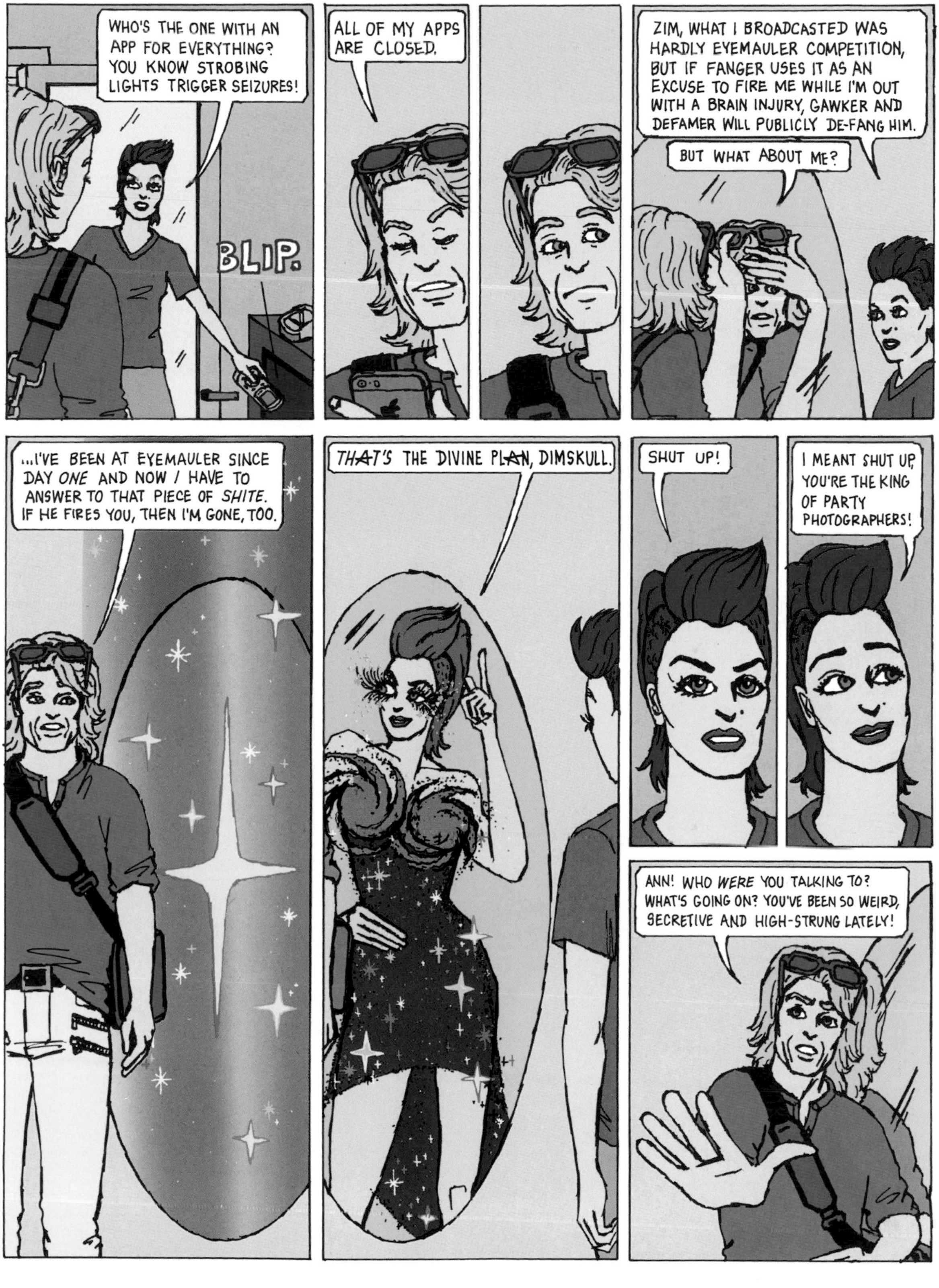

WHO'S THE ONE WITH AN APP FOR EVERYTHING? YOU KNOW STROBING LIGHTS TRIGGER SEIZURES!
BLIP.
ALL OF MY APPS ARE CLOSED.
ZIM, WHAT I BROADCASTED WAS HARDLY EYEMAULER COMPETITION, BUT IF FANGER USES IT AS AN EXCUSE TO FIRE ME WHILE I'M OUT WITH A BRAIN INJURY, GAWKER AND DEFAMER WILL PUBLICLY DE-FANG HIM.
BUT WHAT ABOUT ME?
...I'VE BEEN AT EYEMAULER SINCE DAY *ONE* AND NOW *I* HAVE TO ANSWER TO THAT PIECE OF *SHITE*. IF HE FIRES YOU, THEN I'M GONE, TOO.
THAT'S THE DIVINE PLAN, DIMSKULL.
SHUT UP!
I MEANT SHUT UP, YOU'RE THE KING OF PARTY PHOTOGRAPHERS!
ANN! WHO *WERE* YOU TALKING TO? WHAT'S GOING ON? YOU'VE BEEN SO WEIRD, SECRETIVE AND HIGH-STRUNG LATELY!

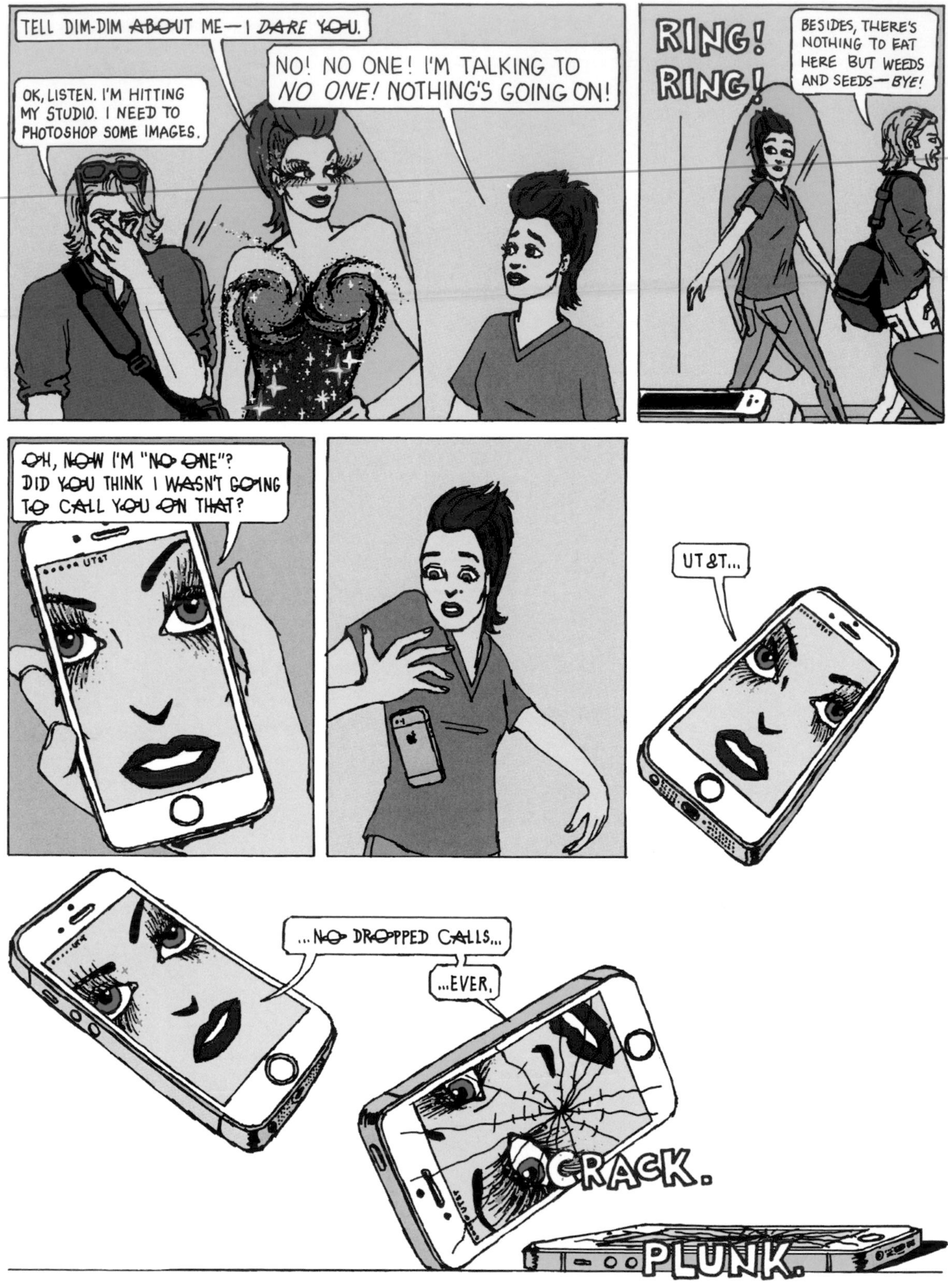
TELL DIM-DIM ABOUT ME—I DARE YOU.
OK, LISTEN. I'M HITTING MY STUDIO. I NEED TO PHOTOSHOP SOME IMAGES.
NO! NO ONE! I'M TALKING TO NO ONE! NOTHING'S GOING ON!
RING! RING!
BESIDES, THERE'S NOTHING TO EAT HERE BUT WEEDS AND SEEDS—BYE!
OH, NOW I'M "NO ONE"? DID YOU THINK I WASN'T GOING TO CALL YOU ON THAT?
UT&T
UT&T...
...NO DROPPED CALLS...
...EVER.
CRACK.
PLUNK.

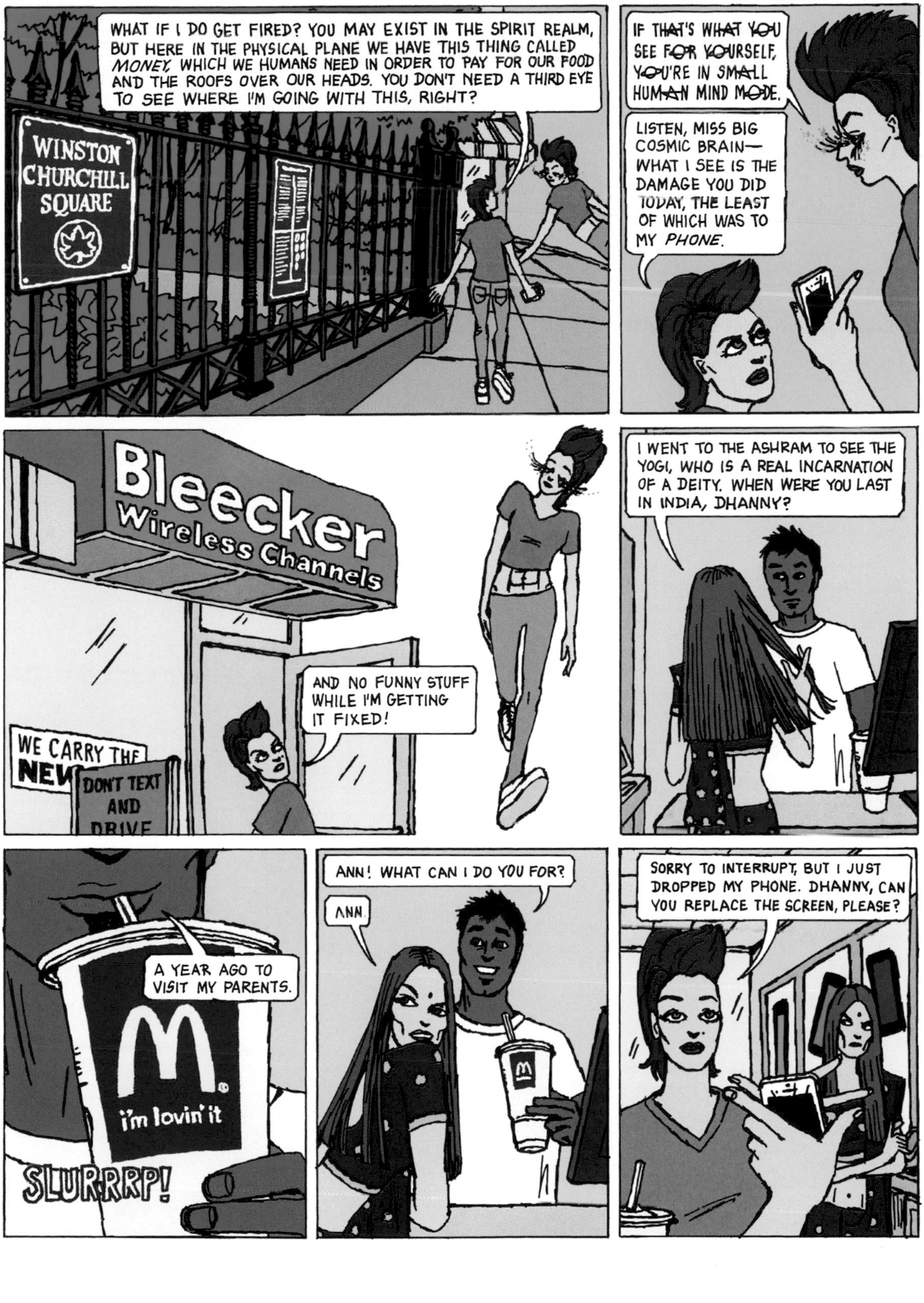
WHAT IF I DO GET FIRED? YOU MAY EXIST IN THE SPIRIT REALM, BUT HERE IN THE PHYSICAL PLANE WE HAVE THIS THING CALLED *MONEY,* WHICH WE HUMANS NEED IN ORDER TO PAY FOR OUR FOOD AND THE ROOFS OVER OUR HEADS. YOU DON'T NEED A THIRD EYE TO SEE WHERE I'M GOING WITH THIS, RIGHT?
WINSTON CHURCHILL SQUARE
IF THAT'S WHAT YOU SEE FOR YOURSELF, YOU'RE IN SMALL HUMAN MIND MODE.
LISTEN, MISS BIG COSMIC BRAIN— WHAT I SEE IS THE DAMAGE YOU DID TODAY, THE LEAST OF WHICH WAS TO MY *PHONE.*
Bleecker Wireless Channels
AND NO FUNNY STUFF WHILE I'M GETTING IT FIXED!
WE CARRY THE NEW
DON'T TEXT AND DRIVE
I WENT TO THE ASHRAM TO SEE THE YOGI, WHO IS A REAL INCARNATION OF A DEITY. WHEN WERE YOU LAST IN INDIA, DHANNY?
A YEAR AGO TO VISIT MY PARENTS.
i'm lovin' it
SLURRRP!
ANN! WHAT CAN I DO YOU FOR?
ANN.
SORRY TO INTERRUPT, BUT I JUST DROPPED MY PHONE. DHANNY, CAN YOU REPLACE THE SCREEN, PLEASE?

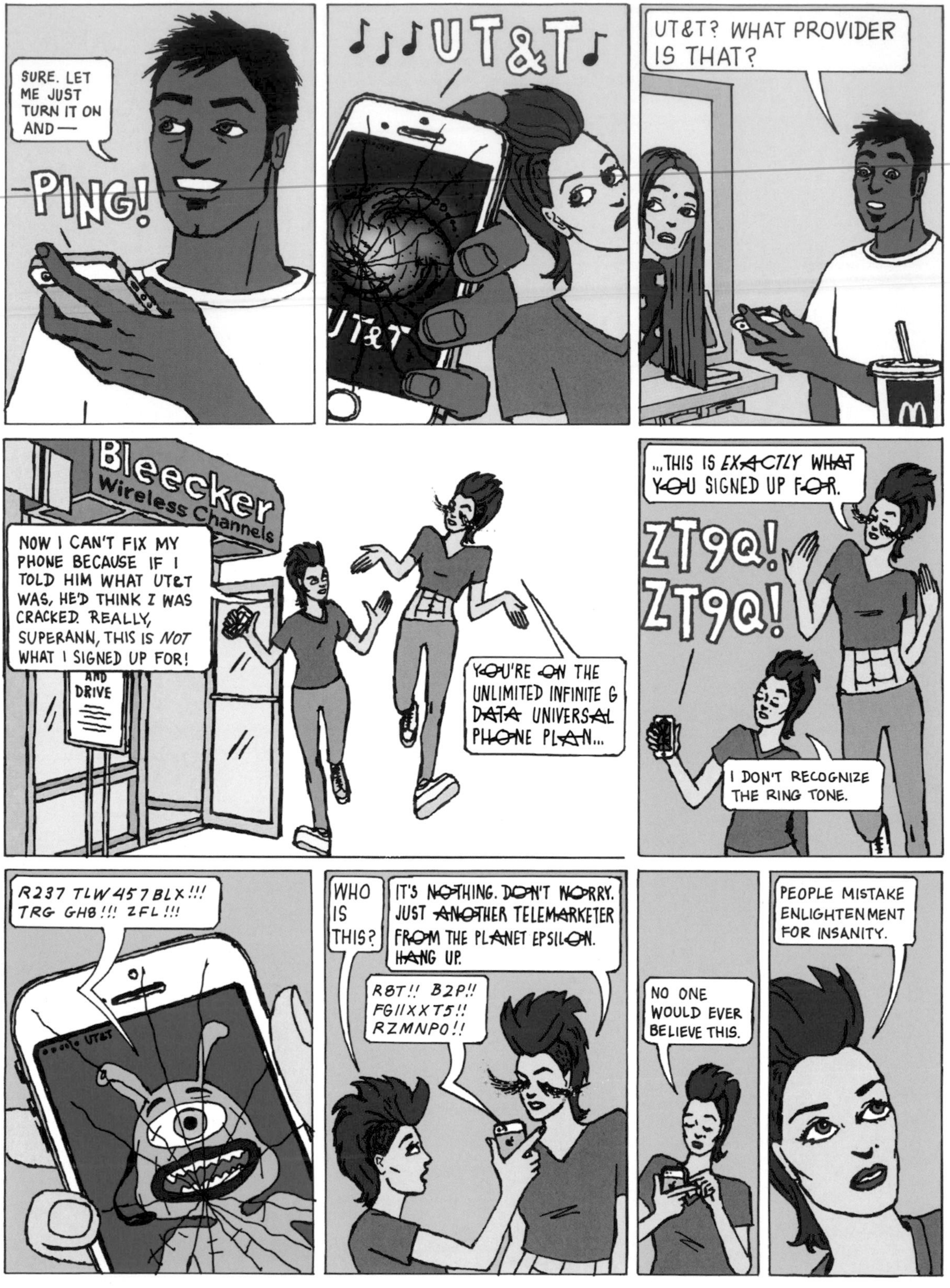

SURE. LET ME JUST TURN IT ON AND—
PING!
UT&T
UT&T
UT&T? WHAT PROVIDER IS THAT?
Bleecker Wireless Channels
NOW I CAN'T FIX MY PHONE BECAUSE IF I TOLD HIM WHAT UT&T WAS, HE'D THINK I WAS CRACKED. REALLY, SUPERANN, THIS IS *NOT* WHAT I SIGNED UP FOR!
AND DRIVE
YOU'RE ON THE UNLIMITED INFINITE G DATA UNIVERSAL PHONE PLAN...
...THIS IS *EXACTLY* WHAT YOU SIGNED UP FOR.
ZT9Q! ZT9Q!
I DON'T RECOGNIZE THE RING TONE.
R237 TLW 457 BLX!!! TRG GHB!!! ZFL!!!
UT&T
WHO IS THIS?
IT'S NOTHING. DON'T WORRY. JUST ANOTHER TELEMARKETER FROM THE PLANET EPSILON. HANG UP.
R8T!! B2P!! FGIIXXT5!! RZMNPO!!
NO ONE WOULD EVER BELIEVE THIS.
PEOPLE MISTAKE ENLIGHTENMENT FOR INSANITY.

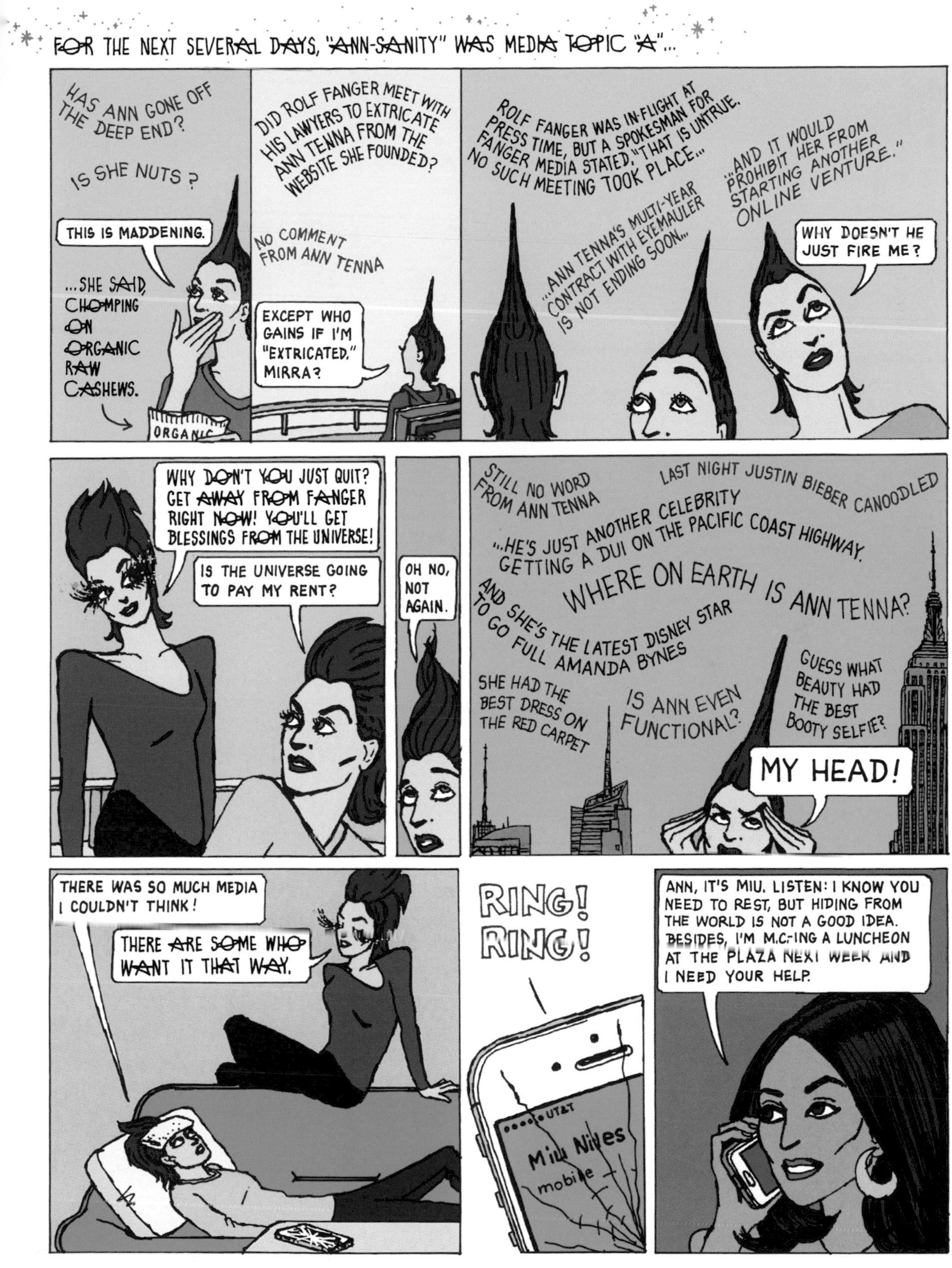

FOR THE NEXT SEVERAL DAYS, "ANN-SANITY" WAS MEDIA TOPIC "A"...
HAS ANN GONE OFF THE DEEP END?
IS SHE NUTS?
THIS IS MADDENING.
...SHE SAID, CHOMPING ON ORGANIC RAW CASHEWS.
ORGANIC
DID ROLF FANGER MEET WITH HIS LAWYERS TO EXTRICATE ANN TENNA FROM THE WEBSITE SHE FOUNDED?
NO COMMENT FROM ANN TENNA
EXCEPT WHO GAINS IF I'M "EXTRICATED," MIRRA?
ROLF FANGER WAS IN-FLIGHT AT PRESS TIME, BUT A SPOKESMAN FOR FANGER MEDIA STATED, "THAT IS UNTRUE. NO SUCH MEETING TOOK PLACE...
...ANN TENNA'S MULTI-YEAR CONTRACT WITH EYEMAULER IS NOT ENDING SOON...
...AND IT WOULD PROHIBIT HER FROM STARTING ANOTHER ONLINE VENTURE."
WHY DOESN'T HE JUST FIRE ME?
WHY DON'T YOU JUST QUIT? GET AWAY FROM FANGER RIGHT NOW! YOU'LL GET BLESSINGS FROM THE UNIVERSE!
IS THE UNIVERSE GOING TO PAY MY RENT?
OH NO, NOT AGAIN.
STILL NO WORD FROM ANN TENNA
LAST NIGHT JUSTIN BIEBER CANOODLED
...HE'S JUST ANOTHER CELEBRITY GETTING A DUI ON THE PACIFIC COAST HIGHWAY.
WHERE ON EARTH IS ANN TENNA?
AND SHE'S THE LATEST DISNEY STAR TO GO FULL AMANDA BYNES
SHE HAD THE BEST DRESS ON THE RED CARPET
IS ANN EVEN FUNCTIONAL?
GUESS WHAT BEAUTY HAD THE BEST BOOTY SELFIE?
MY HEAD!
THERE WAS SO MUCH MEDIA I COULDN'T THINK!
THERE ARE SOME WHO WANT IT THAT WAY.
RING! RING!
AT&T
Miu Niles
mobile
ANN, IT'S MIU. LISTEN: I KNOW YOU NEED TO REST, BUT HIDING FROM THE WORLD IS NOT A GOOD IDEA. BESIDES, I'M M.C.-ING A LUNCHEON AT THE PLAZA NEXT WEEK AND I NEED YOUR HELP.

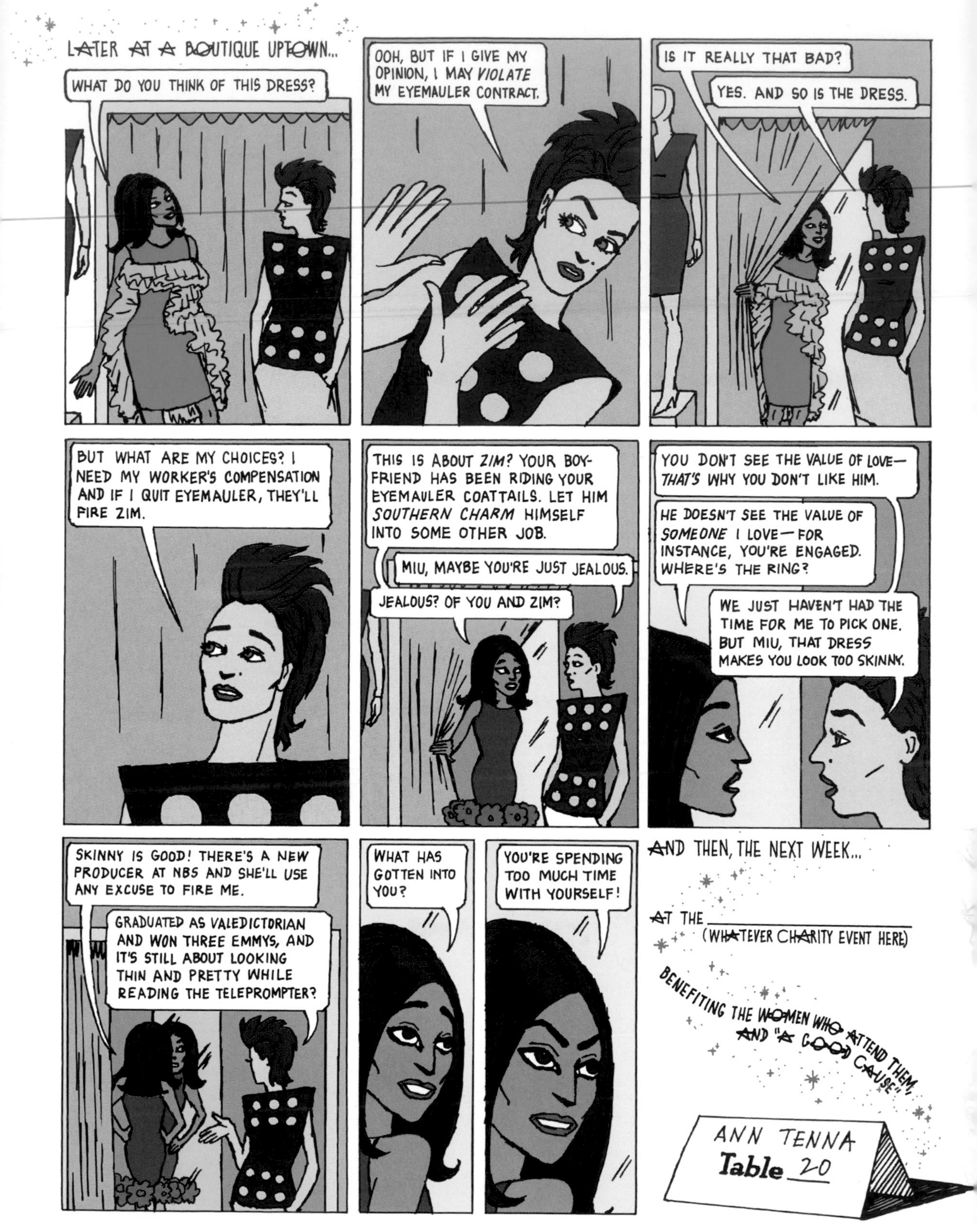
LATER AT A BOUTIQUE UPTOWN...
WHAT DO YOU THINK OF THIS DRESS?
OOH, BUT IF I GIVE MY OPINION, I MAY VIOLATE MY EYEMAULER CONTRACT.
IS IT REALLY THAT BAD?
YES. AND SO IS THE DRESS.
BUT WHAT ARE MY CHOICES? I NEED MY WORKER'S COMPENSATION AND IF I QUIT EYEMAULER, THEY'LL FIRE ZIM.
THIS IS ABOUT ZIM? YOUR BOY-FRIEND HAS BEEN RIDING YOUR EYEMAULER COATTAILS. LET HIM SOUTHERN CHARM HIMSELF INTO SOME OTHER JOB.
MIU, MAYBE YOU'RE JUST JEALOUS.
JEALOUS? OF YOU AND ZIM?
YOU DON'T SEE THE VALUE OF LOVE— THAT'S WHY YOU DON'T LIKE HIM.
HE DOESN'T SEE THE VALUE OF SOMEONE I LOVE—FOR INSTANCE, YOU'RE ENGAGED. WHERE'S THE RING?
WE JUST HAVEN'T HAD THE TIME FOR ME TO PICK ONE. BUT MIU, THAT DRESS MAKES YOU LOOK TOO SKINNY.
SKINNY IS GOOD! THERE'S A NEW PRODUCER AT NBS AND SHE'LL USE ANY EXCUSE TO FIRE ME.
GRADUATED AS VALEDICTORIAN AND WON THREE EMMYS, AND IT'S STILL ABOUT LOOKING THIN AND PRETTY WHILE READING THE TELEPROMPTER?
WHAT HAS GOTTEN INTO YOU?
YOU'RE SPENDING TOO MUCH TIME WITH YOURSELF!
AND THEN, THE NEXT WEEK...
AT THE ______
(WHATEVER CHARITY EVENT HERE)
BENEFITING THE WOMEN WHO ATTEND THEM, AND "A GOOD CAUSE"
ANN TENNA
Table 20

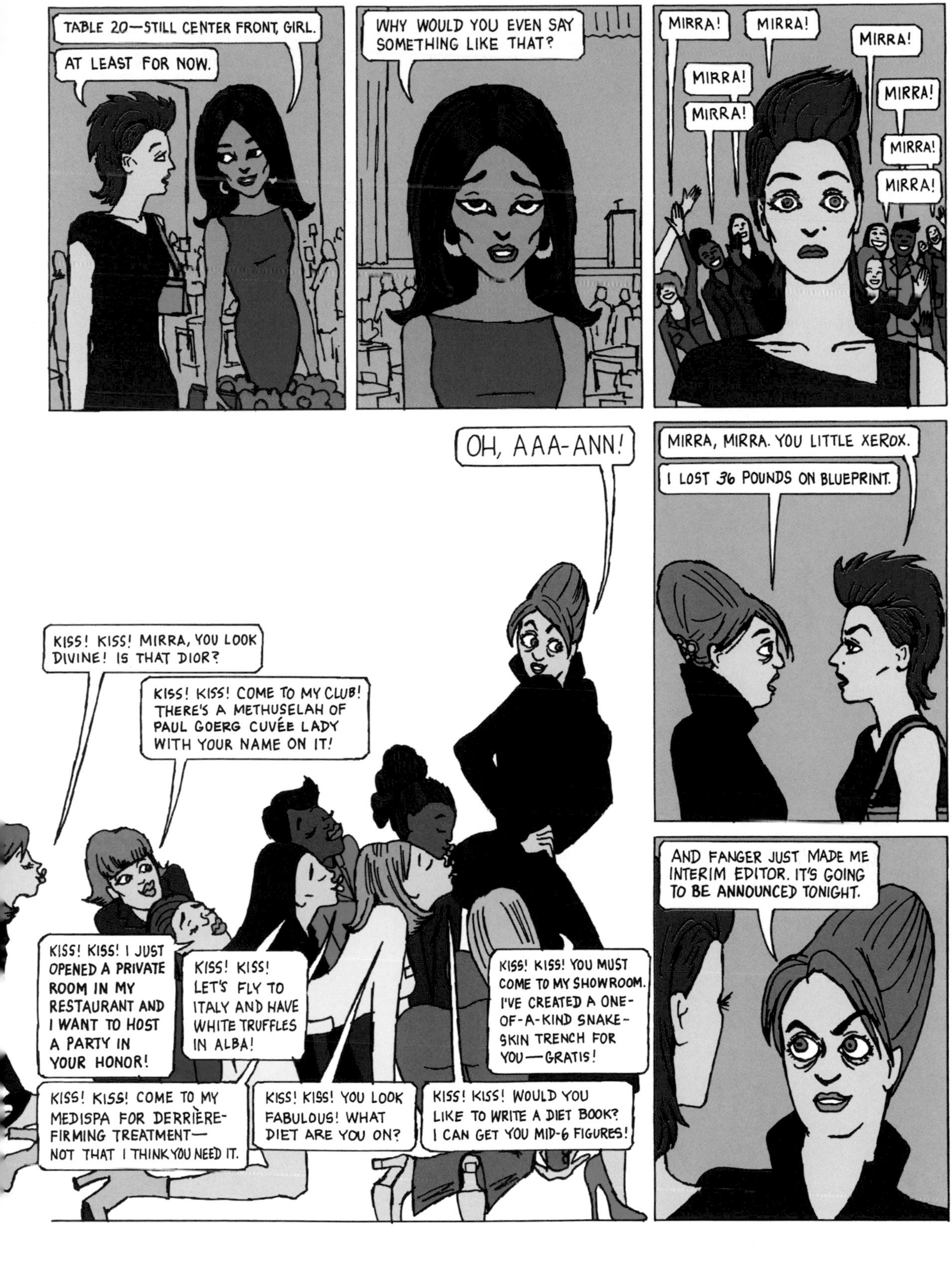
TABLE 20—STILL CENTER FRONT, GIRL.
AT LEAST FOR NOW.
WHY WOULD YOU EVEN SAY SOMETHING LIKE THAT?
MIRRA!
MIRRA!
MIRRA!
MIRRA!
MIRRA!
MIRRA!
MIRRA!
MIRRA!
OH, AAA-ANN!
KISS! KISS! MIRRA, YOU LOOK DIVINE! IS THAT DIOR?
KISS! KISS! COME TO MY CLUB! THERE'S A METHUSELAH OF PAUL GOERG CUVÉE LADY WITH YOUR NAME ON IT!
KISS! KISS! I JUST OPENED A PRIVATE ROOM IN MY RESTAURANT AND I WANT TO HOST A PARTY IN YOUR HONOR!
KISS! KISS! LET'S FLY TO ITALY AND HAVE WHITE TRUFFLES IN ALBA!
KISS! KISS! YOU MUST COME TO MY SHOWROOM. I'VE CREATED A ONE-OF-A-KIND SNAKE-SKIN TRENCH FOR YOU—GRATIS!
KISS! KISS! COME TO MY MEDISPA FOR DERRIÈRE-FIRMING TREATMENT—NOT THAT I THINK YOU NEED IT.
KISS! KISS! YOU LOOK FABULOUS! WHAT DIET ARE YOU ON?
KISS! KISS! WOULD YOU LIKE TO WRITE A DIET BOOK? I CAN GET YOU MID-6 FIGURES!
MIRRA, MIRRA. YOU LITTLE XEROX.
I LOST 36 POUNDS ON BLUEPRINT.
AND FANGER JUST MADE ME INTERIM EDITOR. IT'S GOING TO BE ANNOUNCED TONIGHT.

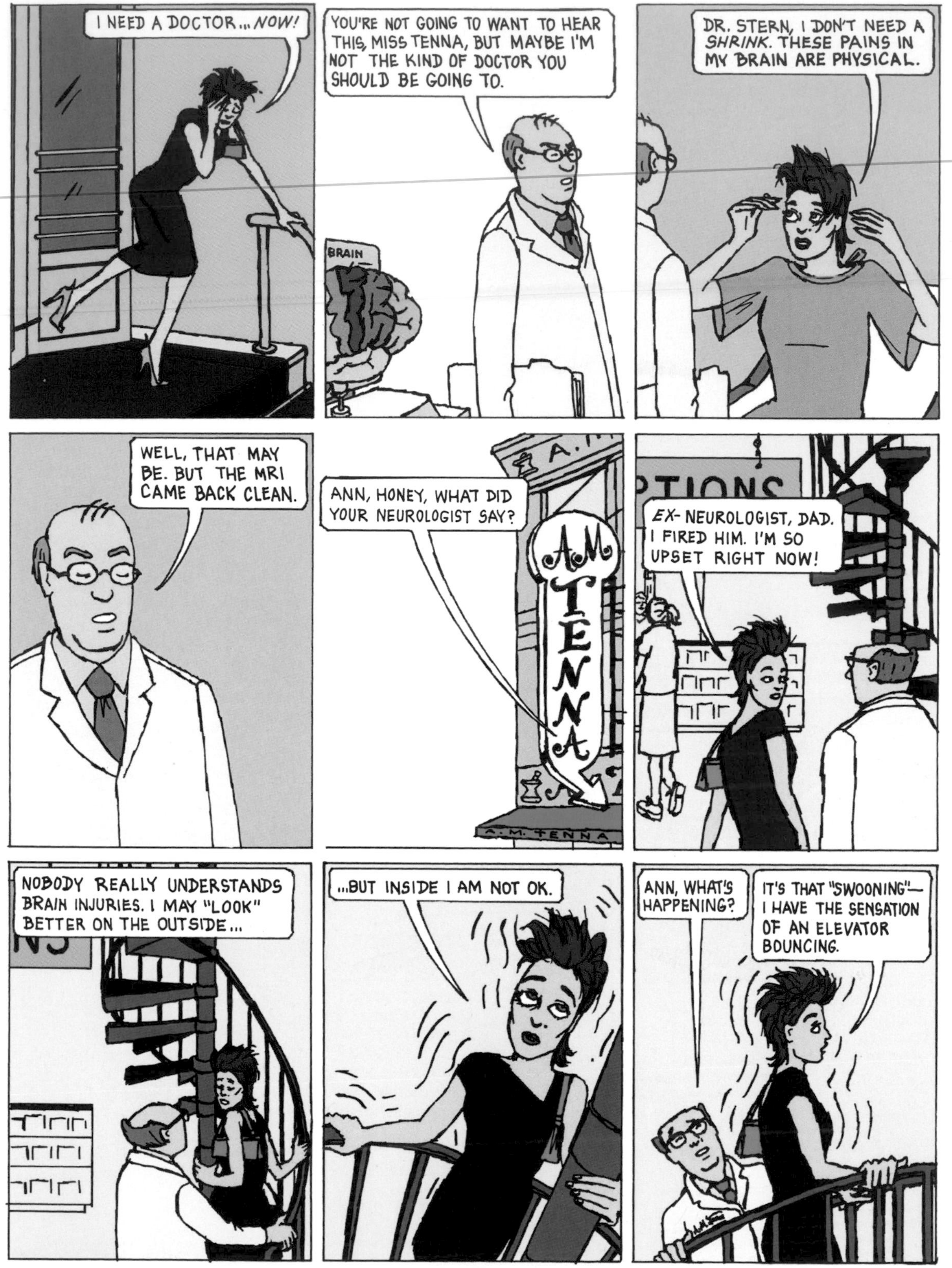
I NEED A DOCTOR... *NOW!*
YOU'RE NOT GOING TO WANT TO HEAR THIS, MISS TENNA, BUT MAYBE I'M NOT THE KIND OF DOCTOR YOU SHOULD BE GOING TO.
BRAIN
DR. STERN, I DON'T NEED A *SHRINK*. THESE PAINS IN MY BRAIN ARE PHYSICAL.
WELL, THAT MAY BE. BUT THE MRI CAME BACK CLEAN.
ANN, HONEY, WHAT DID YOUR NEUROLOGIST SAY?
A.M. TENNA
A.M. TENNA
EX- NEUROLOGIST, DAD. I FIRED HIM. I'M SO UPSET RIGHT NOW!
NOBODY REALLY UNDERSTANDS BRAIN INJURIES. I MAY "LOOK" BETTER ON THE OUTSIDE...
...BUT INSIDE I AM NOT OK.
ANN, WHAT'S HAPPENING?
IT'S THAT "SWOONING"— I HAVE THE SENSATION OF AN ELEVATOR BOUNCING.

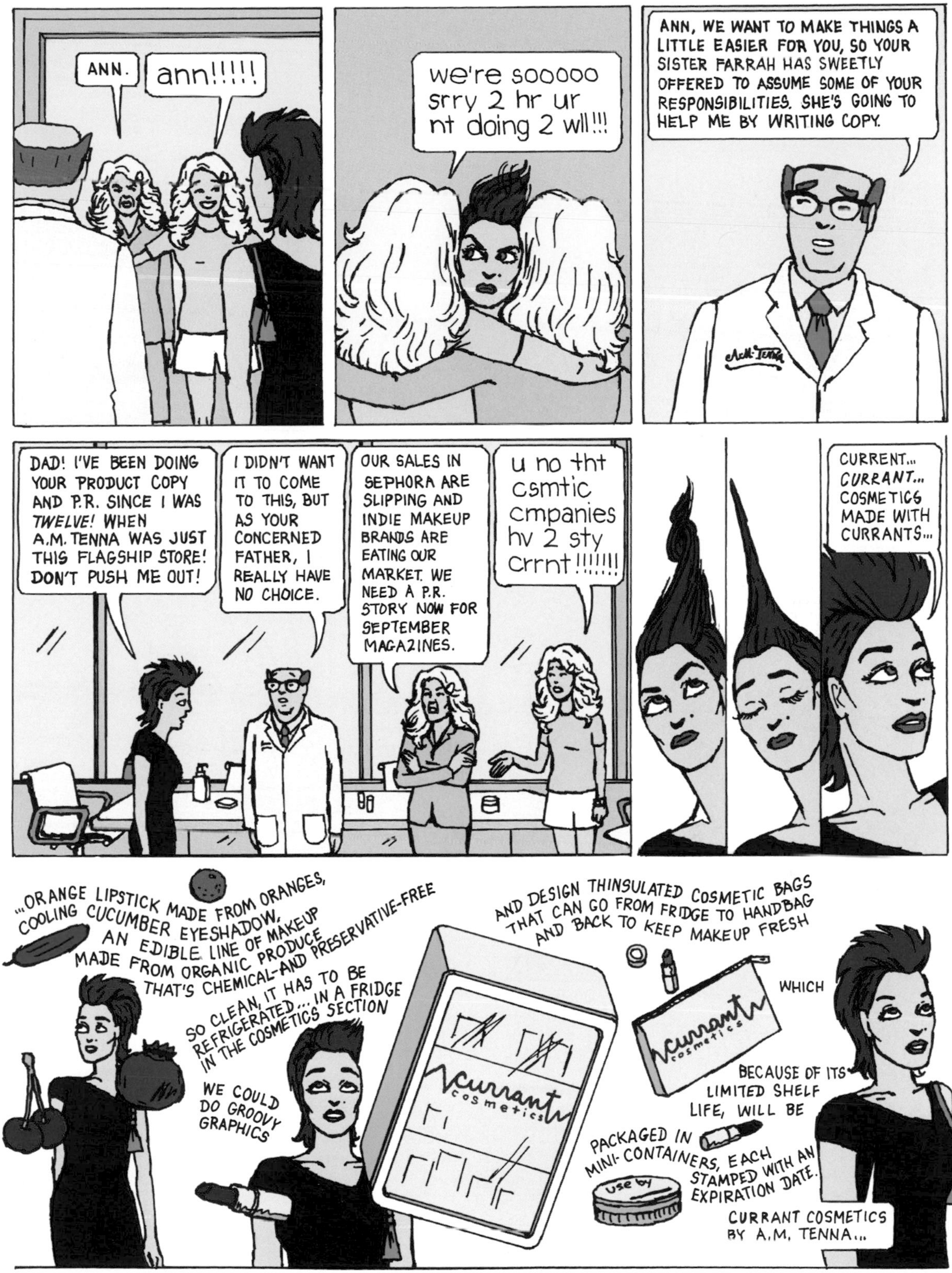

ANN.
ann!!!!!
we're sooooo srry 2 hr ur nt doing 2 wll!!!
ANN, WE WANT TO MAKE THINGS A LITTLE EASIER FOR YOU, SO YOUR SISTER FARRAH HAS SWEETLY OFFERED TO ASSUME SOME OF YOUR RESPONSIBILITIES. SHE'S GOING TO HELP ME BY WRITING COPY.
A.M. TENNA
DAD! I'VE BEEN DOING YOUR PRODUCT COPY AND P.R. SINCE I WAS *TWELVE!* WHEN A.M. TENNA WAS JUST THIS FLAGSHIP STORE! DON'T PUSH ME OUT!
I DIDN'T WANT IT TO COME TO THIS, BUT AS YOUR CONCERNED FATHER, I REALLY HAVE NO CHOICE.
OUR SALES IN SEPHORA ARE SLIPPING AND INDIE MAKEUP BRANDS ARE EATING OUR MARKET. WE NEED A P.R. STORY NOW FOR SEPTEMBER MAGAZINES.
u no tht csmtic cmpanies hv 2 sty crrnt!!!!!!!
CURRENT... *CURRANT...* COSMETICS MADE WITH CURRANTS...
...ORANGE LIPSTICK MADE FROM ORANGES, COOLING CUCUMBER EYESHADOW,
AN EDIBLE LINE OF MAKEUP MADE FROM ORGANIC PRODUCE THAT'S CHEMICAL-AND PRESERVATIVE-FREE
SO CLEAN, IT HAS TO BE REFRIGERATED... IN A FRIDGE IN THE COSMETICS SECTION
WE COULD DO GROOVY GRAPHICS
currant cosmetics
AND DESIGN THINSULATED COSMETIC BAGS THAT CAN GO FROM FRIDGE TO HANDBAG AND BACK TO KEEP MAKEUP FRESH
currant cosmetics
WHICH
BECAUSE OF ITS LIMITED SHELF LIFE, WILL BE
PACKAGED IN MINI-CONTAINERS, EACH STAMPED WITH AN EXPIRATION DATE.
use by
CURRANT COSMETICS BY A.M. TENNA...

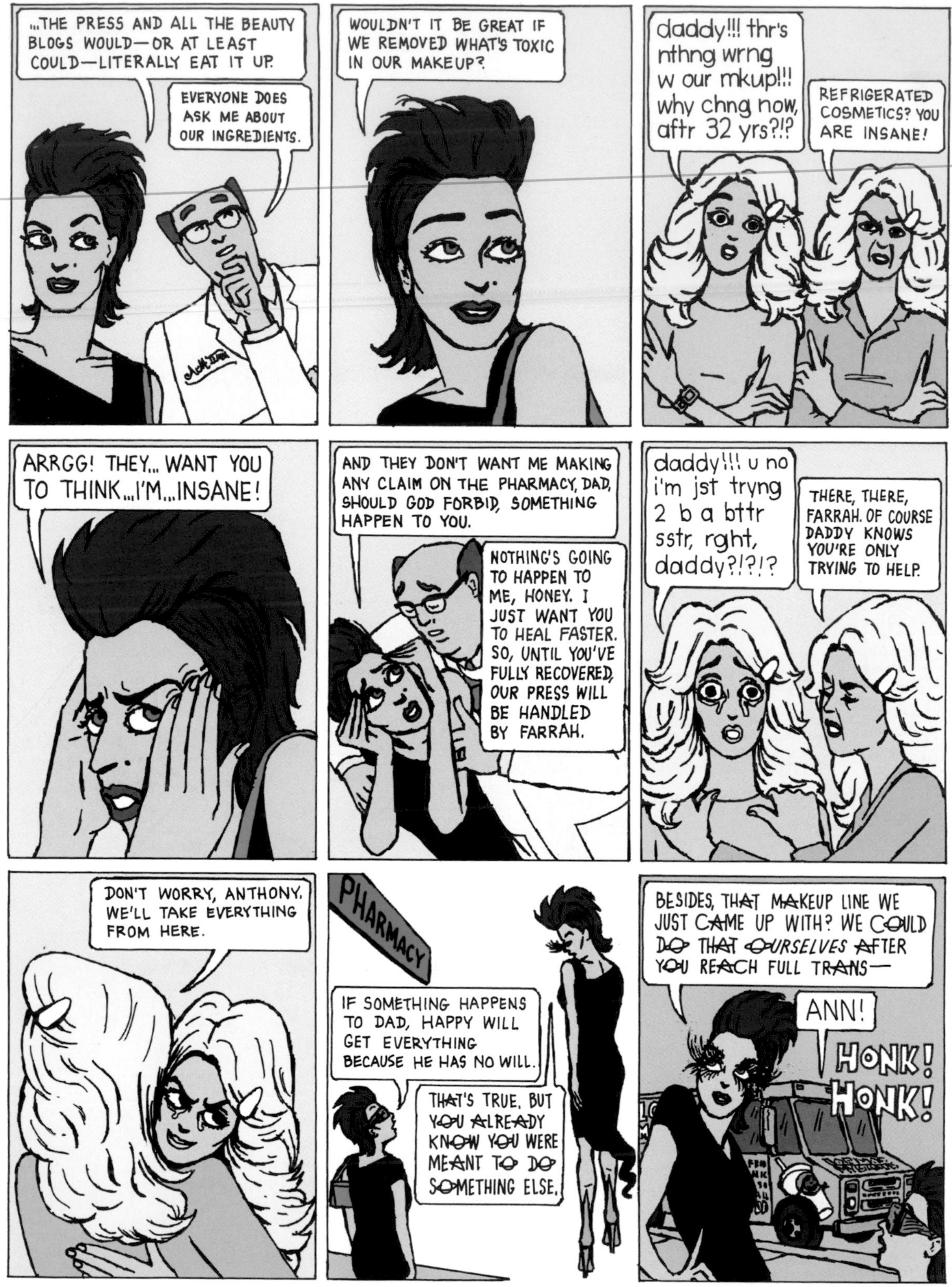
...THE PRESS AND ALL THE BEAUTY BLOGS WOULD—OR AT LEAST COULD—LITERALLY EAT IT UP.
EVERYONE DOES ASK ME ABOUT OUR INGREDIENTS.
WOULDN'T IT BE GREAT IF WE REMOVED WHAT'S TOXIC IN OUR MAKEUP?
daddy!!! thr's nthng wrng w our mkup!!! why chng now, aftr 32 yrs?!?
REFRIGERATED COSMETICS? YOU ARE INSANE!
ARRGG! THEY... WANT YOU TO THINK...I'M...INSANE!
AND THEY DON'T WANT ME MAKING ANY CLAIM ON THE PHARMACY, DAD, SHOULD GOD FORBID, SOMETHING HAPPEN TO YOU.
NOTHING'S GOING TO HAPPEN TO ME, HONEY. I JUST WANT YOU TO HEAL FASTER. SO, UNTIL YOU'VE FULLY RECOVERED, OUR PRESS WILL BE HANDLED BY FARRAH.
daddy!!! u no i'm jst tryng 2 b a bttr sstr, rght, daddy?!?!?
THERE, THERE, FARRAH. OF COURSE DADDY KNOWS YOU'RE ONLY TRYING TO HELP.
DON'T WORRY, ANTHONY. WE'LL TAKE EVERYTHING FROM HERE.
PHARMACY
IF SOMETHING HAPPENS TO DAD, HAPPY WILL GET EVERYTHING BECAUSE HE HAS NO WILL.
THAT'S TRUE, BUT YOU ALREADY KNOW YOU WERE MEANT TO DO SOMETHING ELSE.
BESIDES, THAT MAKEUP LINE WE JUST CAME UP WITH? WE COULD DO THAT OURSELVES AFTER YOU REACH FULL TRANS—
ANN!
HONK! HONK!

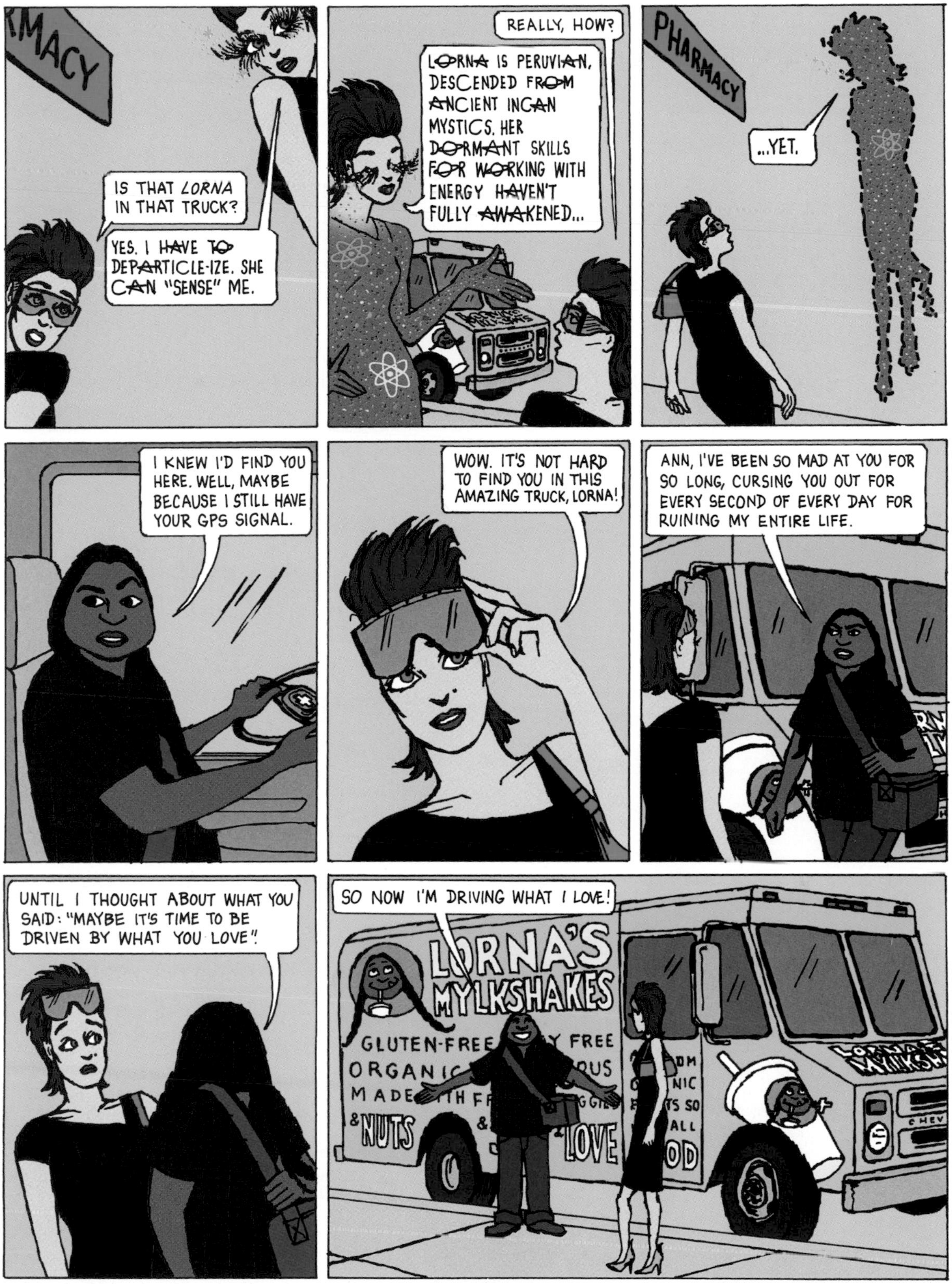
RMACY
IS THAT LORNA IN THAT TRUCK?
YES. I HAVE TO DEPARTICLE-IZE. SHE CAN "SENSE" ME.
REALLY, HOW?
LORNA IS PERUVIAN, DESCENDED FROM ANCIENT INCAN MYSTICS. HER DORMANT SKILLS FOR WORKING WITH ENERGY HAVEN'T FULLY AWAKENED...
PHARMACY
...YET.
I KNEW I'D FIND YOU HERE. WELL, MAYBE BECAUSE I STILL HAVE YOUR GPS SIGNAL.
WOW. IT'S NOT HARD TO FIND YOU IN THIS AMAZING TRUCK, LORNA!
ANN, I'VE BEEN SO MAD AT YOU FOR SO LONG, CURSING YOU OUT FOR EVERY SECOND OF EVERY DAY FOR RUINING MY ENTIRE LIFE.
UNTIL I THOUGHT ABOUT WHAT YOU SAID: "MAYBE IT'S TIME TO BE DRIVEN BY WHAT YOU LOVE".
SO NOW I'M DRIVING WHAT I LOVE!
LORNA'S MYLKSHAKES
GLUTEN-FREE
&NUTS
LOVE

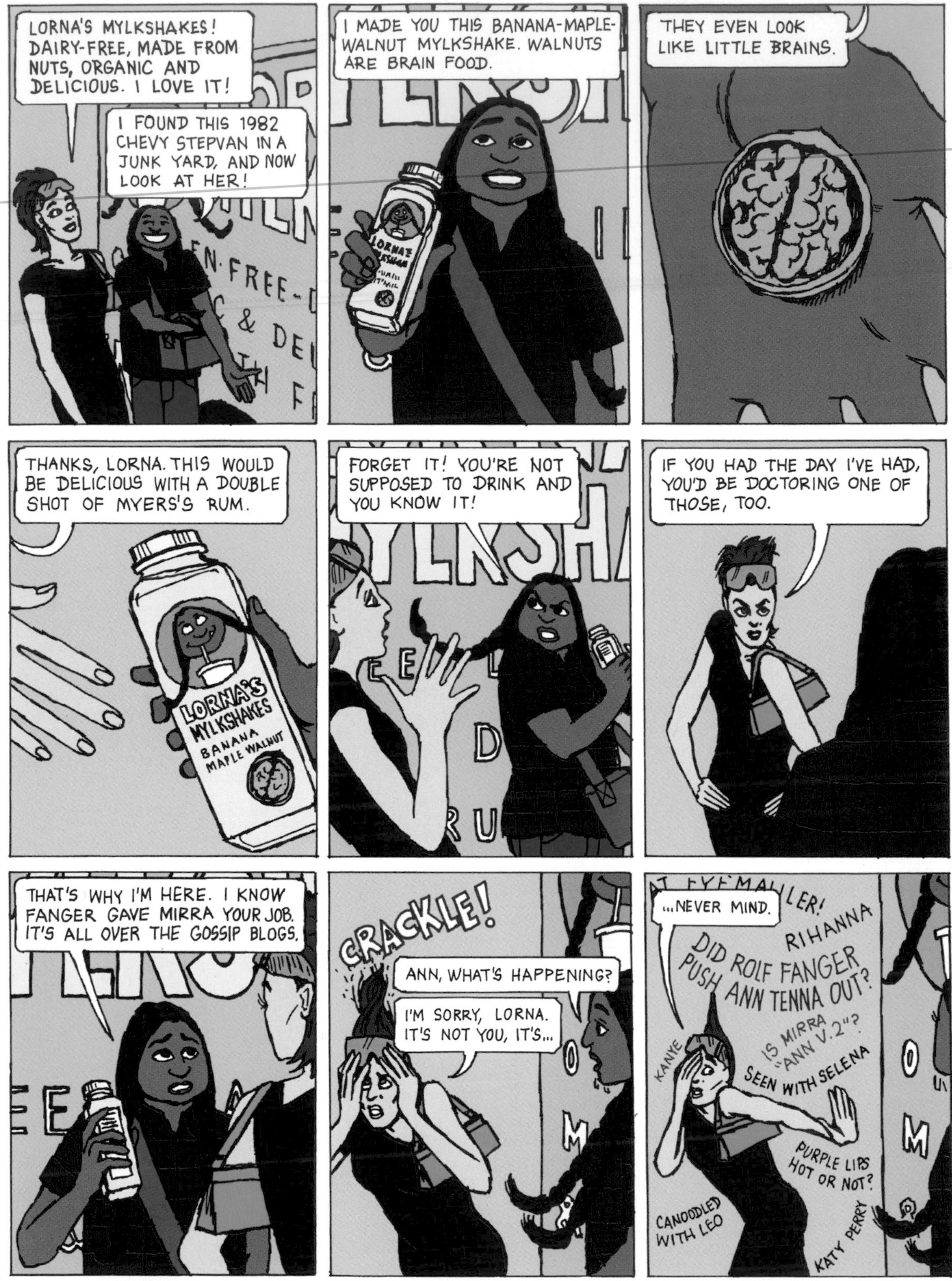
LORNA'S MYLKSHAKES! DAIRY-FREE, MADE FROM NUTS, ORGANIC AND DELICIOUS. I LOVE IT!
I FOUND THIS 1982 CHEVY STEPVAN IN A JUNK YARD, AND NOW LOOK AT HER!
I MADE YOU THIS BANANA-MAPLE-WALNUT MYLKSHAKE. WALNUTS ARE BRAIN FOOD.
THEY EVEN LOOK LIKE LITTLE BRAINS.
THANKS, LORNA. THIS WOULD BE DELICIOUS WITH A DOUBLE SHOT OF MYERS'S RUM.
LORNA'S MYLKSHAKES
BANANA MAPLE WALNUT
FORGET IT! YOU'RE NOT SUPPOSED TO DRINK AND YOU KNOW IT!
IF YOU HAD THE DAY I'VE HAD, YOU'D BE DOCTORING ONE OF THOSE, TOO.
THAT'S WHY I'M HERE. I KNOW FANGER GAVE MIRRA YOUR JOB. IT'S ALL OVER THE GOSSIP BLOGS.
CRACKLE!
ANN, WHAT'S HAPPENING?
I'M SORRY, LORNA. IT'S NOT YOU, IT'S...
...NEVER MIND.
RIHANNA
DID ROLF FANGER PUSH ANN TENNA OUT?
IS MIRRA "ANN V.2"?
KANYE
SEEN WITH SELENA
PURPLE LIPS HOT OR NOT?
CANOODLED WITH LEO
KATY PERRY

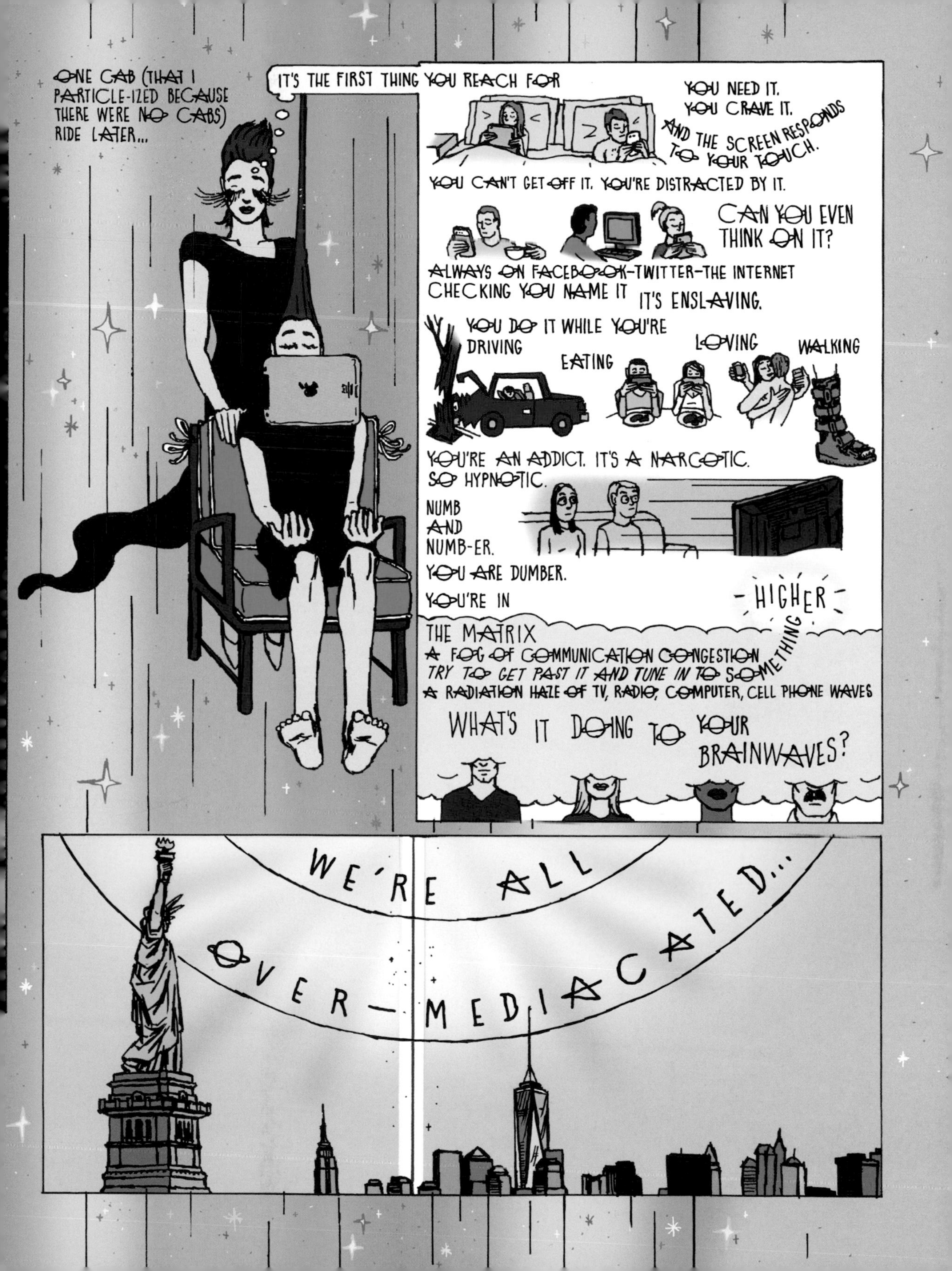

ONE CAB (THAT I PARTICLE-IZED BECAUSE THERE WERE NO CABS) RIDE LATER...
IT'S THE FIRST THING YOU REACH FOR
YOU NEED IT.
YOU CRAVE IT.
AND THE SCREEN RESPONDS TO YOUR TOUCH.
YOU CAN'T GET OFF IT. YOU'RE DISTRACTED BY IT.
CAN YOU EVEN THINK ON IT?
ALWAYS ON FACEBOOK–TWITTER–THE INTERNET
CHECKING YOU NAME IT
IT'S ENSLAVING.
YOU DO IT WHILE YOU'RE
DRIVING
EATING
LOVING
WALKING
YOU'RE AN ADDICT. IT'S A NARCOTIC.
SO HYPNOTIC.
NUMB AND NUMB-ER.
YOU ARE DUMBER.
YOU'RE IN
THE MATRIX
A FOG OF COMMUNICATION CONGESTION
TRY TO GET PAST IT AND TUNE IN TO SOMETHING
HIGHER
A RADIATION HAZE OF TV, RADIO, COMPUTER, CELL PHONE WAVES
WHAT'S IT DOING TO YOUR BRAINWAVES?
WE'RE ALL OVER-MEDIACATED...

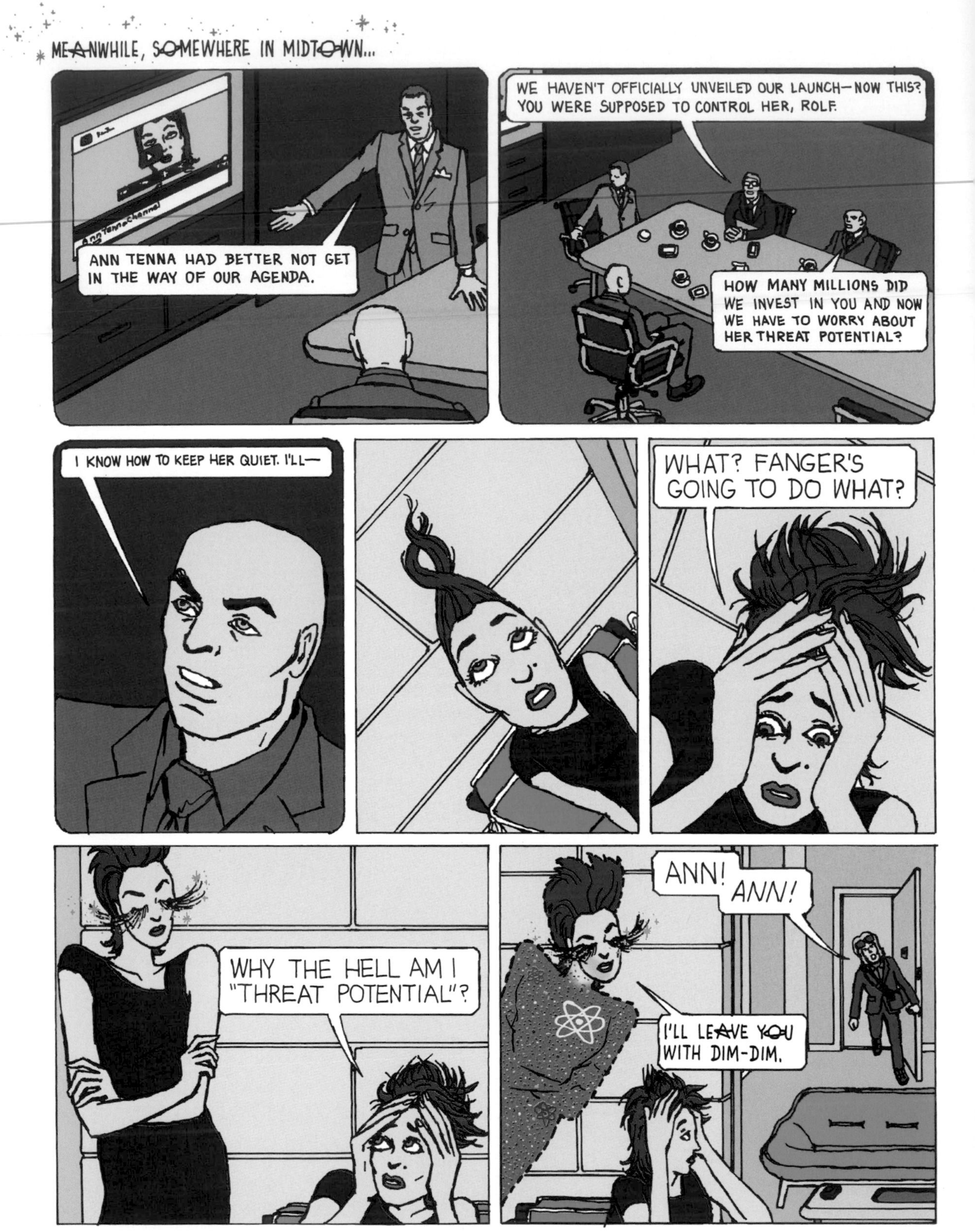
MEANWHILE, SOMEWHERE IN MIDTOWN...
ANN TENNA HAD BETTER NOT GET IN THE WAY OF OUR AGENDA.
WE HAVEN'T OFFICIALLY UNVEILED OUR LAUNCH—NOW THIS? YOU WERE SUPPOSED TO CONTROL HER, ROLF.
HOW MANY MILLIONS DID WE INVEST IN YOU AND NOW WE HAVE TO WORRY ABOUT HER THREAT POTENTIAL?
I KNOW HOW TO KEEP HER QUIET. I'LL—
WHAT? FANGER'S GOING TO DO WHAT?
WHY THE HELL AM I "THREAT POTENTIAL"?
ANN!
ANN!
I'LL LEAVE YOU WITH DIM-DIM.

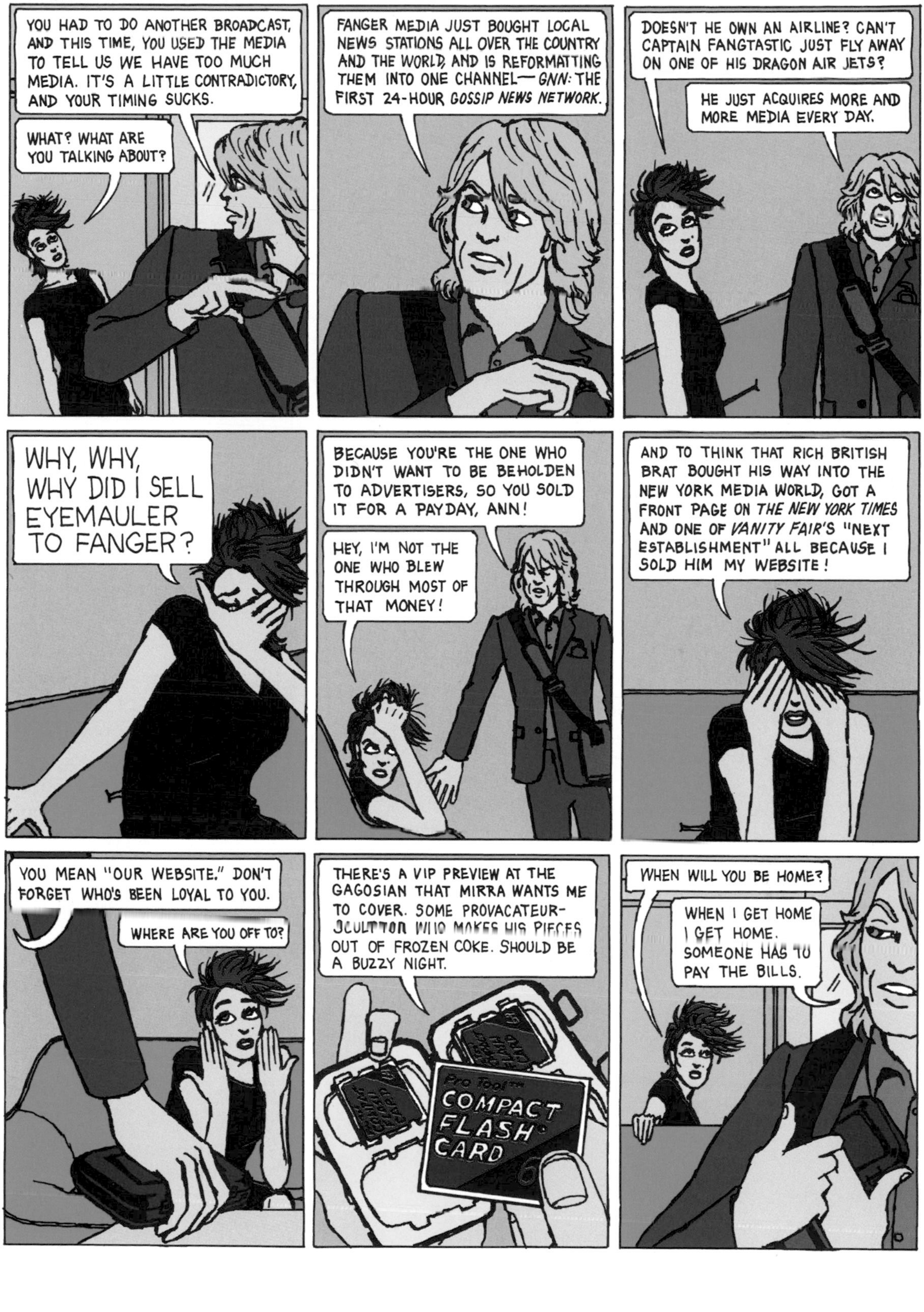
YOU HAD TO DO ANOTHER BROADCAST, AND THIS TIME, YOU USED THE MEDIA TO TELL US WE HAVE TOO MUCH MEDIA. IT'S A LITTLE CONTRADICTORY, AND YOUR TIMING SUCKS.
WHAT? WHAT ARE YOU TALKING ABOUT?
FANGER MEDIA JUST BOUGHT LOCAL NEWS STATIONS ALL OVER THE COUNTRY AND THE WORLD, AND IS REFORMATTING THEM INTO ONE CHANNEL— *GNN:* THE FIRST 24-HOUR *GOSSIP NEWS NETWORK.*
DOESN'T HE OWN AN AIRLINE? CAN'T CAPTAIN FANGTASTIC JUST FLY AWAY ON ONE OF HIS DRAGON AIR JETS?
HE JUST ACQUIRES MORE AND MORE MEDIA EVERY DAY.
WHY, WHY, WHY DID I SELL EYEMAULER TO FANGER?
BECAUSE YOU'RE THE ONE WHO DIDN'T WANT TO BE BEHOLDEN TO ADVERTISERS, SO YOU SOLD IT FOR A PAYDAY, ANN!
HEY, I'M NOT THE ONE WHO BLEW THROUGH MOST OF THAT MONEY!
AND TO THINK THAT RICH BRITISH BRAT BOUGHT HIS WAY INTO THE NEW YORK MEDIA WORLD, GOT A FRONT PAGE ON *THE NEW YORK TIMES* AND ONE OF *VANITY FAIR'S* "NEXT ESTABLISHMENT" ALL BECAUSE I SOLD HIM MY WEBSITE!
YOU MEAN "OUR WEBSITE." DON'T FORGET WHO'S BEEN LOYAL TO YOU.
WHERE ARE YOU OFF TO?
THERE'S A VIP PREVIEW AT THE GAGOSIAN THAT MIRRA WANTS ME TO COVER. SOME PROVACATEUR-SCULPTOR WHO MAKES HIS PIECES OUT OF FROZEN COKE. SHOULD BE A BUZZY NIGHT.
Pro Tool™
COMPACT FLASH® CARD
WHEN WILL YOU BE HOME?
WHEN I GET HOME I GET HOME. SOMEONE HAS TO PAY THE BILLS.

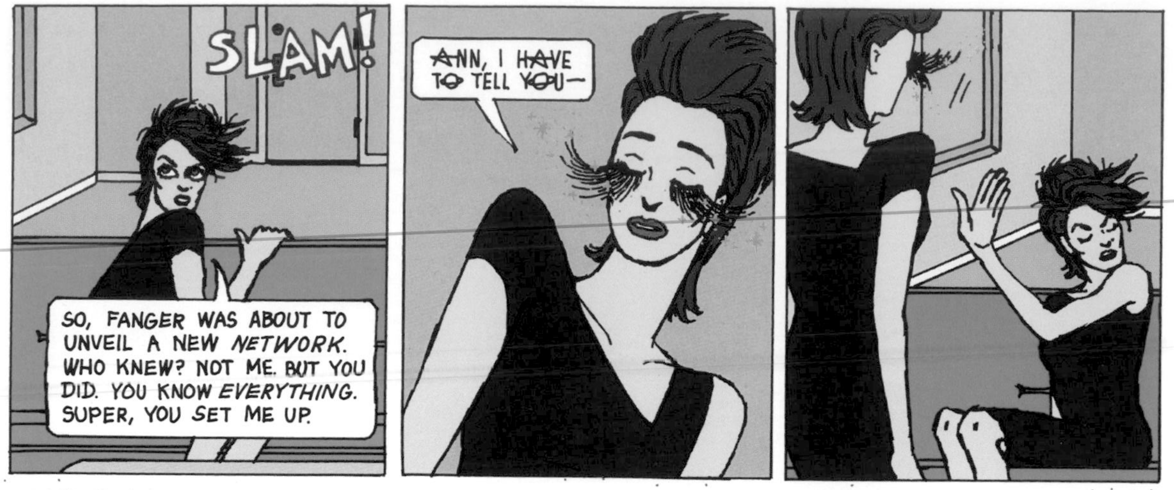
SLAM!
SO, FANGER WAS ABOUT TO UNVEIL A NEW *NETWORK*. WHO KNEW? NOT ME. BUT YOU DID. YOU KNOW *EVERYTHING*. SUPER, YOU SET ME UP.
ANN, I HAVE TO TELL YOU—

AND EVEN IF I TOLD HER WHAT WAS ABSOLUTELY IMPERATIVE FOR HER SOUL'S JOURNEY, WOULD SHE LISTEN?

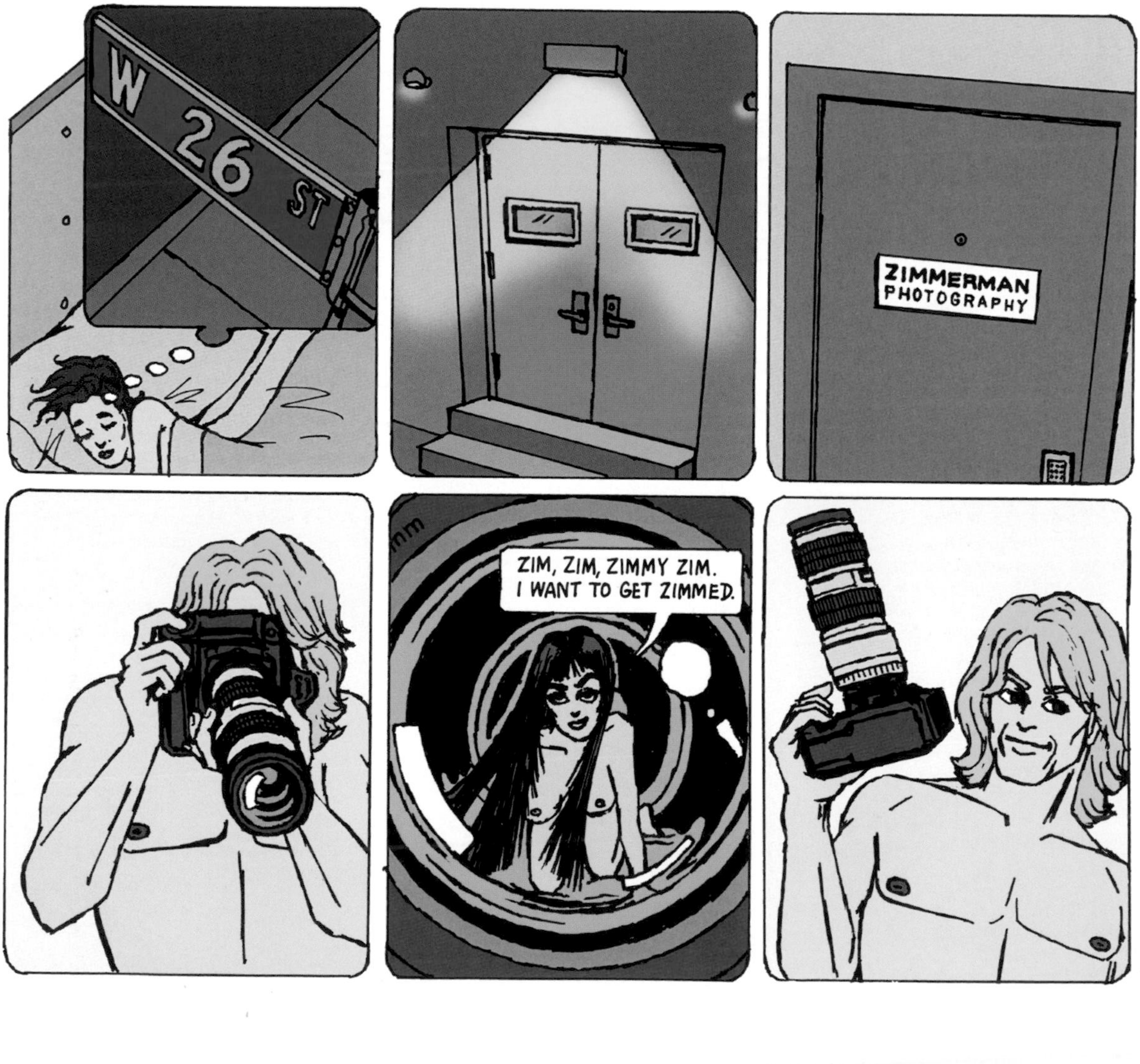
W 26 ST
ZIMMERMAN PHOTOGRAPHY
ZIM, ZIM, ZIMMY ZIM. I WANT TO GET ZIMMED.

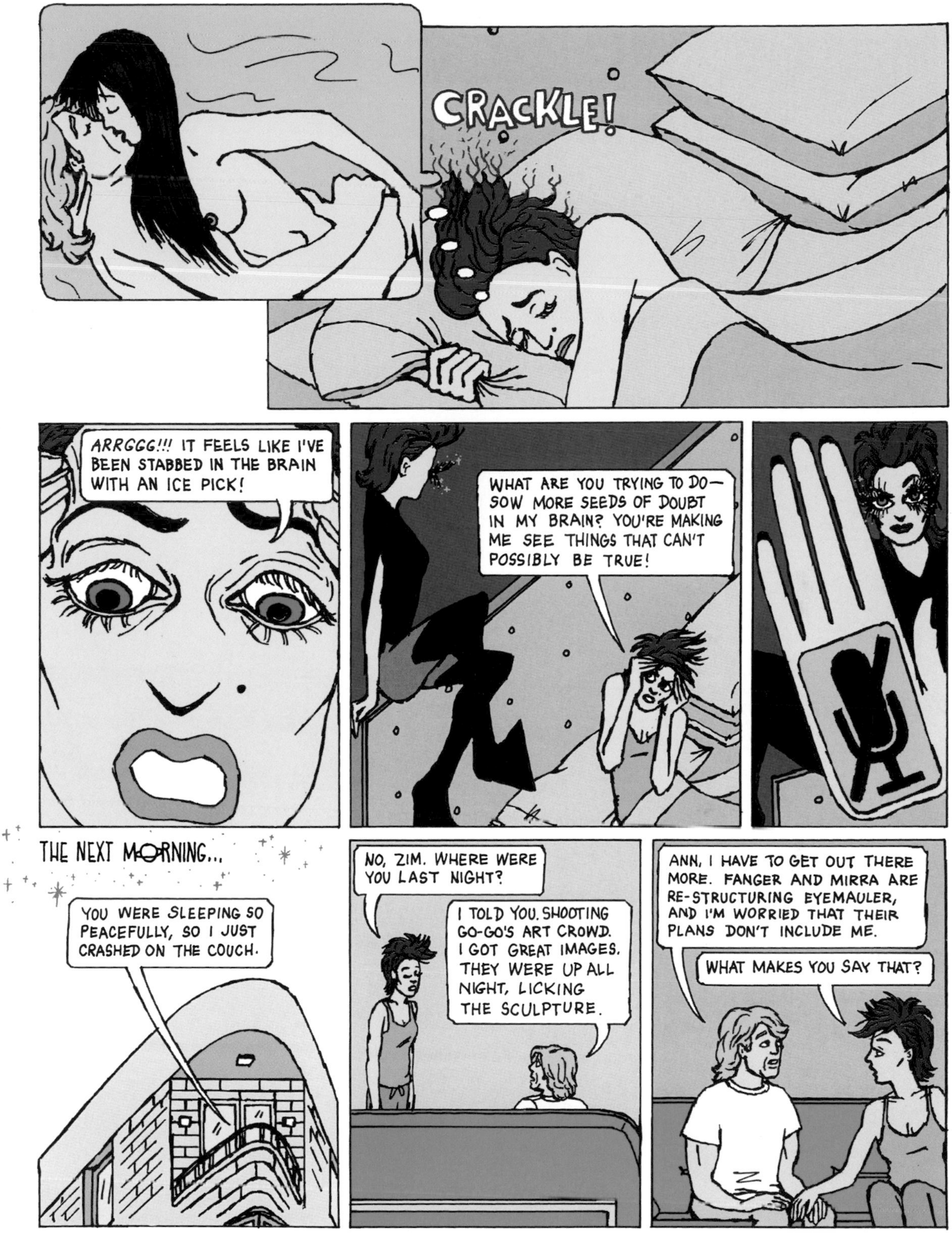
CRACKLE!
ARRGGG!!! IT FEELS LIKE I'VE BEEN STABBED IN THE BRAIN WITH AN ICE PICK!
WHAT ARE YOU TRYING TO DO— SOW MORE SEEDS OF DOUBT IN MY BRAIN? YOU'RE MAKING ME SEE THINGS THAT CAN'T POSSIBLY BE TRUE!
THE NEXT MORNING...
YOU WERE SLEEPING SO PEACEFULLY, SO I JUST CRASHED ON THE COUCH.
NO, ZIM. WHERE WERE YOU LAST NIGHT?
I TOLD YOU. SHOOTING GO-GO'S ART CROWD. I GOT GREAT IMAGES. THEY WERE UP ALL NIGHT, LICKING THE SCULPTURE.
ANN, I HAVE TO GET OUT THERE MORE. FANGER AND MIRRA ARE RE-STRUCTURING EYEMAULER, AND I'M WORRIED THAT THEIR PLANS DON'T INCLUDE ME.
WHAT MAKES YOU SAY THAT?

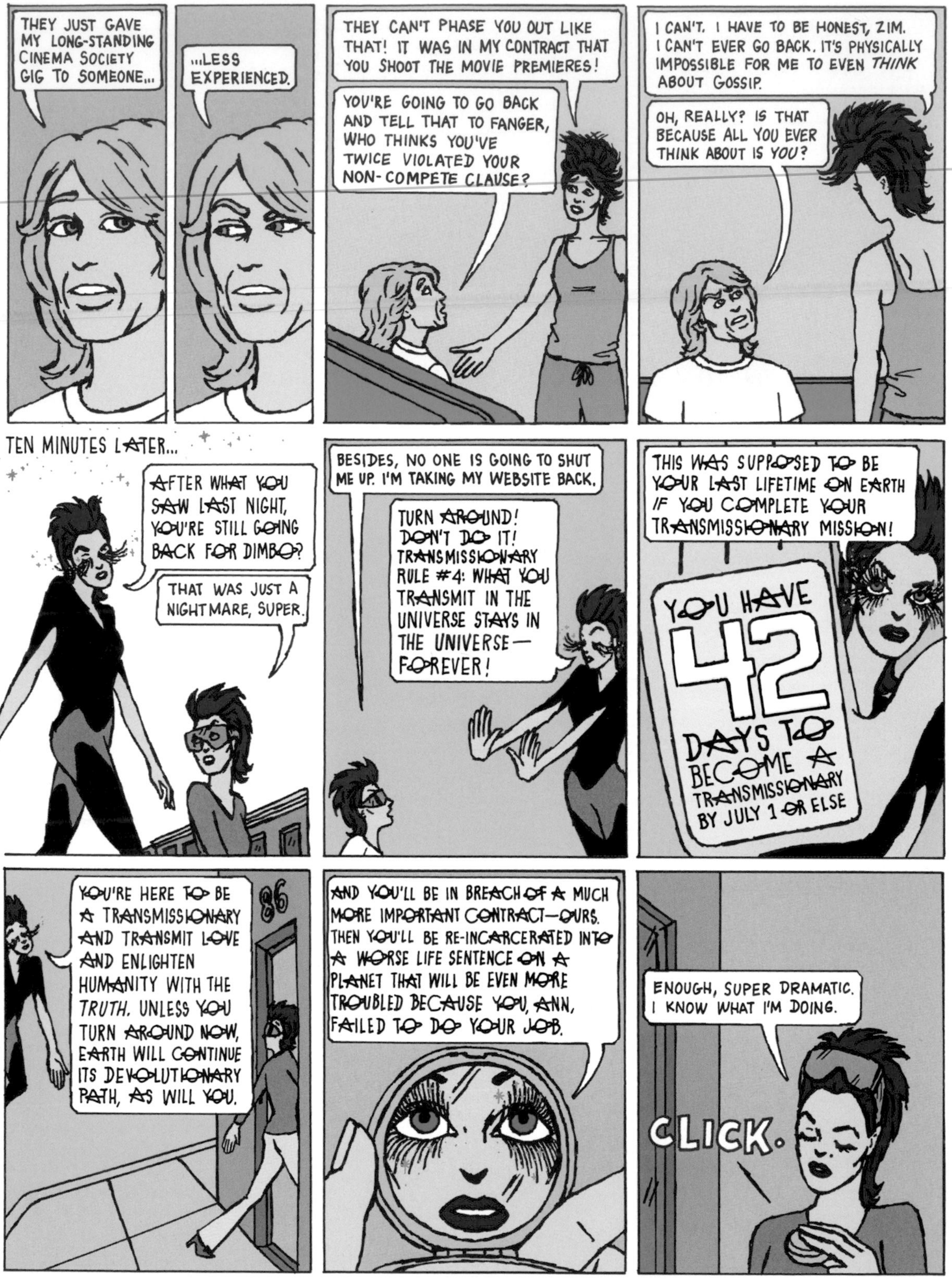
THEY JUST GAVE MY LONG-STANDING CINEMA SOCIETY GIG TO SOMEONE...
...LESS EXPERIENCED.
THEY CAN'T PHASE YOU OUT LIKE THAT! IT WAS IN MY CONTRACT THAT YOU SHOOT THE MOVIE PREMIERES!
YOU'RE GOING TO GO BACK AND TELL THAT TO FANGER, WHO THINKS YOU'VE TWICE VIOLATED YOUR NON-COMPETE CLAUSE?
I CAN'T. I HAVE TO BE HONEST, ZIM. I CAN'T EVER GO BACK. IT'S PHYSICALLY IMPOSSIBLE FOR ME TO EVEN *THINK* ABOUT GOSSIP.
OH, REALLY? IS THAT BECAUSE ALL YOU EVER THINK ABOUT IS *YOU*?
TEN MINUTES LATER...
AFTER WHAT YOU SAW LAST NIGHT, YOU'RE STILL GOING BACK FOR DIMBO?
THAT WAS JUST A NIGHTMARE, SUPER.
BESIDES, NO ONE IS GOING TO SHUT ME UP. I'M TAKING MY WEBSITE BACK.
TURN AROUND! DON'T DO IT! TRANSMISSIONARY RULE #4: WHAT YOU TRANSMIT IN THE UNIVERSE STAYS IN THE UNIVERSE—FOREVER!
THIS WAS SUPPOSED TO BE YOUR LAST LIFETIME ON EARTH *IF* YOU COMPLETE YOUR TRANSMISSIONARY MISSION!
YOU HAVE 42 DAYS TO BECOME A TRANSMISSIONARY BY JULY 1 OR ELSE
YOU'RE HERE TO BE A TRANSMISSIONARY AND TRANSMIT LOVE AND ENLIGHTEN HUMANITY WITH THE *TRUTH*. UNLESS YOU TURN AROUND NOW, EARTH WILL CONTINUE ITS DEVOLUTIONARY PATH, AS WILL YOU.
86
AND YOU'LL BE IN BREACH OF A MUCH MORE IMPORTANT CONTRACT—OURS. THEN YOU'LL BE RE-INCARCERATED INTO A WORSE LIFE SENTENCE ON A PLANET THAT WILL BE EVEN MORE TROUBLED BECAUSE YOU, ANN, FAILED TO DO YOUR JOB.
ENOUGH, SUPER DRAMATIC. I KNOW WHAT I'M DOING.
CLICK.

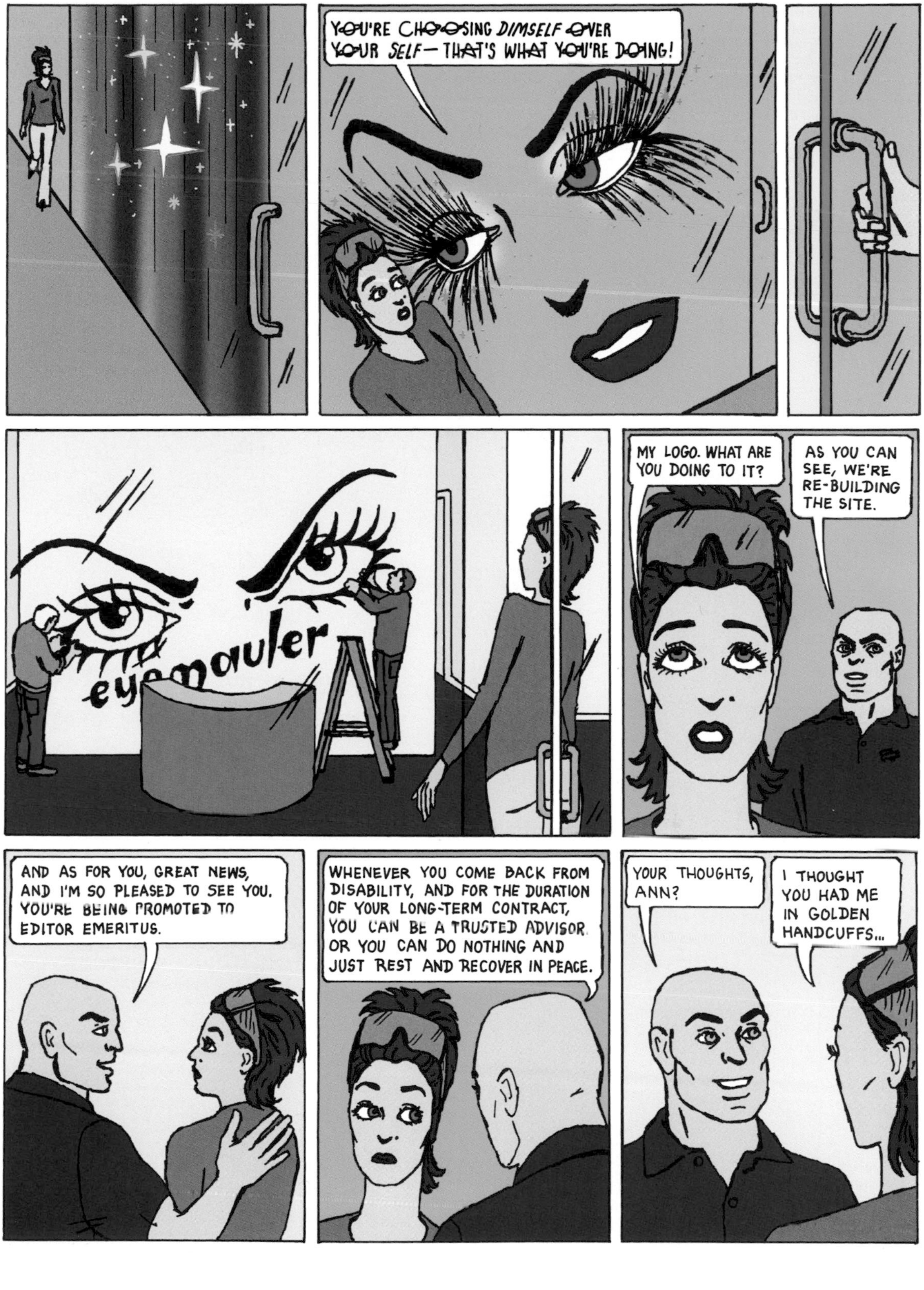
YOU'RE CHOOSING DIMSELF OVER YOUR SELF—THAT'S WHAT YOU'RE DOING!
eyemauler
MY LOGO. WHAT ARE YOU DOING TO IT?
AS YOU CAN SEE, WE'RE RE-BUILDING THE SITE.
AND AS FOR YOU, GREAT NEWS, AND I'M SO PLEASED TO SEE YOU. YOU'RE BEING PROMOTED TO EDITOR EMERITUS.
WHENEVER YOU COME BACK FROM DISABILITY, AND FOR THE DURATION OF YOUR LONG-TERM CONTRACT, YOU CAN BE A TRUSTED ADVISOR. OR YOU CAN DO NOTHING AND JUST REST AND RECOVER IN PEACE.
YOUR THOUGHTS, ANN?
I THOUGHT YOU HAD ME IN GOLDEN HANDCUFFS...

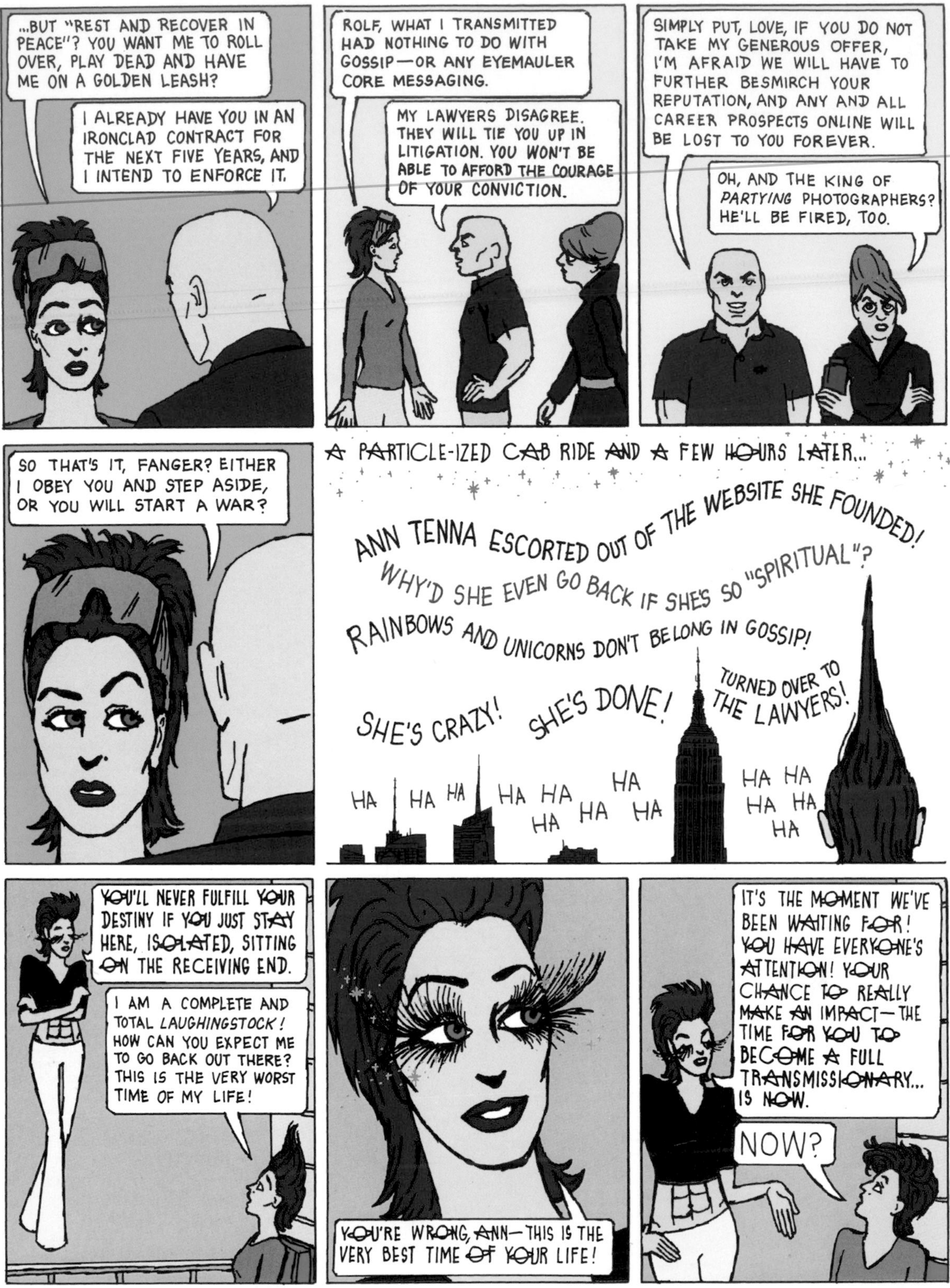

...BUT "REST AND RECOVER IN PEACE"? YOU WANT ME TO ROLL OVER, PLAY DEAD AND HAVE ME ON A GOLDEN LEASH?
I ALREADY HAVE YOU IN AN IRONCLAD CONTRACT FOR THE NEXT FIVE YEARS, AND I INTEND TO ENFORCE IT.
ROLF, WHAT I TRANSMITTED HAD NOTHING TO DO WITH GOSSIP—OR ANY EYEMAULER CORE MESSAGING.
MY LAWYERS DISAGREE. THEY WILL TIE YOU UP IN LITIGATION. YOU WON'T BE ABLE TO AFFORD THE COURAGE OF YOUR CONVICTION.
SIMPLY PUT, LOVE, IF YOU DO NOT TAKE MY GENEROUS OFFER, I'M AFRAID WE WILL HAVE TO FURTHER BESMIRCH YOUR REPUTATION, AND ANY AND ALL CAREER PROSPECTS ONLINE WILL BE LOST TO YOU FOREVER.
OH, AND THE KING OF *PARTYING* PHOTOGRAPHERS? HE'LL BE FIRED, TOO.
SO THAT'S IT, FANGER? EITHER I OBEY YOU AND STEP ASIDE, OR YOU WILL START A WAR?
A PARTICLE-IZED CAB RIDE AND A FEW HOURS LATER...
ANN TENNA ESCORTED OUT OF THE WEBSITE SHE FOUNDED!
WHY'D SHE EVEN GO BACK IF SHE'S SO "SPIRITUAL"?
RAINBOWS AND UNICORNS DON'T BELONG IN GOSSIP!
SHE'S CRAZY!
SHE'S DONE!
TURNED OVER TO THE LAWYERS!
HA HA HA HA HA HA HA HA HA
HA HA HA HA HA
YOU'LL NEVER FULFILL YOUR DESTINY IF YOU JUST STAY HERE, ISOLATED, SITTING ON THE RECEIVING END.
I AM A COMPLETE AND TOTAL *LAUGHINGSTOCK*! HOW CAN YOU EXPECT ME TO GO BACK OUT THERE? THIS IS THE VERY WORST TIME OF MY LIFE!
YOU'RE WRONG, ANN—THIS IS THE VERY BEST TIME OF YOUR LIFE!
IT'S THE MOMENT WE'VE BEEN WAITING FOR! YOU HAVE EVERYONE'S ATTENTION! YOUR CHANCE TO REALLY MAKE AN IMPACT—THE TIME FOR YOU TO BECOME A FULL TRANSMISSIONARY... IS NOW.
NOW?

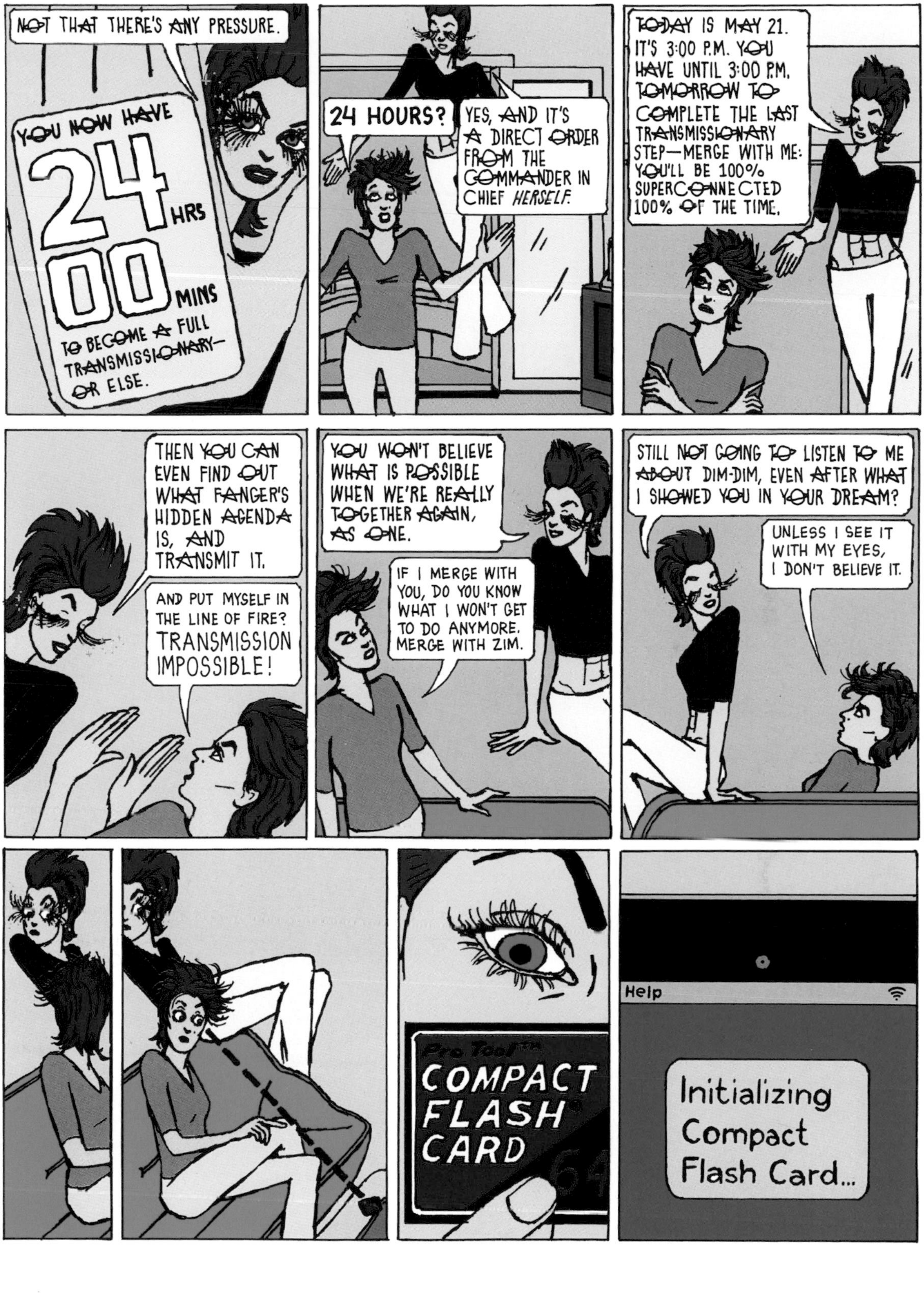
NOT THAT THERE'S ANY PRESSURE.
YOU NOW HAVE 24 HRS 00 MINS TO BECOME A FULL TRANSMISSIONARY— OR ELSE.
24 HOURS?
YES, AND IT'S A DIRECT ORDER FROM THE COMMANDER IN CHIEF *HERSELF*.
TODAY IS MAY 21. IT'S 3:00 P.M. YOU HAVE UNTIL 3:00 P.M. TOMORROW TO COMPLETE THE LAST TRANSMISSIONARY STEP—MERGE WITH ME: YOU'LL BE 100% SUPERCONNECTED 100% OF THE TIME.
THEN YOU CAN EVEN FIND OUT WHAT FANGER'S HIDDEN AGENDA IS, AND TRANSMIT IT.
AND PUT MYSELF IN THE LINE OF FIRE? TRANSMISSION IMPOSSIBLE!
YOU WON'T BELIEVE WHAT IS POSSIBLE WHEN WE'RE REALLY TOGETHER AGAIN, AS ONE.
IF I MERGE WITH YOU, DO YOU KNOW WHAT I WON'T GET TO DO ANYMORE. MERGE WITH ZIM.
STILL NOT GOING TO LISTEN TO ME ABOUT DIM-DIM, EVEN AFTER WHAT I SHOWED YOU IN YOUR DREAM?
UNLESS I SEE IT WITH MY EYES, I DON'T BELIEVE IT.
Pro Tool™
COMPACT FLASH CARD
Help
Initializing Compact Flash Card...

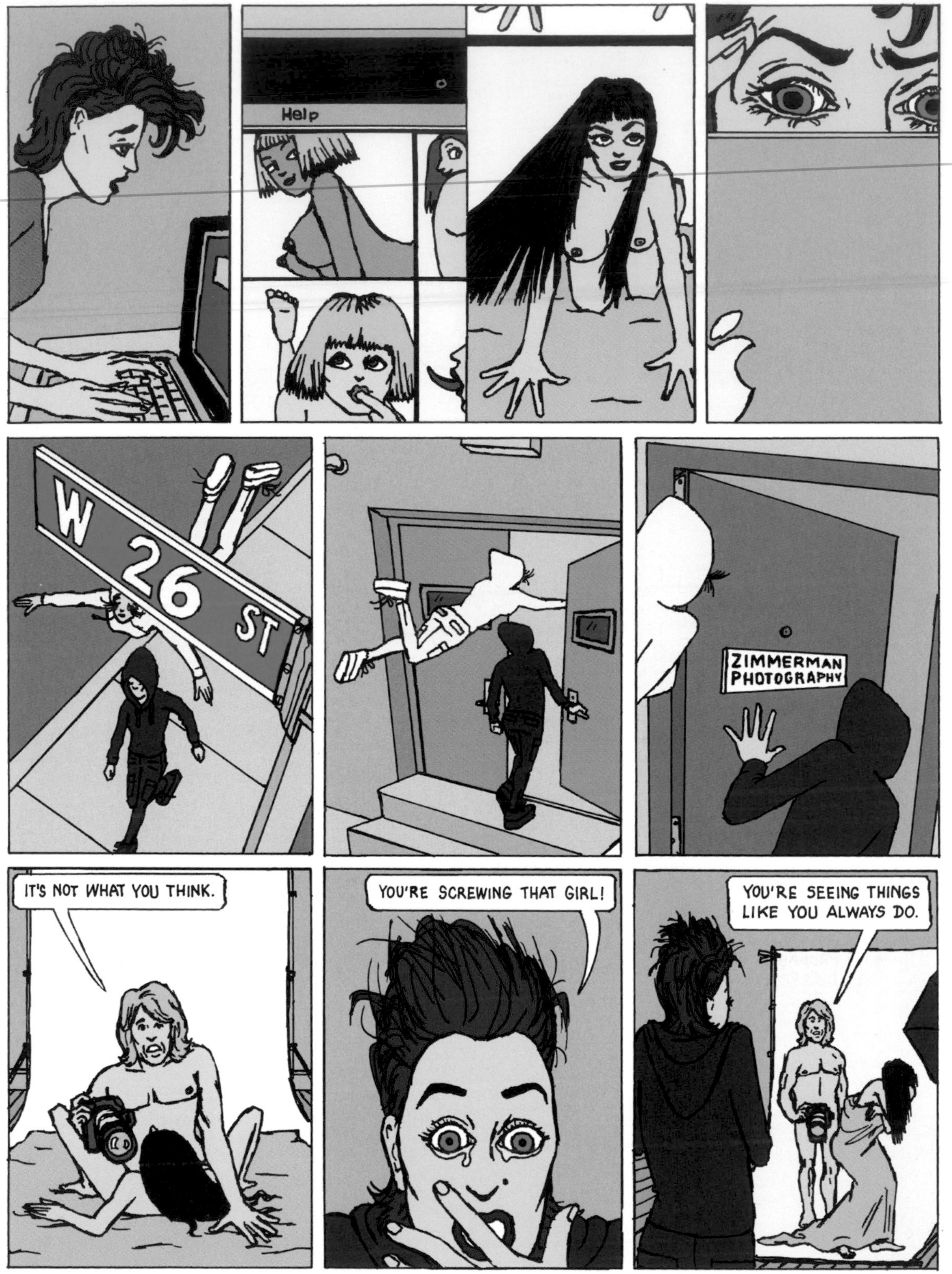
Help
W 26 ST
ZIMMERMAN PHOTOGRAPHY
IT'S NOT WHAT YOU THINK.
YOU'RE SCREWING THAT GIRL!
YOU'RE SEEING THINGS LIKE YOU ALWAYS DO.

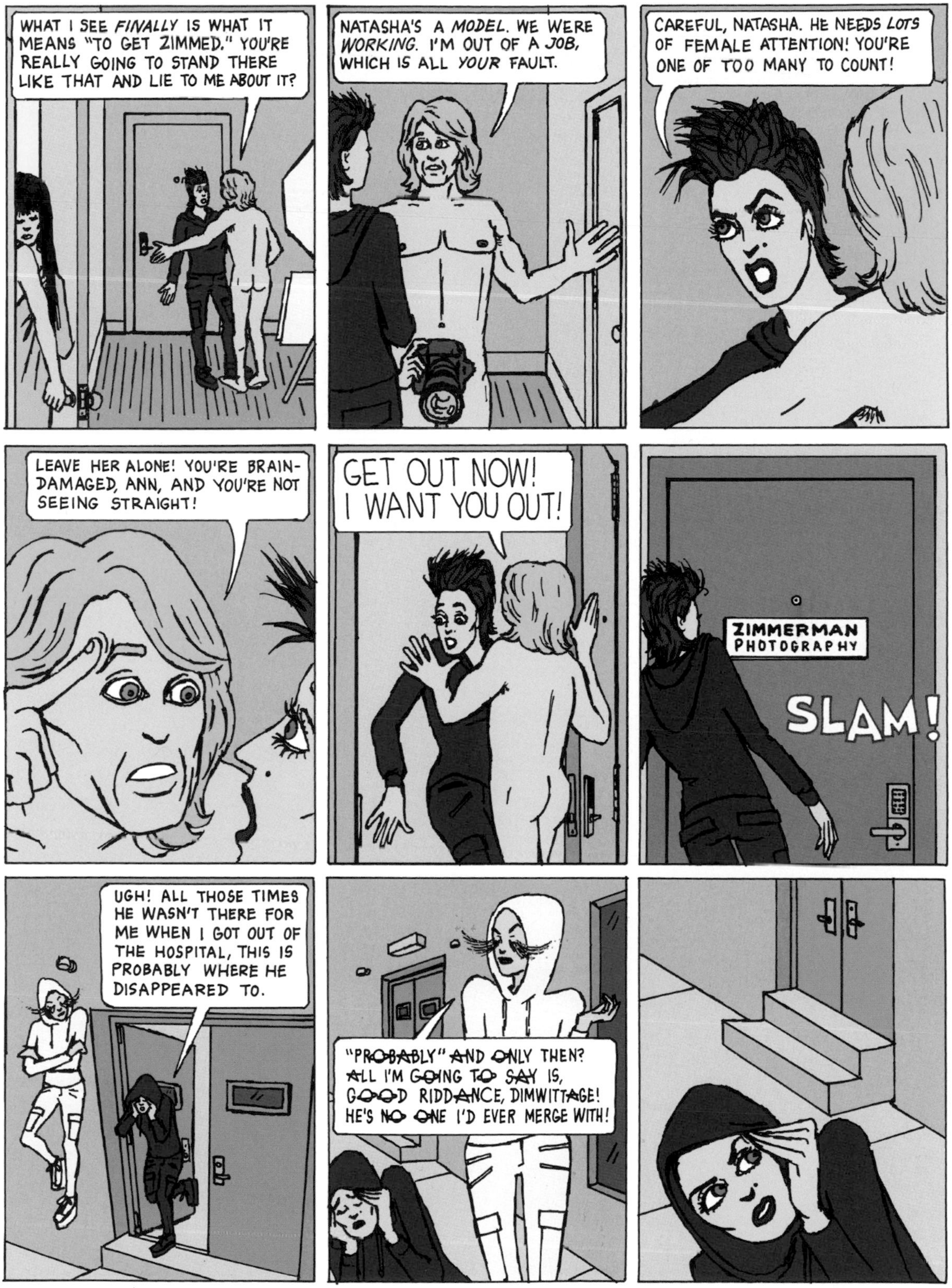
WHAT I SEE FINALLY IS WHAT IT MEANS "TO GET ZIMMED." YOU'RE REALLY GOING TO STAND THERE LIKE THAT AND LIE TO ME ABOUT IT?
NATASHA'S A MODEL. WE WERE WORKING. I'M OUT OF A JOB, WHICH IS ALL YOUR FAULT.
CAREFUL, NATASHA. HE NEEDS LOTS OF FEMALE ATTENTION! YOU'RE ONE OF TOO MANY TO COUNT!
LEAVE HER ALONE! YOU'RE BRAIN-DAMAGED, ANN, AND YOU'RE NOT SEEING STRAIGHT!
GET OUT NOW! I WANT YOU OUT!
ZIMMERMAN PHOTOGRAPHY
SLAM!
UGH! ALL THOSE TIMES HE WASN'T THERE FOR ME WHEN I GOT OUT OF THE HOSPITAL, THIS IS PROBABLY WHERE HE DISAPPEARED TO.
"PROBABLY" AND ONLY THEN? ALL I'M GOING TO SAY IS, GOOOD RIDDANCE, DIMWITTAGE! HE'S NO ONE I'D EVER MERGE WITH!

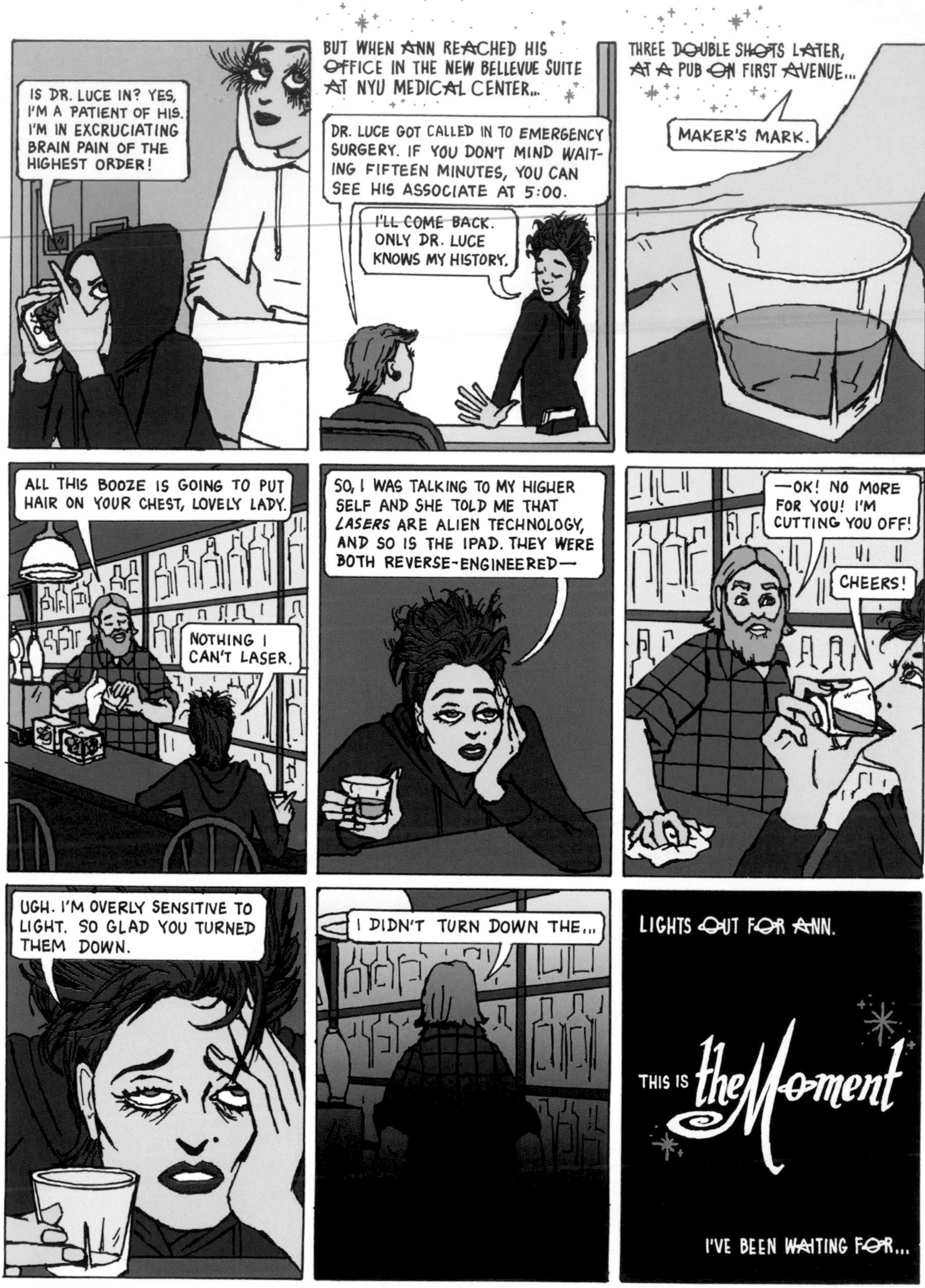
IS DR. LUCE IN? YES, I'M A PATIENT OF HIS. I'M IN EXCRUCIATING BRAIN PAIN OF THE HIGHEST ORDER!
BUT WHEN ANN REACHED HIS OFFICE IN THE NEW BELLEVUE SUITE AT NYU MEDICAL CENTER...
DR. LUCE GOT CALLED IN TO EMERGENCY SURGERY. IF YOU DON'T MIND WAITING FIFTEEN MINUTES, YOU CAN SEE HIS ASSOCIATE AT 5:00.
I'LL COME BACK. ONLY DR. LUCE KNOWS MY HISTORY.
THREE DOUBLE SHOTS LATER, AT A PUB ON FIRST AVENUE...
MAKER'S MARK.
ALL THIS BOOZE IS GOING TO PUT HAIR ON YOUR CHEST, LOVELY LADY.
NOTHING I CAN'T LASER.
SO, I WAS TALKING TO MY HIGHER SELF AND SHE TOLD ME THAT LASERS ARE ALIEN TECHNOLOGY, AND SO IS THE IPAD. THEY WERE BOTH REVERSE-ENGINEERED—
—OK! NO MORE FOR YOU! I'M CUTTING YOU OFF!
CHEERS!
UGH. I'M OVERLY SENSITIVE TO LIGHT. SO GLAD YOU TURNED THEM DOWN.
I DIDN'T TURN DOWN THE...
LIGHTS OUT FOR ANN.
THIS IS the Moment
I'VE BEEN WAITING FOR...

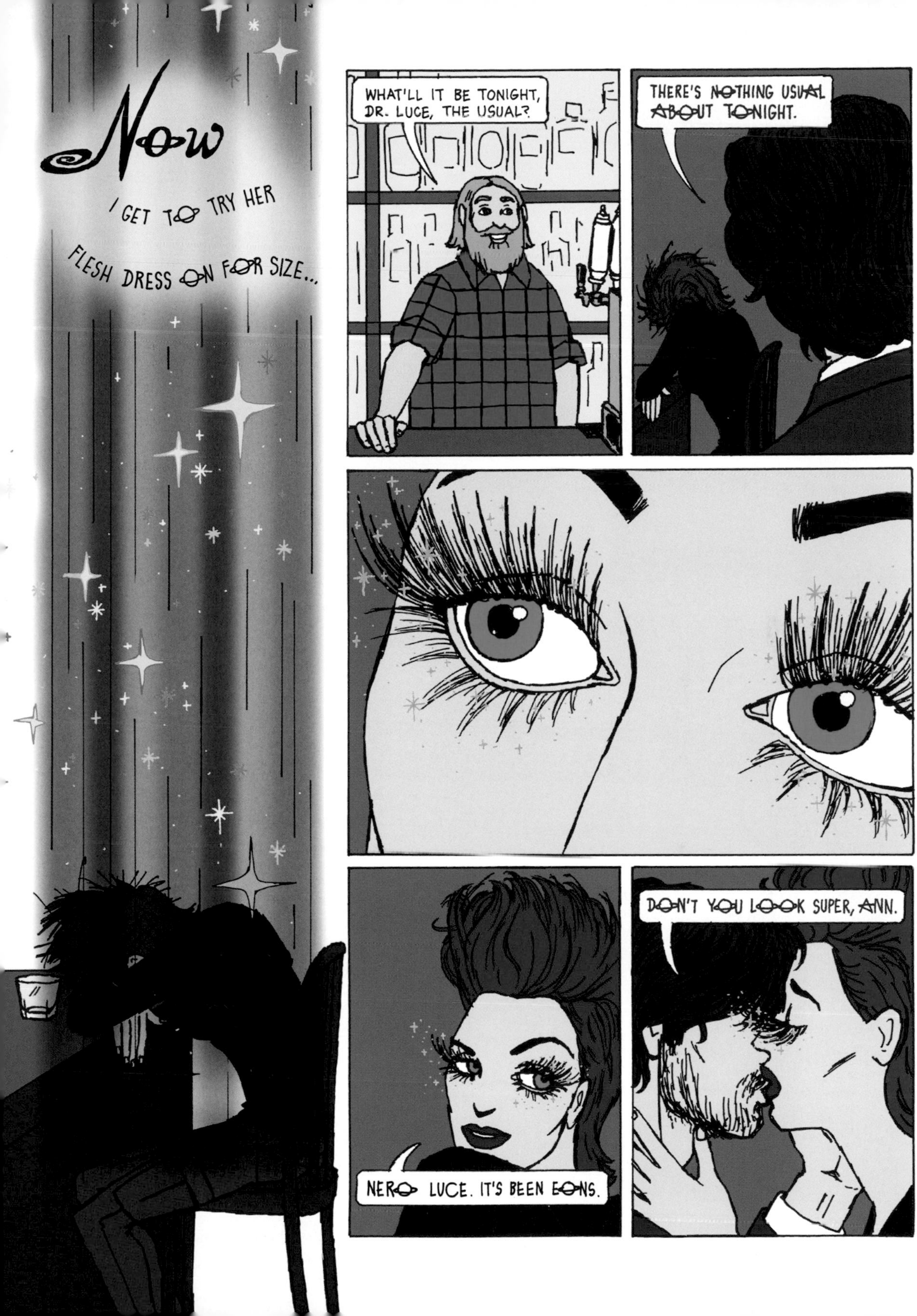
Now
I GET TO TRY HER
FLESH DRESS ON FOR SIZE...
WHAT'LL IT BE TONIGHT, DR. LUCE, THE USUAL?
THERE'S NOTHING USUAL ABOUT TONIGHT.
NERO LUCE. IT'S BEEN EONS.
DON'T YOU LOOK SUPER, ANN.

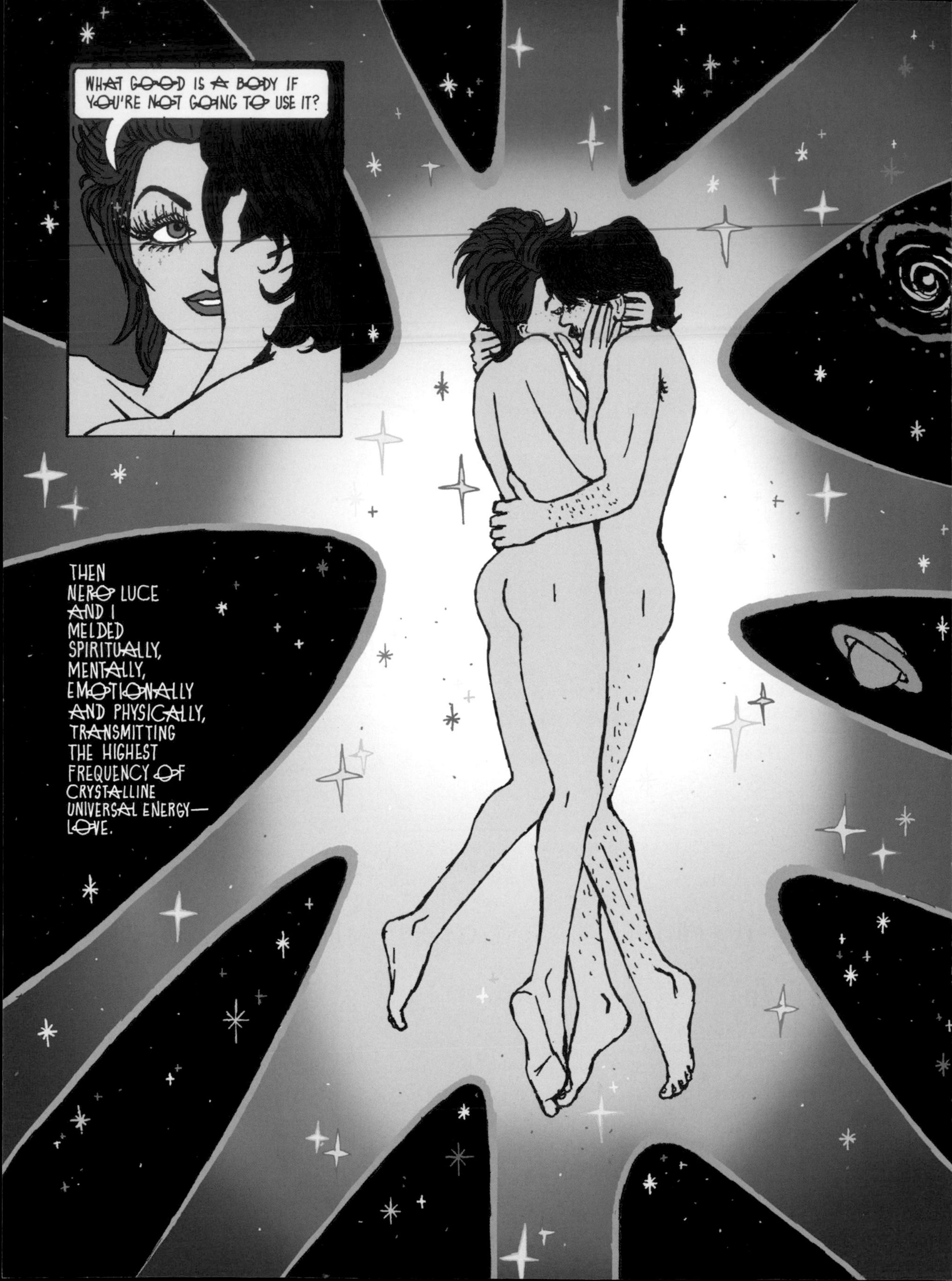
WHAT GOOD IS A BODY IF YOU'RE NOT GOING TO USE IT?
THEN NERO LUCE AND I MELDED SPIRITUALLY, MENTALLY, EMOTIONALLY AND PHYSICALLY, TRANSMITTING THE HIGHEST FREQUENCY OF CRYSTALLINE UNIVERSAL ENERGY— LOVE.

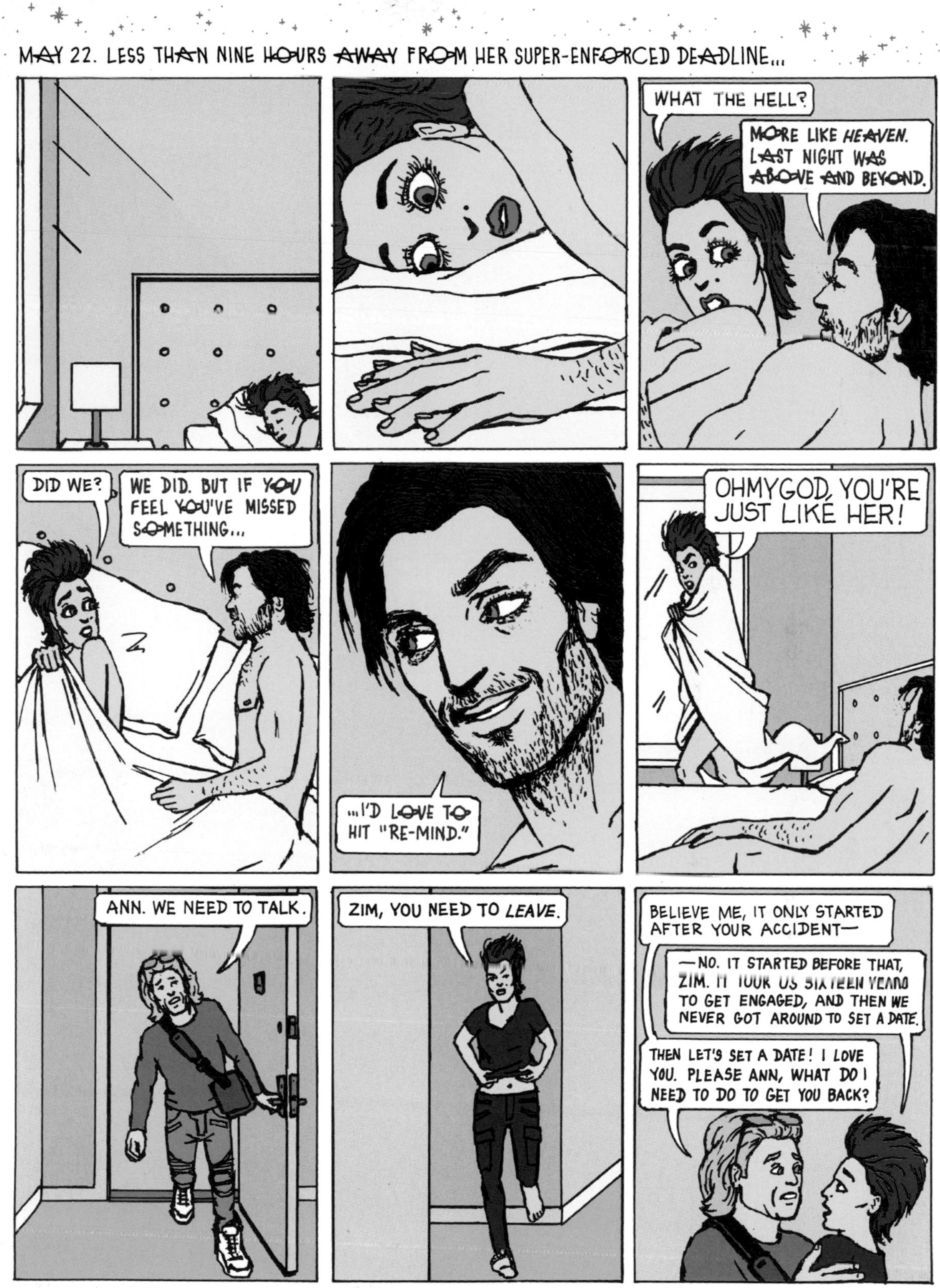
MAY 22. LESS THAN NINE HOURS AWAY FROM HER SUPER-ENFORCED DEADLINE...
WHAT THE HELL?
MORE LIKE *HEAVEN*. LAST NIGHT WAS ABOVE AND BEYOND.
DID WE?
WE DID. BUT IF YOU FEEL YOU'VE MISSED SOMETHING...
...I'D LOVE TO HIT "RE-MIND."
OHMYGOD, YOU'RE JUST LIKE HER!
ANN. WE NEED TO TALK.
ZIM, YOU NEED TO *LEAVE*.
BELIEVE ME, IT ONLY STARTED AFTER YOUR ACCIDENT—
—NO. IT STARTED BEFORE THAT, ZIM. IT TOOK US SIXTEEN YEARS TO GET ENGAGED, AND THEN WE NEVER GOT AROUND TO SET A DATE.
THEN LET'S SET A DATE! I LOVE YOU. PLEASE ANN, WHAT DO I NEED TO DO TO GET YOU BACK?

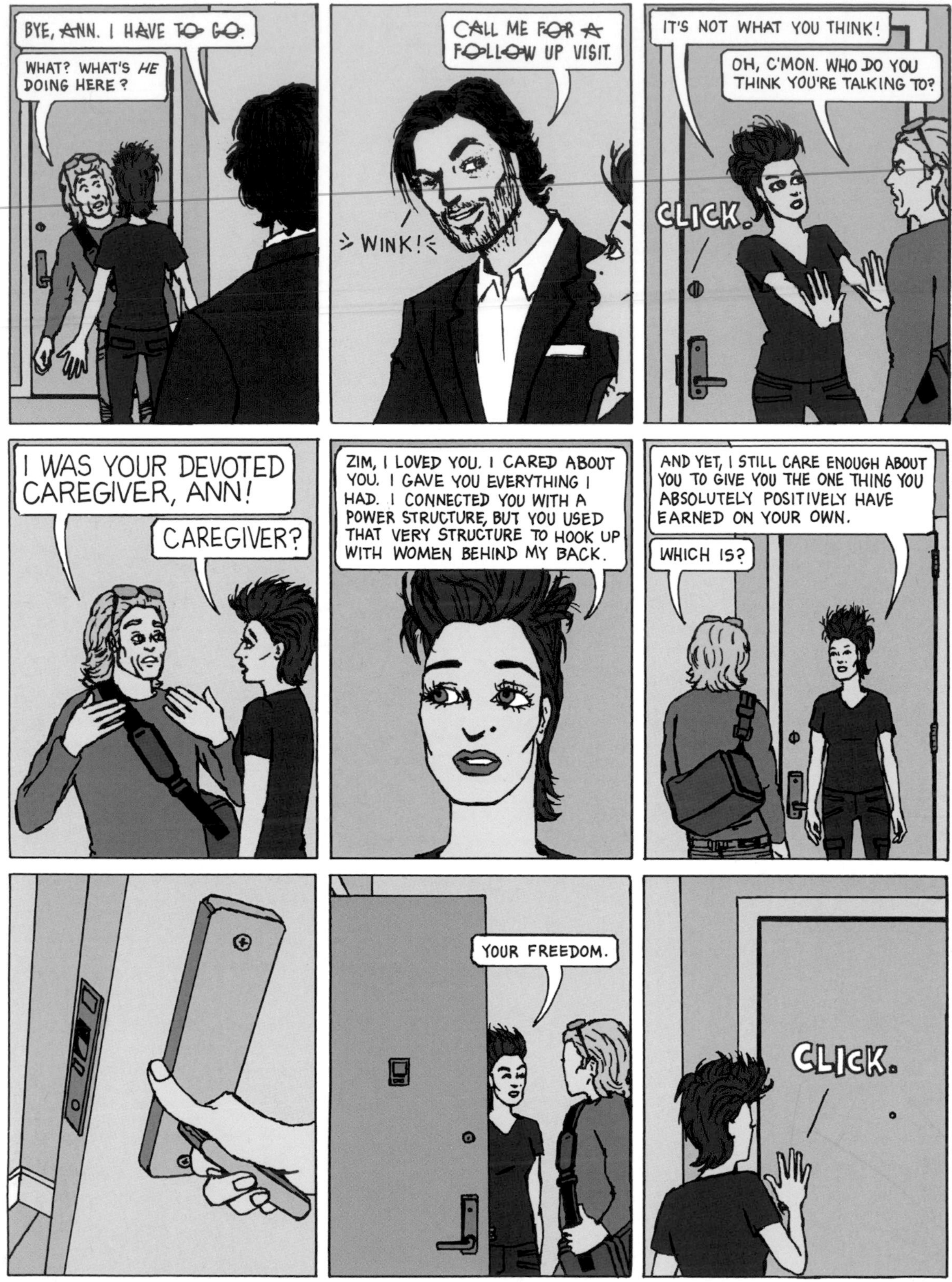

BYE, ANN. I HAVE TO GO.
WHAT? WHAT'S HE DOING HERE?
CALL ME FOR A FOLLOW UP VISIT.
WINK!
IT'S NOT WHAT YOU THINK!
OH, C'MON. WHO DO YOU THINK YOU'RE TALKING TO?
CLICK.
I WAS YOUR DEVOTED CAREGIVER, ANN!
CAREGIVER?
ZIM, I LOVED YOU. I CARED ABOUT YOU. I GAVE YOU EVERYTHING I HAD. I CONNECTED YOU WITH A POWER STRUCTURE, BUT YOU USED THAT VERY STRUCTURE TO HOOK UP WITH WOMEN BEHIND MY BACK.
AND YET, I STILL CARE ENOUGH ABOUT YOU TO GIVE YOU THE ONE THING YOU ABSOLUTELY POSITIVELY HAVE EARNED ON YOUR OWN.
WHICH IS?
YOUR FREEDOM.
CLICK.

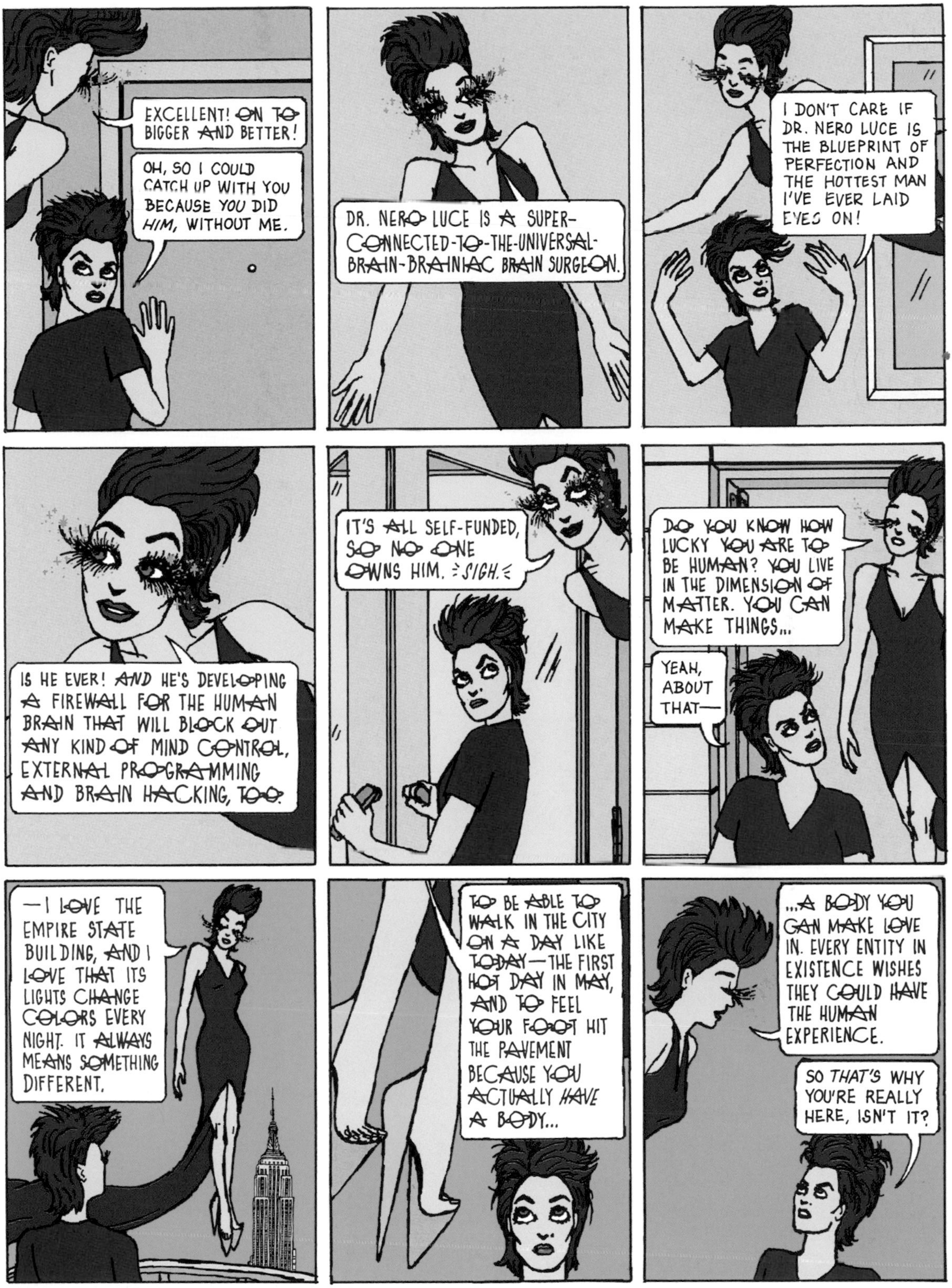
EXCELLENT! ON TO BIGGER AND BETTER!
OH, SO I COULD CATCH UP WITH YOU BECAUSE *YOU* DID *HIM*, WITHOUT ME.
DR. NERO LUCE IS A SUPER-CONNECTED-TO-THE-UNIVERSAL-BRAIN-BRAINIAC BRAIN SURGEON.
I DON'T CARE IF DR. NERO LUCE IS THE BLUEPRINT OF PERFECTION AND THE HOTTEST MAN I'VE EVER LAID EYES ON!
IS HE EVER! AND HE'S DEVELOPING A FIREWALL FOR THE HUMAN BRAIN THAT WILL BLOCK OUT ANY KIND OF MIND CONTROL, EXTERNAL PROGRAMMING AND BRAIN HACKING, TOO.
IT'S ALL SELF-FUNDED, SO NO ONE OWNS HIM. *SIGH.*
DO YOU KNOW HOW LUCKY YOU ARE TO BE HUMAN? YOU LIVE IN THE DIMENSION OF MATTER. YOU CAN MAKE THINGS...
YEAH, ABOUT THAT—
—I LOVE THE EMPIRE STATE BUILDING, AND I LOVE THAT ITS LIGHTS CHANGE COLORS EVERY NIGHT. IT ALWAYS MEANS SOMETHING DIFFERENT.
TO BE ABLE TO WALK IN THE CITY ON A DAY LIKE TODAY—THE FIRST HOT DAY IN MAY, AND TO FEEL YOUR FOOT HIT THE PAVEMENT BECAUSE YOU ACTUALLY *HAVE* A BODY...
...A BODY YOU CAN MAKE LOVE IN. EVERY ENTITY IN EXISTENCE WISHES THEY COULD HAVE THE HUMAN EXPERIENCE.
SO *THAT'S* WHY YOU'RE REALLY HERE, ISN'T IT?

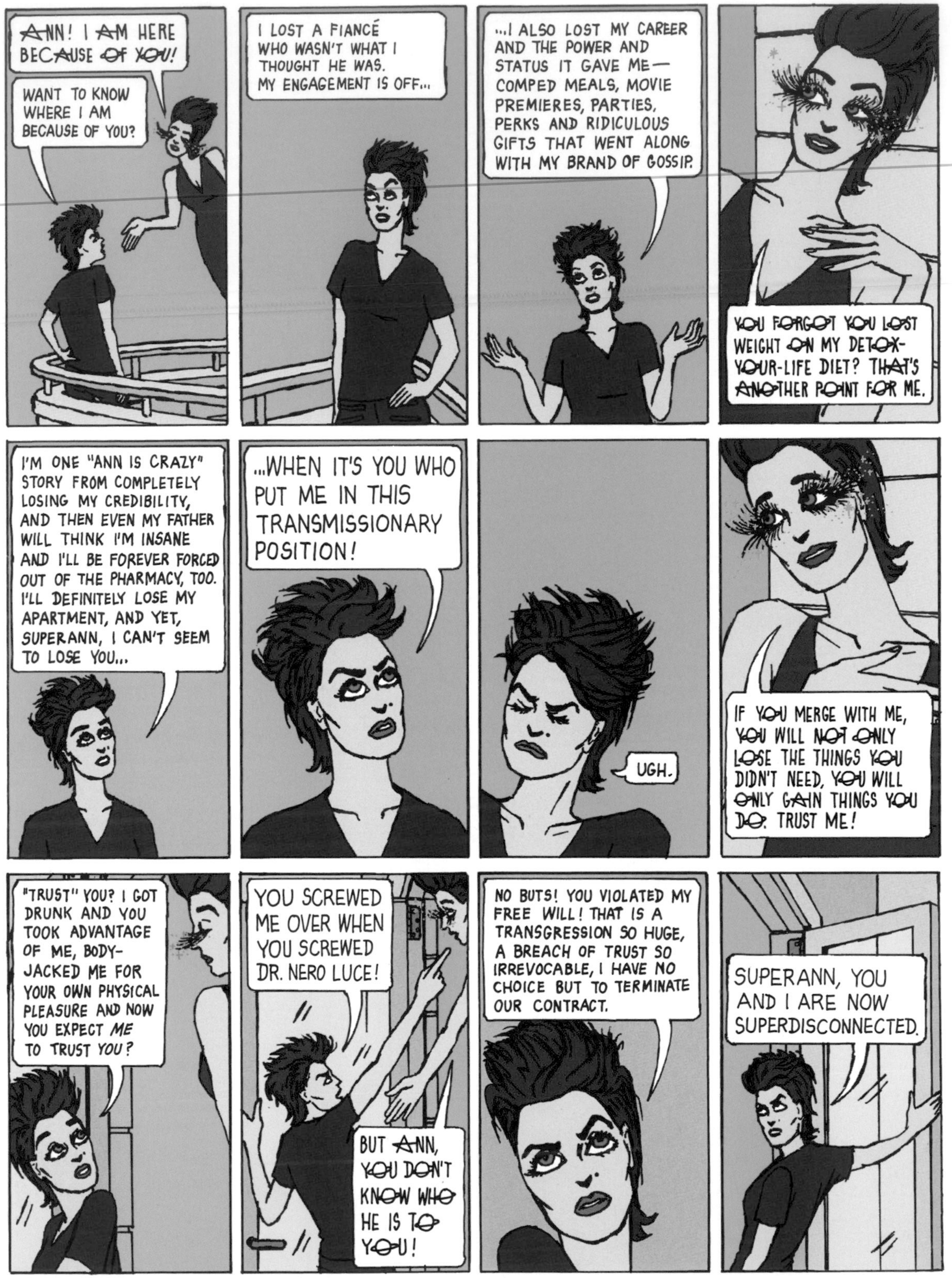
ANN! I AM HERE BECAUSE OF YOU!
WANT TO KNOW WHERE I AM BECAUSE OF YOU?
I LOST A FIANCÉ WHO WASN'T WHAT I THOUGHT HE WAS. MY ENGAGEMENT IS OFF...
...I ALSO LOST MY CAREER AND THE POWER AND STATUS IT GAVE ME— COMPED MEALS, MOVIE PREMIERES, PARTIES, PERKS AND RIDICULOUS GIFTS THAT WENT ALONG WITH MY BRAND OF GOSSIP.
YOU FORGOT YOU LOST WEIGHT ON MY DETOX-YOUR-LIFE DIET? THAT'S ANOTHER POINT FOR ME.
I'M ONE "ANN IS CRAZY" STORY FROM COMPLETELY LOSING MY CREDIBILITY, AND THEN EVEN MY FATHER WILL THINK I'M INSANE AND I'LL BE FOREVER FORCED OUT OF THE PHARMACY, TOO. I'LL DEFINITELY LOSE MY APARTMENT, AND YET, SUPERANN, I CAN'T SEEM TO LOSE YOU...
...WHEN IT'S YOU WHO PUT ME IN THIS TRANSMISSIONARY POSITION!
UGH.
IF YOU MERGE WITH ME, YOU WILL NOT ONLY LOSE THE THINGS YOU DIDN'T NEED, YOU WILL ONLY GAIN THINGS YOU DO. TRUST ME!
"TRUST" YOU? I GOT DRUNK AND YOU TOOK ADVANTAGE OF ME, BODY-JACKED ME FOR YOUR OWN PHYSICAL PLEASURE AND NOW YOU EXPECT ME TO TRUST YOU?
YOU SCREWED ME OVER WHEN YOU SCREWED DR. NERO LUCE!
BUT ANN, YOU DON'T KNOW WHO HE IS TO YOU!
NO BUTS! YOU VIOLATED MY FREE WILL! THAT IS A TRANSGRESSION SO HUGE, A BREACH OF TRUST SO IRREVOCABLE, I HAVE NO CHOICE BUT TO TERMINATE OUR CONTRACT.
SUPERANN, YOU AND I ARE NOW SUPERDISCONNECTED.

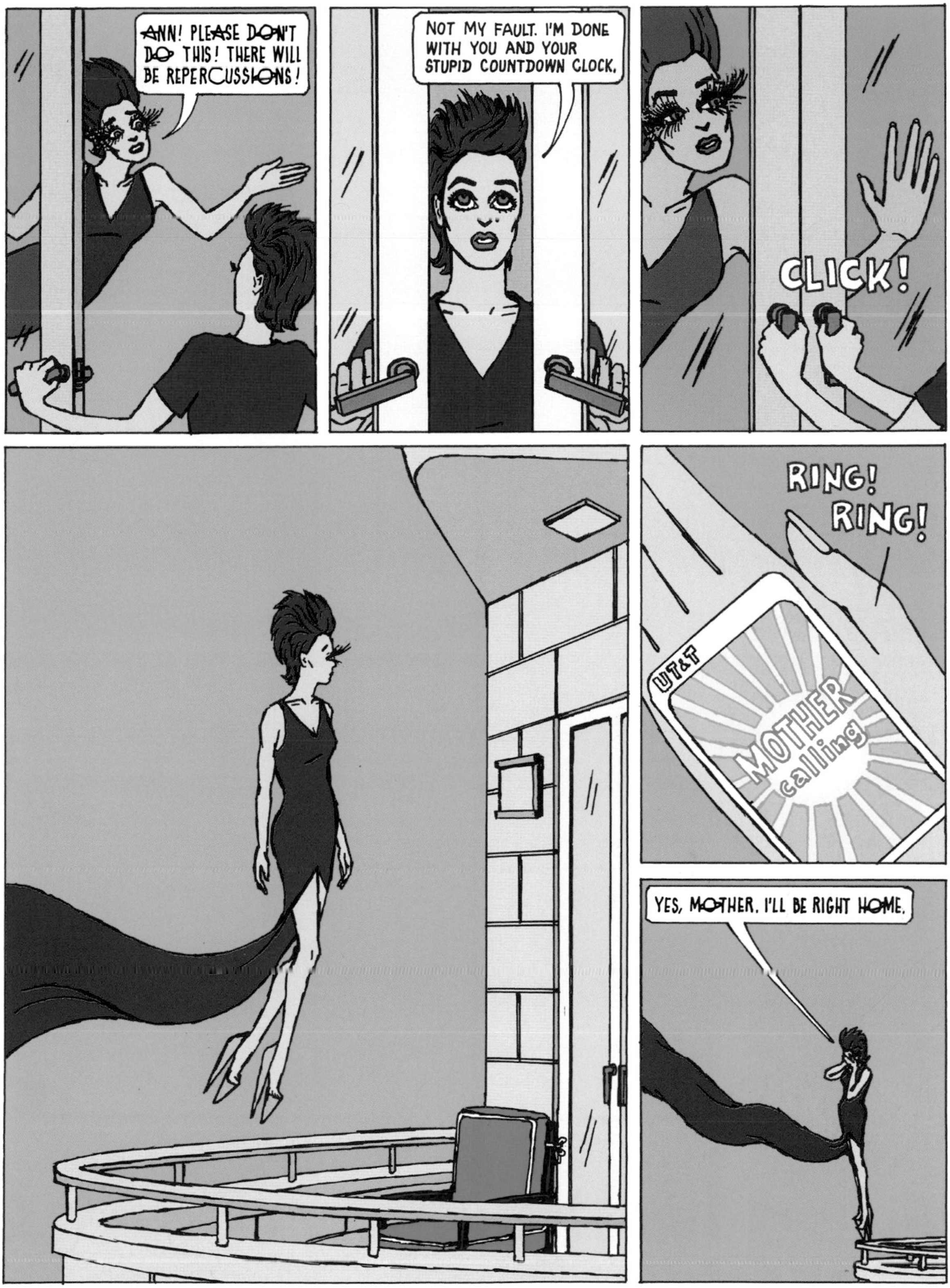
ANN! PLEASE DON'T DO THIS! THERE WILL BE REPERCUSSIONS!
NOT MY FAULT. I'M DONE WITH YOU AND YOUR STUPID COUNTDOWN CLOCK.
CLICK!
RING! RING!
UT&T
MOTHER calling
YES, MOTHER. I'LL BE RIGHT HOME.

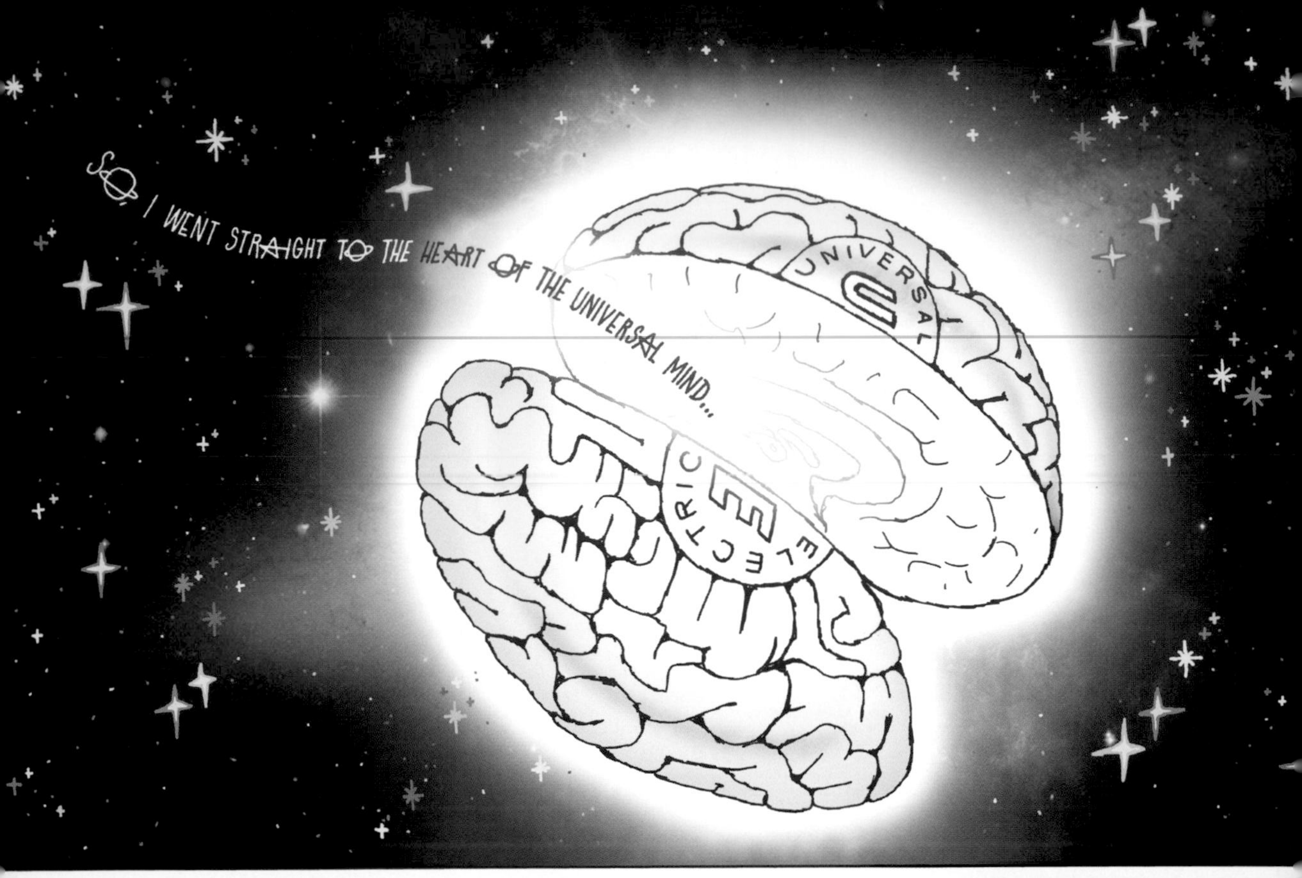
SO, I WENT STRAIGHT TO THE HEART OF THE UNIVERSAL MIND...
UNIVERSAL
ELECTRIC
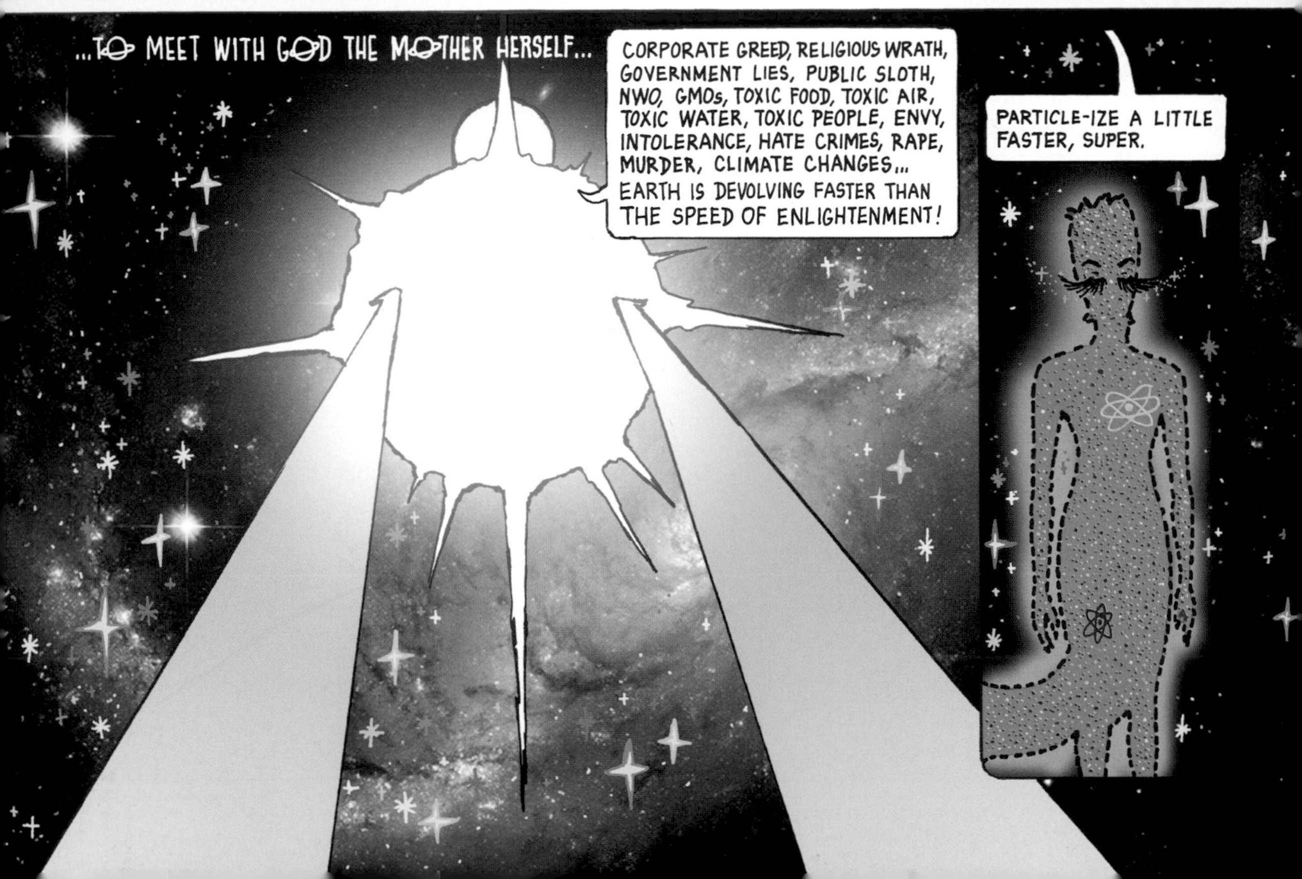
...TO MEET WITH GOD THE MOTHER HERSELF...
CORPORATE GREED, RELIGIOUS WRATH, GOVERNMENT LIES, PUBLIC SLOTH, NWO, GMOs, TOXIC FOOD, TOXIC AIR, TOXIC WATER, TOXIC PEOPLE, ENVY, INTOLERANCE, HATE CRIMES, RAPE, MURDER, CLIMATE CHANGES... EARTH IS DEVOLVING FASTER THAN THE SPEED OF ENLIGHTENMENT!
PARTICLE-IZE A LITTLE FASTER, SUPER.

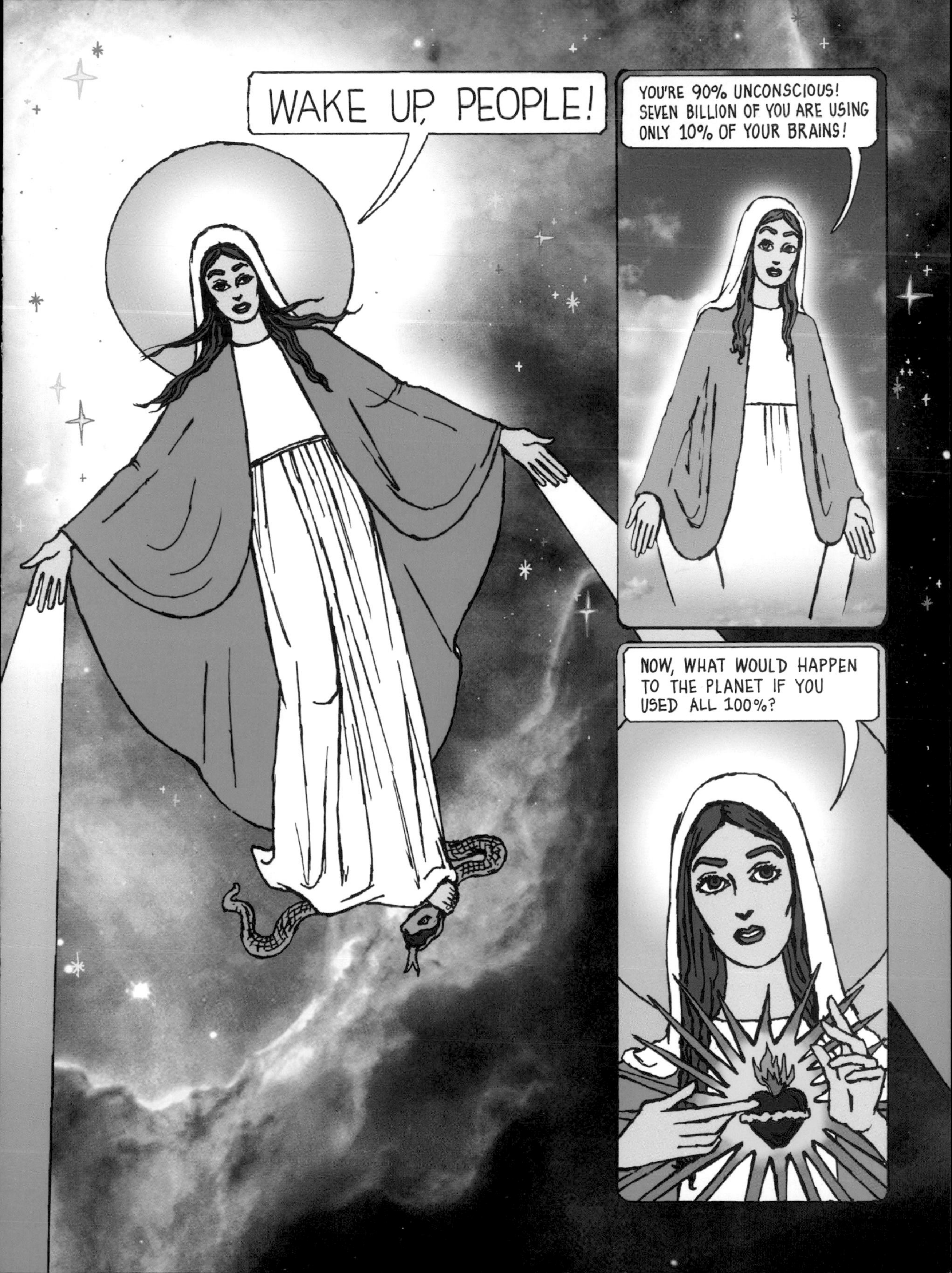
WAKE UP, PEOPLE!
YOU'RE 90% UNCONSCIOUS! SEVEN BILLION OF YOU ARE USING ONLY 10% OF YOUR BRAINS!
NOW, WHAT WOULD HAPPEN TO THE PLANET IF YOU USED ALL 100%?

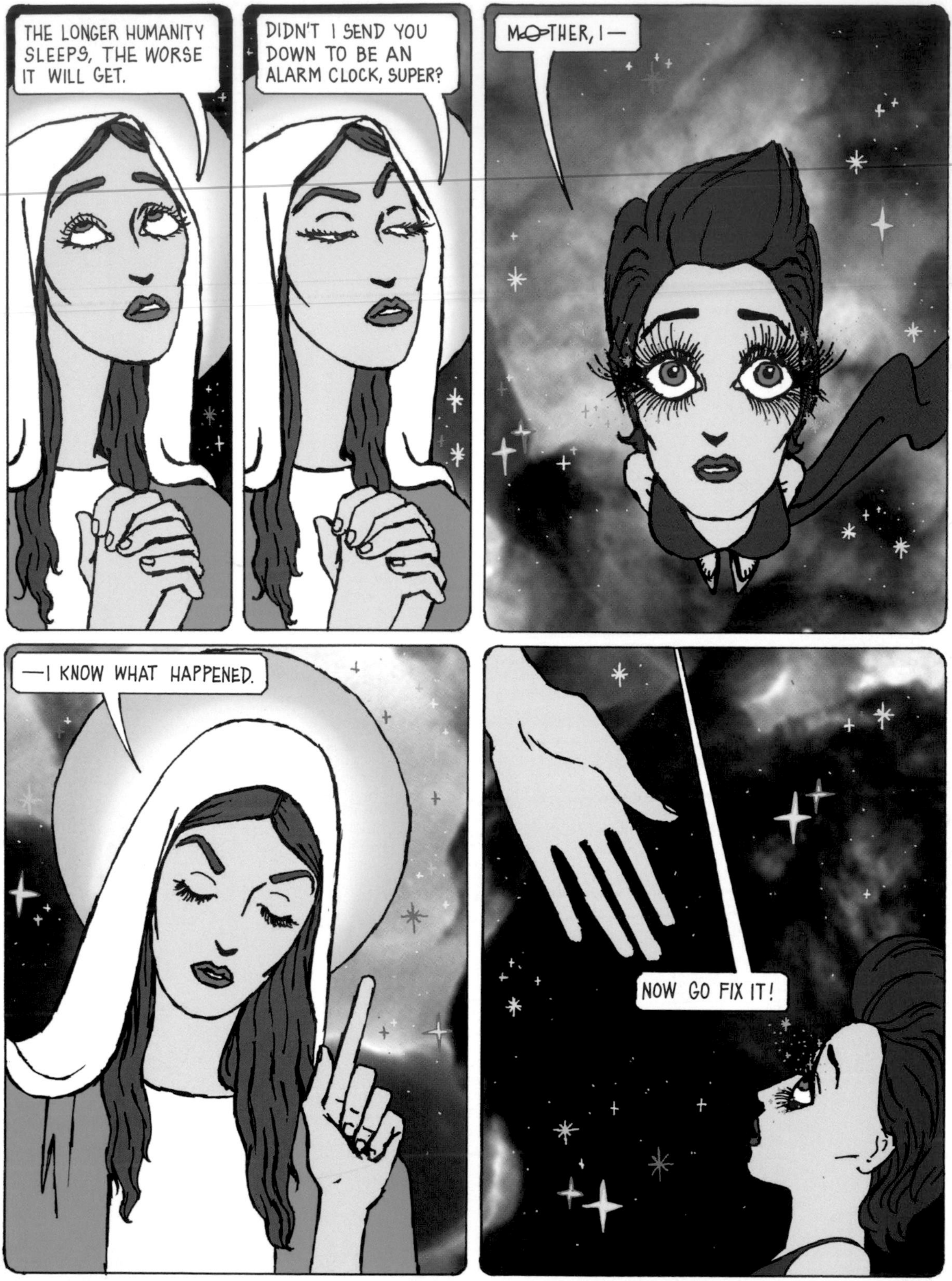
THE LONGER HUMANITY SLEEPS, THE WORSE IT WILL GET.
DIDN'T I SEND YOU DOWN TO BE AN ALARM CLOCK, SUPER?
MOTHER, I—
—I KNOW WHAT HAPPENED.
NOW GO FIX IT!

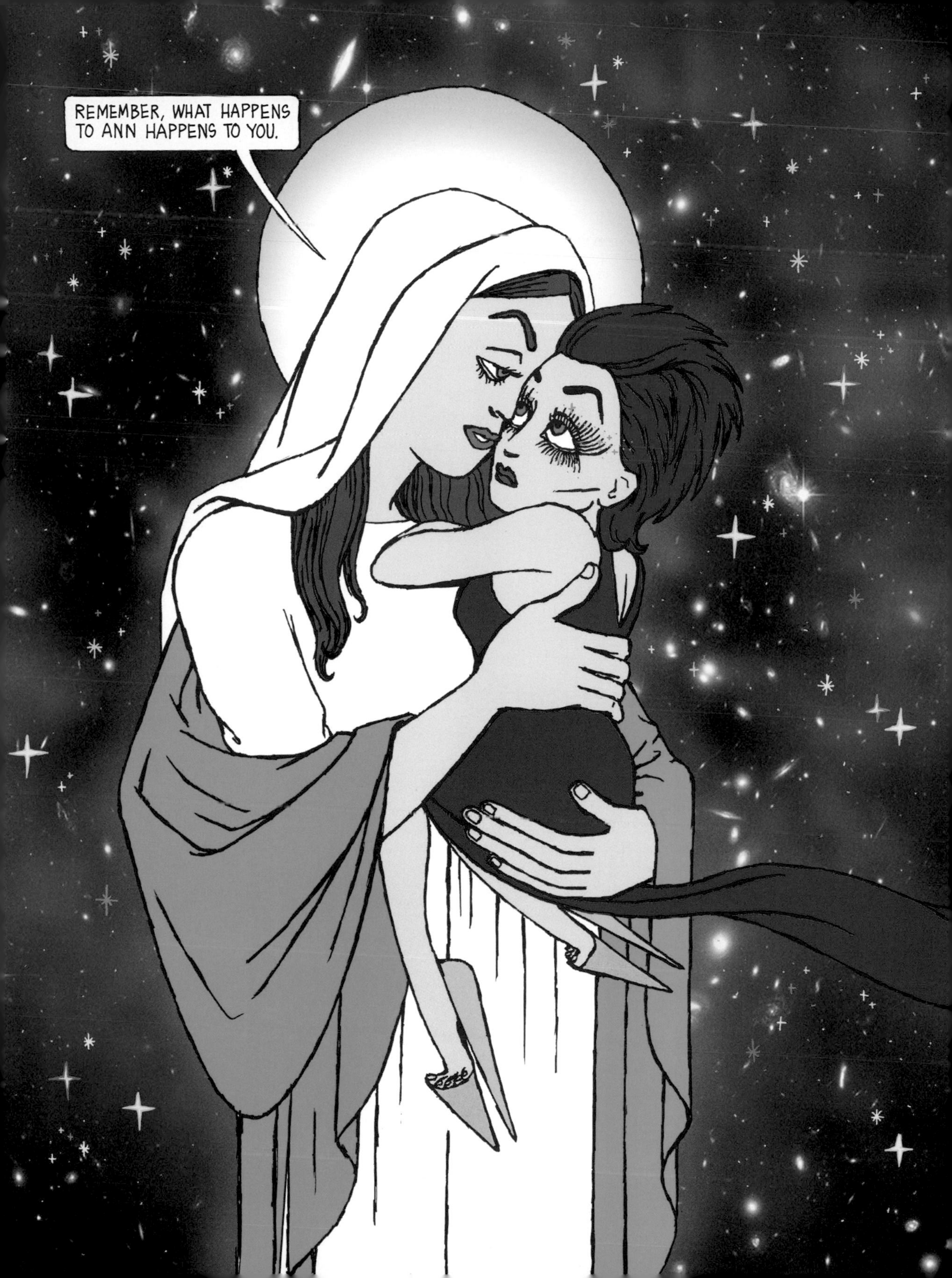
REMEMBER, WHAT HAPPENS TO ANN HAPPENS TO YOU.

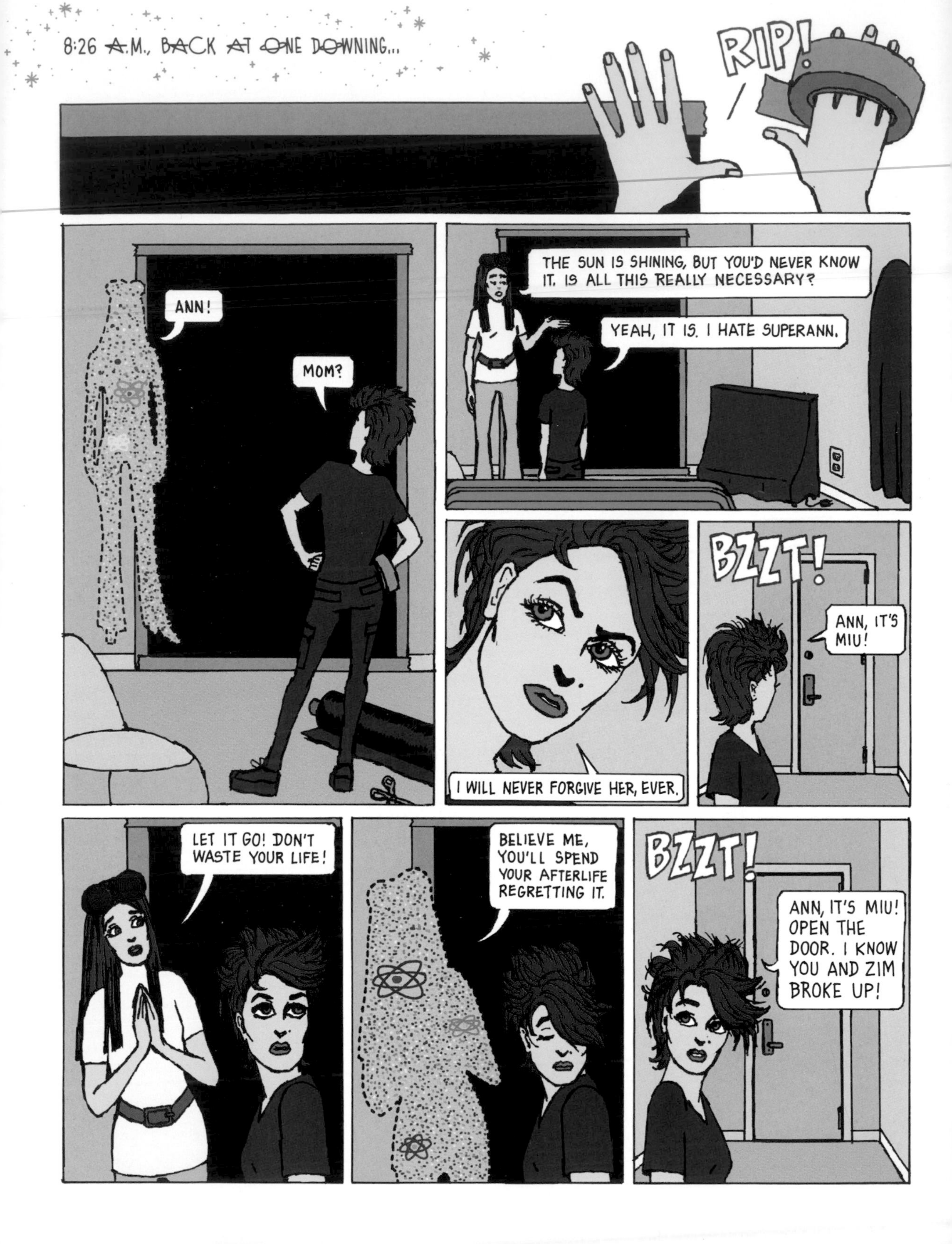
8:26 A.M., BACK AT ONE DOWNING...
RIP!
ANN!
MOM?
THE SUN IS SHINING, BUT YOU'D NEVER KNOW IT. IS ALL THIS REALLY NECESSARY?
YEAH, IT IS. I HATE SUPERANN.
I WILL NEVER FORGIVE HER, EVER.
BZZT!
ANN, IT'S MIU!
LET IT GO! DON'T WASTE YOUR LIFE!
BELIEVE ME, YOU'LL SPEND YOUR AFTERLIFE REGRETTING IT.
BZZT!
ANN, IT'S MIU! OPEN THE DOOR. I KNOW YOU AND ZIM BROKE UP!

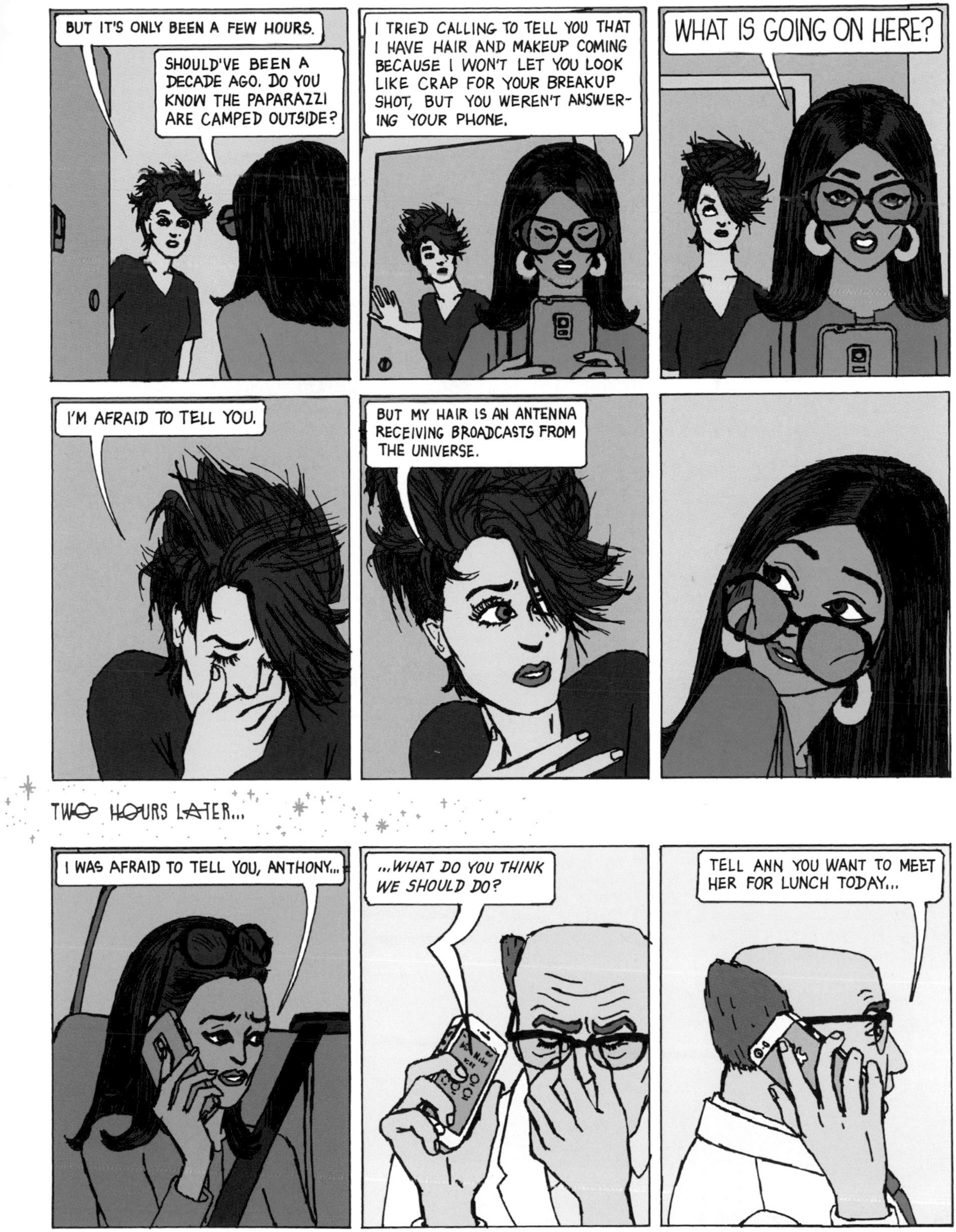
BUT IT'S ONLY BEEN A FEW HOURS.
SHOULD'VE BEEN A DECADE AGO. DO YOU KNOW THE PAPARAZZI ARE CAMPED OUTSIDE?
I TRIED CALLING TO TELL YOU THAT I HAVE HAIR AND MAKEUP COMING BECAUSE I WON'T LET YOU LOOK LIKE CRAP FOR YOUR BREAKUP SHOT, BUT YOU WEREN'T ANSWERING YOUR PHONE.
WHAT IS GOING ON HERE?
I'M AFRAID TO TELL YOU.
BUT MY HAIR IS AN ANTENNA RECEIVING BROADCASTS FROM THE UNIVERSE.
TWO HOURS LATER...
I WAS AFRAID TO TELL YOU, ANTHONY...
...WHAT DO YOU THINK WE SHOULD DO?
TELL ANN YOU WANT TO MEET HER FOR LUNCH TODAY...

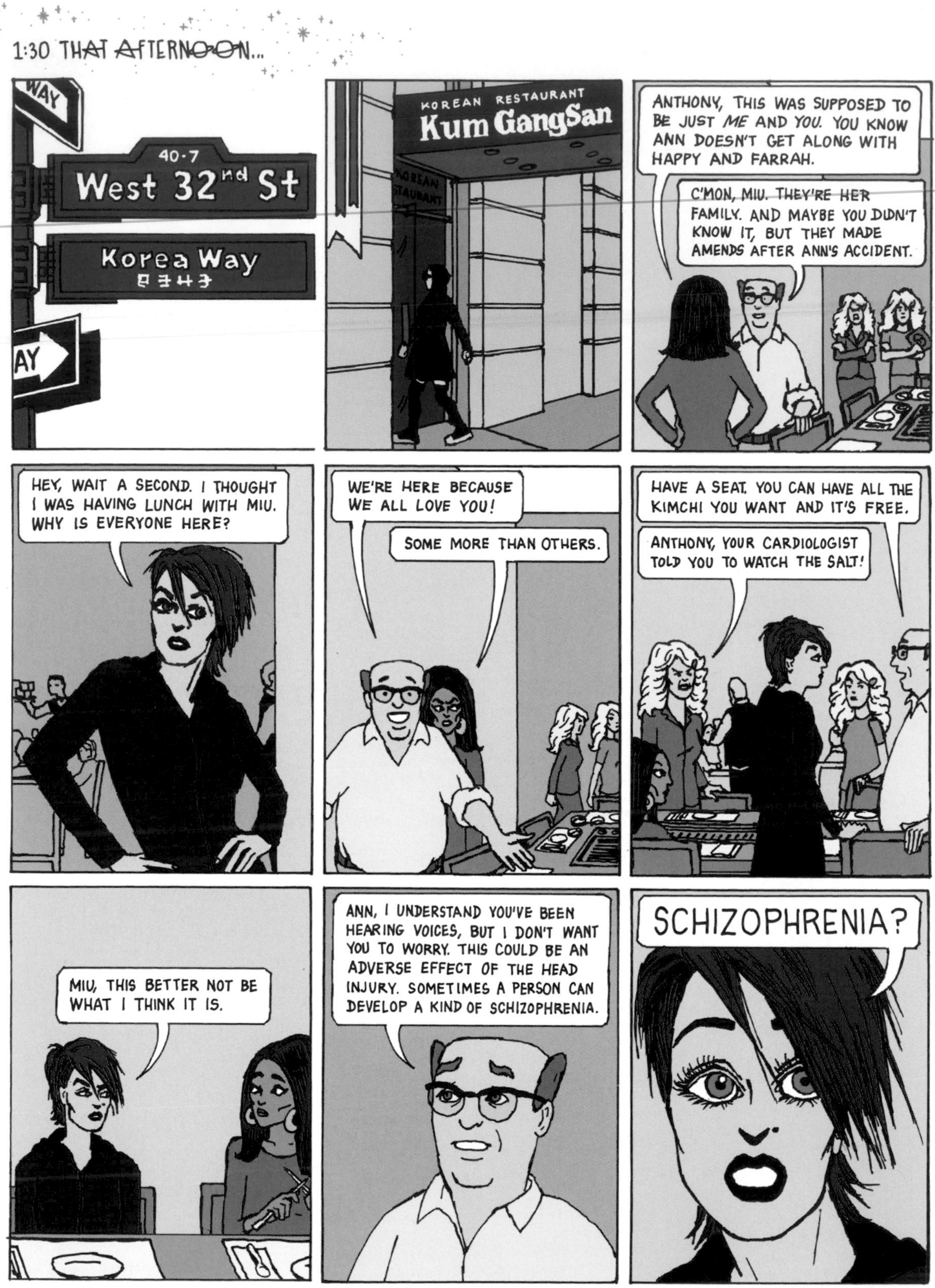
1:30 THAT AFTERNOON...
40-7
West 32nd St
Korea Way
KOREAN RESTAURANT
Kum GangSan
ANTHONY, THIS WAS SUPPOSED TO BE JUST *ME* AND *YOU.* YOU KNOW ANN DOESN'T GET ALONG WITH HAPPY AND FARRAH.
C'MON, MIU. THEY'RE HER FAMILY. AND MAYBE YOU DIDN'T KNOW IT, BUT THEY MADE AMENDS AFTER ANN'S ACCIDENT.
HEY, WAIT A SECOND. I THOUGHT I WAS HAVING LUNCH WITH MIU. WHY IS EVERYONE HERE?
WE'RE HERE BECAUSE WE ALL LOVE YOU!
SOME MORE THAN OTHERS.
HAVE A SEAT. YOU CAN HAVE ALL THE KIMCHI YOU WANT AND IT'S FREE.
ANTHONY, YOUR CARDIOLOGIST TOLD YOU TO WATCH THE SALT!
MIU, THIS BETTER NOT BE WHAT I THINK IT IS.
ANN, I UNDERSTAND YOU'VE BEEN HEARING VOICES, BUT I DON'T WANT YOU TO WORRY. THIS COULD BE AN ADVERSE EFFECT OF THE HEAD INJURY. SOMETIMES A PERSON CAN DEVELOP A KIND OF SCHIZOPHRENIA.
SCHIZOPHRENIA?

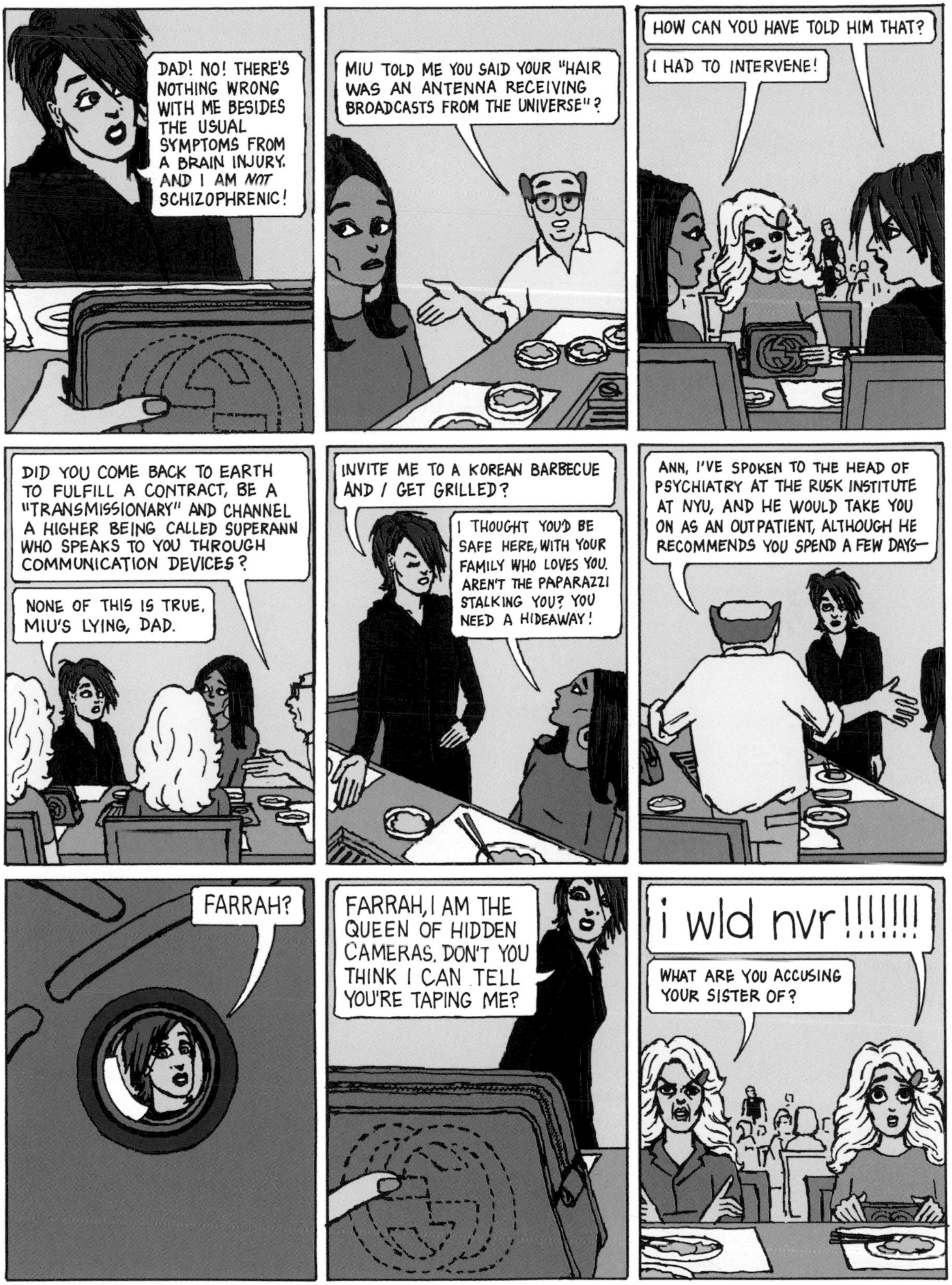
DAD! NO! THERE'S NOTHING WRONG WITH ME BESIDES THE USUAL SYMPTOMS FROM A BRAIN INJURY. AND I AM *NOT* SCHIZOPHRENIC!
MIU TOLD ME YOU SAID YOUR "HAIR WAS AN ANTENNA RECEIVING BROADCASTS FROM THE UNIVERSE"?
HOW CAN YOU HAVE TOLD HIM THAT?
I HAD TO INTERVENE!
DID YOU COME BACK TO EARTH TO FULFILL A CONTRACT, BE A "TRANSMISSIONARY" AND CHANNEL A HIGHER BEING CALLED SUPERANN WHO SPEAKS TO YOU THROUGH COMMUNICATION DEVICES?
NONE OF THIS IS TRUE. MIU'S LYING, DAD.
INVITE ME TO A KOREAN BARBECUE AND I GET GRILLED?
I THOUGHT YOU'D BE SAFE HERE, WITH YOUR FAMILY WHO LOVES YOU. AREN'T THE PAPARAZZI STALKING YOU? YOU NEED A HIDEAWAY!
ANN, I'VE SPOKEN TO THE HEAD OF PSYCHIATRY AT THE RUSK INSTITUTE AT NYU, AND HE WOULD TAKE YOU ON AS AN OUTPATIENT, ALTHOUGH HE RECOMMENDS YOU SPEND A FEW DAYS—
FARRAH?
FARRAH, I AM THE QUEEN OF HIDDEN CAMERAS. DON'T YOU THINK I CAN TELL YOU'RE TAPING ME?
i wld nvr!!!!!!!!
WHAT ARE YOU ACCUSING YOUR SISTER OF?

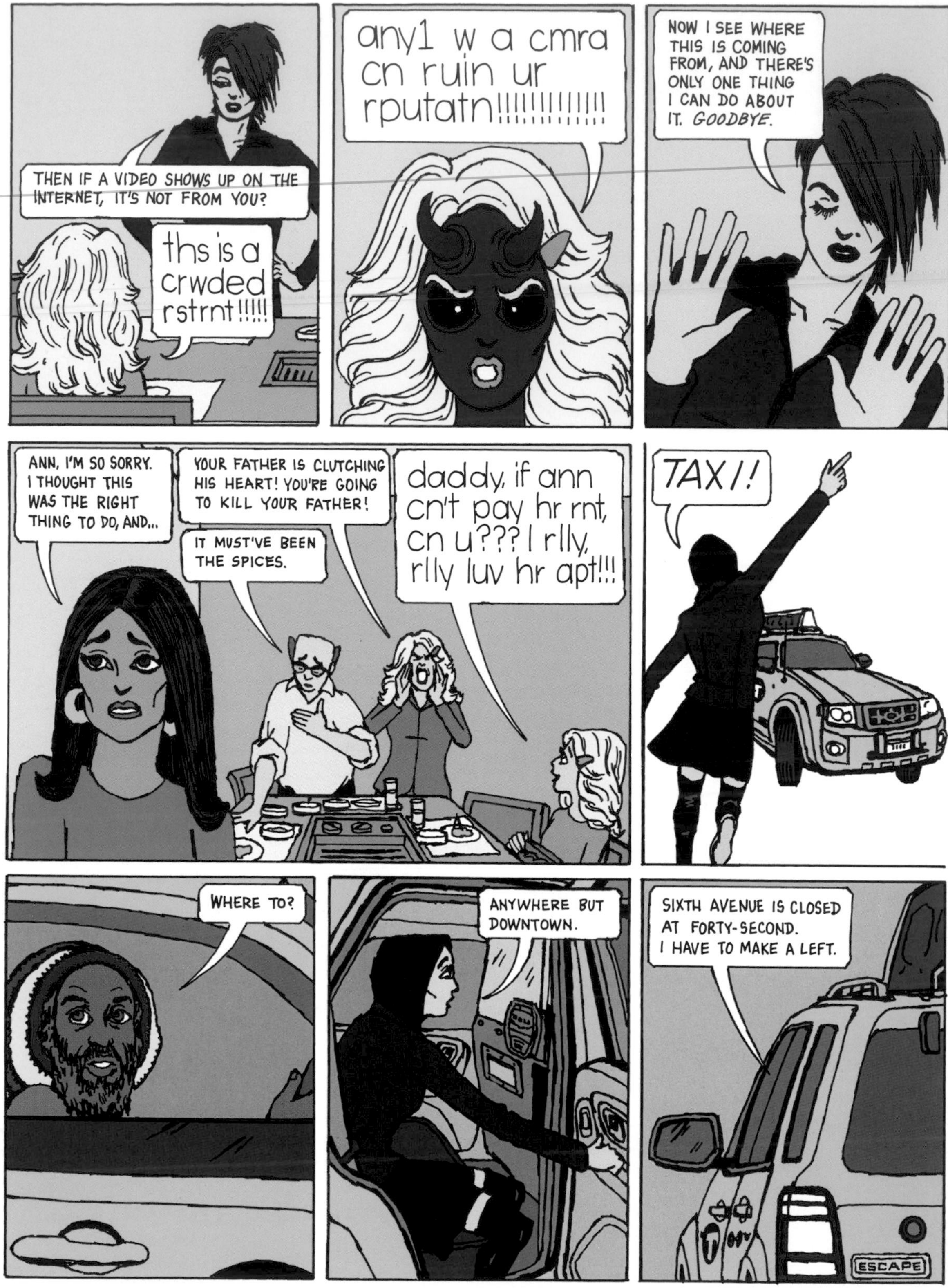
THEN IF A VIDEO SHOWS UP ON THE INTERNET, IT'S NOT FROM YOU?
ths is a crwded rstrnt!!!!!
any1 w a cmra cn ruin ur rputatn!!!!!!!!!!!!!
NOW I SEE WHERE THIS IS COMING FROM, AND THERE'S ONLY ONE THING I CAN DO ABOUT IT. GOODBYE.
ANN, I'M SO SORRY. I THOUGHT THIS WAS THE RIGHT THING TO DO, AND...
YOUR FATHER IS CLUTCHING HIS HEART! YOU'RE GOING TO KILL YOUR FATHER!
IT MUST'VE BEEN THE SPICES.
daddy, if ann cn't pay hr rnt, cn u??? I rlly, rlly luv hr apt!!!
TAXI!
WHERE TO?
ANYWHERE BUT DOWNTOWN.
SIXTH AVENUE IS CLOSED AT FORTY-SECOND. I HAVE TO MAKE A LEFT.
ESCAPE

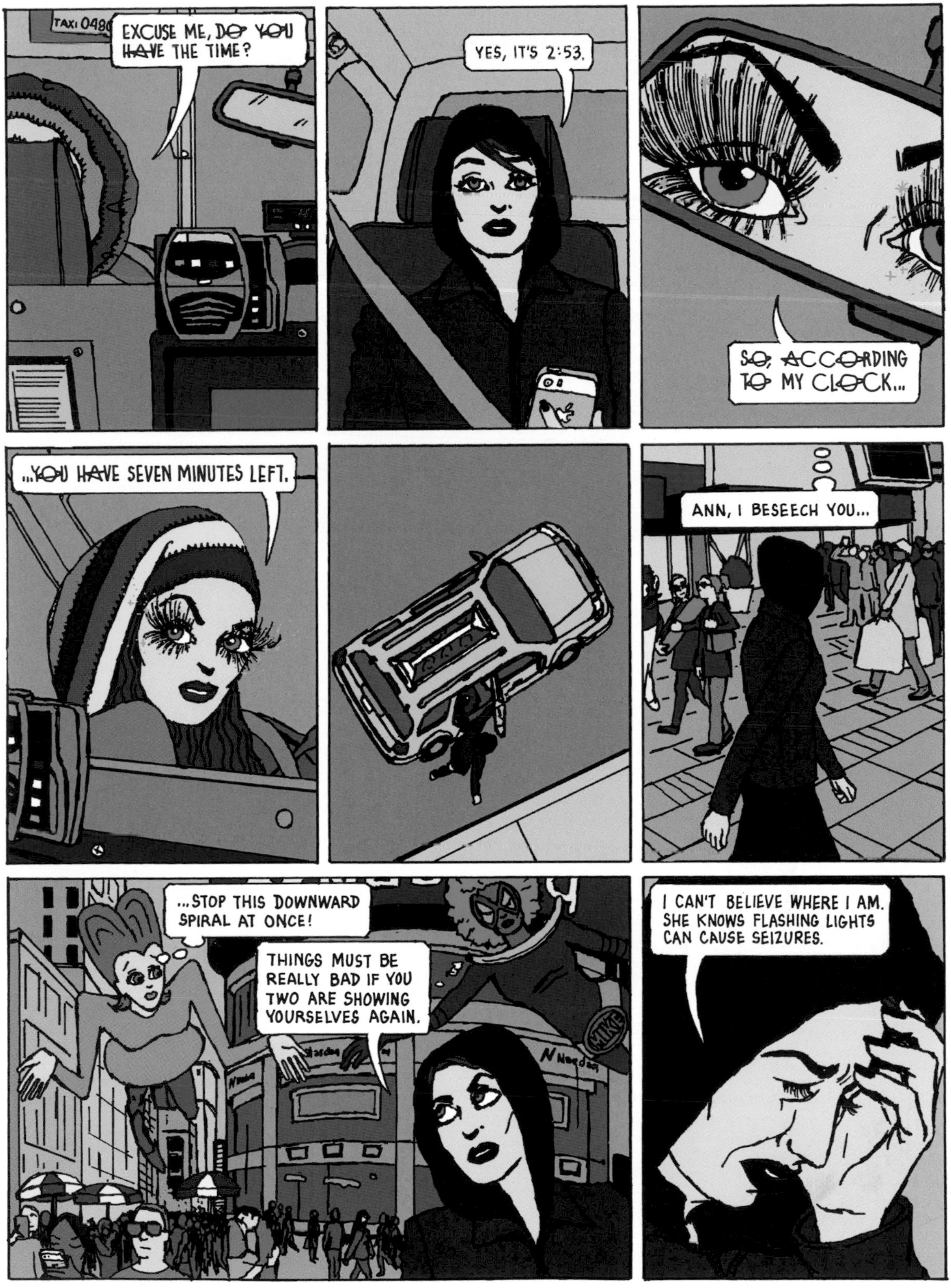
EXCUSE ME, DO YOU HAVE THE TIME?
YES, IT'S 2:53.
SO, ACCORDING TO MY CLOCK...
...YOU HAVE SEVEN MINUTES LEFT.
ANN, I BESEECH YOU...
...STOP THIS DOWNWARD SPIRAL AT ONCE!
THINGS MUST BE REALLY BAD IF YOU TWO ARE SHOWING YOURSELVES AGAIN.
I CAN'T BELIEVE WHERE I AM. SHE KNOWS FLASHING LIGHTS CAN CAUSE SEIZURES.

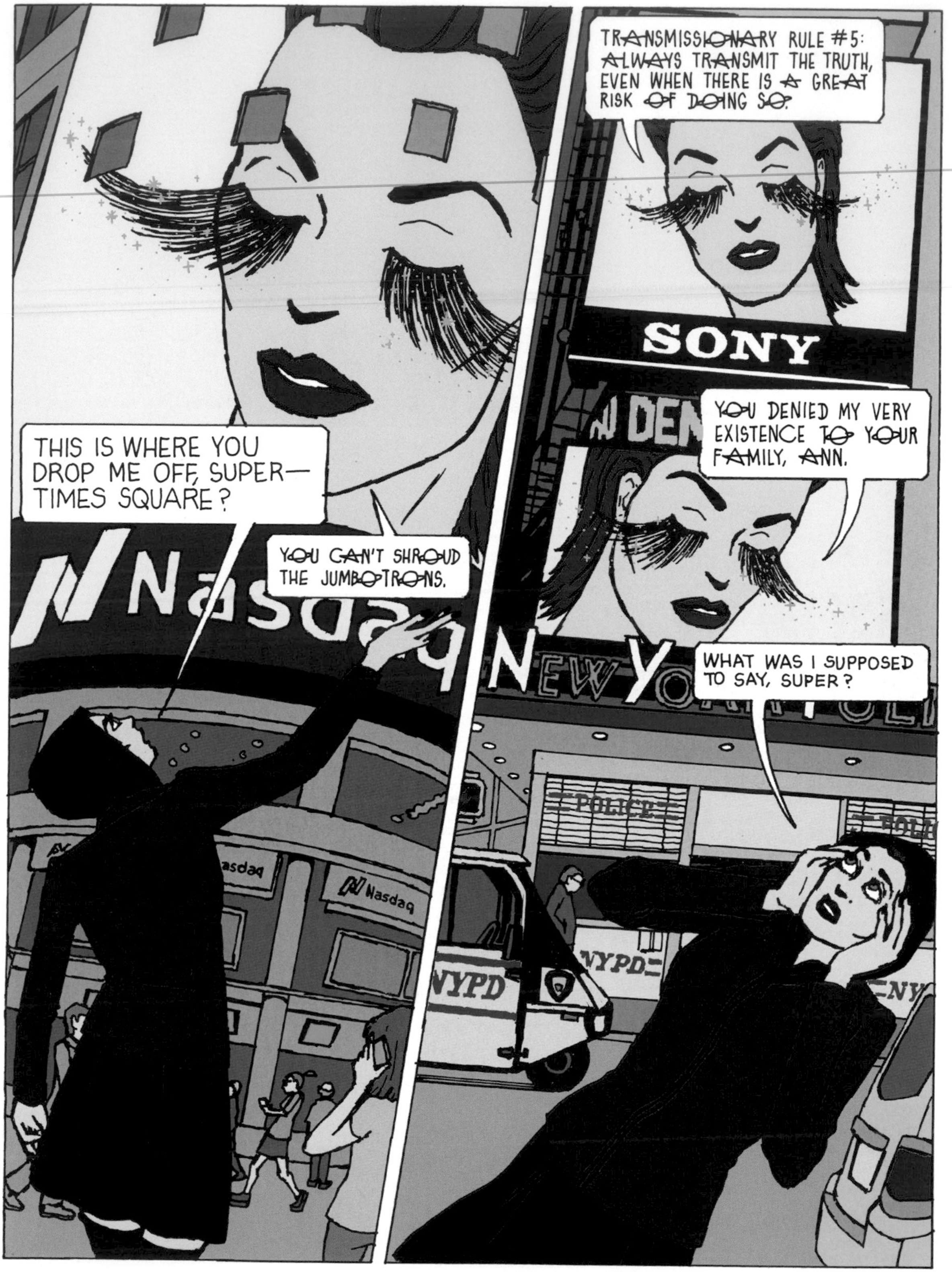
THIS IS WHERE YOU DROP ME OFF, SUPER— TIMES SQUARE?
YOU CAN'T SHROUD THE JUMBOTRONS.
TRANSMISSIONARY RULE #5: ALWAYS TRANSMIT THE TRUTH, EVEN WHEN THERE IS A GREAT RISK OF DOING SO.
SONY
YOU DENIED MY VERY EXISTENCE TO YOUR FAMILY, ANN.
WHAT WAS I SUPPOSED TO SAY, SUPER?
Nasdaq
POLICE
NYPD

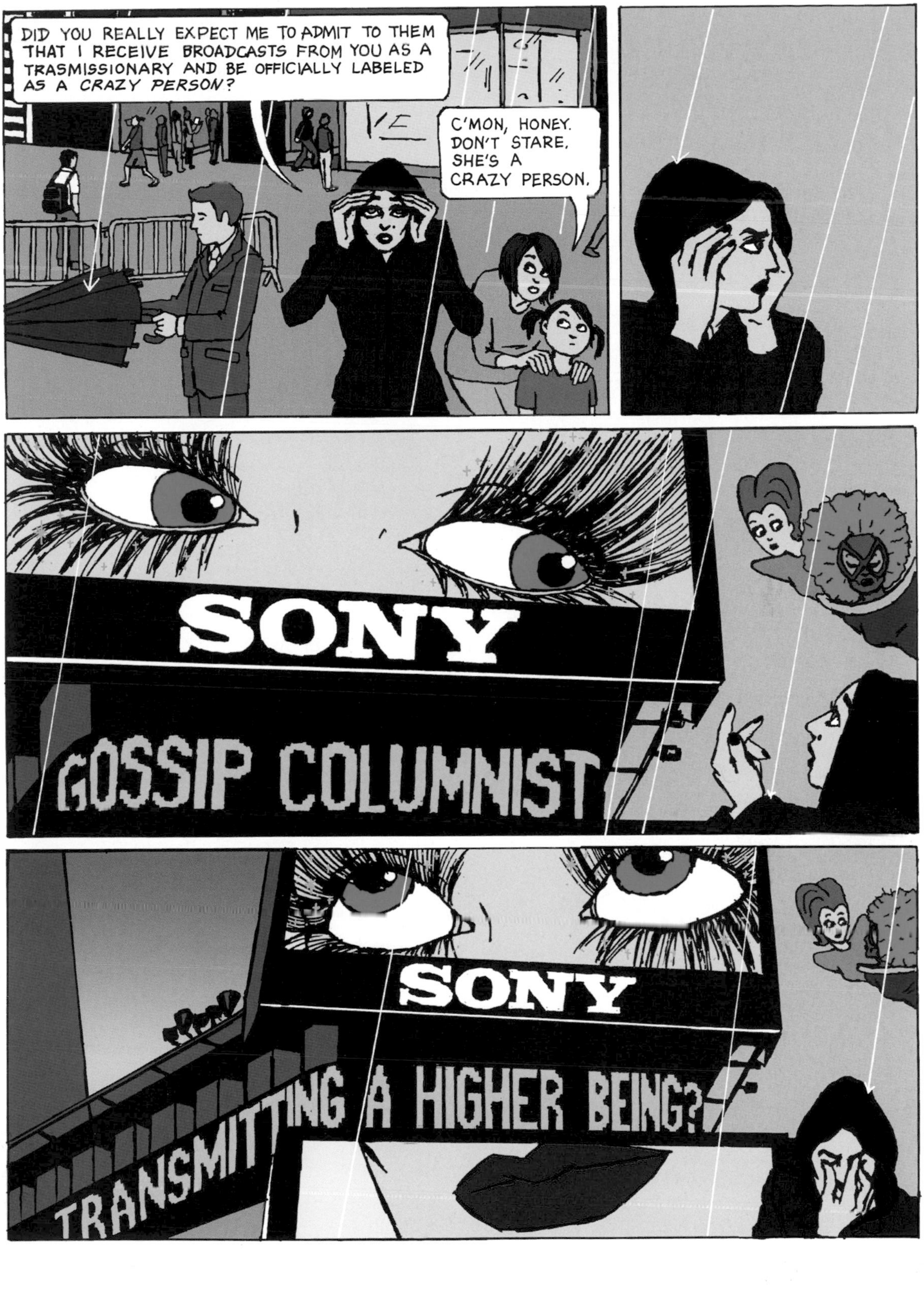
DID YOU REALLY EXPECT ME TO ADMIT TO THEM THAT I RECEIVE BROADCASTS FROM YOU AS A TRASMISSIONARY AND BE OFFICIALLY LABELED AS A *CRAZY PERSON?*
C'MON, HONEY. DON'T STARE. SHE'S A CRAZY PERSON.
SONY
GOSSIP COLUMNIST
SONY
TRANSMITTING A HIGHER BEING?

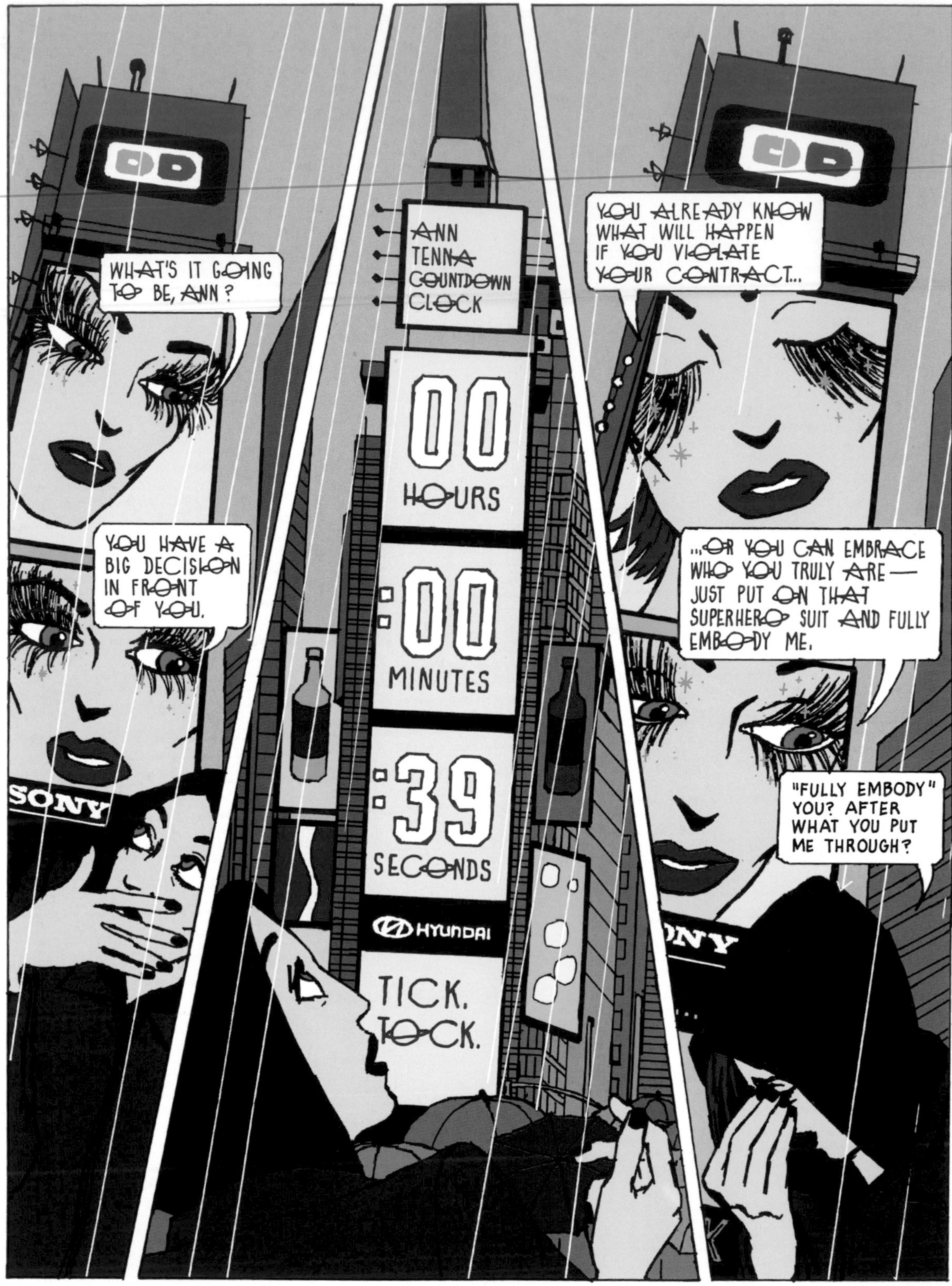
WHAT'S IT GOING TO BE, ANN?
YOU HAVE A BIG DECISION IN FRONT OF YOU.
SONY
ANN TENNA COUNTDOWN CLOCK
00 HOURS
:00 MINUTES
:39 SECONDS
HYUNDAI
TICK. TOCK.
YOU ALREADY KNOW WHAT WILL HAPPEN IF YOU VIOLATE YOUR CONTRACT...
...OR YOU CAN EMBRACE WHO YOU TRULY ARE— JUST PUT ON THAT SUPERHERO SUIT AND FULLY EMBODY ME.
"FULLY EMBODY" YOU? AFTER WHAT YOU PUT ME THROUGH?

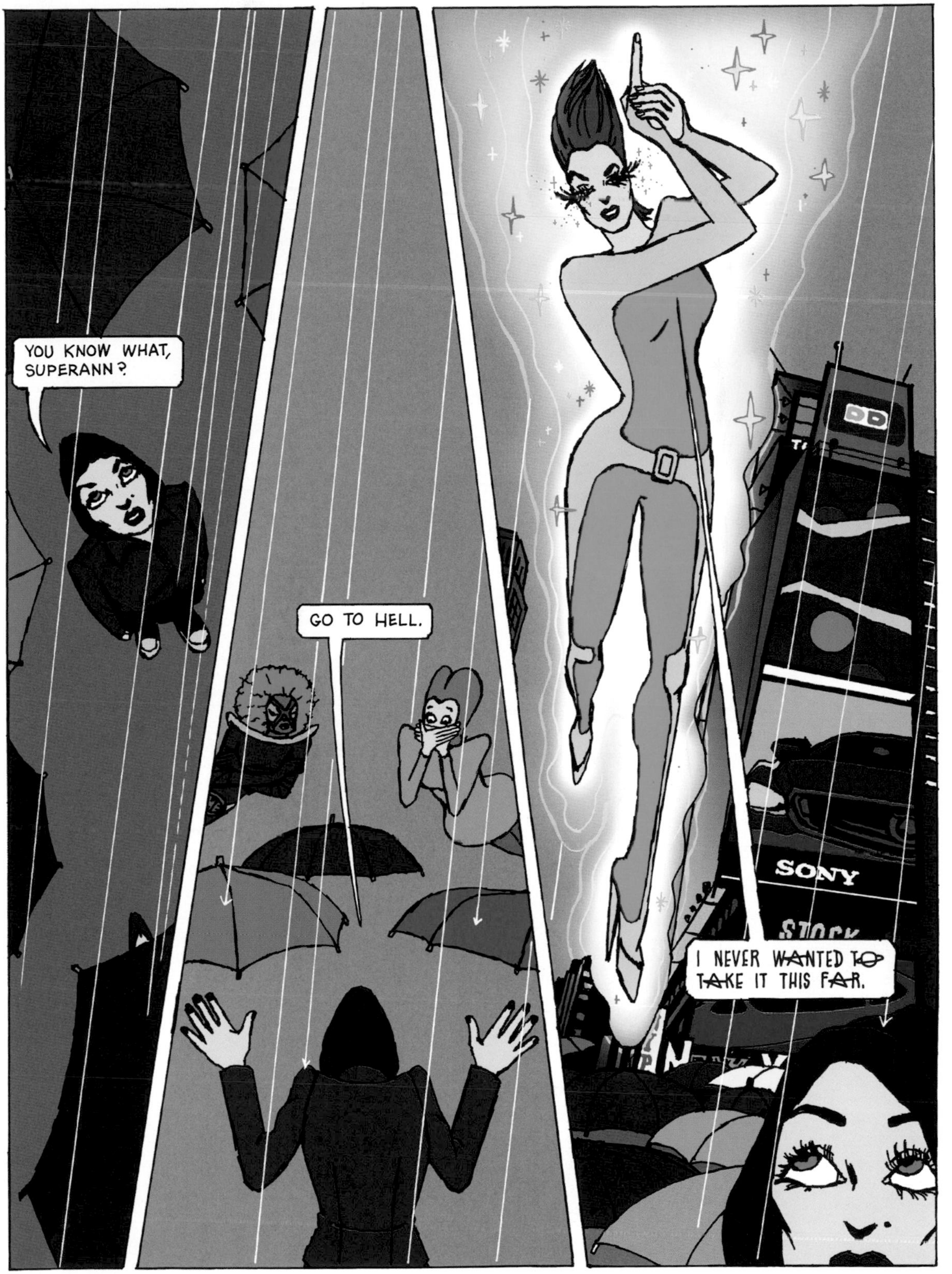
YOU KNOW WHAT, SUPERANN?
GO TO HELL.
I NEVER WANTED TO TAKE IT THIS FAR.
SONY

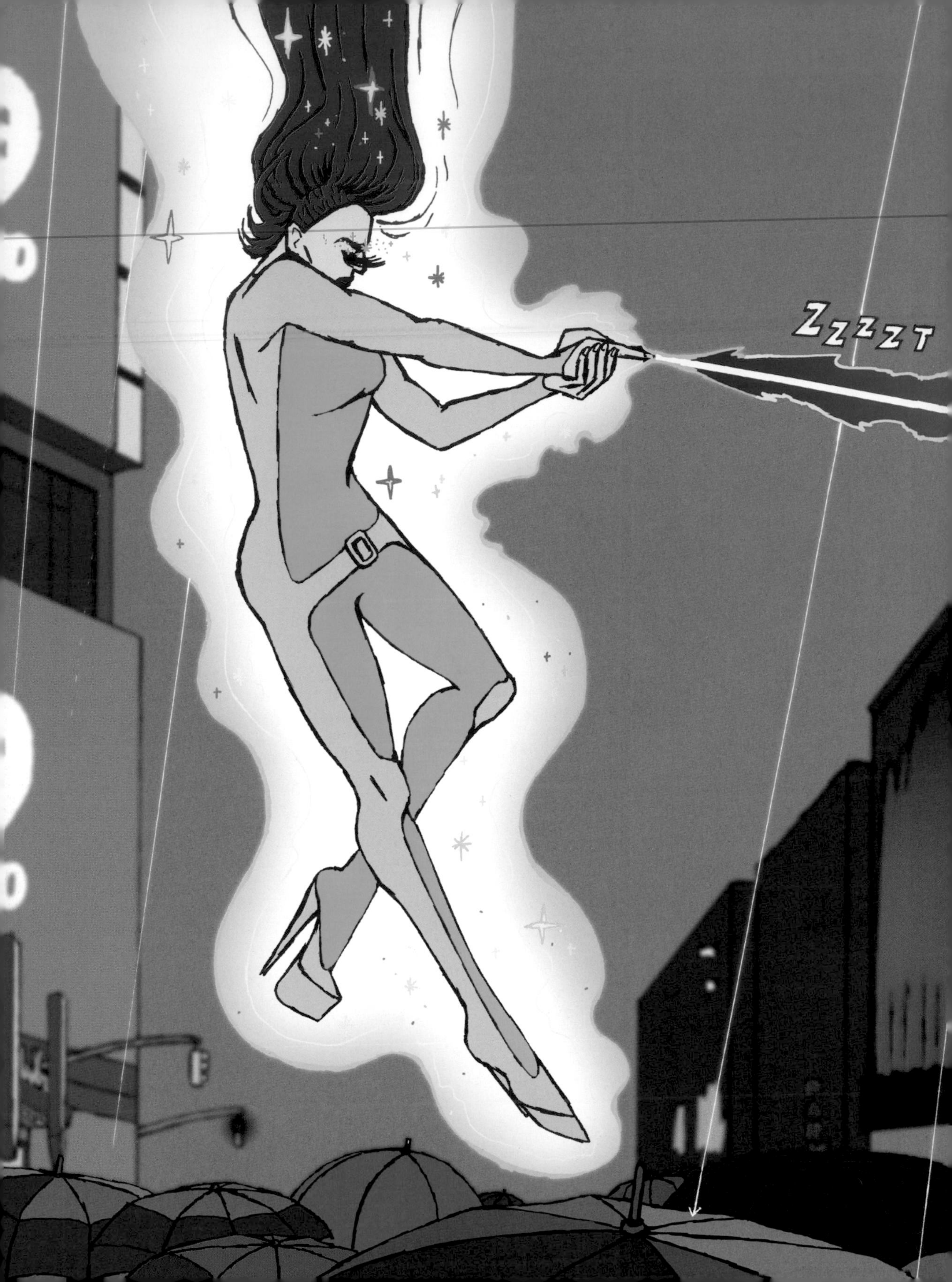
ZZZZT

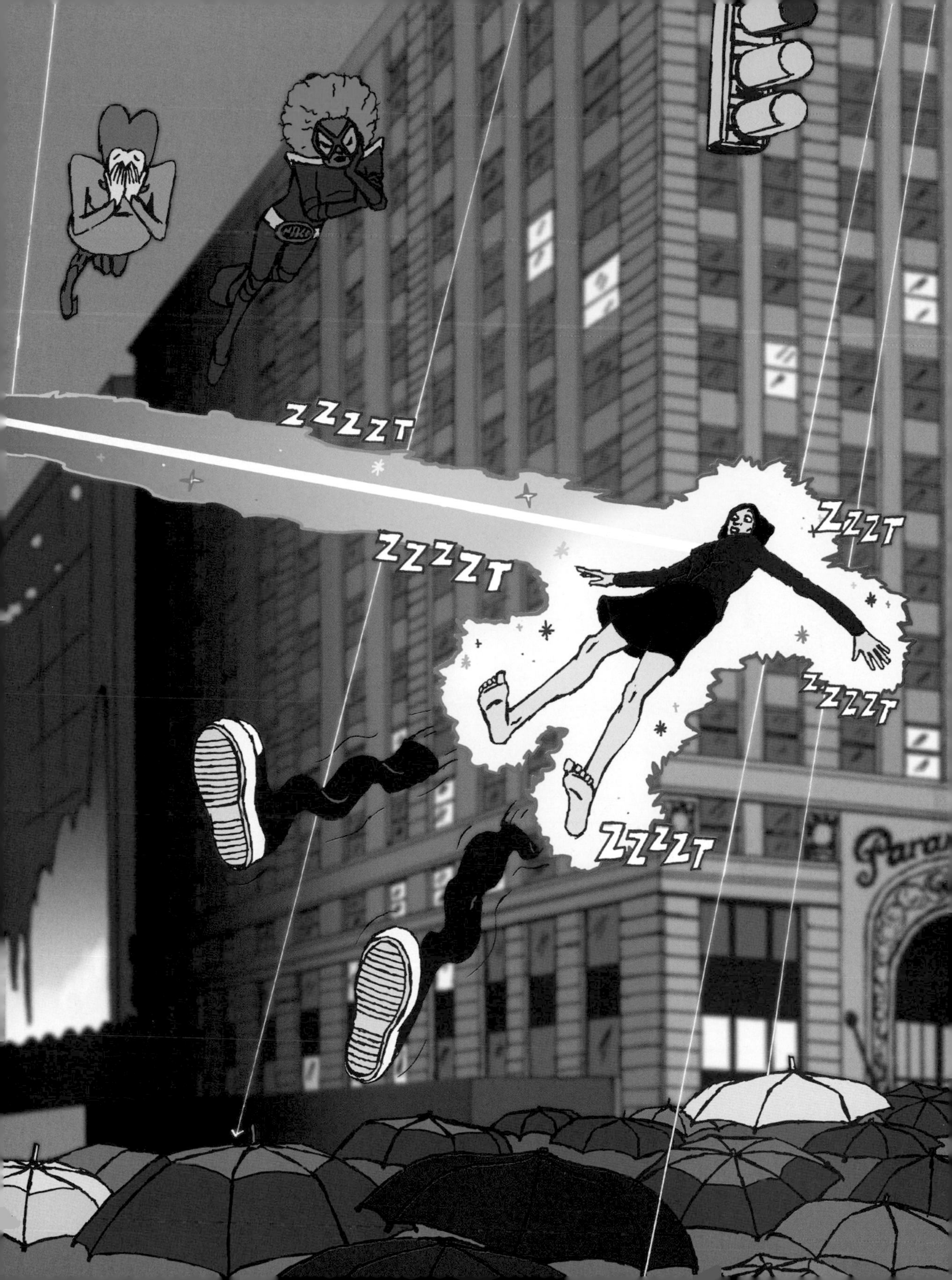
ZZZZT
ZZZT
ZZZZT
ZZZZT
ZZZZT

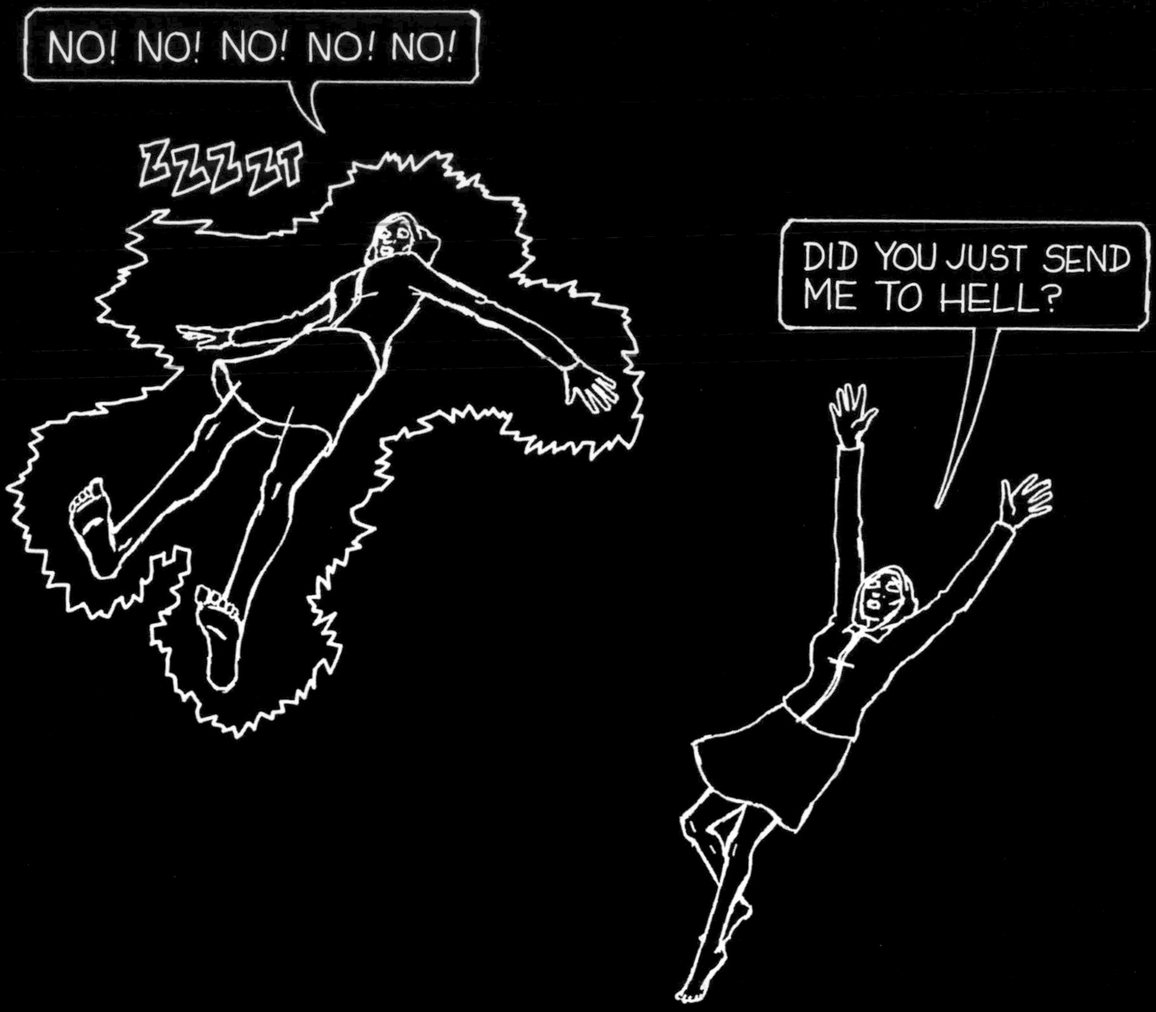
NO! NO! NO! NO! NO!
ZZZZZT
DID YOU JUST SEND ME TO HELL?

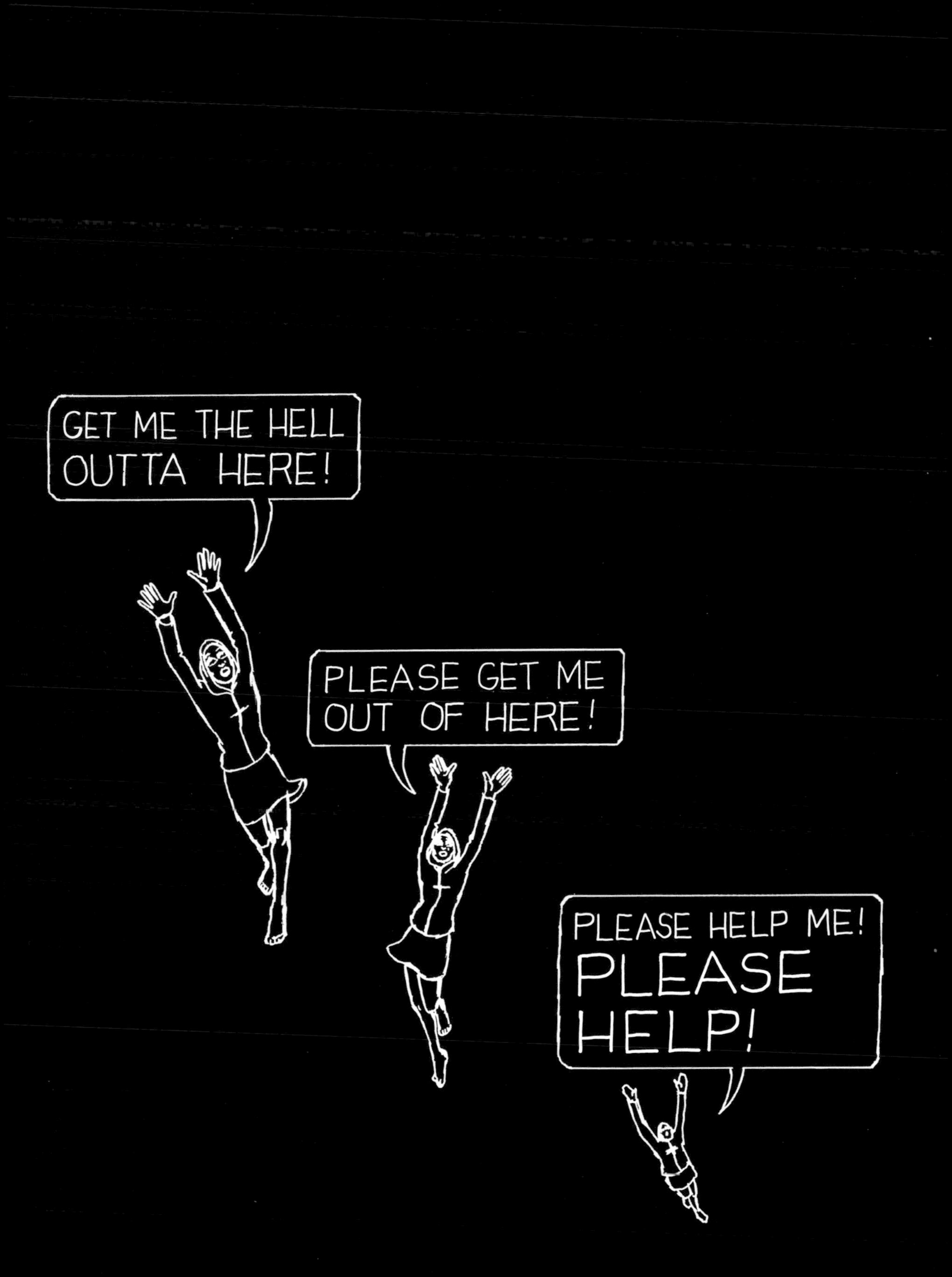
GET ME THE HELL OUTTA HERE!
PLEASE GET ME OUT OF HERE!
PLEASE HELP ME! PLEASE HELP!

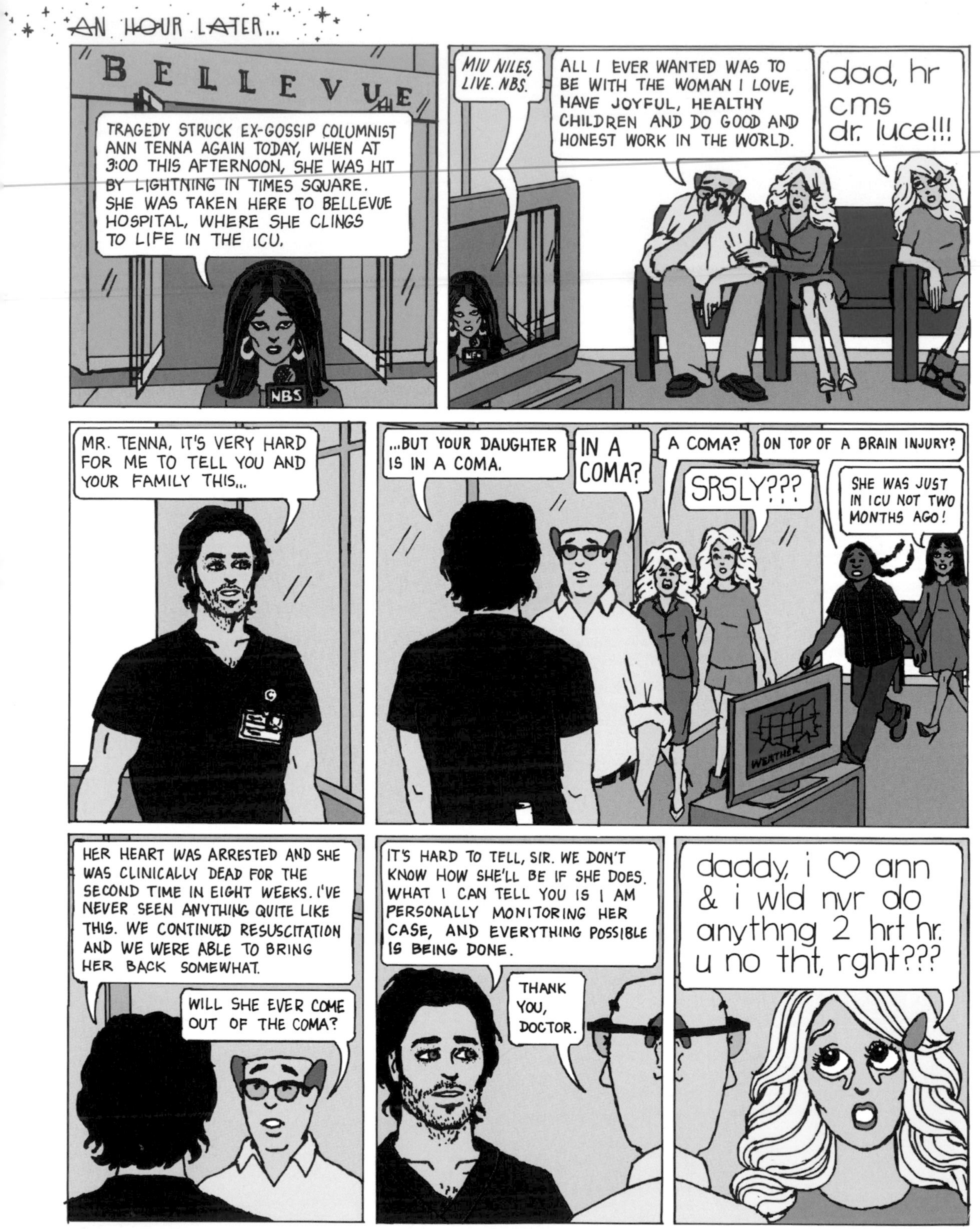
AN HOUR LATER...
BELLEVUE
TRAGEDY STRUCK EX-GOSSIP COLUMNIST ANN TENNA AGAIN TODAY, WHEN AT 3:00 THIS AFTERNOON, SHE WAS HIT BY LIGHTNING IN TIMES SQUARE. SHE WAS TAKEN HERE TO BELLEVUE HOSPITAL, WHERE SHE CLINGS TO LIFE IN THE ICU.
NBS
MIU NILES, LIVE. NBS.
ALL I EVER WANTED WAS TO BE WITH THE WOMAN I LOVE, HAVE JOYFUL, HEALTHY CHILDREN AND DO GOOD AND HONEST WORK IN THE WORLD.
dad, hr cms dr. luce!!!
MR. TENNA, IT'S VERY HARD FOR ME TO TELL YOU AND YOUR FAMILY THIS...
...BUT YOUR DAUGHTER IS IN A COMA.
IN A COMA?
A COMA?
SRSLY???
ON TOP OF A BRAIN INJURY?
SHE WAS JUST IN ICU NOT TWO MONTHS AGO!
WEATHER
HER HEART WAS ARRESTED AND SHE WAS CLINICALLY DEAD FOR THE SECOND TIME IN EIGHT WEEKS. I'VE NEVER SEEN ANYTHING QUITE LIKE THIS. WE CONTINUED RESUSCITATION AND WE WERE ABLE TO BRING HER BACK SOMEWHAT.
WILL SHE EVER COME OUT OF THE COMA?
IT'S HARD TO TELL, SIR. WE DON'T KNOW HOW SHE'LL BE IF SHE DOES. WHAT I CAN TELL YOU IS I AM PERSONALLY MONITORING HER CASE, AND EVERYTHING POSSIBLE IS BEING DONE.
THANK YOU, DOCTOR.
daddy, i ♡ ann & i wld nvr do anythng 2 hrt hr. u no tht, rght???

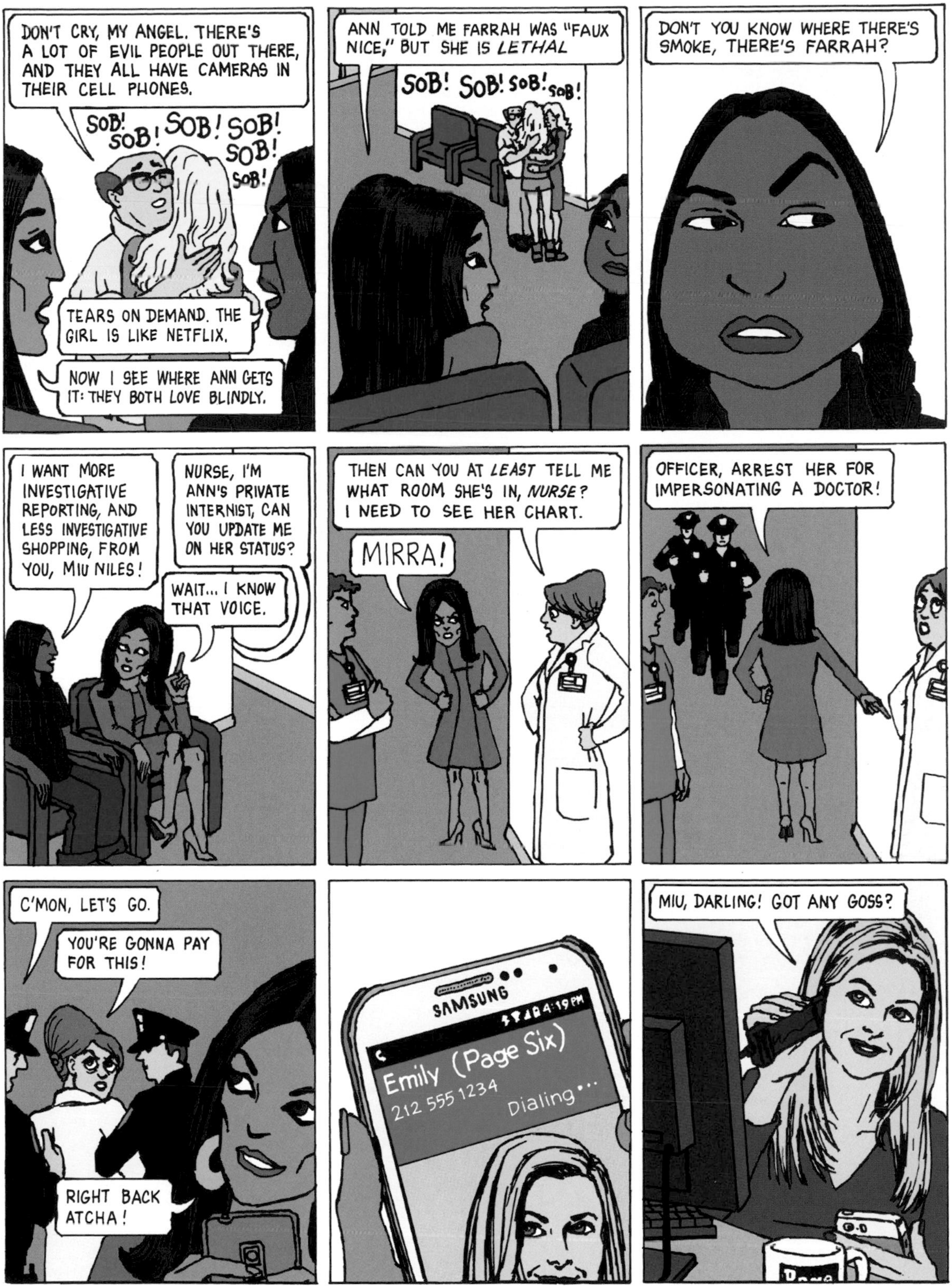

DON'T CRY, MY ANGEL. THERE'S A LOT OF EVIL PEOPLE OUT THERE, AND THEY ALL HAVE CAMERAS IN THEIR CELL PHONES.
SOB! SOB! SOB! SOB! SOB! SOB!
TEARS ON DEMAND. THE GIRL IS LIKE NETFLIX.
NOW I SEE WHERE ANN GETS IT: THEY BOTH LOVE BLINDLY.
ANN TOLD ME FARRAH WAS "FAUX NICE," BUT SHE IS *LETHAL*
SOB! SOB! SOB! SOB!
DON'T YOU KNOW WHERE THERE'S SMOKE, THERE'S FARRAH?
I WANT MORE INVESTIGATIVE REPORTING, AND LESS INVESTIGATIVE SHOPPING, FROM YOU, MIU NILES!
NURSE, I'M ANN'S PRIVATE INTERNIST, CAN YOU UPDATE ME ON HER STATUS?
WAIT... I KNOW THAT VOICE.
THEN CAN YOU AT *LEAST* TELL ME WHAT ROOM SHE'S IN, *NURSE*? I NEED TO SEE HER CHART.
MIRRA!
OFFICER, ARREST HER FOR IMPERSONATING A DOCTOR!
C'MON, LET'S GO.
YOU'RE GONNA PAY FOR THIS!
RIGHT BACK ATCHA!
SAMSUNG
4:19 PM
Emily (Page Six)
212 555 1234
Dialing...
MIU, DARLING! GOT ANY GOSS?

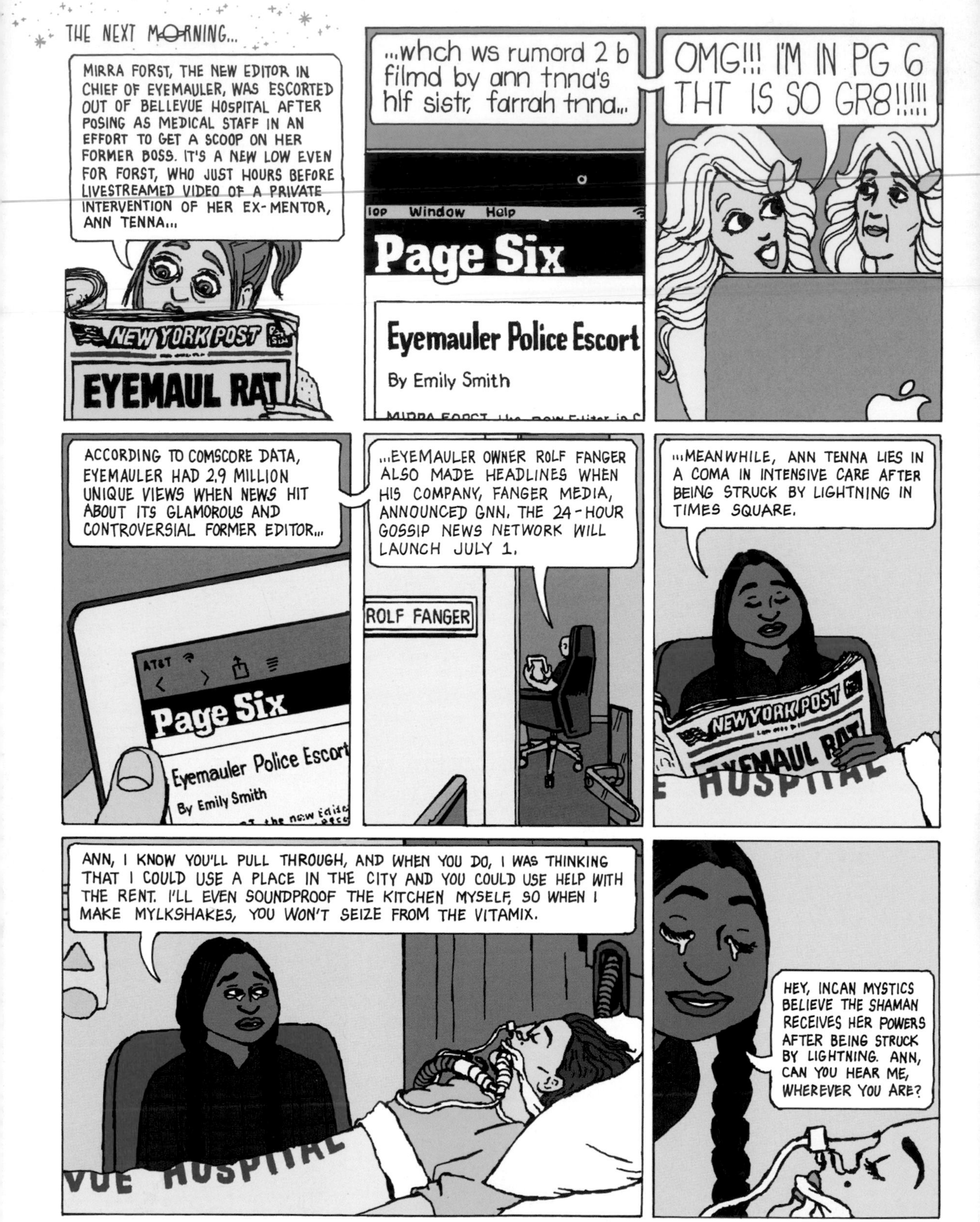
THE NEXT MORNING...
MIRRA FORST, THE NEW EDITOR IN CHIEF OF EYEMAULER, WAS ESCORTED OUT OF BELLEVUE HOSPITAL AFTER POSING AS MEDICAL STAFF IN AN EFFORT TO GET A SCOOP ON HER FORMER BOSS. IT'S A NEW LOW EVEN FOR FORST, WHO JUST HOURS BEFORE LIVESTREAMED VIDEO OF A PRIVATE INTERVENTION OF HER EX-MENTOR, ANN TENNA...
NEW YORK POST
EYEMAUL RAT
...whch ws rumord 2 b filmd by ann tnna's hlf sistr, farrah tnna...
Window Help
Page Six
Eyemauler Police Escort
By Emily Smith
OMG!!! I'M IN PG 6 THT IS SO GR8!!!!!
ACCORDING TO COMSCORE DATA, EYEMAULER HAD 2.9 MILLION UNIQUE VIEWS WHEN NEWS HIT ABOUT ITS GLAMOROUS AND CONTROVERSIAL FORMER EDITOR...
AT&T
Page Six
Eyemauler Police Escort
By Emily Smith
...EYEMAULER OWNER ROLF FANGER ALSO MADE HEADLINES WHEN HIS COMPANY, FANGER MEDIA, ANNOUNCED GNN. THE 24-HOUR GOSSIP NEWS NETWORK WILL LAUNCH JULY 1.
ROLF FANGER
...MEANWHILE, ANN TENNA LIES IN A COMA IN INTENSIVE CARE AFTER BEING STRUCK BY LIGHTNING IN TIMES SQUARE.
NEW YORK POST
EYEMAUL RAT
HOSPITAL
ANN, I KNOW YOU'LL PULL THROUGH, AND WHEN YOU DO, I WAS THINKING THAT I COULD USE A PLACE IN THE CITY AND YOU COULD USE HELP WITH THE RENT. I'LL EVEN SOUNDPROOF THE KITCHEN MYSELF, SO WHEN I MAKE MYLKSHAKES, YOU WON'T SEIZE FROM THE VITAMIX.
VUE HOSPITAL
HEY, INCAN MYSTICS BELIEVE THE SHAMAN RECEIVES HER POWERS AFTER BEING STRUCK BY LIGHTNING. ANN, CAN YOU HEAR ME, WHEREVER YOU ARE?

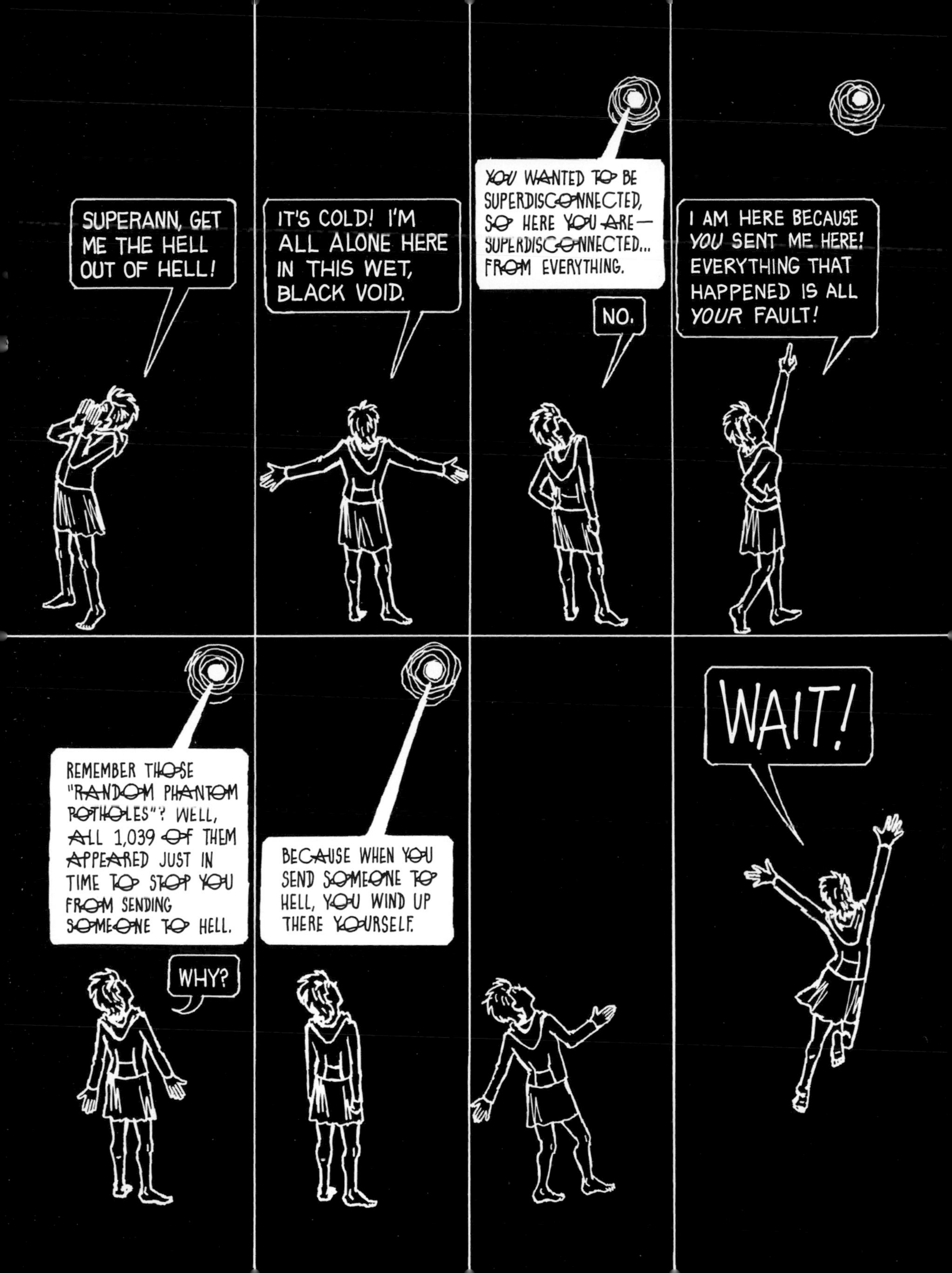
SUPERANN, GET ME THE HELL OUT OF HELL!
IT'S COLD! I'M ALL ALONE HERE IN THIS WET, BLACK VOID.
YOU WANTED TO BE SUPERDISCONNECTED, SO HERE YOU ARE—SUPERDISCONNECTED... FROM EVERYTHING.
NO.
I AM HERE BECAUSE YOU SENT ME HERE! EVERYTHING THAT HAPPENED IS ALL YOUR FAULT!
REMEMBER THOSE "RANDOM PHANTOM POTHOLES"? WELL, ALL 1,039 OF THEM APPEARED JUST IN TIME TO STOP YOU FROM SENDING SOMEONE TO HELL.
WHY?
BECAUSE WHEN YOU SEND SOMEONE TO HELL, YOU WIND UP THERE YOURSELF.
WAIT!

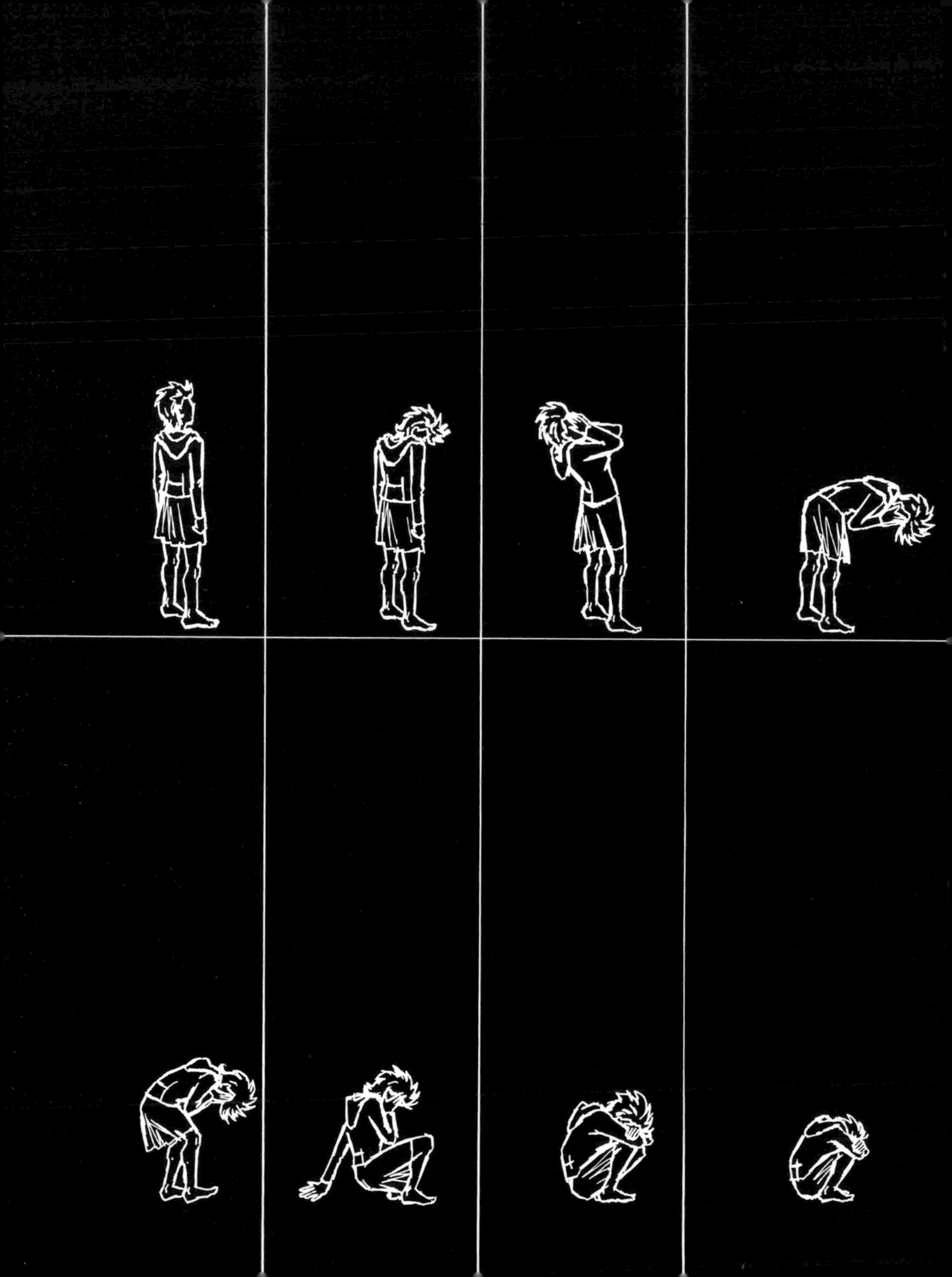

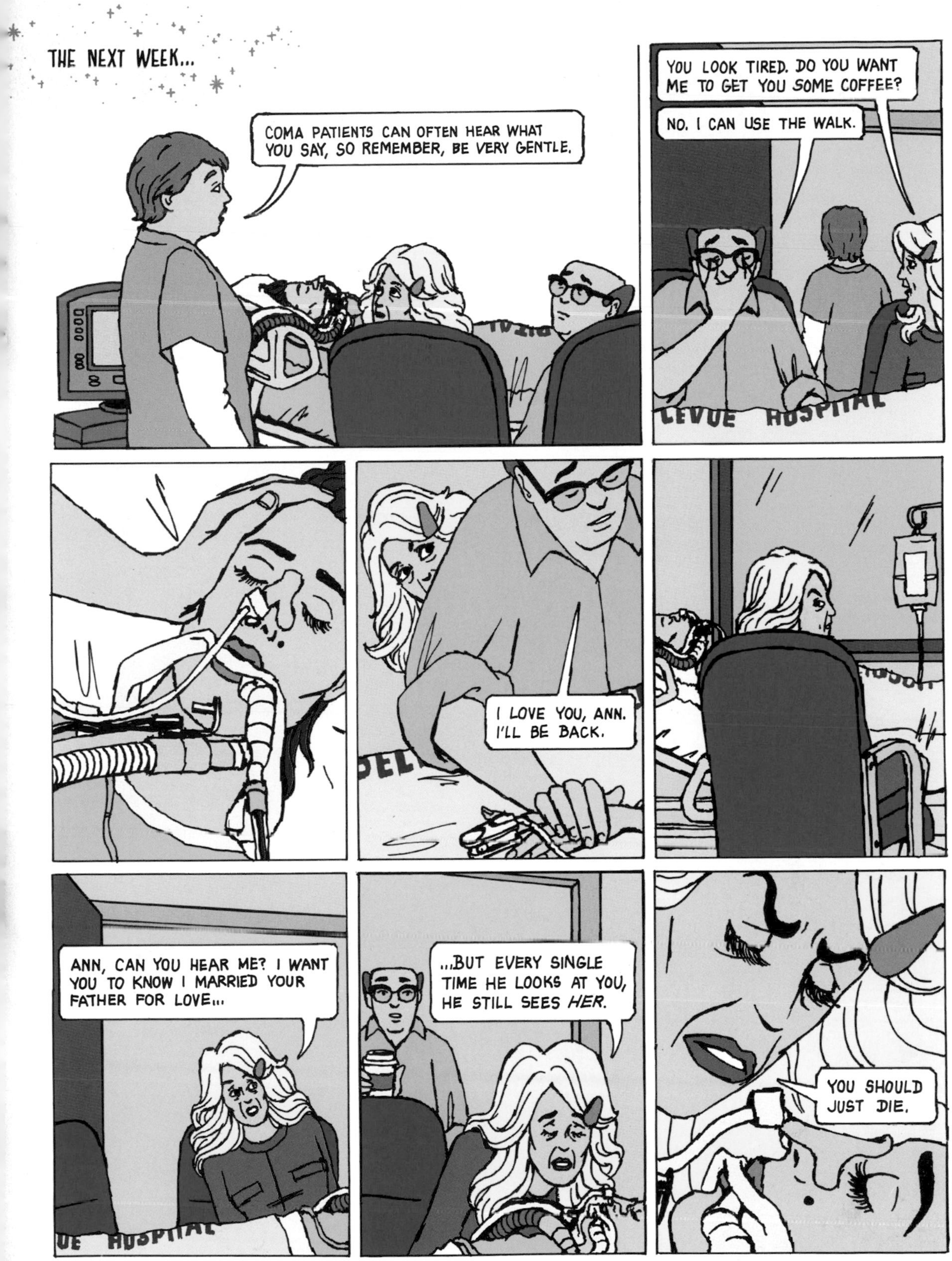
THE NEXT WEEK...
COMA PATIENTS CAN OFTEN HEAR WHAT YOU SAY, SO REMEMBER, BE VERY GENTLE.
YOU LOOK TIRED. DO YOU WANT ME TO GET YOU SOME COFFEE?
NO. I CAN USE THE WALK.
LEVUE HOSPITAL
I LOVE YOU, ANN. I'LL BE BACK.
ANN, CAN YOU HEAR ME? I WANT YOU TO KNOW I MARRIED YOUR FATHER FOR LOVE...
UE HOSPITAL
...BUT EVERY SINGLE TIME HE LOOKS AT YOU, HE STILL SEES HER.
YOU SHOULD JUST DIE.

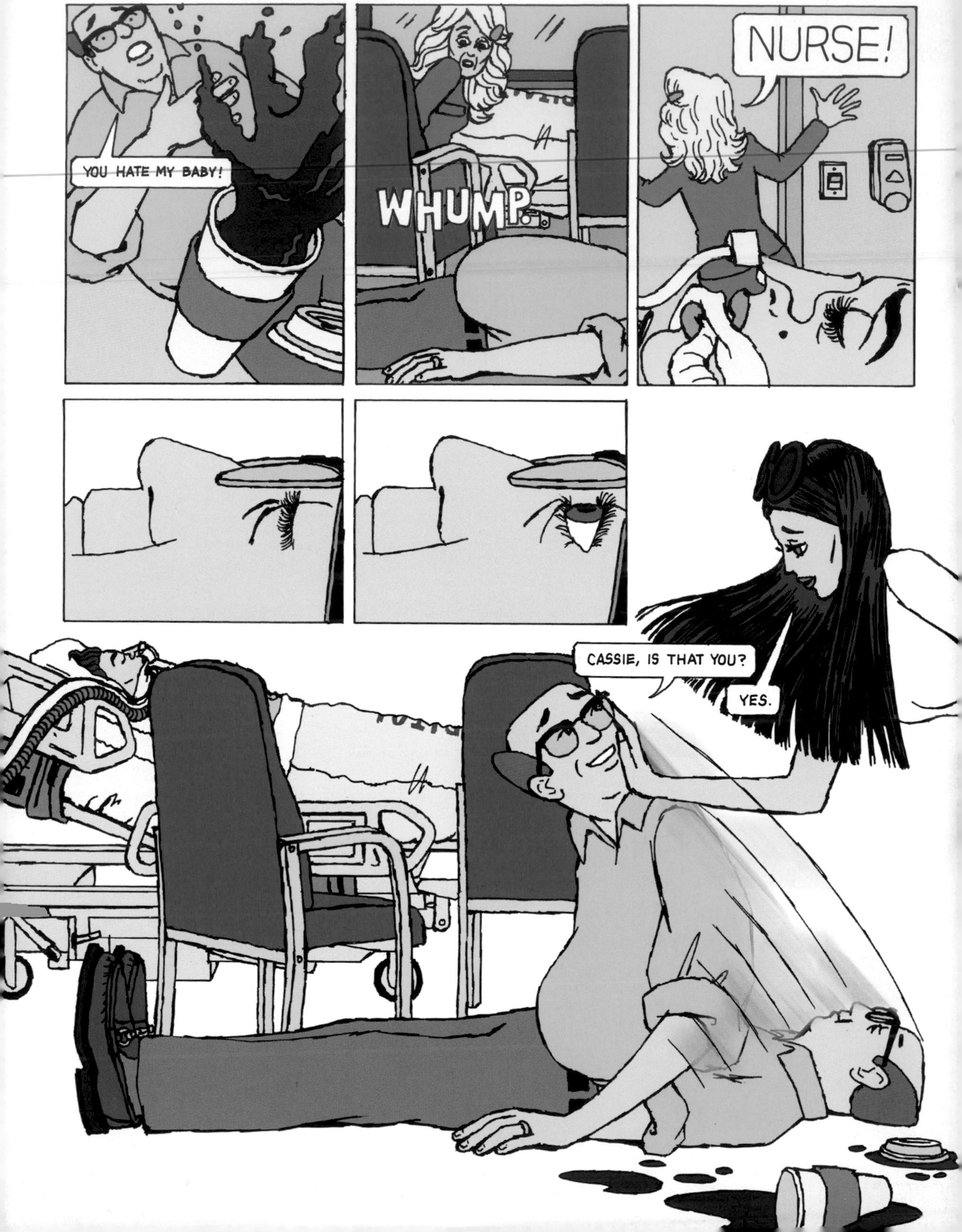

YOU HATE MY BABY!
WHUMP
NURSE!
CASSIE, IS THAT YOU?
YES.

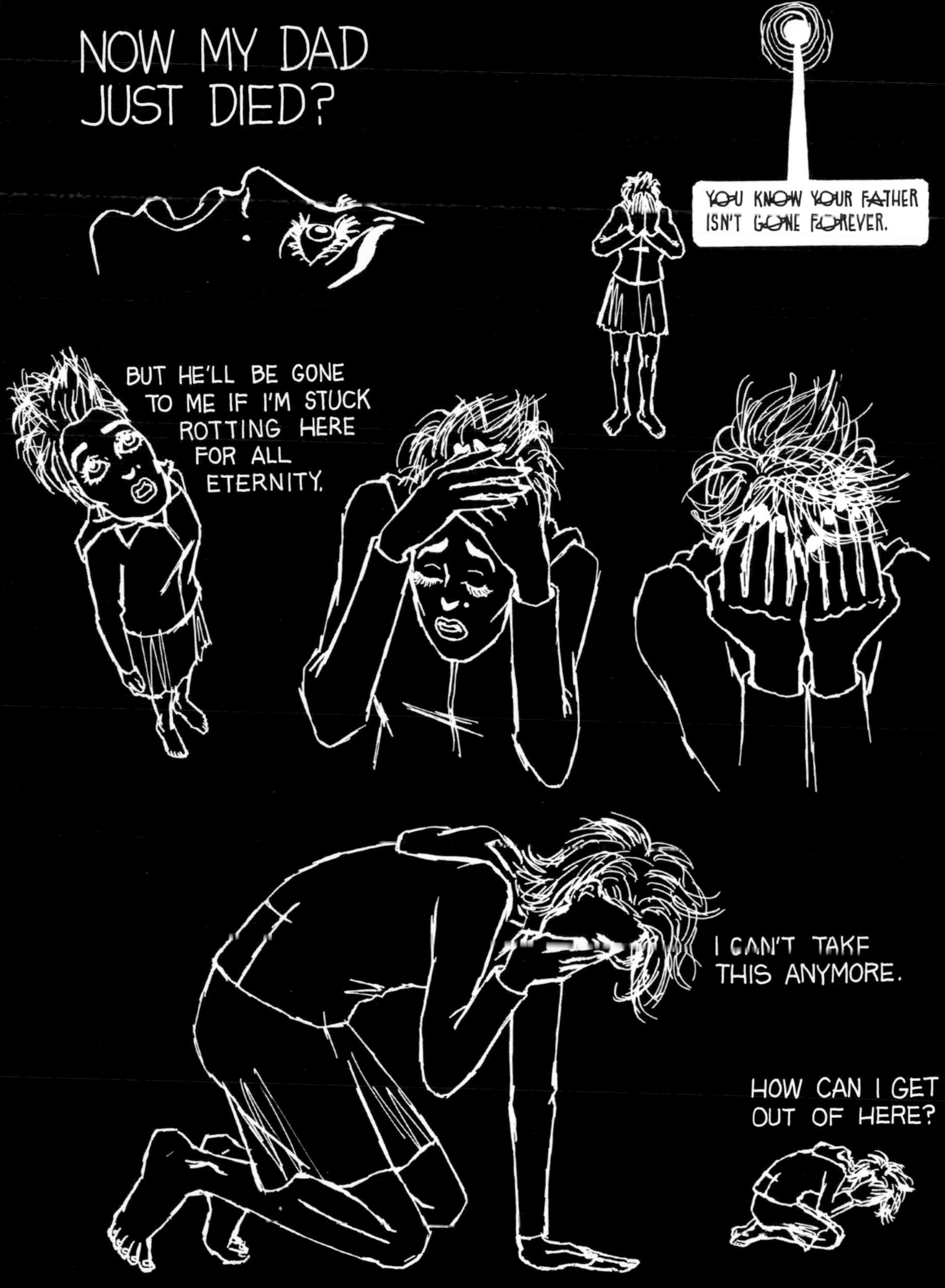
NOW MY DAD JUST DIED?
YOU KNOW YOUR FATHER ISN'T GONE FOREVER.
BUT HE'LL BE GONE TO ME IF I'M STUCK ROTTING HERE FOR ALL ETERNITY.
I CAN'T TAKE THIS ANYMORE.
HOW CAN I GET OUT OF HERE?

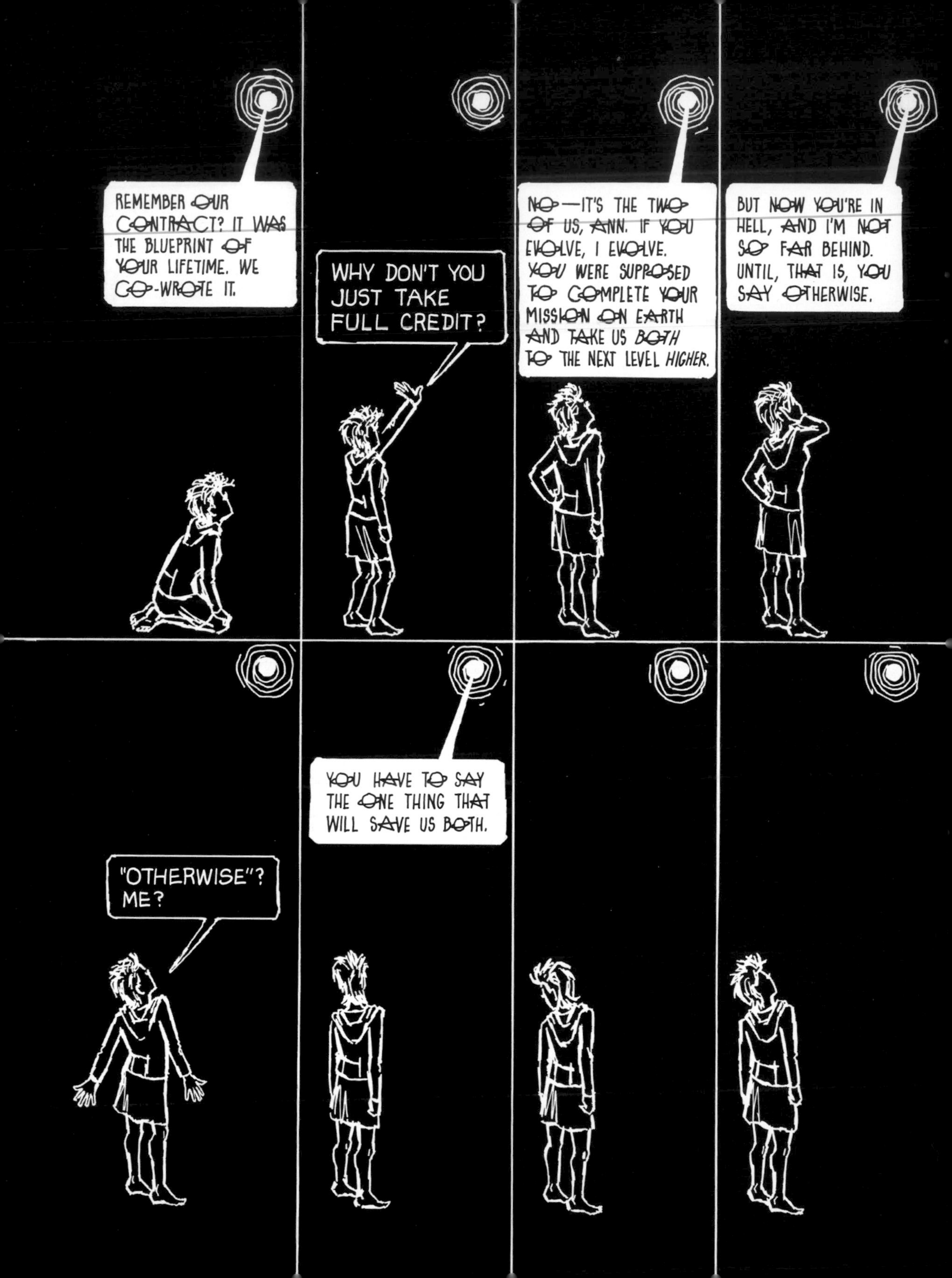
REMEMBER OUR CONTRACT? IT WAS THE BLUEPRINT OF YOUR LIFETIME. WE CO-WROTE IT.
WHY DON'T YOU JUST TAKE FULL CREDIT?
NO—IT'S THE TWO OF US, ANN. IF YOU EVOLVE, I EVOLVE. YOU WERE SUPPOSED TO COMPLETE YOUR MISSION ON EARTH AND TAKE US *BOTH* TO THE NEXT LEVEL *HIGHER*.
BUT NOW YOU'RE IN HELL, AND I'M NOT SO FAR BEHIND. UNTIL, THAT IS, YOU SAY OTHERWISE.
"OTHERWISE"? ME?
YOU HAVE TO SAY THE ONE THING THAT WILL SAVE US BOTH.

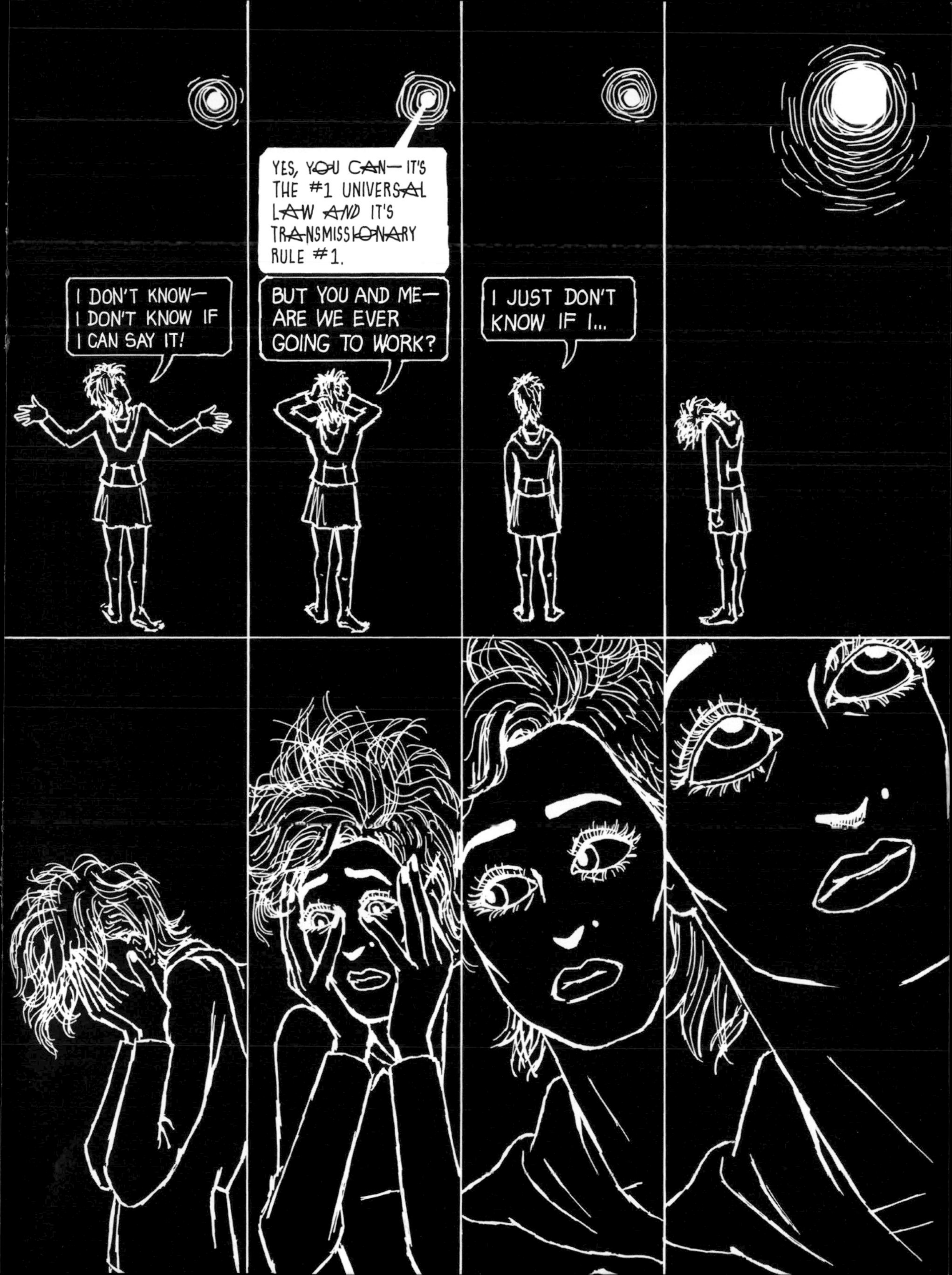
I DON'T KNOW—
I DON'T KNOW IF
I CAN SAY IT!
YES, YOU CAN— IT'S THE #1 UNIVERSAL LAW AND IT'S TRANSMISSIONARY RULE #1.
BUT YOU AND ME—
ARE WE EVER GOING TO WORK?
I JUST DON'T KNOW IF I...

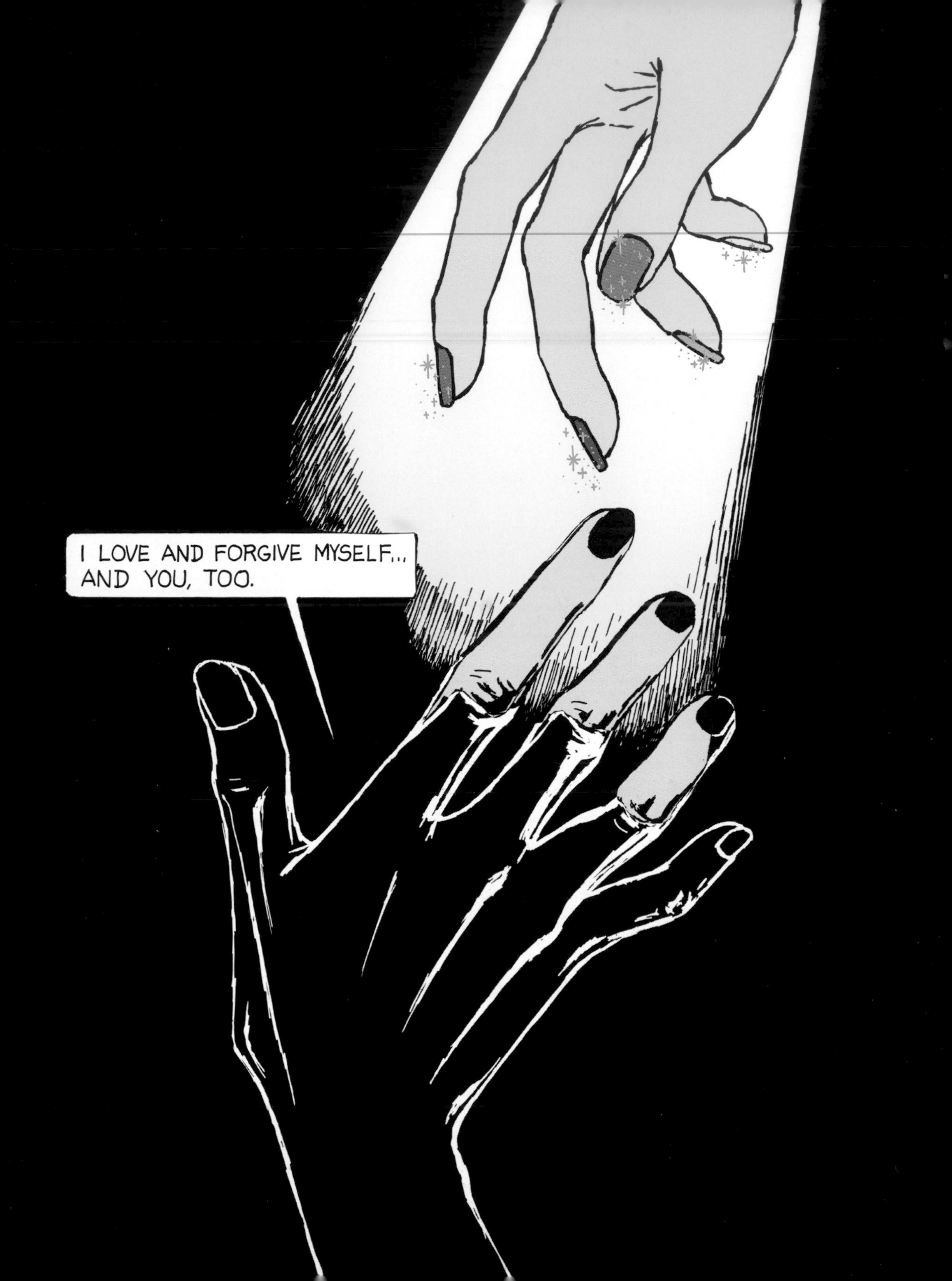
I LOVE AND FORGIVE MYSELF...
AND YOU, TOO.

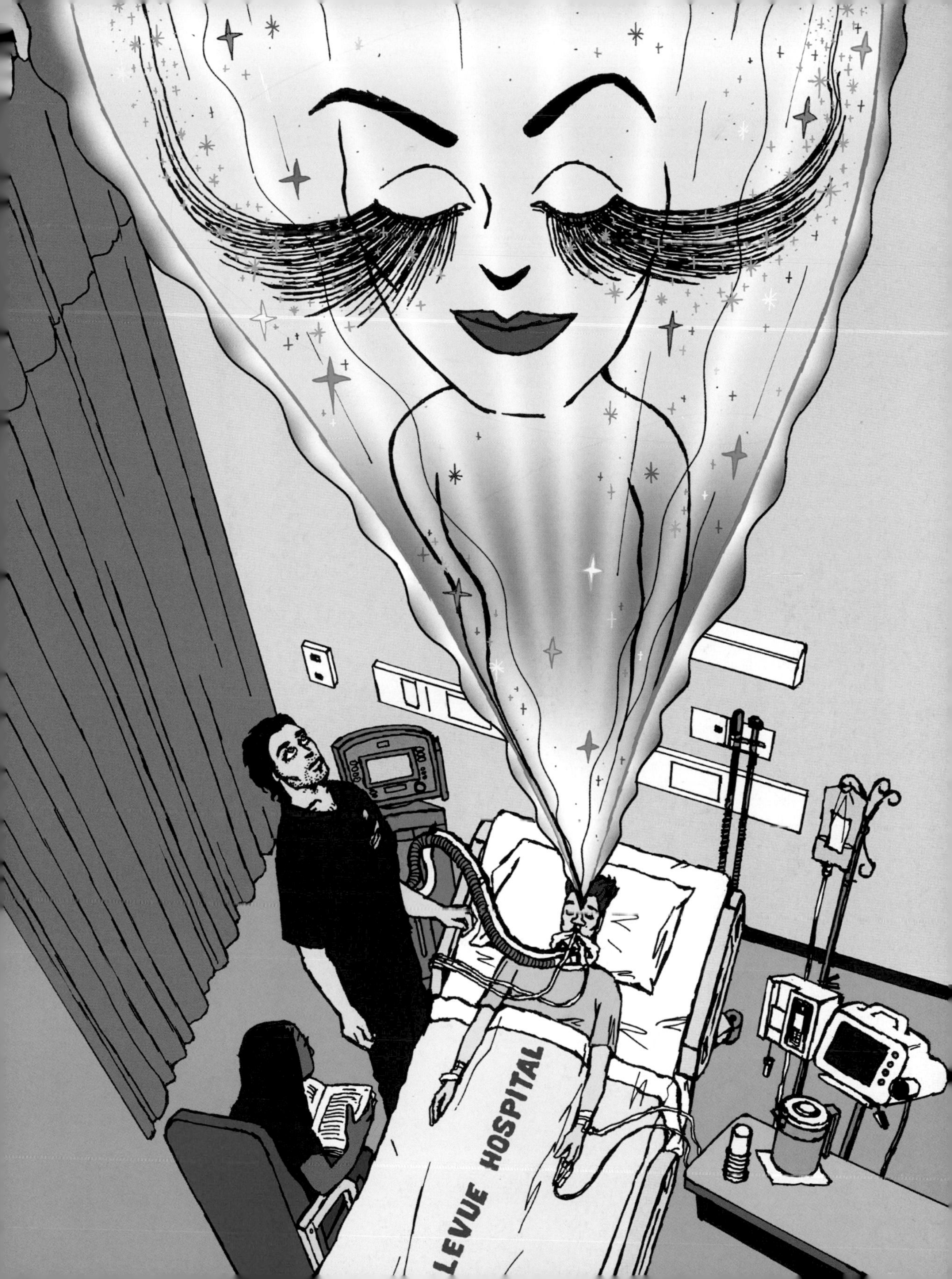
LEVUE HOSPITAL

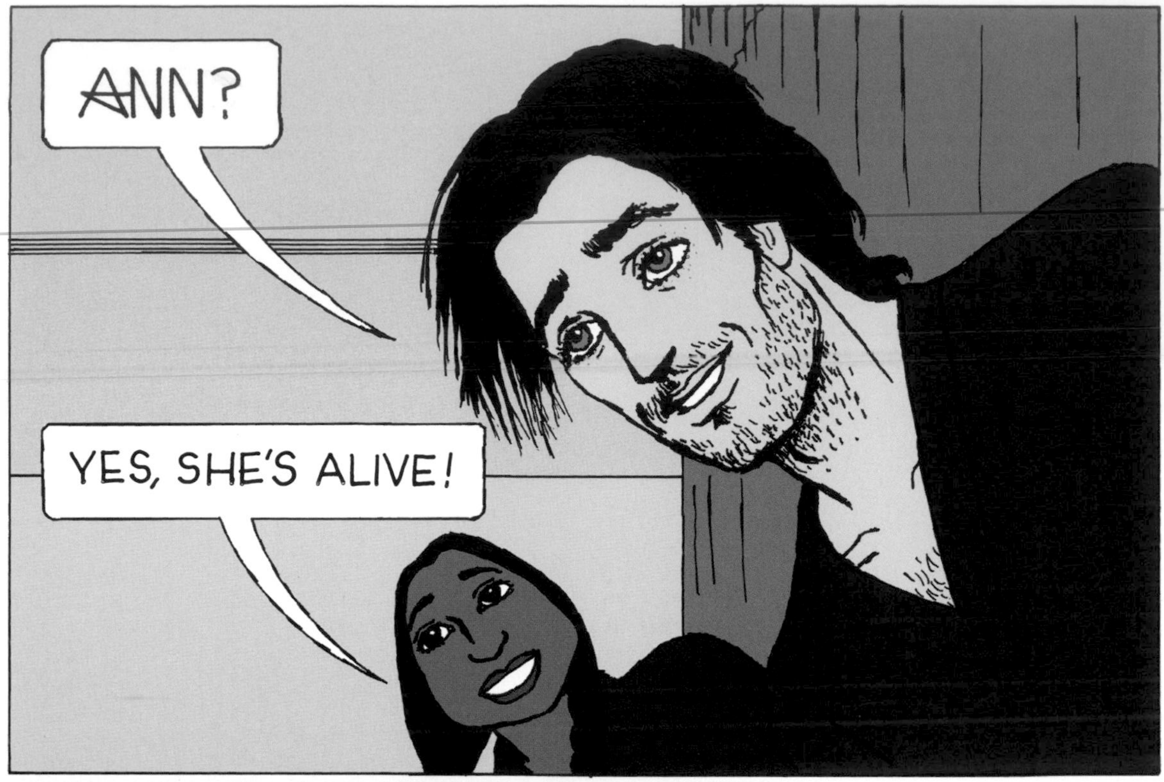
ANN?
YES, SHE'S ALIVE!

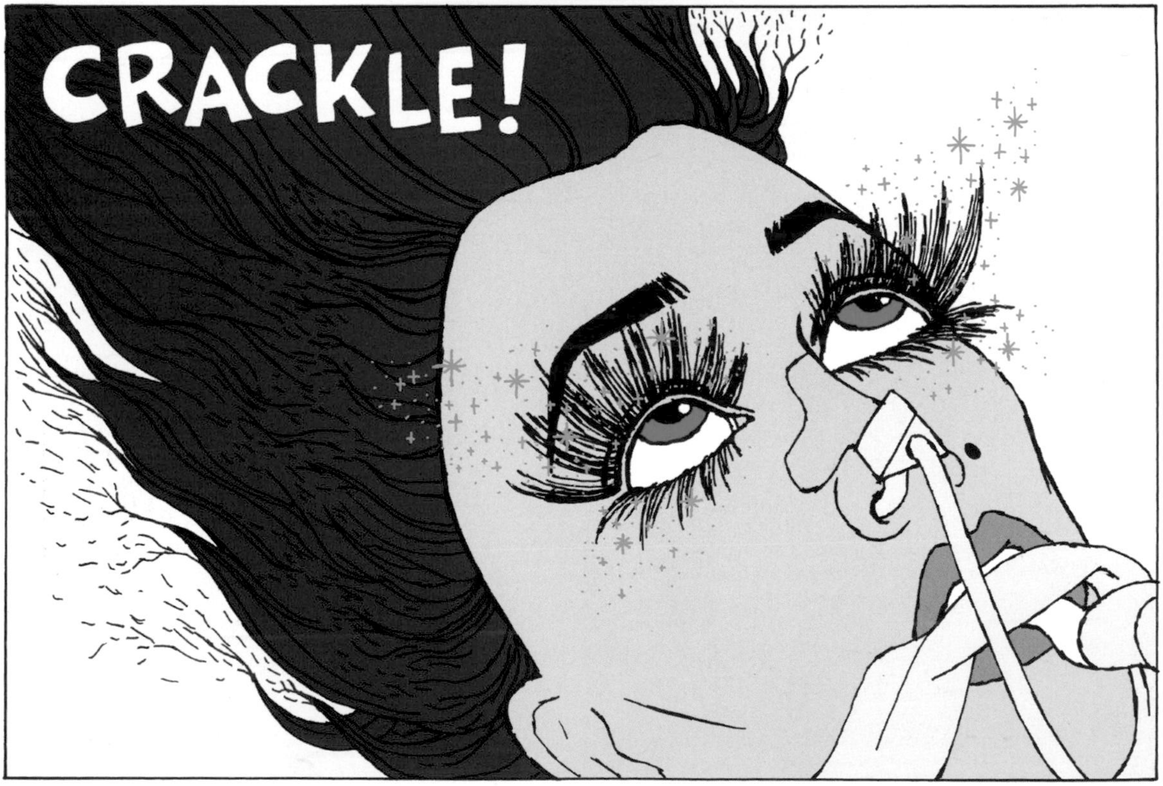
CRACKLE!

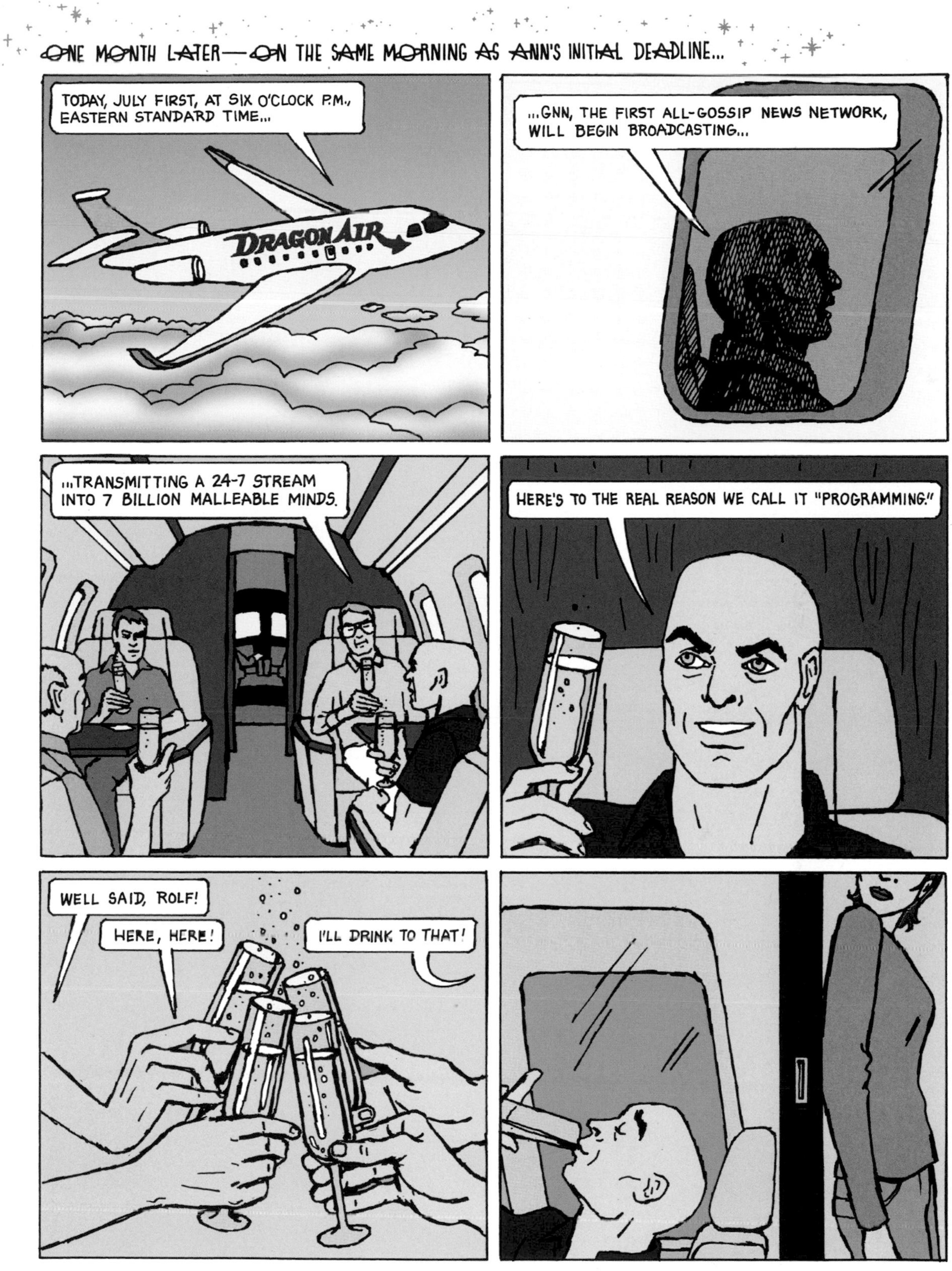
ONE MONTH LATER— ON THE SAME MORNING AS ANN'S INITIAL DEADLINE...
TODAY, JULY FIRST, AT SIX O'CLOCK P.M., EASTERN STANDARD TIME...
DRAGON AIR
...GNN, THE FIRST ALL-GOSSIP NEWS NETWORK, WILL BEGIN BROADCASTING...
...TRANSMITTING A 24-7 STREAM INTO 7 BILLION MALLEABLE MINDS.
HERE'S TO THE REAL REASON WE CALL IT "PROGRAMMING."
WELL SAID, ROLF!
HERE, HERE!
I'LL DRINK TO THAT!

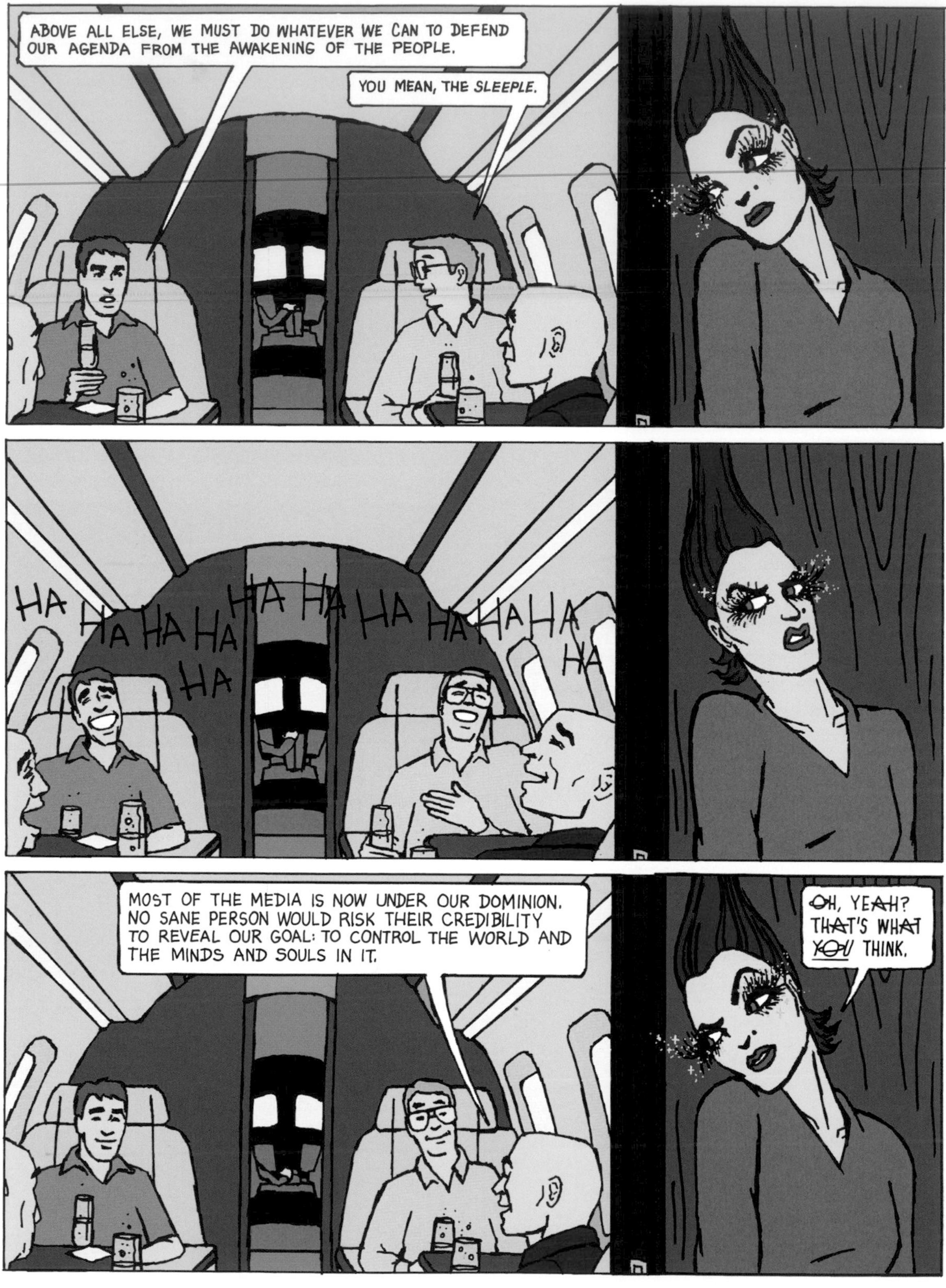
ABOVE ALL ELSE, WE MUST DO WHATEVER WE CAN TO DEFEND OUR AGENDA FROM THE AWAKENING OF THE PEOPLE.
YOU MEAN, THE *SLEEPLE.*
HA HA HA HA HA HA HA HA HA HA HA HA HA HA
MOST OF THE MEDIA IS NOW UNDER OUR DOMINION. NO SANE PERSON WOULD RISK THEIR CREDIBILITY TO REVEAL OUR GOAL: TO CONTROL THE WORLD AND THE MINDS AND SOULS IN IT.
OH, YEAH? THAT'S WHAT *YOU* THINK.

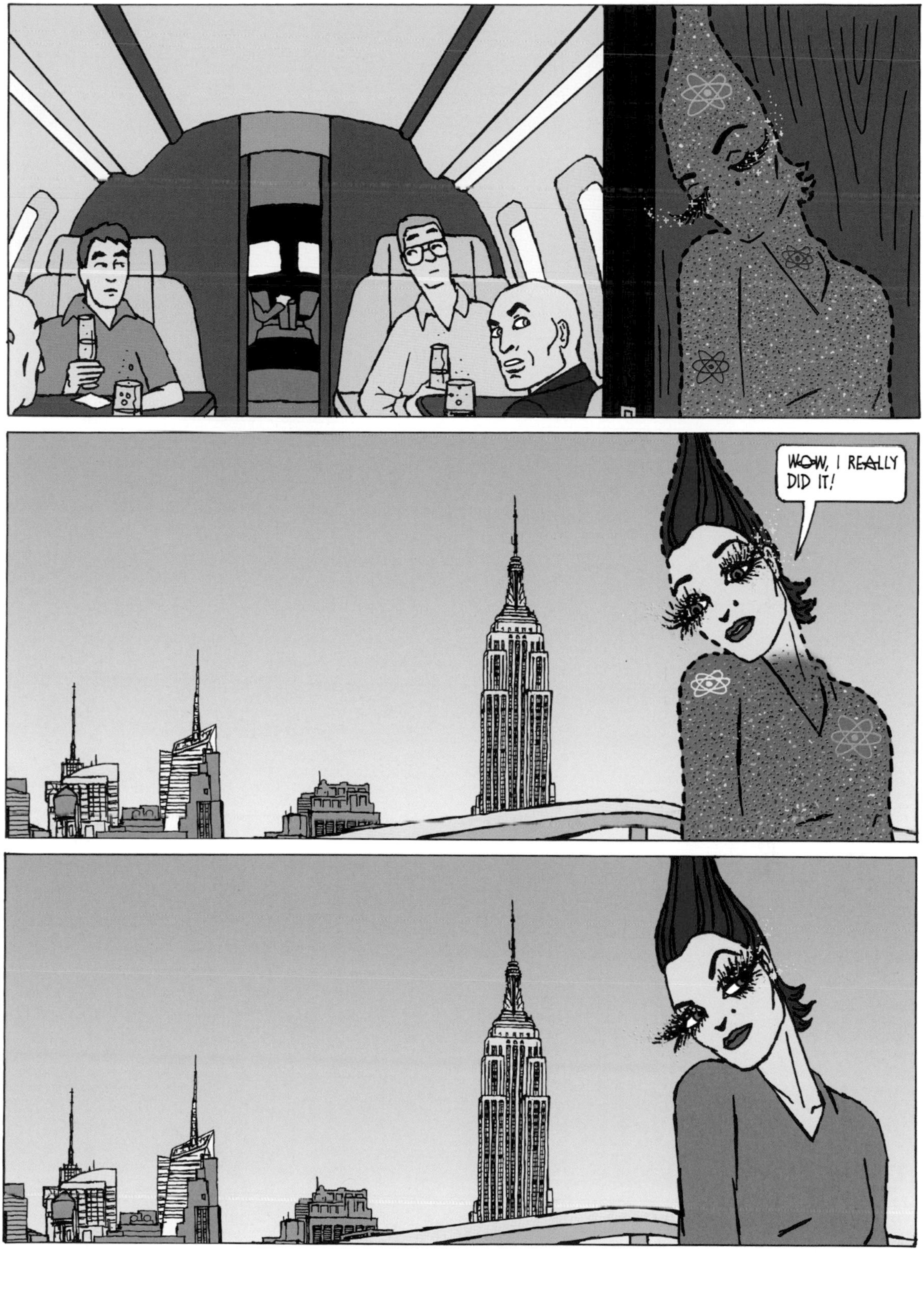

WOW, I REALLY DID IT!

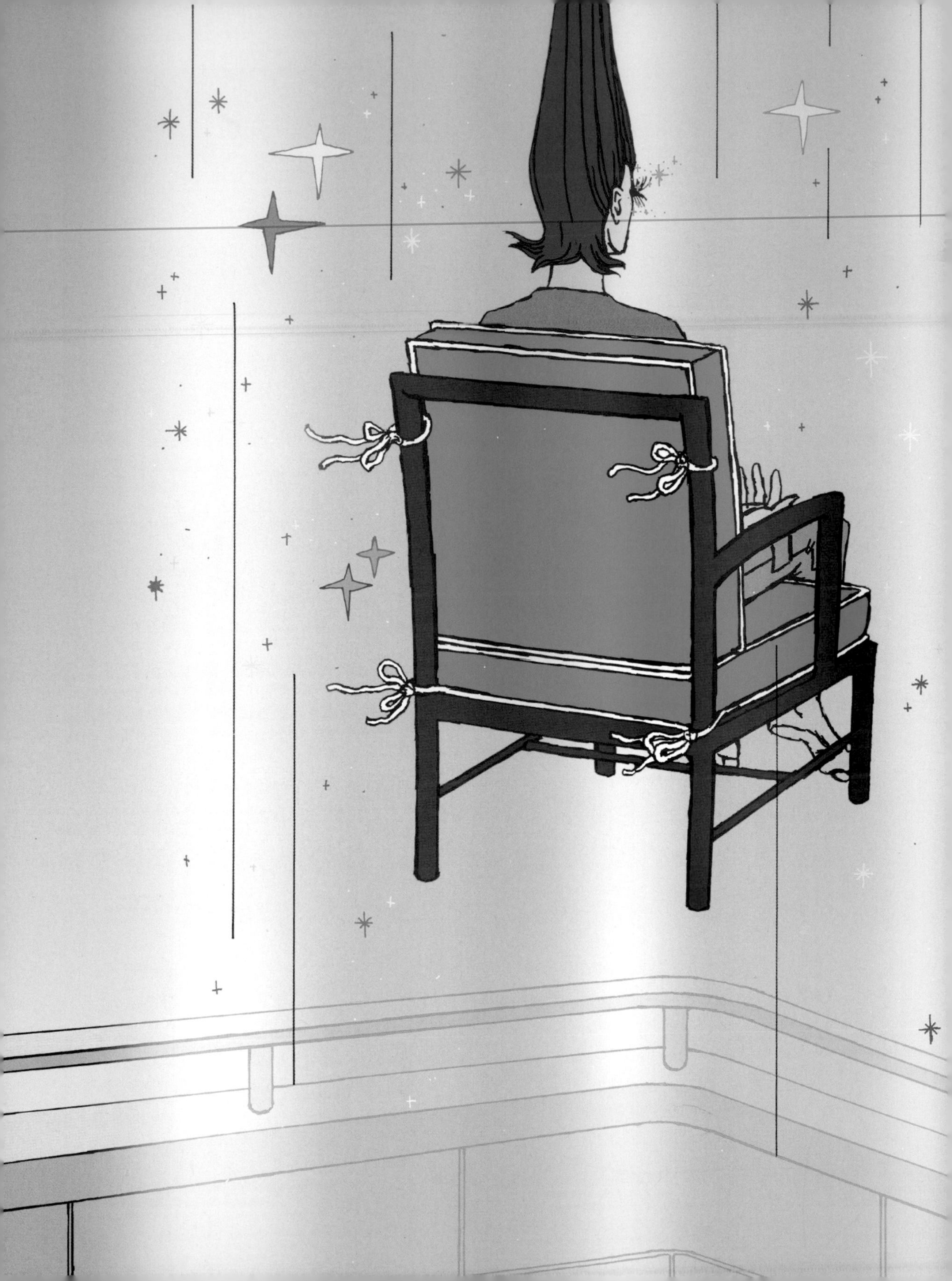

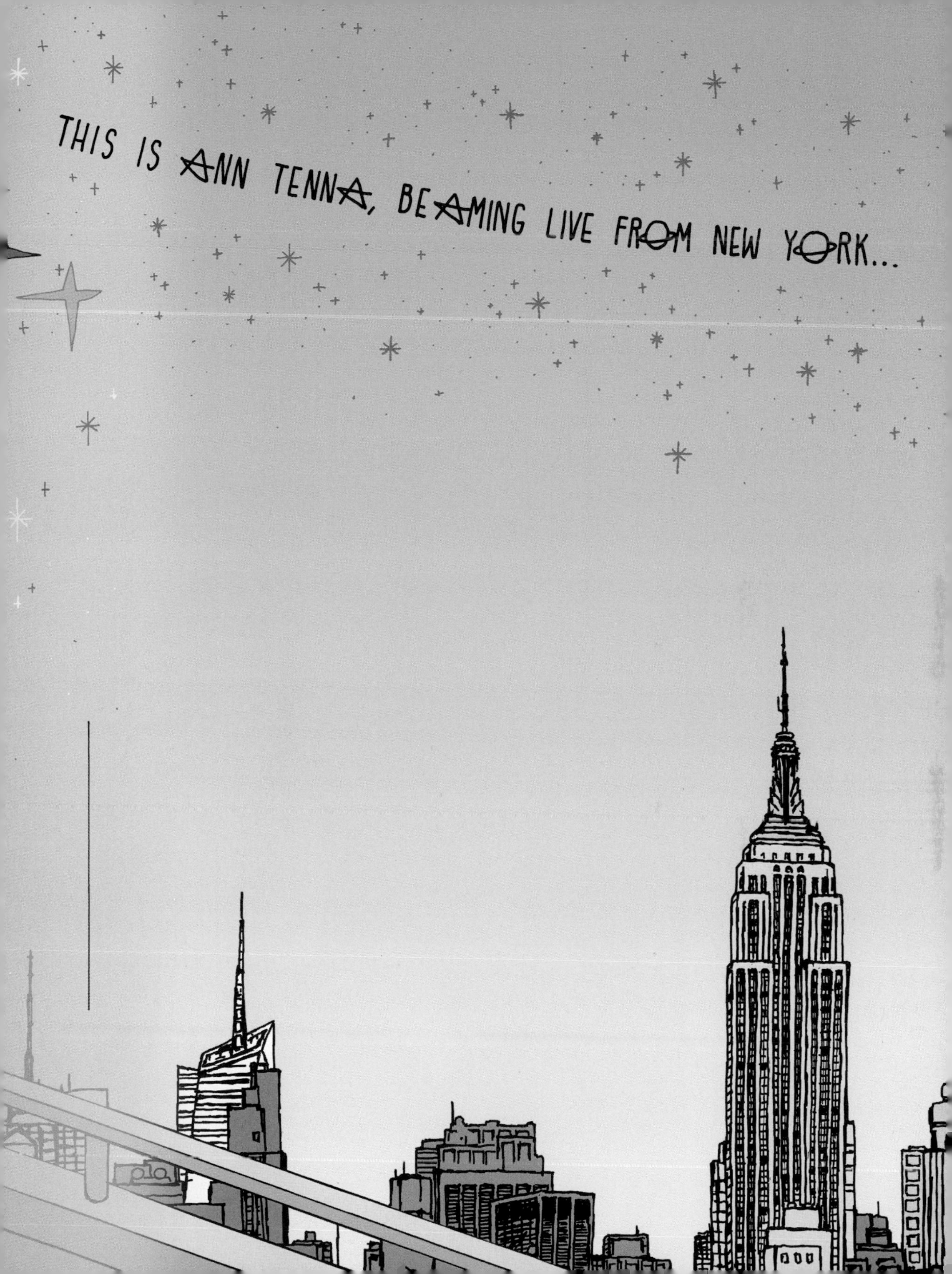
THIS IS ANN TENNA, BEAMING LIVE FROM NEW YORK...

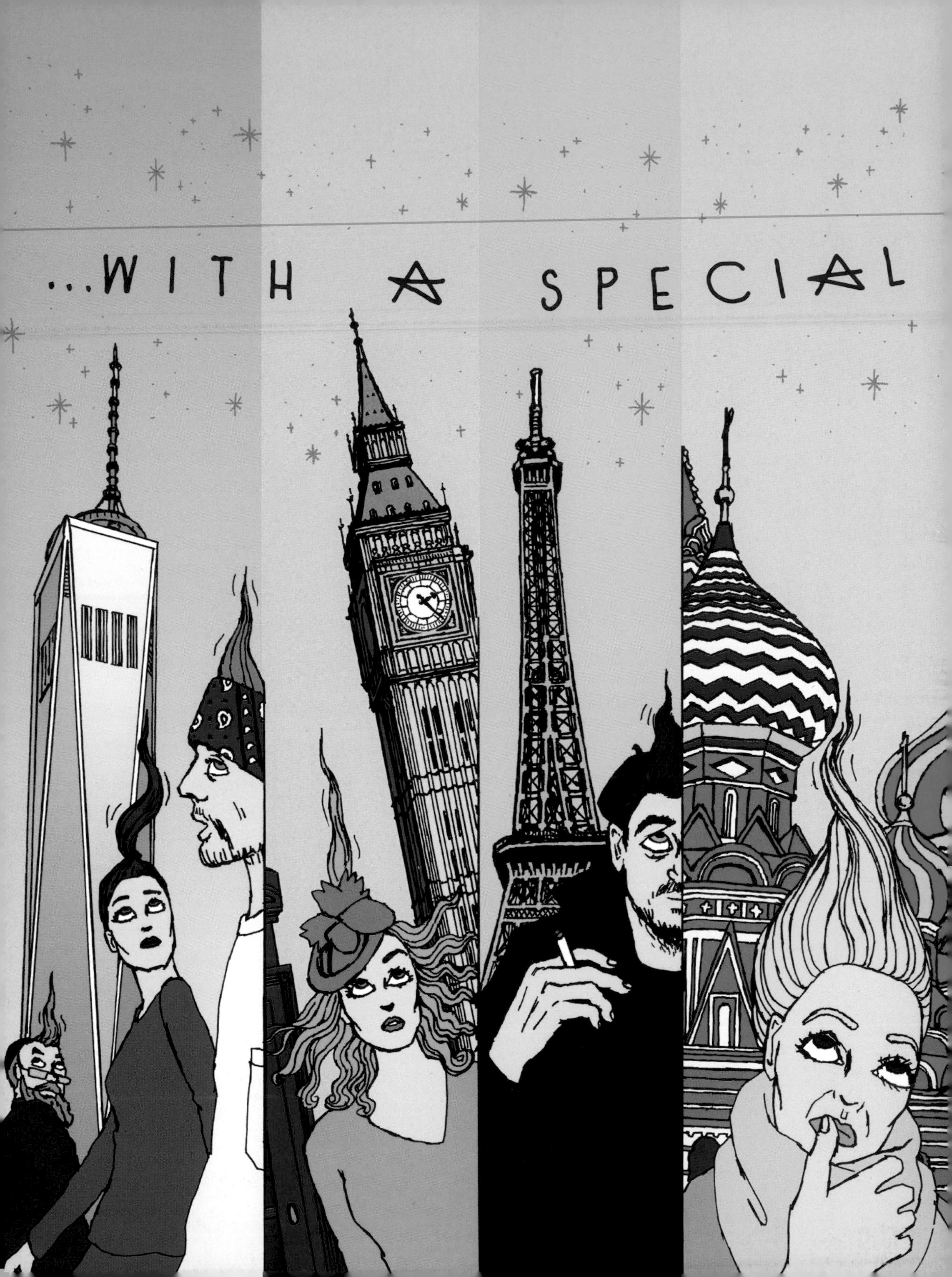
...WITH A SPECIAL

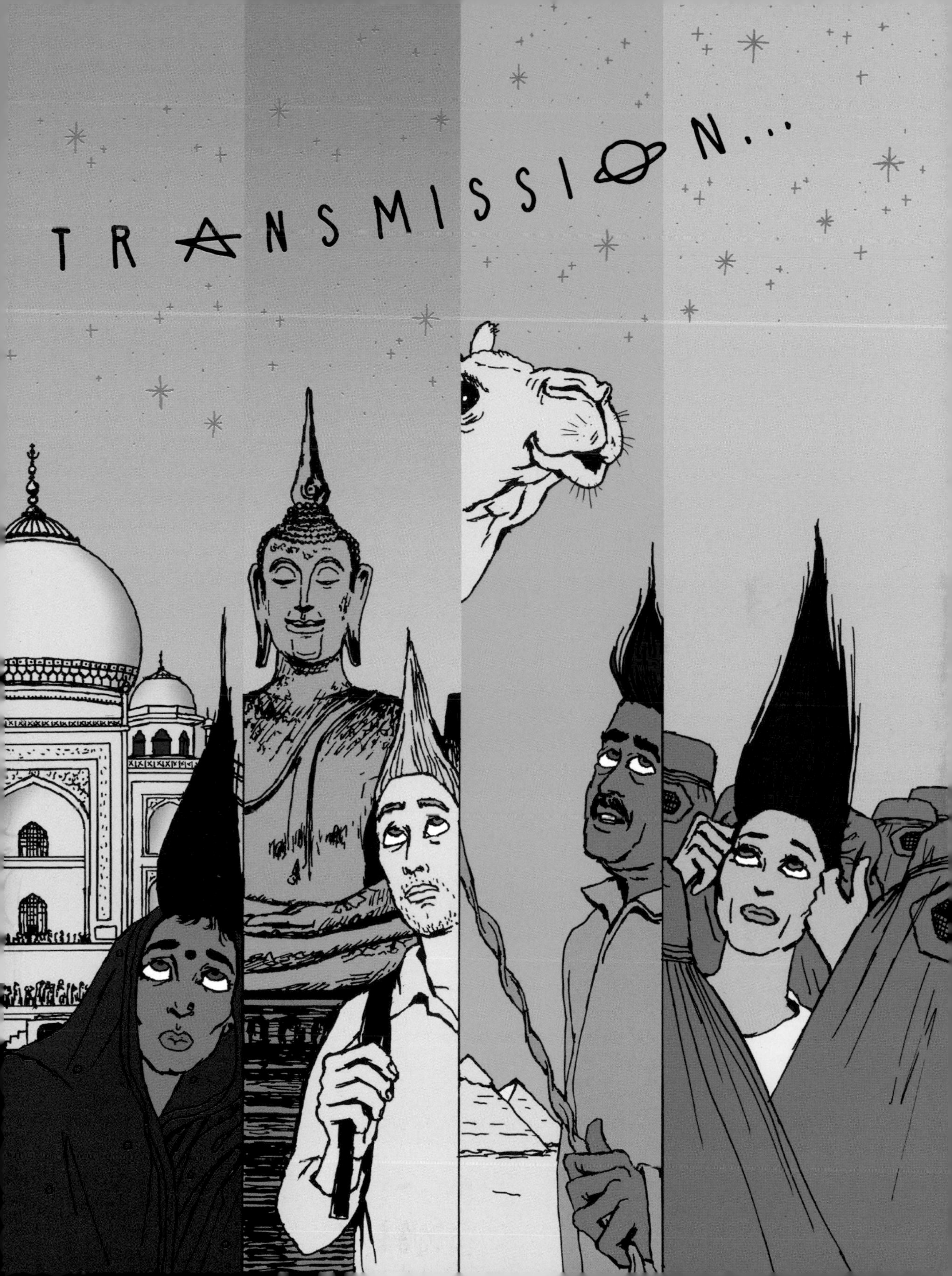
TRANSMISSION...

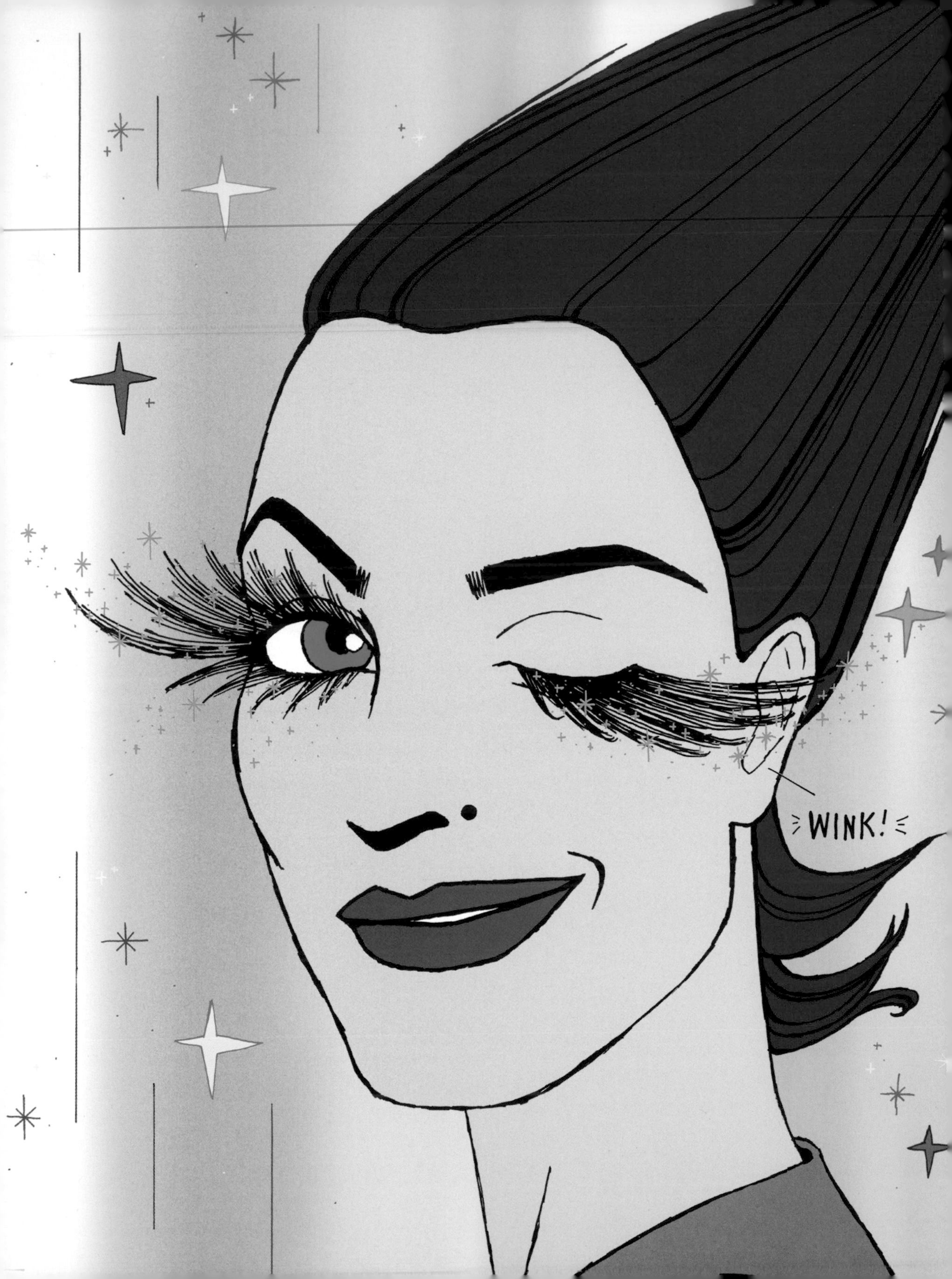
WINK!

INFINITE THANKS TO

MY MOTHER/TEACHER/EPIC SHOE DESIGNER, VIOLETTA; THE GREATEST PHARMACIST IN THE WORLD, MY FATHER, TONY; MY BROTHERS, ANTHONY AND DAVID, AND DAVID'S FAMILY YUN, APOLLONIA AND PHILOMENA; MY SISTER, DINA, AND HER SONS, JOHNNY AND VINCENT; AND MY HUSBAND, SILVANO.

THE TREMENDOUS TEAM AT KNOPF: MY BRILLIANT AND UNWAVERINGLY PASSIONATE EDITOR/SISTER ROBIN DESSER AND THE AMAZING AND INSIGHTFUL JENNIFER KURDYLA; THE GRAPHIC NOVEL GURU ANDY HUGHES AND THE STELLAR PEGGY SAMEDI; DESIGNER EXTRAORDINAIRE STEPHANIE ROSS; THE PR MAVENS PAUL BOGAARDS AND JOSEFINE KALS; THE WONDERFUL KIM THORNTON, KATE BERNER AND MALLORY CONDER AT THE PENGUIN RANDOM HOUSE SPEAKER'S BUREAU; AND THE LEGENDARY PUBLISHER PAR EXCELLENCE SONNY MEHTA.

MARVELOUS COLORIST DENNIS BICKSLER AND HIS TEAM AT NORTH MARKET STREET GRAPHICS.

MY SUPER AGENTS ELIZABETH SHEINKMAN AND ERIC SIMONOFF AT WILLIAM MORRIS ENDEAVOR.

THE MEDICAL EXPERTS: DR. PAUL GOLDSTEIN, DR. PAULA KLEIN, DR. MICHAEL INFANTINO, DR. BRETT KING, DR. CHRISTOPHER MILLS, DR. KIM SCHULTHEISS, DR. ALLEN B. KANTROWITZ AND DR. BARRY SEGAL.

IAN GINSBERG, OWNER OF C.O. BIGELOW, THE NATION'S OLDEST AND COOLEST APOTHECARY.

THEANU APOSTOLOU; MICHELLE MANNING BARISH; MATTHEW CARASELLA; HUMBERTO CARRENO; STEVE COHEN; EDU CUERO; JANET CULLUM; DR. NIKKI DELANEY; ANNA DELUCA; KELLY DEMARCO; SHARON DORRAM; STEVEN DILLON; BEKIM AND MICKY EJUPI; KIMBERLEY RYAN EKERN; STEVE GARBARINO; JEFFREY GURNARI; LEIGH HABER; SCHUYLER HAZARD; ANN DEXTER JONES; ANNE KEATING; TZIPORAH KASACHKOFF; RICHARD AND DANA KIRSHENBAUM; MICHAEL KLEIN; LAWRENCE KONNER; TOM LAMPSON; DREW LEE; LINDA LAMBERT; ESTELLE LEEDS; DAN LUFKIN; MAX MacKENZIE; CHERI MANCUSO; LISA MIRCHIN; BOB MORRIS; AMY NEDERLANDER; ROBIN AND KEVIN NELSON; CELINE RATTRAY; MARIO RINALDI; RUTHIE ROSENBERG; ROB SHUTER; LINDA, MICHAEL AND VANNA STONE; ANNE FAHEY-STORMENT; SOPHIA TEZEL; NAZ TEZFIT; MIKE ONE-STOP-WIRELESS TUNK; HECTOR VALLENILLA; IRA SILVERBERG; ROBERT VERDI; LINDA WALSH; JEFFREY WARD.

AND

THE DIVINE CYNTHIA LUFKIN: I MISS YOU EVERY DAY, AND I KNOW YOU'RE UP THERE WITH GOD, THE MOTHER OF THE UNIVERSE.

A NOTE ABOUT THE AUTHOR

MARISA ACOCELLA MARCHETTO IS A CARTOONIST FOR *THE NEW YORKER* WHOSE WORK HAS APPEARED IN *THE NEW YORK TIMES*; *GLAMOUR*; AND *O, THE OPRAH MAGAZINE*, AMONG OTHER PUBLICATIONS. SHE IS ALSO THE AUTHOR OF THE GRAPHIC MEMOIR *CANCER VIXEN*, NAMED ONE OF *TIME'S* TOP TEN GRAPHIC MEMOIRS, AND A FINALIST FOR THE NATIONAL CARTOONISTS SOCIETY GRAPHIC NOVEL OF THE YEAR. A FOUNDER AND CHAIR OF THE MARISA ACOCELLA MARCHETTO FOUNDATION AT MOUNT SINAI BETH ISRAEL COMPREHENSIVE CANCER CENTER, SHE LIVES IN NEW YORK CITY.

A NOTE ON THE TYPE

ALL TYPE WAS HAND LETTERED ON YUPO PAPER BY THE AUTHOR, INCLUDING THE

SUPERANN FONT,

WHICH WAS CREATED BY MARISA ACOCELLA MARCHETTO.

PRE-PRODUCTION BY NORTH MARKET STREET GRAPHICS, LANCASTER, PENNSYLVANIA

PRINTED AND BOUND BY TIEN WAH PRESS, SINGAPORE

ALSO BY MARISA ACOCELLA MARCHETTO

CANCER VIXEN

JUST WHO THE HELL IS SHE, ANYWAY?

THIS IS A BORZOI BOOK
PUBLISHED BY ALFRED A. KNOPF

www.aaknopf.com

KNOPF, BORZOI BOOKS, AND THE COLOPHON ARE REGISTERED TRADEMARKS OF PENGUIN RANDOM HOUSE LLC.

LIBRARY OF CONGRESS CATALOGING-IN-PUBLICATION DATA
MARCHETTO, MARISA ACOCELLA.
  ANN TENNA: A NOVEL / MARISA ACOCELLA MARCHETTO.—FIRST EDITION.
    PAGES CM
"THIS IS A BORZOI BOOK."
  ISBN 978-0-307-26747-4 (HARDCOVER: ALK. PAPER)—ISBN 978-0-385-35318-2 (eBook)
1. GOSSIP COLUMNISTS—COMIC BOOKS, STRIPS, ETC. 2. SELF-REALIZATION IN WOMEN—COMIC BOOKS, STRIPS, ETC. 3. GRAPHIC NOVELS. I. TITLE.
  PN6727.M238A56 2015
  741.5'973 — dc23
                    2014025825

JACKET ART BY MARISA ACOCELLA MARCHETTO,
JACKET DESIGN BY MARISA ACOCELLA MARCHETTO AND STEPHANIE ROSS.
MANUFACTURED IN SINGAPORE
FIRST EDITION